Liberty and Uni

MW00654698

This, the first of two volumes of *Liberty and Union*, is a comprehensive constitutional history of the United States from the Anglo-American origins of the Constitution through the colonial and antebellum periods, to the Civil War and the consequent restructuring of the nation.

Written in a clear and engaging narrative style, it successfully unites thorough chronological coverage with a thematic approach, offering critical analysis of core constitutional history topics, set in the political, social, and economic context that made them constitutional issues in the first place. Combining a thoughtful and balanced narrative with an authoritative stance on key issues, the authors explain the past in the light of the past, without imposing upon it the standards of later generations.

Authored by two experienced professors of History and Law, this textbook has been thoughtfully constructed to offer an accessible alternative to dense scholarly works—avoiding unnecessary technical jargon, defining legal terms and historical personalities where appropriate, and making explicit connections between constitutional themes and historical events. For students in an undergraduate or postgraduate constitutional history course, or anyone with a general interest in constitutional developments, this book will be essential reading.

Useful features include:

- Full glossary of legal terminology
- Recommended reading
- A table of cases
- Extensive supporting artwork
- Companion website

Useful documents provided:

- Declaration of Independence
- Articles of Confederation
- Constitution of the United States of America
- Chronological list of Supreme Court justices

Edgar J. McManus is Professor Emeritus of History at Queens College, City University of New York.

Tara Helfman is Assistant Professor at Syracuse University College of Law.

"The Constitution of the United States was made not merely for the generation that then existed, but for posterity—unlimited, undefined, endless, perpetual posterity."
—Henry Clay, U.S. Senate (1850)

LIBERTY AND UNION

A Constitutional History
of the United States

VOLUME 1

Edgar J. McManus
and Tara Helfman

Routledge
Taylor & Francis Group

NEW YORK AND LONDON

First published 2014
by Routledge
711 Third Avenue, New York, NY 10017

and by Routledge
2 Park Square, Milton Park, Abingdon, Oxon OX14 4RN

Routledge is an imprint of the Taylor & Francis Group, an informa business

© 2014 Taylor & Francis

The right of Edgar J. McManus and Tara Helfman to be identified as authors of this work has been asserted by them in accordance with sections 77 and 78 of the Copyright, Designs and Patents Act 1988.

Library of Congress Cataloging-in-Publication Data

McManus, Edgar J.
   Liberty and union : a constitutional history of the United States /
by Edgar J. McManus and Tara Helfman.
      pages cm
   Includes bibliographical references and index.
   1. Constitutional history—United States.   2. Liberty—United States.
I. Helfman, Tara.   II. Title.
KF4541.M39 2014
342.7302'9—dc23   2013014080

ISBN: 978-0-415-89282-7 (hbk)
ISBN: 978-0-415-89283-4 (pbk)
ISBN: 978-0-203-43587-8 (ebk)

Typeset in Horley
by Apex CoVantage, LLC

 Certified Sourcing
www.sfiprogram.org
SFI-00453

Printed and bound in the United States of America
by Edwards Brothers Malloy

For Solfrid Cristina Kvernsveen
—EJM

For Pamela Helfman
—TJH

Contents

Figures and Acknowledgments

Preface

This two-volume study of United States constitutional history borrows its title from Daniel Webster's reply to Senator Robert Hayne in their 1830 Senate debate over the nature of our national government. The debate involved tensions that had existed between state and federal government almost from the inception of the Union, and it raised questions about the viability of republican government itself in a country with so many diverse interest groups. Merchants and tradesmen in Webster's Massachusetts had little in common with the slaveholding interests represented by Hayne in South Carolina. Whether national harmony could be preserved in the face of the decentralizing tendencies of sectional politics was an open question. The Founding Fathers had been aware of the problem and of the threat it posed to the Young Republic. Benjamin Franklin gave voice to their concerns at the conclusion of the Philadelphia Constitutional Convention. When asked what sort of government the Convention had given the nation, he replied, with apparent foreboding, "A Republic, if you can keep it."

Franklin's reply reflected reservations that many of the Revolutionary generation had about the durability of republican governments. Historically, republicanism had a bad track record. One of its problems was that it afforded demagogues with temporary majorities opportunities to run roughshod over minority interests and turn popular government into partisan tyranny. The political failures of the late Roman Republic prepared the way for the Caesars, and the phantom republics of Renaissance Italy in the end succumbed to bloody factionalism. Only the Venetian Republic survived into the modern era and then only by turning itself into a de facto gerontocracy. The republic for which Franklin expressed anxiety would be different, however, because it was designed with built-in restraints on the exercise of power. Factionalism need not be fatal if the rights of minorities are protected until the pendulum of power swings in their direction. The success of republican government ultimately depends on acceptance by the losers of government by the winners. With the tragic exception of our fratricidal conflict in the 1860s, the losers in our political wars have been remarkably accommodative. The Constitution that so many doubted back in 1787 is today the oldest and most successful written constitution in history.

No feature of the Constitution contributed more to the stability of republican government than the system of checks and balances restricting the exercise of political power. Although the Philadelphia Convention had convened primarily to strengthen the national government, the Founding Fathers realized that a stronger government increased the possibilities for abuses of power. So they included safeguards, as James Madison noted in *The Federalist*, No. 51, dividing and allocating power among the three branches of government in such a way that each branch acts as a check upon the others. These systems of checks and balances not only discourage factional excesses but also make political accommodation a practical necessity if anything is to be accomplished. The full power of government, in effect, can seldom be brought to bear on one side or the other of truly divisive issues. This aspect of the system has been described by some critics as political gridlock, which is true enough, though a form of gridlock that has served the nation remarkably well over the years. It failed the nation only once, when the election of an antislavery president blinded supporters of slavery to the fact their interests remained protected by the other two branches of government. It was one of the paradoxes of secession that southerners abandoned a government two-thirds of which they still controlled.

Americans had constitutional government long before the Philadelphia Convention gave them a written constitution. The principles of constitutional government arrived here with the English settlers who put government under law and the protection of personal liberty at the very center of their political culture. Ideas about legal due process and individual rights brought over from England underpinned the political development of every colony. The American Revolution was less a repudiation of all things English than an affirmation of a century and a half of Anglo-American constitutional development. Americans were never so English, John Adams famously observed, as when they declared their independence of England. The Constitution drafted at Philadelphia was based on principles of government that Americans of the colonial era had long taken for granted. The separation of powers and checks and balances were features of government in every colony. Perhaps the greatest achievement of the Founders is that they succeeded beyond all expectations in turning this colonial legacy into a successful and republican national state.

This book is not, as its title makes clear, a history of the United States Constitution, but rather a constitutional history of the United States. While that great document is of course central to the story, it is not the whole story. A century and a half of constitutional development preceded the Philadelphia Constitutional Convention. Our aim here is to cover these developments from their English origins, through the colonial and national periods, including a civil war and two world wars, down to the most recent decisions of the United States Supreme Court on contemporary constitutional issues. The growing impact of international law on our constitutional system is also discussed. Without overloading the text with historiographical digressions, alternative points of view on key issues are presented for evaluation. The pivotal role of the Supreme Court as the arbiter of constitutionality is discussed from the standpoint of both proponents and critics of judicial review. Attention is also given to court politics and to the institutional constraints under which the Court operates as a branch of government.

The roles played by Congress and the president in our constitutional history have not been neglected. Some presidents have had a major impact on constitutional developments, not just by appointing justices to the Supreme Court, but by actions of their own that have created constitutional precedents. Nor should we forget that Congress, besides having the power to propose constitutional amendments, can modify and abridge the jurisdiction of federal courts and thus influence constitutional interpretation. What the Constitution means at any given time cannot be separated from the balance of political forces. This has made the Constitution flexible and relevant to changing times and circumstances, but at the same time exposes it to the pressures of majoritarian politics. The Thirteenth, Fourteenth, and Fifteenth Amendments are political legacies of the Civil War and Reconstruction. The Sixteenth and Seventeenth, and to some extent the Eighteenth and Nineteenth as well, are products of the progressive movement that swept the nation at the beginning of the twentieth century. Textual analysis of these amendments makes little sense apart from the political context of their adoption.

But the Constitution does more than just mirror the vagaries of our political culture. It imposes upon the political process constraints on power that even those in power accept. This is because constitutionalism is the most powerful and durable ideology this country has produced. Racial segregation became acceptable in the late nineteenth century by constitutional interpretation, and it became unacceptable and odious by the same route half a century later. The Constitution is the foundation of our nationhood, more important even than language in creating a sense of political community. Americans have no royal family, state religion, or common ethnicity cementing their links with one another. We have only the Constitution and the way of life it guarantees in creating the commonality of nationhood. It is what holds us together and legitimizes our political aspirations.

In the preparation of this text a conscious effort has been made to explain the past in the light of the past and not to impose upon it the standards of later generations. On the other hand, the right to interpret the past has not been abandoned, because history without interpretation is like reading without thinking, analogous to watching television with the sound turned off. But while positions are suggested on controversial issues, we have attempted to avoid the pitfalls of partisanship. We do not think that the past can be forced into the focus of a single point of view or explained exclusively on the basis of one theory without historical distortion. Readers should always keep in mind that the interpretations occasionally offered are by no means the only tenable ones. Our purpose throughout is to provide a readable account of how constitutionalism has functioned over the years and to encourage readers to rethink and make up their own minds about the great issues discussed.

To facilitate additional reading on particular topics, there are recommended readings, a glossary of legal terminology, tables of cases, a list of justices of the Supreme Court, and the texts of the Declaration of Independence, Articles of Confederation, and the Constitution of the United States. Many of the Supreme Court decisions are quoted extensively for the sake of authenticity and for insight into judicial reasoning. Readers of this book also have access to an interactive website providing links to primary and secondary sources, including case law, constitutional and historical documents, and scholarly articles. The website ensures that the text remains on the cutting edge of constitutional law, a field constantly changing and therefore in need of constant updating of the scholarship. Every effort has been made to make this account interesting and accessible without patronizing the reader or oversimplifying the material. Our aim is not to entertain, but neither is it to put readers to sleep in the first chapter.

EDGAR J. McMANUS
QUEENS COLLEGE
CITY UNIVERSITY OF NEW YORK

TARA HELFMAN
SYRACUSE UNIVERSITY
COLLEGE OF LAW

October 14, 1066	December 25, 1066	1166	1215	June 15, 1215	November 1215
Normans Defeat Anglo-Saxons at Battle of Hastings	William the Conqueror Crowned First Norman King of England	Assize of Clarendon	Beginning of First Barons' War	King John Accepts Magna Carta	Fourth Lateran Council Prohibits Clergy from Participating in Trial by Ordeal

December 21, 1620	1628–1644	June 2, 1628	March 25, 1634	January 14, 1639	June 4, 1639
Settlement of Plymouth Colony	Publication of Edward Coke's *Institutes of the Lawes of England*	Charles I Accepts Petition of Right	Settlement of Maryland Colony	Fundamental Orders of Connecticut	Fundamental Articles of New Haven

December 16, 1689	1689	1735	1765–1769		
Enactment of English Bill of Rights	Publication of John Locke's *Second Treatise of Civil Government*	Trial of John Peter Zenger	Publication of William Blackstone's *Commentaries on the Laws of England*		

I   English and Colonial Origins

1263–1264	January 1265	May 14, 1607	1610	August 2–4, 1619	November 11, 1620
Simon de Montfort Begins Leading Second Barons' War	First Elected Parliament Meets in England	Settlement of Jamestown	Dr. Bonham's Case	Virginia House of Burgesses Becomes the First Elected Assembly in the American Colonies to Enact Legislation	Mayflower Compact

December, 1641	January 30, 1649	May 27, 1679	May 5, 1682	April 4, 1687	December 11, 1688	February 13, 1689
Massachusetts Body of Liberties	Execution of Charles I	Charles II Assents to Habeas Corpus Act	Pennsylvania Charter of Liberties	James II Issues Declaration of Indulgence	James II Flees England	William III and Mary II Crowned Co-Regents of England

> "A subject and a sovereign are clear different things."
> —King Charles I on the scaffold, January 30, 1649

The constitutional history of the United States and of English-speaking people everywhere began at the Battle of Hastings in 1066 with the Norman conquest of England. By then the laws and customs of previous invaders had settled into patchworks of local usages providing a basis for political order throughout the country. The Normans did not disturb these systems of customary law immediately. The task of pacifying and reorganizing the country politically left the conquerors little time to meddle with existing legal institutions. Nevertheless, the governmental changes that they brought from the Continent mark the real beginning of Anglo-American constitutional history. Normandy was then the best-governed state in Europe, and the Normans brought to England a superior system of administration than had existed under the Saxons. The laws of the nation did not change overnight, but the stage was set for constitutional developments that over the centuries would become the proud heritage of the descendants of victors and vanquished alike.

Figure I.1 Panel of the twelfth-century Bayeux Tapestry depicting the death of Harold, the last Anglo-Saxon king of England. Harold (left) is depicted at the Battle of Hastings, attempting to pull an arrow from his eye. The imagery is symbolically significant, as Harold was reputed to have broken an oath to William the Conqueror. The customary punishment for bearing false witness was blinding.

Musee de la Tapisserie, Bayeux, France. Erich Lessing / Art Resource, NY

Institutionalizing the Conquest

The first Norman kings worked hard to tighten their political and administrative controls. William the Conqueror brought feudalism to England, but a brand of feudalism strikingly different from that of the European continent. Under the system, all holders of fiefs swore direct allegiance to the king as well as to their immediate suzerains. Their direct oath to the Crown superseded the loyalty that vassals owed to the immediate lord from whom they held their fiefs. The king claimed lordship over all the land in England, a claim at odds with the usual decentralizing tendencies of feudalism. These political arrangements for many years concerned only the ruling classes and had no immediate impact on ordinary people. The latter continued to sort out their affairs as they had in the past according to local customs and usages. Yet the political arrangements introduced by the

Normans represented an approach to government that in time would make the Crown the source of law as well as political power in a truly national state.

William II (r. 1087–1100) continued the task of pacification, stamping out pockets of Saxon resistance and tightening the reins of government. Military force remained the key to power until the time of Henry I (r. 1100–1135) when the first institutional controls came into being in the form of a royal justice system. Henry made his sheriffs (local officers with jurisdiction over a shire or county) responsible for keeping the peace, and he sent itinerant judges through the country to hear appeals for justice directed to the Crown. Since the king claimed jurisdiction over all offenses involving breaches of the peace, his judges gradually took over most of the criminal jurisdiction of the pre-Norman courts. Henry's motives were both pecuniary and political. Since most offenses were then punishable by fines, the royal administration of justice added considerably to Crown revenues. The laws of the country did not change overnight, because the king's judges at first followed existing local laws and customs in the cases brought before them. But the days when laws varied from place to place were now numbered. The growing system of royal courts provided a conduit for a system of uniform laws common to all of England.

The great innovations of Henry's reign came to a halt during the terrible civil war that followed his death. The conflict between his daughter Matilda and his nephew King Stephen (r. 1135–1154) over the succession was a disaster for monarchy and a tragedy for the country. It brought unbridled lawlessness that laid England waste with whole districts terrorized by armed bands pillaging and plundering in the name of one side or the other. Even a ruler more resolute than the ineffectual Stephen would have been powerless to resist the demands of the barons and bishops in exchange for their support. The concessions Stephen made to the bishops in particular weakened the jurisdiction of the emerging royal courts. Stephen not only recognized the right of church courts to adjudicate ecclesiastical affairs but their jurisdiction to try members of the clergy accused of ordinary crimes. This loss of jurisdiction would not be easily recovered, but it was a price Stephen had to pay.

Henry II and the Common Law

The disasters of Stephen's reign underscore the principal weakness of medieval monarchy as a system of government. Too much depended upon the character and capability of the person occupying the throne. The whole network of royal power could collapse like a house of cards during the reign of a weak or vacillating ruler. But this began to change with the ascension to the throne of Henry II (r. 1154–1189), the ablest and best of England's medieval kings. He created a system of administration that functioned efficiently regardless of who occupied the throne. He began by restoring and strengthening the royal courts as instruments of government. This provided the Crown with a steady stream of revenue and bound the nation closer to the king as the ultimate source of justice.

While the royal courts claimed jurisdiction over criminal cases, the adjudication of civil disputes for many years remained in the hands of local courts, which applied local customary law in the cases brought before them. But the royal courts gradually extended their jurisdiction to civil matters as well on the theory that some private offenses involved breaking the king's peace. Trespass, for example, involved direct, intentional wrongs against persons or property and posed a threat to the peace of the community. It was out of trespass that a wide range of intentional civil offenses (modern torts), such as assault, battery, and false imprisonment, developed. Eventually, royal jurisdiction extended to unintentional offenses as well with the emergence of negligence, defamation, and deceit as civil forms of action in the king's courts. Jurisdiction based on acts of misfeasance in time extended to acts of nonfeasance, such as failure to perform an obligation, thus setting the stage for the development of contract law.

The Writ System

The device through which the civil jurisdiction of the king's courts expanded over the years was the so-called writ system. A writ was an order from the king to the sheriff of the county where the dispute arose directing him to bring the party complained against before the next session of the court for adjudication of the matter. Every writ in theory involved some principle of law applicable to the particular case. Writs had a name relating to their purpose and so might be obtained by any plaintiffs having similar problems. Obtaining the appropriate writ was essential in getting the case before the court and invoking the power of the king on behalf of the plaintiff. Until the writ of trespass became available about the middle of the thirteenth century, the owner of land wrongfully taken by another had to rely upon self-help or unpredictable local law in order to recover his property.

An English Barrister Looks Back on the Historical Development of the Writ

"I do suppose that in ancient time the forms of writs were devised by counsel, as are now the pleas . . . But in King Edward I's time it is likely they came in to be registered. For that king . . . caused divers books of the law to be written and purposed to have reformed the law, as it were the English Justinian. Because, therefore, it is a matter of no small moment to begin well, and that the writ is the foundation of the future action, the policy of England hath from the time which I speak of cast this care upon him that is great next to the greatest, adjoining unto him a college of clerks . . . for the framing and bringing into form of those *formulae juris* . . ."

—John Dodderidge, Counsel for the Defense, *Slade v. Morley* (1602)

The writ system brought with it the great innovation of trial by jury. The typical writ ordered the sheriff to bring to court twelve persons familiar with the case. They would be put under oath to tell the truth and then asked whether the plaintiff's version of the case was correct. This was trial by jury in the original and literal sense that the persons under oath (jurors) provided the only evidence considered by the court. The jurors did not weigh evidence presented by others, as they do today, but provided it themselves as panels of official witnesses. The new procedure, which was later extended to criminal trials as well, represented a great improvement over existing trial practices. It shifted the administration of justice away from oaths, ordeals, and combats toward a more rational evaluation of the facts of the case.

The Grand Jury

Henry II also made a key innovation in bringing wrongdoers to justice. Criminal trials had previously begun with the victim or some interested party appealing to the king's judges for justice. But prosecution by appeal proved ineffective against rich and powerful wrongdoers against whom no one dared to bring charges. The situation not only affronted the king's justice system but deprived him of revenue in the form of fines and court fees. At the Assize of Clarendon in 1166, Henry moved decisively to deal with the problem. He instructed his itinerant judges that before holding court, the leading men of the town should be put under oath and required to report any crimes committed there since the last session of the court. Oaths carried so much weight in the Middle Ages that God-fearing people were likely to think twice before swearing falsely. Thus began the grand jury system that down to the present has been a powerful law-enforcement tool in the discovery and prosecution of criminals. Although initially a prosecutorial device, it would also evolve over the centuries into a safeguard against unjustified prosecutions.

Defendants indicted by grand juries were originally tried by oath or ordeal. The latter involved subjecting the accused to some physical test believed to determine guilt or innocence. In trial by water, the accused would be bound hand and foot and thrown into a body of water blessed by a priest. If he floated to the surface, the water was deemed to have rejected him because he was guilty; if he sank, he would be pulled from the water by ropes to which he was attached and declared innocent. Trial by oath was drier and safer for a defendant. He simply brought to court witnesses prepared to swear that he was innocent of the charges against him. Their oath decided the case, and no further evidence would be considered by the court. The process assumed that the witnesses would not risk eternal damnation by swearing falsely. Trial by combat was also available in cases begun by appeal rather than by grand jury indictment. The defendant in such a trial could challenge his accuser to a fight to the death with weapons blessed by a priest. The blessing was necessary to insure that God would not permit a miscarriage of justice. The combat option was not available to defendants tried on a grand jury indictment. The grand jurors spoke for the king, and the king could not be challenged.

But these early forms of trial became obsolete in 1215 when the Fourth Lateran Council forbade the clergy to participate in such proceedings. Without clerical sanction, the underlying assumption that God somehow determined the outcome of the trial became untenable. Consequently, for several years there were no criminal trials in England. Persons indicted by grand juries were simply banished for disturbing the peace of the community. The problem of how to try them was eventually solved by impaneling twelve-member trial juries from the twenty-three member grand juries that had indicted them. Since the latter were already familiar with the case, it was reasonable to assume that they were qualified to try the defendant. Jury trial already existed under the writ system for civil cases, and it now seemed reasonable to extend it to criminal trials as well. Why the number of jurors came to be fixed at twelve is uncertain, but twelve-member juries became a fixed feature of jury trial from the fourteenth century onward. A fairly large number was apparently considered necessary in order to prevent miscarriages of justice. The older system of trial by ordeal had relied upon the infallible judgment of God, but trial by jury involved the very fallible judgment of men. Requiring that all twelve jurors agree on the verdict provided an additional safeguard against human fallibility.

Henry II not only reformed the administration of justice but set in motion sweeping changes in the substantive law of England. He gathered about him eminent lawyers whose opinions, together with the decisions and case precedents of his judges, mark the real beginning of the English common law. This new and growing body of law was "common" in the sense that it applied throughout the realm. The older systems of law were not displaced immediately. The ecclesiastical courts still enforced canon law; the courts merchant applied the *lex mercatoria* in business disputes; and the town and borough courts enforced their own local customary laws. But these were limited and specialized systems of law. The common law alone applied everywhere the royal courts dispensed justice. Its reach and rationality made it an attractive alternative against which the other systems could not in the long run compete.

No one contributed more to the course and content of the common law than the thirteenth-century royal judge Henry de Bracton. His legal treatise *De Legibus et Consuetudinibus Angliae* (*On the Laws and Customs of England*) provided the first comprehensive account of medieval English law based on reports of actual cases. Bracton's access to official records not usually open to the public enabled him to compile a summary of contemporary law and practice that profoundly influenced the development of the common law. He was the first to analyze and compare particular cases and to criticize or praise judicial decisions. Modeled on legal categories drawn from Roman law, *De Legibus* in some ways resembles a modern legal treatise in its case law comparisons and speculations about what the law should be in hypothetical cases. The importance of Bracton's work cannot be exaggerated. Previously, cases had been decided by the courts without reference to earlier cases or precedents; that now changed, and the common law soon assumed its characteristic features as a system of case law based on precedent. The availability of case records now became indispensable to practicing attorneys. Significantly, the first of the Year Books making such materials generally accessible appeared in 1268, the year of Bracton's death.

The only effective rival of the common law was a complementary system of royal justice known as equity. This was actually a system of anti-law designed to correct injustices arising from the mechanical application of the common law. As case precedents hardened into inflexible legal principles, exceptions sometimes had to be made in order to prevent injustice. Contracts, for example, were automatically enforced by the law courts if executed in proper form. It did not matter whether one of the parties had tricked or defrauded the other; all that mattered was technical compliance with the formalities of contract law. When such a case arose, the wronged party could petition the king for relief from the unjust consequences of the law. The petition would be turned over to the chancellor, who

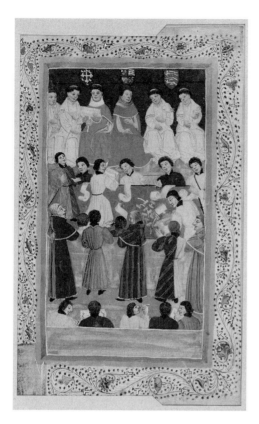

Figure I.2 Manuscript painting of Court of Chancery (c. 1460). Established during the reign of Richard II, the court had jurisdiction over cases in equity.

Reprinted by permission of The Masters of the Bench of the Inner Temple

ran the machinery of royal government, for a determination of its merits. As the volume of petitions grew, the cases were processed by lawyers assisting the chancellor. Since the decision would come from the chancery, as the chancellor's office was known, the process came to be known as a chancery proceeding. Separate courts of chancery were established during the reign of Richard II (r. 1377–1399) to deal with the heavy case load. The principal difference between law courts and chancery courts was that the latter did not use juries. Chancery was not bound by fixed rules in deciding cases but relied instead on general principles of equity in order to reach a fair result. While the two systems sometimes clashed, both were essential for the rational administration of justice. One provided England with uniform laws based on experience and precedent, and the other insured that law itself did not become an instrument of injustice.

The Common Law and Natural Law

Implicit in the development of the common law was the idea that a higher body of immutable law existed upon which judges could draw in settling disputes not covered by statutes or case precedents. Usually judges could deal with the cases before them by deduction and analogy, but occasionally they had to deal with something completely novel for which there were no precedents. When this occurred, they would frame a new rule to cover the facts of the case. This law-finding function assumed the existence of a body of natural law from which they could infer a rule of common law appropriate for the case before them. The alternative to "finding" a new rule of law somewhere in existing but invisible law would have been to admit that they were actually making new law, which was not their function as judges. The concept of a higher body of natural law was consistent with common-law thought and practice in medieval England. Bracton regarded natural law as the source of all law, binding even the king. Although common-law judges did not cite it explicitly, the invisible body of law to which they routinely adverted was conceptually identical.

That both the common law and natural law were unwritten systems of law facilitated crossovers between them. Originally the common law was regarded as declaratory of the natural law, but over time the two became conflated and some common-law rules and doctrines came to be regarded as part of the natural law. The conflation appears fairly clear in the common-law rule that legislation in derogation of the common law must be construed narrowly in order to minimize its impact on the presumably higher body of common law. While judges might deduce virtually anything from the common law, they were strictly limited in what they might deduce from statutes. In *Calvin's Case* (1608), Sir Edward Coke argued that the law of nature was part of the law of England, and to the extent that they coincided, the law of England was also immutable. Two years later in *Dr. Bonham's Case* (1610), Coke declared an act of parliament void as incompatible with the immutable law of England, which could be changed by neither king nor parliament.

The conflation of common-law rights with natural rights had important constitutional consequences. It set the stage for the English civil war of the 1640s and for the complete triumph of parliament over monarchy later in the century. A century later it appears in the assertion in the American Declaration of Independence of the right of Americans to the independence "to which the Laws of Nature and of Nature's God entitles them." The rights claimed by the Declaration had originally been common-law rights, but they had now evolved into natural rights bestowed by God and Nature. For more than a century after Independence had been won, the Supreme Court would read common-law rules and doctrines into the United States Constitution as expressions of natural law.[1]

Magna Carta

The rebellion of the barons against King John (r. 1199–1216) early in the thirteenth century had constitutional consequences that still resonate today. In 1215 the barons forced the king to accept Magna Carta, the Great Charter of Liberties binding him to respect their traditional rights. It included a provision against arbitrary taxation that anticipated by two centuries the principle of no taxation without representation. Equally important was the guarantee that no one might be deprived of life, liberty, or property unless convicted by his peers of violating some law of the land. These provisions bound the king himself to the rule of law, making the government of England, in theory at least, a government of laws and not of men.

Magna Carta and the Origins of Due Process

"No free man shall be taken or imprisoned or disseised or outlawed or exiled or in any way ruined, nor will we go or send against him, except by the lawful judgement of his peers or by the law of the land."

Figure I.3 Fourteenth-century manuscript painting of King John hunting a stag.
© The British Library Board, Cotton Claudius D. II, f.116

Despite what it has come to represent today, Magna Carta originally had nothing to do with the rights of ordinary people. It was essentially a feudal compact between a suzerain and his rebellious vassals. The original document was actually in effect for only about nine weeks. Three separate revisions superseded it over the next twenty years, and only the last, the charter issued by Henry III in 1225, became a permanent part of the law of England. Yet, the Great Charter of 1215 marks a turning point in English history, lighting a torch that still shines brightly across the centuries. Without it, there would have been no later revisions or a final version. Later generations have rightly revered it as one of the seminal texts of English constitutionalism.

Emergence of Parliament

The barons rebelled again during the long reign of Henry III (r. 1216–1272), and they set in motion important structural changes in the government of England. After taking the king prisoner in 1264, Simon de Montfort, the leader of the disaffected barons, convened an assembly purporting to represent the nation. Called a parliament (from the Anglo-Latin *parliamentum*—a conference, or a talking together), it consisted of the lords and bishops of England, two knights from every shire, and two prominent citizens from the most important towns. In 1295, Edward I adopted Montfort's prototype in summoning representatives to what became known as the Model Parliament. Both Montfort and Edward sought to broaden their base of support by including representatives of the common people of England in the government of the country. Their immediate goal was to limit the influence of the lords and bishops, until then the traditional power base in England. Another reason for broadening the political base was the rising cost of government. By the fourteenth century the feudal fees and taxes to which the king was entitled were no longer sufficient to meet the costs of running a national state. The Crown needed new sources of revenue, and the growing prosperity of the townspeople and the country gentry made it logical for the king to look to them both for support and revenue. Inevitably the day would come when these new paymasters of government would play a dominant role in the political life of the nation.

The Tudors

By the late fifteenth century everything was in place for a major realignment of political forces. The changing nature of warfare and the emergence of dynamic new classes in society combined to undermine the old feudal order. Economic power shifted to merchants and manufacturers whose interests coincided with the centralizing goals of monarchy. The feudal regime was marred by turbulence and disorder, which was bad for business, whereas a strong monarchy offered peace and stability. Three decades of internecine conflict during the Wars of the Roses decimated the baronage and made the nation eager for more stable political arrangements. Henry VII (r. 1485–1509), the first of the Tudors, was the immediate beneficiary of the new situation. He offered order and stability to a nation exhausted by civil strife. The price of order was despotic government, but to most of the nation this seemed a fair exchange for the recurring cycles of war and anarchy.

The Tudor monarchs who followed Henry were masters at manipulating the forms of parliamentary government. Both Henry VIII (r. 1509–1547) and Elizabeth I (r. 1558–1603) skillfully created the appearance of popular support for all their major undertakings. They managed to identify their own goals with the wider interests of the nation. Nothing politically risky was undertaken without going through the formality of consulting with parliament. Whether defying the Pope or seizing monastery lands, they found it safer to act with the approval of parliament than to act alone. With only minor exceptions, there was little risk that parliament might oppose them. Elections were rigged, and members of the commons could be flattered or intimidated into doing the Crown's bidding. Still, there was a tacit shift of power insofar as the precedent had been set that parliament should be consulted on all important matters. This turned out to be more important in the long run than all the Tudor manipulations. The very need for manipulation was itself a concession to the growing importance of the classes represented in parliament.

Divine Right Monarchy

The rise of parliament to political dominance ironically began under Stuart monarchs who despised even the forms of parliamentary government. James I (r. 1603–1625), the first of that dynasty, set the stage for conflict by failing to grasp the advantages of Tudor statecraft. He rejected the forms of popular government that had served the Tudors so well and claimed to rule by divine right, asserting that his power to govern came from God, and that no one in the realm might lawfully oppose him. While divine right theory was in vogue on the Continent at the time, England's tradition of limited government made the king's extravagant claims untenable. The Tudors had been absolutists, but they never challenged the traditions of the nation. They shrewdly disguised their despotism in the forms of popular government. James refused to concede even the illusion of limited power. He imposed taxes by decree and dissolved parliament when its leaders protested his actions. His divine right claims raised monarchy to such heights that its fall was inevitable.

James I on the Divine Right of Kings

"The state of monarchy is the supremest thing upon earth. For kings are not only God's lieutenants upon earth, and sit upon God's throne, but even by God himself they are called gods. . . . For if you will consider the attributes to God, you shall see how they agree in the person of the king. God has power to create, or destroy, make, or unmake at his pleasure, to give life, or send death, to judge all, and to be judged nor accountable to none; to raise low things, and to make high things low at his pleasure, and to God are both soul and body due. And the like power have kings . . ."

—Speech to Parliament (1610)

Figure I.4 Portrait of King James I of
England and VI of Scotland by Daniel
Mytens (1621).
© National Portrait Gallery, London

Charles I (r. 1625–1649) inherited his father's divine right pretensions, and
they soon embroiled him in a bitter dispute with parliament. Like his father,
Charles used the prerogative courts of Star Chamber and High Commission
to prosecute political opponents and religious dissenters. Proceedings in these
courts were closed to the public, and defendants could be tortured, mutilated,
and branded by them. When parliament refused to vote funds for a military expedition against France, the king raised money by means that outraged the nation. He extorted forced loans from the gentry and punished those who resisted
by quartering troops in their homes or imprisoning them without trial. The failure of the military expedition forced him to turn to parliament in order to get
more money, and the price of getting it would be high. In 1628 Charles had to
accept the Petition of Right, a document second only to Magna Carta in constitutional importance. The Petition set clear limits on royal power, declaring that
taxes and loans not approved by parliament were illegal, and prohibiting arbitrary imprisonment and the quartering of troops in private houses. This stinging
denunciation of what the king had done widened the breach between him and

parliament. What had begun as a fissure now became a chasm. It set both sides on a collision course that would plunge England into civil war and bring the king to the scaffold.

The English Civil War

In 1642 the conflict between Charles I and parliament plunged England into a civil war that unleashed forces not seen since the peasant revolts of the Middle Ages. It brought down the king, then parliament, and put the country under a decade of military dicta-torship. The conflict produced English democratic thought, notions of equality, and the idea of universal suffrage. On the edge of the revolutionary ferment was a faction known as the Levellers, who from 1647 to 1649 shaped opinion in the all-powerful army, and who favored republicanism over the now-discredited institution of monar-chy. Although suppressed by Oliver Cromwell in the 1650s, the Levellers raised the threshold of political debate on both sides of the Atlantic. They were the precursors of the democratic ideals that promoted revolution both in France and America in the late eighteenth century.

A Leveller Proposes a Democratic Constitution

"I think that the poorest he that is in England has a life to live as the greatest he; and therefore truly, sir, I think it's clear, that every man that is to live under a government ought first by his own consent to put himself under that government; and I do think that the poorest man in England is not at all bound in a strict sense to that government that he has not had a voice to put himself under . . ."

—Colonel Thomas Rainsborough, Putney Debates on the Constitution of England (October 1647)

The execution of the king at the end of the civil war affected political thinking everywhere. Charles had committed no crime for which he could be held legally ac-countable, and the judges who condemned him had no lawful authority to try him. The sovereignty of the people and the equality of all persons before the law were invoked to justify the proceedings against him. His judges rejected the notion that monarchs were above the law and proclaimed a new democratic law that held even anointed kings as accountable as the meanest commoner. English kings had been killed before, but never in public or under color of law. The trial and execution of Charles I perma-nently changed the political consciousness of people everywhere. The spectacle of a sovereign people sending their king to the scaffold forever shattered the mystique of monarchy.

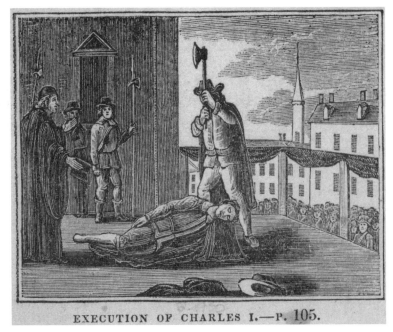

EXECUTION OF CHARLES I.—P. 105.

Figure I.5 Print of the Execution of King Charles I (1649).

Picture Collection, The New York Public Library, Astor, Lenox and Tilden Foundations

The Restoration Monarchy

The restoration of monarchy under Charles II (r. 1660–1685) marked the beginning of a new constitutional order. Charles regained the throne of his executed father only at the price of recognizing parliament as a partner in government. The hated prerogative courts of Star Chamber and High Commission, abolished during the Interregnum, remained abolished under the Restoration, and there were no more claims of divine right absolutism. The Restoration parliament passed numerous laws protecting individual rights and proclaiming its own preeminence in public affairs. One key measure was the Habeas Corpus Act of 1679 requiring judges to issue writs of habeas corpus on demand. The writ directed the officer having custody of the prisoner to produce him in court to justify the legality of his detention. Such writs had been issued since the fourteenth century at the discretion of judges. The Act of 1679 made issuance of the writ mandatory. Any judge refusing to issue one faced a fine of 500 pounds, and any officer failing to comply with one could be fined 100 pounds. The Act applied only in England, but some assemblies in the English colonies adopted it as a model and enacted it almost verbatim.

The death of Charles II set the stage for even more constitutional upheaval. Charles was succeeded by his brother James II (r. 1685–1688), a Catholic who hoped to return England to the Catholic faith. It had been foreseen that James might cause trouble, and in 1679 a faction in parliament known as Whigs made an unsuccessful attempt to exclude him from the succession. On the other side of the issue was a faction known as Tories, who championed the cause of dynastic legitimacy. But James as king alarmed even his Tory supporters by following the same arrogant course that had cost his father his head. He claimed the right in individual cases to suspend the laws barring Catholics from public office. The claim was asserted so frequently that it soon became evident that the king felt free to ignore any law that displeased him. In 1687 he cast all caution aside and issued a Declaration of Indulgence suspending all penal laws against Catholics and dissenting Protestants outside the Anglican religious establishment.

The Glorious Revolution

Parliament put up with these provocations on the assumption that James in a few years would be succeeded by his Protestant daughter Mary, who was married to William of Orange. But these hopes were dashed when James's second wife, Mary of Modena, gave birth to a son in 1688. Confronted with the prospect of a new line of Catholic rulers, a cabal of lords, bishops, and gentry invited William and Mary to replace James and save England from the Catholic menace. To put a gloss of legitimacy on the offer, rumors were circulated that the child was not James's son but an impostor being foisted upon the nation to insure a Catholic succession. In any case, William and Mary accepted the offer, and James, finding himself without any support, fled to France without firing a shot. This bloodless transfer of power was celebrated in England and the colonies as the Glorious Revolution.

The deposition of James II marked the final triumph of parliament over monarchy. William and Mary became king and queen of England not by divine right or dynastic succession but at parliament's invitation. Their coronation in 1689 brought a year of sweeping constitutional changes. Parliament began by limiting all revenue appropriations to one year, thus tightening its control over public spending and putting the Crown on a shorter leash. Then it passed the Toleration Act granting religious freedom to all Christians except Catholics and Unitarians. The most important measure of all was the Bill of Rights, a landmark document in Anglo-American constitutional history. It guaranteed the right of jury trial, affirmed the right of people to petition for the redress of grievances, outlawed cruel and unusual punishments, and prohibited excessive bail or fines for minor offenses. It confirmed the right of the people to keep arms for their own defense and prohibited standing armies in peacetime without parliament's consent. There was also a provision that members of parliament might not be impeached or held accountable for anything said in parliament except by order of parliament itself. While the Bill of Rights applied only in England, its principles resonated across the Atlantic and quickly entered the mainstream of American constitutional thinking.

The American Colonies

The great changes taking place in England in the seventeenth century profoundly influenced the English settlers in America. The conflict between the king and parliament gave tangible meaning to the idea of limited government and the right of people to take up arms in defense of liberty. For more than a decade following the civil war of the 1640s, Americans lived under a home government that had executed an anointed king in the name of the sovereign people. These events struck a responsive chord in the New England colonies where the early Puritan settlers shared the political and religious ideals of their coreligionists in England. Leading English Puritans such as Hugh Peters and Sir Harry Vane had lived for a time in Massachusetts before returning home to support parliament against the king. Most of New England only grudgingly accepted the Stuart Restoration in 1660, and ultra-Puritan New Haven Colony sheltered and protected the regicides John Dixwell, William Goffe, and Edward Whalley from the fate awaiting them in England. All fugitives lived out their lives in New England beyond the reach of royal vengeance.

Their remoteness from England gave the English colonies opportunities for political growth with relatively little interference from the home government. Most of the colonies were founded under charters requiring only that their political arrangements should not be repugnant to the laws of England. This was hardly a burden for people who regarded English law as part of their proud national heritage. Moreover, by then the law of England had become so vast and complicated that the settlers could pick and choose what best served their purpose. There was nothing in their legal baggage preventing them from broadening the base of government far beyond the English model.

Colonial Political Arrangements

Because they were founded at different times and for different reasons, the colonies had a varied political development. Despite institutional similarities, no two were exactly alike or followed identical patterns. Massachusetts was settled by English Puritans who sought to establish a model religious state, while Rhode Island was founded by religious fugitives from Massachusetts. New York was originally the Dutch colony of New Netherland, and Georgia began as a refuge for English paupers and debtors. Some colonies combined with others during the course of their development, and others subdivided into separate jurisdictions. New Hampshire was part of Massachusetts before becoming a separate province in 1679; New Haven Colony combined with Connecticut in the 1660s; and New Plymouth merged with Massachusetts in the 1690s. Before becoming a single province in 1702, the Eastern and Western parts of New Jersey had several decades of separate political development. Not until well into the eighteenth century were the boundaries of the colonies permanently in place.

Legal developments in the colonies largely reflected the circumstances of their settlement. The Massachusetts Puritans originally based most of their criminal laws on Old Testament models, and New Haven Colony, the strictest of the Puritan jurisdictions, made Scripture binding in civil as well as criminal matters. Rhode Island was actually the only New England colony to adhere strictly to English common law from the beginning. Because the settlers needed the support of the home government to remain independent of their hostile Puritan neighbors, they neglected no opportunity to demonstrate their loyalty to England. The rest of New England used English law as well, but much more selectively and not always the common law. By the early seventeenth century England had more than a dozen subsystems of law, so there was plenty to choose from besides the common law. One subsystem from which New Englanders borrowed freely was a body of local town and borough laws known as custumals. Their most distinctive feature, and one with obvious constitutional significance, was that they were in writing and put clear and ascertainable limits on the power of government.

English law entered the colonies mainly through legal handbooks and commentaries readily available in England and the colonies in the early seventeenth century. By far the most influential was Michael Dalton's *The Country Justice*, a summary of contemporary law and procedure in England. Dalton, who was a justice of the peace in Cambridge, wrote the book as a reference work for the numerous justices in England who had no formal legal training. His simple and direct style, with alphabetized entries for the convenience of readers, made the handbook popular in England and America. An earlier unalphabetized handbook, William Lambarde's *Eirenarcha*, was also available, having gone through thirteen editions by 1619. While preparing the colony's first comprehensive law code for publication in 1647, the Massachusetts General Court ordered two copies each of Dalton's *Country Justice*, Sir Edward Coke's *Commentaries upon Littleton*, Coke's *Reports*, the *Book of Entries* (probably by Coke), and *New Terms*, probably by William Rastell, a popular law dictionary that went through numerous editions between 1527 and 1624. The Massachusetts lawmakers thought that these English references would provide "better light for making and proceeding about laws."

Colonial Charters

The English colonies differed from the settlements established in America by other Europeans in one key respect. They were founded not by the government but by companies and individual proprietors with private goals. The cost of establishing settlements was so high that the Crown granted vast tracts of land, along with powers of government, to private investors willing to put up the money and take the risks. The first permanent English settlement at Jamestown was founded in 1607 by the Virginia Company under a royal charter giving it legal title to the entire colony. The first public officials of Virginia were agents of the company, and the first laws of the colony were enacted at Company shareholders' meetings in London. Similarly, Massachusetts was founded by the Massachusetts Bay Company under a charter giving the Company powers of government. Maryland began in 1632 under a proprietary grant to Lord Baltimore, and in 1682 Pennsylvania came into being as a proprietary holding of the Penn family. Even New York, which began as the Dutch colony of New Netherland, went through a stage of private development as a commercial enterprise of the Dutch West India Company.

Rights of Settlers under the First Charter of Virginia

"[W]e do, for Us, our Heirs, and Successors, DECLARE, by these Presents, that all and every the Persons being our Subjects, which shall dwell and inhabit within every or any of the said several Colonies and Plantations, and every of their children, which shall happen to be born within any of the Limits and Precincts of the said several Colonies and Plantations, shall HAVE and enjoy all Liberties, Franchises, and Immunities, within any of our other Dominions, to all Intents and Purposes, as if they had been abiding and born, within this our Realm of England, or any other of our said Dominions."

—April 10, 1606

Figure I.6 Seal of the Virginia Company of London. On one side is the seal of James I enclosing the king's portrait. On the other are the words *Pro Concilio Suo Virginiae* ("For His Council of Virginia"), enclosing the king's arms. The Company's 1606 Letters Patent set out the design of the seal in detail.

Courtesy of the Library of Virginia

Besides granting powers of government to the companies and proprietors, the charters contained guarantees protecting the rights of the settlers. They spelled out the terms under which settlers could acquire title to land, participate in public affairs, and even how they might worship. Since no rights other than those specifically guaranteed could be lawfully claimed, the charters were crucially important in every colony. The charter granted to Lord Baltimore, for instance, required the consent of the freemen to all laws promulgated in the colony. This had the practical effect of giving freeholders the right to vote, not because they were English, but because the colony charter said so. With so much at stake, colonial people had reason to prize their charters. While not constitutions in the modern sense, they underscored from the outset the importance of protecting fundamental rights with written and ascertainable guarantees.

Colonies founded without charters relied on compacts agreed upon by the settlers as a de facto basis for government. The Pilgrims adopted the Mayflower Compact for New Plymouth; the Connecticut settlers adopted the Fundamental Orders; and the founders of New Haven Colony subscribed to a Fundamental Agreement. Only Rhode Island developed without first adopting some constitutional document as a basis for its political arrangements. But this was a deliberate omission because the settlers feared provoking their Puritan neighbors in Massachusetts who claimed jurisdiction over their territory. They prudently waited for political recognition by England, which finally came in the form of a charter in 1644, before venturing to draft a constitution setting up a colony government. The document finally adopted proved to be worth the delay. Besides establishing a democratic colony government under a federal system sharing power with the town governments, it provided for the separation of church and state and guaranteed freedom of conscience. These and other progressive features make it one of the most important documents of American constitutional history.

The early period of private control had a lasting effect on the political development of every colony. More interested in profits than politics, the founding companies and proprietors made political concessions calculated to promote settlement and growth. In 1619 the Virginia settlers got the right to elect an assembly, the House of Burgesses, with general lawmaking powers. Thereafter the Virginia Company retained control of only the executive functions of government. Similar transfers of power occurred in other colonies, either to increase governmental efficiency or to satisfy the demands of the settlers. The reorganization of political arrangements was facilitated by acceptance on both sides of the Atlantic that the taxes needed to pay for government could be levied only by the elected representatives of the people. The relatively easy transfer of legislative power to the settlers would have been far more difficult had the colonies been under the direct control of the English government from the beginning. Governments seldom share power willingly but usually fight tooth and nail to keep and augment it. Fortunately, those who controlled political arrangements in early America were not in the power business. They had other goals and willingly made political concessions in order to achieve them.

These early transfers of power cost England dearly in the long run. They created in every colony systems of government with no links of accountability to the home government. By the time England took direct control and turned the most important colonies into royal provinces, a strong tradition of self-government had taken hold in America. Any attempt to change the existing system at the expense of local rights would have caused serious problems. The English government originally viewed these arrangements as useful in handling local details of government. Colonial assemblies were certainly better informed and able to deal with local problems than officials 3,000 miles away in

London. So the displacement of the companies and proprietors really made little difference in the colonies. Only the executive functions of government were taken over by England directly; control of the legislative functions remained as before on this side of the Atlantic.

The separation of powers would have worked better if both sides had been clear about the ground rules. But England and the colonies never came to terms on the nature of their constitutional relationship. England took the view that colonial institutions of government existed only on sufferance, not as a matter of constitutional right. They were merely governments of political convenience whose functions might be taken over by England at any time. But this was not the way most Americans viewed things. A century of what amounted to virtual autonomy with regard to their internal affairs convinced them that their elected assemblies were a necessary part of the political scheme of things, as essential to constitutional government as parliament was to constitutional government in England. Failure to reconcile these opposing views set both sides on a collision course long before the dispute over taxation and representation precipitated armed conflict.

Protecting Traditional Rights

The colonial assemblies were vigilant in protecting traditional rights brought over from England. They endorsed from the outset the great principle of Magna Carta that no one should be punished unless first convicted by a jury of breaking some known law of the land. Jury trial had by now evolved beyond its medieval procedural origins into a substantive right that protected defendants against biased or highhanded judges. Jurors no longer functioned as panels of official witnesses but as evaluators of evidence presented in court by others, and it was up to them to decide whether the evidence justified a conviction. In most cases a defendant could not be brought to trial unless a grand jury first found that the evidence against him justified a trial. The grand jury process begun by Henry II had by now evolved into a safeguard against unjustified prosecutions. Both the right of jury trial and the right to a grand jury hearing were essential features of the colonial justice system.

The Spirit of Magna Carta in America

"No man's life shall be taken away, no man's honor or good name shall be stained, no man's person shall be arrested, restrained, banished, dismembered, nor any ways punished . . . unless it be by virtue of equity or some express law of the country warranting the same, established by a General Court and sufficiently published . . ."

—Massachusetts Body of Liberties (1641)

Another safeguard brought from England was the common-law rule against double jeopardy. This rule predated even Magna Carta and barred more than one prosecution for the same offense. To harass individuals with endless prosecutions violated fundamental notions of fairness. The resources of the state were so overwhelming that at some point even innocent defendants would be worn down and convicted. So a conviction or acquittal ended the matter completely, and the defendant thereafter could not be retried for any reason. The rule actually provided more protection in the colonies than in England. The English rule applied only to crimes punishable by death, but in the colonies it applied to minor offenses as well. Under no circumstances could a person be tried more than once for the same offense.

Colonial lawmakers also adopted the English privilege against compulsory self-incrimination. The privilege had a tangled history going back to the early days of the common law. One of its sources was the early common-law rule that defendants could not testify under oath on their own behalf. Oaths originally carried so much weight that a defendant who swore to his innocence might be acquitted regardless of the evidence against him. There was also a desire to prevent feudal and canonical practices involved in trials by oath from gaining a foothold in the common-law courts. While the original purpose of the testimonial disability was to prevent the defendant from clearing himself by taking an oath, it logically followed that if he could not testify for himself neither could he be forced to testify against himself.

The privilege in England had particular relevance to the prosecution of religious dissenters because of its association with the so-called ex officio oath. This was the oath that English judges claimed the right to administer by virtue of their office. The ex officio oath became bitterly controversial when the Courts of Star Chamber and High Commission used it to root out and punish religious dissidents. Suspects would be brought to court and required to answer under oath what they really thought about the official Anglican religion. Those who refused to answer under oath were deemed guilty and punished. Since these courts were royal prerogative courts apart from the common-law courts, there was no right to a jury trial. Lying to the court in such cases was not a viable option for persons with sincere religious convictions. An oath called upon God to witness the truth of what was said, and not to speak truly meant risking eternal damnation. The oath was a powerful inquisitorial device in the hands of the state and was regarded by its critics as the moral equivalent of torture.

The English Puritans who had direct experience with the oath brought their hatred of it to New England. In 1637 the Massachusetts General Court created an uproar when it announced that it would proceed "ex officio" in questioning the Antinomian minister John Wheelwright about an allegedly seditious sermon. Wheelwright's outraged supporters loudly protested that the Court meant to force him to incriminate himself in the manner of Star Chamber. Whatever may have been intended, the Court suddenly found itself on the defensive. John Winthrop, the presiding magistrate, hastily explained that the words "ex officio" had been used only to signify the official nature of the inquiry. Wheelwright would not be required to testify under oath but only asked to provide the Court with unsworn information. The incident underscores the revulsion evoked by any hint of compulsory self-incrimination. The General Court settled the issue with finality four years later by expressly prohibiting ex officio oaths.

Demographic Diversity

While their origins were English, the colonies differed from England in numerous ways. For one thing, there was a high degree of ethnic and religious diversity. The open-door policy followed everywhere with regard to immigration, together with opportunities for social and economic improvement, attracted Europeans of virtually every nationality. Dissatisfaction with conditions at home also drew numerous settlers. Wars, political oppression, and religious persecution brought a steady influx of non-English settlers to every colony. The revocation of the Edict of Nantes in 1685 brought large numbers of French Huguenots to New York, Massachusetts, and South Carolina. A descendant of one of these Huguenot refugees became the first chief justice of the United States. The wars of Louis XIV resulted in a heavy migration of Germans that continued throughout the eighteenth century. There was also an influx of Scotch-Irish following the Jacobite revolts of 1715 and 1745 on behalf of the Stuart Pretenders. By the first federal census in 1790, only slightly more than 60 percent of the population could trace their origins to England. These non-English settlers made an easy adjustment to colonial society and quickly adapted to the life and institutions of their new homeland.

One group not assimilated into colonial life was the large slave population brought here from Africa and the West Indies. The acute shortage of free labor that existed in every colony created a demand for slaves and indentured servants. The latter were free settlers who voluntarily bound themselves to labor contracts (indentures) in return for free passage to America; the former were captives whose freedom had been stolen from them and who had no prospect of a better life in the colonies. Indentured servants moved easily into the general population once their term of service expired, but for slaves there was no expiration date on bondage. They and their descendants were condemned to a system of endless exploitation and subordination indelibly defined by race. Their situation was totally at odds with the generally progressive tendencies of colonial society.

English law provided no models for dealing with an institution like slavery. Chattel bondage had disappeared in the countries of northern Europe long before the colonial era, and Americans were essentially on their own in hammering out pragmatic arrangements. The institutional model tying race to slavery originated in the West Indies where race-based slavery had been established by the time the first Africans reached the American mainland. The measures adopted for the management and control of slaves were calculatedly brutal and terroristic. In Pennsylvania slaves were branded, castrated, and put to death for offenses punishable by flogging or imprisonment if committed by whites. Following a slave insurrection in New York in 1712 and a suspected plot in 1741, slaves

"[B]e *it enacted* . . . That all Negroes and Indians, (free Indians in amity with this government, and degrees, mulattoes, and mustizoes, who are now free, excepted,) mulattoes or mustizoes who now are, or shall hereafter be, in this Province, and all their issue and offspring, born or to be born, shall be, and they are hereby declared to be, and remain forever hereafter, absolute slaves, and shall follow the condition of the mother, and shall be deemed, held, taken, reputed and adjudged in law, to be chattels personal, in the hands of their owners and possessors . . ."

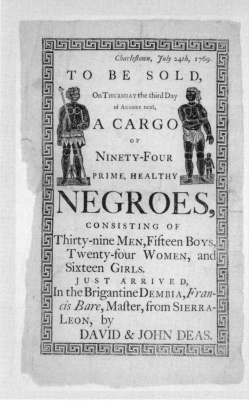

Figure I.7 Slave Auction Notice from Charleston, South Carolina (1769). It is estimated that more than 40 percent of all the Africans brought to America during the colonial period entered through South Carolina.

© *American Antiquarian Society*

were broken on the wheel, burned at the stake, and gibbeted alive in chains. While free whites looked to law for the protection of life and liberty, the African bondsmen learned to fear it as an instrument of repression. The stark reality of slavery was that it precluded a significant part of the population from sharing the values that bound the rest of colonial society together.

Colonial Government

Government in the colonies was characterized by the separation of powers between an executive branch headed by the governor and an assembly elected by the people. The system superficially resembled political arrangements in post-Restoration England where for several decades the lawmaking power of parliament and the executive prerogatives of the king were in rough equilibrium. But the separation of powers was actually more sharply drawn in America where the contending branches of government served different constituencies. Royal governors who were accountable to England often found it difficult to work with assemblies accountable only to the voters who elected them. A measure deemed reasonable in England might not seem reasonable at all to people in New York or Virginia. The problem was systemic and unrelated to particular issues. Even the most routine details of government could cause serious friction between governors and their assemblies.

Tensions between the branches of government were sometimes exacerbated by the appointment of governors totally unqualified for office. Some were flagrantly corrupt, others ignorant or arrogant, but all behaved in ways that brought England and the executive branch into disrepute. Lord Cornbury, governor of New York and New Jersey from 1702 to 1708, was one of the worst. The historian H.L. Osgood described him as "a mean liar, a vulgar profligate, a frivolous spendthrift, an impudent cheat, a fraudulent bankrupt, and a detestable bigot." Osgood thought that Cornbury did more to discredit England in the colonies than any of the royal officials sent to America. But there were others who in some respects may have been worse. Benjamin Fletcher, a governor of New York in the 1690s, was certainly not much better. Graft, corruption, and dealings with pirates marred his administration. William Cosby, governor of New York from 1732–1736, may not have been as bad as Cornbury and Fletcher, but he was bad enough. It was during his administration that John Peter Zenger was tried for seditious libel for publicizing his misconduct in office.

One advantage governors had in dealing with the assembly was that the executive branch of government was never out of session. The governors ran a continuous administration uninterrupted by adjournments and elections. Even when the assembly was in session, the governor had considerable leverage in dealing with it. He could propose laws as well as veto any not to his liking. Moreover, his veto was absolute, so nothing could be enacted without his consent. The governor could also dissolve a troublesome assembly and order new elections in order to get a more compliant one. Finally, his power to appoint public officials gave him a powerful patronage tool with which to influence public events. Skillful use of patronage could work wonders in dealing with the lawmakers.

The most important power of the assembly was its control of the public purse. Only the assembly could levy taxes and appropriate the money needed to carry on the work of government. Since a governor without money could do nothing, the lawmakers actually had enormous power. Assemblies used this power routinely to augment their role in government. They might refuse essential appropriations or even withhold the governor's salary unless he went along with particular measures. Governors were sometimes forced to approve measures despite standing orders from England not to do so. A governor who deviated from his official instructions ran risks, but it was also risky to attempt to govern without sufficient funds. Why the government had been crippled by revenue shortfalls might be more difficult to explain than occasional departures from instructions.

Nor were assemblies above using their revenue powers to encroach upon the governor's prerogatives. Money might be withheld in order to influence or block the appointment of key officials. The New York assembly routinely voted salaries in the name of particular officials rather than for the office, and salary appropriations were usually for no more than a year at a time. This not only put pressure on the governor to appoint officials acceptable to the assembly but underscored for those appointed the importance of remaining on good terms with the lawmakers. Officials who angered their paymasters faced the undesirable prospect of working without salaries.

Popular Government

The colonial assemblies rose to power on the same wave toward popular government that propelled parliament to power in England. Americans saw a parallel in the struggle of their assemblies against particular governors and the struggle of parliament against royal absolutism. But the parallel was not seen in England, particularly after the conflict with monarchy had been won. The official view in England was that the colonial assemblies had no constitutional standing; they had only delegated authority that might be modified or withdrawn at any time. But this sort of thinking ignored completely the political reality that by the eighteenth century most Americans regarded their assemblies as colonial equivalents of the House of Commons.

The general trend toward popular government by no means made the colonies bastions of democracy. Voting was a privilege rather than a right, and there were numerous restrictions on political participation. Property qualifications for both voting and office-holding insured that only the most substantial citizens actually had a voice in government. Six colonies made the ownership of land a prerequisite for voting, and the rest tied the suffrage to the possession of either real or personal property. The system rewarded economic success, but it was by no means aristocratic or exclusionary. Land was so cheap and economic opportunities so numerous that voting qualifications could be met in most of the colonies without great difficulty. Nowhere in the eighteenth century, England included, did government rest upon a broader popular base than in the English colonies.

Besides property qualifications, some colonies had religious tests for voting. Only members of Puritan congregations could originally vote in most of the New England colonies, and five colonies (New York, Rhode Island, Maryland, Virginia, and South Carolina) at one time or another excluded Catholics from the suffrage. The bias against Catholics had more to do with politics than with their religious beliefs. Their support of the Stuart Pretenders after the Glorious Revolution made them politically suspect. Four colonies (New York, Pennsylvania, Rhode Island, and South Carolina) denied Jews the right to vote but did not discriminate against them otherwise. Catholics and Jews were by no means alone in being excluded from political affairs. Large numbers of apprentices and servants had no political voice or representation. And people living on the western frontier were seldom fairly represented in proportion to their numbers. Some districts were grossly underrepresented or not represented at all in the assemblies. But for all its shortcomings and imperfections, government in the English colonies probably reflected the popular will more closely than government anywhere else in the eighteenth century.

Colonial Courts

The checks and balances between the executive and legislative branches of government did not extend to the courts. The judiciary was the weakest branch of government in colonial times. Justice in the early settlements was originally dispensed by general governing bodies in the course of conducting other public business. Even after regular courts had been established, political and judicial functions remained intertwined. In Massachusetts the legislature was the highest court of appeals, while the county courts not only tried cases but performed numerous administrative functions. The governor and executive council of Virginia met twice yearly to try important cases and hear appeals from the lower courts. South Carolina had a Grand Council responsible for trying cases, managing public lands, and providing for the defense of the colony. Not until well into the eighteenth century were judicial matters separated from the other business of government.

Even after separate courts had been established they never became equal partners in government. Judges dared not forget that the governor who appointed them might remove them or that the assembly might withhold their salary. This did not necessarily undermine the administration of justice, but it kept the judiciary mindful of its subordination to the political branches of government. In some colonies judges served at the pleasure of the governor and in others during good behavior. The latter protected judges from arbitrary removal but not against reprisals by the legislature in the form of reduced or withheld salaries. After 1760, England adopted a policy of making judges more accountable to the executive branch, and governors were instructed to appoint them at pleasure in order to make them more politically responsive. This amounted to a double standard, because the 1701 Act of Settlement gave English judges life tenure during good behavior. The refusal of parliament to extend judicial independence to the colonies was later cited in the Declaration of Independence as one of the grievances justifying separation from England.

Political Thought in England and America

Political thought in the colonies was largely shaped by John Locke's natural rights theory of government. In his *Second Treatise of Civil Government* (1689), Locke justified the Glorious Revolution and parliament's final triumph over monarchy. He argued that all power flows from the people who first combined under a social compact to form society and then proceeded to adopt a political compact creating a particular form of government. The second compact could be altered or replaced without dissolving the first and sending people back to the state of nature. Since the purpose of the political compact was to protect life, liberty, and property, which Locke regarded as the natural rights of all people, any government that becomes destructive of these rights might justifiably be overthrown. Although Locke wrote specifically to justify the triumph of parliament in England, his theory of the right of revolution, as Americans understood it, justified resistance to any violation of natural rights, including violations by parliament.

John Locke on the Social Compact

"Whensoever therefore the *Legislative* shall . . . either by Ambition, Fear, Folly or Corruption, *endeavour to grasp* themselves, *or put into the hands of any other an Absolute Power* over the Lives, Liberties, and Estates of the People; By this breach of Trust they *forfeit the Power*, the People had put into their hands, for quite contrary ends, and it devolves to the People, who have a Right to resume their original Liberty, and, by the Establishment of a new Legislative (such as they shall think fit) provide for their own Safety and Security, which is the end for which they are in Society. What I have said here, concerning the Legislative, in general, holds true also concerning the *supreame Executor*, who having a double trust put in him, both to have a part in the Legislative, and the supreme Execution of the Law, Acts against both, when he goes about to set up his own Arbitrary Will, as the Law of the Society."

—*Second Treatise of Civil Government* (1689)

Figure I.8 Portrait of John Locke by Herman Verelst (1689).

© *National Portrait Gallery, London*

Few political theorists have had greater influence than Locke on constitutional government. The special place of life, liberty, and property in the hierarchy of human rights had been proclaimed before, most notably in Magna Carta, but never before as a principle of limited government that elevated the rights of ordinary citizens over the power of the state. Although his treatise specifically condemned the abuses of monarchy, no branch of government could run roughshod over natural rights without triggering the same right of revolution that had transformed England in the seventeenth century. These ideas not only settled into the bedrock of English constitutional thought but affected political thinking in France and America as well. All political ideas to some extent reflect the political change that shaped them. But in time, if they are rational and coherent, these products of change become agents of change. This is precisely why Locke's ideas proved so durable and adaptable, cropping up repeatedly in the Declaration of Independence, key provisions of the Constitution, and in the Due Process Clause of the Bill of Rights.

Next to Locke, Sir Edward Coke probably had the greatest influence on political and legal thought in America. Coke was the greatest English judge and legal scholar of the seventeenth century, and his commentaries on the common law influenced generations of American lawyers. Given the importance of lawyers in political life, this alone would have made him a powerful influence. But Coke's main contribution to constitutional thought in the colonies was his holding in *Dr. Bonham's Case* (1610) that parliament could not pass a valid law contrary to the constitution of England. The law in question had authorized the London College of Physicians to license the practice of medicine in London and to punish physicians who practiced in the city without a license. Coke invalidated the act on the ground that it was repugnant to the constitution for anyone to be tried and punished outside the courts of England. While parliament might be the highest lawmaking body, its legislative power had constitutional limits. Any measures that exceeded these limits were automatically null and void.

The principle asserted in *Dr. Bonham's Case* was essentially the right of the judiciary to strike down acts of parliament on constitutional grounds. Such a claim, dubious even in 1610, would be rendered politically untenable by the great constitutional changes of the seventeenth century. By the end of the century, a triumphant parliament that claimed to embody the national will recognized no limits on its powers. Acts of parliament were automatically constitutional because, as the voice of the nation, parliament could change even the constitution of England. The political upheavals of the seventeenth century turned *Dr. Bonham's Case* into an anachronism, a judicial precedent upon which no English judge would dare to rely. The Glorious Revolution had been precipitated in part by the king's suspension of laws passed by parliament. If a king could be deposed for suspending an act of parliament, what judge in England would dare declare any act of parliament unconstitutional?

While Coke's views on the limits of parliamentary power went largely unnoted in England, they were widely noted in the colonies. Most Americans subscribed to the idea that basic rights could not be abridged or taken away by any branch of government. Neither king nor parliament might lawfully abrogate the constitutional rights of the people. James Otis cited *Dr. Bonham's Case* in the 1760s in challenging the legality of writs of assistance. He declared that not even parliament could authorize search warrants that violated constitutional rights, and any attempt to do so would be null and void. This was precisely what Coke held in ruling for Dr. Bonham. His ruling was the opening shot in the movement for judicial review and the special role of the courts in protecting constitutional rights against the political branches of government.

No one contributed more to the transfer of English law across the Atlantic than the British jurist and legal scholar Sir William Blackstone. When his *Commentaries on the Laws of England* appeared in the 1760s, American subscribers turned the work into an instant bestseller. His four-volume treatise eventually sold more copies in America than in England, becoming the basic textbook for generations of American lawyers. Subscribers to the first edition included John Adams, James Iredell, John Jay, John Marshall, and James Wilson. Blackstone's approach to law was essentially Lockean, with heavy emphasis on the rights of persons, including the "absolute rights" of individuals with respect to life, liberty, and property. His ideas about law dovetailed with the political views of the emergent Revolutionary generation, particularly with respect to taxation and the rights of Englishmen under the British constitution.

The Legal Birthright of All Englishmen

"[The liberties of Englishmen] consist, primarily, in the free enjoyment of personal security, of personal liberty, and of private property. So long as these remain inviolate, the subject is perfectly free; for every species of compulsive tyranny and oppression must act in opposition to one or other of these rights, having no other object upon which it can possibly be employed. To preserve these from violation, it is necessary that the constitution of parliaments be supported in it's full vigor; and limits certainly known, be set to the royal prerogative. And, lastly, to vindicate these rights, when actually violated or attacked, the subjects of England are entitled, in the first place, to the regular administration and free course of justice in the courts of law; next, to the right of petitioning the king and parliament for redress of grievances; and lastly to the right of having and using arms for self-preservation and defence. And all these rights and liberties it is our birthright to enjoy entire . . ."

—Sir William Blackstone, *Commentaries on the Laws of England,*
Vol. I, Bk. I, Ch. I (1765)

Figure I.9 Portrait of Sir William Blackstone, artist unknown (c. 1755).

© *National Portrait Gallery, London*

Blackstone's *Commentaries* made English law more accessible and perhaps even saved the common law from possible extinction in America. His great and lasting achievement is that he succeeded in transforming the common law from a cacophony of case law into a logical and apparently harmonious system of substantive law with clear divisions of subject matter and themes. Volume 1 covers the rights of persons; volume 2, the rights of property; volume 3, private wrongs (torts); and volume 4, public wrongs, including crimes and punishments. Some scholars regard the *Commentaries* as crucial in transforming English law from an archaic writ-bound system mired in procedure into a modern comprehensive system of substantive law. The legal historian W.S. Holdsworth wrote that if the *Commentaries* had not appeared when they did, the United States probably would not have retained the common law. Many Americans of the late eighteenth century, including Thomas Jefferson, favored adopting a civil law system to finalize the break with England. In the early 1800s several states passed statutes barring the adoption of the English common law. That the trend did not take hold and displace the common law completely owes much to the influence of Blackstone's *Commentaries*.

The French political theorist the Baron de Montesquieu also contributed to American political thinking. His *Spirit of the Laws* (1748) argued that the political institutions of nations had to be consistent with their social and cultural life in order to function successfully. This sort of thinking held great appeal for Americans who desired to expand their own rights of self-government beyond the constraints imposed by Britain. Montesquieu also believed that abuses of power could be prevented by separating the functions of government with a built-in system of checks and balances. This would prevent any branch of government from becoming powerful enough to threaten the liberty of the people. Such ideas made particular sense to people whose political arrangements already featured an informal separation of powers. But more to the point, the separation of powers provided a useful rationale for the role in government claimed by the colonial assemblies.

Religious Toleration

Religious toleration became a fact of life in the English colonies at a time people in Europe were killing one another in the name of religion. The open-door immigration policy brought in so many denominations that mutual toleration was a practical necessity. Anglicans, Quakers, Baptists, Congregationalists, Dutch Reformed, Presbyterians, Lutherans, Methodists, Catholics, and Jews managed to live in peace regardless of what they thought of one another's beliefs. Although the English government sought to create an Anglican establishment in the royal colonies, Anglicans were a majority only in Virginia, Maryland, and South Carolina. Despite official support from England, the Anglican clergy had little influence on public policy in any of the colonies. Much more influential were the Congregational (Puritan) clergy of New England who in the seventeenth century were active partners in government. But even here freedom of conscience was respected because it was a tenet of faith among Puritans that matters of conscience were between God and the individual. Only those who proselytized or openly challenged the religious establish-ment faced the wrath of the Puritan state. But by the eighteenth century even Puritan ardor had cooled and religion gradually ceased being a public issue.

Some colonies adopted official declarations of religious toleration. Rhode Island showed the way in 1647 under a constitution guaranteeing both freedom of conscience and separation of church and state. Two years later, Maryland granted religious freedom to all Christians, except Unitarians, and in 1699 New Jersey guaranteed freedom of con-science to all its inhabitants. During the seventeenth century Puritan New England dealt harshly with Quakers and Baptists who proselytized, but no one was punished for pri-vately held beliefs. By the eighteenth century virtually all meddling ceased with regard to the religious convictions of individuals. Even colonies with official churches did not pre-vent members of dissenting denominations from worshipping freely. Although Catholics and Jews incurred civil disabilities, nowhere were they persecuted by the state for their religious beliefs.

Religious dissent sometimes had a sharp political edge. Many of the dissenting clergy disliked English political institutions as intensely as they detested the official Anglican religion. They were not above turning their pulpits into forums of political subversion. Long before Locke justified the right of revolution in his treatise on government, the New England clergy preached resistance to tyranny as a religious duty. In 1687 the Reverend John Wise was jailed in Massachusetts for urging resistance to a tax imposed by the gov-ernor without the consent of the legislature. The numerous sermons preached by gen-erations of clergymen on the virtues of limited government reinforced secular political beliefs. The ideology of revolution took hold in many of the dissenting congregations long before the first shots were fired at Concord and Lexington.

Freedom of the Press

Political sentiment in the colonies overwhelmingly endorsed the idea that a free press was indispensable to accountability in government. Unlike the licensed English press, the co-lonial press had to contend with no official constraints apart from the possibility of prose-cution for seditious libel for overzealous criticism of public officials. The tension between seditious libel and press freedom came into sharp focus in 1735 at the trial of John Peter Zenger for publishing articles critical of New York's Governor William Cosby. The trial was the culmination of a political feud that began when Cosby arrived in New York and proceeded to antagonize some leading members of the colony's political establishment. Cosby's powerful enemies promptly moved to arouse public opinion against him by en-gaging Zenger to wage a newspaper campaign exposing the abuses of his administration. They put up the money and wrote the articles for Zenger's *New-York Weekly Journal*, which from its first issue in 1733 became a thorn in Cosby's side. The upshot was that Zenger was arrested and charged with seditious libel.

The trial caused Cosby more harm than all the hostile newspaper articles combined. Andrew Hamilton, the brilliant attorney brought from Philadelphia to defend Zenger, turned the tables on the prosecution and made the governor's official misconduct the focus of the case. He argued persuasively that the articles were true and that no one should be punished for publishing the truth. Hamilton was well aware that this was not the law, because truth did not matter in a case of seditious libel. The only issue to be determined was whether the publication undermined respect for government. If it did, the defendant was guilty regardless of the truth of the publication. Moreover, it was up to the judges to determine as a matter of law whether the material was libelous; the only function of the jury in such cases was to determine who published the material. Since Zenger admitted publishing the articles, his conviction by judges controlled by Cosby seemed inevitable. But Hamilton refused to play by rules clearly stacked against his client. Disregarding instructions and warnings from the bench, he urged the jury to consider the truth of the articles and bring in a general verdict of acquittal that left nothing for the judges to decide. He coupled his argument with a powerful appeal for freedom of the press as a necessary safeguard against abuses by public officials. None of this had anything to do with seditious libel, but it was sufficient to persuade an already friendly jury to ignore the law and acquit Zenger.

Andrew Hamilton on Freedom of the Press

"[T]he Question before the Court and you, Gentlemen of the Jury, is not of small nor private Concern, it is not the Cause of a poor Printer, nor of *New-York* alone, which you are now trying: No! . . . It is the Cause of Liberty; and I make no Doubt but . . . by an impartial and uncorrupt Verdict, [you] have laid a noble Foundation for securing to ourselves, our Posterity, and our Neighbours, That, to which Nature and the Laws of our Country have given us a Right,—the Liberty—both of exposing and opposing arbitrary Power (in these Parts of the World, at least) by speaking and writing Truth."

—From *A Brief Narrative of the Case and Tryal of John Peter Zenger* (1736)

Figure I.10 Portrait of Andrew Hamilton by Adolph Ulrich Wertmüller (1808).

Independence National Historical Park

Zenger's acquittal did not change the law of seditious libel or establish modern press freedom in America. Truth did not become a legal defense in cases of seditious libel until well into the nineteenth century. But the case nevertheless had a powerful and immediate impact on attitudes about press freedom everywhere. The trial was widely reported both in the colonies and in England, and it destroyed Cosby's reputation. One English commentator remarked that while Hamilton's argument to the jury might not be the law, "it is better than law, it ought to be law, and always will be law wherever justice prevails." Zenger's acquittal went far to discredit the idea that public officials should have protection against criticism while in office. Moreover, Hamilton's trial tactics provided a model for attorneys in seditious libel cases. If playing by the rules did not work, defense counsel could appeal to the fairness and common sense of the jurors in urging jury nullification of the law. No matter what the law might be, juries could ignore it in particular cases regardless of instructions from the bench. Not a single conviction for seditious libel was recorded in any of the colonies following Zenger's acquittal. An important principle had been on trial, and, against heavy odds, the principle had prevailed.

Zenger's acquittal is attributable in part to progressive tendencies in the colonies that favored the rights of individuals over the power of government. Had he been tried in England, an acquittal would have been unlikely. Trial juries in the colonies had considerably more discretion with regard to the law because pressure from the Crown and royal judges to bring in convictions was not a factor in their deliberations. The broader political base of colonial government made jurors less vulnerable to official intimidation. It also fostered in the colonies a bottom-to-top political culture that by the late eighteenth century severely strained relations with England. The public celebrations occasioned by the verdict make it clear that people viewed the acquittal as more than the victory of a local printer over an unpopular governor. The accountability of government was at the heart of the case, and the verdict was a ringing endorsement of that principle. Jurors often represented the will of the community as effectively as members of the legislative branch, and jury nullification of the law in particular cases could deliver a clear political message. The message in Zenger's case carried all the way to London and resulted in Cosby's removal from office.

Note

1. See pages 26–30, 56–57, and 145–151 below.

March 1733	February 10, 1763	October 7, 1763	April 5, 1764	September 1, 1764	March 22, 1765
Molasses Act	Treaty of Paris Ends French and Indian War	Royal Proclamation Relating to Settlement and Organization of Britain's North American Territories	Repeal of Molasses Act; Enactment of Sugar Act	Currency Act	Stamp Act

December 16, 1773	March 31, 1774	May 20, 1774	June 2, 1774	June 22, 1774	September 5, 1774
Boston Tea Party	Boston Port Act	Massachusetts Government Act; Administration of Justice Act	Quartering Act	Quebec Act	First Continental Congress Meets in Philadelphia

II Independence and Nationhood

March 24, 1765	March 17, 1766	1767	March 5, 1770	June 10, 1772	May 10, 1773
Quartering Act	Repeal of Stamp Act	Townshend Acts	Boston Massacre; Partial Repeal of Townshend Acts	Burning of the *Gaspée*	Tea Act

May 10, 1775	July 8, 1775	August 23, 1775	January 1776	July 4, 1776
Second Continental Congress Meets in Philadelphia	Second Continental Congress Adopts Olive Branch Petition	George III Proclaims American Colonies in a State of Rebellion	Publication of Thomas Paine's *Common Sense*	Declaration of Independence

"[T]he people of the colonies are descendents of Englishmen. England, Sir, is a nation which still, I hope, respects, and formerly adored, her freedom. The colonists emigrated from you when this part of your character was most predominant, and they took this bias and direction the moment they parted from your hands. They are therefore not only devoted to liberty, but to liberty according to English ideas and on English principles."

—Edmund Burke, *Speech to Parliament on Reconciliation with the American Colonies* (1775)

Despite the shared tradition of political liberty, relations between England and the colonies took a bad turn after 1760 when the home government attempted to reform colonial administration. If prudently managed, reform might have improved colonial relations, particularly if the home government had recognized political realities in the colonies. The assemblies claimed rights not recognized by parliament, and parliament claimed powers not recognized by the assemblies. Most Americans assumed that their assemblies had a constitutional role in government not unlike the role of parliament in England, while parliament regarded the assemblies as mere institutions of convenience. The contradictions needed sorting out before the competing claims caused serious trouble. But the situation required caution and mutual respect, because any attempt to impose unilateral changes would only make matters worse. The colonies were no longer shaky outposts of empire in the wilderness; they had become thriving centers of population, wealth, and political power with claims that no sensible home government could safely ignore.

The French and Indian War

The French and Indian War, the colonial counterpart of the Seven Years' War in Europe (1756–1763), brought existing problems to a head and created serious new ones as well. In 1763 the home government established the Proclamation Line that excluded Americans from the vast territories won from France in Canada and the Ohio Valley. Since Britain had borne the brunt of the war in North America, the home government saw no reason to take the interests of the colonies into account in organizing the new territory. The war had been fought and won with troops and naval forces from Britain. Not only had there been meager colonial support, but some colonists on the northern frontier had carried on a profitable business selling supplies to the enemy. This helped to prolong resistance in Canada at the cost of British lives. Nor were colonial merchants above carrying on a lucrative trade with the French West Indies, which provided them with essential supplies that helped the French war effort. While most Americans had nothing to do with any of this illegal traffic, a resentful home government did not make fine distinctions. All Americans found themselves tarred by the disloyalty of a few.

The war convinced Britain that colonial relations had to change. Political ties had to be strengthened and the colonies integrated within the imperial system. While the British were probably right on the need for reform, they failed to understand that the cooperation of the colonial assemblies would be needed. Everything that subsequently went wrong can be traced to the failure to involve Americans from the beginning. There could be no real change in the ground rules unless Americans accepted the new relationship. Success demanded a willingness to accept the colonists as partners in a common enterprise. Not to do so would doom reform and call into question for many Americans the legitimacy of the British imperial system.

What made the case for caution particularly compelling was that the war had made Americans more assertive of their rights. The conquest of Canada, which ended the French threat to the northern colonies, had the effect of ending American reliance on British military protection. Americans who had no reason to fear foreign invasion had less reason to accept British interference in their internal affairs. Count Vergennes, the French foreign minister, correctly predicted what was likely to happen. The colonies "stand no longer in need of [England's] protection," he wrote. "She will call on them to contribute towards supporting the burdens they have helped to bring on her, and they will answer by striking off all dependence." If British leaders had been half as perceptive as the French minister, the colonies might not have been lost.

The burden Vergennes had in mind was the greatly increased public debt with which Britain emerged from the war. The conflict added approximately sixty million pounds to the already heavy public debt borne by British taxpayers, and most members of parliament were convinced that an American contribution was long overdue. The debt burden per person was twenty times greater in Britain than in the colonies, and the situation was no longer tolerable. The colonies had prospered under British protection for more than a century without paying a shilling to Britain for their own defense. But the time had now come for them to share in the costs of running an empire. The case for taxing Americans seemed so compelling that few in parliament took into account how the colonies might react. What they failed to realize was that the constitutional issues implicit in taxation had to be addressed before a shilling in revenue could be peaceably collected.

The tightening of colonial controls began even before the war had ended. It started with stricter enforcement of the laws regulating American commerce. While Americans never questioned the right of parliament to regulate trade, the regulations themselves were routinely violated by colonial merchants. Smuggling and the wholesale bribery of customs officials became an accepted part of doing business. Public opinion condoned such practices, because many in colonial society had an interest in the illegalities. Artisans and shopkeepers shared in the profits of the merchants, and the illegal trade brought in specie to pay for needed imports. The prosperity of many communities rested on the assumption that the trade laws existed to be honored in the breach. Why, after all, should Americans sacrifice their vital interests because of regulations made three thousand miles away and over which they had no control?

Tightening of Colonial Controls

The first signs of trouble appeared in the early 1760s when the home government ordered strict enforcement of the Molasses Act. This Act, passed in 1733, imposed a prohibitive duty on molasses and sugar imported from the French West Indies. So profitable was this trade that the law was virtually a dead letter from the beginning. News that the home

Complain and Smuggle, Smuggle and Complain

"During the late War, you *Americans* could not import the Manufactures of other Nations . . . so conveniently as you can in Times of Peace; and therefore, there was no Need of watching you so narrowly, as far as that Branch of Trade was concerned. But immediately upon the Peace, the various Manufactures of *Europe,* particularly those of *France,* which could not find Vent before, were spread, as it were, over all your Colonies, to the prodigious Detriment of your Mother Country; and therefore our late Set of Ministers acted certainly right, in putting in Force the Laws of their Country, in order to check this growing Evil. If . . . the Persons to whom the Execution of these Laws were intrusted, exceeded their Instructions; there is no Doubt to be made, but that all this will be rectified by the present Administration. And having done that, they will have done all that in Reason you can expect from them. But alas! the Expectations of an *American* carry him much further: For he will ever complain and smuggle, and smuggle and complain, 'till all Restraints are removed, and 'till he can both buy and sell, whenever, and wheresoever he pleases."

—Josiah Tucker, *A Letter from a Merchant in London
to His Nephew in North America* (1766)

government now intended to enforce it caused dismay throughout New England. The trade was vital to the region's prosperity. New England distilleries converted the imported molasses into rum, which was sent to Africa and exchanged for slaves, who were then transported to the West Indies and exchanged for specie and molasses. This was the infamous triangular trade from which colonial merchants reaped a golden harvest. Nothing matched its importance in generating profits for reinvestment and economic growth. Merchants in Massachusetts predicted ruin should the West Indian trade be disrupted. Importers would be unable to pay debts owed to British creditors, and capital would be unavailable for business expansion. The prospect of economic disaster hit New England like a thunderbolt.

The upshot was a storm of protests from Boston's leading merchants. Hard pressed to defend smuggling itself, they made the measures adopted for enforcement of the Act the key issue. Because smugglers were unlikely to be convicted by sympathetic local juries, parliament in 1696 had transferred jurisdiction in such cases to vice-admiralty courts where defendants did not have the right to a jury trial. This did not involve discrimination against colonial defendants, because persons accused of smuggling in England were tried the same way. But this did not prevent Massachusetts merchants from making an issue of the process. They loudly attacked the vice-admiralty courts for denying defendants a jury trial.

Writs of Assistance

Another issue exploited by the merchants was the use of writs of assistance to enforce the trade laws. Customs officials found ordinary search warrants almost useless in smuggling cases. They were issued by the courts only on evidence of wrongdoing and only for the search of specified premises for specific goods. Such warrants allowed smugglers time to remove the goods to a place not covered by the warrant. Customs officers needed authority to seize goods without warning in order to deal effectively with smuggling. Thus they turned to the writ of assistance, a general search warrant that allowed them to search any premises suspected of harboring smuggled goods. But the use of such warrants raised real constitutional issues which soon became the focus of opposition to enforcement of the trade laws.

Opponents of the writs charged that they violated traditional rights of privacy. A customs officer armed with a writ of assistance could enter any house, shop, or warehouse on mere suspicion that it contained smuggled goods. The writ got its name from the fact that it required law officers and even ordinary citizens to assist in its execution. Refusal to assist was punishable as contempt of court. Moreover, the writ never lapsed, as ordinary warrants lapsed, upon completion of the search. Once issued, it remained in force during and for six months after the reign of the monarch in whose name it had been issued. An officer with such a warrant had permanent and virtually unlimited powers of search and seizure.

Although writs of assistance had been used earlier in the colonies, they were never much of an issue until Britain moved to crack down on smuggling. They had been only a minor irritant during the period of lax enforcement, but strict enforcement of the trade laws now made them bitterly controversial. The death of King George II in 1760 gave opponents an opportunity to mount a legal challenge of their constitutionality. All writs outstanding at the king's death had to be renewed, and the applications for renewal were handled by the Massachusetts Supreme Court. The issue was joined when Charles Paxton, chief of customs for Boston, applied for new writs in the name of George III, and sixty-three local merchants opposed his application. They challenged the court's jurisdiction to issue such writs, arguing that only the English Court of Exchequer had the requisite jurisdiction. The argument so impressed Chief Justice Samuel Sewall that he ordered a special hearing on the issue at the next full term of the court.

When the full Court met in February 1761, the merchants were represented by Oxenbridge Thacher and James Otis, two of Boston's leading attorneys. Thacher's fame rested on his mastery of legal technicalities, while Otis was noted for his brilliant oratory. They made an excellent team. Thacher focused on the narrow jurisdictional issue, arguing that the acts of parliament authorizing colonial courts to issue the sort of writs ordinarily issued by the Court of Exchequer had neglected to give them the specific Exchequer jurisdiction needed to do so. He did not argue that parliament could not authorize writs of assistance in the colonies, only that the laws passed for that purpose were technically defective. When his turn came, Otis eschewed technical arguments and went straight to the heart of the constitutional issue. He denounced writs of assistance as "the worst instrument of arbitrary power, the most destructive of English liberty and the fundamental principles of law, that ever was found in an English law-book." Freedom from arbitrary intrusions by the state was an ancient liberty that could not be taken away by king or parliament. Citing Coke's holding in *Dr. Bonham's Case* (1610), he urged the court not to issue the writs on the ground that the act of parliament authorizing them was unconstitutional.

Otis argued, as Coke had argued in *Dr. Bonham's Case*, that parliament was bound by the constitution of England, and that laws passed in violation of the constitution were not enforceable in the courts. For the courts to enforce unconstitutional measures would put ancient liberties at the mercy of shifting majorities in parliament, and the constitution itself would soon become a rope of sand. But the Massachusetts Supreme Court declined Otis's invitation to a confrontation with parliament, and so Paxton got his writs. But Otis's arguments electrified the courtroom. John Adams later wrote,

> Every man of a crowded audience appeared to me to go away, as I did, ready to take up arms against Writs of Assistance. Then and there was the first scene of the first act of opposition to the arbitrary claims of Great Britain. Then and there the child Independence was born.

James Otis Argues Against Writs of Assistance

"In the first place, the writ is universal, being directed "to all and singular justices, sheriffs, constables, and all other officers and subjects"; so that, in short, it is directed to every subject in the King's dominions. Every one with this writ may be a tyrant; if this commission be legal, a tyrant in a legal manner, also, may control, imprison, or murder anyone within the realm. In the next place, it is perpetual; there is no return. A man is accountable to no person for his doings. Every man may reign secure in his petty tyranny, and spread terror and desolation around him . . ."

—February, 1761

Figure II.1 Portrait of James Otis, Jr. (1862).

Library of Congress, Prints and Photographs Division, LC-USZ62-48937

Adams recalled that he thereafter found it impossible to read "any section of the acts of trade without a curse." Otis's arguments had ignited in him "a spirit of combined resistance against the encroachments of unlawful power."

Storm Warnings

The uproar over writs of assistance should have alerted the home government that colonial rights would be fiercely defended. There were other storm warnings as well.

The Proclamation Act of 1763, the measure prohibiting settlement in the Ohio Valley, caused much resentment. Massachusetts and Virginia protested that the ban violated their charters, and land speculators in all the colonies were fierce in their denunciations. The Sugar Act of 1764 was also opposed because of its revenue features. While the Act reduced import duties on molasses, the fact that it was designed to produce revenue made it controversial. The colonial assemblies claimed the exclusive right to raise revenue. The Currency Act of 1764 also caused trouble. It prohibited the assemblies from issuing paper money, and it was passed to protect British creditors from being repaid with worthless currency. While the measure was primarily aimed at Virginia, all the colonies protested against it as unjustified meddling in their internal affairs.

The Stamp Act

But colonial resentments did not harden into organized political resistance until parliament passed the Stamp Act in 1765. The measure clearly violated rights claimed by the colonial assemblies. Americans were required to affix revenue stamps to legal documents, insurance policies, ships' papers, licenses, newspapers, almanacs, pamphlets, and even dice and playing cards. The Act taxed people directly and thus challenged the assemblies' control of public revenue. The Sugar Act also produced revenue, but that measure at least took the form of a trade regulation that masked its revenue features. But there was no mistaking the nature of the Stamp Act. It was taxation pure and simple, a direct challenge to rights enjoyed by the colonies for more than a century.

The Stamp Act united Americans as they had never been united before. It was denounced from Massachusetts to Virginia as a gross violation of constitutional rights. The right of British subjects to be taxed only by their elected representatives had been a

Figure II.2 Illustration from *The Pennsylvania Journal and Weekly Advertiser* (October 24, 1765) in protest of the Stamp Act.

Library of Congress, Prints and Photographs Division, LC-USZ62-242

settled constitutional principle since the seventeenth century. So it came as a shock that parliament, a body where colonials were not represented, should attempt to tax them. But parliament took the position that Americans were represented. Although not physically present, they were virtually represented in the sense that every member of parliament represented the whole English nation. Many parts of England had no representatives in parliament, but their interests were nevertheless taken into account when decisions were made. This view of things found little support in the colonies. Many dismissed the idea of virtual representation as nonsense and political humbug. The colonies were so large and contained so many interest groups that only actual constituency representation made sense. Since no Americans sat in parliament, it followed that parliament did not represent them.

> **The House of Commons Questions Benjamin Franklin on Taxation in the Colonies**
>
> Q. Was it an opinion in America before 1763, that the parliament had no right to lay taxes and duties there?
>
> A. I never heard any objection to the right of laying duties to regulate commerce; but a right to lay internal taxes was never supposed to be in parliament, as we are not represented there.
>
> —February, 1766

Parliament added fuel to the fire by passing the Quartering Act in 1765. The measure had been requested by General Thomas Gage, the military commander in America, when the revenue produced by the Sugar Act failed to cover military expenses. The Act required the colonial assemblies to provide British troops with barracks and supplies. A subsequent revision provided for the billeting of troops in taverns, barns, and uninhabited dwellings at the expense of the colonies. The colonies also had to pay for firewood, salt, candles, bedding, and rations of beer and rum for the troops. No taxes were imposed on the colonies, but the measure did impose a revenue burden. Parliament left it to the assemblies to determine how the revenue would be raised.

Most Americans regarded the Quartering Act as unnecessary and potentially dangerous. With the French gone from Canada, they no longer needed a large standing army to protect them. Quite the contrary, given the friction with England, the army might be used against them. In 1766 the Massachusetts assembly challenged the Act by refusing to appropriate money for the troops. A clash in New York City between townspeople and bayonet-wielding soldiers led the assembly to refuse an appropriation. Parliament retaliated by suspending the assembly's legislative powers, leaving New York temporarily without a lawmaking body. Most of the colonies resisted the Quartering Act in one way or another, some by voting appropriations without mentioning it, others by voting less than the amount requested.

But such concerns were minor compared with the Stamp Act. The colonists had long assumed that they could be taxed only by their elected assemblies. Now they faced the prospect of losing this basic right at the heart of constitutional government. Nor could parliament have chosen a more provocative form of taxation. The tax fell directly on lawyers, merchants, and printers, all of whom were politically important because of their ability to influence public opinion. Any form of taxation would have been objectionable, but none could have caused a greater uproar. The Act antagonized the groups and interests most likely to take the lead in organizing a united opposition.

The American Position

The Stamp Act almost immediately ignited debates about the nature of the ties between Britain and the colonies. One theory advanced by Daniel Dulany, a Maryland lawyer, held that there were constitutional limits on the power of parliament in America. While parliament had the right to regulate trade, even in ways that incidentally produced revenue, direct taxes could be imposed only by the colonial assemblies. Parliament's tax power could not be exercised in the colonies because Americans were not represented in parliament. Patrick Henry took a similar stand in the Virginia House of Burgesses. He persuaded the Burgesses to pass a set of resolutions endorsing the principle of no taxation without representation. He went even further and declared that Virginians had the right to manage all their domestic affairs without interference from Britain. Dulany's and Henry's views

The Colonial Response to the Stamp Act

"The Right of Exemption from all Taxes *without their Consent* the Colonies claim as *British subjects*. They derive this Right from the Common Law, which their Charters have declared and confirmed, and they conceive that when stripped of this Right, whether by Prerogative or by any other Power, they are at the same Time deprived of every Privilege distinguishing Free-Men from Slaves . . . On the other Hand, they acknowledge themselves to be subordinate to the Mother-Country, and that the Authority vested in the supreme Council of the Nation may be justly exercised to support and preserve that Subordination."

—Daniel Dulany, *Considerations on the Propriety of Imposing Taxes in the British Colonies* (1765)

"[T]he first adventurers and settlers of this His Majesty's Colony and Dominion of Virginia brought with them, and transmitted to their posterity, and all other of His Majesty's subjects since inhabiting this His Majesty's said Colony, all the liberties, privileges, franchises, and immunities, that have at any time been held, enjoyed, and possessed, by the people of Great Britain . . . [T]he taxation of the people by themselves, or by persons chosen by themselves to represent them, who can only know what taxes the people are able to bear, or the easiest method of raising them, and must themselves be affected by every tax laid on the people, is the only security against a burthensome taxation, and the distinguishing characterstick of British freedom, without which the ancient constitution cannot exist."

—*Virginia Resolves on the Stamp Act,* May 30, 1765

reached a wide audience through the colonial press. They were printed and quoted in every colony to justify resistance to taxes not approved by the representatives of the people. That Dulany would ultimately side with the loyalists and Henry with the patriots in the coming revolution only serves to underscore where conservatives and radicals stood on the issue.

Massachusetts led the resistance to the Stamp Act. On the motion of James Otis, the assembly sent a circular letter to the other assemblies proposing a meeting of representatives from all the colonies to assemble in New York City in October 1765 to consider measures to be taken in common. The Stamp Act Congress, as the meeting was called, was attended by delegates from nine of the colonies. The four colonies not represented were prevented by their governors from sending delegates, but their assemblies nevertheless agreed to be bound by the decisions made by the Congress. This was the first act of organized resistance to the home government. The Congress adopted resolutions denouncing taxation without representation and declaring that the colonists were not and could not be represented in parliament. A Declaration of Rights and Grievances, authored by John Dickinson, was adopted affirming the right of Americans to be taxed only by their elected representatives. Petitions were drawn up and sent to the king and parliament demanding repeal of the Stamp Act as well as repeal of restrictions that had been imposed on colonial commerce the previous year.

The Sons of Liberty

Resistance went beyond petitions and resolutions. Patriotic groups like the Sons of Liberty sprang up to prevent enforcement of the Stamp Act. While the leaders were sometimes persons of wealth and social standing, the rank and file came from the lower classes spoiling for a fight. The latter provided the bone and sinew needed to transform the ideology of resistance into forceful action. The Sons of Liberty forced stamp agents to resign their commissions and pressured merchants into boycotting British goods. Resistance sometimes turned violent. A Boston mob burned the records of the vice-admiralty court and ransacked the home of the comptroller of the currency. Chief Justice Thomas Hutchinson and others who dared support Great Britain were targeted for reprisals. The mob broke into Hutchinson's house and looted his library. The intimidation was so effective that by the time the Stamp Act went into effect in November 1765, every stamp agent in America had been terrorized into resigning.

Economic reprisals were organized to force repeal of the Act. The merchants of Boston, Philadelphia, and New York City adopted non-importation agreements virtually closing American markets to British merchants and manufacturers. Technically, the boycott was voluntary and involved no legal sanctions, but those who broke it faced reprisals. Fear of violence at the hands of the Sons of Liberty made enforcement remarkably effective. American imports from Britain fell by at least £600,000 in 1765, putting heavy pressure on parliament to repeal the Act. The loss of American markets cost thousands of British workers their jobs and created a clamor in Britain for repeal.

Repeal of the Stamp Act

Although repealing the Stamp Act was a bitter pill to swallow, parliament really had no choice. Resistance in the colonies made it clear that the tax could not be collected without using the army. No stamps had been sold, no revenue raised, and the colonies were on the brink of rebellion. The case for repeal became so compelling that even the king supported it. So in March 1766 parliament backed down, not only repealing the Stamp Act but reducing duties under the Sugar Act in order to make them more acceptable. The news was greeted in the colonies with rejoicing and public celebrations. Several towns collected funds for statues of the king and William Pitt, who had supported repeal in parliament. The boycott and the demonstrations ended, and most Americans looked forward to more harmonious relations with Britain.

But one cloud still darkened on the horizon. Parliament had not abandoned the idea of taxing the colonies. The Stamp Act had been repealed not because parliament accepted American constitutional arguments but because the boycott had caused economic hardship in Britain. On the same day it voted repeal, parliament passed the Declaratory Act making it clear that it had not budged on the constitutional question. The Act asserted parliament's "full authority" to bind the colonies "in all cases whatsoever" and rejected the American position that only colonial assemblies could impose taxes. Pitt, who had led the fight for repeal, deplored the Declaratory Act for keeping the controversy alive. For parliament to claim powers that could not be enforced was needlessly provocative and likely to cause future conflict.

Figure II.3 Print titled *A View of the Obelisk Erected Under Liberty-Tree in Boston on the Rejoicings for the Repeal of the Stamp Act 1766.* Allegorical images representing American resistance to the Stamp Act appear on each side of the obelisk as follows: "1. America in distress apprehending the total loss of Liberty. 2d. She implores the aid of her Patrons. 3d. She endures the Conflict for a short Season. 4. And has her Liberty restord by the Royal hand of George the Third." Images of members of the British government and royal family appear on each side of the obelisk.

Library of Congress, Prints and Photographs Division, LC-DIG-ppmsca-05479

The Townshend Acts

The restoration of order in the colonies did not solve Britain's debt problem. The problem worsened in 1767 when parliament reduced British land taxes. And again, despite the Stamp Act fiasco, parliament looked to the colonies for needed revenue. This time, however, taxes were imposed in the form of trade regulations rather than by direct taxation. The idea was the brainchild of Charles Townshend, Chancellor of the Exchequer. Because Americans had not questioned the right of parliament to regulate commerce, Townshend thought that revenue could be raised by taxing colonial imports. The Townshend Duty Acts, as the measures were called, imposed tariffs on paper, lead, glass, tea, and other goods imported in large quantities by Americans. The duties were expected to raise about £40,000 annually, and the money was earmarked by parliament to pay the salaries of the governors and other officials in the colonies. Customs officers were authorized to use writs of assistance to insure strict enforcement of the tariffs.

The American response should have been anticipated. The Townshend duties were denounced as disguised revenue measures that undermined the role of the assemblies in colonial government by putting the governors and other executive branch officials on the British payroll. John Dickinson best summed up the American position when he declared that revenue produced by trade regulations had to be merely incidental to the main purpose of regulation in order to be acceptable. If the real purpose was to raise revenue, then the regulations amounted to direct taxation. The Townshend duties did exactly that and were therefore as unconstitutional as the Stamp Act.

Figure II.4 Mezzotint of Charles Townshend by John Dixon, after Sir Joshua Reynolds (1770).

© *National Portrait Gallery, London*

Massachusetts again took the lead in organizing the opposition. A circular letter calling for concerted action was drafted by Samuel Adams and dispatched by the assembly to the other colonies. In the meantime, a Boston town meeting voted a boycott of some British goods, mostly luxury items, until the Townshend Acts were repealed. Boycotts were also organized in Providence and New York City. These local measures were soon endorsed by the assemblies of New Hampshire, Connecticut, and New Jersey. The resistance spread southward until every colony adopted some kind of boycott. The Stamp Act had taught Americans the effectiveness of economic pressure, and they now used it again to force repeal of the tariffs. In Philadelphia and New York City, imports from Great Britain fell to about one-sixth of pre-boycott levels.

The Boston Massacre

The Sons of Liberty again became active, using the tactics that had been successfully employed against the Stamp Act. There was so much mob violence in Boston that troops had to be sent from Halifax to restore order. The soldiers were insulted and taunted by the townspeople, and fights erupted that further inflamed public opinion. On March 5, 1770, a crowd threatening to overwhelm a troop detachment was fired upon, killing three outright and mortally wounding two other civilians. The radicals denounced the incident as a massacre, and a general uprising was averted only by the withdrawal of the troops from the city to the islands in Boston harbor. Clashes between soldiers and townspeople also broke out in New York City. When the Sons of Liberty attempted to prevent soldiers from posting broadsides, a riot erupted in which clubs, swords, and bayonets were used. No one was killed, but several on both sides were wounded. The incidents demonstrated how easily political opposition could turn into armed conflict.

The boycott and disorders finally forced parliament to concede that it had made another mistake. On the very day of the Boston Massacre, a bill was taken up for repeal of the Townshend Acts. The boycott not only prevented the collection of duties but seriously harmed the British economy. Even the king favored repeal, but there was still reluctance to repeal the Acts unconditionally. Americans might regard total repeal as tacit acceptance of their constitutional claims. So parliament left the tax on tea while repealing the other duties. It obviously sought to save some political face and put the colonies on notice that Britain still claimed the right to tax them. "I am clear there must always be one tax to keep up the right," the king wrote, "and as such I approve the Tea Duty." But the overall mood was conciliatory. Lord North, the new prime minister, pledged that no new taxes would be imposed and he allowed the Quartering Act to expire without calling for its renewal. Only the tax on tea remained, ticking away like a time bomb, and reminding Americans that the underlying issue of taxation remained unresolved.

Moderates vs. Radicals

Partial repeal of the Townshend Acts set off a sharp debate within the colonies. The merchants and shippers who had suffered most from the boycott now favored moderation;

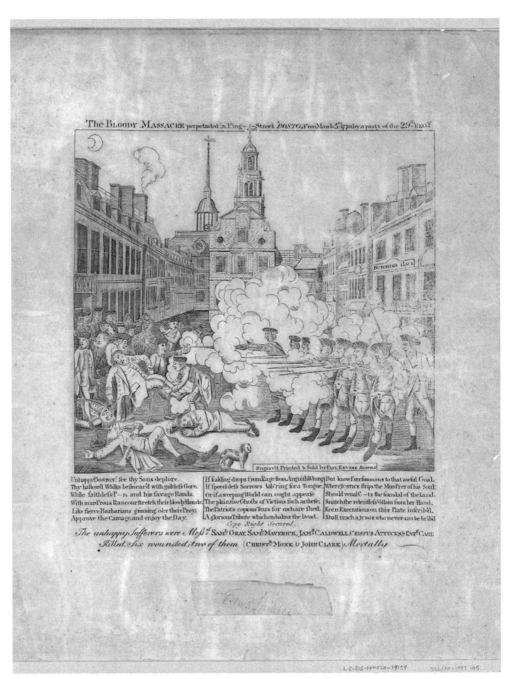

Figure II.5 Engraving titled *The Bloody Massacre Perpetrated in King Street Boston on March 5th 1770 by a Party of the 29th Regt.* by Paul Revere, Boston. Revere, best known for his midnight ride, was an important American craftsman, silversmith, and engraver prior to the War of Independence. Through this image, he helped popularize the events of the Boston Massacre among colonials.

Library of Congress, Prints and Photographs Division, LC-DIG-ppmsca-19159

they would limit the boycott to tea alone because the duties had been removed from everything else. A limited boycott would deny Britain the unconstitutional revenue while allowing untaxed trade to resume. But the radicals insisted upon full repeal before resuming normal relations. They argued that the constitutional rights of Americans would not be safe until parliament abandoned all efforts to tax them. Partial repeal was a step in the right direction but did not go far enough. Americans should not let their guard down, and the full boycott should continue until the last tax was off the books. The boycott had forced partial repeal, and it would soon bring total repeal if the colonies stood firm.

The moderates prevailed in the end, though the radicals were probably right. Only total repeal would have brought permanent reconciliation. But a house-by-house canvass conducted by the moderates in New York City showed that a large majority of the inhabitants favored easing the boycott. The Sons of Liberty challenged the count, claiming that less than half the townspeople had been polled, and Isaac Sears, a radical leader, threatened reprisals against merchants who resumed trade before the other colonies approved. The boycott nevertheless collapsed, and Philadelphia, Boston, and other commercial towns soon followed New York's example. The ban on British imports had caused hardship in the colonies, and most Americans favored relaxing it now that most of their goals had been achieved. Within a year, British imports more than doubled, leading many to believe that trouble with Britain was a thing of the past.

Moderates had reason to work for reconciliation. Many had reason to fear that political agitation in the colonies had gotten out of hand, and that radicals had gained too much influence. The moderates had joined the radicals in opposing parliament on the tax issue, but they had no wish to share power with them on a permanent basis. Most of the radical leaders came from outside the colonial political establishment, and they owed their importance to anti-British militancy. Complete reconciliation with Britain would end political turbulence, restore the status quo, and probably consign the radicals to oblivion. This was precisely what the conservatives and moderates wanted. They saw their own monopoly of political life threatened by street politics and mob violence. The radicals might even win control of the assemblies if the conflict with Britain continued. That would end the rule of the propertied class and put their interests at the mercy of the mob. Some conservatives were less concerned about what parliament had done in the past than with what the radicals might do in the future.

The radicals drew their support from groups with grievances against the ruling classes. Thousands of small farmers, shopkeepers, and artisans resented political domination by the social and economic elite. They resented the unequal representation, restricted suffrage, and unfair taxes to which they were subjected. Success in forcing repeal of the Stamp Act and Townshend Acts demonstrated that entrenched power could be defeated. The principles asserted against Great Britain seemed equally relevant at home. The idea of no taxation without representation had special meaning for the disfranchised workers and farmers who had to pay taxes voted by assemblies in which only the upper classes were represented. They saw no reason to halt their political activity just because the goals of the moderates had been achieved. Indeed, the situation demanded even greater militancy to insure that the gains won would not be lost.

Several issues still remained to keep anti-British sentiment alive. The home government kept troops stationed in the colonies; the trade laws were being more strictly enforced; and parliament still claimed the power to tax Americans. The radicals exploited every grievance and made inflated claims of American rights. Samuel Adams, leader of the Massachusetts radicals, not only denied the right of parliament to impose taxes but also its right to interfere in the internal affairs of the colonies. He declared that Americans had a constitutional right to self-government in matters not involving external relations. Patrick Henry, the Virginia radical, took a similar stand, asserting that the colonies had from the beginning "the inestimable Right of being governed by such Laws, respecting their internal Polity and Taxation, as are derived from their own Consent." Such claims put conservatives on the defensive. Rejecting them seemed unpatriotic, but endorsing them meant taking positions that would make complete reconciliation with Britain impossible.

The *Gaspée* Affair

In 1772 an outbreak of mob violence in Rhode Island dealt the moderates a sharp setback. Rhode Island merchants carried on an extensive business in untaxed tea smuggled in from Holland, and the *Gaspée*, an armed schooner, was sent into Rhode Island waters to halt the illegal trade. Lieutenant William Dudingston, its commander, soon made himself notorious by his vigorous enforcement of the trade regulations. Many questioned the legality of his decision to send property seized in Rhode Island to the vice-admiralty court in Boston for condemnation. The fact that he profited personally from the condemnations did not help matters. Dudingston for a time had to keep his ship at sea in order to avoid local lawsuits arising from his conduct. An opportunity to square accounts came when the *Gaspée* ran aground on a sandbar near Providence. A mob from the town boarded and looted the *Gaspée*, wounded Dudingston, and burned the ship.

The attack was denounced in Britain as an act of treason. An irate home government appointed a commission of inquiry and offered a reward of £500 for apprehension of the culprits. Those responsible would be brought to England for trial, apparently because local juries could not be trusted to bring in a conviction. The plan to try the case in England caused protests even among Rhode Islanders who deplored the incident. The right to a local grand jury hearing was so fundamental that it could not be waived without compromising other constitutional rights. But the issue was rendered moot by the inability of the commission to uncover any evidence. Although their identities must have been well known, witnesses could not be found to testify against those involved. The commission ran into a wall of silence and had to report failure.

Relations with Britain got another jolt in 1772 when news reached Massachusetts that the governor and judges would henceforth be paid directly by the Crown. The assembly would no longer control their salaries. This upset the balance of power in government by making the executive and judicial branches independent of the legislature. Samuel Adams urged immediate resistance, and a committee of correspondence was set up at Boston to keep in touch with radicals in other towns and colonies. Massachusetts soon had a network of committees for concerted political action. The idea quickly spread among radicals in other colonies. In 1773 the Virginia assembly appointed a committee to correspond

A Son of Liberty on the Gaspée Affair

"A court of inquisition, more horrid than that of Spain or Portugal, is established within this colony, to inquire into the circumstances of destroying the Gaspée schooner; and the persons who are the commissioners of this new-fangled court, are vested with most exorbitant and unconstitutional power. They are directed to summon witnesses, apprehend persons not only impeached, but even suspected! and them, and every of them, to deliver them to Admiral Montagu, who is ordered to have a ship in readiness to carry them to England, where they are to be tried . . . Is there an American, in whose breast there glows the smallest spark of public virtue, but who must be fired with indignation and resentment, against a measure so replete with the ruin of our free constitution? To be tried by one's peers, is the greatest privilege a subject can wish for; and so excellent is our constitution, that no subject shall be tried, but by his peers."

—Samuel Adams ("Americanus"), *Providence Gazette* (December 26, 1772)

Figure II.6 Portrait of Samuel Adams by John Singleton Copley (c. 1772).

Photograph © 2013 Museum of Fine Arts, Boston Oil on canvas, 125.73 × 100.33 cm, Museum of Fine Arts, Boston, deposited by the City of Boston (L-R 30.76c)

with other colonies, and assemblies everywhere followed suit. By February 1774, only North Carolina and Pennsylvania had not set up standing committees. Whatever happened now, the radical response would be swift and united.

The Tea Act

Despite radical gains, the moderates and conservatives still firmly controlled the colonial assemblies. What the radicals lacked was an issue that would unite public opinion behind them. There had been no great unifying issue since the repeal of the Townshend Acts. They finally got their issue in 1773 in the form of the Tea Act, a measure passed by parliament to save the British East India Company from bankruptcy. The Act authorized the company to sell tea in the colonies through its own agents and consignees instead of through colonial middlemen. This gave the company a virtual monopoly of the tea market by enabling it to undersell both legal merchants and smugglers. Although the company tea would carry the import duty left over from the Townshend Acts, it would still sell at bargain prices. While consumers in the colonies would get cheap tea, colonial merchants, retailers, and smugglers faced economic ruin.

The Tea Act handed radicals a winning issue. Even conservatives were appalled at its economic implications. Not only would it put colonial merchants out of the tea business but, if successful, it might lead parliament to grant similar monopolies to other companies and drive them out of business completely. Commerce played a key role in the colonial economy, so the issue was easy for ordinary citizens to understand. The issue also had a political aspect which the radicals were quick to exploit. They accused parliament of trying to tempt Americans with tea so cheap that the unconstitutional tea duty would not be noticed. If the strategy worked, other taxes would surely follow. Thus taxation again became an issue, one that would propel the radicals to power.

The Boston Tea Party

Conservatives and radicals joined forces to keep the company tea out of the colonies. This was essential both to prevent the duty from being paid and to protect consumers from the temptation to buy cheap tea. A mass meeting in Philadelphia forced the company's consignee to resign, and mob threats produced the same results in Charleston and New York City. Mobs also forced the tea ships to leave Philadelphia and New York City and return to England without unloading. The radicals prevailed everywhere except Boston,

Figure II.7 Mezzotint titled *A New Method of Macarony Making, as Practised at Boston* (1774). This print depicts two men, one identifiable as a Son of Liberty by the bow in his hat, tarring and feathering a British customs officer. The eighteenth-century epithet "macaroni" referred to a man who dressed in an ostentatious or flamboyant manner.

Library of Congress, Prints and Photographs Division, LC-USZ62-45386

where the company's consignees fled to Castle William in the harbor and refused to re-sign. Moreover, Governor Thomas Hutchinson took a hard line and refused to allow the tea to be sent back to England until the duty had been paid. The Sons of Liberty also took a hard line. Between fifty and sixty of them forcibly boarded the tea ships and dumped their cargoes into Boston harbor. The incident put an end to conciliation and polarized relations between Britain and the colonies.

The Intolerable Acts

The Boston Tea Party brought harsh reprisals from Britain. Parliament was shocked how far British authority had eroded in the colonies. Mobs controlled the major cities, and or-derly processes of government had broken down. Unless the lawless elements were sup-pressed and order restored, the colonies might spin out of control completely. So during the spring and summer of 1774 parliament passed the Coercive Acts, a series of repressive measures that Americans dubbed the Intolerable Acts. One, the Boston Port Act, pun-ished the entire city for the destruction of the tea. Boston was closed to commerce until the East India Company was compensated for its loss. Another, the Administration of Justice Act, provided that British officials charged with capital crimes in the course of suppressing riots or enforcing the trade laws should be sent to England for trial if the governor thought a fair trial could not be held in Massachusetts. A third measure, the Massachusetts Government Act, completely reorganized the provincial government. The governor was granted additional powers, and the authority of the assembly was sharply reduced. No public meetings could be held without the governor's consent, and even then they had to stay within the approved agenda.

Parliament also passed the Quebec Act and the Quartering Act, which although not coercive, Americans considered intolerable. The first extended the boundary of Canada southward to the Ohio River and westward to the Mississippi. It centralized power in the hands of a council appointed by the king and gave the Catholic clergy a privileged position in Canadian society. The political and clerical provisions were completely contrary to En-glish traditions, and the boundary arrangements violated the charter claims of several col-onies to territory in the Ohio Valley. Massachusetts, Connecticut, and Virginia protested that the new boundaries were unlawful. The Quartering Act was even more objectionable. It provided for the billeting of troops not only in taverns and vacant buildings but in oc-cupied dwellings as well. These arrangements would allow troops to be stationed in the towns where they could be used to suppress mob violence quickly. The forced billeting of troops in private households seemed final proof that parliament meant to ride roughshod over the rights of Americans.

The home government sent General Gage to Boston to replace Hutchinson as gover-nor, a clear signal that the army would be used to restore order. On the day of his arrival, a Boston town meeting approved a proposal of the radicals for a boycott of British goods until the Intolerable Acts had been repealed. Fearful that an immediate boycott might make a political settlement impossible, the conservatives tried to buy time. The threat of boycott was a powerful bargaining chip, but using it prematurely might slam the door on reconciliation completely. Moreover, if a boycott failed, Americans would then have to choose between abject submission or armed resistance. In order to create an opportunity for tempers to cool, the merchants of Philadelphia and New York City proposed that the colonies send representatives to a congress to consider measures to be taken in common for the redress of grievances. The Massachusetts assembly approved the proposal and suggested that the congress meet in the fall of 1774 in Philadelphia.

First Continental Congress

Georgia was the only colony not represented when fifty-six delegates from the colonies convened in September for the First Continental Congress. The numerical balance between radicals and moderates was about even, but the radicals were better organized and more effectively led. They scored a major victory with the adoption of Joseph Warren's Suffolk Resolves declaring the Coercive Acts unconstitutional. The Resolves advised the people of Massachusetts to ignore the Acts and form a new government. The radicals also pushed through a non-importation agreement known as the Continental Association. The Association took the form of a pledge by the delegates that their colonies would boycott British goods, discontinue the slave trade so profitable to Britain, and halt all exports to England, Ireland, and the West Indies. Adoption of these measures left little room for political maneuver; parliament could either back down or face the economic consequences. Committees were to be elected in every town and county to enforce the Association and to punish violators by publicity and social ostracism. Any colony refusing to join the Association would itself be boycotted.

The importance of the Continental Congress went beyond the measures adopted. It served notice on Britain that the colonies stood united and that an attack on one would be resisted as an attack on all. The Congress also gave colonial leaders their first real exposure to national politics. Delegates from different colonies learned to work together and form alliances on particular issues. Radicals from Massachusetts discovered that they had more in common with Virginia radicals than with Massachusetts conservatives. "The more We conversed," John Adams wrote, "the more We were encouraged to hope for a general Union of the Continent." The idea of a national union, though still inchoate, first appeared at the Congress. Before adjourning in October, the delegates voted to meet again in May of the following year if American grievances had not been redressed.

Meanwhile, the situation in Massachusetts went from bad to worse. British authority was openly defied as the radicals made preparations for armed conflict. Thousands of militiamen marched on Cambridge in September when British troops seized military supplies belonging to the colony. No fighting had yet broken out, but General Gage began to fortify Boston. Defying the Massachusetts Government Act, the assembly met in October and proclaimed itself a Provincial Congress. It took over executive functions belonging to the governor and delegated them to a Committee of Public Safety. Thus the colony had two governments: the legal one headed by the governor and an extralegal one which wielded more real power. Gage's power did not reach beyond the troops under his command. The situation had deteriorated so badly that in February 1775 parliament declared Massachusetts to be in a state of rebellion. Two months later fighting broke out at Concord and Lexington, plunging the colony into armed conflict.

Second Continental Congress

When the Second Continental Congress met in May, the delegates had few options. Thousands of militiamen besieged the British in Boston, and the other New England colonies had already voted to assist the rebels. Indeed, the conflict had spread beyond New England. Forces from Vermont seized Fort Ticonderoga in New York on the day the Congress convened. So there was never any doubt that the delegates would stand by their embattled countrymen. They promptly voted to join in the struggle and authorized the raising of a Continental Army with George Washington as commander in chief. They also voted two million dollars in bills of credit to cover the cost of military operations. But amidst these preparations for war, Congress made one last appeal for a political settlement. The so-called Olive Branch Petition was sent to the king urging him to halt the fighting while there was still time. The delegates affirmed their loyalty to the Crown while denouncing parliament for forcing them into armed resistance. The resistance would cease, they declared, if the king curbed parliament and redressed their grievances.

The appeal to the king was based on a theory rapidly gaining ground in the colonies about relations with England. This was the idea that the colonists owed allegiance to the king alone and that parliament had only limited jurisdiction over them. It was argued that the colonial assemblies had complete control of taxation and other internal affairs, subject only to the king's veto. Americans took the position that parliament, not the king, had caused the trouble, and that their loyalty to the Crown remained intact. This was a politically safe and self-serving position, because the Crown posed no threat to colonial rights. Affirming their loyalty to the king probably also reassured Americans that their resistance stopped short of treason.

But the refusal of George III to receive the Olive Branch Petition demolished any pretense that the colonies were not in a state of rebellion. This was a tactical mistake on the king's part because it cut the ground from under the Americans who still hoped for a political settlement. They were left with no option but armed resistance. Congress appointed a committee to fit out warships, authorized two battalions of marines, and issued letters of marque and reprisal for the seizure of British ships. A committee was even appointed to solicit foreign military assistance, an incongruous move for supposedly loyal subjects of the king. Still, Congress persisted in the fiction that only parliament was the villain, a fiction that at least kept the door open for a possible political solution.

The door remained open for more than a year, but the force of events made a political settlement increasingly difficult. British forts and arsenals were seized, Canada invaded, and the royal governors driven from the colonies. By the end of 1775 the whole structure of colonial government had collapsed, and only a semblance of the old system remained. The colonial assemblies reconstituted themselves into provincial congresses or conventions with no ties to Britain. The colonies became independent and self-governing states in everything but name. Sentiment for independence, once the dream of only ultra-radicals, spread rapidly among all classes of people. The anomaly of avowing loyalty to the king while resisting his authority could not be ignored indefinitely. It fostered confusion at home and made it difficult to form foreign alliances, particularly with the French whose assistance was desperately needed. A war for American rights within the British Empire had much less appeal to France than one to disrupt the Empire.

Declaration of Independence

Thousands of Americans were converted to the idea of independence by Thomas Paine's famous pamphlet *Common Sense*. The pamphlet was one of the most remarkable and influential best-sellers in American history. It sold perhaps as many as 500,000 copies at a time the country probably had fewer than three million people. No author has ever reached a greater proportion of the population. When the pamphlet appeared in January 1776, many in Congress already favored independence. But most of the general public remained uncertain and confused. While constitutional rights clearly had to be defended,

Severing the Tie with Britain

"Ye that tell us of harmony and reconciliation, can ye restore to us the time that is past? Can ye give to prostitution its former innocence? Neither can ye reconcile Britain and America. The last cord is now broken, the people of England are presenting addresses against us. There are injuries which nature cannot forgive[.]"

—Thomas Paine, *Common Sense* (1776)

Figure II.8 Portrait of Thomas Paine by Matthew Pratt (c. 1785–1795).

Kirby Collection of Historical Paintings, Lafayette College, Easton, PA

a complete break with England might not be possible or even desirable. Paine's arguments made the case for independence politically compelling. He rejected the idea that Americans had no grievances against the king, the one remaining hope for redress and reconciliation, denouncing him as a "Royal Brute" whose machinations were responsible for the unconstitutional measures passed by parliament. By discrediting the king, he discredited the basis for a political solution.

Congress took up the issue during the spring of 1776. North Carolina took the lead by instructing its delegates to vote for independence. On June 7, Richard Henry Lee of Virginia proposed a formal resolution that "these United Colonies are, and of right ought to be, free and independent States." On July 2, Congress voted to adopt Lee's resolution after an intense debate dominated by the radicals. The actual drafting of the Declaration of Independence, formally adopted two days later, was the work of Thomas Jefferson. Only a few minor changes were made in his draft before its adoption. The Declaration, though at the time only a political document framed to rally support for independence, is perhaps the most important document of American constitutional history. It set forth with stirring clarity not only the reasons for the break with Britain but the principles to which American committed themselves as a free and independent nation.

In drafting the Declaration of Independence, Jefferson drew heavily upon John Locke, so much so that Richard Henry Lee, one of the document's signers, remarked that most of it might have been "copied from Locke's Treatise on Government." The influence of Lockeian social compact theory is certainly clear enough in the Declaration's assertion that "Governments are instituted among Men, deriving their just powers from the consent of the governed . . . [W]henever any Form of Government becomes destructive of these ends, it is the Right of the People to alter or to abolish it." What Americans were doing had happened before. As in late seventeenth-century Britain, the Crown's attempt to govern arbitrarily without the consent of the governed had resulted in its loss of political legitimacy.

The grievances enumerated in the Declaration reiterate many of the complaints listed in the English Bill of Rights of 1689. Both documents include a litany of the Crown's crimes against its subjects, holding the king personally culpable for offenses against liberty and for abuses of power. Both also denounce the quartering of troops among civilians, violations against the jury system, and the imposition of taxes without the approval of the people's representatives. Most important of all, both documents justify the overthrow of arbitrary government by recognizing the governed as the ultimate source of legitimate political power. The similarities between the two documents would not have been lost on Americans acutely aware of their constitutional heritage. The Declaration of Independence proclaimed their commitment to the same traditions of liberty and limited government vindicated in Britain a century earlier by the Glorious Revolution.

March 1, 1781	September 3, 1783	March 1785	May 20, 1785	August 1786	September 1786	May 25, 1787
Articles of Confederation	Treaty of Paris Ends Revolutionary War	Mount Vernon Conference	Land Ordinance	Outbreak of Shays's Rebellion	Annapolis Convention	Constitutional Convention Convenes in Philadelphia

April 1788	May 1788	June 1788	July 1788	November 1789	May 1790
Maryland Ratifies the Constitution	South Carolina Ratifies the Constitution	New Hampshire and Virginia Ratify; the Constitution Goes Into Effect	New York Ratifies the Constitution	North Carolina Ratifies the Constitution	Rhode Island Ratifies the Constitution

III   A More Perfect Union

July 13, 1787	September 17, 1787	October 27, 1787	December 1787	January 1788	February 1788
Northwest Ordinance	Signing of the Constitution	First of *The Federalist* Papers Appears	Delaware, Pennsylvania, and New Jersey Ratify the Constitution	Georgia and Connecticut Ratify the Constitution	Massachusetts Ratifies the Constitution

"The people in America have now the best opportunity and the greatest trust in their hands that Providence ever committed to so small a number since the transgression of the first pair."

—John Adams (1787)

For all its clarity and eloquence as a statement of national principles, the Declaration of Independence articulated no new ideas about government. John Adams, a member of the drafting committee, commented on its lack of originality, noting "there is not an idea in it but what has been hackneyed in Congress for two years before." The political philosophy of the Declaration can be traced to John Locke, whose views on government held sway in America long before the break with England. Some of its ideas predated Locke, going back across the centuries to the Magna Carta and the guarantees of the early English common law. The Declaration was essentially a restatement of principles long held by Americans and to which they now recommitted themselves as an independent people.

State Constitutions

The Declaration triggered a wave of political reorganization at the state level. Even before its adoption by the Continental Congress, several colonies had severed all political links with Britain. The rest now followed suit, adopting constitutions as sovereign and independent states. Connecticut and Rhode Island accomplished this simply by deleting references to British authority from their colonial charters. The others got new constitutions which, with only one exception, were promulgated by the provincial congresses and conventions that had assumed power at the outbreak of hostilities. Only Massachusetts held a constitutional convention and submitted the document to the voters for ratification. The need for written charters of government was taken for granted by all Americans, their colonial experience having taught them to trust no other political arrangements.

John Adams on the Drafting of State Constitutions

"[W]e had a people of more intelligence, curiosity, and enterprise, who must be all consulted, and we must realize the theories of the wisest writers, and invite the people to erect the whole building with their own hands, upon the broadest foundation . . . [T]his could be done only by conventions of representatives chosen by the people in the several colonies, in the most exact proportions . . . [I]t was my opinion that Congress ought now to recommend to the people of every Colony to call such conventions immediately, and set up governments of their own, under their own authority; for the people were the source of all authority and original of all power."

—Autobiography

Figure III.1 Portrait of John Adams by Henry Houston (c. 1797).

National Portrait Gallery, Smithsonian Institution / Art Resource, NY

While honoring the separation of powers in principle, the new state constitutions made the legislative branch the dominant branch of government in practice. This was partly because legislatures were by far the most trusted branch of government, but also because the legislators who drafted them had no desire to relinquish power. They had been the popular branch of government during the colonial period, defending local interests against an executive branch controlled by Britain. All the states except Pennsylvania provided for bicameral legislatures similar to those of the colonial era. The lower house was more frequently elected than the upper, and property qualifications for voting and holding office were lower. Most of the real power was exercised by the lower house, which controlled both taxation and appropriations. Its prototype was the colonial assembly, which had also governed through the power of the purse.

The memory of arrogant royal governors made the Revolutionary generation distrustful of the executive branch. There was no desire to replace them with powerful officials who might develop similar tendencies. New Hampshire and Pennsylvania provided for plural executives instead of a single governor, and most of the other states subordinated their governors to the legislature. In five states the entire legislature elected the governor, and in two he was chosen by the lower house alone. Most states limited the governor to a single one-year term, gave him no veto, and made the legislature a partner in executive appointments. The executive branch was strongest in the four states where governors were elected by the people. Only two states, Massachusetts and New York, allowed them to veto measures passed by the legislature. Distrust of the executive branch caused Pennsylvania to write a warning against "the danger of establishing an inconvenient aristocracy" into its state constitution.

Every state had property qualifications for voting and holding public office. Some made the payment of taxes sufficient, but most required ownership of specific amounts and kinds of property. The right to vote in Virginia, for example, was limited to owners of twenty-five acres of settled land or five hundred acres of unsettled land. North Carolina made just being on the tax rolls sufficient to vote in elections for the lower house but required ownership of fifty acres to vote for candidates to the upper house. Property qualifications for holding public office usually varied with the office. New Jersey and Maryland required at least one thousand pounds for candidates to the upper house and only half as much for candidates to the lower house. The highest property qualifications were set for the office of governor. The flagrant avarice of some royal officials during the colonial era suggested that only the most substantial citizens could be trusted with the office. In South Carolina, where the property test was highest, candidates for governor had to be worth at least £10,000.

Although the judiciary was more independent than in colonial times, it remained inferior to the political branches of government. Judges were appointed either by the legislature or with its approval, but thereafter could be removed only for official misconduct. The appointment of judges at the pleasure of the Crown had been a grievance listed in the Declaration of Independence, and the new state constitutions put an end to the practice. Judicial tenure for fixed terms or during good behavior became the rule, giving judges a degree of independence that would have been unthinkable in colonial times. Fixed terms for judicial tenure ran from one year in Connecticut and Rhode Island to seven in New Jersey and Pennsylvania. Judges appointed for only one year obviously had less independence than those appointed for seven, but at least they could not be removed until their year expired. While the fear of not being reappointed may have influenced some, most displayed an independence that would have been difficult in colonial times. In 1786 and 1787 the courts of Rhode Island, New Jersey, and North Carolina overturned state laws on the ground that they violated their respective state constitutions. This established judicial review at the state level more than a decade before John Marshall extended it to the federal government.

All the state constitutions contained a bill of rights, usually in the form of a preamble at the beginning of the document. Many of the rights listed had long been taken for granted by Americans as part of their English constitutional heritage. These included guarantees that no one would be deprived of life, liberty, or property without due process of law; the right to a jury trial; the rule against double jeopardy and compulsory self-incrimination; the right to bail and the protection of habeas corpus; and the prohibition of cruel and inhuman punishments. Some rights, such as freedom of speech, press, and religion, were products of the colonial period. Others are traceable to Revolutionary idealism. The new state constitution of Vermont outlawed slavery, and the Massachusetts bill of rights declared, "All men are born free and equal," a provision later construed by the state supreme court to abolish slavery. These lists of fundamental rights and declarations of principle set limits on government beyond which those in power could not venture without risking the loss of legitimacy.

The Articles of Confederation

The adoption of state constitutions left only the central government without a constitutional mandate. The second Continental Congress was only a de facto government whose powers might be modified or cancelled by the states at any time. Many Americans had reservations about the desirability of a permanent central government. But this state of affairs made it difficult for Congress to manage the war and deal with foreign governments effectively. So when Richard Henry Lee proposed his resolution for independence in 1776, he also proposed that Congress prepare a plan for creating a de jure federal union for submission to the states. A committee headed by John Dickinson was appointed to work on the project, and a draft entitled "Articles of Confederation and Perpetual Union" was submitted to Congress on July 12, 1776. But military setbacks and more urgent matters delayed formal consideration until the fall of 1777 when Congress finally gave its full attention to the Articles.

Many Americans doubted the wisdom of establishing a permanent central government. A wartime union of the states was obviously needed, but making the union "perpetual" might not be a good idea. The whole thrust of the Revolution was against central authority and toward local government. Many feared central government as the natural enemy of individual liberty. The problem was systemic. Every central government regardless of form tends to become arbitrary as power is concentrated beyond the reach of the people. Parliament, the popular branch of government in England, at a distance of three thousand miles had become a form of tyranny in America. Because the country was so large, any central government set up here would be similarly difficult to control. Having rid themselves of one central authority, Americans could not be blamed for hesitating to replace it with another.

While agreeing on the need for a de jure federal union, Congress divided sharply on such issues as representation and taxation under the proposed Articles. Delegates from the larger states argued for proportional representation based on population, while those from the small states insisted upon equal representation for the states. The principle of state equality finally prevailed when it became clear that the small states would accept no other arrangement. The tax issue was resolved by leaving the tax power completely in the hands of the states. The Confederation government would have authority to requisition taxes, but only the states could actually levy and collect them. The requisitions would be apportioned according to the value of all the land granted or surveyed by the states, which meant that the states would contribute according to their ability to pay. But since the Confederation government could not enforce its requisitions, its revenues would depend on the willingness of the states to comply.

The most difficult obstacle of all turned out to be the western land claims of some of the states. Six states claimed extensive territory on the basis of their colonial charters, and one, New York, claimed most of the Northwest on the basis of its jurisdiction over the lands of the Iroquois Indians. The six states without any western claims naturally had doubts about the wisdom of a permanent union with states that might one day become super-states. The delegates from these states argued that the western lands should be ceded to the Confederation government in order to provide it with a source of revenue and keep all the states within their current boundaries. They pointed out that the western lands were not actually controlled by the states claiming them, and that the war effort of all the states would be needed to wrest them from the British. Therefore it was only fair that all states should share in the benefits as well as the burdens of the struggle. But such arguments fell on deaf ears. Before voting to accept the Articles of Confederation, the land-rich states forced Congress to agree that nothing would be done to limit their western claims.

Congress finally approved the Articles on November 15, 1777 and sent them to the states two days later for ratification. Most of the states ratified them within a year, but Maryland announced that it would withhold approval until the western lands had been ceded to the Confederation government. Virginia's offer to donate all the land needed to pay for military bounties failed to win Maryland over. So the deadlock continued until early 1780 when New York broke ranks and agreed to cede its land claims to the new Confederation government. When Connecticut ceded its claims in October, the others came under heavy pressure to fall into line. The war itself might yet be lost if the states

Constituting the United States of America

Art. I. The Stile of this confederacy shall be "The United States of America."

Art. II. Each State retains its sovereignty, freedom and independence, and every Power, Jurisdiction and right, which is not by this confederation expressly delegated to the United States, in Congress assembled.

Art. III. The said States hereby severally enter into a firm league of friendship with each other, for their common defence, the security of their Liberties, and their mutual and general welfare, binding themselves to assist each other, against all force offered to, or attacks made upon them, or any of them, on account of religion, sovereignty, trade, or any other pretence whatever.

—The Articles of Confederation (1781)

squabbled prematurely over the spoils of victory. Virginia finally yielded, ceding its claims in January 1781, whereupon Maryland ratified the Articles. Congress made ratification official on March 1, and the new government went into effect the following day.

The Confederation Government

Although the United States now had a constitution, the new government in some ways remained indistinguishable from the old. Substantively, the Articles did little more than legalize the existing central government. The second Continental Congress now became the Congress of the Confederation, but its organization and powers remained essentially the same. Its authority did not go much beyond what the colonies had considered proper for king and parliament. It could declare war, make peace, manage foreign relations, establish post offices, standardize weights and measures, regulate Indian affairs, and deal with piracy. But since the states controlled taxation, it was difficult for Congress to exercise even these delegated powers without state approval. The states also retained control of foreign and interstate commerce, thus undercutting the Confederation's ability to deal effectively with foreign governments.

The Articles made no provision for the separation of powers found in the state constitutions. Such provisions were not needed, because the Confederation government was too weak to require formal checks and balances. Each state had one vote in Congress, and a supermajority of nine out of thirteen was required for decisions on such important matters as declaring war, borrowing money, and raising armed forces. The executive functions of government were delegated to departments appointed by and accountable to Congress. A committee consisting of one delegate from each state managed things between sessions of Congress, though it could not act in matters requiring more than a simple majority.

The Confederation government was also weakened by the absence of a judiciary. The state courts had to be relied upon to enforce laws passed by Congress. This undermined central authority because of the natural tendency of the state courts to favor their own laws when conflicts arose. Nor could the Confederation government be strengthened by interpreting its delegated power broadly. Article II specifically limited its functions to powers "expressly" granted, a limitation precluding any possible claim of implied powers. Further complicating matters, the government could not realistically be strengthened by constitutional amendment. Article XIII required the consent of all the states for amendments, which had the practical effect of making the constitution virtually unamendable. A single state could hold the welfare of the entire nation hostage to its own local interests.

Still, the Articles of Confederation changed the course of American history. Their adoption marked the beginning of a federal union that has endured for more than two centuries. The Articles also contained many innovative features that prepared the way for the Constitution adopted in 1787. Article IV provided for the interstate extradition of fugitives from justice, guaranteed the right of free movement across state lines, and provided for full faith and credit among the states with regard to public acts and judicial decisions. Article XIII anticipated the Supremacy Clause of our present Constitution, declaring that "the Articles of this Confederation shall be inviolably observed by every state, and the union shall be perpetual." The Articles turned what had been a wartime coalition of independent states into a lasting federal union.

Successes and Failures of the Confederation

The Confederation government scored some notable successes. It prosecuted the war against Britain successfully and handled wartime diplomacy with considerable skill. The Treaty of Paris ending the war in 1783 was negotiated and ratified by Congress, not by the states. This was the single most important treaty in American history and the single greatest achievement of the Confederation government. Britain not only recognized the independence of the former colonies but ceded to them vast western territories between the Allegheny Mountains and the Mississippi River. The territorial provisions set the stage for the ultimate expansion of the United States across the continent to the Pacific Ocean. American history would have been vastly different had Congress settled for less.

The two most important peacetime achievements of the Confederation government also related to the western territories. One was the Land Ordinance of 1785 passed by Congress for the disposition and settlement of the western lands. The Ordinance was passed primarily to raise money, because land sales were the only reliable source of federal revenue. The states were slow in paying their tax requisitions, so land had to be sold to cover the expenses of government. The Ordinance provided for the division of the western lands into townships of thirty-six sections, each section containing 640 acres. Section 16 in every township was reserved for the support of public education, and several sections were reserved for the United States. The land would be surveyed and then sold at auction in parcels of townships and sections at a minimum price of one dollar an acre. Since the minimum purchase required an outlay of at least $640, then a considerable sum of money, the plan favored investors and speculators over actual settlers. Nevertheless, the surveys and sales created marketable land titles and opened the West to settlement. The system worked so well that it remained the basic public land policy of the United States until the Civil War.

Congress also made arrangements for the government of the western territories. In 1787 the Northwest Ordinance was passed for the territories north and west of the Ohio River. Settlers in these territories were guaranteed religious freedom, the right of habeas corpus, jury trial, and the protection of the common law. Cruel and unusual punishments were prohibited, as were slavery and involuntary servitude except as punishment for crime. Politically, the territory would go through three stages of development. In the beginning, all power would be vested in a governor, secretary, and judges appointed by Congress. Then, when the population of a territory reached five thousand adult males, the settlers would elect a legislature and send a delegate to Congress. The delegate would participate in debates but not have the right to vote. Finally, when the total population reached sixty thousand, the settlers would draft a state constitution and apply to Congress for admission to the Union. If Congress approved, the territory would become a state on an equal footing with the original thirteen states.

The importance of the Northwest Ordinance cannot be exaggerated. It established policies for the national territories which would be followed by the United States for more than a century. The decision to prepare the western territories for statehood was by no means automatic. They could have been kept under Confederation control permanently as political dependencies of the national government. But that course was rejected both on grounds of principle and as an invitation to trouble. The war against Britain had demonstrated the pitfalls of colonialism, and Congress wisely decided against turning the territories into colonial dependencies. By conceding the right of self-government from the beginning, Congress guaranteed the integration of the West within the existing political system. The Ordinance also gave a gloss of legitimacy to future westward expansion. Territories acquired by the United States would not be inhabited by subject peoples but by citizens whose rights matched those of people in any part of the nation.

Problems with Great Britain

The worst failures of the Confederation government came in the field of foreign affairs. The Treaty of Paris bound Congress to recommend that the states compensate loyalists for property confiscated during the war and to remove legal impediments to the recovery of pre-Revolutionary debts owed to British creditors. When several states ignored the recommendations, the British charged bad faith and refused to withdraw their garrisons from the Northwest. Since the decision not to withdraw had been made before the Treaty went into effect, the charge of bad faith was really just a pretext to remain. Many in Britain believed that the Confederation would collapse and that British control of the Northwest would then become permanent and enable Britain to control the lucrative fur trade of the territory. This trade, which amounted to about a million dollars a year, made the occupation profitable in the short term even if the Northwest could not be held permanently.

Britain's postwar trade policies were hostile and costly to American commerce. American ships were barred from the British West Indies, and the export of rum, sugar, and molasses to the United States was prohibited. Moreover, American lumber and agricultural products were excluded from Britain in order to protect the market for Canadian imports. These measures created serious problem because the United States had to export raw materials and farm produce in order to pay for needed imports. The fact that most of the manufactured goods imported came from Britain should have given the United States leverage in negotiating trade concessions. But that was not the case, as John Adams discovered when he arrived in London to secure a trade treaty and withdrawal from the Northwest. The British refused to make any concessions. They had no reason to fear reprisals from a government without power to regulate commerce or money to pay for a military expedition against their garrisons in the Northwest.

"There is no truth more clear to me than this, that the great interest of our two countries is a thorough reconciliation. Restraints on the freedom of commerce and intercourse between us can afford no advantage equivalent to the mischief they will do by keeping up ill humour and promoting a total alienation."

—Benjamin Franklin to David Hartley, September 6, 1783

Figure III.2 Portrait of Benjamin Franklin by Edward Fisher (c. 1763–1785).

Library of Congress, Prints and Photographs Division, LC-DIG-ppmsca-09851

Problems with Spain

Equally serious problems existed with Spain. The Treaty of Paris fixed the boundary of Spanish Florida at the thirty-first parallel, but Spain claimed territory at least a hundred miles north of this line. The territory claimed included most of the land west of Georgia and south of the Cumberland River. Like the British in the Northwest, the Spaniards maintained military posts in the disputed territory and incited the Indians of the Southwest against American settlers. While Spain's ultimate goal was control of the entire territory, there were short-term goals as well. The fur trade of the Southwest was highly profitable and helped pay for the military occupation. And should the Confederation collapse, the territory would become permanently Spanish. No matter what happened in the long run, Spain had much to gain and nothing to lose in opposing the United States.

Control of the lower Mississippi and the port of New Orleans gave Spain a powerful weapon against the United States. The Treaty of Paris granted Americans the right of navigation on the whole Mississippi, but that right meant nothing unless New Orleans could be used as a port of deposit. Western farmers in the Ohio Valley sent their goods downriver to New Orleans for shipment by ocean vessels to eastern markets. When Spain revoked the right of deposit in 1784, the West faced economic ruin. The revocation posed a greater threat to American interests than anything that had yet happened on the frontier. The hostility of the Indians had slowed but not halted the influx of settlers. The opportunities offered by the frontier made the risks worth taking. But the closing of the Mississippi meant an end to the economic progress and promise of a better life that attracted settlers in the first place.

Westerners appealed to Congress for assistance in reopening the Mississippi. In 1785 John Jay, the Secretary for Foreign Affairs, opened negotiations with Diego de Gardoqui, the Spanish minister to the United States. But Jay had nothing to offer in return for the concessions sought. Moreover, Gardoqui had orders from Madrid not to yield on the boundary question or the closing of the Mississippi. The best Jay could get was a treaty providing some benefits for American shipping but which contained a proviso that the Mississippi would remain closed to Americans for twenty-five years. The proviso threw the West into an uproar. Westerners felt that they had been betrayed for the benefit of the commercial interests of the East. Some favored severing ties with the Confederation and dealing with Spain directly. Fortunately for the Union, the southern states, which had close ties with the West, forced Congress to drop the treaty. While this ended the immediate threat of western secession, the problems with Spain remained unresolved.

The angry reaction of the West sent a clear signal that clashing sectional interests might wreck the Union. Eastern leaders had apparently been willing to sacrifice the interests of the frontier for trade concessions from Spain. Westerners came out of the affair deeply alienated. George Rogers Clark, John Sevier, James Wilkinson, and other western leaders began negotiating with Spain directly. Wilkinson actually shifted allegiance and accepted Spanish subsidies to promote western secession from the Confederation. The idea had powerful appeal to people convinced that the interests of the East and West were basically irreconcilable. "The western settlers," George Washington wrote in 1785, "stand as it were on a pivot. The touch of a feather would turn them any way." The future of the nation also stood on that pivot.

Domestic Troubles

The domestic problems facing the United States were just as serious as the foreign ones. The country had been fairly prosperous during the Revolution, but the end of the war brought an economic downturn. With military needs no longer absorbing surpluses, farmers found themselves trapped in a cycle of oversupply and falling prices. Manufacturers lost their wartime markets completely. Cheap British manufactures flooded the country and drove many of them out of business. Merchants found themselves excluded from normal markets by hostile British trade policies. While British goods flooded American markets, Americans had only limited access to British markets. Staggering trade deficits resulted, and specie rapidly left the country to pay for imports. The ratio of imports to exports was roughly three to one, and the difference had to be made up in gold and silver. In 1784 alone nearly $15 million in specie left the United States to pay for British imports. The imbalance called for trade controls, but the Confederation government could not regulate commerce.

The loss of specie greatly reduced the money supply, sending the country into a deflationary spiral that sharply reduced the general price level. Some classes benefited while others suffered. Debtors who had borrowed to buy goods, tools, or land at peak prices now had to repay their creditors with scarcer money of much greater purchasing power than the money borrowed. The deflation caused widespread suffering among farmers, tradesmen, and workers who found it difficult to pay their taxes and other obligations. The creditors, on the other hand, stood to make windfall profits at the expense of their debtors. The latter turned to their state legislatures for relief. They demanded the issuance of paper money to replace the specie that had left the country to redress trade imbalances. They also demanded the postponement of debt payments to prevent foreclosures until the economy revived.

Such proposals were denounced by creditors as confiscatory, but they nevertheless prevailed in seven states. The debtors scored their greatest successes in states with the most democratic political systems. In Rhode Island, where the lower house was elected every six months, the legislature issued a flood of paper money. When the creditors refused to accept it, a law was passed making it legal tender and refusal became a criminal offense. The law further provided for trial without jury, "according to the law of the land," for those refusing to accept paper money. In *Trevett v. Weeden* (1786) the Rhode Island Superior Court struck this provision down on the ground that the right to a jury trial was the law of the land. One of the judges denounced the whole law as unconstitutional. The judiciary was the only branch of government with the resolve to resist the clamor for debt relief.

Shays's Rebellion

Disreputable elements in society exploited the grievances of hard-pressed debtors for purposes of their own. The idle and shiftless agitated for the outright cancellation of all debts and for the redistribution of property. The New Hampshire militia had to be called out to keep order when the legislature refused to give in to the debtors' demands. In 1786 mob violence erupted in western Massachusetts when the lawmakers adjourned without authorizing more paper money or protecting homes and farms against foreclosure. Armed bands prevented the courts from holding foreclosure proceedings. One of the leaders, Daniel Shays, a former captain in the Continental Army, tried to seize the arsenal at Springfield, but his forces were repulsed by state militia. This turned the tide against the rebels, and order was finally restored early in 1787. The uprising sent a shockwave through the entire country. What had happened in Massachusetts could happen anywhere, and the next time the outcome might be different. Moderates and conservatives everywhere began to think seriously about the possibility of class insurrection.

The disorders convinced many that a stronger central government was needed to back up the state governments in such emergencies. Massachusetts had appealed to the Confederation government for help against the Shays rebels, but the Confederation could do nothing. Standing alone without any prospect of outside assistance, most of the states had shown themselves to be vulnerable to mob pressures. Some had given in and appeased the agitators with laws undermining the rights of creditors. But paper money and debt postponements only sharpened the appetite of malcontents whose real goal was the redistribution of private property. All in all, there had been a serious erosion of values and loss of political will under the weak Confederation government. It was in fact a phantom government without real power, and its weakness reduced respect for government at every level. Many feared a slide into anarchy unless the process was reversed by strengthening government at the center.

A Contemporary Reflects on Shays's Rebellion

"The people, thrown suddenly into passion, whilst this paroxysm, whilst this fit of insanity continues, commit a thousand enormities . . . Had the commotion, which Shays excited in Massachusetts, happened in a state of *small territory*, what would have been the probable consequences? Before the people had recovered from their madness, perhaps all would have been lost."

—John Stevens, Jr., writing as Americanus,
Daily Advertiser (New York), November 2, 1787

Figure III.3 Engraving titled *Looking Glass for 1787* by Amos Doolittle. A wagon symbolizing the state of Connecticut, loaded with debt, is depicted sinking in mud. "Federals" and "Antifederals" pull it in opposite directions while the driver exclaims, "Gentlemen this Machine is deep in the mire and you are divided as to its releaf."
Library of Congress, Prints and Photographs Division, LC-USZC4-1722

But the obstacles to a stronger government seemed almost insuperable. Nothing could be achieved by attempting to amend the Articles, because amendments required the approval of all the states. Several attempts had been made, and none succeeded in getting unanimous consent. In 1781 Rhode Island and Virginia blocked a proposal to authorize Congress to impose a five percent import duty for the purpose of paying the national debt. A similar amendment was proposed in 1783, and this time a single state, New York, voted it down. In 1784 a proposal to grant Congress power to regulate foreign commerce for fifteen years was defeated by the southern states. Any of these amendments would have been a step in the right direction, but all failed because of petty and sometimes parochial opposition. New York, for example, had opposed federal import duties because its landowners feared higher land taxes if the state gave up customs revenues to the Confederation government. The system in some cases held the whole nation hostage to the selfish interests of the few.

Proponents of political change had to wage an uphill battle against defenders of the status quo. Opponents of a stronger national government believed that only local government could be kept under popular control. The more remote the levers of power, the more likely power would be wielded by the social and economic elite. Many ordinary citizens had cause to fear strengthening the federal government at the expense of the states. Debtors, for example, were more likely to get relief from their own legislatures than from a Congress too far away to be pressured. Keeping power at home seemed so obviously in the interest of the many that the odds heavily favored the status quo.

But proponents of change made up in political skill what they lacked in numbers. The movement for strengthening the central government had the support of Alexander Hamilton, George Washington, James Madison, and others with impeccable political credentials. Moreover, they did not have to win over a mass electorate in order to promote their agenda. Broad popular support was not needed in the 1780s to effect major political changes. Property qualifications for voting and office holding put control of public affairs firmly in the hands of the middle and upper classes. The enfranchised part of the population could make changes regardless of the wishes of the disfranchised classes. Changing the system would not be easy, but it would be much easier than if the masses had been a serious political factor.

Mount Vernon Conference

Movement toward a stronger central government began in 1785 when commissioners from Maryland and Virginia met to discuss navigation problems on Chesapeake Bay and the Potomac River. The negotiations were completed at Mount Vernon, where Washington acted as host, and the commissioners issued a joint request that their legislatures invite Pennsylvania to participate in establishing a water link between Chesapeake Bay and the Ohio River. Maryland not only approved but proposed including Delaware; Virginia went even further and proposed a meeting of all the states at Annapolis to discuss uniform rules of commerce. Nothing was said about changing the Articles of Confederation, but the need for concerted state action on matters of national importance was hardly a vote of confidence for the status quo.

Although nine states accepted the invitation, only five were actually represented when the Annapolis Convention met in 1786. The delegates elected John Dickinson as chairman, but nothing substantive was accomplished because of the small representation. Instead, the Convention called upon the states to send delegates to a convention to be held at Philadelphia the following year for the purpose of proposing constitutional changes. This went well beyond the Annapolis agenda and raised for the first time the prospect of sweeping political reforms. The proposed convention would not be limited to commercial discussions but would consider broad proposals "to render the constitution of the Federal Government adequate to the exigencies of the Union." The resolution was sent to Congress and the governors of every state for official action.

The proposal was strongly supported by advocates of political change and equally opposed by defenders of the status quo. Virginia and New Jersey approved the plan without much difficulty, and the other states soon followed their lead and appointed delegates to attend the convention. The response at the state level left Congress no alternative but to endorse the idea as well. The endorsement emphasized, however, that the convention was to meet "for the sole purpose of revising the Articles of Confederation, and reporting to Congress and the several legislatures such alterations and provisions therein." Since any proposed revisions would require the consent of Congress and ratification by all the states, nothing radical was expected to come out of the convention. This assumed of course that the delegates stayed within their official mandate. Rhode Island, anticipating that they might not, rejected the proposal and refused to participate in the convention.

The Philadelphia Constitutional Convention

Rhode Island's absence caused hardly a ripple when the delegates arrived in Philadelphia in 1787. The assemblage included the most distinguished statesmen and political leaders in America. Twenty-nine of the fifty-five delegates present had attended college, over half were lawyers, and the rest were drawn from the ranks of the merchants, planters, and professional people. Some had broad experience in government. Thirty-nine had served in Congress, eight had signed the Declaration of Independence, and seven had been governors of states. The delegates elected George Washington, the most revered person in America, as president of the Convention. Other luminaries included Benjamin Franklin, George Mason, Edmund Randolph, Gouverneur Morris, James Wilson, John Dickinson, Roger Sherman, Alexander Hamilton, William Patterson, Oliver Ellsworth, and Elbridge Gerry. Together, they represented the greatest gathering of political talent in American history.

While the delegates agreed on the need for a stronger central government, they disagreed sharply on the nature and extent of the changes needed. Although there were no formal alignments, most of the delegates could be accurately characterized as either nationalists or supporters of states' rights. The nationalists, who included Madison, Hamilton, Wilson, and Morris, favored a major shift of power from the states to the federal government. The states' rights delegates, led by Patterson, Sherman, and Ellsworth, sought to keep any increases of federal power within the framework of state sovereignty.

Figure III.4 *Washington as Statesman at the Constitutional Convention* by Junius Brutus Stearns (1856).

Virginia Museum of Fine Arts, Richmond. Gift of Edgar William and Bernice Chrysler Garbisch. Photo: Katherine Wetzel. © Virginia Museum of Fine Arts

Both sides shared the same conservative views, and both deplored the drift of public affairs under the weak Confederation government. They differed only on how much change was needed. The states' rights delegates performed a valuable service by keeping the trend toward nationalism within bounds. The existing system probably could not have been changed without the compromises they forced upon the nationalists.

The Virginia Plan

Because some delegates arrived late, the Convention began eleven days behind schedule on May 25, 1787. The Virginia delegates, having arrived earlier, used the delay to draft their own plan for a strong federal government. The plan, which was largely the work of Madison, called for a bicameral congress with proportional representation in both houses based on population or taxes paid, a national executive appointed by Congress, and a federal judiciary, also appointed by Congress, whose members would serve during good behavior. Congress would have power to legislate on all matters with national ramifications, as well as power to invalidate state laws in conflict with the federal Constitution. The executive would enforce federal laws and handle the administrative details of government. There would also be a council of revision consisting of the executive and several federal judges who together could suspend state or federal laws deemed by them to be unwise. Finally, the use of force was authorized against states which acted against the national interest.

The Virginia Plan went far beyond the Convention's mandate from Congress. It called for a massive transfer of power under a new constitution that would make the Union national rather than federal in character. The plan completely ignored the Articles of Confederation, though the purpose of the Convention was supposedly to propose changes in the Articles. Edmund Randolph, who presented the plan to the Convention, began with a denunciation of the Confederation government for failing to protect essential national interests. The country needed a new constitution, he declared, "to provide for the common defense, security of liberty, and general welfare." Randolph did not have to remind the delegates of the obvious fact that nothing could be accomplished by trying to amend the Articles. A single state could block changes, and Rhode Island's refusal to send delegates signaled the fate awaiting any amendments proposed by the Convention. Unless the delegates acted boldly, their deliberations would be an exercise in political futility.

While the idea of a new constitution had broad support, the Virginia Plan itself sharply divided the Convention. The delegates from the small states rejected proportional representation as a device for handing control of the new government over to the large states. The arrangement would all but obliterate the small states as political entities. The delegates from the small states agreed that a stronger federal government was needed, but they saw no reason it had to be created at the expense of the political equality of the states. The proposal for proportional representation had more to do with strengthening the position of the large states within the union than with increasing federal power. The result would be a unitary national state with the ability to trample the interests of the smaller states.

The New Jersey Plan

Opponents of the Virginia Plan rallied behind an alternative plan proposed by the New Jersey delegation. This called for a unicameral congress in which the states would be represented equally. Congress would have power to levy import duties, regulate foreign and interstate commerce, and allocate taxes among all the states on the basis of population. There would be a plural executive appointed by Congress and removable by Congress at the request of a majority of state governors. There would be a federal judiciary appointed by the executive to serve during good behavior. State courts would be bound to enforce federal laws and treaties in case of conflicts with state laws. Finally, the federal government might use armed force if necessary to compel submission to federal authority.

Although both plans strengthened the federal government, the differences between them were enormous. The Virginia Plan called for a truly national government standing on a broad popular base, while the New Jersey Plan rejected popular representation in favor of the existing system of equal voting by the states. The Virginia Plan proposed a single national executive not accountable to the states, while the New Jersey Plan called for a plural executive removable by a majority of the states. The Virginia Plan called for an extensive system of federal courts, while the New Jersey Plan provided for only one federal court of limited jurisdiction and relied instead upon the state courts to enforce federal laws and treaties. After three days of heated debate, the Convention rejected the New Jersey Plan and voted to organize a federal government along the lines of the Virginia Plan.

The Connecticut Compromise

Defeat of the New Jersey Plan did not end the debate over representation in congress. The plan for a bicameral Congress passed without difficulty, but the small states still bitterly resisted the idea of proportional representation. The deadlock was finally broken by a compromise proposed by Roger Sherman of Connecticut (hence the Connecticut Compromise), which called for proportional representation in one house of Congress and equal representation in the other. The House of Representatives would be popularly elected on the basis of the total number of free inhabitants of the states plus three-fifths of the slave population, and the Senate would consist of two senators from each state who would be elected by their state legislatures. The three-fifths formula for representation in the House was an accommodation between the North and South. The latter had wanted slaves to be counted fully in apportioning representation, and the former had sought to limit representation to free inhabitants. So, in effect, they split the difference. However politically necessary it may have been at the time, this fractionalization of people by race and class augured ill for the future of the country.

The Connecticut Compromise did not please everyone. Madison argued until the end for proportional representation in the Senate as well as in the House of Representatives. Voting equality for the states was a mistake, he declared, for state boundaries were accidents of history and had nothing to do with the real interests of the country, which were regional and national in character. To allow an appointed Senate bearing no relation to population or property to thwart the will of an elected majority was not a good basis for government. While Madison was right in theory, he may have underestimated the practical need for compromise on the issue. Americans who equated state government with popular government were not yet ready for a truly national state where majority rule prevailed. The task of the Convention was not to draft a perfect constitution but rather one that could be ratified. Without the compromise with respect to Congress, there would have been little chance of ratification.

The operational details of the new government were hammered out in the course of debate. Members of the House of Representatives would serve for two years, senators for six, and the president for four years. Congress would have power to impose duties on imports but not on exports, to tax imported slaves at no more than ten dollars a head, and to prohibit the importation of slaves completely after 1808. The president might veto bills passed by Congress, but the veto could be overridden by a two-thirds majority in both houses. The three-fifths formula for representation in Congress also became the basis for apportioning direct taxes among the states. These arrangements were not the product of political theory. They were pragmatic compromises needed to defuse real conflicts that might have wrecked the Convention.

Slavery and the Constitution

The Three-Fifths Compromise had as much to do with proportional representation as with the future of slavery in the United States. Antislavery delegates to the Convention feared that counting slaves for the purpose of representation would give Southern states an indirect incentive to continue importing and acquiring new slaves. The more slaves a state had, the more representatives it could send to Congress; and the more representatives slave states sent to Congress, the less likely the slave trade would be abolished in the new nation. Besides, the law of Southern states classified slaves as chattel property and not as human beings. Antislavery delegates pointed out the paradox of representing slaves at the federal level when they were not represented in state governments.

Gouverneur Morris Opposes the Three-Fifths Compromise

"Upon what principle is it that the slaves shall be computed in the representation? Are they men? Then make them Citizens and let them vote. Are they property? Why then is no other property included? . . . The admission of slaves into the Representation when fairly explained comes to this: that the inhabitant of Georgia and S.C. who goes to the Coast of Africa, and in defiance of the most sacred laws of humanity tears away his fellow creatures from their dearest connections & damns them to the most cruel bondages, shall have more votes in a Govt. instituted for protection of the rights of mankind, than the Citizen of Pa. or N. Jersey who views with laudable horror, so nefarious a practice."

—*Debates on the Federal Convention*, August 8, 1787

GOVERNEER MORRIS ESQ.ᴿ
Member of Congress.

Figure III.5 Portrait of Gouverneur Morris by Pierre Eugène du Simitiére (1783).

Library of Congress, Prints and Photographs Division, LC-USZ62-45482

Many Northern delegates were nevertheless unwilling to take a principled stand against slavery or the slave trade. Taxes on imported slaves would send needed revenue into federal coffers and ensure that Southern states helped shoulder the burden of funding the new national government. Nor, for that matter, were Northern delegates prepared to risk breaking up the already fragile union on the slavery issue. In the end, another compromise was struck. The Constitution would include a provision barring Congress from prohibiting the slave trade until 1808, but in the meantime allowing the national government to tax slave imports at a rate of up to ten dollars per person.

The Electoral College

The selection of the president produced the most complicated compromise of all. While delegates from the large states generally favored election by Congress or by popular vote, those from the small states had different ideas. Some contended that the voters were not qualified to make such an important decision, and that election by Congress would breach the separation of powers. The Convention finally settled on a compromise that provided for the election of the president by an Electoral College in which each state would have as many electors as it had senators and representatives in Congress. The large states, having more representation in Congress, would have more presidential electors than the small states. Each elector would have two ballots to cast for any two candidates, and the candidate receiving the most votes, provided they amounted to a majority of electors, became president. The runner-up in the balloting became vice president. If no one had the necessary majority, the election would go to the House of Representatives, where the state delegations, voting as states, would elect the president from the five candidates with the most electoral votes. The provision for voting as states rather than by head guaranteed that the small states would not be outvoted by the large states. It also balanced the scales for the advantage the large states had in the Electoral College. As a practical matter, it was expected that most elections would be decided in the House. Since the electors could vote for any candidates, only the most outstanding candidates were likely to have majority support. Candidates who were not truly outstanding would have to face a runoff in the House of Representatives.

The Federal Judiciary

While the Convention recognized the need for a federal judiciary, creating one required great political tact. A network of powerful federal courts enforcing federal laws directly throughout the country would be perceived as a threat to states' rights and perhaps prevent ratification of the Constitution. So the Convention finessed the issue and provided only that judicial power should be vested in "one supreme court, and in such inferior courts as the Congress may from time to time ordain and establish." The only court actually established by the Constitution was the Supreme Court, and most of its jurisdiction was left for Congress to determine after the Constitution had been ratified. Judges in the federal courts would be appointed by the president with the consent of the Senate, and they would hold office during good behavior. Their independence was guaranteed by providing that judges' salaries might not be reduced while they remained in office. The most important thing from the standpoint of federal power was that the new government would have its own courts for the enforcement of its laws.

The Convention did not make the mistake of turning the new constitution into a straitjacket that would defeat the ends of government. The Articles of Confederation had made the mistake of specifically limiting the Confederation government to powers "expressly" granted. The new constitution contained no limiting language. On the contrary, the so-called Elastic Clause of Article I authorized Congress to do all things "necessary and proper" to implement the powers expressly granted. This would later be construed by the Supreme Court to create a government that had implied powers as well as the powers expressly granted. The new government, unlike the old, would have the flexibility needed to deal with the changing circumstances of national life.

Omission of a Bill of Rights

The new constitution did not contain a bill of rights. The omission was not an oversight but a policy decision made by the Convention. The delegates had assembled in Philadelphia to create a stronger central government, and to saddle the new government with restrictions from the outset might be counterproductive. There was also the risk that the Convention might become bogged down in lengthy debates as to which rights should be protected. It would be a time-consuming process, and many delegates were convinced that they had no time to spare. There was a sense of urgency that the task at hand was too important to permit unnecessary distractions.

Only late in the Convention was a motion proposed by George Mason of Virginia to include a bill of rights in the new constitution. Mason thought that it "would give great quiet to the people" to know that their traditional rights would be safe under the new government. The task would not be difficult, he assured the delegates, because the state bills of rights could serve as models for a set of federal guarantees. But the Convention, voting by states, unanimously rejected the idea. Opponents contended that guarantees were not needed and might actually be counterproductive. The new government would be a limited government of delegated powers, none of which authorized interference with the traditional rights of the people. Moreover, the enumeration of particular rights might prove invidious to other rights not enumerated. Their omission might imply that they were less important and therefore subject to modification or abridgment. Because it would be impossible to enumerate every right, all rights would be safer if no particular rights were singled out for protection.

Although a formal bill of rights was not included, some basic rights were specifically protected in the main body of the Constitution. The right of habeas corpus could not be suspended in peacetime, and bills of attainder and ex post facto laws were prohibited completely. Moreover, persons accused of federal crimes had the right to a jury trial in the state where the crime was committed. Venue could not be transferred to another state in order to improve the government's chances of getting a conviction. Treason was defined so strictly that the charge could not be used for political purposes. The crime could be proved only by the testimony of two or more witnesses to the same overt act or by the confession of the defendant in open court. The high evidentiary standards protected defendants against the abuses perpetrated under English treason law.

The rights of property were also protected. The states might not issue bills of credit or make anything except gold and silver legal tender. This protected creditors against the sort of paper money inflation that in some states had scaled down the value of debts under the Confederation. The states were also forbidden to abridge the obligations of contract, which meant no more debt postponement laws could be passed for the benefit of debtors. The holders of federal bonds were guaranteed that all such obligations "shall be as valid against the United States under this Constitution, as under the Confederation." These provisions had a powerful appeal to constituencies whose support would be needed for ratification.

The worst defect of the Articles of Confederation was an amending process that could not work. The unanimous consent requirement made the Articles virtually unamendable. That mistake would not be repeated. The Convention struck a balance between stability and flexibility. The new constitution could be changed by amendments proposed by a two-thirds vote of both houses of Congress and ratified by three-fourths of the states. Or the states might take the initiative and propose amendments of their own. If two-thirds of the states so petitioned, Congress would call a convention to propose amendments, which would then be referred to the states for ratification. Although amending the Constitution would not be easy, the process was at least politically feasible when change was really needed.

After the details of government had been settled, the Convention turned to the practical problem of getting the Constitution ratified. The delegates had no illusions about the obstacles to be overcome or the possibility that it might be rejected. The plan adopted provided that ratification would be effective when the Constitution had been approved by nine state conventions called for that purpose. It would have been risky to leave the decision to state legislatures, which stood to lose power to the federal government, and riskier still to leave it to a popular referendum. Special state conventions were the best bet for winning approval. They could be managed in ways that a referendum could not, and they had no powers of government to lose by voting approval. While it might be unfair to say that the deck was stacked, supporters of the Constitution were certainly dealt the best cards.

The provisions for ratification really amounted to a political coup. The Articles of Confederation had created a perpetual union which could be changed only with the consent of all the states. What was now proposed was a new union to take effect upon the approval of only nine of the thirteen states. In effect, the Convention preferred a smaller union of only nine states to the existing Confederation. If the new government worked, the other states would probably fall into line and eventually ratify the Constitution. The union might have to be broken up and reconstructed in order to make it workable. There were risks, of course, because some states might choose to go their separate ways. But the need for a more effective national government seemed compelling enough to justify the gamble.

The Final Document

The drafting of the Constitution was entrusted to a Committee on Style and Arrangement, which put everything together in logical order. Most of the actual writing was done by Gouverneur Morris, whose final draft with only minor changes was approved on September 17, 1787. The Convention's four months in session had been the most politically productive four months in American history. Only three of the forty-two delegates present refused to sign the document. Elbridge Gerry refused to sign for reasons still unclear, and George Mason and Edmund Randolph did not sign because it did not include a bill of rights. The omission would become a major issue in the fight for ratification.

The Constitution was unquestionably a conservative document. The president would not be elected directly by the people and therefore would not be accountable to them; the Senate would be small, powerful, and also not directly elected; and federal judges would be appointed for life and were removable only for official misconduct. The undemocratic character of the Constitution reflected the Founding Fathers' profound distrust of democracy. Democratic government was thought to lack stability and to provide opportunities for demagogues and tyrants. "The evils we experience flow from the excess of democracy," Elbridge Gerry warned the Convention, and most of the delegates shared this view. They assumed that only the propertied class with its interest in stability could be trusted to govern responsibly. The country had been misgoverned during the Confederation period partly because idlers and malcontents had too much influence in public life. The prevailing view among the delegates was that governments built on a popular base stood on quicksand.

When Congress received the Constitution on September 20, some members proposed censuring the Convention for exceeding its mandate. It had been authorized only to propose changes in the Articles of Confederation, not to scrap them completely. But such a move was politically untenable because it would have meant censuring some of the most respected leaders in America. The idea of censuring George Washington, for instance, was simply unthinkable. His reputation stood higher in the country than all of Congress combined. Besides, the Constitution had many desirable features that deserved consideration. Even if the Convention had gone too far, there was really nothing Congress could do about it. The states would have the final say regardless of what Congress did. After a week of pointless debate, the Constitution was submitted to the states for consideration by special conventions.

The Fight over Ratification

Supporters of the Constitution hoped for speedy approval. Well organized and ably led, they counted on support from the propertied class of every state. Voting qualifications gave property owners an influence disproportionate to their numbers in the election of delegates to the ratifying conventions. But it soon became evident that ratification would not be easy. Opponents of the Constitution tried to block the call for a state convention in Pennsylvania by staying away and breaking the quorum in the legislature. A pro-Constitution mob finally dragged them from their lodgings to the Assembly so that the motion could be passed for holding a convention. The affair served notice that the opposition to ratification would be formidable.

The contest for ratification had some of the features of a class struggle. The Federalists (as supporters of the Constitution called themselves) generally represented wealth, talent, and education. They drew their support from merchants, land speculators, businessmen, and professionals. The Antifederalists (as the Federalists dismissively dubbed them) had the backing of small farmers, debtors, and ordinary citizens who were naturally wary of anything favored by the rich and powerful. They were not opposed to constitutional change in principle, but they were convinced that the document drafted by the Philadelphia Convention needed drastic revisions. Their leaders were Patrick Henry, Samuel Adams, Richard Henry Lee, and other radicals of the Revolutionary era. Amos Singletary, a leader of the opposition in Massachusetts, warned that the upper classes would control the new federal government, "and then they will swallow up all us little folks, like the great Leviathan."

The Federalists tried to take the high ground, arguing that a stronger central government was needed to protect essential national interests and preserve the federal union. The weak Confederation government could not deal effectively with foreign governments, and more domestic upheavals, like the rebellion in Massachusetts, were likely if the power vacuum continued. While most Antifederalists conceded the need for change, they contended that the Philadelphia Constitution went too far in centralizing authority. They charged that the Federalists had become so obsessed with the idea of a national state that they were prepared to risk the freedom of the people. Why, they asked, did the Constitution have no bill of rights protecting traditional liberties? It spelled out new and sweeping powers for the federal government but apparently had no space for a bill of rights to prevent abuses of power. This was a difficult question to answer; Federalists could only respond that a bill of rights was not needed because the new government had only delegated powers. Antifederalists knew that they had a popular issue in the omission of a bill of rights, and they used it effectively during the struggle for ratification.

Nevertheless, supporters of the Constitution had a momentum that the opposition could not match. The Federalists offered an alternative to the existing system, while their opponents offered nothing but a continuation of the status quo. Time also favored the Federalists, because every victory in a state convention promoted ratification in the other states. Delaware ratified first, unanimously, on December 7, 1787, and Pennsylvania ratified next, on December 12, despite the opposition of delegates from the rural areas. The New Jersey convention ratified the Constitution unanimously six days later. Georgia gave its unanimous approval on January 2, 1788, and a week later Connecticut voted overwhelmingly for ratification. These quick victories over weak opposition created a bandwagon effect for ratification in the more difficult states.

The first real test came in Massachusetts. The smoldering resentments left by Shays's Rebellion gave the Antifederalists a broad popular base. The small farmers, debtors, and ordinary citizens had learned to distrust the lawyers, merchants, and businessmen who

An Antifederalist Opposes the Proposed Constitution

"[T]his new constitution is, in its first principles, highly and dangerously oligarchic; and it is a point agreed that a government of the few, is, of all governments, the worst. The only check to be found in favour of the democratic principle in this system is, the house of representatives; which I believe may justly be called a mere shred or rag of representation . . . Yet there is no restraint in form of a bill of rights, to secure (what Doctor Blackstone calls) that residuum of human rights, which is not intended to be given up to society, and which indeed is not necessary to be given for any good social purpose."

—Richard Henry Lee to Edmund Randolph, October 16, 1787

Figure III.6 Portrait of Richard Henry Lee by Charles Willson Peale (1784).

Library of Congress, Prints and Photographs Division, LC-USZ62-92331

supported ratification. Led by Samuel Adams, the Antifederalists had a majority of approximately 192–144 when the convention began, and had they pressed for an early vote the Constitution would probably have been rejected. But they were outmaneuvered by the Federalists whose delaying tactics in the end split the opposition. First, the Federalists won over John Hancock, who had been wavering, and then they won over Adams by agreeing to support amendments to the Constitution. Only when every possible deal had been cut was the Constitution put to a vote and narrowly approved by a margin of 187 to 168. Federalist skill and intrigue turned what first looked like certain defeat into a signal victory.

But success in Massachusetts was followed by a sharp setback in Rhode Island. Although the Constitution had strong support among merchants, businessmen, and professionals, the legislature refused to call a ratifying convention. Instead, the Constitution was submitted directly to the people, which was precisely what the Federalists did not want.

They denounced the referendum as illegal and refused to participate on the ground that the matter could only be decided by a convention. Still, nearly half the state's voters cast ballots, and they overwhelmingly rejected the Constitution by a count of 2,708 to 237. Even had the boycotters participated, the outcome would not have been different. The lack of popular enthusiasm for ratification could not have been clearer.

The setback in Rhode Island did not prove fatal. The Federalists got back on track in April 1788 when Maryland ratified by a comfortable margin. South Carolina followed suit in May, which left the Constitution just one state short of going into effect. This set the stage for the final push for ratification in the New Hampshire convention. Although the Antifederalists had a majority at the outset, the delaying tactics of the Federalists prevented a vote until ratification in other states turned the tide in their favor. As in Massachusetts, they won over wavering delegates by promising to support amendments to the Constitution. Their victory in the ninth state gave the country a new federal union whether the remaining states ratified or not.

But the success of the new government still depended heavily on what happened in Virginia and New York. Both states were needed to give the union permanence and stability. It might unravel without them at any time, and the prospects for ratification were not promising in either state. If the Antifederalists had pressed for an early vote in Virginia, the Constitution would have been easily defeated. But they allowed themselves to be drawn into debates, which gave the Federalists time for political maneuver. While the Antifederalists were scoring debating points, the Federalists lobbied and picked up votes. When finally put to a vote on June 25, the Constitution was ratified by the narrow margin of 89 to 79. A shift of only five votes would have kept Virginia out of the union.

The prospects for ratification in New York were even worse. The Antifederalists were led by Governor George Clinton, and opposition was particularly strong in all the rural districts. Aware they faced an uphill fight, the Federalists launched a newspaper campaign even before the convention met. Beginning on October 27, 1787, a series of eighty-five articles under the pseudonym *Publius* appeared in support of the Constitution. The actual authors were John Jay, who contributed five articles on foreign affairs; Madison, who wrote twenty-nine on the operation of the new federal government; and Hamilton, who contributed fifty-one on the economic benefits of the Constitution. The articles were published in book form as *The Federalist* the following May. Although polemical in purpose, the collection provided a clear and authoritative explanation of the Constitution and how the new government was intended to function. Even Antifederalists conceded its essential fairness and candor. Whether or not it won many converts in 1788, it soon became an indispensible guide for constitutional interpretation.

The Federalist addressed a general public that had every reason to believe that an experiment in republican government at the national level was doomed to failure. History taught that republics were prone to faction, corruption, public apathy, and private ambition. What was to prevent the same from happening to the new republic proposed for the United States? And what was to prevent a strengthened federal government from using its power against the people rather than for them? The authors of *The Federalist* addressed these concerns head on. "If men were angels," Madison wrote, no government would be necessary . . . In framing a government which is to be administered by men over men, the great difficulty lies in this: you must first enable the government to control the governed; and in the next place, oblige it to control itself.

The new Constitution's system of checks and balances would keep the respective branches of government under control. No branch of the federal government could usurp the powers of the other branches, nor could the federal government usurp the powers reserved by the Constitution to the states. Political faction and personal ambition would be kept in check by the size and diversity of the fledgling nation, which no individual or group could dominate completely.

Opponents had a clear majority when the New York convention met in June, but supporters of the Constitution used their well-honed delaying tactics to prevent an immediate vote. With votes pending in New Hampshire and Virginia, Hamilton argued that it would be unwise to reject the Constitution without knowing the outcome there. When news arrived that New Hampshire had ratified, the issue before the convention changed completely. It was no longer a question of whether to form a new federal union but whether to join one that New Hampshire's ratification had already brought into being. Rejecting the Constitution now meant severing political ties with the rest of the country. Thrown on the defensive by the force of events, Antifederalists shifted ground and argued for conditional ratification contingent on changes in the Constitution. The Federalists rejected this because it would have required the agreement of the other states, possibly unraveling victories already won. Delegates from the rural counties were warned that New York City, which strongly favored ratification, might secede and join the union on its own if the convention refused to ratify. When finally put to a vote on July 26, the Constitution was approved by a margin of 30 to 27.

The importance of ratification by Virginia and New York cannot be exaggerated. If either had rejected the Constitution, the new federal Union probably would have failed. Had they gone their independent ways, they would have disrupted the territorial integrity of the Union and destabilized it politically. It was inevitable that some decisions of the new government would not be popular with all the states. Those on the losing side of a bitterly contested issue would have been sorely tempted to leave the Union if an independent Virginia or New York had demonstrated the feasibility of political independence. Both had the population and resources to manage their own affairs successfully without federal assistance. The narrow margins by which they entered the Union may have been the most important ballots cast in American history.

Except for Rhode Island, only North Carolina failed to ratify the Constitution. The Constitution was not actually rejected, but neither was it approved. The state convention called for a bill of rights and other changes before voting ratification. But once the new government was established, public opinion turned against further delay. A second convention met in November 1789 and ratified the Constitution by an overwhelming majority. Rhode Island joined the Union the following year, though with less enthusiasm.

Threats of federal trade reprisals forced the state legislature to summon a ratifying convention. The convention met in January but debated until May before voting approval by a margin of 34 to 32, the closest vote in any state convention. But the closeness of the vote was not really important. The important thing was that the Federalists had won. They had succeeded in bringing all thirteen states of the Confederation under a new central government. The national era of American constitutional history had now truly begun.

April 30, 1789	September 24, 1789	October 19, 1789	December 15, 1791	February 18, 1793	April 22, 1793	July 1794
George Washington Sworn in as President of the United States	Judiciary Act	John Jay Becomes First Chief Justice of the United States	Ratification of Bill of Rights	Chisholm v. Georgia	Proclamation of Neutrality	Outbreak of Whiskey Rebellion

1798	November 10, 1798	December 24, 1798	September 30, 1800	February 4, 1801	March 4, 1801
Alien and Sedition Acts	Kentucky Resolutions	Virginia Resolutions	Treaty of Morfontaine	John Marshall Becomes Chief Justice of the United States	Thomas Jefferson Sworn in as President of the United States

IV Launching the New Government

November 19, 1794	April 1795	August 12, 1795	March 7, 1796	March 8, 1796	March 4, 1797
Jay's Treaty	Vanhorne's Lessee v. Dorrance	John Rutledge Becomes Chief Justice of the United States	Ware v. Hylton	Hylton v. United States	John Adams Sworn in as President of the United States

"No man who ever held the office of President would congratulate a friend on obtaining it."
—John Adams to Josaiah Quincy (1825)

The Constitution adopted at Philadelphia provided only a paper framework for government; whether it succeeded or failed would be up to those responsible for its implementation. The possibility of failure hung like a cloud over the first federal elections as opponents of ratification made furious efforts to win control of the new government. Elections to Congress were contested in every state except Georgia, causing some Federalists to fear that the declared enemies of a strong central government would be in a position to subvert it. Rumors even circulated that some presidential electors planned to cast one of their ballots for Patrick Henry, who had opposed the Constitution in the Virginia ratifying convention. Alexander Hamilton took the precaution of urging the electors in Connecticut and Pennsylvania to cast no second ballot in order to insure that no one received as many votes as George Washington. While Washington was certain to get one ballot from every elector, the system of double voting prescribed by the Constitution made an electoral deadlock theoretically possible.

Hamilton's apprehensions turned out to be unfounded. No other candidate was ever in serious contention. Washington received sixty-nine electoral votes, and John Adams, the runner-up, became vice president with thirty-four. John Jay and John Hancock appeared on some ballots, and George Clinton, the only opponent of ratification, received only three votes from Virginia. The method of selecting electors, having been left to the states by the Constitution, was not uniform. They were chosen by popular vote in six states, by the legislature in three, and in one, New Jersey, by the governor and his council. A deadlock between the Antifederalist majority in the assembly and the Federalist-controlled senate prevented the appointment of electors in New York. But the outcome of the balloting was overwhelmingly popular: the election of the greatest living American to head the new government.

The Federalists also prevailed in the congressional elections, winning control of the Senate and House of Representatives by wide margins. So the new government would not be, as some had feared, at the mercy of those who had opposed it. Most members of the first Congress had been delegates to the Constitutional Convention or to the state ratifying conventions, and all but seven had supported ratification. Federalists also controlled the judiciary, for Washington appointed only supporters of the Constitution to the new federal courts. Whatever happened, those who had wanted the new government would be responsible for its success or failure.

When the first Congress met, the federal government existed mainly on paper. The Confederation government left behind only a dozen unpaid clerks, an empty treasury, no navy, and an army consisting of 672 officers and men. Congress quickly imposed a tariff to raise money, but months passed before customs officials were appointed to collect the

George Washington on the New Constitution

"The merits and defects of the proposed Constitution have been largely & ably discussed. For myself, I was ready to have embraced any tolerable compromise that was competent to save us from impending ruin; and I can say there are scarcely any of the amendments, which have been suggested, to which I have *much* objection . . . It is nearly impossible for any body who has not been on the spot to conceive (from any description) what the delicacy and danger of our situation have been. Though the peril is not past entirely; thank God! the prospect is somewhat brightening."

—Letter to Thomas Jefferson, August 31, 1788

Figure IV.1 Portrait of George Washington by Rembrandt Peale (1795).

National Portrait Gallery, Smithsonian Institution / Art Resource, NY

duties. Nor could other federal laws be enforced until a judiciary had been set up and judges appointed. But there was a positive side to building from the ground up. The government began with a wide range of choices unencumbered by past failures or entrenched interests. Except for the public debt inherited from the Confederation, the slate had been wiped clean for a new beginning.

Organizing the New Government

Setting guidelines for relations with the executive branch had a high priority with the first Congress. Some issues involved protocol, such as how the president should be addressed and whether Congress should hear his addresses standing or seated. Others were substantive and touched on the separation of powers. There was uncertainty, for instance, about what the Constitution meant in authorizing the president to make treaties "by and with the Advice and Consent of the Senate." Washington assumed this required prior consultation with the Senate, but he got a cold reception when he appeared there personally to discuss treaty proposals with the senators. They made it clear that they regarded his participation in formal Senate deliberations as a breach of the separation of powers. Their touchiness had lasting consequences, for Washington never solicited their advice again. The precedent thus set was followed by his successors, with the result that the "Advice" provision became largely meaningless. While the consent of the Senate to treaties would still be needed, no formal consultation would be held on their negotiation. This would be exclusively an executive prerogative.

The small size of the first Congress allowed both houses to dispense with standing committees and deal with legislation directly. Only nine Senators were present for the election of John Langdon as first president pro tempore, and only thirty Representatives for the election of Frederick A. Muhlenburg as first speaker of the House. Bills were debated informally in both houses as committees of the whole before being put to a formal vote. If approved, the measure would be turned over to a select committee for drafting. At this point the head of the executive department responsible for its implementation would be consulted on matters of detail and invited to make suggestions. The measure would then be submitted to the full house for debate and possible amendment before a final vote was taken. If passed, it went to the other house for approval.

Although both houses were theoretically equal, the House of Representatives originally had more real power than the Senate. It was the popular branch of government, indeed the only branch of government directly elected by the people. The Senate represented the states as political entities, and senators were accountable only to the state legislatures that had chosen them. Despite its lawmaking functions, the Senate more closely resembled an executive council than a legislative body. Its regular presiding officer was the vice president, and important executive functions, such as treaties and judicial appointments, required its consent. Moreover, as the popular branch of government, the House of Representatives had control of the purse. The provision in the Constitution requiring all tax measures to originate in the House gave the Representatives special leverage. The Senate could block or force compromises on tax proposals but it could not initiate them.

The upshot was that every department of government had to look primarily to the House for funding.

While the president ran the executive branch, the Constitution did not authorize him to set up separate executive departments of government. Congress assumed responsibility for this under the provision in Article I authorizing it to enact all laws "necessary and proper" for implementing powers granted to the federal government. The first departments set up were the Department of Foreign Affairs (later renamed the State Department), the Treasury Department, and the War Department. The offices of Attorney General and Postmaster General soon followed. The president, as head of the executive branch, had the power to fill executive posts with the consent of the Senate, but it was not clear at the outset whether his power to remove executive officials also required Senate consent. On the advice of Madison, who had been elected to the House, Congress set up the executive departments with no restrictions on the power of removal. But the constitutional issue itself remained unresolved. In 1833 Andrew Jackson's dismissal of Secretary of Treasury William Duane sharply divided Congress, and Andrew Johnson's removal of Secretary of War Edwin Stanton in 1867 led to his impeachment. The issue would not be resolved until the twentieth century when the Supreme Court declared the power of removal an executive prerogative.[1]

The only strings on executive power imposed by the first Congress involved the Treasury Department. Because the Department would play such a key role in government, some congressmen thought it safer to divide the functions of the office among several commissioners. But the final decision was to have a single Treasury Secretary who would be required to make reports personally or in writing to either house of Congress. This deviation from the separation of powers was justified by the constitutional responsibility of Congress to control public expenditures. The Secretary's reports would enable it to monitor Treasury operations and prevent unauthorized spending. Congress took the additional precaution of creating the separate offices of comptroller, auditor, treasurer, and register to keep track of disbursements.

Judiciary Act of 1789

No task facing the first Congress was more important than creating a system of federal courts. The Constitution provided for a Supreme Court but left it to Congress to set up lower courts and to spell out their jurisdiction. The Judiciary Act passed in 1789 created a comprehensive court system that freed the federal government from dependence on the state courts for the enforcement of federal laws. At its apex stood the Supreme Court with a chief justice and five associate justices; next came three circuit courts which met twice yearly to try cases involving citizens from different states, as well as certain federal cases; and at the base of the system were thirteen district courts whose geographic jurisdiction was approximately coextensive with a state. Appeals could be taken from the district courts to the circuit courts and from the circuit courts to the Supreme Court. Each of the district courts had one judge, but the circuit courts had none. They consisted of two justices of the Supreme Court and one judge from the district courts in the circuit. Since the case load would be light in the beginning, the Supreme Court justices and district judges were expected to do double duty at the circuit level. Having district judges on the circuit bench also ensured that local rules and procedures were followed when federal jurisdiction was based on diversity of citizenship.

Section 25 of the Judiciary Act extended the judicial power of the United States over the state courts. It allowed appeals to be brought from the state courts to the Supreme Court when the case involved the supremacy of the Constitution, a treaty, or a federal law. Specifically, appeals could be brought if the highest court of a state declared a federal law or treaty unconstitutional, or if it upheld a state law which had been challenged under a federal law, treaty, or the Constitution. Federal authority would have been seriously compromised if state courts had the final word on federal constitutional issues. The Supreme Court was more likely than the state courts to uphold federal power and see to it that the laws and treaties of the United States were uniformly enforced. The Constitution did not expressly authorize such appeals, but nationalists considered Section 25 within the power granted to Congress to regulate the Supreme Court's appellate jurisdiction. To others, however, it seemed a serious intrusion upon the judicial sovereignty of the states.

The Bill of Rights

Congress also lost no time making good on the Federalist promise made during the struggle for ratification that the first order of business would be to add a bill of rights to the Constitution. Five states had ratified with the understanding that there would be amendments protecting traditional liberties against federal abridgment. Washington alluded to the matter in his inaugural address, and most assumed prompt action by Congress. On June 8, 1789, James Madison proposed the first amendments to his colleagues in the House of Representatives. A Bill of Rights, he argued, would help win the support of Americans apprehensive of the powerful federal government created by the new Constitution. It would also shore up the political liberties implicitly enshrined in the Constitution.

After extensive debate during the summer of 1789, the House of Representatives proposed seventeen amendments protecting various individual rights against the states as well as against the federal government. But the Senate rejected this intrusion upon the sovereignty of the states and limited the reach of the protection to the federal level. With the exception of a proposal protecting those "religiously scrupulous of bearing arms" from being compelled to render military service, the House-Senate conference accepted the Senate's position and consolidated everything into twelve amendments. Ten were finally ratified as the American Bill of Rights. The two amendments not ratified were essentially technical and did not involve traditional liberties. One dealt with representation in Congress, and the other related to congressional salaries. The latter would eventually be ratified as the Twenty-seventh Amendment two centuries later, but the former still languishes in the political limbo of unratified amendments.

Adoption of the Bill of Rights added to the popularity of the new government by placing it squarely on the side of traditional rights and liberties. The First Amendment guaranteed freedom of speech, press, and religion, as well as the right of assembly and

"[S]o far as a declaration of rights can tend to prevent the exercise of undue power, it cannot be doubted but such declaration is proper. But I confess that I do conceive, that in a Government modified like this of the United States, the great danger lies rather in the abuse of the community than in the legislative body. The prescriptions in favor of liberty, ought to be levelled against that quarter where the greatest danger lies, namely, that which possesses the highest prerogative of power. But it [is] not found in either the executive or legislative departments of government, but in the body of the people, operating by the majority against the minority."

—Address in Congress (June 8, 1789)

petition. The Second protected the right to keep and bear arms, and the Third restricted the quartering of troops in private houses. The Fourth prohibited unreasonable searches and seizures. Warrants could be issued only "upon probable cause, supported by oath or affirmation, and particularly describing the place to be searched, and the person or things to be seized." The Fifth, Sixth, and Seventh Amendments spelled out some of the basic features of common-law due process. The Fifth guaranteed criminal defendants a grand jury hearing, prohibited compulsory self-incrimination, barred double jeopardy, and forbade arbitrary punishments. The Sixth guaranteed the right to a jury trial, to confront one's accusers in open court, and to have the assistance of counsel. The Seventh provided for a jury trial in civil cases involving more than twenty dollars. The Eighth, which was also part of the English Bill of Rights, prohibited excessive bail, fines, and cruel and unusual punishments.

The Ninth and Tenth Amendments imposed general restraints on the federal government. The Ninth provided that the enumeration of rights in the previous eight should not be construed to authorize interference with other rights not enumerated. The Tenth reinforced the Ninth, providing that powers not granted by the Constitution to the federal government, nor prohibited by it to the states, are reserved to the states or to the people. The wording of this provision turned out to be more important than just about anything else in the Constitution. Although based on the resolve of the Massachusetts ratifying convention that the new government should have only the powers expressly granted by the Constitution, the word "expressly" was omitted from the amendment. The Articles of Confederation had limited the old government to powers expressly delegated and thereby precluded any possible claim of implied powers. The nationalists in Congress had no desire to tie their own hands. So they left the door open for more expansive interpretations of federal power by leaving out the limiting adverb.

Washington's Presidency

No one contributed more to the success of the new government than George Washington as president. The prospect of having him head the government caused many to support ratification who otherwise might have opposed the Constitution. He stood higher in public esteem than the new government itself. His journey from Mount Vernon to New York City for the inauguration became a triumphal procession replete with banquets, parades, and flowers strewn in his path. He was greeted in New York City with two thirteen-gun salutes, and the buildings were festooned with decorations bearing his name. After Chancellor Robert R. Livingston had administered the oath of office, bells rang and shouts of "Long live George Washington" filled the air. The prestige and dignity almost immediately surrounding the presidency had more to do with the eminence of the first president than with the office itself.

Washington strove to make the presidency a unifying institution. He traveled extensively and put all parts of the country in touch with the new government through his personal presence. He carefully avoided the appearance of partisanship and tried to remain above the political fray in order to preserve his office as a symbol of national unity. Although Washington delegated considerable authority to his department heads, he personally controlled public policy and steadfastly pursued particular goals. His highest priority was to keep the country at peace, because he was convinced that taking sides in foreign conflicts might divide Americans to the point of wrecking the Union. He also recognized that prosperity would strengthen the government politically and so supported measures to promote economic growth. Fortunately, an economic revival already underway when Washington took office gave his administration an aura of success from the beginning. Great men tend to be lucky, and the first president was no exception.

The most important department head was Alexander Hamilton, Washington's brilliant Secretary of the Treasury. Congress had made the office special by reserving the right to call on the Secretary for advice and information. Hamilton used this relationship to the utmost and soon involved himself in every phase of public policy. A first-rate administrator, he took over management of most of the everyday business of government. Washington did nothing to discourage him but rather sought his advice on a wide range of matters having nothing to do with the Treasury. This sometimes caused friction with other department heads who resented Hamilton's influence and growing power. They were all strong-willed and ambitious, and Washington had to employ great tact to prevent resignations. Thomas Jefferson, Hamilton's principal critic in the administration, was particularly hard to handle. But Washington managed to keep the two men together, harnessing their special skills for the success of the government.

The Constitution did not provide for a cabinet or any council of trusted advisors with whom the president could discuss policy and politics. Still, a cabinet system soon evolved out of Washington's practice of consulting with department heads individually and requesting written opinions from them. But they did not meet as a group until 1791 when Washington suggested that during his absence from the capital they should consult together with Vice President Adams on any problems that arose. These meetings thereafter became so common that by 1793 the term "cabinet" came into common usage. The system gave the president a forum for frank deliberations before committing the administration to a particular course of action.

The Whiskey Rebellion

In 1794 the new government faced its first domestic crisis with the so-called Whiskey Rebellion. Western farmers had long disposed of their surplus grain by distilling it, and they resented the excise tax levied by Congress in 1790 on whiskey. They viewed the levy as a tax on the grain itself. Although Congress reduced the excise in 1792, their resentment turned violent in western Pennsylvania where Treasury agents were prevented from collecting taxes. Washington acted decisively to restore order and uphold federal authority. When the insurgents ignored his order to desist, he called out the Pennsylvania militia and troops from neighboring states to suppress them. The uprising soon collapsed and order was restored. Two of the rebel leaders were convicted of treason, but Washington wisely pardoned them. Political martyrs were the last thing the new government needed. The show of force had been sufficient to put malcontents on notice that the government would deal swiftly with those who defied it.

Executive Prerogatives

Washington set several important precedents in foreign affairs. In 1793 he took it upon himself to receive "Citizen" Edmond Genêt as minister of the new French Republic despite objections that Congress should have been consulted before recognizing the new government. Though opponents of the French Revolution grumbled, Congress did not challenge the president's right to act on his own authority. Another precedent was set the same year when Washington issued a proclamation of neutrality in the war that had erupted between France and Great Britain. Those who sympathized with the French protested that treaties of alliance dating from 1778 bound the United States to assist France. But the failure of Congress to challenge the proclamation amounted to a tacit recognition of the president's prerogative to interpret the treaty obligations of the United States. Washington set another precedent by rejecting a demand from the House of Representatives for papers relating to the unpopular Jay Treaty of 1794. He took the position that the Constitution made the president responsible for negotiating treaties, and that the details of negotiation were therefore protected by executive privilege. The House finally backed down and voted by a narrow margin to drop the demand.

But Washington was never overbearing or patronizing in his dealings with Congress. He respected Congress as an institution and never tried to intimidate it or bend it to his will. Although the Constitution gave him a veto over legislation, he refrained from using it unless he considered the measure in question unconstitutional. In 1791, for example, he vetoed a law giving some states more representation in Congress than authorized by the Constitution precisely for that reason. But he never used his veto power as a weapon or bargaining chip to influence the legislative process. Until the administration of Andrew Jackson, Washington's successors followed his example and kept the veto out of politics.

The Supreme Court

Washington's Supreme Court appointments set precedents that endured into the twenty-first century. He appointed only justices who shared his political views, particularly on the need for a strong federal government. He also took geographic factors into account and tried to give all parts of the country judicial representation. Overweighting the Court with justices from one section would have been divisive in an era when states' rights and local pride were powerful forces. Regional balance made good political sense. Except for John Rutledge, whose case was special, all of Washington's appointees were confirmed by the Senate without difficulty. The senators never claimed, as some would later contend, that their Article II function to give "advice and consent" made them partners in the appointment process.

The chief justiceship went to John Jay, the aristocratic New Yorker who had served as Secretary of Foreign Affairs in the Confederation government. Jay had only limited judicial experience, but his unusual qualities of character and mind might have made him a great chief justice. That he did not become one can be attributed to the original limitations of the office. The Supreme Court played an insignificant role in the early political life of the nation. It would take time for cases to work their way up through the lower federal and state courts for Supreme Court action. In the meantime, the Court remained on the periphery of power, overshadowed by Congress and the president. Jay, whose ambitions matched his talents, soon lost interest in an office that kept him on the sidelines. He resigned after six years to become governor of New York.

Having appointed a New Yorker chief justice, Washington named southerners to three of the five associate justiceships. The first went to John Rutledge, a former governor of South Carolina and a signer of both the Declaration of Independence and the Constitution. Rutledge had wanted the chief justiceship, and he accepted the lesser post with some reluctance. He remained on the Court for only two years and did not attend a single session. The Court handled so little business in the beginning that the trip from Charleston to New York City and later to Philadelphia did not seem worth making. Rutledge's decision to resign in 1791 in order to become chief justice of South Carolina is a fair gauge of where the court stood in the hierarchy of national power.

The second justiceship went to William Cushing, a former royal judge and the first chief justice of the State of Massachusetts. Cushing was so conservative that critics complained that in his heart he always remained a royal judge. His conduct at debtor trials immediately before Shays's Rebellion caused many to regard him as a tool of the creditor class. But Cushing on some occasions put liberty over the claims of property. His charge to the jury as chief justice of Massachusetts in *Commonwealth v. Jennison* (1783) had the effect of abolishing slavery in that state by judicial interpretation. He instructed the jury that a clause in the state constitution declaring that "all men are born free and equal" meant exactly what it said and thus abolished slavery as a legal institution. "The idea of slavery," he declared, "is inconsistent with our own conduct and Constitution . . . there can be no such thing as perpetual servitude of a rational creature."

Washington's next appointee was James Wilson of Pennsylvania. Like Rutledge, he had signed both the Declaration of Independence and the Constitution. He had authored the Contract Clause of the Constitution and had assisted Gouverneur Morris in drafting the final document. Wilson may have later regretted his concern for the rights of creditors under the Contract Clause. His unsuccessful speculations left him hopelessly in debt, and his last days were spent dodging creditors. He had to stay out of Pennsylvania while still on the Court in order to avoid imprisonment for debt. But his misfortunes came later; at the time of his appointment he was prosperous and successful, and no one contributed more to the early development of the Court. Wilson's reputation as a legal and constitutional expert stood so high that Washington placed his nephew Bushrod Washington in his office to study law. Had Wilson's later problems with creditors not gotten in the way, he probably would have been promoted to chief justice when Jay resigned.

John Blair of Virginia got the fifth justiceship. Although a close friend of the president, he was not Washington's first choice for the post. He was appointed only after John Wythe, also a Virginian, declined in order to remain a state court judge. Blair had been a delegate to the Philadelphia Convention and had signed the Constitution. Like Wilson, he speculated heavily while on the Court, with the difference that his speculations were highly profitable. The last appointment went to Robert Harrison, whose tenure was the shortest in the Court's history. Five days after being confirmed by the Senate, he was chosen chancellor of Maryland, a position he preferred to his Supreme Court seat. Because he simply returned his commission to Washington without resigning, it is arguable whether he ever really became a member of the Court. In any case, the appointment then went to James Iredell, who had led the fight for ratification in North Carolina. Iredell was thirty-eight years old when appointed and the youngest member of the Court.

Only two of Washington's original appointees remained on the Court for the duration of his administration. The rapid turnover had much to do with the burdensome circuit court duties imposed on the justices by the Judiciary Act of 1789. They had to spend considerable time traveling about their circuits under conditions sometimes crude and primitive. Washington had difficulty finding a replacement when Rutledge resigned in 1791. This was partly because he wanted only first-rate appointees for a Court which had not yet become a first-rate institution. He first offered the post to Edward Rutledge, the justice's nephew, who declined in order to remain in the South Carolina legislature. Charles C. Pinckney turned down the job for the same reason. The president then turned to Thomas Johnson, a federal district judge in Maryland, who was persuaded to accept on the assurance that Congress would make the circuit court duties less onerous. Congress did provide some relief, but not enough to satisfy the sixty-one-year-old Johnson. He resigned after serving for little more than a year. The vacancy was finally filled by Senator William Paterson of New Jersey, who was sixteen years younger than Johnson and more willing to take on circuit duties. Paterson served for thirteen years, about twice the average tenure of Washington's other appointees.

Chief Justice Jay was the next to leave. He had been dissatisfied from the beginning but reluctant to leave until a better position in government became available. In 1792, while still chief justice, he ran unsuccessfully for the governorship of New York, and he would have run again the following year had not the president dissuaded him. Washington appointed him special ambassador to Great Britain in 1794 to negotiate the settlement of grievances that had brought the country to the brink of war. The result was a widely unpopular treaty that even supporters of the administration thought made too many concessions to the British. The Senate debate was conducted behind closed doors, and the treaty was ratified in secrecy. When its text was finally published, a wave of revulsion swept

George Washington to the First Supreme Court
of the United States

"I have always been persuaded that the stability and success of the national government, and consequently the happiness of the people of the United States, would depend in a considerable degree on the interpretation and execution of its laws. In my opinion, therefore, it is important that the Judiciary system should not only be independent in its operations, but as perfect as possible in its formation."

—Letter to the Chief Justice and Associate Justices, April 3, 1790

Figure IV.2 Portrait of John Jay by Gilbert Stuart (1794).

National Portrait Gallery, Smithsonian Institution / Art Resource, NY

the country. The Federalists found themselves on the defensive, and the chief justice was denounced as a traitor and burned in effigy. But Jay's days on the Court were already numbered. In 1795 he resigned to become governor of New York. Given the status of the Court in 1795, this was considered a step upward. Congress was not in session when Jay resigned, so Washington made a recess appointment. Hamilton, his first choice, declined the chief justiceship in order to pursue his law practice and political interests in New York. Before the president made another choice, he received a letter from former Justice Rutledge offering to take the post. Given his attendance record during his previous tenure, the offer must have come as a surprise. But Washington was pleased to get someone with Rutledge's credentials. Qualified candidates were hard to find, and Rutledge was certainly qualified. So Washington appointed him with a request that he preside over the next session of the Court. No one doubted that the Senate would confirm him when it reconvened.

But Rutledge was not confirmed. Before leaving for Philadelphia to take up his duties as chief justice, he delivered a wild harangue against the Jay Treaty at a public meeting in Charleston. He heaped abuse on everyone connected with the treaty and suggested that the senators who ratified it had been out of their minds or bribed with British gold. Actually, it was Rutledge who was losing his mind, and the tirade was the first indication that his mental breakdown had begun. Nevertheless, he presided over the August term of the Court even handing down a significant holding in *Talbot v. Janson* (1795) that a United States citizen could become a citizen of a foreign country without forfeiting his United States citizenship. Rutledge then left Philadelphia for his round of circuit court duties. Although uneasy about the Charleston speech, Washington was reassured enough to send the nomination to the Senate when Congress reconvened. But the Senate was less forgiving than the president and refused to confirm him. In retrospect, the rejection turned out to be providential. Rutledge's condition deteriorated rapidly, and by the time of his death in 1800 he was completely insane. A lunatic chief justice was the last thing the early Court needed.

Washington had difficulty finding a new chief justice. He first offered the post to Patrick Henry, whose growing conservatism made him acceptable to Federalists. But Henry, who was sixty years old, declined on grounds of age. Justice Cushing, who was the president's next choice, declined for the same reason. The post finally went to Senator Oliver Ellsworth of Connecticut, who had played a leading role in drafting the Judiciary Act of 1789. Ellsworth served for only four years before resigning in 1800 to make way for John Marshall.

While seeking a replacement for Rutledge, Washington found another vacancy on his hands with the resignation of Justice Blair. Blair's seat went to Samuel Chase, an ardent Federalist whose combative temperament made him one of the most controversial justices

Figure IV.3 Portrait of Oliver Ellsworth by W.R. Wheeler after Ralph Earl.

Collection of the Supreme Court of the United States

in the Court's history. Chase, who previously served as chief judge of Maryland, had a sharp analytical mind and a matchless understanding of the Constitution. Until eclipsed by Marshall, he was easily the most brilliant and influential member of the Court. But his overbearing partisanship at times turned the federal bench into a political forum. His critics called him the "hanging judge" because of his harsh and biased rulings while on circuit court duty.

The justices appointed by Washington staunchly supported an independent judiciary. When Congress authorized members of the circuit courts to serve as commissioners to review the claims of war veterans, they objected to the assignment as nonjudicial. In 1792 the matter came to a head in *Hayburn's Case* where the federal circuit court for Pennsylvania refused to review the claims of a veteran. In a letter to the president, the judges declared that they could only perform such duties "as are properly judicial, and to be performed in a judicial manner." The law was repealed a few months later, so there was no confrontation with Congress. They also drew the line the following year when the president solicited an opinion from the Supreme Court on issues of international law. The justices replied that they could not give advisory opinions or take positions on political questions without compromising the independence of the Court and their own judicial responsibilities. How could they rule impartially on an issue on which they had already given an advisory opinion? They were not precluded however from performing nonjudicial functions voluntarily as individuals, as they had offered to do in *Hayburn's Case*. Although both Jay and Ellsworth represented the United States on diplomatic missions while serving as chief justice, these were individual assignments which did not compromise the institutional independence of the Court.

Staying out of politics was not easy, because even issues of law sometimes had unavoidable political ramifications. Defenders of state sovereignty objected strongly to a circuit court ruling in *Champion & Dickason v. Casey* (1792) that Rhode Island's debt postponement law impaired the obligations of contract and was therefore unconstitutional. A Virginia debt sequestration law was invalidated by the Supreme Court in *Ware v. Hylton* (1796) on the ground that it violated provisions in the Treaty of Paris protecting the rights of British creditors. Proponents of states' rights denounced these decisions as intrusions into the domestic affairs of the states. Upholding federal sovereignty was one thing, but putting private rights over the sovereign powers of the states was quite another.

One decision of the Supreme Court caused such a political backlash that it was overturned by constitutional amendment. In *Chisholm v. Georgia* (1793) the Court upheld the right of citizens of South Carolina to sue the State of Georgia in the federal courts. Article III of the Constitution gave the federal courts jurisdiction over controversies between a state and citizens of another state. The purpose of this provision, Madison had assured the Virginia ratifying convention, was judicial fairness. If a state wanted to sue a citizen of another state it could not do so in its own courts but would have to use a neutral federal forum. The Supreme Court declared this provision to be a two-way street and upheld the right of a private citizen to sue Georgia despite the latter's claim of sovereign immunity. The Georgia legislature denounced the decision and ordered the death penalty for any official who attempted to enforce it in Georgia. Numerous states joined in the protest, pointing out that nothing in the Constitution superseded the common-law right of the sovereign not to be sued without its consent. The clamor resulted in the Eleventh Amendment depriving the federal courts of jurisdiction in suits brought by private citizens against states.

In *Hylton v. United States* (1796) the Supreme Court for the first time ruled on the constitutionality of an act of Congress. The law in question imposed a tax on carriages, and the constitutionality of the levy turned on whether it was a direct tax or an excise. If a direct tax, it would have violated the Article I provision that direct taxes must be apportioned among the states on the basis of population. The Court upheld the law, ruling that only poll taxes and land taxes are direct levies. The case had important implications. If the Court could uphold acts of Congress, why could it not invalidate them as well? The decision had no immediate repercussions, because Congress had been upheld. But if the Court had struck down the law, the attack on Congress's legislative power almost certainly would not have gone unchallenged.

Most of Washington's judicial appointees subscribed to the Lockean vested rights doctrine that natural rights should be protected by the courts whether the Constitution expressly protected them or not. The right to possess property, for instance, was so fundamental that any law to the contrary would automatically be null and void. But political prudence kept the courts from embracing the doctrine openly as a rule of decision. The states almost certainly would have objected to the expansion of federal judicial power beyond the provisions of the Constitution. The Eleventh Amendment had demonstrated that the courts were not free to do as they pleased. The principle of vested rights could best be promoted by wrapping it in the mantle of some specific constitutional guarantee. In *Vanhorne's Lessee v. Dorrance* (1795), for example, the federal circuit court for Pennsylvania invalidated a state law that transferred some disputed land from one person to another. While declaring the possession of property "one of the natural, inherent, and unalienable rights of man," the Court based its decision on the Contract Clause of the Constitution. This stretched the Clause somewhat, but it was safer than not citing it at all. The coupling of natural rights with contract rights over the years became one of the guiding principles of federal jurisprudence.

The Social Compact and the Constitution

"Men have a sense of property: Property is necessary to their subsistence, and correspondent to their natural wants and desires; its security was one of the objects, that induced them to unite in society. No man would become a member of a community, in which he could not enjoy the fruits of his honest labour and industry. The preservation of property then is a primary object of the social compact . . . The constitution expressly declares, that the right of acquiring, possessing, and protecting property is natural, inherent, and unalienable. It is a right not *ex gratia* from the legislature, but *ex debito* from the constitution."

—*Vanhorne's* Lessee v. Dorrance *(1795)*

No Federal Common Law

While the federal courts clearly had jurisdiction to enforce federal law, there was some uncertainty as to the nature of federal law. The basic issue was whether federal judges could apply the common law in cases not covered by statutes. The answer was important both for the courts and for the government. Could the government, for example, prosecute defendants for crimes not covered by the Constitution or laws passed by Congress? The Washington administration assumed that the answer was yes, and federal prosecutors sought common-law indictments against persons who violated the president's neutrality proclamation of 1793. The Supreme Court did not rule on the issue directly, but their circuit court opinions reveal that the justices were sharply divided. Justice Chase rejected the idea completely, noting that the common law had been adopted only selectively by the states, and that adopting it at the federal level would create conflicts between state and federal law. Chief Justice Ellsworth argued the opposite, citing frequent allusions to the common law in the Constitution and Bill of Rights. This certainly seemed to imply the existence of a national common law. The issue was not settled with finality until *United States v. Hudson & Goodwin* in 1812, when the Supreme Court ruled that there was no federal common law.

The Federalists in charge of the new government were not an organized party in the beginning. They were simply persons who, despite many differences among themselves, had supported the Constitution during the struggle for ratification. The emergence of national parties had not been anticipated by the Founding Fathers, because they thought the country too large for its diverse interest groups to sort out their differences and organize nationwide parties. The original Federalists had actually warned against the formation of parties and factions as incompatible with the ideals of republican government. The common good, not partisanship, should be the only guide for public policy. But the first federal elections were no sooner over than the definition of what made a Federalist began to narrow into support for particular policies and programs. Within a few years, many who had called themselves Federalists during the fight for ratification found themselves on opposite sides of the most important issues.

Hamilton's Financial Program

Political lines began to harden during the debate over Hamilton's bold financial program for the new government. The brilliant Treasury Secretary was convinced that commerce and manufacturing were the dynamic forces in American economic life, and that the government should support them in order to promote prosperity and strengthen the country's political foundations. He called for funding the national debt, assuming responsibility for the unpaid war debts of the states, and establishing a national bank. Paying the state and federal debts would establish the credit of the new government and also make capital available for economic expansion. A national bank would facilitate interstate business and provide the government with a reliable financial agent. His goal was a prosperous nation governed by a powerful national state.

Alexander Hamilton on Public Finance

"[T]hough a funded debt is not, in the first instance, an absolute increase of capital, or an augmentation of real wealth; yet, by serving as a new power in the operations of industry, it has, within certain bounds, a tendency to increase the real wealth of a community, in like manner, as money, borrowed by a thrifty farmer, to be laid out in the improvement of his farm, may, in the end, add to his stock of real riches . . . And, as the vicissitudes of nations beget a perpetual tendency to the accumulation of debt, there ought to be in every government a perpetual, anxious, and unceasing effort to reduce that which at any time exists, as fast as shall be practicable, consistently with integrity and good faith."

—*Report on the Subject of Manufactures* (1791)

Figure IV.4 Portrait of Alexander Hamilton by John Trumbull (1806).

National Portrait Gallery, Smithsonian Institution / Art Resource, NY

All of Hamilton's proposals encountered bitter opposition in Congress. While the idea of paying the federal debt had broad support, Madison denounced the plan to pay only current bondholders as a windfall for the speculators who had purchased bonds from their original owners at steep discounts during the hard times of the Confederation period. He proposed instead to pay speculators the highest price that had prevailed on the market and to pay the original owners the difference between the highest market price and the face value of the bonds. Southerners in Congress also opposed federal assumption of state war debts. The North would benefit more from this than the South because the proportion of debt to population was less in the South than in the North. Besides, most of the southern states had already funded their debts, so southerners would have to take on the double burden of having to help pay off northern debts in the form of higher federal taxes. Southerners also objected to the proposal for a national bank. Since the money supply of the country was mainly in the financial centers of the North, northerners would end up owning most of the bank's stock and controlling its operations. The South had cause for apprehension about creating a powerful financial institution over which it would have almost no control. But in the end, a divided Congress passed all three measures as Hamilton had proposed them.

The National Bank

The debate over the bank was not only bitter but raised serious constitutional issues. Madison contended that Congress had no authority to charter such an institution, because power to do so had not been granted by the Constitution. The constitutional issue led Washington to request written opinions from his cabinet before signing the bill. The cabinet split evenly, with Hamilton and Knox supporting the bank, and Jefferson and Randolph opposing it as unconstitutional. Jefferson and Hamilton were the main antagonists, and their opinions proposed fundamentally different theories of constitutional interpretation. Jefferson argued that the Constitution created a government of only delegated powers, and that only powers expressly delegated could be legitimately exercised. The bank could not be justified under the "necessary and proper" clause of Article I because it was not necessary for governmental operations. That it might facilitate governmental operations did not make it necessary, and the constitutional standard was necessity, not convenience. The Constitution had to be interpreted strictly, Jefferson declared, because the Tenth Amendment reserved all powers not delegated to the federal government to the states or the people. He warned that any reading of the Constitution which allowed the government to exercise powers beyond those expressly delegated would lead in the end to federal absolutism.

Hamilton rejected Jefferson's strict constructionism as a constitutional straitjacket. He contended that the federal government had implied powers as well as those expressly granted. Authority to establish a national bank was implied by the power expressly granted to Congress to levy and collect taxes. He argued that every grant of express power carries with it implied power to employ such means as are useful and proper for its implementation:

> If the end be clearly comprehended within any of the specified powers, and if the measure have an obvious relation to that end, and is not forbidden by any particular provision of the constitution—it may safely be deemed to come within the compass of the national authority.

As for the "necessary and proper" clause, Hamilton argued that the word "necessary" does not always mean essential; it often means "no more than *needful, requisite, incidental, useful, or conducive to.*" Although not fully convinced by Hamilton's parsing of the clause, Washington signed the bill anyway because it most directly concerned Hamilton's department. But the constitutional debate did not end there. It continued until the bank was finally destroyed during the Jackson administration.

Although Hamilton's ideas prevailed in the long run, the winning side is not always the correct side. Jefferson's strict constructionism was not the political straitjacket that

Hamilton made it out to be. For one thing, it would not have denied the federal government the implied powers necessary for its operations. Jefferson insisted only that the framers of the Constitution intended the word "necessary" to mean more than just useful or convenient. Hamilton's looser usage opened up vast vistas of federal power unimagined in the eighteenth century. This is probably what Hamilton wanted, but it was not what the framers intended. Making convenience rather than necessity the test of constitutionality gave the government almost unlimited scope in defining its own authority. Self-restraint and internal checks and balances would be the only practical limits on the exercise of federal power. Although Jefferson as president also practiced loose constructionism when it suited his purposes, he may have been more on the mark when he originally opposed it for opening up, as he put it, "a boundless field of power, no longer susceptible of any definition."

Foreign Relations

The political debate extended beyond domestic issues into foreign affairs. The French Revolution precipitated a general European war that raged almost continuously until the defeat of Napoleon at Waterloo in 1815. The conflict divided Americans ideologically. Some, like Jefferson and Madison, saw the French cause as another round in the continuing struggle for human rights and republican government begun by Americans in 1776. Others, like Hamilton and most Federalists, saw revolutionary France as the enemy of religion, constitutional government, and property rights. Although under heavy pressure to take sides, Washington decided to steer a neutral course. The country was so sharply divided on events in Europe that any other course might have wrecked the Union.

Maintaining neutrality was complicated by American treaty commitments to France dating from 1778. When the French went to war with Great Britain in 1793, the cabinet was sharply divided on what to do. Hamilton argued that treaties made with the government of Louis XVI did not oblige the United States to assist revolutionaries who had overthrown the monarchy and executed the king. Moreover, the treaties bound the United States to assist only in a defensive war, and it was the French who had declared war on Britain. Jefferson countered with the argument that treaties are made between nations, not governments, and that the treaties with France were still in force. Although he did not favor armed intervention, he opposed repudiating the treaties or doing anything likely to weaken the French cause. Washington took Jefferson's advice not to renounce the treaties, but he followed Hamilton's advice against siding with the French. Over Jefferson's objections, he issued a neutrality proclamation that had the practical effect of denying France any assistance.

The proclamation outraged American supporters of the French Revolution and became the first test of the president's power over foreign affairs. Some argued that the proclamation usurped the constitutional authority of Congress to declare war by foreclosing the option. Hamilton defended the proclamation as a proper exercise of the president's executive prerogative in foreign affairs. While Congress had the power to declare war, the president had a duty to maintain peaceful relations until war was declared. Jefferson rejected this completely. He contended that Congress should have been consulted because of its constitutional responsibilities in anything relating to war and peace. The disagreement culminated in the Pacificus-Helvidius debates on the constitutionality of the proclamation.

The debates reflected ideological and political rifts within the administration. Hamilton, writing under the pseudonym "Pacificus," justified the Neutrality Proclamation as within the president's constitutional powers. He wrote that while Congress alone can declare war, "it is . . . the duty of the Executive to preserve Peace until war is declared." Madison entered the fray as "Helvidius" at the behest of Jefferson, who as a member of the cabinet could not openly oppose administration policy. "For God's sake, my dear Sir, take up your pen," he urged, "select the most striking heresies, and cut him to pieces in the face of the public. There is nobody else who can and will enter the lists with him." Although initially reluctant, Madison wrote a series of articles attacking Hamilton personally and denouncing anyone supporting the Proclamation as a secret monarchist and enemy of republican government. The Jeffersonian and Hamiltonian visions for America had sharply diverged, with executive power the immediate point of contention. History has sided with Hamilton of course, and today the executive branch wields almost unlimited power with respect to foreign policy, subject only to Congress's power to declare a formal state of war.

Citizen Genêt

The controversy over the neutrality proclamation convinced Edmond Genêt, the French minister to the United States, that Washington's policy lacked popular support. So he threw caution to the wind and commissioned privateers to prey on British shipping. He also plotted military expeditions against Florida and Louisiana. When warned by Jefferson to desist, Genêt threatened to appeal over the president's head directly to the people. This was a serious blunder, because Washington's public esteem transcended both politics and policy. The challenge to the president backfired and increased support for neutrality. Jefferson and Madison regarded Genêt as a liability to the French cause, and the cabinet voted to demand his recall. The Jacobins, who had just taken power in France, were glad to comply. An order for Genêt's arrest was issued, and he almost certainly would have gone to the guillotine had Washington not refused to extradite him.

The neutrality proclamation caused Jefferson to leave the administration. Washington's tilt toward Hamilton in foreign as well as domestic affairs left him without real influence in the cabinet. The proclamation was the final straw because Jefferson had been overruled on a matter involving his own department. Since he could not oppose the administration while still a part of it, he submitted his resignation to take effect at the end of 1793. Edmund Randolph, who succeeded him as Secretary of State, had to take over the difficult task of steering a neutral course between belligerents who increasingly scorned the rights of neutrals. Jefferson's departure to join in the opposition made the task even more difficult.

President Washington on Citizen Genêt

"Is the Minister of the French Republic to set the Acts of this Government at defiance, *with impunity*? and then threaten the Executive with an appeal to the People? What must the world think of such conduct and of the Government of the U States in submitting to it?"

—Letter to Thomas Jefferson, July 11, 1793

CITIZEN GENET.[1]

Figure IV.5 Portrait of Edmond-Charles Genêt.

Emmet Collection, Miriam and Ira D. Wallach Division of Art, Prints and Photographs, The New York Public Library, Astor, Lenox and Tilden Foundations

Violations of American Neutrality

The most serious foreign problems confronting the United States involved the British. They not only maintained military garrisons on American soil in the Northwest but flagrantly violated American neutral rights on the high seas. France, having lost most of her merchant marine, opened her ports to neutral shipping, but Britain soon slammed the door shut on this lucrative trade by issuing orders for the seizure of neutral vessels carrying French goods. The British revived the controversial Rule of 1756 under which trade not permitted in peacetime could not be carried on in time of war. This was contrary to contemporary norms of international law and, to make matters worse, the Royal Navy began implementing the new policy even before the United States learned of its existence. About three hundred American ships were seized in violation of the neutral rights of the United States. Adding insult to injury, American sailors on many of the vessels were impressed into British naval service on the pretext that they were deserters from the Royal Navy.

These outrages inflamed public opinion in the United States. The administration came under heavy pressure to take reprisals ranging from the sequestration of British property to a declaration of war. Jefferson had recommended a boycott of British goods, but

Hamilton argued successfully that this would reduce needed tariff revenues and cause serious economic problems. A declaration of war would have the worst consequences of all. It would cut off British investment in the United States and totally disrupt American commerce. The arguments against war were compelling, but anti-British sentiment ran high nevertheless. Congress for its part prepared for the worst by voting appropriations for harbor fortifications and military supplies.

Jay's Treaty

Washington, hoping for a diplomatic solution, appointed John Jay as special envoy to Britain. His first choice had been Madison, but because Hamilton objected (Madison was regarded as pro-French), he turned to Jay, a skilled negotiator. Although the Constitution did not prohibit such an appointment, Jay's assumption of executive functions while still chief justice made a dent in the separation of powers. He was instructed to secure a treaty providing for the removal of British garrisons from the Northwest, restoration of the rights of neutral shipping on the high seas, and compensation for the American vessels already seized. Jay was to make no concessions which conflicted with the treaty obligations of the United States to France. Washington hoped for peace but not at the price of national dishonor.

Jay's negotiating position could not have been weaker. He really had nothing to offer the British for the concessions he sought. Hamilton made his situation worse by informing George Hammond, the British minister to the United States, that the cabinet had secretly voted not to join the League of Armed Neutrality being organized in Europe to resist British naval provocations. How much damage this actually did cannot be assessed, but the possibility that the United States might join the League was Jay's only real bargaining chip. So the British were under no pressure to concede anything. The most Jay could obtain was an agreement to withdraw from the Northwest by June 1, 1796 and some trading concessions in the British West Indies. But the latter were granted on condition that American vessels carried no West Indian staples, British or non-British, to any ports except their own. The treaty also provided for a mixed commission to settle the payment of pre-Revolutionary debts owed to British creditors, fix the boundary between New England and Canada, and compensate American shippers for illegal seizures made by the Royal Navy. British trade with the United States would be on a most-favored-nation basis, and there would be no economic reprisals by the United States against British trade restrictions. The treaty said nothing about the impressment of American sailors into the Royal Navy or the naval blockade that had precipitated the crisis.

The treaty did so little to redress the main grievances of the United States that there was a public outcry when its terms became known. It was so unpopular that for a time it seemed the Senate might reject it. Jay was not alone in bearing the brunt of public outrage; Hamilton was stoned when he tried to defend the treaty at a public meeting. Although the Senate ratified the treaty at Washington's urging, its restrictive provisions regarding the West Indian trade were deleted. Some members of the House of Representatives tried to block enforcement of the treaty by refusing to vote the appropriations needed to

"The result of my negotiations will doubtless produce fresh disputes, and give occasion to much declamation . . . [M]en are more apt to think of what they wish to have, than of what is in their power to obtain."

—Letter to President Washington, March 6, 1795

implement some of its provisions. They took the position that no money would be voted until the president provided the House with all documents and correspondence relating to the treaty. Washington turned them down flat, insisting that the materials demanded were protected by executive privilege, which could not be waived without breaching the separation of powers. The House finally backed down and voted the needed funds. But the outcome and the fate of executive privilege might have been different had the president been anyone but Washington.

Although Washington had hoped for something better, the Jay Treaty well served the long-term interests of the country. It confirmed American sovereignty over the Northwest and prevented a war that the United States was not politically or militarily prepared to fight. The treaty also set the stage for settling long-standing differences with Spain. It convinced Spain, which by now was the ally of France in Europe, that an Anglo-American alliance might be in the making. Such an alliance would pose a threat to Florida and Louisiana unless relations with the United States improved. Spain's apprehensions enabled Thomas Pinckney to negotiate the highly favorable Treaty of San Lorenzo in 1795. The treaty settled every issue of the past decade, from the Florida boundary dispute to navigation rights on the Mississippi, on American terms.

Party Politics

The policy debates of the 1790s set the stage for the emergence of national political parties. The framers of the Constitution had not anticipated such a development. They assumed that the country was too large for its diverse interest groups to organize effectively beyond state or regional boundaries. Party politics had not gone beyond the state level during the Confederation, and most Americans expected things to remain the same under the Constitution. Hamilton and Madison predicted that a stronger federal union would actually reduce factionalism by bringing people together for common national goals. They could not have been more mistaken, for every act of the new government occasioned bitter debate. Within a year, Hamilton and Madison were on opposite sides of issues that split the country politically. On one side were the businessmen, merchants, and professionals who stood to benefit from Hamilton's policies; on the other were the southern planters, small farmers, and town workers who would not benefit from the policies but would nevertheless have to pay for them with their taxes.

The debate over foreign policy gave factionalism an added ideological edge. The Federalists regarded the French Revolution as a threat to law and order everywhere. They feared the spread of Jacobinism and therefore supported Great Britain as the last bulwark of the established order in Europe. The Republicans, as the Antifederalists came to be known because of their support of the French Republic, saw things differently. They regarded the Revolution as part of a millenary struggle for progress and social justice. A defeat for human rights and equality in Europe, they believed, would strengthen the forces of reaction everywhere. Republicans accused Federalists of harboring monarchial sentiments and of plotting to impose an oligarchy on the country. They had ignored the interests of ordinary citizens and run the government for the benefit of a political and economic elite. Their support for royalist Britain against revolutionary France exposed them as enemies of real republicanism.

The key to power was control of the federal government, and this required political collaboration across state lines. The presidency could only be won by imposing party discipline on presidential electors in all the states. Electoral majorities could not be obtained unless electors committed themselves in advance to particular candidates. If they continued to cast ballots for candidates of their own choice, as the Constitution had intended, most elections would have to be decided in the House of Representatives. Winning the presidency, the source of so much power and patronage, became the driving force behind national political organization. Putting electoral majorities together created the national party system.

Control of the national government gave the Federalists an advantage in party organization. Hamilton's Treasury agents were everywhere, not just collecting taxes and performing official functions, but building a national political network. Since the interest groups that benefited from the Hamiltonian program could be counted on for support, a political constituency existed from the beginning. The Republicans had a much more difficult time welding their disparate elements into a cohesive political force. They initially lacked the political skill of their opponents and did not have the power of the federal government behind them. It took the Republicans until about 1792 to establish a political network throughout the country.

The Adams Administration

Washington's decision not to accept a third term in 1796 set the stage for the first contested presidential election. Although the election was fought by party candidates, there were no party conventions or formal nominations. Everything on both sides was arranged by state party leaders who relied mainly on correspondence to choose party candidates. Then party electors were chosen to cast the state's electoral votes for the party candidates. The Federalists agreed to back John Adams for president and Thomas Pinckney for vice president, and the Republicans chose Thomas Jefferson and Aaron Burr, a leading New York Republican.

Both tickets had regional balance with a northerner and a southerner to insure party harmony. After a bitter campaign fought mainly in the press, Adams won a narrow victory. If the Federalist electors had maintained strict party discipline, Pinckney would have been elected vice president. But this was not the case. Disappointed that Adams had been chosen over Hamilton, some of them broke ranks and cast their second ballot for Jefferson instead of Pinckney. This made the outcome uncomfortably close. Adams won by only three votes, and Jefferson, finishing second, became his vice president.

Adams would have had a difficult presidency under any circumstances because of the rise of partisan politics. But some of his problems sprang from his refusal or inability to play the role of party leader. Washington had been able to remain above the political fray because his personal prestige made his leadership virtually unassailable. Adams made the mistake of thinking that as president he would be accorded the same deference and respect. He soon learned to his chagrin that the presidency without Washington was just another public office as well as a target for political invective. The Republicans almost immediately unleashed a torrent of abuse against him. Adams himself made a perfect target. Although a great patriot and one of the architects of American independence, he had the manner and appearance of a stiff-necked aristocrat. Nor could he count on a united party to support him, partly because he did nothing to unite it. Too self-righteous for political intrigue, he made no attempt to win over the Hamiltonians who had opposed his nomination. His essentially nonpolitical approach to government was out of step with the times, for running a successful administration now required a high degree of political leadership.

The most pressing problems facing Adams involved foreign affairs. While the Jay Treaty improved relations with Great Britain and led to a favorable treaty with Spain, it brought the country to the brink of war with France. The French were furious that the United States had seemingly waived its neutral rights on the high seas and granted most-favored-nation status to Great Britain. The Americans had not only reneged on their treaty obligations to France but had adopted what amounted to a pro-British brand of neutrality. So the French decided to take reprisals. In July 1796 the French government declared that in the future France would treat American commerce as the British had treated it. Orders were issued for the seizure of American ships trading with British ports or carrying British goods. Diplomatic relations were broken, and the American minister, Charles C. Pinckney, was ordered to leave French soil.

The X, Y, Z Affair

Although most Federalists favored a declaration of war on France, Adams hoped for a diplomatic settlement. He appointed a commission consisting of Charles C. Pinckney, John Marshall, and Elbridge Gerry to negotiate a treaty restoring normal relations. The French government refused to receive them officially. Instead, the commissioners had to negotiate informally with three agents appointed by Talleyrand, the French foreign minister. The agents, identified only as X, Y, and Z in dispatches to the United States, demanded a loan for France and a bribe of $240,000 for the members of the ruling Directory. The commissioners refused and informed Adams, who reported to Congress on March 19, 1798 that negotiations had failed. When the X, Y, Z correspondence and bribe demand were revealed, the country exploded with anger. The Hamiltonian Federalists, led by Secretary of State Timothy Pickering, called for an immediate declaration of war. Congress hastily enacted defense measures, and Washington was appointed commanding

Figure IV.6   Print titled *A New Display of the United States* by Amos Doolittle (1799). A portrait of John Adams is encircled by state seals and bears caption, "Millions for Defense and Not One Cent for Tribute."

Library of Congress, Prints and Photographs Division, LC-DIG-ppmsca-15716

general with Hamilton second in command. The treaties of 1778 were abrogated, and an undeclared naval war against France broke out on the high seas.

But Adams had not given up on peace. In February 1799, having gotten assurances that an envoy would be respectfully received, he appointed William Vans Murray as minister to France. The war faction was dismayed, and Federalist senators threatened to block Murray's appointment. Adams responded by threatening to resign and turning the presidency over to Jefferson, who was the last person Federalists wanted in charge. So a compromise was hammered out for the appointment of a commission consisting of Murray, Chief Justice Ellsworth, and Governor William R. Davie of North Carolina. By the time the commissioners reached Paris, a new French government headed by Napoleon was in power and ready for a settlement. The negotiations culminated in the Treaty of Morfontaine (also known as the Convention of 1800), which cancelled the treaties of 1778 and endorsed the principle that neutral ships make neutral cargoes. The treaty prevented a war but cost Adams the support of the Hamiltonian wing of his party.

The Alien and Sedition Acts

In preparing for war in 1798, Congress passed the Alien and Sedition Acts as internal security measures. Both laws restricted and punished political dissent. The Alien Act authorized the deportation of any foreign resident deemed by the president to pose a danger to the United States. The Sedition Act made it a misdemeanor, punishable by fine and imprisonment, to publish any "false, scandalous and malicious writing" which brought the government, members of Congress, or the president into disrepute. The Alien Act was mainly directed against foreigners in the United States who engaged in partisan politics, particularly those who published attacks on the administration. The Sedition Act sought to muzzle the Republican press. Federalists believed that attacks on the administration had crossed the line between reasonable dissent and outright sedition.

Both measures set off a fierce constitutional debate. They were attacked by Republicans as despotic and unconstitutional. The arbitrary deportation of aliens violated rudimentary notions of due process, and the restraints on political dissent abridged freedom of speech and press. The Republicans had cause for concern, because their opponents now had a legal weapon to use against them. Although the Alien Act was not enforced, enforcement of the Sedition Act was partisan and vigorous. Twenty-five persons were prosecuted and ten convicted, all of them Republican editors or printers. Republicans charged that the prosecutions violated freedom of speech and press, while Federalists contended that the First Amendment did not guarantee absolute freedom of expression but only barred Congress from imposing prior restraints on the right to speak and publish. Nothing protected the press, Federalists argued, against the consequences of libel. The Sedition Act protected legitimate dissent by making truth a defense. What critics of the administration wanted, Federalists charged, was not freedom to publish the truth but freedom to destroy public trust in government by malicious falsehoods.

Some Federalists took the position that the government did not need a statute to prosecute seditious libel. They claimed the authority to prosecute offenses punishable at common law as well as those prohibited by statute. Several common-law indictments had been obtained in the 1790s, and the courts in most cases had upheld them. The Sedition Act, Federalists argued, gave the press more freedom than it had at common law by making truth a defense and leaving the issue of libel to the jury. Indeed, the Act only authorized the federal government to do what the states had long done in suppressing sedition. The press guarantees of the state constitutions had not prevented the states from punishing such offenses.

The Republicans rejected common-law precedents as irrelevant. They insisted that there was no federal common law and that the government only had powers granted by the Constitution. Whatever standing the common law might have among the states, there were no federal crimes except those covered by statute or the Constitution. The Constitution would not have mentioned treason if the crime had been punishable as a common-law offense. The Republicans declared that the First Amendment had abolished the common-law crime of seditious libel and barred federal prosecutions for the offense. What the states did was their own affair because they were not bound by the First Amendment. But even without the amendment, the Sedition Act would be unconstitutional because nothing in the Constitution authorized Congress to pass such a law. Not even the implied powers theory could be stretched to cover the measure. The suppression of dissent, they argued, was hardly "necessary and proper" for the exercise of any of the government's delegated powers.

Kentucky and Virginia Resolutions

Although upheld by the federal circuit courts as constitutional, the Sedition Act put the Federalists on the defensive politically. They were accused of attempting to destroy freedom of speech and turn the government into a one-party oligarchy. Jefferson and Madison staked out the Republican position in sets of Resolutions passed by the Kentucky and Virginia legislatures. The Resolutions declared that the Constitution was a compact among the states, and that the states therefore had the right to judge whether it had been violated. They also declared that when the federal government oversteps its constitutional authority, the states "have the right, and are in duty bound, to interpose for arresting the progress of the evil[.]" In effect, state power could be used to prevent the enforcement of federal laws deemed by the states to be unconstitutional. Although neither state actually attempted to prevent enforcement, both claimed the sovereign right to do so.

The Kentucky and Virginia Resolutions were denounced by the Federalists as a formula for anarchy. If each state could judge for itself whether a federal law should be enforced, federal authority would be shredded. A law held constitutional and enforceable in one state might be declared unconstitutional and unenforceable in another. Federalists attacked the compact theory of the Constitution as historically untenable. The Constitution had not been ratified by the state governments but by conventions acting directly for the people. But the Republicans were not persuaded. They argued that if the states could not resist unconstitutional acts of the federal government, both the states and the people would be at its mercy. How could the federal government or any government be trusted as the sole judge of its powers? Such an approach would render the guarantees of the Bill of Rights meaningless, because the government would be free to bend them to its own convenience. Whatever the merits of their arguments, the debate put Federalists on the defensive. Their opponents were perceived to stand for free speech and liberty, while the Federalists were in the position of having to defend an unpopular law. The debate dealt Republicans a winning hand for the coming presidential election.

Election of 1800

The federal elections of 1800 were the most bitterly contested that the country had yet seen. Republicans warned that a renewed lease on power for the Federalists would result in oligarchy, and the Federalists predicted ruin and anarchy should the Republicans win. When the electoral votes of New York turned out to be decisive, an effort was made to deny its electoral votes to Jefferson despite the fact that the Republicans had carried the state. Since state law provided that the presidential electors would be chosen by the legislature elected in 1800, the victorious Republicans could be counted on to appoint Republican electors when they took office. Hamilton sought to prevent this by changing the law. He urged Governor Jay to call a special session of the outgoing Federalist legislature to repeal the law and appoint Federalist electors. "[T]he scruples of delicacy and propriety," he wrote, "ought not to hinder the taking of a *legal* and *constitutional* step to prevent an atheist in religion, and a fanatic in politics, from getting possession of the helm of state." But Jay refused to be a party to changing the rules after the game had been played. So the electors were chosen by the incoming legislature, which gave the Republicans an eight-vote margin of victory.

Electoral Deadlock

Although the Republicans had won, it was not immediately clear who would be president. The electoral count revealed a serious defect in the electoral process. The Founding Fathers had not anticipated that national parties would contest presidential elections. They had assumed that presidential electors would vote as individuals rather than as representatives of organized parties. But the party system that emerged in the 1790s changed all this and turned the electors into rubber stamps for party candidates. Party discipline was so effective in 1800 that every Republican elector cast one ballot for Jefferson and the other for Burr, thus creating an electoral tie and sending the election to the House of Representative. The deadlock remained unresolved for a week until Hamilton intervened and urged Federalists in the House to vote for Jefferson as the lesser evil. This tipped the balance to Jefferson, who finally won on the thirty-sixth ballot. The affair led to the adoption of the Twelfth Amendment, ratified in 1804, which provides for the election of the president and vice president on separate ballots. The electors retained two ballots but in the future would cast them for the particular office.

Judiciary Act of 1801

The Federalists remained in office for nearly four months after losing the elections. They made use of the time to entrench themselves in the judiciary. Over Republican objections, they hurriedly passed the Judiciary Act of 1801 to reorganize the courts and create new judicial posts for the party faithful. The Act reduced the Supreme Court to five members, which would deny Jefferson an appointment when the first vacancy opened; it created sixteen circuit courts with regular circuit judges, which relieved Supreme Court justices of their circuit duties; and it provided for numerous federal attorneys, marshals, clerks, and justices of the peace. Although the Act improved judicial efficiency and made Supreme Court appointments more attractive, its purpose was transparently political: to pack the judiciary with Federalists. It was under this law that Adams made his so-called midnight appointments during the final days of his administration. One of them, the chief justice-ship, went to John Marshall, who for the next three decades would uphold Federalist principles of government long after the party itself had vanished from the political scene.

When the Federalists left office in 1801, they left behind a record of political achievement unparalleled in American history. They had turned a shaky confederation of states into a strong federal union capable of protecting the essential interests of the nation. They gave the country twelve years of brilliant leadership, negotiated vital treaties, settled boundary disputes, and opened up the West for American expansion. No party has ever had a clearer vision of national goals or done more to promote them. The Federalists never regained power after their defeat in 1800. The tide of history had already begun to run strongly against them. They stood for a political elitism incompatible with the democratizing tendencies of American life. But even Republicans who decried their principles acknowledged Federalist achievements by leaving in place the successful structure of government they had created.

Note

1. Myers v. United States, 272 U.S. 52 (1926).

			March 1799	May 14, 1801	April 29, 1802
			Outbreak of Fries's Rebellion	Tripoli Declares War on United States	Judiciary Act of 1802

April 18, 1806	January 20, 1807	May 4, 1807	June 22, 1807	August 3, 1807	September 1, 1807
Non-Importation Act	Brockholst Livingston Becomes Associate Justice of Supreme Court	Thomas Todd Becomes Associate Justice of Supreme Court	Leopard-Chesapeake Incident	Treason Trial of Aaron Burr Begins	Acquittal of Aaron Burr

January 4, 1815	January 8, 1815	March 4, 1817	September 1, 1823	June 16, 1826	
Report of the Hartford Convention	Battle of New Orleans	James Monroe Takes Office as President of the United States	Smith Thompson Becomes Associate Justice of Supreme Court	Robert Trimble Becomes Associate Justice of Supreme Court	

V   Jeffersonian Republicanism

March 2, 1803	April 30, 1803	March 12, 1804	May 7, 1804	March 1, 1805	June 4, 1805
Stuart v. Laird	Louisiana Purchase Treaty	Conviction of District Judge John Pickering	William Johnson Becomes Associate Justice of Supreme Court	Senate Acquittal of Justice Samuel Chase	Signature of Peace Treaty with Tripoli

December 22, 1807	March 1809	March 4, 1809	November 23, 1811	February 3, 1812	December 24, 1814	June 18, 1812
Embargo Act	Repeal of Embargo Act	James Madison Takes Office as President of the United States	Gabriel Duvall Becomes Associate Justice of Supreme Court	Joseph Story Becomes Associate Justice of Supreme Court	Treaty of Ghent	War of 1812 Declared

"[N]o society can make a perpetual constitution, or even a perpetual law. The earth belongs always to the living generation. They may manage it then, and what proceeds from it, as they please, during their usufruct."

—Jefferson to Madison (1789)

The rivalry between Thomas Jefferson and Alexander Hamilton was one of the most influential in American history. It was more than a mere political contest. It was a philosophical rivalry between two visions of the republic created by the Constitution. Although never president himself, Hamilton helped give shape and purpose to the new federal republic. Its strong national government, energetic executive, and vigorous economic policy owed much to Hamilton's efforts. But when Thomas Jefferson became president in 1801, he brought a new political philosophy with him. He rejected the Federalist ideal of a powerful national state. He favored states' rights on the ground that state government was closer to the people and therefore more responsive to their interests. The whole point of government, he believed, was to safeguard personal freedom while promoting the interests of the majority. Centralized power worked primarily for the benefit of interest groups with the skill and resources to influence public policy from a distance. Hamilton's funding of the public debt, for instance, had benefited wealthy bondholders and speculators with a windfall to be paid by taxing workers and farmers.

Jefferson also rejected the Hamiltonian vision of a powerful commercial and industrial state, hoping instead for a nation of self-sufficient farmers independent of powerful economic interests. In a letter to John Jay, he observed, "Cultivators of the earth are the most valuable citizens. They are the most vigorous, the most independant, the most virtuous, & they are tied to their country & wedded to it's liberty and interests by the most lasting bonds." Having observed firsthand the degraded condition of the masses in the crowded cities of Europe, Jefferson wanted something better for the United States. "The mobs of great cities," he wrote, "add just so much to the support of pure government, as sores do to the strength of the human body." If government promoted an agrarian way of life that kept people economically free to make their own political choices, personal liberty would be safe, and peace and general prosperity would naturally follow. Although he was not naive about human nature or the pitfalls of democracy, Jefferson believed wholeheartedly in the ability of people to govern themselves. Without majority rule, republican government would soon degenerate into oligarchy and the tyranny of the few over the many. "Sometimes it is said that man cannot be trusted with the government of himself," Jefferson noted in his inaugural address. "Can he, then, be trusted with the government of others? Or have we found angels in the form of kings to govern him? Let history answer this question."

Jeffersonian Government

Although he would later refer to his election as the Revolution of 1800, Jefferson left intact the Federalist structures of government. The national bank that he had strongly opposed continued to operate, and the public debt that he had once sharply criticized was not repudiated. As president, Jefferson recognized the importance of continuity and moderation in building lasting political foundations. "We are all republicans; we are all federalists," he declared in his inaugural address, a conciliatory approach that led even Hamilton to comment that "the new President will not lend himself to dangerous innovations." Jefferson sought balance and consensus in his cabinet appointments. Two members came from Massachusetts and one from Connecticut, both Federalist strongholds which had not given him a single electoral vote. Nor did he fire Federalist officeholders in order to make room for Republicans. He removed some for political reasons and filled vacancies with Republicans, but his use of the patronage power was not ruthlessly partisan. By the middle of his second term Federalists still held 130 of the 316 offices directly controlled by the president.

But while the system remained essentially intact, the style of the new administration differed markedly from the old. The new president abandoned his predecessors' practice of delivering messages to Congress in person. He considered such addresses uncomfortably close to royal pronouncements from the throne and unsuitable for a republic. His messages were read to Congress by a clerk without pomp or ceremony, setting a precedent that was followed until the Wilson administration. Jefferson also put an end to Federalist formality at public ceremonies, and his two inaugurations were models of republican simplicity. He pointedly ignored protocol at White House dinners and insisted on simplicity at public receptions. Anthony Merry, the British minister to the United States, was shocked when the president received him in slippers when he made his first official call at the White House. Merry took it for an insult, though no insult had been intended. Republican slippers and informality simply reflected the new style of government.

Jefferson moved swiftly to correct what he considered Federalist abuses of power. He pardoned everyone convicted under the Sedition Act on the ground that the law was "in palpable and unqualified contradiction to the Constitution." Since the federal circuit courts had upheld the law as constitutional, this served notice that he did not feel himself bound by the constitutional interpretations of judges. Jefferson also moved to reduce both taxes and the national debt. The British admiralty helped him out by ruling in the *Polly* case (1800) that American ships could carry on trade between French ports if the voyage was interrupted by a stop in an American port. This "broken voyage" ruling opened the French West Indies to American shipping and greatly increased tariff revenues as American vessels touched base at American ports. The new flow of revenue enabled Congress to repeal the unpopular excise taxes enacted by the Federalists to pay the debt. At the same time, spending cuts by the administration made it possible to reduce the debt from about $83 million to $57 million. Jefferson gave debt reduction a high priority because he considered it a burden on taxpayers and an undesirable link between government and powerful financial interests. Albert Gallatin, his brilliant Secretary of the Treasury, persuaded Congress to abandon the practice of voting general

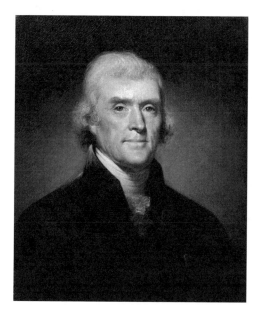

Figure V.1 Portrait of Thomas Jefferson by Rembrandt Peale (1800).

White House Historical Association (White House Collection): 55

appropriations and vote itemized ones instead in order to keep the budget balanced. The item system also ensured that funds appropriated for one purpose would not be used for another.

Judiciary Act of 1802

The elections of 1800 put the Republicans in control of both the executive branch and Congress but left the Federalists in control of the courts. Adams used his last days in office filling the judicial posts created by the Judiciary Act of 1801 with Federalists. The court-packing enraged Jefferson, and Republicans denounced the Federalist appointees as "midnight judges." The new Congress moved to cancel some of the appointments by repealing the Act and abolishing the circuit court judgeships. The repealing measure, the Judiciary Act of 1802, restored the Supreme Court to six members and again assigned circuit court duties to the justices. The circuit courts would now consist of one Supreme Court justice and a district court judge from within the circuit. The constitutionality of assigning Supreme Court justices to the circuit courts was upheld by the Supreme Court in *Stuart v. Laird* (1803) on the ground of long-standing practice. So, with only minor modifications, the federal judiciary reverted to the system originally established by the Judiciary Act of 1789.

Federalists in Congress opposed the abolition of the circuit court judgeships as unconstitutional. They contended that it amounted to dismissal of the newly appointed judges in violation of the life-tenure provisions of Article III. The Republicans rejected the constitutional argument as completely without merit. While the Constitution protected judges from removal, it also authorized Congress to regulate the courts. This authority could not be held hostage to the tenure expectations of judges. The existence of every federal court, except the Supreme Court, depended upon the will of Congress. And the Republican Congress now imposed its will as ruthlessly in abolishing the judgeships as the Federalists had in creating them. To forestall a judicial appeal on the constitutionality of the measure, Congress postponed the next term of the Supreme Court until 1803. The new arrangements by then would be a *fait accompli*.

Thomas Jefferson on President Adams's Midnight Appointments

"I can say with truth, that one act of Mr. Adams's life, and only one, ever gave me a moment's personal displeasure. I did consider his last appointments to office as personally unkind. They were from among my most ardent political enemies, from whom no faithful co-operation could ever be expected; and laid me under the embarrassment of acting thro men whose views were to defeat mine . . . It seemed but common justice to leave a successor free to act by instruments of his own choice."

—Letter to Abigail Adams, June 13, 1804

Purging the Judiciary

The president also took aim at Federalists already on the bench with a view to removing those guilty of partisan excesses. Jefferson distrusted the federal judiciary as an institution, partly because the provision for life tenure made judges politically unaccountable. He rejected the idea of an independent judiciary as incompatible with republican government. Judges had to be made accountable or the country would eventually find itself under the heel of a judicial oligarchy. Although the Constitution granted them life tenure, Congress still had the power to impeach and remove them. Jefferson believed that the power should be used to remove judges who abused their powers of office. The system of checks and balances that kept the political branches in line should also apply to the courts. That judges alone among all federal officials should be free to act with impunity was a preposterous notion promoted by enemies of republicanism.

Jefferson regarded the impeachment of judges as a legitimate device for the achievement of political goals. Although Article II of the Constitution authorizes the removal of federal officials for high crimes and misdemeanors, Article III apparently holds judges to a higher standard by granting them tenure during good behavior. This makes them removable, Jefferson reasoned, for improprieties falling short of actual criminality. Impeachment was the only device available for keeping the judiciary within bounds and preventing abuses of judicial power. Not to use it would subject the nation to a judicial absolutism alien to traditional notions of constitutional government.

John Pickering of the district court for New Hampshire was the first federal judge targeted by Jefferson for removal. An ardent Federalist who happened to be mentally unbalanced, he offered the Republicans a perfect opportunity to establish the principle that impeachment was essentially a political device. The charges filed against him in the House of Representatives included allegations of "loose morals and intemperate habits," appearing on the bench "in a state of intoxication," and invoking "the name of the Supreme Being . . . in a most profane manner." Pickering's most glaring defect, his mental derangement, was not mentioned in the impeachment. Because insanity is a legal defense in criminal proceedings, the House did not want to raise an issue that might prevent the Senate from convicting him. Although nothing in the impeachment amounted to a high crime or misdemeanor, the Senate voted to convict and remove him from office. Jefferson regarded the outcome as a victory for the political accountability of judges. Pickering's removal put all federal judges on notice that the good behavior required by the Constitution meant more than strict legality.

Impeachment of Justice Chase

Jefferson next took aim at the Supreme Court itself, marking Justice Samuel Chase, its most vulnerable member, for removal. Chase was a great authority on the Constitution and a first-rate judge, but he was also fiercely partisan and overbearing on the bench. He had staunchly defended the unpopular Sedition Act and harshly treated Republican defendants and attorneys who appeared before him. In 1804 Chase gave the administration an opening by delivering a partisan harangue to a Baltimore grand jury. He attacked the president and congressional Republicans as enemies of freedom and property. Jefferson seized the opportunity to start the impeachment process. "You must have heard of the extraordinary charge of [Chase] to the Grand Jury at Baltimore," he wrote to Congressman Joseph Nicholson. "Ought this seditious and official attack on the principles of our Constitution, and on the proceedings of a State, to go unpunished? And to whom so pointedly as yourself will the public look for the necessary measure?" Nicholson, who was regarded as Jefferson's choice to replace Chase, referred the matter to the Speaker of the House, and impeachment proceedings were begun.

The House voted eight articles of impeachment against Chase. The first accused him of arbitrary and unjust rulings during the treason trial of John Fries, leader of the so-called Fries Rebellion against a federal property tax in 1799. The next five charged him with various improprieties during the trial of James Callender for violating the Sedition Act. "It is a pity," Chase had remarked after the trial, "that they had not hanged the rascal." The seventh accused him of abuse of power for refusing to discharge a grand jury until it indicted a Republican printer for sedition. The eighth, a blatantly political article, involved his speech to the Baltimore grand jury, the incident that had precipitated the proceedings against him. He was accused of "prostituting the high judicial character with which he was invested to the low purpose of an electioneering partisan." Although all the charges were serious and for the most part accurate, none constituted an offense punishable under law. He could be removed from office only if the Senate accepted the House's theory that impeachment was a political proceeding requiring no proof of criminal offenses. That he had behaved improperly in office was enough to justify his conviction.

Chase's trial in 1805 was a landmark event in the history of the federal courts. His conviction almost certainly would have been followed by the impeachment of Chief Justice Marshall and other justices targeted by Jefferson for removal. John Randolph, one of the House prosecutors, argued that impeachment was a proper and necessary device to keep judges accountable. The "high crimes and misdemeanors" standard for impeachment prescribed by Article II of the Constitution had to be construed broadly to include noncriminal improprieties. The mere fact that a judge could not be sent to jail should not prevent his removal from the bench. If the "good behavior" standard for judicial tenure prescribed by Article III meant only noncriminal behavior, then the standard would be deplorably low. After all, Judge Pickering had not been guilty of any punishable offense, yet the Senate had convicted and removed him from office.

Chase was ably defended by Luther Martin and Charles Lee, and they rejected the House theory of impeachment completely. They argued that the Senate could not convict him without finding him guilty of some legal offense. Improprieties not covered by law were not sufficient grounds for removal. To remove him on such grounds would subordinate the judicial tenure provisions of the Constitution to the whim of partisan majorities in Congress. Martin argued that some of the alleged misconduct was only the impatience of a learned judge who did not suffer fools gladly. If a judge could be removed for possessing

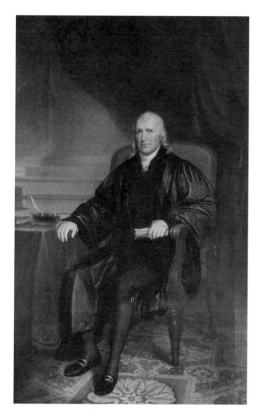

Figure V.2 Samuel Chase by John Beale
Bordley (1836).
Collection of the Maryland State Archives

superior legal talent, then legal ignorance would become a prime requisite for holding
judicial office.

Martin emphasized that more was at stake than the removal of a single justice. The
proceedings amounted to an attack on the independence of the judiciary. Vice President
Aaron Burr, who presided at the trial, was so impressed by the argument that he retained
Martin to manage his defense against treason charges the following year. But the outcome
for Chase depended on whether Republicans in the Senate would support Jefferson's
assault on judicial independence. Since they outnumbered Federalists by twenty-five to
nine, a straight party vote would have produced the two-thirds majority needed for a conviction. In the end, enough northern Republicans broke ranks to acquit Chase. There was
a majority for conviction on three of the articles, but it fell short of the two-thirds majority required by the Constitution. So Chase stayed on the Court, and Jefferson suffered a
stunning political defeat.

Chase's acquittal had far-reaching consequences. The Republican defections in the
Senate convinced Jefferson that impeachment could not be used as a political device.
Chief Justice Marshall's position now became secure for the first time since his appointment. The outcome demonstrated, Jefferson wrote, that impeachment was "an impractical thing, a mere scarecrow" without substance. Judges could now "consider themselves

secure for life" and free to "skulk from responsibility." There would never be another attempt to remove a judge for holding views opposed to those of the party in power. On the other hand, the case permanently dampened the partisan enthusiasm of judicial appointees. It served as a warning that the judiciary could not claim independence unless judges maintained at least the appearance of political neutrality. Since the Chase trial, the Senate has tried seven judges impeached by the House and convicted four of them. Two of those removed were convicted of abuses of office not amounting to criminal offenses.[1] So the "high crimes and misdemeanors" standard that saved Chase has not always prevailed. What has prevailed though is the principle that judges should not be removed for political reasons unrelated to their behavior as judges.

Supreme Court Appointments

Jefferson finally got an opportunity to fill a Supreme Court vacancy when Justice Moore resigned in 1804. The president wanted someone who would maintain his independence of the Federalist justices, particularly Chief Justice Marshall, and speak out for Republican principles on the Court. He chose William Johnson of South Carolina, a close friend and political supporter. Johnson's numerous dissents broke the solidarity of the Court, but his influence on constitutional law was slight. He voted with the Federalist majority on many key issues, and Marshall remained firmly in charge. Jefferson made two other appointments. In 1808 he appointed Brockholst Livingston of New York to the vacancy created by the death of Justice Paterson. Congress created another opening the following year by increasing the membership of the Court to seven. The new seat went to Thomas Todd, a Kentucky Republican. Both Livingston and Todd soon fell under Marshall's influence, so the voting balance of the court was not disturbed. Jefferson later warned his successor Madison that in making appointments it would be difficult to find "a character of firmness enough to preserve his independence on the same bench with Marshall."

The First Barbary War

While domestic issues concerned him most, Jefferson from the outset of his administration had to deal with an overseas challenge posed by the Barbary pirates. For centuries pirates from the North African states of Algiers, Morocco, Tripoli, and Tunis (the so-called Barbary Coast) had seized ships and crewmen in the Mediterranean with virtual impunity. The European nations most affected by these state-sponsored depredations found it cheaper and politically expedient to pay tribute for the safe passage of their commerce than the alternative of taking concerted military action. Before the break with England, American commerce in the Mediterranean had been protected under British treaties with the pirate regimes and by the power of the Royal Navy. But the protection ended when the United States became an independent nation. Throughout the Confederation period, American ships and sailors were seized in the Mediterranean, and Congress had neither the power to take reprisals nor the money to ransom the captives. The emergence of a stronger national government under the Constitution did not appreciably alter the situation. Both the Washington and Adams administrations paid tribute to the Barbary States to buy safe passage for American shipping in the Mediterranean. By the time Jefferson became president, nearly one-fifth of the national revenue had been paid either to ransom captives or to buy protection against the seizure of American vessels.

The situation came to a head in 1801 when the Bashaw (or Pasha) of Tripoli demanded additional tribute that Jefferson was not prepared to pay. The president decided instead to send a naval force to the Mediterranean and confront the pirates directly. But before taking action he consulted with his cabinet on how to proceed. In a meeting held on May 15, 1801, the cabinet unanimously agreed that a naval squadron should be dispatched, though there was some disagreement on the nature and scope of the mission. Attorney General Levi Lincoln advised that the squadron should defend itself if attacked, but should not act offensively and hunt down the enemy. Secretary of State James Madison and Treasury Secretary Albert Gallatin argued for a more aggressive strategy, including hot pursuit into enemy harbors. Gallatin raised the question of congressional approval since the Constitution clearly vests the power to wage war in Congress. But Congress was then in recess, and it would have taken weeks for it to assemble in a special session. Gallatin personally held the view that approval was not needed because the president as commander in chief had all the authority needed under Article II to take defensive action against enemies of the United States. Jefferson and his cabinet were unaware as they deliberated that the country was already at war. The day before, on May 14, the Bashaw declared war on the United States in typical Barbary fashion by sending soldiers to chop down the flagpole of the American consulate in Tripoli.

When Congress convened, Jefferson justified the actions taken as purely defensive. He acknowledged that under the Constitution he had no authority to declare a state of war between the United States and Tripoli. Congress responded with a resolution tacitly approving all that had been done and authorizing the president "to cause to be done all such other acts of precaution or hostility as the state of war will justify." This functional equivalent of a declaration of war bears a striking similarity to the Gulf of Tonkin Resolution under which Congress endorsed American involvement in the Vietnam conflict a century and a half later. In response to Jefferson's request for more specific authority with regard to hostilities, Congress in 1802 authorized him to "employ such of the armed vessels of the United States as may be judged requisite" for the protection of American ships and crew members. For all practical purposes, the president was given what amounted to a free hand to deal with the pirates.

The war itself dragged on until 1805 with neither side gaining a decisive advantage. When the naval campaign failed to bring the Bashaw to terms, a land expedition was launched from Egypt with the object of replacing him with his older brother from whom he had usurped the throne. A mixed force of American marines and Greek, Arab, and Berber mercenaries crossed the Libyan desert and captured the stronghold of Derna. The loss of Derna shocked the Bashaw into negotiating a treaty acceptable to the United States. In June 1805 the Bashaw signed a Treaty of Peace and Amity ending hostilities and releasing 300 Americans from captivity. For releasing the captives, the Bashaw received a ransom of $60,000. Although important in establishing the credibility of the United States on the international scene, neither the war nor the treaty put an end to Barbary piracy. Pirates sponsored by the other rogue regimes of North Africa were not affected. The extortions would continue until the Second Barbary War in 1815 ended all tribute payments to the Barbary States.

Apart from the naval skirmishes with France in the 1790s, the conflict with Tripoli was the first of the many undeclared wars fought by the United States. The war underscored for the first time the ambiguity of the war power under a Constitution that makes the president as commander in chief responsible for defending the nation while assigning to Congress authority to declare a formal state of war. Where the authority of one branch of government ends and the other begins is the heart of the problem. While the president obviously has authority to defend the nation against aggression without first consulting Congress, does the power to defend also include authority to commit the armed forces to combat thousands of miles from home without congressional approval? Jefferson thought that the answer was yes, and the presidents who followed him in office have all agreed. The minor war waged against Tripoli became a precedent for most of the subsequent undeclared wars fought by this nation. That Congress subsequently approved Jefferson's actions is beside the point. What else can any Congress do once the armed forces of the nation are committed to combat? It might have been better had Jefferson's Congress asserted its Article I powers by formally declaring war on Tripoli instead of tamely acquiescing to the exercise of presidential war power. That would have reclaimed for Congress power delegated to Congress alone by the Constitution. The course pursued conceded

Figure V.3 Print titled *Bombardment of Tripoli* by Currier and Ives (c. 1846).
Library of Congress, Prints and Photographs Division, LC-USZC4-2705

far too much to the executive branch and set an unfortunate precedent for the future. In retrospect, Jefferson's war against the pirates goes far to confirm the adage that history essentially chronicles old ways of dealing with modern problems.

The Louisiana Purchase

Jefferson's purchase of Louisiana from France in 1803 precipitated a major political storm. Federalists attacked the purchase on the ground that the Constitution made no provision for the purchase of foreign territory, and the president therefore had no authority to make such a treaty. Jefferson defended the purchase on the ground that the sovereignty of the national government includes the power to acquire territory and expand the nation's boundaries. The debate actually had more to do with politics than with constitutional theory. The Federalists realized that westward expansion would upset the balance of political power in the United States. As new western states entered the Union, they would join the agrarian South and render the eastern strongholds of Federalism powerless.

The Debate on the Louisiana Purchase

Jefferson Makes the Case for the Purchase

"[We have] not been unaware of the danger to which our peace would be perpetually exposed while so important a key to the commerce of the western country remained under foreign power . . . While the property and sovereignty of the Mississippi and its waters secure an independent outlet for the produce of the western States, and an uncontrolled navigation through their whole course, free from collision with other powers and the dangers to our peace from that source, the fertility of the country, its climate and extent, promise in due season important aids to our treasury, an ample provision for our posterity, and a wide-spread field for the blessings of freedom and equal laws."

—Third Annual Message to Congress, October 17, 1803

A Federalist Senator Opposes the Purchase

"Louisiana must and will become settled, if we hold it, and with the very population that would otherwise occupy part of our present territory. Thus our citizens will be removed to the immense distance of two or three thousand miles from the capital of the Union, where they will scarcely ever feel the rays of the General Government; their affections will become alienated; they will gradually begin to view us as strangers; they will form other commercial connections, and our interests will become distinct . . . We already have territory enough, and when I contemplate the evils that may arise to these States, from this intended incorporation of Louisiana into the Union, I would rather see it given to France, to Spain, or to any other nation of the earth, upon the mere condition that no citizen of the United States should ever settle within its limits . . ."

—Senate Speech of Samuel White of Delaware (1803)

Ohio, when admitted in 1803, immediately joined the Republican camp, and the new states to be formed from Louisiana would probably do the same. The egalitarian spirit that prevailed on the western frontier virtually guaranteed it. To many eastern Federalists, the prospect of becoming a permanent minority because of territorial expansion was completely unacceptable.

Some ultra-Federalists in New England hatched a plot to pull the Northeast out of the Union. The Essex Junto, as the plotters were known, hoped to establish a confederacy consisting of the five New England states along with New York and New Jersey. When Hamilton would have nothing to do with the scheme, they turned to Aaron Burr to bring New York into the confederacy. Burr had carried New York for the Republicans in 1800, but they had dropped him from the presidential ticket in 1804 in favor of George Clinton. So the vice president decided to seek the governorship of New York and, in return for Federalist support, agreed to swing New York into the confederacy and become its president. Burr's defeat in the gubernatorial election dealt the conspiracy a fatal blow. But even had he won, it seems unlikely that the plotters could have pulled their states out of the Union. The acquisition of Louisiana was overwhelmingly popular, even in New England, where Jefferson carried every state except Connecticut in winning reelection in 1804. His victory gave the acquisition political legitimacy, and the Supreme Court subsequently confirmed its constitutionality on the ground that the power of Congress to govern the national territories implies the power to acquire them.[2]

Burr's Western Conspiracy

Having broken with the Republicans, Burr lost his Federalist supporters by killing Alexander Hamilton in a duel resulting from the bitter gubernatorial race. His political career in ruins and facing murder charges in New York and New Jersey, he moved west in 1805 to recoup his fortunes. Westerners, duelists themselves, were dazzled by Burr, whose personal charm and magnetism were conceded even by his enemies. From his base in the Ohio Valley, the former vice president organized a far-flung conspiracy that has puzzled historians down to the present. This is probably because he had no fixed goal but was prepared to shift course with his opportunities. Only one thing is certain: He raised military forces and prepared for war against either Spain or the United States. Whether he planned to detach the western territories of the United States or carve out an empire at the expense of Spain remains an open question. He obtained money from Spain to set up a buffer state in Louisiana and sought money and naval assistance from Great Britain for the same purpose. But this does not prove that Burr actually intended what he proposed. It proves only that he would take money from any source in order to promote his schemes. All sorts of people became involved in his machinations, including the bishop of New Orleans and General James Wilkinson, commander of the American forces in Louisiana. Westerners were a bold breed, and Burr had no difficulty raising troops for some sort of military adventure.

But before Burr could implement his plans, General Wilkinson decided that he had more to gain by betraying him. So he sent a letter to Jefferson accusing Burr of organizing "a deep, dark, wicked, and widespread conspiracy" to seize the western territories of the United States. He explained that he had become involved only to discover Burr's plans and protect the interests of the United States. This was transparent nonsense, but it served Jefferson's purpose to believe him. He ordered Burr's arrest and threatened "condign punishment" for those involved in the conspiracy. When informed of Wilkinson's betrayal, Burr disbanded his forces and attempted to reach the safety of Spanish soil in Florida. But he was apprehended in Alabama and brought to Richmond, Virginia, for trial on charges of treason against the United States.

Burr's Treason Trial

The administration made every effort to get a conviction. "Go into *any* expense necessary," Jefferson wrote to George Hay, the federal attorney prosecuting the case, "and meet it from the funds provided by the Attorney General for other expenses." A conviction would not only settle old grievances against Burr but also enable the president to claim credit for saving the West. General Wilkinson's self-serving explanation was accepted at face value so that he could testify for the government against Burr. Efforts were made to inflame public opinion against the defendant. A biased account of the affair was sent to Congress, and Republican newspapers attacked Burr as the American Catiline.

Defaming Burr turned out to be easier than proving him guilty. Treason, unlike other federal crimes, is defined by the Constitution itself. Article III limits it to acts of war against the United States or giving aid and comfort to its enemies. Proof of the crime must be clear and unambiguous. "No person shall be convicted of treason," Article III provides, "unless on the testimony of two witnesses to the same overt act, or on confession in open court." The drafters of the Constitution rejected the English common-law notion of constructive treason. Under English law, disloyal intentions and even thoughts were as treasonous as disloyal acts. This opened the door for treason prosecutions for political purposes. Under Article III, a defendant could not be convicted unless proven guilty of overt acts against the United States.

Burr's trial began in the spring of 1807 before the federal circuit court for Virginia. Chief Justice Marshall presided, and he strictly construed the constitutional definition of treason. Had the repeal of the Judiciary Act of 1801 not put Supreme Court justices back on circuit court duty, Marshall would not have been on the bench to complicate things for the prosecution. The chief justice fully grasped the politics of the case, and his rulings probably saved Burr from the gallows. He ruled that none of Burr's statements or actions implying treasonous intent were admissible against him unless they related to specific acts of treason. He held that since the Constitution required proof of overt acts, the only evidence of intent admissible was "the intention with which the overt act itself was committed–not a general evil disposition, or an intention to commit a distinct fact." These rulings made it impossible for the jury to bring in a conviction. While there was ample proof that Burr had plotted treason, the government could not prove that specific acts of treason had been committed.

Jefferson on Burr's Conspiracy

"It appeared that [Burr] contemplated two distinct objects, which might be carried on either jointly or separately, and either the one or the other first, as circumstances should direct. One of these was the severance of the Union of these States by the Allegheny Mountains; the other an attack on Mexico . . . He collected from all the quarters where himself or his agents possessed influence all the ardent, restless, desperate, and disaffected persons who were ready for any enterprise analogous to their characters. He seduced good and well-meaning citizens, some by assurances that he possessed the confidence of the Government and was acting under its secret patronage, a pretense which procured some credit from the state of our differences with Spain, and others by offers of land . . ."

—Message to Congress (January 22, 1807)

Figure V.4 Portrait of Aaron Burr by John Vanderlyn.

Yale University Art Gallery, New Haven, CT

One of the most important issues raised by the case related to executive prerogative. When Burr learned that Wilkinson had altered some documents before sending them to Jefferson, he demanded that the president be called to testify and be required to bring the papers with him to court. After a heated debate over the power of the Court to subpoena the president, Marshall ruled that the Court had the power to do so. The Constitution, he said, gave every accused person the right "to compel the attendance of his witnesses" at the trial, and nothing exempted the president from this provision. But Jefferson claimed exemption on the grounds of executive privilege, contending that the separation of powers barred the courts from issuing orders against the executive branch. He made essentially the same argument that Washington had made in refusing to send Congress papers relating to the Jay Treaty. In the end, however, Jefferson sent copies of the papers to the federal attorney, though not to the Court, and with instructions to withhold anything not material to the case. Refusal to cooperate at all would have created the impression that the administration had something to hide. Marshall, realizing that this was the most he could get, settled for partial compliance. But his ruling on the Court's subpoena powers set a precedent that would be cited by the Supreme Court 167 years later in compelling President Richard Nixon to turn over the Watergate tapes.[3]

Burr's acquittal angered the public, and Marshall was bitterly assailed for his handling of the case. The Republican press noted that during a court recess Marshall had attended a dinner party at which Burr (who had been released on bail) was also a guest. Jefferson sent Congress a copy of the trial record along with a message suggesting Marshall's impeachment. He asked Congress to consider whether Burr had been acquitted for reasons of law and lack of evidence or because Marshall had twisted the law to prevent his conviction. Jefferson made it clear that he thought the law had been deliberately misconstrued. While Marshall was not impeached, public opinion ran strongly against him. A Baltimore mob hanged Burr and the chief justice in effigy while a band played "The Rogue's March."

The trial permanently settled the law of treason in the United States. It stands today exactly the way Marshall construed it in 1807. The government must prove that the defendant actually committed, not just plotted, specific acts of treason. In effect, conspiracies or plots unrelated to specific acts do not count in treason cases. Marshall rejected the idea of constructive treason and set a standard so high that treason prosecutions thereafter became much less common. This does not mean that the government cannot protect itself, only that it must carry a heavy burden of proof in treason cases. Congress still has ample power to pass statutes punishing those who conspire to overthrow the government by

Jefferson Asserts Executive Privilege

"With respect to papers, there is certainly a public & private side to our offices. To the former belong grants of land, patents for inventions, certain commissions, proclamations, & other papers patent in their nature. To the other belong mere executive proceedings. All nations have found it necessary, that for the advantageous conduct of their affairs, some of these proceedings, at least, should remain known to their executive functionary only. He, of course, from the nature of the case, must be the sole judge of which of them the public interests will permit publication. Hence, under our Constitution, in requests of papers, from the legislative to the executive branch, an exception is carefully expressed, as to those which he may deem the public welfare may require not to be disclosed; as you will see in the inclosed resolution of the H of Representatives, which produced the message of Jan 22, respecting this case. The respect mutually due between the constituted authorities in their official intercourse, as well as sincere dispositions to do for every one what is just, will always insure from the executive, in exercising the duty of discrimination confided to him, the same candor & integrity to which the nation has in like manner trusted in the disposal of its judiciary authorities."

—Thomas Jefferson, Letter of June 17, 1807

unlawful means. The fact that plotters cannot be punished as traitors does not mean that they cannot be punished at all. Nothing in Marshall's opinion prevents the prosecution and punishment of criminal conspiracies under appropriate statutes.

Failure to Acquire West Florida

Jefferson let no opportunity pass to expand the territory of the United States. His vision of a great agrarian republic required space for a growing population of citizen-farmers. The acquisition of Louisiana gave him a pretext for further expansion. He claimed that the purchase included West Florida, then in the possession of Spain. When direct negotiations with Madrid failed, the president tried a more devious approach. In 1805 he asked Congress for a military appropriation to deal with what he described as the threat of Spanish aggression. There was no threat at all, but he claimed one existed in order to put pressure on Madrid. At the same time, Jefferson also requested a secret appropriation of $2 million for what he called diplomatic purposes. The money would actually be used to bribe Napoleon to support the American claim to West Florida. The military appropriation would signal our readiness to use force, and the pressure from France would leave the Spanish government isolated in Europe. Spain in the end would have to capitulate and cede West Florida to the United States.

Some Republicans in Congress regarded Jefferson's tactics as less than honorable. If the United States had a legitimate claim to West Florida, it was wrong to pay a bribe to get it; if the territory rightly belonged to Spain, obtaining it by bribery and military threats was equally wrong. Led by John Randolph, they demanded to know the purpose of the secret appropriation, a disclosure that would embarrass the administration and probably wreck the scheme. The dissidents were states' rights supporters and extreme agrarians who thought Jefferson had not gone far enough in reversing Federalist policies. They used the secrecy issue to challenge the president and put the administration on the defensive. Jefferson's congressional supporters rejected their demand on constitutional grounds, citing the president's prerogative in foreign affairs to justify not revealing how the money would be spent. Randolph responded that secret appropriations were incompatible with the constitutional authority of Congress to control public expenditures. Jefferson in the end got his secret appropriation, but he did not get West Florida. The debate made it impossible for him to pay a bribe, and so the territory remained under Spanish control. The affair underscored one of the gray areas in the separation of powers where both Congress and the president had conflicting but legitimate claims.

Trouble with Great Britain

The "broken voyage" rule under which American commerce had prospered since 1800 was abandoned by the British in 1804. There had been so many abuses of the rule by American shippers that the British restored the earlier Rule of 1756 prohibiting all trade between ports under French control. This was the policy that had brought the United States to the brink of war with Britain in the 1790s. American ships would be seized unless the captain could prove that the voyage from the French port would terminate at an American port. Otherwise, the voyage would be deemed a continuous voyage between enemy ports, and the ship and cargo would be confiscated. Relations with Britain soon returned to the days immediately preceding the Jay Treaty. The seizure of American ships increased sharply, and the number of American sailors impressed into the Royal Navy rose dramatically. The foreign crisis that had confounded Federalists in the 1790s now returned to plague Republicans.

Jefferson believed that economic pressure could force the British to abandon their naval violations. In 1806 Congress gave him some diplomatic leverage by passing a law banning the importation of numerous British goods. Enforcement of the law was suspended while the president attempted to negotiate a settlement. But diplomacy failed to win concessions, and the situation steadily worsened. Both Britain and France had tightened their European blockades. The British issued Orders-in-Council prohibiting trade with ports under French control and requiring neutral ships to stop at a British port and pay a tax before entering neutral ports in Europe. Napoleon, in turn, issued the Berlin and Milan Decrees ordering the seizure of ships which complied with the British regulations. Neutral vessels stopping at a British port to pay the tax would be deemed denationalized and subject to seizure as British property. American shippers found themselves in an impossible situation. Compliance with the Orders-in-Council subjected them to seizure by the French, while failure to comply meant likely seizure by the British.

Although ships and cargos were lost, American commerce nevertheless prospered. Strict enforcement of the regulations was impossible, and the volume of American trade by 1807 was greater than at any time before 1835. If it had just been a matter of lost ships and cargos, the administration might have pursued a policy of protest and profit. But the British impressments of American seamen made this impossible. An incident in the summer of 1807 brought the United States and Britain to the brink of war. The British warship *Leopard* fired on and boarded the American frigate *Chesapeake* to search for alleged deserters from the Royal Navy. The attack outraged Republicans and Federalists alike and brought the nation to the brink of war. Many were convinced that only a declaration of war could redeem the nation's honor.

But Jefferson did not want war. His economy measures had left the United States militarily unprepared, and he still believed economic reprisals would work if given a chance. So in December 1807 he persuaded Congress to pass the Embargo Act in a final effort to force Britain and France to respect American neutral rights. The Act forbade American vessels to leave United States ports for Europe. By cutting off American trade completely, Jefferson believed France and Britain could be brought to terms. The measure not only failed but turned out to be the worst policy blunder of his administration. Britain managed to replace goods previously shipped from the United States with goods from South America, and British shippers also profited from the absence of American competition. The French turned the Act to their own advantage. Napoleon ordered the seizure of American ships in French ports on the pretext that they could not really be American because United States law barred American vessels from Europe. His self-serving cynicism cost Americans about $10 million in goods and shipping between 1807 and 1809.

The Embargo Act had disastrous consequences for the United States. Shipbuilding and commerce languished, throwing thousands of Americans out of work. Merchants, insurers, and warehousemen faced economic ruin. Farmers also suffered. Many faced foreclosure as the domestic oversupply created by the loss of foreign markets drove prices down. The embargo was unpopular everywhere, but its worst effects were felt in New England. Town meetings denounced the measure, and state legislatures attacked its constitutionality. Governor John Trumbull of Connecticut declared it unconstitutional and urged the state governments to block its enforcement. The theory underlying the constitutional attack was that the commerce power of Congress authorizes only the regulation of commerce, not its destruction. Several state governors responded to Trumbull's appeal by refusing to provide militia to enforce the embargo. Senator Timothy Pickering, leader of the ultra-Federalists in Massachusetts, proposed calling a New England convention for the purpose of declaring the law unconstitutional and resisting its enforcement. The backlash convinced even Republicans in Congress that the embargo had to end. Jefferson finally yielded to the pressure and signed a repeal measure in 1809, just three days before leaving office. The failure of economic pressure left the United States with few options in dealing with France and Britain.

Although Jefferson left office on a note of failure and frustration, his presidency left a permanent mark on constitutional government. The separation of powers had not been previously tested in the crucible of party politics. Jefferson's attack on the judiciary put the system of checks and balances to its first real test. The refusal of Congress to remove judges for political reasons not only affirmed the independence of the courts but served notice that a party leader in the White House could not automatically count on the support of party members in Congress. The Republicans had ample votes in the House and Senate to remove Chase, Marshall, and other Federalist judges; but they put the institutional independence of the courts over loyalty to the president. Jefferson's defeat strengthened Congress as well as the judiciary. If party discipline had prevailed, both Congress and the courts would have been equal losers. A precedent would have been set for a parliamentary system of government unintended by the Constitution.

The Madison Administration

Jefferson was succeeded by his friend James Madison, who brought to the presidency a superb understanding of constitutional government. He had been the principal author of the Virginia Plan at the Constitutional Convention, and his efforts during the struggle for ratification earned him the title "Father of the Constitution." Along with Hamilton and Jay, he had authored *The Federalist* explaining the operation of the new federal government. But Madison's understanding of constitutional government was not matched by his practical skills in the art of government. For all his brilliance, he turned out to be a poor politician and a second-rate administrator. Most of his public career had been spent in Jefferson's shadow, the shadow of a master politician. When called upon to run his own administration, Madison proved to be a mediocre president. His failure to lead as effectively as Jefferson had led caused power to shift gradually to Republican leaders in Congress.

Figure V.5 Portrait of James Madison by John Vanderlyn (1816).

White House Historical Association (White House Collection): 24

The War Hawks

Madison inherited all the problems that had plagued Jefferson's final years as president. Every effort to persuade Great Britain and France to respect American neutral rights had failed. The insults suffered by the United States were a national disgrace, and many believed that nothing short of war could set things right. The congressional elections of 1810 demonstrated the extent of popular discontent. Nearly half the members of the House and Senate were voted out of office, and a new breed of aggressive leaders, mainly from the South and West, replaced them in Congress. Among them were Henry Clay, John C. Calhoun, Langdon Cheves, Felix Grundy, and Richard M. Johnson. They would all leave their mark on government. Although they disagreed on many issues over the years, they had one thing in common in 1810: an ardent nationalism that demanded the use of military force against the British. John Randolph dubbed them "war hawks," and the label stuck because it fit them like a glove. Their growing influence in Congress limited Madison's options and forced him into positions ultimately making war inevitable.

While France had also violated American neutral rights, the violations committed by the British were much more serious. The impressment of American sailors inflamed public opinion much more than the seizure of ships and cargoes. Moreover, France was remote and less vulnerable to attack, while Britain and Britain's ally Spain offered excellent targets in Canada and Florida. Westerners coveted Canada, both for expansion and to halt the flow of military supplies to the Indians of the Northwest. Southerners viewed Florida in the same light. Its conquest would expand southern boundaries and end the Indian raids, which Spanish colonial authorities seemed unable or unwilling to prevent. Even if they had no grievances, Americans had a golden opportunity to profit from the war in Europe. With Britain fully committed to the war against Napoleon, Canada and Florida appeared ripe for the taking.

War of 1812

By the summer of 1812 pressure from congressional Republicans forced a reluctant Madison to ask for a declaration of war against Great Britain. The House and Senate divided along sectional lines, with the South and West voting for war, and New England and most of the Middle States voting against it. The sectional split reflected sectional interests. The South and the West had something to gain through territorial expansion, while the Northeast faced almost certain destruction of its commerce at the hands of the British navy. Governor Caleb Strong of Massachusetts proclaimed a day of public fast to protest the declaration, and Connecticut's General Assembly predicted that the war would bring disaster. The war became the major issue in the fall elections, splitting Republicans and giving Federalists a popular issue in the Northeast. Antiwar Republicans backed DeWitt Clinton of New York for president in the 1812 election, rejecting Madison as a pawn of the "war hawks." Although Madison won a second term, the party came out of the election sharply divided. Clinton, who had Federalist support, carried every northern state except Pennsylvania and Vermont, leaving Madison with only the South and the West. This was enough to keep him in the White House but not enough of a mandate to wage war successfully.

The administration had led the country into war without adequately preparing for it. The result was defeat and humiliation on every front. American forces invading Canada were defeated, and the British occupied northern New York and parts of Maine. The City of Washington was captured and the capitol burned, and most of the American merchant marine was destroyed by the Royal Navy. The disruption of commerce sharply reduced tariff revenues, and the government lacked money for military operations. By 1814 poor leadership and mismanagement had brought the United States to the brink of collapse. New England bankers refused to market the federal bonds issued to pay for the war, and military enlistments fell far short of manpower needs. Congress authorized the enlistment of 50,000 volunteers, but only 10,000 could be raised, mainly in the South and West. New Englanders in Congress opposed conscription and voted against military appropriations. They dubbed the conflict "Mr. Madison's War" and challenged its constitutionality. The war power had been abused, they asserted, to serve the interests of the French, not to defend the United States.

The antiwar faction openly flouted federal authority. When Madison called the state militia into national service, as he had authority to do under a federal statute passed in 1795, the New England states refused to comply. They contended that the order was unconstitutional because the Constitution did not expressly authorize Congress to determine whether the requisite circumstances for federalizing the militia existed. The Massachusetts Supreme Court issued an advisory opinion that the power to make the determination, not having been expressly granted to the federal government, was reserved to the states by the Tenth Amendment. The legislature of Connecticut took a similar stand, declaring that state militia could be called into national service only to suppress insurrection or repel a foreign invasion. Both states not only withheld their militia but actively obstructed federal enlistments. They passed laws directing state judges to release from

Figure V.6 Drawing titled *U.S. Capitol After Burning by the British* by George Munger (1814). At the time the British invaded the United States, the Capitol Building was still under construction. On August 24, 1814, British forces set it afire, along with other public buildings in Washington, D.C. This drawing depicts fire damage to the House and Senate Wings. The shell of the rotunda is visible.

Library of Congress, Prints and Photographs Division, LC-DIG-ppmsca-23076

service any minors who enlisted without the written consent of their parents. Since federal law allowed enlistments without parental consent, these measures had the effect of nullifying federal laws.

The Hartford Convention

The unpopularity of the war revived the political fortunes of the New England Federalists. Their party had lost ground since 1800, but they now rode the wave of public resentment to regain power in the region. By 1813 they had regained control of all the state governments in New England. The following year, the Massachusetts legislature issued a call for the New England states to hold a convention to form a common front for dealings with the federal government. Although extremists had proposed the idea, moderates were in control when the convention met at Hartford in December 1814. No plans were entertained for breaking up the Union. The main goal was to propose constitutional changes protecting the interests of the Northeast against a national government increasingly dominated by southern and western Republicans. One of the key resolutions was a states' rights declaration much like the Kentucky and Virginia Resolutions of 1798. It asserted the right of every state to protect its citizens against abuses of federal power in violation of the Constitution. States' rights theory thus came full circle. A doctrine once endorsed by Madison when the Federalists were in power was now invoked by Federalists against his administration.

The Hartford Convention compiled a list of political and constitutional demands to be presented to the administration. The political demands called for guarantees against conscription, for the allocation of federal revenues collected locally to local defense, and for interstate arrangements, independent of federal arrangements, for resisting foreign invasion. One of the key constitutional demands called for elimination of the Three-Fifths Compromise under which slaves were fractionally counted for the allocation of representation in Congress. Others called for a two-thirds majority of both houses for the admission of new states to the Union, and for a prohibition against declarations of war when the United States had not been actually invaded. One of the proposed amendments would have barred naturalized citizens from holding federal office, and another would have limited the president to a single term. Commissioners were appointed to negotiate with the Madison administration, and the delegates agreed to hold another convention if their proposals were rejected. The resolution to meet again was an implied threat that rejection would have serious consequences.

By the time the commissioners reached Washington, events had cut the ground from under them. The country was euphoric with the news of General Andrew Jackson's victory over the British at New Orleans and that the Treaty of Ghent had ended the war. Everything had suddenly changed, and the commissioners abandoned their mission as hopeless. The brilliant victory and a favorable peace treaty bolstered the prestige of the administration and threw its critics on the defensive. Administration spokesmen now charged that Federalist obstructionism, not Republican bungling, had caused the military setbacks. The fact that the Hartford Federalists met in secrecy enabled the Republicans to charge that they had plotted secession and disunion. There was no hard evidence to support such charges, but the suspicion nevertheless took hold of Federalist disloyalty. The return of peace enabled people to forget how unpopular the war had been; soon even those who had opposed it found it politically expedient to forget their wartime opposition. Pilloried by Republicans for alleged disloyalty and torn by internal factionalism, the Federalists soon disintegrated as a national political party.

The War of 1812 had severely strained national unity. It brought to the surface long-standing grievances between the sections. But the war also strengthened the Union by affirming the traditions that bound Americans together. For all the antiwar rhetoric, only Federalist extremists contemplated secession. While its authority had been seriously challenged, the federal government emerged from the war stronger than before. The key constitutional issues were ultimately resolved in its favor. A decade later, the Supreme Court ruled that the president, with the consent of Congress, has sole authority to determine when the state militia should be called into national service.[4] The return of peace sent a surge of pride through the country for having come through the first war fought as an independent nation. Forgotten were the blundering and political disarray that had brought the country to the brink of ruin. All that mattered was that the United States had defended its sovereign rights, won a great victory at New Orleans, and concluded peace on honorable terms. The unpopular war that achieved no major goals turned out, in retrospect, to have been remarkably successful.

New Supreme Court Appointments

The political ascendancy of the Republicans at the national level insured that no more Federalists would be appointed to the federal courts. Jefferson and his successors appointed only party loyalists to the Supreme Court. Madison made two appointments, and one of them was a great one. Following the death of Justice Cushing in 1811, the president sought to maintain the Court's geographic balance by appointing a New Englander. His first choice was Levi Lincoln, who had been Jefferson's attorney general, but Lincoln declined on grounds of age. Alexander Wolcott, his second choice, accepted, but the Senate refused to confirm him because of his meager credentials. When John Quincy Adams, who was then ambassador to Russia, also declined the appointment, Madison finally nominated Joseph Story of Massachusetts. Story, who had Federalist connections, had joined the Republican Party when it became clear that the Federalists were marked for political extinction. Jefferson had misgivings about Story's real convictions and warned Madison that he was only a "pseudorepublican." But by now too many Republicans had Federalist roots for the party to make invidious distinctions between true believers and political pragmatists. So Story got the appointment, and the Court got one of its greatest justices.

Jefferson's apprehensions about Story proved correct. He sided with John Marshall from the beginning, and a close collaboration developed between them. The chief justice could not have hoped for a better ally, for Story had a matchless grasp of the technical operation of the law. Perhaps the greatest legal scholar ever to sit on the Court, he complemented Marshall's political and analytical skills perfectly. His books on constitutional law became standard texts for law professors and judges. Story taught law at Harvard during his years on the Court and influenced a whole generation of legal practitioners. His impact on contemporary law, particularly with respect to equity jurisdiction and the law of conflicts, was greater than that of any American jurist with the possible exception of Chancellor Kent. Story put his vast erudition and prestige at Marshall's service. Marshall would have been a great chief justice without Story, but whether he would have become our greatest chief justice without him is doubtful.

Madison's second appointment went to Gabriel Duvall of Maryland. Duvall filled the vacancy created by the death of Justice Chase in 1811, and his tenure was largely undistinguished. He later became totally deaf, an infirmity that prevented him from hearing oral arguments and participating fully in Court conferences. Monroe, who succeeded Madison, made only one appointment to the Court. It went to Smith Thompson of New York following the death of Justice Livingston in 1823. Monroe's successor, John Quincy Adams, appointed Robert Trimble of Kentucky on the death of Justice Todd in 1826. Trimble died in 1828 after a brief and uneventful tenure. Though all these appointees were nominal Republicans, they all succumbed to Marshall's influence.

Joseph Story on the Constitution and the Courts

"[The Constitution is not] a mere compact, or league, or confederacy, existing at the mere will of any one or more of the States, during their good pleasure; but, (as it purports on its face to be,) . . . a Constitution of Government, framed and adopted by the people of the United States, and obligatory upon all the States, until it is altered, amended, or abolished by the people, in the manner pointed out in the instrument itself. It is to be interpreted, as all other solemn instruments are, by endeavoring to ascertain the true sense and meaning of all the terms; and we are neither to narrow them, nor to enlarge them, by straining them from their just and natural import, for the purpose of adding to, or diminishing its powers, or bending them to any favorite theory or dogma of party. It is the language of the people, to be judged of according to common sense, and not by mere theoretical reasoning. It is not an instrument for the mere private interpretation of any particular men. The people have established it and spoken their will; and their will, thus promulgated, is to be obeyed as the supreme law. Every department of the Government must, of course, in the first instance, in the exercise of its own powers and duties, necessarily construe the instrument. But, if the case admits of judicial cognizance, every citizen has a right to contest the validity of that construction before the proper judicial tribunal; and to bring it to the test of the Constitution. And, if the case is not capable of judicial redress, still the people may, through the acknowledged means of new elections, or proposed amendments, check any usurpation of authority, whether wanton, or unintentional, and thus relieve themselves from any grievances of a political nature."

—*A Familiar Exposition of the Constitution of the United States* (1840)

Era of Good Feeling

The demise of the Federalists as a national party was followed by a brief period of one-party government in the United States. After Monroe's smashing electoral victory in 1816, the Federalists ceased to contest presidential elections. So Monroe ran unopposed for reelection in 1820. One political commentator described this absence of interparty rivalry as the "era of good feeling." But factionalism was far from dead; it had simply become less open and apparent. As the now dominant party, the Republicans attracted persons of every political persuasion. Many of the new recruits had nothing in common except the desire to belong to the party of patronage and power. Splits within the party soon developed as different groups and leaders struggled for control. Before Monroe left the White House, the stage was set for the emergence of a new two-party system.

The West played an important role in redrawing the political map. The population west of the Alleghenies more than doubled between 1810 and 1820, increasing from about one million to over 2.2 million. Five new states joined the Union, shifting the balance of power away from the East. The political process also became more democratic as property qualifications on voting and office holding were reduced or eliminated. No part of the country escaped the democratizing trends. Politicians everywhere competed for popular support by extending the suffrage to people previously disfranchised. By the 1820s government at every level had a broader popular base than at the turn of the century.

The democratization of political life turned politicians into brokers who negotiated alliances between competing groups and interests. This resulted in a more pragmatic brand of politics that had little to do with principle or ideology. Republicans now sponsored Federalist programs that the Jeffersonians had strongly opposed a generation earlier. In 1816 they reestablished the national bank, and Madison, who had once opposed it, signed the bill into law. They even enacted parts of Hamilton's program that had been rejected in the 1790s. In 1816 the Republican-controlled Congress passed the first protective tariff in American history. The measure was designed to protect the growing textile industry of New England against foreign competition. This was the sort of Republicanism that even Hamilton would have applauded.

Some of the political changes reflected the changing ethnic and social composition of the nation. A flood of immigration and the growth of commerce, manufacturing, and transportation innovations transformed the foundations of national life. The country became more diverse but also more difficult to govern. The most important force holding it together was the commitment of all groups and classes to the principle of constitutional government. As the clash of interests intensified, the Constitution assumed almost talismanic importance in balancing interests and preventing abuses of power. Despite sharp disagreements over its interpretation, the document itself acquired the aura of Holy Writ. Once a controversial political document, it had become a covenant between the generations, a link between what the nation had been and aspired to become, and welding together the most diverse and dynamic society in history.

Notes

1. Judges Archbald and Ritter in 1913 and 1936, respectively.
2. American Insurance Co. v. Canter, 26 U.S. (1 Pet.) 511 (1828).
3. United States v. Nixon, 418 U.S. 683 (1974).
4. Martin v. Mott, 25 U.S. (12 Wheat.) 19 (1827).

February 25, 1791	August 8, 1798	February 24, 1803	March 4, 1809	March 16, 1810	March 4, 1811
First Bank of the United States Chartered	Calder v. Bull	Marbury v. Madison	James Madison Takes Office as President of the United States	Fletcher v. Peck	Charter of the First Bank of the United States Expires

February 25, 1819	March 6, 1819	February 16, 1820	March 5, 1821	February 17, 1823	March 2, 1824
Dartmouth College v. Woodward	McCulloch v. Maryland	Houston v. Moore	Cohens v. Virginia	Green v. Biddle	Gibbons v. Ogden

March 12, 1830	March 22, 1830	February 16, 1833	July 6, 1835
Craig v. Missouri	Providence Bank v. Billings	Barron v. Baltimore	Death of Chief Justice Marshall

VI John Marshall and Judicial Nationalism

March 3, 1812	March 15, 1813	March 14, 1816	March 20, 1816	March 4, 1817	February 17, 1819
New Jersey v. Wilson	Fairfax's Devisee v. Hunter's Lessee	Congress Charters the Second Bank of the United States	Martin v. Hunter's Lessee	James Monroe Takes Office as President of the United States	Sturges v. Crowninshield

March 19, 1824	March 4, 1825	March 12, 1827	March 13, 1827	March 4, 1829	March 20, 1829
Osborn v. Bank of the United States	John Quincy Adams Takes Office as President of the United States	Brown v. Maryland	Ogden v. Saunders	Andrew Jackson Takes Office as President of the United States	Willson v. Black Bird Creek Marsh Co.

"[R]emembering that you cannot separate a man from his place, remember also that there fell to Marshall perhaps the greatest place that ever was filled by a judge."
—Justice Oliver Wendell Holmes, Jr., *Collected Legal Papers* (1920)

The political dominance of the Republicans after 1800 left the Supreme Court as the last bastion of Federalism in government. During his thirty-four years as chief justice, John Marshall stood firm against localizing tendencies and wrote the Federalist commitment to strong national government into the constitutional law of the nation. He shaped constitutional development more than all the presidents and congresses combined prior to the Civil War. Years after the Federalists had disappeared as a political party, their ideas survived in Marshall's constitutional rulings. His decisions came to be regarded as great state papers, far more important and permanent than the pronouncements of elected political leaders.

While Marshall was a great judge, probably our greatest, his talents were primarily political. A leading Federalist, he had been appointed by President Adams to keep the chief justiceship out of Republican hands. His Federalist predecessor, Oliver Ellsworth, was in poor health, and party leaders persuaded him to resign so that Jefferson would not have the opportunity to replace him later. If Ellsworth had not resigned, his death in 1807 would have delivered the office to the Republicans. Marshall, who enjoyed excellent health, kept the chief justiceship safely Federalist for more than three decades.

He outlived most of his opponents and denied a whole line of Republican presidents the pleasure of replacing him.

The Supreme Court was already Federalist and nationalist when Marshall became chief justice, so he had no need to make political conversions. The Court had already ruled against states' rights in *Chisholm v. Georgia*, causing a political backlash that culminated in the adoption of the Eleventh Amendment. Three years later, in *Ware v. Hylton* (1796), the Court invalidated a Virginia statute on the ground that it conflicted with a federal treaty. The only concession to states' rights was the ruling in *Calder v. Bull* (1798) that the constitutional ban against state ex post facto laws applied only to criminal statutes. Except for the *Chisholm* decision, handing down nationalist decisions had been politically safe. The Court could count on the support of a Federalist president and Congress. But everything changed in 1800 when the Federalists were routed at the polls. The Court now faced a hostile president and a Congress bent on reducing its influence and independence.

Marshall proved to be a brilliant strategist in deflecting attacks upon the Court. Given the intensely partisan political climate, this was not easy, particularly because the principle of judicial independence had yet to win broad public acceptance. Jefferson and most congressional Republicans rejected the idea as antirepublican. The Federalists themselves had politicized the judiciary with their partisan appointments, so Republicans could not be blamed for taking political reprisals. The Court was not held in particularly high esteem when Marshall became chief justice. In 1789 Robert Harrison had declined appointment in order to become Chancellor of Maryland, and John Jay, the first chief justice, resigned in 1795 in order to become governor of New York. Even when President Adams offered to reappoint Jay before offering the post to Marshall, Jay declined. Jay had left the Court, he explained, convinced that it lacked "the energy, weight, and dignity which was essential to its affording due support to the national government." What Jay found lacking, Marshall would more than amply provide.

Marshall Takes the Helm

Marshall's political astuteness showed from the very beginning. He persuaded the justices to abandon the practice of delivering individual *seriatim* opinions in favor of consensus opinions giving the Court the appearance of speaking with a single voice. Disagreements would be resolved in conference behind closed doors, and then the decision would be announced as the unanimous decision of all the justices. This strengthened the Court's credibility by creating the impression that no other decision was possible. Jefferson was quick to grasp the implications of the innovation, and he sharply condemned it. "Another most condemnable practice of the supreme court," he wrote, "is that of cooking up a decision in Caucus & delivering it by one of their members as the opinion of the court, without the possibility of our knowing how many, who, and for what reasons each member concurred." That so many of the decisions were written by Marshall himself probably contributed to the president's chagrin. He wrote a total of 519 opinions as chief justice, and in nearly two-thirds of them spoke for a unanimous Court. Until Jefferson appointed Justice Johnson in 1804, there was not a single dissenting opinion.

Figure VI.1 Portrait of John Marshall by
Henry Inman (1832).
Courtesy of the Library of Virginia

Jefferson did not have to wait long to open his attack upon the courts. The opportunity, when it came, was the result of Marshall's own negligence. As secretary of state in the waning days of the Adams administration, he had failed to deliver the commissions of forty-two persons appointed by the president as justices of the peace. The oversight gave Jefferson the opportunity to prevent some of the appointees from taking office. The new president directed his Secretary of State, James Madison, to deliver twenty-five of the undelivered commissions but to withhold the other seventeen. These were the "midnight" appointments made by Adams after his defeat, after, as Jefferson put it, "he knew he was not appointing for himself." The president announced that he would treat these appointments as "mere nullities."

Marbury v. Madison

William Marbury and three of the other "nullities" turned to the Supreme Court for help in securing their commissions. They applied for a writ of mandamus ordering Madison to deliver them. The Court had been authorized to issue the writ against federal officials by Section 13 of the Judiciary Act of 1789. The petitioners were represented by Charles Lee, who had been Attorney General under Adams. Levi Lincoln, the new Attorney General, represented the administration. The appearance of Lee as counsel for the petitioners made *Marbury v. Madison* political from the outset. While Republicans expressed open contempt for the suit, Federalists saw it as an opportunity to score points against Jefferson for abuse of power. Marbury won the first round in December 1801 when the Court agreed to take the case under consideration by issuing a preliminary rule to show cause why the writ should not be granted. Formal arguments were set for the new term of the Court. The granting of the rule suggested that a mandamus might be issued ordering the administration to deliver the commissions.

Republicans in Congress denounced the proceedings as a breach of the separation of powers. The idea that one branch of government could issue orders to another branch was rejected on constitutional grounds. The case also underscored for Republicans the anomaly of a judiciary still controlled by a party rejected by the voters at the polls. William Giles, a leading Republican in the House, declared that their victory would not be complete "so long as that strong fortress is in possession of the enemy." That the Supreme Court dared to contemplate issuing an order against the executive branch aroused indignation. Senator John Breckenridge, later to become Jefferson's attorney general, condemned the preliminary rule as "the most daring attack which the annals of Federalism have yet exhibited." Even before formal arguments were heard, the political backlash made it clear that more was at stake than the undelivered commissions.

The Court found itself on the horns of a dilemma. If it granted Marbury a mandamus, there was no way it could be enforced. Jefferson would almost certainly ignore the order, and his defiance would humiliate the Court and perhaps expose some of the justices to the threat of impeachment. But a decision against Marbury would be equally damaging. The Court would be perceived as fearful of a confrontation with the political branches of government and powerless to deal with a defiant president. It seemed likely that respect for the Court as an institution would diminish no matter how the case was decided.

Marshall fully anticipated reprisals against the Court if Marbury won. Caesar Rodney spoke for most Republicans in the House of Representatives when he declared that the courts had to submit to "the strong arm of Legislative authority. We shall discover who is master of the ship," he warned. The impeachment of Justice Chase was already underway,

Figure VI.2 Portrait of William Marbury.

Early nineteenth century. Attributed to Rembrandt Peale, Collection of the Supreme Court of the United States

and rumors circulated that the chief justice would be next. Many Republicans hoped to replace Marshall with Judge Spencer Roane of the Virginia Court of Appeals, a jurist who shared Jefferson's constitutional views. There was support in Congress for legislation subordinating all the federal courts to the political branches. The debate over repeal of the Judiciary Act of 1801 revealed that there was little support in Congress for the idea of judicial independence or the right of the courts to review the constitutionality of acts of the political branches. Senator Breckenridge took the position that only Congress could interpret the Constitution as it related to legislative matters. He rejected completely the notion that judges should have the final say on constitutional issues. "Who checks the courts," he asked, "when they violate the Constitution?"

The administration behaved contemptuously when the case came up for argument in February 1803. Madison refused to furnish information on the undelivered commissions, and Attorney General Lincoln would not tell the Court what had happened to them. Without proof of their existence, the Court could issue no orders for their delivery. Some State Department clerks were finally found who testified that they still existed. When the attorney general refused to argue the merits of the case, it became apparent that the administration would defy any order issued against it. Such tactics almost dared Marshall to issue the mandamus. Jefferson fully expected Marbury to win, because he could not imagine Marshall backing down with the Court's prestige on the line. He would then disregard the order, and Congress would have grounds to proceed against the justices for abusing their authority.

But Marshall confounded the administration with a ruling that not only extricated the Court from its predicament but actually enhanced its prestige. Speaking for a unanimous Court, he declared that Marbury had a right to his commission and that Jefferson had acted unlawfully in withholding it. He went on to lecture the president about his executive duties, warning that he "cannot at his discretion sport away the vested rights of others." Jefferson had abused his powers of office in keeping Marbury's commission from him. Marshall pulled no punches in deploring what the president had done. "The government of the United States has been emphatically termed a government of laws," he said. "It will certainly cease to deserve this high appellation, if the laws furnish no remedy for the violation of a vested legal right."

Having ruled that Marbury was entitled to his commission, all that remained was for the Court to issue the mandamus ordering Madison to deliver it. But knowing that the order would be ignored, Marshall did not fall into the trap of issuing it. He ruled instead that although Marbury was entitled to a mandamus, the Court did not have jurisdiction to issue one. He declared that Section 13 of the Judiciary Act of 1789, which conferred such jurisdiction on the Court, was unconstitutional. It was unconstitutional because it sought to increase the Court's original jurisdiction (trial jurisdiction) beyond the scope of Article III. Because the original jurisdiction of the Court is spelled out in Article III, it can be neither increased nor decreased by Congress. While the Court's appellate jurisdiction can be regulated by Congress, its original jurisdiction can be changed only by constitutional amendment. Although the administration had acted unlawfully, the Court unfortunately lacked the jurisdiction needed to grant the relief requested.

Since this was the first time the Court declared an act of Congress unconstitutional, Marshall supported his holding with a forceful defense of its right to do so. "It is emphatically the province and duty of the judicial department to say what the law is," he wrote.

> If two laws conflict with each other, the courts must decide on the operation of each. So if a law be in opposition to the constitution; if the law and the constitution apply to a particular case, so that the Court must either decide that case conformably to the law, disregarding the constitution; or conformably to the constitution, disregarding the law, the Court must determine which of these conflicting rules governs the case. This is of the very essence of judicial duty.

He went on to argue that any law in conflict with the Constitution must be disregarded because the Constitution is the supreme law of the land. Taking dead aim at opponents of judicial review, he declared that persons who demanded automatic enforcement of laws passed by Congress "close their eyes on the constitution, and see only the law." Judges cannot do this, he contended, because their oath of office binds them to uphold the Constitution, even over acts of Congress. He asked,

> Why does a judge swear to discharge his duties agreeably to the Constitution of the United States, if that constitution forms no rule for his government?—if it is closed upon him, and cannot be inspected by him? If such be the real state of things, this is worse than solemn mockery. To prescribe, or to take this oath, becomes equally a crime.

What it came down to, according to Marshall, was that the oath taken by judges to uphold the Constitution prevents them from enforcing unconstitutional acts of Congress.

Marshall's argument for judicial review was brilliant, but the rest of his opinion was shot through with politics. If the Court indeed lacked jurisdiction to grant the relief requested, Marbury's petition should simply have been dismissed without any discussion of the merits of the case. The usual order of things is for the Court to decide jurisdictional

---

Marshall on Judicial Review

"Those then who controvert the principle that the constitution is to be considered, in court, as a paramount law, are reduced to the necessity of maintaining that courts must close their eyes on the constitution, and see only the law . . . This doctrine would subvert the very foundation of all written constitutions. It would declare that an act, which, according to the principles and theory of our government, is entirely void; is yet, in practice, completely obligatory. It would declare, that if the legislature shall do what is expressly forbidden, such act, notwithstanding the express prohibition, is in reality effectual. It would be giving to the legislature a practical and real omnipotence, with the same breath which professes to restrict their powers within narrow limits. It is prescribing limits, and declaring that those limits may be passed at pleasure."

—Marbury v. Madison (1803)

issues first, because lack of jurisdiction makes it unnecessary to decide anything else. But Marshall reversed things and ruled for Marbury on the merits before holding that the Court lacked jurisdiction to issue a mandamus. His obvious motive was to discredit the administration for abuse of power in withholding the commission. Only then did he rule on the jurisdictional issue in a way that denied the administration an opportunity to defy the Court.

The decision caused a political uproar, and some Republicans called for Marshall's impeachment. Although the Court had already reviewed the constitutionality of a federal law in *Hylton v. United States* (1796), this was the first time it had declared one unconstitutional. The decision enraged Republicans in Congress who viewed it as an attack on the separation of powers. But nothing could be done about the decision itself, because the Court had not required Congress or the president to do anything. Technically, the administration had won, but on grounds that infuriated most Republicans. Marshall's opinion arrogated to the Court the right to invalidate acts of the political branches of government. "All wrong, all wrong," John Randolph declared in the House of Representatives, "but no man in the United States can tell why or wherein."

Jefferson resented Marshall's attack on his administration more than the holding on judicial review. Federalists had been advocating judicial review since the struggle for ratification. In Number 78 of the *Federalist*, Hamilton had argued that a vigorous and independent federal judiciary would be a check on legislative power. As a delegate to the Virginia Convention in 1788, Marshall himself had argued, "If [Congress] were to make a law not warranted by any of the powers enumerated, it would be considered by the judges as an infringement of the Constitution which they are to guard." While the chief justice had a right to his opinions on judicial review, Jefferson did not think he had the right to turn the Court into a political forum for attacks on his administration. The president rejected Marshall's ruling on the lawfulness of withholding Marbury's commission as a mere "obiter disquisition" that did not belong in the Court's opinion. A proper judicial determination would have ended the case with a dismissal for lack of jurisdiction. "But the Chief Justice," Jefferson complained, "went on to lay down what the law would be, had they jurisdiction of the case[.]"

Modern commentators have been equally critical of Marshall's handling of the case. Declaring Section 13 unconstitutional because it enlarged the original jurisdiction of the Court by authorizing the issuance of writs of mandamus deftly conflated the issue of jurisdiction, which relates to persons and subject matter, with judicial remedies available to the Court in the exercise of its jurisdiction. The authority to issue writs of mandamus did not increase the Court's original jurisdiction; that remained the same with respect to persons and cases. The authority granted by Section 13 related only to the remedies that might be employed by the Court in the exercise of its existing jurisdiction. Confounding the two allowed Marshall to dismiss the case on grounds that enhanced the status of the Court as a branch of government. That he wanted such an outcome would explain his somewhat strained interpretation of the mandamus provision. While the text is far from clear, on the basis of context, the provision could have been construed to authorize the writs in cases of appellate jurisdiction. This would have been entirely within the power

> **Section 13 on Writs of Mandamus**
>
> "The Supreme Court shall also have appellate jurisdiction from the circuit courts and courts of the several states, in the cases herein after specially provided for; and shall have power to issue writs of prohibition to the district courts, when proceeding as courts of admiralty and maritime jurisdiction, and writs of mandamus, in cases warranted by the principles and usages of law, to any courts appointed, or persons holding office, under the authority of the United States."

of Congress under Article III of the Constitution. Since *Marbury* was a case of original jurisdiction, this would have left the Court without an appropriate remedy, and the outcome would have been the same. But the case then would have been decided as a matter of statutory construction and without declaring an act of Congress unconstitutional. The politics of the case made the latter the desired outcome and may also explain the questionable reasoning employed to produce it.

The Case against Judicial Review

Marshall's argument for judicial review ultimately rests on the theory that the oath of office taken by judges to uphold the Constitution binds them not to enforce laws in conflict with the Constitution. The most persuasive rebuttal of this theory was expounded by Justice John Gibson of the Pennsylvania Supreme Court in *Eakin v. Raub* (1825). He wrote:

> The oath to support the constitution is not peculiar to judges but is taken indiscriminately by every officer of the government, and is designed rather as a test of the political principles of the man, than to bind the officer in the discharge of his duty[.]

What effect, for example, does such an oath have on the duties of a recorder of deeds whose work has nothing to do with the Constitution?

> But granting it to relate to the official conduct of a judge, as well as every other officer, and not to his political principles, still it must be understood in reference to supporting the constitution, *only as far as that may be involved in his official duty*; and, consequently, if his official duty does not comprehend an inquiry into the authority of the legislature, neither does his oath.

Gibson's point was that the oath taken by judges to uphold the Constitution only binds them not to violate the Constitution themselves; it does not bind them to prevent Congress from violating the Constitution. Judges do not violate their oath to uphold the Constitution if they enforce unconstitutional laws passed by Congress. Congressmen take their own oath to uphold the Constitution, and how they discharge it is their own responsibility, not the responsibility of judges.

Jefferson rejected judicial review on constitutional grounds. Judges had no mandate to set themselves up as arbiters on issues of constitutionality. For them to negate the will of the people as expressed in Congress was not compatible with republican government. It should be up to the majority to determine at the polls how the Constitution should be interpreted. "To consider the judges as the ultimate arbiters of all constitutional questions," he warned, "would place us under the despotism of an oligarchy." He feared that judicial review would turn the Constitution into "a mere thing of wax" that judges could twist "into any form they please." Jefferson noted that the Constitution created no single forum for settling constitutional issues. "It has more wisely made all the departments co-equal and co-sovereign within themselves." He did not think that constitutional government needed the protection of the courts. "When the legislative or executive functionaries act unconstitutionally, they are responsible to the people in their elective capacity. The exemption of the judges from that is quite dangerous enough." Judicial review really meant judicial supremacy, something Jefferson regarded as the enemy of popular government.

> I know no safe depository of the ultimate powers of the society, but the people themselves; and if we think them not enlightened enough to exercise their control with a wholesome discretion, the remedy is not to take it from them, but to inform their discretion by education. This is the true corrective of abuses of constitutional power.

Marshall's views prevailed in the long run not because they were correct but because they served the practical needs of government. It was important to settle constitutional disputes with some degree of finality rather than leave them undecided in the political arena. The courts were better suited for this task than either of the political branches of government. Although the Supreme Court did not declare another act of Congress unconstitutional until the *Dred Scott* case in 1857, the right of the Court to do so became less controversial over the years. It provided a means of settling constitutional disputes without transparent partisanship or bias. The acceptance of judicial review also had a great deal to do with the growth of public confidence in the courts and diminished respect for the political branches of government. Constitutional interpretations that would have split the country if announced by Congress were received with relative calm because of confidence in the fairness and integrity of judges. Jefferson would have lamented this development, but the reality of popular government is that people have reason to distrust the politicians they elect to represent them.

State Sovereignty and the Court

The same Republicans who denounced the Court for invalidating part of the Judiciary Act of 1789 also denounced it for upholding Section 25 of the Act. Section 25 gave the Supreme Court jurisdiction to hear appeals from the state courts in cases where rights claimed under the Constitution, federal laws, or treaties of the United States had been denied. This grant of jurisdiction had been opposed by states' rights supporters as unconstitutional. They contended that the Constitution expressly made the state courts responsible for upholding federal supremacy in such matters, and that Congress had no power to subject their decisions to federal review. Such review was incompatible with the judicial independence of the states and turned their courts into subdivisions of the federal system. The desire for uniformity in the enforcement of federal rights did not justify unconstitutional encroachments upon the sovereignty of the states.

The constitutionality of Section 25 was challenged in the courts for the first time in *Fairfax's Devisee v. Hunter's Lessee* (1813). The case grew out of a conflict between a Virginia law under which the Fairfax estate had been confiscated during the Revolution and a provision in the Treaty of Paris calling for the restoration of confiscated property. Part of the confiscated land had been sold to David Hunter and a number of other buyers, including John Marshall and his brother James. Thomas Martin, one of the Fairfax claimants, challenged Hunter's title on the ground that the confiscation law conflicted with the restoration provisions of the peace treaty. When the Virginia Court of Appeals upheld Hunter's title in 1810, the Fairfax claimants appealed to the United States Supreme Court under Section 25.

Marshall's personal interest in the case prevented him from participating in the deliberations. Since two other justices were absent and another dissented, the case was decided by less than a majority of the full Court. Justice Story, in a plurality opinion, reversed the Virginia Court of Appeals on the ground that the recovery provisions of the Treaty of Paris superseded rights created under the state confiscation law. The Constitution makes treaties part of the supreme law of the land, and state laws to the contrary were therefore unconstitutional. So Story ruled in favor of the Fairfax claimants and directed the Virginia Court of Appeals to carry out the order. This was the first time a state court had been overruled under the controversial Section 25. The Court had invalidated a Virginia debt sequestration law in *Ware v. Hylton* (1796), but Section 25 had not been involved. The case had begun in the federal courts and came to the Supreme Court within the federal system; state courts were not involved. The *Fairfax* appeal directly involved the Virginia courts and challenged the state's judicial independence.

Story's order provoked an angry response from the Virginia Court of Appeals. Led by Chief Judge Spencer Roane, who had first consulted with Jefferson and Madison, the Virginia judges refused to enforce the order. Roane rejected the idea that any federal court could constitutionally overturn a state court decision. The state courts were institutions of state government, and the state governments were sovereign within their spheres of operation. Their courts could no more be subject to federal review than the federal courts could be subject to state review. Congress had acted beyond its constitutional power in passing Section 25, and the provision for appeals from the state courts to the United States Supreme Court was a legal nullity. This was the most forceful declaration of states' rights since the Kentucky and Virginia Resolutions of 1798.

Roane's stand brought the case back to the Supreme Court for a second appeal in *Martin v. Hunter's Lessee* (1816). This time, the constitutionality of Section 25 was the main issue, because the Virginia court had declared it unconstitutional. All the justices except Marshall participated, so Story was able to write a majority opinion from which there was only one dissent. Story upheld the constitutionality of Section 25 on the ground that under Article III of the Constitution Congress could have given the federal courts exclusive jurisdiction over cases involving federal issues and deprived state courts of concurrent jurisdiction in such cases completely. Section 25 simply had the effect of treating the state courts as part of the federal system in cases presenting federal issues. There was no encroachment upon state sovereignty, because the right of appeal was limited to matters clearly under federal jurisdiction. He again reversed the Virginia Court of Appeals and ruled in favor of the Fairfax claimants.

But this time Story did not remand the case to the Virginia Court of Appeals. Anticipating defiance, he remanded it instead to the trial court where it had originated. Although this prevented Judge Roane from blocking enforcement of the order, it did not

Story on the Constitutional Powers of the States

"[T]he constitution . . . is crowded with provisions which restrain or annul the sovereignty of the states in some of the highest branches of their prerogatives. The tenth section of the first article contains a long list of disabilities and prohibitions imposed upon the states . . . The language of the constitution is also imperative upon the states as to the performance of many duties. It is imperative upon the state legislatures to make laws prescribing the time, places and manner of holding elections for senators and representatives, and for electors of president and vice-president. And in these, as well as some other cases, congress have a right to revise, amend, or supercede the laws which may be passed by state legislatures. When, therefore, the states are stripped of some of the highest attributes of sovereignty, and the same are given to the United States; . . . and in every case are, under the constitution, bound by the paramount authority of the United States; it is certainly difficult to support the argument that the appellate power over the decisions of state courts is contrary to the genius of our institutions."

—Martin v. Hunter's Lessee (1816)

Figure VI.3 Portrait of Joseph Story by George Peter Alexander Healy (c. 1855).

Collection of the Supreme Court of the United States

prevent him from denouncing the decision. He attacked the decision in a series of articles denying the right of the federal government to be the final judge of its own powers. The Constitution established a federal union, not a unitary state, and the states retained their sovereignty except for the powers delegated to the federal government. Because state courts were official instruments of the states, Congress could not subordinate them to the federal courts for any purpose. The Supreme Court's decision upholding Section 25 was not binding on the sovereign states. They would be defenseless against federal encroachments, Roane warned, if the reach of federal power was ultimately up to the Supreme Court, which was itself an instrument of the federal government. Such were the views of the jurist who probably would have been Jefferson's choice to replace Marshall as chief justice.

Section 25 and the Eleventh Amendment

Section 25 came before the Court again in *Cohens v. Virginia* (1821). The Cohen brothers had been convicted and fined in the Virginia courts for selling lottery tickets in violation of state law. Because the lottery had been authorized by Congress to raise money for public improvements in the District of Columbia, the Cohens appealed to the Supreme Court under Section 25 on the ground that the Virginia law conflicted with the act of Congress. The appeal was different from the previous Section 25 appeals because it was brought against a state and not, as in the *Fairfax* and *Martin* cases, against a private party. Virginia challenged the jurisdiction of the Court to hear the appeal on two grounds. The first attacked the constitutionality of Section 25, an argument already rejected by the Court. The second contended that the Eleventh Amendment barred the appeal by immunizing the states against suits in federal courts. Even if Section 25 was constitutional, counsel for Virginia argued, the Amendment precluded its use against the states.

The Court ruled against Virginia on both counts. Marshall upheld the constitutionality of Section 25 and rejected the argument that the Eleventh Amendment precluded appeals to the Supreme Court against the states. He used the case to expound on the nature of the Union and the jurisdiction of the federal courts. The states could no longer claim complete sovereignty, he said, because part of their sovereignty had been surrendered in creating the federal government. They became "members of one great empire—for some purposes sovereign, for some purposes subordinate." This abridgment of sovereignty made Section 25 constitutional. Nor did the Eleventh Amendment prevent appeals against the states under Section 25. The Amendment only prevented private parties from suing the states in federal courts. But it did not prevent them from appealing to the federal courts in suits begun by the states. The Cohens had not brought proceedings against Virginia; the proceedings had been brought by Virginia against the Cohens. The immunity from lawsuits granted to the states by the Eleventh Amendment did not apply in cases begun by the states.

Having ruled against Virginia on the constitutional issues, Marshall upheld the conviction of the Cohens under the state antigambling statute. He ruled that the statute was a valid exercise of the State's police powers. Since Congress had not expressly authorized the sale of lottery tickets outside the District of Columbia, there was no conflict with federal law. The outcome of the case bears a tactical resemblance to Marshall's handling of *Marbury v. Madison.* He balanced a technical victory for Virginia against a major assertion of jurisdiction for the Court. Had he invalidated the antigambling statute and overturned the convictions, Virginia probably would have defied the Court and ignored the decision. But since the statute had been upheld, there was no opportunity to challenge the Court's authority. Even so, the political response was bitter. Jefferson joined Judge Roane and most other Virginia Republicans in attacking the Court for another encroachment upon the sovereignty of the states.

Although history has come down on Marshall's side of the argument, Jefferson and Roane raised important issues. The constitutionality of Section 25 was not as self-evident then as the passage of time has made it today. Marshall and Story were correct in arguing that Congress, instead of providing for appeals from the state courts to the Supreme Court, could have given the federal courts complete jurisdiction over federal issues. But that was really beside the point. The issue was whether Section 25 encroached upon the judicial independence of the states. The authority of Congress to provide for the uniform enforcement of federal law did not necessarily authorize it to put the state courts under federal tutelage. Authorizing federal appeals undermined the state courts as instruments of state government. Would it be constitutional, for example, to require state governors to refer their executive decisions to the president for review? If the answer is no, as it surely must be, what makes federal encroachments on state judicial functions different? Jefferson and Roane saw no logical difference, and that put them at odds with both Marshall and history.

Marshall's views prevailed mainly because of their practicality. They guaranteed the uniformity and supremacy of federal law without forcing the federal government to assume judicial work best performed by the state courts. Many cases involving federal issues do not turn on the federal issue; their outcome often depends on the interpretation of state laws. To have consigned such cases to the federal courts for trial would have been costly and cumbersome. Section 25 provided a device for federal involvement only when the federal issue was decisive. Marshall's interpretation of the Eleventh Amendment was also pragmatic. If the Amendment had prevented appeals against the states, the Supreme Court would have had no jurisdiction to review criminal cases that raised constitutional issues. Since every criminal case is brought in the name of the state against the defendant, it would have been impossible to bring a federal appeal no matter how flagrantly federal rights had been violated. Jefferson and Roane did not misread the Constitution, but they both ignored the practical aspects of their interpretations.

Expanding Federal Power

Marshall pushed the limits of federal power far beyond the letter of the Constitution in *McCulloch v. Maryland* (1819). The case involved an attempt by Maryland to prevent the national bank from operating within the state. The legislature imposed a prohibitive tax on the operations of all banks not chartered by the state, but the real target was the Second

Bank of the United States. Congress had chartered the latter in 1816 to succeed Hamilton's first national bank, whose charter had expired in 1811. The South and West regarded the bank as a northern financial monopoly ultimately hostile to agrarian interests. Several states sought to exclude it, and Maryland attempted to do so by imposing a $15,000 tax for the privilege of issuing bank notes. When James McCulloch, cashier of the Baltimore branch, refused to pay, Maryland sued in its state courts to enforce collection. The bank challenged the constitutionality of the tax on the ground that it conflicted with the act of Congress granting its charter. When the Maryland courts upheld the tax, the case was appealed to the United States Supreme Court.

The Court had to decide two separate issues. The first was the constitutionality of the act of Congress chartering the bank, and the second was Maryland's right to tax it. Maryland contended that the charter was invalid because nothing in the Constitution expressly authorized Congress to charter a national bank. Jefferson had made the same argument in the 1790s in opposing the first national bank, and Hamilton had argued that Congress had implied as well as expressly delegated powers. The Court now had to decide whether Jefferson's strict constructionism or Hamilton's loose constructionism prevailed as a rule of constitutional interpretation. Even if the Court upheld the constitutionality of the charter, there was still a strong case for the right of Maryland to tax it. Taxation is an incident of sovereignty, and Maryland within its own borders was sovereign.

A unanimous Court ruled against Maryland on both issues. Marshall began by upholding the constitutionality of the charter. In an opinion that vindicated Hamilton completely, he held that the "necessary and proper" clause of Article I gave Congress powers beyond those expressly granted by the Constitution. The express power to levy and collect taxes carried with it the implied power to create financial agents, like the national bank, to implement the delegated power. "Let the end be legitimate," he wrote, "let it be within the scope of the Constitution, and all means which are appropriate, which are plainly adapted to that end, which are not prohibited, but consist with the letter and spirit of the constitution, are constitutional." Hamilton's theory about the scope of federal power now ceased being theory and became settled constitutional law.

Marshall then proceeded to declare the Maryland tax unconstitutional on the ground that it violated the sovereignty of the national government. Because the bank had been chartered to implement delegated federal powers, the states could not interfere with it in any way. Holding that the power to tax involves the power to destroy, Marshall ruled that the tax posed a threat to federal governmental operations. The bank had been chartered to assist in governmental functions, and Maryland therefore might do nothing to interfere with it. "If the States may tax one instrument," he wrote, "they may tax any and every other instrument. They may tax the mail; they may tax the mint; they may tax patent rights; they may tax the papers of the custom-house; they may tax judicial process[.]" Such encroachments on governmental functions were incompatible with the sovereignty of the national government.

The South and West denounced the decision as still another abridgment of state sovereignty. Two former presidents, Jefferson and Madison, joined in the protests. The decision was roundly attacked in Congress, and five state legislatures called for a constitutional amendment allowing them to exclude the national bank from their borders. The case probably would have caused controversy regardless of how it was decided. The Court could have invalidated the bank's charter only by declaring that the act of Congress which incorporated it was unconstitutional. How Republicans might have reacted to that can be gauged from their angry reaction to the *Marbury* decision. Nor did state sovereignty come out on the losing side completely. Marshall's ruling that a sovereign government and its instruments cannot be taxed also prevented the federal government from taxing the states.

A Federal Government of Enumerated Powers

"This government is acknowledged by all to be one of enumerated powers . . . That principle is now universally admitted. But the question respecting the extent of the powers actually granted, is perpetually arising, and will probably continue to arise, as long as our system shall exist . . . If any one proposition could command the universal assent of mankind, we might expect it would be this—that the government of the Union, though limited in its powers, is supreme within its sphere of action. This would seem to result necessarily from its nature. It is the government of all; its powers are delegated by all; it represents all, and acts for all. Though any one State may be willing to control its operations, no State is willing to allow others to control them. The nation, on those subjects on which it can act, must necessarily bind its component parts . . . The government of the United States, then, though limited in its powers, is supreme; and its laws, when made in pursuance of the constitution, form the law of the land . . ."

—Chief Justice John Marshall, *McCulloch v. Maryland* (1819)

The Court had to reiterate much of its *McCulloch* holding in *Osborn v. Bank of the United States* (1824). Ohio attempted to circumvent *McCulloch* by authorizing the state auditor to seize bank property for nonpayment of a state tax. The state would then be protected by the Eleventh Amendment against a suit in the federal courts to recover the property. The bank countered by obtaining an injunction in the federal circuit court for Ohio ordering the auditor, Ralph Osborn, not to collect the tax. Osborn ignored the order and seized bank assets, which he then turned over to the state treasury. The bank thereupon sued Osborn for damages in the federal circuit court. When the court awarded damages to the bank, Osborn appealed to the Supreme Court on the ground that he had acted only in his official capacity as state auditor. In effect, the suit was really against Ohio and therefore barred by the Eleventh Amendment from being brought in the federal courts. Marshall ruled against Osborn on the ground that state officials who act under an obviously unconstitutional state law cannot claim official immunity for their actions. While the Eleventh Amendment immunized Ohio from suit in the federal courts, it did not immunize state officials whose actions made them personally liable. The ruling restricted the protection afforded by the Amendment by making state officials personally accountable in the federal courts.

The Monetary Clause

While construing the Constitution loosely in favor of federal power, Marshall construed it strictly with respect to the powers of the states. He went out of his way in *Craig v. Missouri* (1830) to turn the monetary clause into a tight constitutional constraint. Missouri had authorized the issuance of loan certificates which might be used for the payment of state taxes and debts, as well as to compensate state officials for their salaries and fees. The certificates were challenged on the ground that Article I of the Constitution prohibited the states from issuing bills of credit or making anything except gold and silver legal tender for the payment of debts. The Missouri law did not appear to violate the prohibition because it did not make its certificates legal tender, which was the whole point of the constitutional ban. But Marshall, speaking this time for a sharply divided Court, nevertheless declared the law unconstitutional. Three of the seven justices dissented on the ground that the law was a legitimate exercise of the State's borrowing power and not a provision for unconstitutional legal tender. The dissent signaled a growing willingness on the part of some justices to give the states the benefit of the doubt on close constitutional issues.

The Commerce Power

The Constitution put foreign and interstate commerce under the control of Congress, but it did not define commerce or its relation to the internal trade carried on within the states. The Court attempted to do both in *Gibbons v. Ogden* (1824). The case grew out of an exclusive license granted by New York to Robert Fulton and Robert Livingston in 1805 to operate steamships in state waters. Fulton and Livingston later issued a sublicense to Aaron Ogden who, along with Thomas Gibbons, established a ferry service between New York and New Jersey. Gibbons later broke with Ogden and established a ferry service of his own under a federal license obtained under the Coasting Act of 1793. Ogden thereupon sued in the New York courts and obtained an injunction forbidding Gibbons to infringe upon his exclusive license. Gibbons appealed to the United States Supreme Court on the ground that the state license violated his rights under federal law.

The case posed two separate questions. The first was whether the federal commerce power covered navigation and transportation as well as the exchange of goods. The second was whether the states had any concurrent power to regulate commerce under federal control. All commerce had intrastate ramifications for which the Constitution provided no guidelines. Ogden contended that his exclusive state license was constitutional because it covered only navigation and transportation and did not extend to the buying and selling of goods. Even if the federal commerce power included navigation and transportation, it covered only transportation between states. The New York license granted exclusive rights only in state waters and therefore did not interfere with interstate commerce. Nothing in the Constitution, he contended, prevented the states from regulating their internal waterways.

These were powerful arguments, so persuasive that Chancellor James Kent had upheld Ogden's license in the New York courts. But Marshall was not convinced, and he ruled against Ogden on both issues. First, he held that commerce includes navigation and transportation as well as the exchange of goods. He then ruled that the federal commerce power extends to all coastal and inland waters on which foreign and interstate commerce could be carried. Although commerce wholly within a state was outside federal jurisdiction, the federal commerce power did not stop at state lines. It extended to all aspects of intrastate commerce relating to interstate and foreign commerce. While Ogden's New York license covered only state waters, its impact on interstate commerce was obvious. There would be no commerce at all between the states if each state had exclusionary power over its own waters. Such a state of affairs would render the commerce powers of Congress meaningless. Marshall left unanswered, as not essential to the decision, the question whether in the absence of federal regulations the states had any concurrent powers to regulate foreign and interstate commerce.

The decision came at a time when many states were granting monopolies to transportation companies. The constitutionality of such grants had been far from clear when *Gibbons v. Ogden* came before the Court. The unconstitutionality of Ogden's license did not then seem as obvious as it appears today. After all, it had been upheld by Chancellor Kent, one of the great jurists of the age. There was no reason, except for Marshall's expansive view of federal power, why the decision could not have gone the other way. But history would again prove the chief justice correct. A decision upholding steamship monopolies in the 1820s would have been a precedent for state railroad monopolies a generation later. The decision favored national systems of transportation unobstructed by state monopolies.

Original Package Doctrine

In *Brown v. Maryland* (1827) Marshall held that the Commerce Clause limited the states' powers of taxation. The case grew out of a Maryland law requiring wholesale dealers in foreign goods to pay a license fee to the state. The law was challenged as an unconstitutional interference with commerce. Roger B. Taney, Maryland's Attorney General, made a persuasive case for the constitutionality of the measure by arguing that it was a legitimate exercise of the state's licensing power. It applied to a wide range of wholesalers and did not specifically target those engaged in foreign and interstate dealings. Marshall nevertheless declared the law unconstitutional. He had to concede, however, that licensing was a valid state function. So his opinion provided guidelines to reconcile it with federal jurisdiction over foreign and interstate commerce. He held that imported goods were not subject to state taxes or licensing fees while they remained in their original form or package. Only after they had been "mixed up with the mass of property in the country" were they subject to state and local taxes. Marshall conceded the right of the states to regulate imports in the course of exercising their ordinary police powers. But he ruled that the Maryland law had nothing to do with police powers. It primarily involved taxation, and taxes could not be imposed on imported goods until they entered the general stream of commerce.

State Police Powers and Commerce

Marshall made a significant concession to the police powers of the states in *Willson v. Black Bird Creek Marsh Co.* (1829). The case was brought by a steamship operator doing business under a federal license similar to the one upheld in *Gibbons v. Ogden*. Willson, the steamship operator, challenged the constitutionality of a Delaware law for the damming of a navigable creek. He contended that the dam would obstruct interstate commerce and abridge rights granted by his federal license. The case was different from *Gibbons* insofar as the Delaware law had nothing to do with commerce. The state had sought only to manage its marshes and inland waters for the general welfare. Whether it could do so in a way that incidentally interfered with interstate commerce was the issue before the Court.

The Court upheld the law as constitutional. Marshall ruled it a valid exercise of the State's police powers and not an encroachment upon the federal commerce power. What also distinguished the case from *Gibbons* was that Congress had not acted with respect to the creek in question, so there was no federal-state conflict to resolve in an area of federal jurisdiction. "If Congress had passed any act which bore on the case," Marshall wrote, "we should feel not much difficulty in saying that a state law coming in conflict with such act would be void." He held, in effect, that federal jurisdiction is paramount but not necessarily exclusive with respect to interstate commerce. Delaware had a legitimate interest in damming the creek, and the damming violated no federal law. Marshall noted that property values in the region "must be enhanced by excluding the water from the marsh, and the health of the inhabitants probably improved." The states were free to promote local public interests to the extent that what they did involved no conflict with federal commerce policy.

The Contract Clause and Property Rights

Marshall's interpretation of the Contract Clause of Article I left a permanent mark on property law in the United States. The Articles of Confederation had left property rights at the mercy of the states by allowing them a free hand to issue worthless legal tender and postpone the payment of debts. The Constitution put an end to this by forbidding the states to impair the obligations of contract or to make anything except gold and silver legal tender. The Contract Clause had ramifications for more than contractual obligations. The federal circuit court for Pennsylvania cited it in *Vanhorne's Lessee v. Dorrance* (1795) to invalidate a state law transferring title to some disputed land. The court construed the Clause broadly to protect all sorts of property rights. But the holding was only a prelude to the creative uses Marshall would find for the Clause during his tenure as chief justice.

The Clause came before the Supreme Court for the first time in *Fletcher v. Peck* (1810). The case grew out of the most notorious land fraud in American history. In 1795 the Georgia legislature granted about 35 million acres of land along the Yazoo River to four land companies. The grant, which covered nearly all of what later became the states of Alabama and Mississippi, had been procured by the wholesale corruption of the state legislature. Georgia received only $500,000 for the grant, less than 1.5 cents per acre. When word got out that all but one member of the legislature had been bribed, the corrupt lawmakers were voted out in the next state elections. The new legislature revoked the grant under a law restoring all the land to Georgia. In the meantime, some of the land had been resold by the companies to buyers who had not been involved in the fraud. The rescinding legislation wiped out their rights as well as the rights of the offending companies.

The case posed several issues that had no clear-cut answers. First, did Georgia as a sovereign state have the power to revoke rights that it had granted, or would such action violate the Contract Clause? The Clause clearly covered private contracts, but did it also apply to contracts involving sovereign states? Second, did the corruption of the Georgia legislature invalidate the grant from the outset and thereby prevent the perpetrators of the fraud from passing title to the subsequent buyers in good faith? There was no question that the land still held by the companies could be recovered, but what about the land resold to buyers not involved in the fraud? Third, were land grants, which actually created no contractual obligations, even within the purview of the Clause? Any approach the Court took in resolving these issues would have important ramifications.

Speaking for a unanimous Court, Marshall upheld the rights of the subsequent buyers against the rescinding legislation. He ruled that states were as bound by the Contract Clause as were private parties, and the rights of the subsequent buyers in good faith were constitutionally protected. Though not contracts in the technical sense, land grants created implied obligations that put them within the coverage of the Clause. They bound the grantor not to do anything invidious to the title conveyed to the grantee. "The state of Georgia was restrained," Marshall wrote, "from passing a law whereby the estate of the plaintiff in the premises so purchased could be constitutionally and legally impaired[.]" The original grant could be rescinded for fraud, but the land resold to buyers not involved in the fraud could not be recovered.

The decision was immediately attacked by states' rights supporters as a misconstruction of the Constitution. They contended that the sole purpose of the Contract Clause was to prevent the states from impairing rights created by private contracts. It had never been intended to deprive states of their sovereign power to revoke their own grants. Marshall had put public grants on the same footing as private contracts and given the Clause far more scope than the framers of the Constitution intended. He was attacked personally as a land speculator (though he had not speculated in Yazoo lands), and his detractors charged that this influenced his opinion. The charge of bias may have had something to do with the vehemence of the decision. In declaring the Georgia statute unconstitutional, Marshall cited the Contract Clause, the doctrine of vested rights, and the constitutional ban against ex post facto laws and bills of attainder. So much overkill suggested that the grounds of the decision might indeed be shaky.

Critics of the decision were probably correct on the issue of original intent. Marshall seems to have stretched the Contract Clause beyond its original meaning. Its purpose had been to protect the sort of private obligations which had been abridged by the states during the Confederation period. Marshall's interpretation of the Clause cut deeper into the powers of the states than the framers had probably intended. He essentially put the states on the same footing as private individuals with respect to obligations of contract. The decision not only deprived Georgia of some land along the Yazoo River but cost all the states some of their sovereignty.

The Court stretched the Contract Clause even further in *New Jersey v. Wilson* (1812). The case grew out of a pre-Revolutionary treaty under which New Jersey exempted the Delaware Indians from paying taxes on tribal lands. Whites who subsequently purchased the land claimed that the tax exemption passed from the Indians to them along with title to the land. New Jersey contended that the exemption applied only to the Indians and did not attach to the land itself for the benefit of subsequent buyers. Marshall ruled that the exemption did pass with the land and that the Contract Clause barred the state from rescinding it. Although widely denounced as another abridgment of state sovereignty, the decision had only limited consequences. The states thereafter protected themselves by prescribing strict time limits when they granted tax exemptions.

Dartmouth College Case

Marshall gave the Contract Clause an added dimension in *Dartmouth College v. Woodward* (1819). At issue was the charter granted in 1769 by King George III to the founders of Dartmouth College. The charter provided for a board of twelve trustees who had power to govern the College in perpetuity and to fill board vacancies among themselves. In 1816 the New Hampshire legislature abrogated the charter under a law putting the College under public control. The board was enlarged from twelve to twenty-one, the additional members to be appointed by the governor and council. A new board of twenty-five overseers, also appointed by the governor and council, was created with veto power over the trustees. The reorganization of the College was politically motivated. Its president, John Wheelock, had been dismissed in 1815 by the trustees after a bitter dispute involving political and religious differences. Wheelock led the Presbyterian and Republican faction at the College, while the trustees were Federalists and Congregationalists. When the Republicans won the state elections the following year, they moved to take over the College and restore Wheelock to office. Dartmouth was reorganized as a public institution with Wheelock as president.

The reorganization was resisted by the old board of trustees who for a time continued to run the College. The new trustees eventually ousted them from the campus and took over the College buildings and records. But the old trustees did not give up. They rented some rooms in nearby Hanover and continued to operate as a college with the support of loyal faculty and students. They also began legal proceedings to recover the seal, records, and account books of the College. William Woodward, the Secretary and Treasurer of the College, sided with the new board and refused to turn over the items requested. So the old trustees sued him in the name of the College to recover them. When Woodward cited the state law reorganizing the College as a defense, the old trustees challenged the constitutionality of the reorganization. The state courts predictably upheld the law, and the old trustees appealed to the United States Supreme Court.

The appeal was handled by Daniel Webster, and never was a case argued more eloquently. Webster had been on the winning side in *Gibbons v. Ogden* and *McCulloch v. Maryland*, and his arguments were sometimes incorporated almost verbatim in Marshall's opinions. No attorney of any generation has had a greater influence on the interpretation of the Constitution. He argued that the Dartmouth College charter was a contract and constitutionally protected against abrogation by the state. The College was not a public institution, as the state contended, but a private one created and sustained by the efforts of private citizens. He reminded the Court that what the legislature had done had serious implications for all educational institutions. Upholding what New Hampshire had done would discourage the founding of private colleges everywhere. This argument turned the tables on the state, which claimed to represent the public interest, by showing that the reorganization actually disserved the public interest.

Webster's efforts continued even after the Court adjourned to consider its decision. He revised and polished his written brief, had it privately printed, and sent copies to his friend Justice Story for distribution among the justices. He also sent a copy to Chancellor Kent of New York, knowing that Kent had influence with some of the justices. The possibility that Kent might be consulted was certainly worth a copy. Webster spared no effort on behalf of the College. A Dartmouth graduate himself, he felt personally involved in the case. By today's standards, he may have gone too far in promoting the interests of his client. But professional and ethical standards were looser then, and out-of-court contacts between attorneys and judges were not unusual. Even so, Webster's efforts are almost unique in the annals of American advocacy.

The Court ruled for Dartmouth, declaring the revocation of its charter unconstitutional. Marshall's opinion, from which only one of the justices dissented, held that the law making it a public institution violated the Contract Clause. He ruled that the charter was a contract and therefore constitutionally protected against abridgment by the state. He rejected the argument that the Constitution protected only privately created rights, and not publicly created rights granted by charter. Charters had all the elements of contracts, Marshall declared. The time and money its founders had invested in the College in reliance on the charter formed the legal consideration (the quid pro quo) essential to any contract. As a contract, the charter had the full protection of the Constitution.

The decision had important consequences for American economic development. The case was decided at a time when state governments were chartering numerous corporations

Figure VI.4 Portrait of Daniel Webster by Francis Alexander (1835). Also known as the "Black Dan" portrait, this painting was commissioned in honor of Webster's work in Dartmouth College v. Woodward. It hangs in Dartmouth's Baker Library to this day.

National Portrait Gallery, Smithsonian Institution / Art Resource, NY

Expanding the Contract Clause

"It is more than possible, that the preservation of rights of this description was not particularly in the view of the framers of the Constitution, when the clause under consideration was introduced into that instrument. It is probable, that interferences of more frequent occurence, to which the temptation was stronger, and of which the mischief was more extensive, constituted the great motive for imposing this restriction on the state legislatures. But although a particular and a rare case may not, in itself, be of sufficient magnitude to induce a rule, yet it must be governed by the rule, when established, unless some plain and strong reason for excluding it can be given . . . It is not enough to say, that this particular case was not in the mind of the convention when the article was framed, nor of the American people, when it was adopted. It is necessary to go further, and to say that, had this particular case been suggested, the language would have been so varied, as to exclude it, or it would have been made a special exception. The case, being within the words of the rule, must be within its operation likewise, unless there be something in the literal construction, so obviously absurd, or mischievous, or repugnant to the general spirit of the instrument, as to justify those who expound the Constitution in making it an exception."

—Chief Justice John Marshall, *Dartmouth College v. Woodward* (1819)

for enterprises requiring large amounts of capital. The corporate form made it possible for American entrepreneurs to raise capital quickly and efficiently in a young nation undergoing rapid expansion and economic growth. Between 1783 and 1801 alone, almost 350 business corporations were chartered in the United States, dwarfing in less than twenty years the number of corporations that had been chartered in England during the entire eighteenth century. The *Dartmouth College* decision reassured investors that the Constitution protected their corporations from state interference. Once chartered, a corporation could not arbitrarily be put out of business by the state. Justice Story noted in his concurring opinion that states might protect the public interest by writing exceptions and limitations into charters of incorporation. But only to the extent that states protected themselves in advance could they subsequently interfere with rights granted by the charter.

A few years later, in *Green v. Biddle* (1823), the Court held that even political agreements between states came within the scope of the Contract Clause. The case involved a 1792 accord between Virginia and Kentucky validating land grants previously made in the then-territory of Kentucky by Virginia. Later, in order to resolve overlapping claims, Kentucky passed laws invalidating some of the Virginia titles guaranteed by the accord. In an opinion written by Justice Bushrod Washington, the Court held that the Kentucky laws violated the Contract Clause. Obligations between states as well as those between private parties were protected by the Constitution. The decision was denounced by states' rights supporters as political meddling, and there was talk in Congress of limiting the Court's jurisdiction in such cases. But the decision did not have much practical significance, because in the future the states could include escape clauses in their accords. In the end, the holding made no practical difference; Kentucky simply ignored it and continued settling land disputes under its own laws.

The Court finally drew a line on the Contract Clause in *Providence Bank v. Billings* (1830) in rejecting a claim that the Clause restricted the states' general powers of taxation over corporations. The Providence Bank challenged a Rhode Island law subjecting it to taxation on the ground that because it had not been subject to taxes at the time of its incorporation, the subsequent imposition of taxes violated the Contract Clause. This argument pushed the theory of the *Dartmouth* case beyond all reasonable limits. Marshall ruled against the Bank, holding that a corporation was not exempt from taxes unless expressly exempted from taxation by the terms of its charter. Any implied rights claimed under a charter had to be clearly connected to the rights expressly granted. Since nothing in its charter suggested any intent by the state to exempt the Bank from taxation, the exemption could not be claimed as a contractual right. A different outcome would have put corporations beyond the tax power of the states unless their charters expressly allowed them to be taxed.

Bankruptcy Laws

From the beginning, the Contract Clause had been on a collision course with state bankruptcy laws. Although the Constitution authorized Congress to pass uniform laws of bankruptcy, neither the Federalists nor Republicans showed much enthusiasm for establishing national standards. Only two bankruptcy laws were enacted by Congress prior to the Civil War, and both were soon repealed. So the states filled the bankruptcy vacuum with laws of their own providing relief for insolvent debtors. The New York law was challenged on constitutional grounds in *Sturges v. Crowninshield* (1819). The law granted relief from debts contracted both before and after its enactment. The case, which involved a debt contracted before its enactment, raised two issues: whether the relief granted violated the Contract Clause and whether the power of Congress over bankruptcy was exclusive. If the power was exclusive, the states could not act even in the absence of federal regulations. But even if the states could legislate on the subject, the Contract Clause still bound them not to violate the rights of creditors.

Marshall ruled that while the power of Congress over bankruptcy was paramount, it was not exclusive. The states had concurrent power to regulate bankruptcy so long as their laws did not conflict with federal law. Since there was no federal law, the New York law could not be challenged on that ground. But it could be challenged under the Contract Clause for unconstitutionally impairing obligations of contract. Granting relief for debts contracted before its enactment clearly violated existing rights of contract. Because the case involved only an existing debt, the Court did not have to rule on the constitutionality of laws discharging debts contracted after their enactment. Since the justices were divided on the question, the issue was not addressed.

But the issue had to be addressed in *Ogden v. Saunders* (1827) when a creditor challenged a New York bankruptcy law discharging debts contracted after its enactment. The Court voted 4–3 to uphold the law, with Marshall on the losing side of a major decision for the first and only time during his tenure as chief justice. In an opinion written by Justice Washington, the majority held that bankruptcy laws granting prospective relief to creditors did not violate the Contract Clause. Washington reasoned that because all rights of contract arise under the law of the state where they are made, existing state law becomes an implied term of every contract. The only rights that can be created by contract are those recognized by the laws in force. No one, for instance, could enforce a gambling contract made in a state where gambling is prohibited. Similarly, creditors who lend money in states with bankruptcy laws do so knowing that their debtors may obtain relief from their obligations. That contingency becomes an implied limitation of the contractual rights created. The only constraints imposed by the Constitution are that state bankruptcy laws must be prospective in operation and that they do not discharge debts owed to citizens of other states. The latter would create conflicts between the states and impair the diversity jurisdiction of the federal courts over interstate litigations.

Marshall wrote a dissent joined in by Justices Story and Duvall. He argued that the Contract Clause protects all legal contracts, future as well as past, against abridgment by the states. While state law governs what rights parties to a contract can lawfully create, it cannot prevent the enforcement of rights lawfully created. The protection of the Clause is absolute, Marshall contended. If it protected only existing obligations, the same argument could be made for the legal tender prohibition. Could the states pass prospective paper money laws for the payment of debts contracted after their enactment? The answer was obviously no, but why in one case and not the other? The dissent was one of Marshall's most brilliantly reasoned opinions, but it put logic over practicality. The failure of Congress to act on bankruptcy left thousands of insolvent debtors desperately in need of state relief.

The Bill of Rights

The most important victory for states' rights during the Marshall era came in *Barron v. Baltimore* (1833). The case involved a lawsuit by a Baltimore wharf owner against the city for damages to his wharf caused by city excavations and street repairs. He contended that the Fifth Amendment prohibition against taking property without just compensation required Baltimore to compensate him for the damages. Having lost in the state courts, he appealed to the Supreme Court on the ground that the Fifth Amendment applied to the states as well as the federal government, because it embodied "principles which regulate the legislation of the states, for the protection of people in each and all of the states[.]" This was the most sweeping claim of federal constitutional protection yet asserted before the Court. If sustained, the states would be bound by the same Fifth Amendment constraints that bound the federal government, and by implication other constraints enumerated in the Bill of Rights as well.

Marshall spoke for a unanimous Court in rejecting the claim. He ruled that the Fifth Amendment and the rest of the Bill of Rights applied only to the federal government. The states were not bound by the federal guarantees. He wrote: "Had the framers of these amendments intended them to be limitations on the powers of the state governments, they would have imitated the framers of the original constitution, and have expressed that intention." Marshall ruled that the Constitution was "ordained and established by the people of the United States for themselves, for their own government; and not for the government of the individual states." The states had their own constitutions which imposed such restraints on state government as the citizens of the states deemed appropriate. But the states were no more bound by the federal Bill of Rights than the federal government was bound by bills of rights adopted by the states.

The case really could not have been decided differently without ignoring the early history of the Constitution. The rights guaranteed by the Bill of Rights were first proposed in the state ratifying conventions by delegates who feared that the new federal government might interfere with traditional liberties. Their purpose was not to limit the state governments but to keep the federal government within bounds. The First Amendment did not prevent Connecticut from maintaining a tax-supported church until 1816, nor did it prevent Massachusetts from having one until 1833. The legislative history of the Bill of Rights demonstrated that the guarantees were not intended to apply to the states. The original version passed by the House of Representatives did apply against the states, but the Senate deleted the restrictions on state power and approved a version that applied only to the federal government. This was the version adopted by Congress and ratified by the states.

Although its reasoning was sound, *Barron* ran counter to Marshall's judicial nationalism and to the importance he ascribed to protecting property rights against state abridgment. He could have plausibly ruled in favor of Barron by looking to the text of the Bill of Rights rather than to its legislative history. A strictly textual analysis might have produced a different result. The fact that the guarantees of the First Amendment were made specifically applicable to the federal government, while the guarantees of the other amendments were not, made it possible to argue that some of the latter applied against the states as rights of national citizenship. He might also have argued that one of the purposes of the Constitution was to protect property rights from the sort of state abridgments that occurred during the Confederation period. This line of argument would have been controversial, but not much more so than some of Marshall's other rulings on the limits of state sovereignty.

John Marshall on the Bill of Rights

"[I]t is universally understood, it is a part of the history of the day, that the great revolution which established the constitution of the United States, was not effected without immense opposition. Serious fears were extensively entertained that those powers which the patriot statesmen, who then watched over the interests of our country, deemed essential to union, and to the attainment of those invaluable objects for which union was sought, might be exercised in a manner dangerous to liberty. In almost every convention by which the constitution was adopted, amendments to guard against the abuse of power were recommended. These amendments demanded security against the apprehended encroachments of the general government—not against those of the local governments."

—Barron v. Baltimore (1833)

Constitutional historians such as Akhil Reed Amar have pointed out that prior to *Barron* a considerable body of judicial opinion assumed that some provisions of the Bill of Rights did apply to the states as well as to the federal government. In *Houston v. Moore* (1820), Justice William Johnson, one of Jefferson's appointees to the Court, suggested that the double jeopardy prohibition of the Fifth Amendment bound the states, and the state courts of New York, Massachusetts, and Mississippi reached the same conclusion. While sitting on the federal circuit court for Pennsylvania, Justice Henry Baldwin implied that the Second and Fourth Amendments applied to the states, and he referred to the religion clauses of the First Amendment in interpreting a state law. These holdings were based on the so-called negative-implication theory propounded by the influential legal commentator William Rawle, who argued that virtually all the general provisions of the Bill of Rights bound the states. Rawle reasoned that since the First Amendment specifically applied to Congress, the general language of the other amendments indicated that, unlike the First, they applied also to the states. So the outcome in *Barron* was by no means a foregone conclusion when the issue came before the Court.

Marshall also had available an earlier federal circuit court holding in *Bonaparte v. Camden & Amboy Railroad Co.* (1830) that he might have cited as a precedent for extending the federal just compensation guarantee to the states. The suit had been brought by Joseph Bonaparte, brother of Napoleon, for an injunction against a railroad that claimed the right to lay tracks across his New Jersey estate. The railroad contended that its charter from the state gave it a right of way across privately owned land. But the court held otherwise. In granting the injunction, Justice Baldwin expounded on the rights of owners whose property is taken for a public use. He declared that while every government has the sovereign right to take private property for a public use, "the obligation to make just compensation is concomitant with the right." Noting that this principle of law was recognized in the Fifth Amendment, he declared that it did not require specific recognition, because the right of the owner to just compensation runs with the power of the state to take private property. Baldwin also held that the owner of property taken for public use is protected by the Contract Clause of the Constitution because his right to the property rests upon a lawful purchase contract.

Bonaparte provided Marshall with a plausible argument that just compensation for property taken by the state was so essential to constitutional government that it was generally applicable to the states even though the Fifth Amendment might not have made it explicitly applicable. Such a holding would have had far-reaching consequences, because if one of the federal guarantees essential to constitutional government could be extended to the states by implication, other essential guarantees would likely follow. But the political climate at the time did not favor such a bold assertion of judicial power restrictive of state sovereignty. The national government had just come through a nullification crisis over the protective tariff, and any attempt to nationalize even one of the guarantees of the federal Bill of Rights would probably have precipitated another. Nor could the Court count on the support of the executive branch if Maryland defied the Court. President Andrew Jackson had already made that clear by refusing to enforce Marshall's holding in *Worcester v. Georgia* (1832) that Georgia had no jurisdiction over the lands of the Cherokee nation.

The chief justice was too astute to involve the Court in a power struggle that could not be won. So Barron got no compensation for his damaged wharf, and the guarantees of the Bill of Rights remained applicable only to the federal government.

The Slave Trade and the Court

Following the prohibition of slave imports after 1808, Congress passed a series of laws forbidding United States citizens to engage in the overseas slave trade. The trade was outlawed as a form of piracy punishable by death, and American vessels were authorized to seize slave ships suspected of being owned by Americans. These measures and the seizures that followed opened up the larger question of the status of the maritime traffic in slaves under international law. The reach of the statutes depended upon whether federal prize courts enforced them as declaratory of the law of nations or as mere expressions of United States municipal law. If enforced as municipal law, their impact would be limited only to ships belonging to Americans; the citizens of nations that had not prohibited the trade would not be affected. But if enforced as declaratory of the law of nations, the slave trade of all nations would be effectively outlawed. Since it was universally agreed that slavery was a creature of municipal law and contrary to the law of nature, it ultimately came down to whether natural law or municipal law shaped the law of nations. The Marshall Court had cited natural law in Contract Clause cases, leading opponents of slavery to hope that it would also prove applicable with respect to the slave trade.

The idea that the slave trade was contrary to the law of nations required no great stretch of contemporary jurisprudence. The notion had already been advanced aggressively by Robert Thorpe, Chief Judge of the British Court of Vice Admiralty in Sierra Leone. Thorpe enforced Britain's Act of 1807 for the abolition of the slave trade against British and foreign slave traders alike in proceedings that set in motion the destruction of the African slave trade itself. From his Court of Vice Admiralty at Freetown, Thorpe enforced a policy that rendered any slave ship not explicitly protected by treaty with Britain subject to seizure and condemnation as prize property. He regarded Britain's prohibition of the slave trade as no mere measure of municipal law but rather an authoritative declaration of the unlawfulness of the trade under the law of nations. Because the Act recognized the fundamental injustice and inhumanity of the trade, it compelled him to enforce the ban not only against British ships but against the ships of any nation not expressly authorized by treaty to engage in the traffic. Since only Portugal had treaty protection, Thorpe's expansive interpretation of the 1807 Act and of the law of nations put the Royal Navy and the Court of Vice Admiralty at Sierra Leone in the forefront of enforcing a universal ban on the slave trade.

Similar views on the slave trade and international law were expressed by Justice Story in *La Jeune Eugenie* (1822), a case that tested the reach of the American statutes outlawing the traffic in slaves. The *Eugenie*, a vessel flying the French flag, was seized by an American ship off the coast of Africa and brought to the federal circuit court at Boston presided over by Story. The captured vessel carried no slaves but was outfitted with manacles and chains obviously intended for the slave trade. The French government filed a claim that the *Eugenie* was a French ship and therefore subject only to the jurisdiction of French courts. Story rejected the claim, holding that jurisdiction depended not on ownership but whether the vessel had engaged in the slave trade and whether the trade itself violated the law of nations. He then proceeded to answer both questions in the affirmative, ruling that the ship was indeed a slaver and that the trade violated the law of nations. He closely identified the latter with natural law, holding that it embodied general principles of right and justice as well as the practices of civilized nations and the positive laws regulating international relations. Declaring the slave trade repugnant to "the dictates of natural religion, the obligations of good faith and morality, and the eternal maxims of social justice," he held that the trade could claim no protection under international law. How these views on the slave trade and the law of nations would have fared on appeal can only be conjectured. At the request of the Monroe administration, Story agreed to turn the *Eugenie* over to the French government, which prevented a review of the case by the Supreme Court.

The issues raised in *Eugenie* reached the high court three years in *The Antelope* (1825). The case involved a Venezuelan privateer, the *Columbia*, which captured the *Antelope* and several other slavers with more than 250 African slaves on board. When the *Columbia* was subsequently wrecked off the coast of Brazil, the crew transferred the surviving Africans to the *Antelope*, which in turn was captured by a United States naval vessel and brought to Savannah, Georgia, for condemnation proceedings before a federal circuit court presided over by Justice William Johnson. The case presented complex factual issues of ownership, but the key legal issue was the status of the slave trade under the law of nations. The claimants for the ship and its human cargo included the Spanish and Portuguese governments whose ships had been captured by the privateer, and the captain of the privateer who claimed that the seizures were justified because the slave trade was illegal under the law of nations. The British and American statutes against the trade were cited in support of the claim. Taking a different position from the one taken by Justice Story in *Eugenie*, Justice Johnson rejected the privateer's claim on the ground that the British and American prohibitions applied only to the citizens of both nations. The prohibitions were expressions of municipal laws no more binding on citizens of other nations than the ordinary trade laws of the nation enacting them. Since the slave trade was not prohibited by Spanish or Portuguese law, the Africans taken from Spanish and Portuguese vessels were the property of Spain and Portugal. Only the Africans taken from British and American ships had a claim to freedom under the law of nations.

When the case reached the Supreme Court, the outcome depended upon whether the Court followed Justice Story's or Justice Johnson's circuit court holdings on the reach of slave trade prohibitions. Speaking for a unanimous Court, Chief Justice Marshall upheld Johnson's view that, however abhorrent, the slave trade was legal under the law of nations. Its legality, he declared, "derived from long usage, and general acquiescence." Marshall made a sharp distinction between the slave trade as a violation of natural and moral law and the slave trade as a violation of international law. He described the latter as a body of usages, national acts, and general assents of nations, holding that the traffic in slaves remained lawful for those governments that had not forbidden it. The law of nations in effect followed the vagaries of municipal law with no moral imperatives of its own. Clearly

Marshall on the Slave Trade and the Law of Nations

"That the course of opinion on the slave trade should be unsettled, ought to excite no surprise . . . However abhorrent this traffic may be to a mind whose original feelings are not blunted by familiarity with the practice, it has been sanctioned in modern times by the laws of all nations who possess distant colonies, each of whom has engaged in it as a common commercial business which no other could rightfully interrupt . . . That trade could not be considered as contrary to the law of nations which was authorized and protected by the laws of all commercial nations; the right to carry on which was claimed by each, and allowed by each."

—The Antelope (1825)

uncomfortable with the outcome, Marshall went out of his way to distance himself personally from his own ruling. He noted that as a judge he had to follow the law and resist feelings "which might seduce [him] from the path of duty." That the slave trade was contrary to the law of nature and norms of morality simply did not matter, because the law of nature had nothing to do with the law of nations.

Given his holdings in the *Eugenie* case, it seems surprising that Justice Story did not dissent. But it would have been out of character for him to break ranks and oppose the chief justice on an issue that might have undermined the solidarity of the Court. Moreover, although Marshall's legal rulings upheld the rights of the slave traders, his rulings on the facts of the case largely cancelled the legal rights conceded. He required proof of ownership that wiped out the Portuguese claims completely, and he then proceeded to assume that because Portuguese ownership could not be proved, the slaves likely belonged to United States citizens acting through Portuguese proxies. This made them the property of the United States and eligible for repatriation to Africa under American statutes prohibiting the slave trade. Only the Spanish claims were upheld, but these involved only a fraction of the surviving slaves. Of the 150 survivors, 120 were returned to Africa and freedom, while only 30 were turned over to Spanish claimants and eventually sold into slavery in Florida. It was not a perfect outcome, but Story still got 80 percent of what he wanted, and for Marshall there was the satisfaction of managing another of the unanimous decisions he prized so highly.

Marshall's Legacy

Marshall provided the Court with matchless leadership during his long tenure as chief justice. Although he left his mark on almost every area of constitutional law, two main themes run through his major decisions: that the United States was a nation and not a mere confederation of states, and that private property had to be protected as a fundamental principle of constitutional government. He resisted encroachments upon national sovereignty with a determination matched only by his zeal in defending property rights. The passage of time never diminished his commitment to Federalist principles of government. He opposed Andrew Jackson as resolutely as he had once opposed Jefferson, and for the same reasons. Both stood for a philosophy of government fundamentally at odds with his vision for the nation. While his opponents won ephemeral victories at the polls, in the long run his vision shaped the course of constitutional government in the United States.

One of the reasons Marshall had such a lasting impact on constitutional development is that there were few constitutional precedents when he became chief justice. He began with what amounted to a blank slate that gave him a virtually free hand in matters of constitutional interpretation. Unfettered by case precedents, he was free to create his own precedents that would bind the Court long after he was gone. Later Courts would not be free to ignore his precedents because they would be bound by the rule of *stare decisis* not to reopen issues that he had already settled. While *stare decisis* protected Marshall's key constitutional decisions, it ironically put him on the losing side in *Ogden v. Saunders*, his only defeat on a major constitutional issue. Justice Washington, who wrote the majority opinion, believed that Congress had exclusive jurisdiction over bankruptcy and that state legislation on the subject was therefore unconstitutional. But when Marshall and the rest of the Court ruled to the contrary in *Sturges v. Crowninshield*, he considered the issue settled and the Court's decision binding in future cases. Had Washington considered the issue still open, he would have voted with Marshall in the *Ogden* case to declare the New York bankruptcy law unconstitutional. He felt bound by the *Sturges* precedent even though he disagreed with it. The irony is that Marshall wrote the opinion in the first case that prevented Washington from voting with him in the second.

But Marshall's decisions had more than *stare decisis* to commend them to posterity. They were written in a solemn, magisterial style that implied no other outcome was possible in the case. His constitutional interpretations seemed to have an inexorable logic that defied refutation. Marshall's literary style infuriated Jefferson almost as much as his rulings. The president was too good a stylist himself not to recognize the power of form over substance. Marshall's prestige grew over the years until his constitutional opinions acquired the aura of infallible texts, almost corollaries of the Constitution itself. Although some would be modified by his successors, most turned out to have the durability of granite. They are still with us today as part of the bedrock of our constitutional culture.

The history of the United States might have been vastly different had Marshall not become chief justice. If Ellsworth had not resigned to clear the way for his appointment, Jefferson probably would have appointed Judge Spencer Roane to lead the Court. Although no one can predict with certainty what a chief justice will do after joining the Court, Roane's public statements make it clear that his disagreements with Marshall were fundamental. A brilliant jurist with a forceful personality, he almost certainly would have led the Court in a different direction. As an ardent Jeffersonian, he would have had the backing of the president and Congress. Our constitutional law would probably be very different today if Roane rather than Marshall had shaped it. Strict constructionism probably would have triumphed, with federal authority limited to powers expressly granted by the Constitution. That Marshall rather than Roane was at the helm made a decisive difference in our constitutional development.

The most serious flaw in Marshall's brand of constitutionalism was his tendency to politicize key issues in ways that made his decisions unnecessarily controversial. Some were so broadly crafted that they resemble political pronouncements rather than judicial holdings. *Marbury*, his most celebrated case, was flawed by his transparent hostility to the Jefferson administration and by the semantic legerdemain employed to achieve the desired result. *Gibbons v. Ogden*, his controversial Commerce Clause decision, could have been decided solely on the basis of Gibbons's federal license without the expansive disquisition on the power of Congress over matters not at issue in the case. Similarly, in *McCulloch*, the constitutionality of the national bank could have been upheld without putting the bank, a private corporation, completely beyond the regulatory power of the states. He not only ruled on issues immediately before the Court but tended to anticipate others that might arise in the future. While Jefferson regarded constitutional government as a work in progress to be shaped by every generation, Marshall regarded it as a finished product. It might be said that he sought to bind the future by the scope of his decisions. Marshall had difficulty adjusting his essentially static constitutional jurisprudence to changing times and circumstances. In *Craig v. Missouri* he needlessly restricted the credit of the states because the loan certificates at issue apparently reminded him of the worthless fiat money that ruined creditors under the Articles of Confederation. The Constitution prohibited only the issuance of paper money as legal tender, and the certificates were not legal tender; but for Marshall the resemblance was too close to be permitted. His concern for the rights of property contributed to the *Dartmouth College* holding that corporations have essentially the same rights as natural persons under the Constitution, a principle that today gives them enormous influence over the outcome of elections. A close reading of even his most admired decisions makes it clear why the great chief justice was so controversial in his own time.

Yet, he was indisputably a great chief justice, probably our greatest. John Marshall stands in the select company of the few indispensible figures of American history. He was as important as any of our presidents, with the possible exceptions of Washington and Lincoln. It would be a mistake to assume that he succeeded just because he happened to be on the winning side of history. History has no predetermined winners or losers in the unfolding of events that drive human affairs. The Jeffersonians probably would have prevailed against a lesser adversary. They, not Marshall, seemed to have history on their side. They rode the tide toward popular government that had drowned Federalism at the polls. Marshall managed to withstand the tide by sheer force of will and intellect. He left a legacy of accomplishment unmatched by any of his adversaries, Jefferson included. His biographer Albert Beveridge may not have been far off the mark in noting that he set a standard so high "that all the future could take bearings from it, so enduring that all the shocks the Nation was to endure could not overturn it." Hyperbole, perhaps, but hyperbole inspired by a lifetime of matchless achievement.

January 1, 1808	1819	March 3, 1820	January 24, 1826	July 1827	May 19, 1828	December 20, 1828
Act Prohibiting the Importation of Slaves	Financial Panic	Missouri Compromise	U.S. and Creek Indians sign Washington Treaty	Cherokee Constitution Ratified	Enactment of "Tariff of Abominations"	Georgia Annexes Cherokee Lands

March 2, 1833	July 6, 1835	1836	March 28, 1836	1837	July 4, 1840
Compromise Tariff & Force Act Approved by Jackson	John Marshall Dies	Charter of Second Bank of the United States Expires	Roger B. Taney Becomes Chief Justice of the United States	Financial Panic	Independent Treasury Act

VII Majority Rule and Sectional Rights

March 4, 1829	May 28, 1830	March 18, 1831	March 3, 1832	November 24, 1832	December 10, 1832
Andrew Jackson Takes Office as President of the United States	Andrew Jackson Signs Indian Removal Act	Cherokee Nation v. Georgia	Worcester v. Georgia	South Carolina Passes Ordinance of Nullification	Jackson's Proclamation to the People of South Carolina

"If liberty is ever lost in America, it will be necessary to lay the blame on the omnipotence of the majority that will have brought minorities to despair and will have forced them to appeal to physical force."

—Alexis de Tocqueville, *Democracy in America* (1835)

Chief Justice Marshall's constitutional nationalism was not applauded by many of his contemporaries. Some critics justifiably charged him with steering a course that too often ignored local interests and concerns. The decentralizing tendencies of Jeffersonian politics to some extent reflected the need for greater reliance on state government. As the country expanded and the population increased, many problems had to be addressed that were not dealt with by the federal government. The need for public solutions brought state authority into new areas of governance. The growing importance of state government in turn promoted the growth of sectionalism in politics at the national level. Groups of states with similar interests formed alliances that polarized the federal government on particular issues, one of which, slavery, would ultimately plunge the nation into civil war. The brief infatuation with nationalism that followed the War of 1812 soon gave way to an era of intense regional conflicts which at times threatened the survival of the Union.

The most serious issues dividing the country were the national bank, protective tariffs, and the slavery question. All three had constitutional aspects that would sorely tax the abilities of Congress and the president. Despite its enhanced prestige under Marshall, the Supreme Court had not yet emerged as the accepted arbiter of constitutionality, so most constitutional issues were settled by the political branches of government. The decision of the Court upholding the constitutionality of the national bank did not prevent Andrew Jackson from denying its constitutionality and refusing to be bound by the holding. Nor would Abraham Lincoln later consider himself bound by a Court decision giving slavery constitutional protection in the national territories. The country was still a century away from the day when the political branches would defer to the judgment of the Court on constitutional issues. Before the Civil War, the political branches of government were dominant, and the country looked to politicians, not to judges, for leadership.

The Second National Bank

The first national bank had split the country from its inception, and Congress allowed it to go out of business when its charter expired in 1811. But the bank was reestablished for another twenty-year period in 1816, mainly because its financial services had been missed by the government during the War of 1812. The second bank turned out to be even more controversial than the first. By far the most powerful private corporation in American history, it performed some key financial functions performed today by the Federal Reserve System. It could, for instance, control the money supply by forcing independent banks to withdraw some of their banknotes from circulation. This could be accomplished by threatening to withdraw federal deposits from banks whose notes were not sufficiently backed by gold and silver. The same tactics were used to dictate interest rates and the availability of credit. While this had the beneficial effect of stabilizing the currency and curbing inflationary excesses, it was also bitterly controversial. In the South and West, where money was scarce, the bank was widely unpopular. Both sections regarded it as a monster whose policies harmed the agrarian interests of the country for the benefit of the financial centers of the Northeast.

Western opposition to the bank intensified after the financial panic of 1819. A wild spree of land speculation had set the stage for economic disaster. The speculation drew in farmers who became overextended and fell deeply into debt to their local state banks. The state banks helped inflate the bubble by issuing loans freely, and the national bank abetted the excesses by discounting the notes recklessly. Then, in 1818, the national bank suddenly reversed course. Orders went out to its branch offices to accept no notes but their own, to demand immediate payment on all state notes, and to renew no personal loans or mortgages. The new policy caught the western banks completely by surprise. Many could not clear their accounts and collapsed, dragging down with them thousands of borrowers and depositors. Their assets in the form of vast amounts of land and mortgages went to the national bank to make good the defaults.

Many westerners believed that the bank had deliberately created the panic. It had certainly profited from the western collapse by taking over local bank assets at a fraction of their real value. Although unpopular in the South as well, the bank thereafter became particularly odious in the West. "All the flourishing cities of the West are mortgaged to this money power," Senator Thomas Hart Benton of Missouri complained. "They may be devoured by it at any moment. They are in the jaws of the Monster! A lump of butter in the mouth of a dog! One gulp, one swallow, and all is gone." Nor could the "monster" be regulated or even taxed by the states. The Supreme Court had held in *McCulloch v. Maryland* that the states could neither tax nor exclude it, a holding that confirmed for many in the West that the bank was omnipotent.

The Protective Tariff

The protective tariff turned out to be an even more explosive issue than the bank. Tariffs had originally been levied only to raise money, but in 1816 Congress passed one to protect New England textile manufacturers from foreign competition. The measure had support in all sections of the country, and even southerners with no industries to protect endorsed it as a desirable step toward economic independence. But the South soon discovered the disadvantages of protectionism. The rise of cotton as the great southern staple made planters dependent on overseas markets, and they understandably came to oppose a policy directed against their best customers. Anything that reduced the importation of European textiles into the United States reduced the demand for southern cotton in Europe. Protective tariffs also hurt the South by increasing the price that southerners had to pay for imported goods.

Westerners viewed the tariff in a different light. While they had almost no manufacturing that needed protection, they also had few overseas customers who would be adversely affected by high import duties. Their markets were primarily in the northeastern states where the growth of manufacturing increased demand for western food and raw materials. So the West supported protectionism on the theory that what was good for eastern manufacturers was also good for western farmers. Senator Henry Clay of Kentucky made the tariff part of his so-called American System for promoting national unity and prosperity. High tariffs would increase manufacturing and purchasing power in the Northeast and thus expand the market for western goods. Tariffs would also generate federal revenue with which to pay for transportation improvements linking the West with its eastern markets.

But southerners opposed such schemes as harmful to their interests. They thought that Clay's grand design amounted to nothing more than a system of regional exploitation. Congressional votes on the tariff reflected the intransigence and growing isolation of the South on the issue. Southerners voted 49 to 5 against the Tariff of 1820, and 57 to 1 against the Tariff of 1824. But the alliance between the West with the Northeast put them hopelessly on the losing side of the issue. With the political arithmetic stacked against them, southerners began to attack the tariff on constitutional grounds. They contended that Congress only had power to regulate commerce for the benefit of the entire country, not for the benefit of some states at the expense of others. Protectionism was unconstitutional, they declared, because Congress had no authority to impose hardships on particular states. The only legitimate tariffs were those designed to raise revenue without bias or favor. Turning the issue into a question of southern constitutional rights set the stage for the possible disruption of the Union.

"The great principle, which lies at the foundation of all free government, is, that the majority must govern; from which there is or can be no appeal but to the sword. That majority ought to govern wisely, equitably, moderately, and constitutionally, but govern *it must*, subject only to that terrible appeal. If ever one, or several states, being a minority, can by menacing a dissolution of the Union, succeed in forming an abandonment of great measures deemed essential to the interests and prosperity of the whole, the Union, from that moment, is practically gone. It may linger on, in form and name, but its vital spirit has fled forever!"

—Speech to the Senate (February 1832)

Figure VII.1 Portrait of Henry Clay by John Sartain.

Library of Congress, Prints and Photographs Division, LC-USZ62-51067

The Slavery Issue

The sectional debate over slavery took several decades to develop into a serious national issue. At the outset, the Constitution recognized the legality of the institution and even gave special protection to slaveholding interests. The Three-Fifths Compromise gave the slave states additional representation in Congress and limited the extent to which slaves could be counted in apportioning federal taxes. Article I prohibited any restrictions on the importation of slaves until 1808, at which time the slave trade came under the general commerce powers of Congress. Provision was even made for the return of runaway slaves who fled across state lines. Article IV required the states to which they had fled to return them to their lawful owners. Regardless of the wishes of their own people, the northern states could not grant asylum to fugitive slaves. The Constitution extended the reach of slavery across state lines.

Slavery did not become a serious national issue until the northern states abolished it within their own borders. This had been a gradual process that eliminated slavery slowly by attrition without much cost or inconvenience to northern interests. New York began to phase out slavery by freeing the children born to slaves after July 4, 1799 while leaving their parents in bondage. The children remained in service for a statutory period to reimburse the owner for the expense of raising them. Similar laws in other northern states consigned slavery to gradual extinction. The emancipation laws were generally prospective in operation and did not apply to slaves born before their enactment, which meant that vestiges of the institution survived for many years after slavery was formally abolished. As late as 1860 the federal census reported slaves still living in New Jersey, though their legal designation had technically changed to "servants for life."

The demise of slavery in the North did not immediately put northerners and southerners on a collision course. Northern society remained fundamentally racist, and the extinction of slavery in some states had almost nothing to do with racial justice. "The common people," John Adams wrote of emancipation in Massachusetts, "would not suffer the labor, by which alone they could obtain a subsistence, to be done by slaves." Emancipation in some states resulted in economic displacement for African Americans who lost skilled jobs they had held as slaves. It also brought a tightening of racial controls and greater social segregation to the North. Massachusetts and Rhode Island prohibited interracial marriages, and New Jersey forbade blacks from other states to remain permanently. Connecticut discouraged black immigration by barring nonresident blacks from attending its

Figure VII.2 Photograph of Peter Lee (c. 1880). Lee was born a slave to the Stevens family in New Jersey but was subsequently freed by New Jersey law. Notwithstanding his emancipation, he continued to serve five generations of the family, dying at the age of 99.

Hoboken Public Library

public schools. While northern blacks got legal freedom, nowhere did the freedom gained afford them the rights and opportunities available to whites in northern society.

Slavery in the Territories

While the federal government had no jurisdiction over slavery in the states, it did have jurisdiction over the national territories. Whether this jurisdiction authorized the prohibition of slavery in the territories raised issues that would ultimately disrupt the union. Congress had prohibited slavery in the Northwest Territory during the Confederation period, and it was generally assumed that it had the power to do so in all the national territories. That assumption was challenged in 1818 when Missouri, which had been part of the Louisiana Purchase, applied for admission to the Union as a slave state. While the application was before the House of Representatives, James Tallmadge, an antislavery Republican from New York, attached a proviso requiring Missouri to make arrangements for the gradual abolition of slavery as a condition of statehood. The proviso was bitterly denounced by southerners and finally rejected by the Senate. But the House refused to back down, so Congress adjourned in 1819 without admitting Missouri. The deadlock marked the emergence of slavery as a major sectional issue.

The debate over Missouri soon spread beyond Congress into state legislatures and political meetings throughout the country. The key issue at this point was not the morality of slavery but the power of the South in Congress. Northerners considered the issue crucial to the sectional balance of power. Missouri lay completely west of the Mississippi, and its admission as a slave state could set a precedent for the rest of the western territories. Free states and slave states were then in exact balance at eleven each, and another slave state would shift the balance of power to the South. It would reduce the northern majority in

Representative Tallmadge on Slavery in Missouri

"[E]xtend your view across the Mississippi, over your newly acquired territory . . . Look down the long vista of futurity . . . Behold this extended empire, inhabited by the hardy sons of American freemen, knowing their rights, and inheriting the will to protect them—owners of the soil on which they live, and interested in the institutions which they labor to defend; with two oceans laving your shores, and tributary to your purposes . . . [R]everse this scene; people this fair dominion with the slaves of your planters; extend *Slavery*, this bane of man, this abomination of heaven, over your extended empire, and you prepare its dissolution; you turn its accumulated strength into a positive weakness; you cherish a canker in your breast; you put poison in your own bosom; you place a vulture on your heart—nay, you whet the dagger and place it in the hands of a portion of your population, stimulated to use it by every tie, human and divine! The envious contrast between your happiness and their misery, between your liberty and their slavery, must constantly prompt them to accomplish your destruction."

—Speech in the House of Representatives, February 15, 1819

Figure VII.3 Portrait of James Tallmadge, Jr.
© istockphoto.com

the House of Representatives and give the South control of the Senate. The shift of power could determine the outcome of other important issues, such as the national bank and the protective tariff, which already divided the country along sectional lines. The real struggle was not over slavery in Missouri but over control of the federal government.

The Missouri Compromise

The growing bitterness of the debate made many northern Republicans willing to compromise. Some feared that Federalists would exploit the controversy to rebuild their political base in the North. Federalists played a leading role in the northern antislavery movement and had far better credentials on the issue than most Republicans. If the debate continued, it might also drive a wedge between northern and southern Republicans and disrupt the national party. So there was broad support within the party for the compromise proposed by Henry Clay when Congress reconvened in 1820. Clay's compromise called for admission of Missouri as a slave state; the admission of Maine, which would be separated from Massachusetts, as a free state, thus keeping the free and slave states in balance; and the prohibition of slavery in the rest of the Louisiana Territory north of the line 36°30'. The last had great constitutional significance as the first federal prohibition of slavery since the Articles of Confederation. The power of Congress to keep slavery out of the national territories was tacitly recognized by the Compromise. Southerners would have second thoughts about this concession over the coming decades.

The Compromise resolved the political issues but did not end the debate. The controversy over Missouri had provided northern antislavery groups with an opportunity to focus attention on the injustice of slavery. Many questioned the morality of a political union between free and slave states. Jefferson likened the antislavery polemics attending the Missouri debate to a fire bell in the night. "In the gloomiest hour of the Revolutionary war," he wrote, "I never had any apprehensions equal to those which I feel from this source." Many southerners came out of the affair convinced of the need to defend slavery aggressively rather than apologize for it. Apologies would hand the North an ideological club that could be used against the South on issues other than slavery. The debate also weakened the agrarian ties binding the South to the Northwest. The states of the Northwest sided with the North, leaving the South almost isolated on the slavery issue.

Sectional Politics

By far the most important fact about sectional politics was that no section by itself could control the national government. Power shifted between shaky coalitions that were difficult to organize and almost impossible to hold together. The South and West opposed the Northeast on the national bank; the Northeast and West stood together against the South on the protective tariff; and the South usually found itself standing alone on the slavery issue. Political credit gained on one issue might sometimes help on others, but sectional coalitions were inherently unstable. This was partly because the democratization of politics turned party leaders into ambassadors for regional interests and reduced national policy to makeshift accommodations. But the alternative to accommodation would have been polarization and possible disunion.

A New Political Order

New party alignments began to emerge toward the end of James Monroe's administration. The demise of the Federalists as an effective opposition brought to the surface rivalries and contradictions within the dominant Republican Party. The party leaders who came to power after the War of 1812 could not govern as their predecessors had governed at the turn of the century. The country had changed dramatically in the course of only two decades. New states had entered the Union and shifted power away from the East; suffrage reforms had broadened the popular base of government; and the growth of literacy had made newspapers more important in political campaigns. The new politics put party leaders under heavy pressure and lessened the opportunity for calm deliberation. Decisions had to be made quickly and pragmatically before issues changed and today's allies became tomorrow's adversaries. The stakes were now higher and the system less forgiving. Success brought quick rewards in the form of power and political advantage; failure brought repudiation at the polls and political oblivion. The era of the statesmen who had successfully launched the federal union gave way by the 1820s to the era of the politicians who would have to struggle hard to preserve it.

Republican unity was shattered by a bitter struggle among party leaders to succeed Monroe as president. Three of the leading contenders were cabinet members whose political maneuvering made his last days in office somewhat hectic. They included Secretary of State John Quincy Adams, who had strong support in the Northeast; William Crawford, whose patronage power as Secretary of Treasury had won him a loyal party following; and John C. Calhoun, who as Secretary of War was a rising star in national politics. From outside the administration, Henry Clay, one of the most successful power brokers in Congress, and Andrew Jackson, hero of the Battle of New Orleans, also prepared bids for the presidency. The profusion of candidates and the sectionalization of politics now combined to tear the Republicans apart.

From 1804 onward both Republicans and Federalists had chosen their presidential candidates in caucuses of their respective delegations in Congress. The caucus system promoted party solidarity and harmony between the executive and legislative branches. But by the 1820s the caucus was no longer workable due to the localizing tendencies of party politics. Although Crawford was the choice of the Republican caucus in 1823, his selection settled nothing. Only 66 of the 216 Republicans in Congress attended, not enough to carry much weight with the rest of the party. Clay and Jackson were nominated by their respective state legislatures, and Adams launched his candidacy at a Boston town meeting. All the candidates were Republican, but their candidacies split the party into hostile factions.

A paralytic stroke effectively removed Crawford from the field, and Calhoun removed himself by deciding to seek the vice presidency instead. This narrowed the race to three

Figure VII.4 Portrait of John Quincy Adams by Gilbert Stuart (1818).

White House Historical Association (White House Collection): 32

active contenders, but still too many for anyone to win an electoral majority. Jackson finished first with 99 electoral votes, Adams second with 84, Crawford third with 41, and
Clay finished last with 37. Clay's poor showing can be attributed to the loss of his western
political base to Jackson, whose military exploits made him the idol of the frontier. Since
no candidate had a majority, the election went to the House of Representatives, which
would choose from among the three candidates with the most electoral votes. Although
out of the running himself, Clay had enough power in the House to influence the outcome. He threw his support behind Adams, who won on the first ballot. Clay's reward
came three days later when Adams appointed him Secretary of State.

The Adams-Clay alliance was denounced by Jackson's followers as a "corrupt bargain." They charged that Jackson had been cheated out of the presidency and the will of
the people frustrated. Despite their fulminations, there is no evidence of a bargain, much
less a corrupt one. The alliance between Adams and Clay simply made good political
sense. Both shared the same views on national policy, and their collaboration strengthened
the political ties between the West and the Northeast. Besides, they both regarded Jackson
as an ignorant war hero who was totally unqualified for the presidency. Adams, on the
other hand, had all the qualities, experience, and background needed for the office. That
Clay should prefer him to Jackson had nothing to do with corrupt bargains. Nevertheless,
Jackson's supporters found the charge politically useful in putting the new administration
on the defensive. It also kept Jackson's candidacy alive for the next election.

New Party Alignments

The election marked the reemergence of two-party politics in the United States. The Republicans split into two rival factions: the National Republicans, as the Adams-Clay supporters called themselves; and the Democratic Republicans, the party label taken by the
Jacksonians. Although both claimed to be true heirs of the old Jeffersonian Republicans,
the National Republicans stood for things that were more Hamiltonian than Jeffersonian.
They favored a strong central government, high protective tariffs, and federal funds for
national transportation improvements linking the East with the West. They also supported
the national bank as a stabilizing force in the financial and business life of the nation. The
Democratic Republicans could usually be found on the opposite side of these issues. They
favored states' rights, opposed the national bank, and, in the South, denounced the tariff
and federal transportation improvements. Although less sharply drawn than in the 1790s,
the new alignments closely approximated the rivalries between the Federalists and the
Jeffersonian Republicans. There were differences, of course, because the country was now
larger and political constituencies often overlapped. The democratization of politics also
forced party leaders to tone down party positions in order to be all things to the voters.

The new parties had to deal with internal contradictions. The interests of the West
seemingly lay with the National Republicans on such issues as the protective tariff and
transportation improvements. But the West bitterly opposed the national bank, an institution strongly supported by the eastern wing of the party. The bank issue lessened
the appeal that the rest of the National Republican program held for westerners. Besides,
the West idolized Jackson, whose personal popularity gave him considerable leeway on

divisive issues. But the Democratic Republicans also had difficulty holding their coalition together. Western support for the tariff and transportation improvements clashed with the stand of the South on these issues.

Georgia and Indian Land Titles

No event of the Adams administration more clearly demonstrated the president's commitment to principle than his defense of the treaty rights of the Georgia Indians. He put the honor of the nation over politics in opposing the state seizure of lands belonging to the Creek and Cherokee nations. Treaties with the federal government recognized both tribes as independent nations and confirmed their title to vast amounts of land. But the growth of population put heavy pressure on these arrangements as settlers clamored for access to the Indian lands. Between 1810 and 1830, the population of Georgia, Ohio, and Tennessee nearly tripled from 745,000 to over two million. Georgia had repeatedly urged the federal government to extinguish Indian land titles in favor of white settlers. When federal cooperation was not forthcoming, Georgia took direct action in 1825. Amid allegations of bribery and corruption, a minority of Creek chiefs agreed to sell 25 million acres of tribal land for about $400,000. The sale was immediately repudiated by the Creeks as fraudulent and in violation of their federal treaty rights. President Adams agreed and sent troops to protect them. Georgia denounced the action as an unconstitutional intrusion into state affairs, and preparations were made to dispossess the Creeks by force. A possible clash between federal and state troops was averted when Georgia negotiated more favorable agreements with the Creeks in 1826 and 1827. Adams did not prevent their implementation. But his intervention outraged Georgians and drew widespread criticism throughout the South.

Georgia's next target was the Cherokee nation. State action was triggered by the adoption of a tribal constitution that made it clear that the Cherokees were determined to retain their federal treaty status as a separate self-governing community. In 1828, without federal consent, Georgia annexed all Cherokee lands within the state. The annexation statute provided that after June 1, 1830 all Cherokee laws would be null and void, and persons living on Cherokee lands would be subject to the laws of Georgia. The Cherokee leaders denounced the state action as unconstitutional and asserted their right of self-government under their treaty with the United States. But this time they would get no help from the federal government. Jackson's victory over Adams in the 1828 election brought to office a new and totally unsympathetic administration. The rights of Indians and the federal treaty guarantees had a low priority with most Jacksonians.

Tariff of Abominations

Adams's final year in office brought a worsening of the tariff controversy. The growth of manufacturing in the Northeast had gradually raised duties to higher and higher levels. But the protectionists suffered a setback in 1827 when the Mallory Bill raising duties on woolen textiles was defeated in the Senate by the tie-breaking vote of Vice President Calhoun. The defeat not only alarmed textile manufacturers in the East but also western sheep-raisers who produced the raw wool. Only the South was pleased by the outcome.

The Georgia, Alabama, and South Carolina legislatures marked the setback for protectionism by passing resolutions condemning protective tariffs as unconstitutional.

The defeat of the Mallory Bill gave Jackson's supporters in Congress an opportunity to fish in troubled waters. Since Jackson's position on the tariff was far from clear, they decided to work both sides of the issue to promote his presidential candidacy. His western supporters sponsored a bill imposing high duties on raw wool, flax, hemp, and iron. These were western products, and protecting them would be rewarded at the polls by western voters. But the measure was not expected to pass because of anticipated eastern opposition. The proposed duties would hurt New England manufacturers, who favored protection for finished goods but not for raw materials. Since Adams was likely to carry New England anyhow, antagonizing voters there made no political difference. The Jacksonians expected that their bill would be defeated in the end by the combined opposition of New England and the South. Then they could claim credit in the West for supporting it, while Jackson's southern supporters claimed credit for defeating it. As Senator John Randolph correctly put it, the sole purpose of the bill was "the manufacture of a President of the United States."

To the surprise of everyone, particularly the Jacksonians, the measure was enacted. The New Englanders in Congress ended up voting for it on principle. Their support for protectionism won out over their reservations about the unfavorable features of the bill. Although Jacksonians on both sides of the issue got the political credit they sought, the South as a whole exploded with anger. The measure was denounced as the Tariff of Abominations, and the Georgia, Virginia, and Mississippi legislatures attacked its constitutionality. Boycotts were organized against the northern manufacturers and western farmers who had supported it. Extremists in South Carolina threatened secession unless the law was repealed. But Calhoun, the state's most respected leader, called for restraint. He had joined the Jacksonians, and he assured his followers that a Jackson administration would bring the South tariff relief.

Calhoun's *Exposition and Protest*

While publicly urging moderation, Calhoun privately published an attack on the tariff in his famous *Exposition and Protest*. Although he had voted for the nation's first protective tariff in 1816, he now denounced all protective tariffs as unconstitutional. While Congress had power to enact tariffs for the benefit of the entire nation, it had no power to enact discriminatory ones that benefited some states at the expense of others. He argued that a constitutional power exercised for an unconstitutional purpose had no legal standing. Building on the constitutional theory proposed by Jefferson and Madison in the Kentucky and Virginia Resolutions, Calhoun asserted that the states had the right and duty to prevent enforcement of unconstitutional acts passed by Congress. State power could be interposed against such acts in order to protect citizens of the states against federal lawlessness. Since the states had created the federal government, it was up to them to determine whether it had overstepped its constitutional mandate. The political vehicle for making this determination was the state convention, the direct voice of the people and the source of all sovereign power.

Calhoun on the Southern Economy

"We are the serfs of the system, out of whose labor is raised, not only the money paid into the Treasury, but the funds out of which are drawn the rich rewards of the manufacturer and his associates in interest. Their encouragement is our discouragement. The duty on imports, which is mainly paid out of our labor, gives them the means of selling to us at a higher price; while we cannot, to compensate the loss, dispose of our products at the least advance. It is then, indeed, not a subject of wonder, when understood, that our section of the country, though helped by a kind Providence with a genial sun and prolific soil, from which spring the richest products, should languish in poverty and sink into decay, while the rest of the Union, though less fortunate in natural advantages, are flourishing in unexampled prosperity. The assertion, that the encouragement of the industry of the manufacturing States is, in fact, discouragement to ours, was not made without due deliberation."

—*South Carolina Exposition and Protest* (1828)

From a Miniature by Blanchard   Engraved by A.L. Dick

J. C. Calhoun

Figure VII.5 Portrait of John Calhoun by A. L. Dick.

Library of Congress, Prints and Photographs Division, LC-DIG-ppmsca-19251

Calhoun's *Exposition and Protest* marked not only a turning point in his own career but a turning point in the politics of the nation. He served notice that nationalism was no longer compatible with the interests of his state and section. Southern interests now sharply diverged from those of the rest of the country. The South had no industries needing protection from foreign competition. Overseas markets for southern cotton were more important than domestic ones, and southerners had no need for federal transportation improvements linking them to the West, because they produced no goods for western consumption. Calhoun knew that the South would be outvoted in Congress on such issues by the alliance of western and northeastern interests. His states' rights theory was the South's last line of defense against the tyranny of the majority.

The weakening of national cohesion did not prevent the growth of popular participation in government. The idea that ordinary people could govern themselves had been tacitly rejected at the Constitutional Convention. Believing that democracy was not compatible with good government and the rights of individuals, the Founding Fathers made every effort to restrict its influence. The Electoral College, an appointed Senate, the separation of powers, and life tenure for judges were some of the devices adopted to stabilize government against dramatic shifts in public opinion. Distrust of popular government at the state level took the form of property qualifications, which kept the electorate small and generally conservative. No leader in the early national period really trusted the masses, not even Jefferson, who as president made no effort to liberalize the suffrage or give the common man a voice in government. Jefferson's quarrel with Hamilton was essentially over how power should be used by the governing elite. Both believed that only the educated and able were fit to govern. While Jefferson would have government serve the interests of the many, he did not trust the many to govern directly.

Democratization of Political Life

The democratization of political life after 1800 owed a considerable debt to the West. Although changes in eastern society abetted the process, the West took the lead in opening up politics to the masses. The democratic social climate of the frontier carried over into political life and promoted popular participation in government. The western states entered the Union under constitutions providing for broadly based suffrage, frequent elections, and popular control of all branches of government. The example of the West put pressure on the East where democratic forces were already at work for political reform. Property and religious qualifications for voting were abolished as politicians vied with one another for the support of an expanding electorate. The trend toward empowering ordinary voters caused state legislatures to transfer the selection of presidential electors directly to the people. By 1828 only Maryland and South Carolina had not provided for the popular election of electors.

These changes had a dramatic impact on federal and state politics. Politicians could no longer lead as they had in the era of the Founding Fathers. They could not win the support of the newly enfranchised masses by rational persuasion but had to rely instead on appeals to their emotions and short-term interests. Party leaders took on new importance in dispensing patronage and favors in return for political support. They manipulated issues and essentially turned the substance of politics into a bag of political tricks. One of the most successful practitioners of the new politics, Martin Van Buren of New York, earned renown as the "little magician," both for his stature and his ability to manipulate elections. Attitudes toward public office changed for the worse under the pressure of the new politics. Positions in government were no longer viewed as offices of trust and civic responsibility but as rewards for political services. Senator William L. Marcy, a Van Buren ally, summed it all up with the remark "To the victor belongs the spoils." Party leaders did not apologize for the spoils system but openly defended it as an effective device for keeping government accountable to the electorate.

These changes in political life combined to make Andrew Jackson's presidential candidacy not only possible but inevitable. A generation earlier, in the days of Hamilton and Jefferson, his candidacy would have been a national joke. As a self-made man with almost no formal education, he would have been considered unfit for the office. But the new politics made him an ideal candidate who could rally the masses into a cohesive political force. Ordinary voters could identify with Jackson and take pride that a person like themselves had achieved great things. His candidacy was energetically promoted by the new party leaders. Van Buren organized a pro-Jackson coalition in Congress to prepare the way for victory in 1828.

Senator Marcy of New York Defends the Spoils System

"It may be, sir, that the politicians of The United States are not so fastidious as some gentlemen are, as to disclosing the principles on which they act. They boldly *preach* what they *practice*. When they are contending for victory, they avow their intention of enjoying the fruits of it. If they are defeated, they expect to retire from office. If they are successful, they claim, as a matter of right, the advantages of success. They see nothing wrong in the rule that to the VICTOR belongs the spoils of the ENEMY."

—Senate Speech in Response to Henry Clay, who accused Van Buren of introducing New York's spoils system into national politics (1831)

Figure VII.6 Portrait of William Marcy (c. 1855–1865).

Library of Congress, Prints and Photographs Division, LC-DIG-cwpbh-02789

Jackson's second bid for the presidency began early, in 1825, when the Tennessee legislature nominated him immediately after his defeat by Adams. He thereupon resigned from the Senate in order to devote his full attention to the campaign to make him president in 1828. The resignation protected him against the risk of having to take sides on controversial issues in Congress. Out of government, he could be all things to all people and avoid the traps of sectional politics. Meanwhile, his supporters in Congress could harass the Adams administration while he remained seemingly above the political fray. Adams was no match for the Jacksonians. He thought that dedicated service, which he gave in abundance, would be recognized by the voters and rewarded at the polls. The Jacksonians entertained no such illusions. They knew that perceptions now counted more than substance, and they were masters at manipulating public perceptions.

Election of 1828

The election of 1828 turned out to be the wildest the country had yet seen. The pro-Jackson press, which numbered about 600 newspapers, played a key role in undermining confidence in the Adams administration. The most ridiculous lies were printed about the president. For providing the White House with a billiard table and chess set, which he paid for himself, Adams was accused of buying gambling equipment at public expense. The Adams forces responded in kind with a personal attack on Jackson, who made an easy target. His frontier brawls, duels, and military executions were matters of public record and needed no fabrication or distortion. Even Jackson's marriage was dragged through the political mud. Altogether, it was one of the most disgraceful campaigns in American history. But when it was over, Jackson had scored a stunning victory, carrying most of the South, West, and the Middle States. The electoral count was 178 to 83, with Adams carrying only New England.

Jackson was the first westerner elected president, and he was unlike any of his predecessors in office. Personally, he was a study in contradictions, reflecting in a way the strengths and weaknesses of westerners in general. While generous to a fault with his friends, Jackson was ruthless and vindictive toward those who opposed him. He was irascible, stubborn, and opinionated, but also coldly calculating and highly intelligent. To John Quincy Adams, he was "a barbarian who could not write a sentence of grammar and hardly could spell his name," but to others he was the greatest American since Jefferson. There was one thing at least on which both friend and foe could agree: Jackson was iron-willed and fearless, and he had an instinct for being on the popular side of most public issues.

Jacksonian Democracy

Jackson's presidency fundamentally changed the nature of the office. He considered himself a sort of national tribune with a mandate to impose the will of the people upon government. Whereas members of Congress represented only particular districts and states, he alone spoke for the entire nation. Jackson ran his administration as though accountable only to the people and made no attempt to work closely with Congress as his predecessors had done. He refused to defer to Congress in legislative matters and used his veto power

Figure VII.7 Portrait of Andrew Jackson by James Barton Longacre (1820).

National Portrait Gallery, Smithsonian Institution / Art Resource, NY

more freely than any president before him. Jackson was the first president to use the veto for political purposes. His predecessors had used it only when they had doubts about the constitutionality of acts passed by Congress. Jackson used it to influence legislation and control public policy. He vetoed more bills during his first four years in office than had been vetoed during the previous forty years. Critics who accused him of usurping the powers of Congress dubbed him King Veto and King Andrew I.

The Spoils System

While Jackson did not invent the spoils system, he used it to a far greater extent than it had been used before. He considered public office a form of property at the disposal of the party in power. About twenty percent of all federal officeholders were replaced for political reasons during his two terms as president. Previous presidents had done the same on a more limited scale, but Jackson was the first to proclaim political firings a positive good. He saw rotation in office as a necessary device for implementing the will of the people expressed at the polls. It was the only way government could be made responsive and accountable. The alternative was an official bureaucracy beyond the reach of the political process, and this would be totally incompatible with republican government. The spoils system also strengthened the political parties, which had now become essential to orderly government, by providing party workers with public employment.

Cherokee Nation v. Georgia

The new administration inherited the bitter dispute over the treaty rights of Indians in the South. Georgia's annexation of Cherokee lands in 1828 emboldened Alabama to assert jurisdiction over the lands of the Choctaws and Chickasaws. Like the Cherokees, both tribes had treaties with the United States which recognized them as self-governing nations and guaranteed their land titles. Jackson made it clear from the outset that he sided with the states on the issue. The Cherokee emissaries in Washington were warned that they would have to submit to Georgia law or leave the state and settle beyond the Mississippi. Jackson favored the latter and made Indian relocation the policy of his administration. He took the position that the eastern tribes would be better off if they resettled in the empty territories available in the West. If they remained in the East, they would inevitably be overwhelmed by a rapidly increasing white population. Only distance could save them from extinction as a separate nation. If they chose to stay, they could count on no help from his administration. The states coveting their lands had all contributed to Jackson's election.

Rebuffed by the president, the Cherokees turned to the Supreme Court for protection. They petitioned the Court for an injunction prohibiting Georgia from interfering with rights guaranteed by their treaty with the United States. Before the case was heard, Georgia asserted its jurisdiction over Cherokee lands in a particularly forceful way. An Indian named Corn Tassel was convicted by a state court and sentenced to death for killing another Indian on Cherokee territory. The conviction was appealed to the United States Supreme Court on the ground that Georgia had no jurisdiction to punish crimes committed on Cherokee lands. The Cherokee treaty with the United States gave the tribe exclusive jurisdiction in such matters. The Court issued a stay of execution in December 1830, and ordered Georgia to appear for formal argument of the case the following month. Georgia boldly defied the Court. The state legislature ordered state officials to ignore all federal orders and proceed with the case under Georgia law. Corn Tassel was hanged despite the stay of execution, and the constitutional issue died with him.

Georgia's brutal defiance of the Court was applauded by states' rights supporters in Congress. The Jacksonians joined in the applause and proposed measures that would have limited the Court's jurisdiction in such cases. The House Judiciary Committee even called for repeal of the Court's authority to hear appeals from the state courts. This would have turned the clock back to before 1789 and made it impossible for the Court to overturn state court decisions for any reason. Not since *Cohens v. Virginia* did the Court come under such sustained assault. But turning back the clock had so many undesirable implications for federal-state relations that even critics of the Court had second thoughts. The uproar nevertheless sent a warning to the Court that judicial interference in political matters might bring reprisals.

Corn Tassel's ghost haunted the proceedings when *Cherokee Nation v. Georgia* came before the Court in 1831. The Cherokees claimed that the Court had authority to grant them an injunction under Article III of the Constitution. The Article gave the Court original jurisdiction in cases involving foreign nations, and the Cherokees claimed foreign-nation status under their treaty with the United States. The Court rejected the claim and dismissed the suit on jurisdictional grounds. Speaking for the Court, Chief Justice Marshall ruled that the Cherokees were not a foreign nation within the meaning of Article III. They were instead a "domestic dependent" nation subject to the United States. Therefore, they had no standing to sue in the Supreme Court as a court of original jurisdiction. But Marshall made clear that his sympathies were with the Indians. "If courts were permitted to indulge their sympathies," he wrote, "a case better calculated to excite them can scarcely be imagined." He made it clear that Cherokee treaty rights would be upheld if brought before the Court in a case over which it had jurisdiction.

Worcester v. Georgia

The Court got such a case the following year in *Worcester v. Georgia* (1832). Two New England missionaries, Samuel Worcester and Elizur Butler, had been convicted and sentenced to prison for ignoring a Georgia law requiring them to obtain a state license in order to reside in Cherokee territory. They appealed to the Supreme Court on the ground that the Cherokee treaty with the United States precluded Georgia from asserting jurisdiction over Cherokee lands. The Court agreed and overturned their convictions. The opinion written by Marshall declared that the treaty gave the federal government exclusive jurisdiction over the lands and that the laws passed by Georgia with regard to the lands were unconstitutional. The decision recognized the Cherokees as a separate community within the state, "with boundaries accurately described, in which the laws of Georgia can have no force, and which the citizens of Georgia have no right to enter but with the assent of the Cherokees themselves."

Georgia again defied the Court by refusing to release the missionaries. The governor and attorney general threatened armed resistance if the federal government attempted to enforce the decision. But Jackson had no intention of backing up the Court. He was committed to a policy of Indian removal regardless of Indian treaty rights. "John Marshall has made his decision," the president reportedly remarked, "now let him enforce it!" The comment, though probably apocryphal, accurately reflects the power relationship then existing between the Court and the political branches of government. So the administration did nothing while Georgia defied the judicial power of the United States. Worcester and Butler were eventually released but only after they agreed to leave the state. In the coming century, the case would become the foundation of federal Indian law. But for the

---

Andrew Jackson on Indian Removal

"The plan of removing the aboriginal people who yet remain within the settled portion of the United States to the country west of the Mississippi River approaches its consummation. It was adopted on the most mature consideration of the condition of this race, and ought to be persisted in till the object is accomplished, and prosecuted with as much vigor as a just regard to their circumstances will permit, and as fast as their consent can be obtained. All preceding experiments for the improvement of the Indians have failed. It seems now to be an established fact that they can not live in contact with a civilized community and prosper. Ages of fruitless endeavors have at length brought us to a knowledge of this principle of intercommunication with them."

—Annual Message to Congress, December 7, 1835

time being, Georgia had clearly won the federal-state confrontation abetted by the President of the United States.

Meanwhile, Jackson set in motion his Indian relocation plans. In 1830 Congress passed the Indian Removal Act authorizing him to offer the eastern tribes federal compensation if they abandoned their lands and moved west. Since they could not hope for federal protection, the Indians soon collapsed under state pressure and accepted the offer. Even the Cherokees capitulated and surrendered all their eastern lands for about $5 million in return for new land west of the Mississippi. The administration forced a total of ninety-four treaties of evacuation on the eastern tribes in violation of solemn pledges made to them by

Chief of the Cherokee Nation on Indian Removal

"I still strongly hope we shall find ultimate justice from the good sense of the administration and of the people of the United States. I will not even yet believe that either the one or the other would wrong us with their eyes open. I am persuaded they have erred only in ignorance, and an ignorance forced upon them by the misrepresentation and artifices of the interested . . . The Cherokees, under any circumstances, have no weapon to use but argument. If that should fail, they must submit, when their time shall come, in silence, but honest argument they cannot think will be for ever used in vain. The Cherokee people will always hold themselves ready to respect a *real* treaty and bound to sustain any treaty which they can feel that they are bound to respect . . . But, on one point, you may be perfectly at rest. Deeply as our people feel, I cannot suppose they will ever be goaded by those feelings to any acts of violence. No, sir. They have been too long inured to suffering without resistance, and they still look to the sympathies and not to the fears, of those who have them in their power."

—Letter from Chief John Ross, July 2, 1836

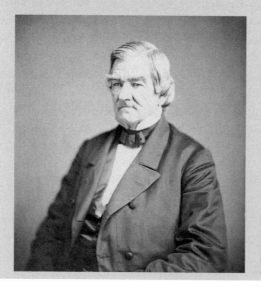

Figure VII.8 Portrait of Cherokee Chief Guwisguwi, a.k.a. John Ross (1858).

National Anthropological Archives, Smithsonian Institution [BAE GN 00988A 06211000]

the United States. The expulsion of the tribes to the western wilderness in what came to be known as the Trail of Tears strengthened the administration in the states coveting tribal lands and caused no problems with white voters in other states. More than twenty-five percent of the Cherokees perished during that trek. What happened was despicable and tragic, but it was also good politics. Only the Supreme Court salvaged a shred of national honor in this deplorable chapter of American history.

Nullification Crisis

Jackson's tariff policy was much more circumspect than his dealings with Indians. While affirming the constitutionality of protective tariffs, he recommended to Congress a downward revision of import duties. The Tariff of Abominations had set duties so high that by 1832 the Treasury had a surplus. All sides agreed that the revenue-producing features of the tariff had to be adjusted. While the South favored a general across-the-board reduction of all rates, the protectionists, led by Henry Clay, favored selective cuts consistent with protectionism. The reductions would be limited to imports that did not compete with home industries. Any Treasury surplus accruing after such reductions could be used to pay for transportation improvements. Clay had his way, and the tariff passed by Congress in 1832 was a protectionist measure that fell far short of southern expectations.

The South was bitterly disappointed with the new tariff, and in South Carolina states' rights extremists took direct action. A state convention was elected to rule on the constitutionality of the measure. The delegates met in November and adopted an ordinance declaring the tariffs of 1828 and 1832 unconstitutional. The ordinance prohibited the collection of duties in the state after January 31, 1833, barred appeals to the Supreme Court on the issue, and threatened secession if the federal government attempted to use force to collect the duties. The state legislature prepared for the worst by voting military appropriations for the expected confrontation.

While again recommending tariff reductions to Congress, Jackson responded to the challenge decisively and without equivocation. His Proclamation to the People of South Carolina, the most important state paper of his administration, denounced nullification and secession as unconstitutional. The nullifying of federal laws, he declared, was "incompatible with the existence of the Union, contradicted expressly by the letter of the Constitution, unauthorized by its spirit, inconsistent with every principle on which it was founded, and destructive of the great object for which it was formed." The president left no doubt that force would be used to prevent secession. "Disunion, by armed force, is TREASON," he warned the people of South Carolina. "Are you really ready to incur its guilt? If you are, on the heads of the instigators of the act be the dreadful consequences; on their heads be the dishonor, but on yours may fall the punishment." The Union was the repository of too many hopes to permit its destruction. That would be a blow to the cause of popular government everywhere. "Its enemies have beheld our prosperity with a vexation they could not conceal; it was a standing refutation of their slavish doctrines, and they will point to our discord with the triumph of malignant joy." Jackson's stand was the strongest pronouncement on the permanence of the Union by any president before Lincoln.

Congress gave Jackson the backing he requested by passing the Force Act authorizing him to use troops to enforce federal revenue laws. He sent warships to Charleston and put Forts Sumter and Moultrie in the harbor on the alert for action. The South Carolina legislature responded with a stinging denunciation of his threat to use force against a sovereign state. It pointed out that Jackson's stand contradicted the position he had previously taken when Georgia defied federal authority on the rights of the Cherokees.

> The President . . . silently, and as it is supposed, with entire approbation, witnessed our sister state of Georgia avow, act upon, and carry into effect, even to the taking of life, principles identical with those now denounced by him, in South Carolina.

The state made preparations to meet force with force. Troops were mobilized and munitions collected for an armed confrontation.

Compromise of 1833

But even while the Force Act was being debated, efforts were underway in Congress to resolve the crisis by compromise. Henry Clay took the lead in working out a settlement for the gradual reduction of duties exceeding twenty percent and for expansion of the free list. Calhoun supported the compromise and urged South Carolina to suspend its ordinance of nullification. The state government welcomed a political settlement when support expected from the rest of the South failed to materialize. Resolutions passed in neighboring states condemning nullification and secession made it clear that South Carolina would stand alone if hostilities broke out. Having moved precipitously without first bringing in neighboring states, the nullifiers found themselves isolated. Clay's compromise saved them from political humiliation and possibly the gallows.

The compromise enabled both sides to claim victory. While federal authority had been upheld, South Carolina had forced a change in national tariff policy. The settlement kept the Union together but weakened it politically. It strengthened the hand of southern extremists by demonstrating that a single determined state could accomplish by threat of force what a decade of conventional political effort had failed to achieve. The lesson would not be forgotten in the South. In retrospect, it is not unreasonable to conclude that the compromise may have been a mistake. In 1833 the situation was ideal to deal with states' rights extremists once and for all. Had South Carolina been forced to submit unconditionally, and surrender was the only alternative to certain military defeat, it might have been less ready a generation later to lead the South into secession. A little armed force in 1833 might have prevented all-out conflict in the 1860s.

The Bank War

Jackson's opposition to the national bank allowed no room for compromise. He denounced it in his first two messages to Congress as a wicked monopoly with too much power for the good of the nation. The bank's charter would expire in 1836, and it seemed likely that

Jackson would veto any extension should he be reelected in 1832. Knowing that he could win on personal popularity alone, Jackson hoped to keep the issue out of the campaign. But his plans were upset by Henry Clay, the candidate of the National Republicans, who thought the bank issue would be perfect for contesting the election. The bank had strong support in business and financial centers, and opposing it would certainly cost Jackson votes. So Clay shepherded a bill through Congress extending the bank's charter for another fifteen years. This put Jackson in the position of having to sign a bill opposed by the West and South, or vetoing it and losing votes in the Northeast where the bank had many supporters. Clay hoped for a veto, knowing it might give him the issue he needed to win the election.

Jackson did not hesitate for a moment. He vetoed the bill and sent Congress an explanatory message identifying his administration with radicalism. The message was drafted by Attorney General Roger B. Taney, and it denounced the bank as "subversive of the rights of the States, and dangerous to the liberties of the people." Moreover, the bank was unconstitutional. The Supreme Court had been wrong in upholding its constitutionality in *McCulloch v. Maryland,* a mistake that certainly did not bind the other branches of government. Jackson declared: "The opinion of the judges has no more authority over Congress than the opinion of Congress has over the judges, and on that point the President is independent of both." The Court was only one of the three branches of government, and nothing in the Constitution made it the final arbiter of questions of constitutionality. "The Congress, the Executive, and the Court must each for itself be guided by its own opinion of the Constitution." He insisted that judges were not the only guardians of constitutional government. "Each public officer who takes an oath to support the Constitution swears that he will support it as he understands it, and not as it is understood by others." Jackson's message was a classic restatement of Jeffersonian principles and a flat rejection of judicial supremacy with respect to constitutional interpretation.

The veto message included a detailed refutation of Marshall's opinion in the *McCulloch* case. Even if Congress did have the implied power to charter a national bank, it did not follow that the sweeping powers granted to the bank were constitutional. The right to establish branch offices in every state for anything but public business could hardly be justified under the "necessary and proper" clause. Jackson rejected Marshall's argument that the bank could not be taxed by the states because it performed financial services for the federal government. While services performed for the government clearly could not be taxed, there was no reason why its private business could not be taxed. Such taxation would not encroach in any way upon the sovereignty of the national government. These were the views of both the president and his attorney general, the man who in a few years would succeed Marshall as chief justice.

Clay considered the veto message a major political blunder. He did not think that responsible citizens would vote for a demagogue who claimed the right to interpret the Constitution as he pleased. Clay may have been right about how responsible citizens would vote, but he was wrong in assuming they would be in the majority. Many voters indeed understood the role of the bank in stabilizing financial markets and the importance of the Supreme Court in developing a uniform system of constitutional law. But they were heavily outnumbered by those who knew nothing about finance or constitutional theory. Most voters knew only that the bank was a powerful monopoly controlled by the rich for the benefit of a business and financial elite. These were the voters Jackson counted on, and they did not disappoint him. He won a landslide victory with an electoral majority of 219 to 49.

Since the election had been fought over the bank, Jackson regarded his stunning victory as a mandate to destroy it. This could be accomplished by withdrawing the federal deposits essential to the bank's operations. But such withdrawals might be unlawful because the bank had the right to hold all federal funds under the charter granted by Congress. Secretary of Treasury Louis McLane had such strong reservations about issuing the order that Jackson called a cabinet meeting and read a statement, drafted by Attorney General Taney, which narrowly limited the discretion of cabinet officers. He informed them that they had no discretion in matters of policy and held office only to implement the will of the president. When McLane remained unconvinced, he was replaced by William Duane. But Duane also developed doubts about the legality of the withdrawals. So he was replaced by Taney, whose loyalty to the president was unconditional. Since Jackson's plans had by now become public knowledge, he shrewdly put off sending Taney's nomination to the Senate for confirmation until the withdrawals were well underway. By the end of 1833 about three-fourths of the federal deposits had been transferred to state banks, many having close ties to the administration.

Jackson's highhandedness was denounced in Congress. The Senate requested a copy of his statement on the responsibilities and duties of cabinet officers, a request Jackson rejected as a breach of the constitutional separation of powers. The executive branch was no more accountable to the legislature than the legislative branch was to the executive. The Senate then passed two resolutions drawn up by Henry Clay censuring the president. One condemned the Treasury Secretary for ordering the withdrawals, and the other condemned the president for usurping power "not conferred by the constitution and laws, but in derogation of both." Although Jackson's supporters in the House pushed through resolutions endorsing his actions, the president nevertheless stood rebuked by the Senate. The Senate followed through by rejecting Taney's nomination as secretary of treasury. But the damage had already been done. Most of the federal deposits had been transferred from the national bank, crippling it as an institution.

Emergence of the Whig Party

Opposition to Jackson brought his opponents together in a broadly based political coalition. It consisted of National Republicans, states' rights Democrats outraged by his threat to use force against South Carolina, westerners angered by his opposition to federal transportation improvements, business groups in the Northeast who supported the national bank, and southern planters who resented their loss of influence in national affairs. The attack on the bank became the catalyst bringing them all together. They called themselves Whigs to dramatize their opposition to a president who, they claimed, put himself above constitutional principles of government. Just as the English Whigs had resisted royal absolutism, so American Whigs would resist presidential absolutism.

The sudden demise of the national bank destabilized the economy. The withdrawal of federal deposits forced the bank to call in loans and liquidate investments. This contracted credit and put pressure on borrowers and state banks in debt to the national bank. While sound credit contracted, the transfer of federal funds to less responsible but politically favored state banks set off an inflationary boom. Known as "pet banks," they issued a flood of paper banknotes that the national bank would no longer be able to force them to redeem in specie. The currency inflation encouraged speculation in public lands. By 1836 the government had sold so much land that the Treasury reported a surplus of $35 million. The money was distributed among the states and spent on transportation improvements that promoted even more land speculation. Investors threw caution to the winds, and the country enjoyed several years of unprecedented but illusory prosperity.

Panic of 1837

The bubble burst in 1836 when Jackson ordered federal officials to accept nothing but gold and silver in payment for public lands. The order precipitated a run on state banks by depositors seeking to exchange their banknotes for the specie now needed to cover their land purchases. But the banks had issued far too much in paper to meet the sudden demand for gold and silver. Their reserves had already come under pressure by the withdrawal of government specie for distribution of the Treasury surplus among the states. Bank after bank failed, precipitating a financial collapse that rocked the economic foundations of the nation. The western banks failed first, then the eastern banks, and by the summer of 1837 not a single bank in the country could meet its obligations in specie. The failure of the banks triggered a downward spiral of bankruptcies and foreclosures. Farms and businesses were lost, and thousands of workers lost their jobs. Aptly called the Panic of 1837, the collapse marked the beginning of the worst economic depression Americans had yet experienced.

Fortunately for the Democrats, the downturn had not become serious enough by 1836 to affect the outcome of the presidential election. So Martin Van Buren, the party candidate, was able to defeat three Whig opponents. The Whigs, who had been unable to agree on a single candidate, adopted a strategy of backing regional candidates with strong local followings. Their plan was to prevent the Democrats from winning an electoral majority, thereby throwing the election to the House of Representatives. Although the strategy failed, the Whigs made an excellent showing in their first bid for national power. Van Buren won with an electoral majority of 170 to 124, far short of Jackson's majority in 1832, and with a popular majority of only 25,000 votes. The Whigs even in defeat demonstrated that they would be a formidable opposition.

Van Buren's administration was ruined from the outset by the worsening economic condition of the country. There was little that government could then do to turn things around, but the party in power was nevertheless blamed when times were bad. The most important measure of his administration, the Independent Treasury Act of 1840, came too late and lacked the popular appeal to compensate for the political damage done by three years of economic hardship. The Act created a subtreasury system under which the

Figure VII.9 Portrait of Martin Van Buren by George Healy (1858).

White House Historical Association (White House Collection): 40

government would manage its own finances without the assistance of state banks or financial monopolies like the national bank. Subtreasury offices throughout the country would keep federal funds on deposit and free the government of dependence on financial intermediaries. Taking federal funds out of private markets was highly controversial, and passage of the Act was a signal victory for Van Buren. But it would not be nearly enough to keep him in office.

Supreme Court Appointments

More than any presidents before them, Jackson and Van Buren regarded appointments to the Supreme Court as just another form of political patronage. Previous presidents had also appointed justices who agreed with them, but Jackson carried things to extremes. He put party loyalty over all other considerations. In 1829 he appointed John McLean of Ohio to the vacancy created by the death of Justice Trimble. McLean, a former state judge and federal postmaster general, used the Court to promote his presidential ambitions. Law took a back seat to politics in most of his major opinions. A second vacancy occurred on the death of Justice Washington in 1829. Jackson appointed Henry Baldwin, a Pennsylvania congressman with an uncontrollable temper. Some doubted his sanity, but his political loyalty was unquestioned. With the death of Washington, Marshall became the last member of the Court appointed by a Federalist president.

Jackson's next appointment went to James M. Wayne, a Georgia congressman who had supported the president during the nullification crisis. Wayne filled the vacancy created by the death of Justice Johnson in 1834. Jackson not only rewarded loyalty but rewarded it quickly. Justice Duvall's resignation in 1835 created an opening for Roger B. Taney, who had helped Jackson destroy the national bank. But the Whigs in the Senate had their revenge by rejecting Taney, so the vacancy was filled by Philip Barbour, a states' rights Democrat from Virginia. In 1836 the most important vacancy of all occurred upon the death of Chief Justice Marshall. With loyal Democrats now in control of the Senate, Jackson nominated Taney for the post. After a fierce partisan debate, the Senate narrowly confirmed him. It was a remarkable reversal of fortune for Taney. Within a year of being rejected for an associate justiceship, he became chief justice of the United States.

Just a day before he left office, the Democratic Congress gave Jackson two more appointments by enlarging the Supreme Court to nine members. The appointments went to John Catron, a Tennessee judge, and William Smith of Alabama. Both were confirmed, but only Catron accepted, leaving the other vacancy to be filled by Van Buren. The appointment went to John McKinley, also of Alabama, so the state lost nothing by Smith's refusal. Van Buren made one more appointment, and it was bitterly controversial. He had been defeated in his bid for reelection in 1840, and the government would soon be controlled by the victorious Whigs. The vacancy occurred with the death of Justice Barbour just a week before Van Buren was due to leave office. To keep the seat Democratic, the president appointed Peter V. Daniel, a federal district judge for Virginia, the following day. The unseemly haste enraged the Whigs, who charged the administration with ruthless partisanship. Although Daniel was confirmed by the Democratic Senate, the affair poisoned the air for future appointments.

Election of 1840

The Whig campaign that defeated Van Buren in 1840 was one of the most cynical in American history. William Henry Harrison, the party candidate, was nominated primarily because he was a newcomer to national politics and had few political enemies. The vice presidential candidate, John Tyler of Virginia, was chosen mainly to attract southern votes to the ticket. The fact that he was out of step with the national party on key issues was less important than the strength he brought to the ticket in the South. The campaign itself was wild and theatrical. The Whigs avoided issues that might cost votes and ran a safe campaign of hoopla and political slogans. They staged parades and political rallies, flooded the country with party emblems and buttons, and distributed plenty of hard cider to keep the crowds enthusiastic. Their strategy was to portray Harrison, who had defeated the Indians of the Northwest at Tippecanoe, as a homespun hero whose log-cabin origins made him the candidate of ordinary citizens. Van Buren, on the other hand, was denounced as an eastern aristocrat who dined in the White House off gold plate while his countrymen went hungry. It was nonsense, of course, but it worked like a charm in the new era of popular politics. Harrison won decisively, defeating Van Buren by an electoral margin of 234 to 60.

The campaign permanently lowered political standards. The Democrats had been expected to lose because of the depression, but they had not been expected to lose so badly. The Whigs turned the election into a complete political rout, winning control of Congress as well as the presidency. Their colorful and exciting campaign brought twice as many voters to the polls as had turned out in 1836. They convincingly demonstrated the importance of style over substance and proved that slogans carried more weight than rational political debate. The Democrats learned from their defeat and put the Whig techniques to work for themselves in future elections. The degradation of political life in the United States thereafter became a bipartisan enterprise.

The Jacksonians left a mixed legacy of good precedents along with the bad. Jackson's use of the veto in dealing with Congress tilted the balance of power permanently toward the executive branch. The device was extremely effective and would be used by all his successors to influence legislation. Jackson's forceful defense of national sovereignty during the nullification crisis became the standard by which all presidents would be judged in their stewardship of the Union. His views on the duties and responsibilities of cabinet officers are now settled constitutional doctrine. Far more than most presidents, he influenced the future through his Supreme Court appointments. Only George Washington and Franklin D. Roosevelt appointed more justices to the Court. Among those appointed was a new chief justice who would keep faith with Jackson's brand of Republicanism just as faithfully as the great chief justice he replaced had with Federalism.

March 12, 1830	March 22, 1830	February 11, 1837	February 14, 1837	February 16, 1837	March 4, 1837	March 9, 1839
Craig v. Missouri	Providence Bank v. Billings	Briscoe v. Bank of Kentucky	Charles River Bridge v. Warren Bridge	New York City v. Miln	Martin Van Buren Takes Office as President of the United States	Bank of Augusta v. Earle

March 15, 1844	December 27, 1844	March 4, 1845	September 2, 1845	August 10, 1846	March 6, 1847	January 3, 1849
Louisville, Cincinnati & Charleston Railroad Co. v. Letson	Ex parte Dorr	James K. Polk Takes Office as President of the United States	Levi Woodbury Becomes Associate Justice of Supreme Court	Robert Grier Becomes Associate Justice of Supreme Court	License Cases	Luther v. Borden

March 4, 1853	May 24, 1854	April 8, 1856	March 4, 1857
Franklin Pierce Takes Office as President of the United States	Ohio Life Insurance & Trust Co. v. Debolt	Dodge v. Woolsey	James Buchanan Takes Office as President of the United States

VIII More Power to the States

> "[A] State has the same undeniable and unlimited jurisdiction over all persons and things, within its territorial limits, as any foreign nation, when that jurisdiction is not surrendered or restrained by the constitution of the United States."
>
> —Justice Philip Barbour, *New York City v. Miln* (1837)

Roger B. Taney, the chief justice appointed by Jackson, was in some ways more complicated than the great jurist he replaced. He entered politics as a Maryland Federalist but broke with the party over Federalist opposition to the War of 1812. Establishing himself in state politics over the next decade, he joined the Jacksonians and became Jackson's attorney general in 1831. He had a brilliant analytical mind, and his loyalty to the president was unconditional. Taney drafted most of Jackson's veto message on the bank bill, including the assertion that the president and Congress are not bound by the constitutional interpretations of the Supreme Court. He assisted in the destruction of the national bank by issuing the Treasury orders for the transfer of federal deposits. The Senate refused to confirm him as Treasury Secretary for his role in the affair, and it subsequently rejected his nomination for the Supreme Court vacancy created by the resignation of Justice Duvall. Had the Jacksonians not regained control of the Senate in 1836, he would have been rejected again for the chief justiceship. Few appointments to the Court have occasioned fiercer debate or raised more questions about the judicial suitability of the

Figure VIII.1 Portrait of Roger Taney by George Peter Alexander Healy (1858).

Collection of the Supreme Court of the United States

appointee. "Judge Story thinks the Supreme Court is gone," wrote Daniel Webster of the appointment. "I think so too."

Like Marshall, Taney joined a Court that shared his basic political views. Five of the justices had been appointed by Jackson, and a sixth by Van Buren, so he had a solid Democratic majority. Only Justices Story and Thompson remained from the Marshall era. Nor did the political branches of government pose the challenges to Taney that Marshall had to face when he became chief justice. The Court had become a more powerful institution over the years mainly as the result of Marshall's efforts to increase its importance and prestige. In 1826 Van Buren commented, not approvingly, on the growth of "a sentiment . . . of idolatry for the Supreme Court which claims for its members an almost entire exemption from the fallibilities of our nature." Even Marshall's death promoted the institutional interests of the Court. Death brought instant canonization, and politicians who had opposed him in life now paid unconditional homage to his memory. This wave of reverence following his death strengthened the Court as an institution to the extent that by 1840 judicial review had become one of the accepted premises of constitutional government.

Retreat from Judicial Nationalism

Without directly challenging the key decisions of his predecessor, Taney skillfully led the Court away from the nationalism of the Marshall era. The case for shifting some power back to the states had become compelling because immigration and economic development created problems that could best be addressed by local government. Between 1830 and 1850 almost 2.5 million immigrants came to America, primarily from Europe. Cheap Western land, the factories of the Northeast, and the promise of employment offered opportunities to skilled and unskilled workers seeking a new beginning. The expansion of railroads, canal systems, and steamboats allowed for greater mobility of people and products alike. Under Taney, the states were given a freer hand to manage their own affairs in business and commercial matters. The first clear sign that a new period of federal-state relations had begun appeared in *Briscoe v. Bank of Kentucky* (1837) with the modification of an important Marshall decision. Kentucky had established a state-owned banking corporation with authority to issue banknotes. Its constitutionality was challenged under the provision in Article I forbidding the states to issue bills of credit. The ban had been strictly enforced by the Marshall Court. In *Craig v. Missouri* (1830), it invalidated a Missouri law authorizing the issuance of certificates to be receivable for taxes and debts owed to the state. Since the certificates were ultimately redeemable by the state, Marshall held that they were unconstitutional as bills of credit even though they were called by a different name. The decision served notice that the ban on state paper money could not be circumvented.

While not overturning *Craig*, the Court upheld the Kentucky law as constitutional. Justice McLean, speaking for the majority, made a careful if specious distinction between the cases. He pointed out *Craig* involved certificates issued by Missouri directly, while *Briscoe* involved banknotes issued not by Kentucky but by a corporation chartered by the state. Kentucky had not issued the notes directly or pledged its credit to redeem them. It had created instead a banking corporation not different from other banks. That it was state-owned and state-managed did not make it part of state government. Unlike an agency of government, it had no sovereign immunity and could be sued like any other corporation. As a separate corporation, it was not subject to constitutional constraints applicable to the states.

Justice Story wrote a scathing dissent. For the Court to distinguish between an official state bank and a bank wholly owned and managed by the state was transparent casuistry. The banking corporation set up by Kentucky was clearly an instrument of the state and therefore a part of state government. The issue was exactly the same as in *Craig*, so the Court had for all practical purposes overturned *Craig*. But this was the last thing that the majority wanted to do, or to be perceived as doing, partly out of deference to *stare decisis*, but also because Marshall had written the *Craig* opinion. The late chief justice was so widely revered that it was more politic to circumvent than overturn his decision. *Briscoe* had precisely that effect, because the states could now get around the currency constraints of the Constitution by acting through corporate proxies. With capital nearing $400 million, the state banks now had a firmer constitutional foothold than ever before.

Two years later, in *Bank of Augusta v. Earle* (1839), the states got the right to prevent out-of-state corporations from doing business within their borders. The case involved some Alabama merchants who had issued bills of exchange that were acquired by a Georgia bank doing business in the state. The merchants later refused to pay the bank on the ground that it had no legal authority to carry on business in Alabama. The Alabama courts upheld the merchants, and the case was appealed to the United States Supreme Court. Daniel Webster, who represented the bank, argued that corporations were "citizens" within the meaning of Article IV of the Constitution, and that their privileges and immunities as citizens were as fully protected by the Constitution as those of natural persons. Alabama could no more exclude a Georgia corporation than it could prevent natural citizens of Georgia from entering the state. The Georgia bank had a constitutional right to do business in Alabama and could therefore enforce the bills of exchange.

The Court upheld the rights of the bank but at the same time rejected Webster's key constitutional argument. Chief Justice Taney ruled that corporations had a general right to do business across state lines under principles of interstate comity. But he denied that they had a constitutional right to do so under the Privileges and Immunities Clause of Article IV. Only natural persons were citizens within the meaning of the Article; corporations were artificial entities that the states might exclude from doing business within their borders. But since Alabama had not specifically excluded out-of-state banks, the Georgia bank had standing under principles of comity to do business in the state. In other words, Alabama had the constitutional power to do what in practice it had not yet done. The decision allowed the states to regulate out-of-state corporations as a condition of doing business there or to exclude them completely.

The States and the Contract Clause

Taney's opinion in *Charles River Bridge v. Warren Bridge* (1837) sharply checked Marshall's expansive interpretation of the Contract Clause. The case involved a charter granted by Massachusetts in 1785 to the Charles River Bridge Company to build and operate a toll bridge between Boston and Cambridge. The bridge proved highly profitable as traffic across the Charles River increased over the years. By 1828 the flow of traffic became too heavy for one bridge to accommodate, so the legislature granted a charter to the Warren Bridge Company to build a second bridge near the first. The Warren Bridge Company would collect tolls for six years to recover the cost of construction and operation, after which the bridge would become free to the public. The arrangement would eventually put the Charles River Bridge Company out of business. Since its charter still had many years to run, the company challenged the constitutionality of the second charter as a violation of rights protected by the Contract Clause.

Although its charter did not expressly provide for exclusivity, the Charles River Bridge Company argued that it clearly implied that no subsequent charter would be granted authorizing a competing bridge. The legal merits of the argument were compelling. The implied terms of a contract are as binding as those expressly stated, and the implication of exclusivity was undeniable. No company would have undertaken building such a bridge had the construction of a competing bridge been within the contemplation of the parties. The courts enforce contracts according to the apparent intent of the parties, and the contract suggested that exclusivity had been intended. When the state courts refused to grant the Charles River Bridge Company an injunction against construction of the second bridge, an appeal was brought to the United States Supreme Court.

The case first came up for argument in March 1831 while Marshall was chief justice. But the absence of Justices Johnson and Duvall prevented an immediate decision. Marshall, Story, and Thompson thought that construction of the second bridge violated the contract rights of the Charles River Bridge Company. Justice McLean thought that the Court lacked jurisdiction to review the case, and Justice Baldwin believed that what Massachusetts had done was constitutional. So the absence of Johnson and Duvall precluded a majority opinion. Although a plurality would have been enough, Marshall did not want to invalidate a state law with less than a majority of the full Court. Expecting this would not take too long, he ordered the case reargued, but delays and new appointments put off the decision to 1837. By the time final arguments were heard, Marshall was dead, and the Court had a new chief justice less committed to the protection of private contract rights.

The key issue before the Court was whether the first charter granted an implied right of exclusivity to the Charles River Bridge Company. Daniel Webster, who represented the company, contended that it did, citing *Fletcher v. Peck* (1810) and *Dartmouth College v. Woodward* (1819) as precedents. The latter held that corporate charters were protected by the Contract Clause, and the former held that what a state grants by contract it impliedly promises not to take away. Taking away rights granted under the first charter was precisely what Massachusetts had done in authorizing the second bridge. Construction of the second bridge would render worthless rights granted under the first charter. Webster also argued that the action of Massachusetts' legislature threatened the rights of property everywhere.

A decade earlier, Webster's arguments might have prevailed. But times had changed, and new constitutional thinking had taken hold. Taney's majority opinion upheld the constitutionality of the second bridge. He held that rights claimed under contracts with a state had to be construed strictly in favor of the public interests represented by the state. The states had to be given the benefit of the doubt in resolving ambiguities, and no rights not expressly created by the contract could be asserted against them. "While the rights of private property are sacredly guarded," he wrote, "we must not forget that the community also have rights, and that the happiness and well-being of every citizen depends on their faithful preservation." The Court refused to bind Massachusetts to an obligation it had not expressly assumed. He declared that the power of a state to promote the public welfare "shall not be construed to have been surrendered or diminished by the State, unless it shall appear in plain words, that it was intended to be done." In other words, implied rights of contract could not be claimed against a state as they might be claimed against a private party.

Taney cited practical reasons for his decision. A decision against Massachusetts, he argued, would adversely affect the development of transportation throughout the country. Science and technology were rendering old systems obsolete, and the states needed leeway to take advantage of the changes. Reading implied exclusivity into old charters would block innovation by allowing old transportation companies to claim monopoly rights never expressly granted. The proprietors of an old turnpike, for instance, might prevent construction of a canal or railroad along the same route. Whole communities would be permanently tied to obsolete systems of transportation. "This court," Taney declared, "are not prepared to sanction principles which must lead to such results."

Although the decision clearly limited the protection of the Contract Clause, Taney tried to tie it to contract precedents of the Marshall era. He cited *Providence Bank v. Billings*

(1830) to support his argument that corporate charters created no rights by implication. In that case the Court held that in chartering a bank the state had not impliedly promised to exempt it from general taxation. "The case now before the court," Taney declared, "is, in principle, precisely the same." But the cases were not the same, and Taney had to know it. The Providence Bank lost because immunity from taxation had nothing to do with banking and therefore could not have been an implied term of the charter. The right of exclusivity, on the other hand, had everything to do with building and operating a bridge across the Charles River. While the proprietors of the Providence Bank had no reason to assume they would not be subject to taxation, the bridge proprietors had every reason to assume that a competing bridge would not be authorized during the period of their charter. That Taney grasped for a precedent so far off the mark demonstrates the pressure he must have felt to harmonize his constitutional rulings with those of the Marshall era.

Justice Story wrote a dissent joined in by Justice Thompson. He declared that contracts involving states as parties stood on the same ground as contracts between private parties. The Constitution did not distinguish between public and private contracts and neither should the Court. The charter granted to the Charles River Bridge Company had clearly implied exclusivity or the bridge would never have been built. To violate rights impliedly granted was as unconstitutional as impairing rights expressly granted. Story rejected Taney's claim that construing contracts narrowly in favor of the states promoted the public interest. "I can conceive of no surer plan to arrest all public improvements, founded on private capital and enterprise, than to make the outlay of that capital uncertain and questionable, both as to security and as to productiveness." But such arguments no longer carried the same weight as in the past. The claims of the state now stood higher than private contract rights in the view of the Court.

The decision was attacked by conservatives everywhere and drew fire from Whigs in Congress. "The intelligent part of the profession will all be with you," Webster wrote to Justice Story, "but then the decision of the Court will have completely overturned, in my judgement, one great provision of the Constitution." Chancellor James Kent of New York expressed similar views in a letter to Story. "I have lost my confidence and hopes," he wrote, "in the constitutional guardianship and protection of the Supreme Court." Whig newspapers pilloried Taney for abandoning the great principle of the sanctity of contracts. But the Jacksonians praised him and defended the Court for putting the welfare of the public over the claims of private interests.

The case generated more heat than the outcome really justified. Partisans on both sides magnified the decision beyond its practical importance. Ever since the *Dartmouth* case, the states had been cautious in granting charters of incorporation. By the 1830s they routinely limited the rights of corporations to those expressly granted, carefully reserving all their general powers of government. The Charles River Bridge charter was an anachronism with no relation to contemporary practices. The case had symbolic rather than practical significance. Still, symbols matter, and Taney's opinion, the first written by him as chief justice, signaled that the Marshall era was definitely over. The interests of the public came first, and the states were now freer to promote the general welfare according to their own lights.

Chancellor Kent on *Charles River Bridge* Decision

"[A] gathering gloom is cast over the future. We seem to have sunk suddenly below the horizon, to have lost the light of the sun[.]"

—*New York Review* (1838)

Figure VIII.2 Portrait of James Kent, Chancellor of New York (c. 1855–1865).

Library of Congress, Prints and Photographs Division, LC-BH82-5142 A

Taney reiterated these views in *Ohio Life Insurance & Trust Co, v. Debolt* (1854). The case turned on the constitutionality of a tax Ohio imposed on a corporation subsequent to its incorporation. Taney upheld the tax on the ground that no express exemption from taxation had been granted by the charter. He wrote:

> The rule of construction, in cases of this kind, has been well settled by this court. The grant of privileges and exemptions to a corporation are strictly construed against the corporation, and in favor of the public. Nothing passes but what is granted in clear and explicit terms. And neither the right of taxation nor any other power of sovereignty . . . will be held by the court to be surrendered, unless the intention to surrender is manifested by words too plain to be mistaken.

The double standard between private contracts and those involving states could not have been clearer.

The issue of rights explicitly granted by a state came before the Court two years later in *Dodge v. Woolsey* (1856). In 1845 Ohio granted a charter to a bank with a provision that the state would receive six percent of the bank's profits in lieu of taxes. Six years later, Ohio adopted a new state constitution requiring all banks to pay property taxes. The legislature then passed a law making the tax-exempt bank liable for more than would have been due under its charter. Woolsey, one of the shareholders, brought suit to enjoin the state from collecting the tax. He contended that the law impaired contract rights protected by the Constitution. The Taney Court agreed and declared the law unconstitutional. The decision, written by Justice Wayne, held that rights expressly granted by the states created binding obligations of contract regardless of their impact on the public interest.

The Court also protected rights created by private contracts against abridgment by the states. Two Illinois statutes impairing the rights of creditors in foreclosure proceedings were invalidated in *Bronson v. Kinzie* (1843). The laws protected debtors at foreclosure sales by giving them repurchase rights detrimental to their creditors. The repurchase rights had the effect of reducing the proceeds that could be raised at the sale and thereby impaired obligations of contract protected by the Constitution. The states could regulate foreclosure proceedings, but the regulations adopted could not impair the rights of creditors. The Court made it clear that private contract rights remained as fully protected as during the Marshall years.

Federal Commerce Power and the States

Some of the most controversial issues argued before the Taney Court related to the Commerce Clause of the Constitution. Even the Marshall Court had difficulty deciding where the internal police powers of the states left off and the commerce powers of the federal government began. Taney inherited the problem along with a particularly difficult case. A New York law dealing with immigration was challenged in *New York City v. Miln* (1837) as an unconstitutional encroachment upon an area of unquestioned federal jurisdiction. The law required the masters of vessels entering the port of New York to provide the local authorities with information about the age, origins, and health of any immigrants on board, and also to post a bond that they would not become a public charge. Waves of immigrants were entering the country through the port cities of the East. Those who were sick and indigent posed a threat to public health as well as a heavy financial burden to municipal governments. The New York law simply gave local officials authority to deal with what had become a serious local problem. But it was immediately challenged as an unconstitutional intrusion into matters reserved to the federal government.

When the case first came up for argument in 1834, the Court was sharply divided. Three of the justices thought the law constitutional as a legitimate exercise of state police powers, and three agreed with Marshall that it was an unconstitutional intrusion into an area of federal jurisdiction. But two of the justices who sided with Marshall had not been present at the arguments and therefore abstained from voting. This left a 3–2 plurality for upholding the law, an outcome Marshall avoided by ordering a reargument of the case. He took the position, as he had in the *Charles River Bridge* case, that constitutional issues should not be decided by less than a majority of the whole Court. By the time the case was finally decided in 1837, the voting balance had shifted. Taney had become chief justice, and the Court had become more sympathetic to the claims of the states.

Justice Barbour delivered a majority decision upholding the law as a constitutional exercise of New York's police power. Every state had the power and duty, he wrote, "to advance the safety, happiness, and prosperity of its people, and to provide for its general welfare, by any and every act of legislation, which it may deem to be conducive to these ends." These basic functions of state government remained "complete, unqualified and exclusive" within the federal system. The fact that the New York law related to matters over which Congress had jurisdiction made no difference. The law addressed legitimate state concerns and was therefore constitutional.

> We think it as competent and as necessary for a State to provide precautionary measures against the moral pestilence of paupers, vagabonds, and possibly convicts; as it is to guard against the physical pestilence, which may arise from unsound and infectious articles imported[.]

State and Federal Authority

"[W]hilst a state is acting within the legitimate scope of its power as to the end to be attained, it may use whatsoever means, being appropriate to that end, it may think fit; although they may be the same, or so nearly the same, as scarcely to be distinguishable from those adopted by Congress acting under a different power: subject, only, say the court, to this limitation, that in the event of collision, the law of the State must yield to the law of Congress. The court must be understood, of course, as meaning that the law of Congress is passed upon a subject within the sphere of its power."

—Justice Philip Barbour, *New York City v. Miln* (1837)

Figure VIII.3 Portrait of Philip Barbour by Kate Flournoy Edwards (1911).

Collection of the U.S. House of Representatives

Story alone dissented. While conceding that the law addressed legitimate state concerns, he thought that it nevertheless encroached upon powers reserved to the federal government. The fact that Congress had not exercised the powers made no difference. Federal jurisdiction over immigration was absolute and exclusive, and the states were precluded from acting for any purpose. Story did not regard state police powers as "unqualified and exclusive," as Barbour described them, but as modified and qualified by the powers delegated by the Constitution to the federal government. Story's analysis was correct, though it took nearly four decades for his view to prevail. *Miln* was ultimately overturned in *Henderson v. New York* (1876) on the ground that federal jurisdiction over immigration is exclusive. But that would be the constitutional law of a later era after the Civil War and Reconstruction had greatly reduced state sovereignty. Until then, *Miln* became a precedent for the expansion of state police powers into areas of federal jurisdiction.

The Court built on the *Miln* precedent in three cases known collectively as the *License Cases* in 1847. Massachusetts, New Hampshire, and Rhode Island had passed laws restricting and taxing the sale of alcoholic beverages. All three were challenged as unconstitutional encroachments upon the federal commerce power. The New Hampshire law seemed particularly vulnerable to attack for violating the "original package" doctrine formulated by Marshall in *Brown v. Maryland*. It taxed imported liquor that had not yet entered the internal stream of commerce of the state. While all three statutes addressed legitimate state concerns, they also imposed restraints on interstate commerce. Separating what was constitutionally permissible from what was not permissible was not easy for the justices. Although a majority voted to uphold the laws, there was no agreement on why they had upheld them. Nine separate opinions were written to explain the decision.

Taney wrote a sort of consensus opinion holding that the federal commerce power did not prevent the states from exercising their ordinary police powers. "It appears to me," he wrote, "that the mere grant of power to the general government cannot, upon any just principles of construction, be construed to be an absolute prohibition to the exercise of any power over the same subject by the States." In other words, the states had concurrent power with the federal government to regulate commerce in the course of exercising their police powers for the protection of the health and welfare of their citizens. Such regulations would be valid unless they conflicted with laws passed by Congress. All three state laws were constitutional, Taney reasoned, because Congress had passed no laws to the contrary. *Brown v. Maryland* had involved a conflict between state and federal laws, he noted, whereas no conflict existed in the present cases.

The Passenger Cases

How far the states might go in exercising their police powers remained an open question. In 1849 a line of sorts was drawn in the *Passenger Cases*. New York and Massachusetts imposed head taxes on immigrants entering the country through their ports. Massachusetts required shipmasters to pay two dollars for every immigrant landed, the proceeds to be used to care for those who became a public charge. New York imposed a tax of one dollar on immigrants arriving in steerage, the way most paupers traveled, and earmarked the money for a hospital to care for those who were sick. While both laws addressed legitimate state concerns, they also dealt with matters under the jurisdiction of Congress.

New York and Massachusetts defended their laws as legitimate exercises of state police power. They pointed out that sick and indigent immigrants created serious problems for local government, and that the measures taken to reduce the financial burden were reasonable and constitutional. Similar laws had been upheld in the *Miln* case, and that precedent clearly covered the present cases. The measures had been enacted to protect the health, safety, and welfare of the community, a legitimate state function according to *Miln*, and therefore constitutional. Neither state had attempted to regulate commerce or immigration or to interfere in any way with the jurisdiction of Congress. Since Congress had not seen fit to act on the subject, there could be no conflict between state and federal laws.

The Court split sharply in declaring both laws unconstitutional. The 5–4 decision had no common focus, with eight of the nine justices writing concurring or dissenting opinions. Justice McLean made the strongest case for invalidating the statutes. He rejected the notion of concurrent state power in areas of federal jurisdiction, arguing that the Constitution gave Congress exclusive jurisdiction over foreign and interstate commerce. "A concurrent power in two distinct sovereignties, to regulate the same thing," he wrote, "is as inconsistent in principle as it is impracticable in action." State police powers could not be exercised in areas of federal jurisdiction. That there was no conflict between state and federal laws made no difference. The states had no power over immigration even in the absence of federal regulations. "Except to guard its citizens against diseases and paupers, the municipal power of a State cannot prohibit the introduction of foreigners brought to this country under the authority of Congress." In other words, local laws dealing with the sick and indigent were permissible, but not measures affecting immigration in general. Federal jurisdiction over the latter was absolute and exclusive.

Taney wrote a vigorous dissent defending the laws as a legitimate exercise of state police powers. He argued that the laws promoted the general welfare of the people of Massachusetts and New York and imposed no restraints on immigration or commerce. They merely refused landing permission to incoming vessels "until the security demanded by the State for the protection of its own people from the evils of pauperism has been given." Since the states had the right to expel persons who threatened the general welfare, Taney reasoned that they might also "meet them at the threshold and prevent them from entering." He found nothing in the Constitution to prevent such an exercise of state police power.

Selective Exclusiveness Doctrine

Since the outcome of the *Passenger Cases* was at odds with *Miln* and the *License Cases*, the decision caused considerable confusion. Two years later, in *Cooley v. Board of Wardens of the Port of Philadelphia* (1852), the Court attempted to reconcile the case law under a general theory of federal-state relations in areas of competing jurisdiction. The case involved a Pennsylvania law that required vessels entering the port of Philadelphia to employ a local pilot to navigate the harbor or else to pay half the pilot's fee to a local benevolent society. Congress had previously asserted jurisdiction over pilotage but had prescribed no regulations; it instead authorized the states to enforce their own regulations until federal rules were promulgated. Since Congress had not yet prescribed rules, there was no conflict between state and federal laws. The statute was nevertheless challenged because of the holding in the *Passenger Cases* that federal commerce jurisdiction was sometimes exclusive even in the absence of federal legislation. The fact that Congress had authorized the states to regulate pilotage made no difference. Congress could no more waive its constitutional powers than the states could usurp them.

The Court upheld the law in a split decision. Justice Curtis, speaking for the majority, held that the pilotage regulation was constitutional because Congress had not yet legislated on the subject. He held that the federal commerce power is always paramount but not necessarily always exclusive. It encompasses matters primarily of local concern as well as others that are clearly national in character. While Congress has exclusive jurisdiction over the latter, the states have concurrent jurisdiction over the former, provided that the measures adopted do not conflict with federal law. This formulation of the federal commerce power came to be known as the "selective exclusiveness" doctrine. Under it, federal jurisdiction was exclusive in matters of national concern, such as immigration, and concurrent, though paramount, in matters primarily of local concern, such as pilotage. Three of the justices rejected the formulation. Justice Daniel concurred with the majority but contended that state power over matters of local concern was absolute and not subject to any paramount federal power. Justices McLean and Wayne took the opposite view and dissented on the ground that the commerce power of the federal government was absolute and exclusive over all aspects of foreign and interstate commerce.

Although selective exclusiveness fell somewhat short of his own expansive views of state police powers, Taney accepted the doctrine as a reasonable accommodation between federal and state interests. That the federal commerce power was paramount even in areas of concurrent state jurisdiction was reiterated by the Court in *Pennsylvania v. Wheeling & Belmont Bridge Company* (1851). The case involved a bridge to be built across the Ohio River under Virginia law. Pennsylvania charged that the bridge would interfere with interstate river navigation in violation of federal law. Although Congress had taken jurisdiction over river navigation in several measures, construction of the bridge was not specifically prohibited. The Court nevertheless ruled against the bridge. Speaking for the majority, Justice McLean held that Congress by taking general jurisdiction over river navigation had precluded the states from acting. Taney and Daniel dissented. They argued that since Congress had not specifically legislated on the subject, the Court should not presume to legislate for it. State measures not in conflict with federal laws should be upheld until conflicts actually arose. Congress agreed with the dissenters. A law was passed authorizing the bridge and overturning the decision. But this did not alter the case precedent that even a general assertion of federal jurisdiction precluded the states from asserting concurrent jurisdiction.

Political Questions and the Court

Taney steered clear of cases presenting essentially political issues. The cases that arose from the so-called Dorr Rebellion in Rhode Island brought several such issues before the Court. The democratization of political life in the rest of the country had little impact in

Rhode Island. The state remained something of a political backwater tied to its colonial past. The old colonial charter, amended in 1776 to provide for independence, served as the state's constitution. The suffrage was restricted to freeholders and their eldest sons, an arrangement that deprived more than half the adult male population and most of those living in urban areas of the right to vote. By the 1840s the political system of the state was two centuries out of date. When it became clear that the charter government would not reform itself, some Democrats led by Thomas Dorr called a convention at Providence in 1841 and drafted a "People's" Constitution enfranchising all adult white males. This goaded the state legislature into proposing charter changes broadening the suffrage. But when submitted to the freeholders for ratification, the proposals were rejected. The enfranchised part of the population made it clear that they would not share power.

Both sides conducted separate elections in 1842 for control of the state government. Dorr was elected governor by the popular party, and a de facto government was set up at Providence. The charter party reelected Governor Samuel King, who took office at Newport. The Dorrites controlled most of northwestern Rhode Island, and the charter government ran the rest of the state. When disorders broke out between supporters of the rival governments, the Newport legislature declared Dorr and his followers in a state of insurrection. It proclaimed martial law and called out the state militia to suppress the insurgency. After an unsuccessful attempt to capture the state arsenal, the Dorrite rebellion collapsed. Dorr fled the state, but some of his supporters were arrested and charged with treason.

The Dorrites had lost a battle but not the war. Their insurgency shocked the freeholders into adopting a new constitution giving most male adults the right to vote. The new

Figure VIII.4 Portrait of Thomas Wilson Dorr by James S. Baillie (1845).

National Portrait Gallery, Smithsonian Institution / Art Resource, NY

An Eyewitness Account of the Dorr Rebellion

"[O]n said morning of the 28th of June, as I was standing in my office, I saw a number of armed men running across the lots west of [the] main street, apparently having an object in view to shoot at, and crying out in a loud tone, "Stop, or we'll shoot you;" and others in the street vociferating "Shoot the d——d scoundrel." . . . These shouts were thickly interspersed with discharges of muskets, one of which took effect in the object pursued, viz: in the leg of a young man . . . The other principal incidents of the day, (to wit, the 28th,) were the making arrests under martial law; breaking into and searching the dwellings, stores, and other buildings of suffrage men. What amount of plunder was carried off from said village, I am unable to state, but have no doubt it was large."

—Clovis Bowen, Proprietor of the Chepachet Meeting House
(Providence, Rhode Island), Deposition taken May 17, 1844

constitution would go into effect in 1844, but the old government in the meantime was anything but conciliatory. When Dorr returned to Rhode Island, he was arrested, convicted of treason, and sentenced to prison. Most Democrats throughout the country sympathized with Dorr, and efforts were made to secure his release. A petition for habeas corpus was filed with the United States Supreme Court in *Ex parte Dorr* (1844) on the ground that treason could only be punished by the federal government. Since the Court was packed with Democrats, it was generally assumed that some reason would be found to order his release. But the petition was dismissed on technical jurisdictional grounds. The Court held that it could not issue writs of habeas corpus on original petitions from prisoners sentenced by state courts.

The legitimacy of the charter government was also challenged in *Luther v. Borden* (1849). Luther, one of Dorr's supporters, sued Borden, a member of the state militia, for breaking into his house to arrest him. Borden's defense was that he had acted lawfully as an officer of the lawful government. The legality of the charter government was precisely the issue that the Dorrites wanted decided in the federal courts. They denied that the government for which Borden had acted was the lawful one. Dorr's government was the lawful government, because the people who elected him had the sovereign right to overturn the archaic system that retained power by disfranchising a majority of the citizens. The Dorrites argued that the American Revolution had been fought for the principle of self-government and that people had a natural right to resist political oppression. Furthermore, the Constitution of the United States guaranteed the people of every state a republican form of government, and the oligarchic charter government hardly met that standard. Luther's suit against Borden was dismissed by the federal circuit court for Rhode Island, thereby setting the stage for an appeal to the United States Supreme Court.

Since the Supreme Court this time presumably had jurisdiction, the case could not be dismissed on technical grounds. But by the time the case was argued, events in Rhode Island had rendered the outcome essentially moot. Dorr had been granted amnesty and released, and the legislature subsequently annulled his conviction. But the question of

> ## Political Questions and the Supreme Court
>
> "Much of the argument on the part of the plaintiff turned upon political rights and political questions, upon which the court has been urged to express an opinion. We decline doing so. The high power has been conferred on this court of passing judgment upon the acts of the State sovereignties, and of the legislative and executive branches of the federal government, and of determining whether they are beyond the limits of power marked out for them respectively by the Constitution of the United States. This tribunal, therefore, should be the last to overstep the boundaries which limit its own jurisdiction. And while it should always be ready to meet any question confided to it by the Constitution, it is equally its duty not to pass beyond its appropriate sphere of action, and to take care not to involve itself in discussions which properly belong to other forums."
>
> —Chief Justice Roger Taney, *Luther v. Borden* (1849)

which government had been the legal one remained open, and any decision on this had serious constitutional ramifications. The Republican form of government guaranteed by Article IV declares: "The United States shall guarantee to every State in this Union a Republican Form of Government." The Article says nothing about how the guarantee shall be enforced. Whether the responsibility lies with the president, congress, or the courts is not made clear. There is nothing in the text indicating which branch shall make the determination whether the government of a particular state meets the constitutional standard.

Taney wisely avoided leading the Court into what could have been political quicksand. Speaking for the majority, he dismissed the appeal on the ground that the issues raised were political and therefore not appropriate for judicial determination. Political questions should be settled by politicians, not by judges. He wrote:

> [C]ertainly it is no part of the judicial functions of any court of the United States to prescribe the qualifications of voters in a State, giving the right to those to whom it is denied . . . or taking it away from those to whom it is given.

Article IV gave the Court no jurisdiction over such matters. It was up to Congress, he ruled, "to decide what government is the established one in a State." Why Congress? Because Congress in seating the senators and representatives of the states recognizes the legitimacy of the state authority under which they are chosen. That finding then becomes "binding on every other department of the government, and could not be questioned in a judicial tribunal." Taney's opinion would later be cited to assert congressional control over post–Civil War Reconstruction in the South.

Federal Diversity of Citizenship Jurisdiction

Taney's states' rights jurisprudence did not prevent him from presiding over the expansion of federal judicial power. In 1844 the Court reconsidered two of Marshall's decisions limiting the diversity of citizenship jurisdiction of federal courts over corporations. In

Strawbridge v. Curtiss (1806) and *Bank of the United States v. Deveaux* (1809), Marshall had held that in diversity cases federal courts had jurisdiction only when all the shareholders of a corporation were citizens of states different from the states of the adversary parties. He rejected the idea that the Constitution gave corporations standing to sue and be sued as "citizens" of the states where they were incorporated. Their standing in the federal courts depended upon the citizenship of the shareholders who owned them. This made it difficult and sometimes impossible for the federal courts to take jurisdiction of many cases best tried at the federal level. A corporation with shareholders in every state would automatically be excluded even if only one of them were a citizen of the state of the adversary party. While the nationwide growth of corporations and shareholding made federal jurisdiction desirable, Marshall's diversity holding made it difficult for the courts to exercise it.

Both of Marshall's decisions were overturned in *Louisville, Cincinnati & Charleston Railroad Co. v. Letson* (1844). Justice Wayne, speaking for the Court, upheld the right of a citizen of New York to sue a South Carolina corporation in the federal courts despite the fact that some of the corporation's shareholders were citizens of New York. "The suit is against the corporation," Wayne wrote, so "nothing must be looked at but the legal entity." A corporation's standing to sue and be sued in the federal courts depended not on the citizenship of its shareholders, as Marshall had held, but on the state of its incorporation. Incorporation had the effect of conferring a form of citizenship upon corporations for purposes of federal diversity jurisdiction. Wayne declared:

> A corporation, created by a State, to perform its functions under the authority of that State . . . seems to us to be a person, though an artificial one, inhabiting and belonging to that State, and therefore entitled, for the purpose of suing and being sued, to be a citizen of that State.

The expansion of federal diversity jurisdiction gave corporations a more favorable judicial forum for bringing suits. State courts were generally hostile to their interests, and access to the federal courts had long been a corporation goal. Although satisfied with the result, Wayne felt uncomfortable about overruling two of Marshall's precedents. He noted in his opinion that the precedents had never found favor with the bar or even with Marshall himself. They had been followed over the years because of *stare decisis*, not because they were deemed correct. "By no one was the correctness of them more questioned," Wayne wrote, "than by the late chief justice who gave them. It is within the knowledge of several of us, that he repeatedly expressed regret that these decisions had been made." Wayne thus paid Marshall the compliment of citing him as authority for overturning his own decisions.

Maritime Jurisdiction

The Court also overturned a Marshall precedent limiting the admiralty jurisdiction of the federal courts. In the case of *The Steamboat Thomas Jefferson* (1825), Marshall held that the admiralty jurisdiction of the United States extended only to seas and coastal rivers. He adopted the long-established rule of English law that admiralty jurisdiction was limited to the ebb and flow of the tide and did not include inland bodies of water. In 1845 Congress acted on the heavy increase of traffic on the Great Lakes by giving the federal district courts admiralty jurisdiction over the lakes and the navigable rivers connecting them. In *Propeller Genessee Chief v. Fitzhugh* (1851), the constitutionality of the act was challenged on the ground that the lakes were not tidewater and therefore not within the admiralty jurisdiction of the federal government. Marshall's tidewater decision was cited as a binding precedent on the issue.

The case had great importance. If the Court followed Marshall's precedent, federal courts would have jurisdiction over the inland waters only in cases where there was diversity of citizenship between the parties. They could not take jurisdiction if the parties were citizens of the same state. The Court put pragmatism over precedent and overturned Marshall's decision. Taney, speaking for the Court, held that the tidewater rule made no sense in the United States. It worked well enough in England, where tidewater and navigable water were almost synonymous, but not in the United States where there were vast bodies of navigable inland waters. Marshall's decision had been made before the great western lakes and rivers had become vital arteries of commerce. "We are convinced,"

Figure VIII.5 Map of trade routes linking the Northwest with the Atlantic seaboard, including railroads, canal systems, and natural waterways (1853).

Library of Congress, Geography and Map Division, G3701P Rr000820

Taney wrote, "that if we follow it, we follow an erroneous decision into which the Court fell." Changing conditions often require changes in law, and precedents of the past must sometimes yield to the needs of the present. Taney was above saying so, but Marshall himself probably would have agreed.

Federal Common Law

Federal judicial power expanded under Taney, as did the reach of federal law itself. Section 34 of the Judiciary Act of 1789 provided that in trials at common law—that is, trials not involving federal statutes—federal courts exercising diversity of citizenship jurisdiction must apply the laws of the states in which they were sitting. While this clearly bound federal judges to follow state statutes in such cases, it was not clear whether they were also bound to follow state case law as well. Case law, also known as decisional law, was the common law of the states, and it was binding in state courts until judicially overturned or superseded by statute. Despite the mass of statutes enacted over the years, decisional law still comprised the bulk of all state law. Whether Section 34 required the federal courts to follow it or allowed them to develop and apply federal case law became an important issue in diversity cases.

There had been sharp disagreement over whether federal common law even existed in the 1790s. The early focus of the debate had been whether federal courts could apply English common law in order to punish sedition in the absence of federal sedition statutes. Passage of the Sedition Act of 1798 rendered the debate moot by giving the federal courts statutory power to try such cases. But the larger issue of whether federal judges could act on common law precedents remained unresolved. The Marshall Court provided a partial answer in *United States v. Hudson and Goodwin* (1812) and in *United States v. Coolidge* (1816), holding that in criminal cases the federal courts could punish only acts declared by Congress to be criminal. This settled once and for all that there was no federal criminal common law, but it left open the question whether there was a federal common law with respect to civil litigations. Dicta in *Hudson* suggested that there was not, but that hardly settled the issue.

While the issue remained technically open, it was generally assumed that the Judiciary Act of 1789 obliged federal judges to apply state common law in diversity of citizenship cases. This meant that in a suit brought by a citizen of New York against a citizen of Massachusetts, the federal courts in Massachusetts would try the case exactly as the Massachusetts state courts would try it. The decisional law of Massachusetts would be followed as well as the Massachusetts statutes. Federal courts trying diversity cases became, in effect, part of the state judicial system. This had the advantage of ensuring that the outcome would be the same whether cases were tried in the state courts or in the federal courts. But there were also disadvantages. Uniformity of law within the states was offset by the growing diversity of law among the states. The full enforcement of state law by the federal courts meant that the outcome of a case frequently varied according to where the case was tried. Instead of promoting legal harmony among the states, the federal courts fostered diversity and conflict instead.

The practice of following all the decisional law of the states was finally abandoned in *Swift v. Tyson* (1842). Speaking for the Court, Justice Story held that the Judiciary Act of 1789 did not require federal courts to apply all the common law of the states in diversity cases. They were bound to follow state decisional law only insofar as it had purely local consequences, for instance, state court decisions on land titles and interpretations of state statutes. Otherwise, federal judges were free to follow whatever decisional precedents they thought most suitable. A federal judge in Maryland did not have to look only to Maryland's state court decisions. He might follow federal court decisions or court decisions in other states instead. Taney hoped that once federal courts were no longer constrained by state decisional law, they would develop a coherent body of federal common law applicable throughout the country. He expected that the states would eventually bring their own systems of case law into line with the federal system for the sake of harmony. The example of federal uniformity would put them under heavy pressure to conform their own common law to the national standard. *Swift v. Tyson* marked the beginning of an experiment with federal common law that would last for nearly a century.

Supreme Court Appointments

New appointments did not disturb the solid Democratic majority on the Court during Taney's tenure as chief justice. Van Buren's midnight appointment of Justice Daniel in 1841 prevented the Whigs from making an appointment for almost two years. By the time the opportunity came with the death of Justice Thompson in 1843, President Tyler had broken with the Whigs in Congress. Whigs in the Senate thereafter blocked his nominees in order to keep the post open until the anticipated election of Henry Clay the following year. The death of Justice Baldwin in the spring of 1844 created another vacancy, but the Senate Whigs again refused to confirm a nominee. Their strategy backfired, however, when the Democratic candidate James K. Polk defeated Clay in the fall election. Polk's victory meant that the appointments might go to a Jacksonian Democrat unless the Senate confirmed Tyler's nominees. Having nothing to lose, the Senate Whigs confirmed Samuel Nelson, a moderate Democrat. Nelson, a former chief judge of New York, was the first justice appointed by a president not a member of his own party.

The second vacancy was left for Polk, who soon had another with the death of Justice Story in 1845. He filled the Story vacancy first, appointing Levi Woodbury, a New

Hampshire Democrat with a distinguished career in state and federal government. Woodbury was easily confirmed, but Polk's nomination of George W. Woodward for Baldwin's seat was rejected. Woodward, a Pennsylvania Democrat, was highly qualified, but conservative Democrats found his liberal record unacceptable. After offering the post to Secretary of State James Buchanan, who declined, Polk appointed Robert C. Grier, a Pennsylvania state court judge. Grier, a loyal Democrat, was confirmed without difficulty.

No Whig joined the Court until President Millard Fillmore appointed Benjamin R. Curtis in 1851. Curtis, who filled the vacancy created by the death of Justice Woodbury, was a highly successful Boston attorney. Daniel Webster recommended his appointment, and he was young enough, at age forty-two, to keep the seat in Whig hands for many years. But the breakup of the Whig party a few years later made this irrelevant. Curtis resigned in 1857 after a bitter dispute with Taney over the *Dred Scott* case. Fillmore got another vacancy with the death of Justice McKinley in 1852, but partisan politics prevented him from filling it. The Democrats had just won the presidential election behind Franklin Pierce, and Senate Democrats blocked Fillmore's nominees in order to keep the post open for a Democrat.

Pierce filled the vacancy with John A. Campbell of Alabama. Campbell, a states' rights Democrat, was the only southern justice to resign from the Court in order to support the Confederacy during the Civil War. President James Buchanan made the last pre–Civil War Court appointment on the resignation of Justice Curtis in 1857. The appointment went to Nathan Clifford of Maine. Clifford, a loyal Democrat, had served in Congress and as attorney general during Polk's administration. Republicans in the Senate fought hard to prevent his confirmation, but the Democrats prevailed in the end. The fight had less to do with Clifford's qualifications than with the polarization of the nation over the slavery issue. Anything at all could precipitate a confrontation, and Clifford just had the bad luck to be caught in the middle of a conflict that would soon engulf the whole nation.

Taney's Legacy as Chief Justice

Taney presided over the Court during a period of adjustment and consolidation. The nationalism of the Marshall years was slowed, and the states got a freer hand in the management of their own affairs. Taney successfully reconciled national sovereignty with the expansion of state police powers at a time when local government had to assume new responsibilities. Marshall had been wary of sharing federal power with the states, fearing that any concessions might erode the foundations of national sovereignty. His concern was completely valid at a time when national sovereignty had to be defended against encroachments by the states. More than half the states passed laws that he invalidated for encroaching upon federal functions, so he had cause to regard state government with suspicion. The national government was new and vulnerable to attack, while state government was old and steeped in tradition. All this had changed by the time Taney became chief justice, and the change was in part the legacy of his great predecessor. The principle of national sovereignty had come to be almost universally accepted and no longer had to be defended with inflexible judicial zeal. The time had come when the states could play a larger role in government without undermining the foundations of national power.

The issues that confronted Taney were far more complex than those of Marshall's time. Most could not be settled categorically on general principles of constitutional law, making it difficult for the Court to reach the sort of consensus opinions favored by Marshall. Concurring and dissenting opinions became more common as the cases became more complicated. Some issues had no clear-cut answers and made solidarity impossible. Taney provided the Court with excellent leadership, but circumstances made it impossible for him to lead as Marshall had led. For one thing, the members of Taney's Court were far more combative and prone to march to their own drumbeat. The justices appointed by Jackson and his successors were mainly politicians who forgot neither their constituencies nor their political ambitions. Taney led as best he could, but no chief justice, Marshall included, could have made team players of such a group.

Had the slavery issue not tarnished his chief justiceship, Taney's reputation would stand higher today. His contributions to constitutional law and federal judicial power are indisputable and survive as lasting legacies. Taney took the lead in developing a pragmatic theory of state police powers that enabled the states to deal effectively with local problems without encroaching upon the jurisdiction of the federal government. His opinion in the *Charles River Bridge* case added a dimension to the Contract Clause as important as any of Marshall's contract rulings. Taney had a powerful intellect, and his technical grasp of the law was superior to that of any of his predecessors, Marshall included. His closely crafted opinion in *The Propeller Genessee Chief* is as brilliant a piece of legal reasoning as any in the annals of the Court. He extended the reach of the federal courts and federal law beyond the confines of the Marshall era, and his contributions to admiralty law and the diversity jurisdiction of the federal courts have stood the test of time. By any reckoning, Taney was an outstanding jurist, and certainly, after Marshall, our most important chief justice of the nineteenth century.

February 12, 1793	May 26, 1836	March 9, 1841	March 10, 1841	April 4, 1841	March 1, 1842	December 3, 1844
First Fugitive Slave Act	House Passes Gag Rule	The Schooner Amistad	Groves v. Slaughter	John Tyler Takes Office as President of the United States	Prigg v. Pennsylvania	Gag Rule Repealed

July 6–13, 1854	March 6, 1857	August–October 1858	March 7. 1859	October 16, 1859	December 18, 1860	March 4, 1861
Emergence of the Modern Republican Party	Dred Scott v. Sandford	Lincoln-Douglas Debates	Ableman v. Booth	John Brown's Raid on Harpers Ferry	The Crittenden Amendment	Abraham Lincoln Takes Office as President of the United States

IX Slavery and the Constitution

March 1, 1845	April 25, 1846	August 8, 1846	February 2, 1848	September 18, 1850	January 6, 1851	May 30, 1854
Annexation of Texas	Outbreak of Mexican War	The Wilmot Proviso	Mexican War Ends	Fugitive Slave Act of 1850	Strader v. Graham	Kansas-Nebraska Act

"The right of property in a slave is distinctly and expressly affirmed in the Constitution . . . in plain words—too plain to be misunderstood."
—Chief Justice Roger B. Taney, *Dred Scott v. Sandford* (1857)

Of all the issues that divided Americans during the antebellum period, the most bitter and persistent was the controversy over slavery. Organized opposition to the institution began during the Revolutionary War. Sentiment against slavery during the colonial period had been fragmented and typically took the form of religious and moral opposition. The natural rights idealism of the Revolutionary era brought it into sharper focus, making it difficult for white Americans to claim freedom for themselves while denying it to African Americans. Most did not try, not even in the South, where slavery had its deepest roots. Washington, Jefferson, and Madison, southerners and slaveholders as well, supported the idea of gradual emancipation. Jefferson's first draft of the Declaration of Independence deplored the slave trade and condemned Great Britain for disallowing colonial laws against the "execrable commerce." Luther Martin considered the existence of slavery "inconsistent with the principles of the Revolution, and dishonorable to the American character." John Jay, a leader of the antislavery movement in New York, thought that unless Americans took steps to end it, their own "prayers to heaven for liberty will be impious."

The Antislavery Movement

Sentiment against slavery spread so rapidly in the North that by 1806 every northern state had made some provision for abolishing it. There was broad agreement among northerners that besides being unjust slavery posed a threat to society. As one colonial abolitionist wrote, "Instead of being a defence and support of the common-wealth, [slaves] are often its terror, and sometimes its destruction. For it must be constantly expected, that a slave will improve every opportunity to throw off his burthen, and imposition."[1] The movement toward freedom in the North marked the point at which the country split into distinct and separate societies, one with a commitment to freedom and progress, the other suspended in time and tied to a way of life morally indefensible.

A Former Slave on Slavery

"I have observed this of my experience with slavery,—that whenever my condition was improved, instead of its increasing my contentment, it only increased my desire to be free, and set me to thinking of plans to gain my freedom. I have found that, to make a contented slave, it is necessary to make a thoughtless one. It is necessary to darken his moral and mental vision, and, as far as possible, to annihilate the power of reason. He must be able to detect no inconsistencies in slavery; he must be made to feel that slavery is right; and he can be brought to that only when he ceases to be a man."

—*Narrative of the Life of Frederick Douglass, An American Slave: Written by Himself* (1845)

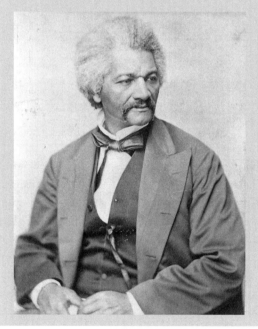

Figure IX.1 Portrait of Frederick Douglass (c. 1850–1860).
Library of Congress, Prints and Photographs Division, LC-USZ62-15887

The survival of slavery in the South probably had more to do with racial demographics than with the profitability of the institution. The numerical insignificance of African Americans in the North made it possible for northern legislatures to emancipate them without disturbing the privileged status of whites in society. The situation was different in the South where the balance between the races was closer. Southern slavery over time became essentially a system for organizing the races in a way that guaranteed the supremacy of whites. This explains why non-slaveholding whites so strongly supported an institution that was often at odds with their economic interests. Only one in four white southerners owned slaves, yet they defended slavery as though their lives depended on it. And their support was strongest precisely in those areas where the concentration of blacks was largest. The idea of freeing the black masses boggled the minds of most southern whites. Even if it adversely affected their economic well-being, slavery was essential to a southern way of life based upon white supremacy.

A South Carolina Congressman on Slavery

"To such a country [slavery] is as natural as the climate itself—as the birds and beasts to which that climate is congenial. The camel loves the desert; the reindeer seeks everlasting snows; the wild fowl gather to the waters; and the eagle wings his flight above the mountains. It is equally the order of Providence that slavery should exist among a planting people, beneath the southern sun . . . [I]t is not the interest of the planters of the South to emancipate their slaves, and it never can be shown to be so . . . [A]ny species of emancipation with us would be followed instantly by civil war between the whites and blacks. A bloody, exterminating war, the result of which could not be doubtful, although it would be accompanied with horrors such as history has not recorded."

—James Henry Hammond, Speech in the House
of Representatives, Feburary 1, 1836

Figure IX.2 Portrait of James Henry Hammond (1859).

Library of Congress, Prints and Photographs Division, LC-DIG-ppmsca-26689

Most whites in the South paid a high price for slavery because the system was at odds with the overall interests of society. It locked the South into a circular economy where planters produced more and more in order to buy more land and slaves in order to produce even more. The wealth created did not improve the material well-being of the community, because no one benefited but the planters. While extremes of wealth and poverty existed in the North, the profits of productive enterprise were at least diffused through society in the form of wages paid to free workers. This diffusion of wealth facilitated class mobility in ways that did not exist in the South. Slavery kept whites as well as blacks in their assigned place in the social order. That so many whites neverthe-less supported it underscores the extent to which race overwhelmed all other concerns in the slave states.

Slavery and the Political Parties

Because slavery divided the nation so sharply, the major political parties tried to keep it out of politics. The Whigs and Democrats were national parties, and party unity could best be served by taking no position at all. This was easy enough at the national level because the Constitution gave Congress only limited jurisdiction over slavery. The only areas of federal concern were the return of fugitive slaves who had fled to other states, the overseas slave trade, and the status of slavery in the national territo-ries. Congress had already acted in all three areas. A fugitive slave law had been passed in 1793; the foreign slave trade and importation of slaves had been outlawed after 1808; and the status of slavery in the national territories had been settled by the Northwest Ordinance of 1787 and the Missouri Compromise of 1820. With national policy in these areas already set, Congress had no reason to become involved when the issue heated up in the 1830s.

Slavery nevertheless surfaced in national politics in unexpected ways. The use of the federal mails to get antislavery propaganda into the South caused a furor during Jackson's administration. Georgia made it a crime to bring in material likely to incite the slaves, and in South Carolina a Charleston mob seized and burned abolition tracts being sent through the mails. The Charleston affair led Postmaster General George Kendall to direct southern postmasters to intercept antislavery material. The president supported Kendall on the ground that the federal government's responsibility not to disturb the peace of local communities transcended its obligation to deliver the mail. Jackson asked Congress for a law prohibiting the circulation of antislavery publications through the mail, but he did not get it. The failure of Congress to take a stand made no practical difference. Southern postmasters simply assumed de facto authority not to deliver antislavery material.

The "Gag Rule"

Efforts to keep the slavery issue out of national politics sometimes backfired. In the 1830s Congress received a flood of petitions urging prohibition of the slave trade in the District of Columbia. Because of its location, the nation's capital had become a major artery for the shipment of slaves from Maryland and Virginia to the Lower South. Northerners re-garded slave trading in the federal capital a national disgrace, and petitions were sent to Congress urging its prohibition. Although the petitions got nowhere, southern congress-men were annoyed that they still kept coming. So in 1836, at the insistence of southern members, the House of Representatives adopted a so-called "gag rule" under which all petitions relating to slavery were tabled without discussion. This abridgment of the right of petition handed opponents of slavery a popular issue. A right guaranteed by the First

Figure IX.3 Broadside titled *Slave Market of America* (1836) depicting a slave coffle in Washington, D.C. Under the caption, "The Home of the Oppressed," a figure carrying a whip leads slaves past the Capitol Building as they cry, "Hail Columbia." Columbia was the female personification of liberty.

Library of Congress, Prints and Photographs Division, LC-DIG-ppmsca-19705

Amendment had been effectively cancelled by the slave power in Congress. What was the point of petitioning when there was no chance the petition would be considered? The "gag rule" was an issue for which radical opponents of slavery could count on the support of moderates who did not generally share their radical views.

The fight against the "gag rule" was led by former President John Quincy Adams. He had been elected to the House of Representatives and served there for eight consecutive terms after leaving the presidency. Though not a radical, Adams opposed slavery, and he believed that rights guaranteed by the Constitution had been impaired by shutting off debate on antislavery petitions. He fought the "gag rule" with every parliamentary device available, and his persistence made it a national issue. He hammered away until public opinion in the North forced northern Representatives to join him. Victory came in 1844 when the House, over bitter southern resistance, dropped the rule. Repeal did not free a single slave, but it was still a great victory for antislavery. The long struggle convinced many moderates in the North that the slave power was prepared to trample the rights of all Americans. Repeal of the rule enraged the South, and a leading Whig newspaper in South Carolina urged secession on the day repeal was voted.

While the House of Representatives debated the "gag rule," the whole country debated whether Texas should join the Union. In 1836, after a successful rebellion against Mexico, American settlers in Texas established an independent republic. They also adopted a constitution legalizing slavery, which became an obstacle to their real goal of annexation by the United States. Most northerners did not want another slave state, partly because it would increase the power of the South in Congress, but also because it would become a precedent for the admission of more slave states in the future. Southerners, on the other hand, were determined that Texas should be annexed. Not to do so, they contended, would be a setback for westward expansion and a blow to the national interests of the United States. The debate so sharply divided the country that party leaders tried to avoid taking sides. Taking any position on the issue would cost the parties votes somewhere.

Manifest Destiny

Despite the efforts to avoid it, slavery erupted as a major political issue with the outbreak of the Mexican War in 1846. The vast territories won in the war compelled Congress to deal with the question of whether the new lands should be open to slavery. The war itself grew out of the strident nationalism of the 1840s and the infatuation of Americans with the idea of Manifest Destiny. The phrase first appeared in an 1845 magazine editorial by John L. O'Sullivan urging the annexation of Texas. Not to annex Texas, he contended, would prevent "fulfillment of our manifest destiny to overspread the continent allotted by Providence for the free development of our yearly multiplying millions." The phrase entered the political vocabulary at the end of the joint Anglo-American occupation of the Oregon Territory. Congressman Robert C. Winthrop of Massachusetts declared that American claims to Oregon rested on "our manifest destiny to spread over the whole continent."

The idea of Manifest Destiny had broad popular appeal. It was thoroughly chauvinistic, but chauvinism and national pride were difficult to distinguish in the nineteenth century on both sides of the Atlantic. American nationalists believed that the United States stood for a new political order destined to liberate the common man from the shackles of inherited class status. Never before had a society of such limitless opportunities for human improvement existed. What had happened on these shores was no accident, many believed, but rather the unfolding of God's plan for the fulfillment of human destiny. The United States had a holy mission to occupy the continent and create the political conditions for an era of unprecedented progress and prosperity. Americans were on the side of history, and no power on earth could resist them.

The main obstacle to Manifest Destiny was Mexico, which blocked the American march westward to the Pacific. Most of the Mexican territories coveted were sparsely populated and vulnerable to settlement and seizure. Texas went first when American settlers declared their independence and set up a separate republic. Only the slavery issue prevented them from joining the Union as a state. Still, Congress lost no time passing resolutions calling for official recognition of the new republic. President Jackson, not wanting to complicate things for the Democrats in the 1836 elections, delayed action until Van Buren was elected. Only then did he establish diplomatic relations with Texas and bring Texans a step closer to their goal of becoming United States citizens.

The slavery issue delayed the annexation of Texas for nearly a decade. A political breakthrough came in 1844 when President Tyler, having broken with the northern Whigs, tried to use Texas to unite the South behind him. His administration negotiated a treaty of annexation making Texas a territory of the United States, an arrangement that would defuse the issue of adding another slave state to the Union. But Tyler committed a major blunder in his message to the Senate recommending ratification of the treaty. Instead of making a broad appeal on behalf of the national interest, he cited the threat posed to the South by British efforts to forge an economic alliance with an independent Texas. Britain had offered Texas generous incentives to become Britain's chief North American cotton source if only Texas would free its slaves. Tyler's appeal to Southern slaveholding interests enabled opponents of slavery to mobilize the North against the treaty. Secretary of State Calhoun compounded the blunder by sending the British minister a note forcefully defending slavery. The note provided just enough additional ammunition to prevent ratification after a furious debate.

Rejection of the treaty did not end the debate. The Democrats kept the issue alive by endorsing annexation at their national convention in 1844. They might not have done so if Martin Van Buren, the leading contender for the party's presidential nomination, had not made a preconvention blunder. To keep his northern supporters in line, he came out against immediate annexation. Henry Clay, the Whig candidate, made a similar announcement, but in a way not likely to offend southern Whigs. Enough southern Democrats were annoyed to block Van Buren's nomination. He had a clear majority of the delegates, but not the two-thirds majority then needed at Democratic conventions. The Democrats deadlocked before finally nominating James K. Polk as a compromise candidate. Polk, a former governor of Tennessee, was hardly known outside his state, but the Democrats gave him a winning platform. It called for the annexation of Texas and the occupation of Oregon. The first had strong appeal in the South, and the second appealed to nationalists in the North. By linking Texas and Oregon, the Democrats cleverly lifted Texas out of its slavery context and made themselves the party of Manifest Destiny in both sections.

The Democrats ran an aggressive campaign, promising to settle for nothing less than all of Oregon. They hammered home their commitment to push the American frontier to the Pacific even if it meant a war with Great Britain. Polk won a close election that was decided by the electoral votes of New York. He carried New York only because of the 15,000 votes cast for the Liberty Party candidate James G. Birney. Since the Whigs and Democrats avoided the issue, opponents of slavery organized the Liberty Party to get the issue on the ballot. Birney had no chance of winning, but the 15,000 votes he received in New York prevented Clay from becoming president. If Birney had not been on the ballot, the votes he siphoned off would almost certainly have been cast against Polk, who carried the state by only 5,000 votes. Clay was the lesser evil from the standpoint of antislavery. He had not endorsed the annexation of Texas, whereas Polk had endorsed it without reservation. The irony was that opponents of slavery had helped elect the candidate who supported the goals of the slave power.

The Mexican War

Polk's victory amounted to a national referendum on territorial expansion. Manifest Destiny had been put to a vote and had emerged triumphant. Congress passed a joint resolution in March 1845 bringing Texas into the Union. Mexico still claimed sovereignty over Texas and responded by breaking diplomatic relations with the United States. This played into the hands of the Polk administration, which had designs on California and the New Mexico territory as well as Texas. Polk's grand scheme for American expansion to the Pacific encompassed the acquisition of half the national territory of Mexico. Since Mexico could hardly be expected to surrender the territory peaceably, the severance of diplomatic relations presented opportunities for political maneuver. If the Mexicans could be provoked into doing something foolish, Polk could not be blamed for the consequences.

Polk's diplomatic overtures to Mexico were hardly conciliatory. He sent John Slidell to Mexico City as minister plenipotentiary with authority to settle all outstanding problems. The most immediate problem was the southwestern boundary of Texas, which Mexico claimed was the Nueces River, but which Texas insisted was the Rio Grande. If the negotiations had been confined to the boundary dispute, a diplomatic settlement probably would have been arranged. But the main goal of the Slidell mission was to negotiate the purchase of New Mexico and California for $5 million and $25 million, respectively. In addition, if Mexico accepted the Rio Grande boundary, the United States would assume responsibility for $2 million in claims against Mexico by American citizens. That Polk expected the mission to succeed seems improbable. No Mexican government could have survived such a deal. Certain disgrace and perhaps a firing squad would probably have been the fate of any leader who ceded away half of the nation's territory. But the diplomatic effort still had to be made if only for the sake of appearances. Then, when diplomacy had failed, the administration would be on firmer ground to take more forceful action.

Predictably, Mexico refused to receive a plenipotentiary for the purpose of negotiating the sale of its national territory. The Mexican government insisted that negotiations be confined to the Texas boundary dispute. Polk thereupon ordered American forces to enter the disputed territory and take up positions along the Rio Grande. If the move had been intended to provoke the Mexicans into doing something rash, it worked perfectly. Mexican forces crossed the Rio Grande and attacked an American cavalry patrol, giving Polk the pretext he needed to ask Congress for a declaration of war. His war message asserted that Mexico had committed aggression against the United States and "shed American blood upon the American soil." The reality was that a weaker nation was about to be despoiled. The stage had been set for the great leap westward that would bring the United States to the Pacific.

War with Mexico made Polk eager for a settlement of the Oregon dispute with Great Britain. When the British proposed dividing the territory along the 49th parallel, a line considerably south of the boundary claimed by the Democrats during the election campaign, Polk took the unprecedented step of referring the offer to the Senate for its advice. The normal procedure is for the president to send proposed treaties to the Senate with a message recommending approval. Polk turned things around and asked the Senate for its recommendation before taking a position himself. He obviously did not want to make himself vulnerable to the charge of betraying campaign promises. The Senate gave him what he wanted by recommending acceptance, and the treaty was formally ratified in June 1846. The settlement foreclosed any possibility of British intervention in the war against Mexico.

The war set off a fierce partisan debate in the United States from the moment the first shot was fired. The Whigs accused Polk of provoking the conflict in order to seize new territory for the expansion of slavery. Congressman Garrett Davis of Kentucky spoke for most of the party when he charged "It is our own President who began this war." That Polk, a Tennessee slaveholder himself, had compromised with Britain while taking a hard line with Mexico made the charge plausible. Some northern Democrats agreed and opposed the war as a slaveholders' conspiracy. The Massachusetts legislature declared the war unconstitutional, and abolitionists urged the free states to leave the Union. Henry Thoreau became a hero in the North by going to jail rather than pay taxes levied for the war. Some Americans openly sided with Mexico. "Every heart worthy of American liberty had an impulse to join the Mexicans," a Whig editorial declared, and Whig Senator Thomas Corwin expressed the hope that Mexico would welcome American troops to hospitable graves.

Whig charges that the war was a slaveholders' conspiracy have no real substance. The most ardent expansionists were northerners with no axe to grind for slavery. Secretary of State James Buchanan was the leading expansionist in Polk's cabinet, and he came from Pennsylvania. Senator Lewis Cass, the most forceful spokesman for Manifest Destiny in Congress, came from Michigan. If the war had been a slaveholders' conspiracy, why did Calhoun, the leading apologist for slavery in the Senate, abstain from voting on the declaration of war? The most likely reason was the realization that the acquisition of new territory would intensify the slavery controversy and polarize the country. Far from being a sectional conspiracy, the war was a truly national enterprise designed to push the American frontier to the Pacific.

The Wilmot Proviso

The war added a new dimension to the slavery debate. It began before the war was four months old when President Polk asked Congress for a $2 million appropriation to pay for expected Mexican territorial cessions to the United States. While the bill was before the House, David Wilmot, an antislavery Democrat from Pennsylvania, added a rider providing that "neither slavery nor involuntary servitude shall ever exist in any part of the territory." The Senate rejected the rider, but the issue had been joined. The principle of the Wilmot Proviso won wide support in the North. Opponents of slavery took the position that it would be a national disgrace to allow slavery in territory from which it was excluded by Mexican law. Although repeatedly rejected by the Senate, the Proviso passed the House of Representatives time after time as an expression of northern opposition to the expansion of slavery. Abraham Lincoln was a member of the House from 1847 to 1849, and he estimated that he voted for it more than forty times.

Northern support for the Wilmot Proviso enraged the South. Calhoun, Jefferson Davis, and other southern leaders denounced it as unconstitutional. Their arguments made the protection of slavery in the territories a matter of constitutional rights. They contended that the national territories were the joint and common property of the states, and that Congress had no authority to enact prohibitions which discriminated against citizens of the slave states. The South even contested the status of slavery in Oregon. When the House of Representatives attempted to extend the antislavery provisions of the Northwest Ordinance to the territory, the Senate blocked the proposal. While the southern senators had no desire to carry slavery into Oregon, they denied the authority of Congress to exclude it. This amounted to a major shift in the South's position on slavery in the territories. What had previously been a matter for negotiation and compromise now became a matter of southern constitutional rights.

Calhoun took the lead in promoting the theory that the Constitution protected slavery in the territories. Slaves were property, no different from other forms of property, and the Constitution protected property in the territories. Nothing in the Constitution authorized Congress to exclude slavery in order to prevent the formation of additional slave states. Calhoun noted that the South had already become a minority section in national politics. If the balance of power shifted completely to the North, disunion and civil war would be inevitable. The South had to protect its institutions from attack by the North. The exclusion of slavery from the territories would lead to an overwhelming preponderance of free states and political vassalage for the South. Southerners, Calhoun warned, would never submit to northern domination cloaked in the ideology of antislavery.

The deadlock in Congress between the House and Senate prevented the organization of the new territories. Oregon finally became a free territory, but no progress was made on California and the New Mexico territory. The issue was so explosive that both parties tried to keep it out of the elections of 1848. The Democrats adopted a platform declaring that Congress had no authority to interfere with slavery in the states, something no one in Congress had seriously proposed. The real issue was whether Congress could interfere with slavery in the territories. The Whigs also avoided the issue. They nominated General Zachary Taylor, one of the heroes of the Mexican War, and made his military exploits the focus of their campaign. The Democrats nominated Lewis Cass, whose unabashed nationalism had strong appeal in both sections.

Since the Whigs and Democrats refused to take positions, opponents of slavery organized a new political coalition to get the issue before the voters. The Free-Soil Party, as the coalition was called, brought together antislavery Whigs, Democrats, and members of the Liberty Party. The Free-Soilers held a national convention at Buffalo attended by delegates from eighteen states. They adopted a platform based on the Wilmot Proviso and nominated Martin Van Buren for president. The new party had broad support in the North and a candidate with solid political credentials. Van Buren split the Democratic vote in New York, drawing off enough votes to throw the state to Taylor and give him an electoral majority. Thus, for the second time in four years, a national election was decided by a third party brought into being by the slavery controversy. The political life of the country had become hostage to a single issue.

The election settled nothing about the status of slavery in the new territories. California and New Mexico remained unorganized, and pressure mounted on Congress to break the impasse. Antislavery groups demanded the prohibition of slavery, while the South closed ranks to oppose them. In January 1849 Calhoun and a caucus of sixty-eight southern congressmen issued an ultimatum to the North. They demanded that the territories be kept open to slavery, that runaway slaves be returned to their owners, and that the flow of antislavery propaganda to the South cease. Southerners began to talk about seceding and forming a southern confederacy if their demands were not met. The hardening of attitudes raised the prospect that the Union might dissolve unless a political settlement could be arranged.

Compromise of 1850

No one was more alarmed by the threat to the Union than Henry Clay, who now used his matchless political skills to save it. No longer driven by fierce personal ambition, Clay threw himself wholeheartedly into an effort to avert the impending disaster. In January 1850 he presented the Senate with a set of proposals for settling differences between the North and South. First, he proposed admitting California to the Union as a free state in accordance with the wishes of the settlers. Second, the rest of the territory taken from Mexico would be organized without any restrictions on slavery. The status of slavery would be decided by the settlers themselves under the principle later called "popular sovereignty." Third, the slave trade would be prohibited in the District of Columbia, a ban long sought by the North. Fourth, a strong fugitive slave law would be passed for the return of slaves who had escaped to the North.

Clay's proposals brought on the greatest debate in the history of Congress. Although weakened by age and needing assistance to climb the steps of the capitol, he argued for his compromise with great force and skill. Clay spoke for two days, and his theme was conciliation and moderation for the sake of the Union. To the North, he offered California as a free state, plus his assurance that the rest of the territory ceded by Mexico would almost certainly be free. Climate and geography made an explicit prohibition of slavery unnecessary. The compromise would also achieve the northern goal of ending the slave trade in the nation's capital. To the South, Clay offered a more effective fugitive slave law and the organization of the Utah and New Mexico territories with no restrictions on slavery. While the compromise might not be perfect, it might be the last chance to save the Union.

Calhoun spoke next, and he rejected compromise. Sick and dying, he delivered his last warning to the North. His speech, which had to be read for him by Senator James M. Mason of Virginia, contended that makeshift compromises would settle nothing. What Clay proposed were temporary expedients that would not save the Union. It could be saved only by halting agitation against slavery. Southerners wanted nothing from the North save recognition of their rights under the Constitution. The North alone was to blame for putting the Union in peril. Northern institutions had not been

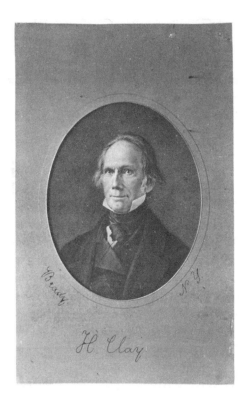

Figure IX.4 Portrait of Henry Clay by Mathew B. Brady.

Collection of the U.S. Senate

attacked by the South, nor had southerners attempted to subvert domestic order in the North. Since the South was already a minority in the Union, its rights would always be vulnerable to attack by the northern majority. Clay's compromise did not address this fundamental problem. Instead of a compromise almost certain to fail, Calhoun proposed a constitutional amendment giving both sections a veto in matters of national legislation. Only then would the South be secure and the threat to the Union permanently ended.

However farfetched the idea may seem today, Calhoun's proposal for sectional vetoes might have averted civil war. Since national legislation was the principal source of sectional strife, conflict could be avoided only by giving each section a protective veto. The protective tariff had threatened the Union in the 1830s just as slavery threatened it in the 1850s. A national government that subjected one section to political domination by the other was inherently unstable. Only a system of dual sovereignty with provisions for concurrent majorities in domestic matters could bring permanent peace between the sections. No basis for conflict would then exist because neither section could dominate the other. This was the solution proposed by the South's greatest political thinker. It probably would have preserved the Union, but at the price of turning the political clock back to the era of the Articles of Confederation.

Webster followed Calhoun, and his position on the compromise was crucially important. If he rejected it, other northern congressmen would have difficulty supporting it. Most of his New England admirers expected a ringing denunciation of slavery, but he disappointed them by supporting the compromise unconditionally. In what was probably the best speech ever delivered in Congress, he appealed for conciliation for the sake of the Union. The appeal turned northern extremists against him, and abolitionists impugned his motives. They accused him of putting personal ambition over principle in order to win southern support for his presidential candidacy. James Russell Lowell charged him with "mean and foolish treachery," and others used even stronger language. Ralph Waldo Emerson remarked, "The word 'honor' in the mouth of Mr. Webster is like the word 'love' in the mouth of a whore."

Senator William Seward of New York spoke for the many northern Whigs who opposed the compromise. He declared that Congress had the power and the duty to prohibit slavery in the territories. The compromise amounted to a pact with evil and had to be rejected. Seward declared that there was a higher law than the Constitution with respect to slavery, and he rejected all political compromises on the issue as "wrong and essentially vicious." With extremists on both sides against it, the fate of the compromise was long uncertain. President Taylor's opposition to the immediate organization of Utah and the New Mexico Territory did not help its chances. Taylor's death in the summer of 1850 ended the uncertainty. His successor Millard Fillmore supported the compromise and helped to bring reluctant southern Whigs into line. His support provided the swing votes needed to get the compromise through Congress.

The compromise was a victory for moderates in both sections and a defeat for extremists who had been prepared to wreck the Union. The South as a whole accepted the

Daniel Webster on the Constitution and the Union

"[I]nstead of speaking of the possibility or utility of secession, instead of dwelling in those caverns of darkness, instead of groping with those ideas so full of all that is horrid and horrible, let us come out into the light of day; let us enjoy the fresh air of Liberty and Union . . . Never did there devolve on any generation of men, higher trusts than now devolve upon us for the preservation of this Constitution, and the harmony and peace of all who are destined to live under it. Let us make our generation one of the strongest, and brightest links, in that golden chain which is destined, I fully believe, to grapple the people of all the states to this Constitution for ages to come. It is a great, popular, constitutional government, guarded by legislation, by law, and by judicature, and defended by the whole affections of the whole people . . . This Republic now extends, with a vast breadth, across the whole continent. The two great seas of the world wash the one and the other shore. We realize, on a mighty scale, the beautiful description of the ornamental edging of the buckler of Achilles,—

Now the broad shield complete, the artist crowned
With his last hand, and poured the ocean round:
In living silver seemed the waves to roll.
And beat the buckler's verge, and bound the whole."

—Speech of March 7, 1850

settlement on assurances from Clay and Webster that the North was ready to respect the rights of southerners. Most northerners also accepted it as a reasonable way to settle the status of slavery in the territories. It seemed to make sense, on paper at least, to leave the issue to the settlers who would have to live with their decision. Popular sovereignty had the double appeal of being democratic and keeping the question out of national politics. Moderates hoped that the compromise would be the final word on the slavery issue.

The Fugitive Slave Law

The part of the compromise that most northerners found difficult to accept was the new fugitive slave law. The law was so heavily weighted in favor of slaveholders that free African Americans in the North were put in jeopardy of enslavement. Alleged runaways who claimed to be free were denied the right to a jury trial, and their testimony on the issue was inadmissible as evidence. The slaveholder or his agent had only to present an affidavit of ownership to a federal judge or commissioner in order to obtain an order of return to the South. The law also compelled northern police and even private citizens to assist in the capture of fugitives. They could not, as under the old law, refuse to cooperate. Any assistance given to runaways was punishable by fine and imprisonment as well as civil damages to the owner.

The law handed abolitionists a popular issue, and they exploited it effectively. When a fugitive named Anthony Burns was captured in Boston in 1854, a mob led by the Rev.

Figure IX.5 Lithograph titled *Effects of the Fugitive-Slave-Law* by Theodor Kaufmann (1850). Four African Americans are fired upon by six armed white men. On the bottom left of the image reads a passage from Deuteronomy: "Thou shalt not deliver unto the master his servant which has escaped from his master unto thee. He shall dwell with thee. Even among you in that place which he shall choose in one of thy gates where it liketh him best. Thou shalt not oppress him." On the bottom right are words from the Declaration of Independence: "We hold that all men are created equal, that they are endowed by their Creator with certain unalienable rights, that among these are life, liberty and the pursuit of happiness."

Library of Congress, Prints and Photographs Division, LC-USZC4-4550

Thomas Higginson stormed the courthouse in an attempt to rescue him. Federal troops had to be deployed to keep Burns in custody. An artillery unit, four platoons of marines, and a sheriff's posse were needed to get him down to the harbor and aboard ship for Virginia. The cost of returning him came to about $100,000, making him the most expensive slave in the country. Similar incidents throughout the North kept the issue alive and exacerbated sectional tensions.

Dissension among the Whigs

The national parties had long been a powerful force in holding the Union together. Both the Whigs and Democrats endorsed the compromise at their conventions in 1852.

242 Slavery and the Constitution

But the Whigs deadlocked when the time came to nominate a presidential candidate. The two leading contenders were Fillmore and Webster, but both were unacceptable to the antislavery Whigs led by Seward. Because Fillmore and Webster split the moderate vote, neither could be nominated. The convention deadlocked for over fifty ballots before finally nominating General Winfield Scott as a compromise candidate. The outcome infuriated southern Whigs. An incumbent president and a distinguished statesman had been denied the nomination by radicals because of their support for the compromise. Nor was General Scott the kind of candidate behind whom the party could unite. Pompous in manner, he was widely regarded as Senator Seward's puppet. That perception would prove fatal to his candidacy in the South.

Southern Whigs defected by the thousands to vote for the Democratic candidate Franklin Pierce. This gave the lackluster Pierce an unexpected landslide victory. He carried all but four of the states and became the first candidate in twelve years to win a majority of the popular vote. The Whig defections in the South were not attributable to Scott's candidacy alone. The party had been falling into disrepute there even before the convention because of the antislavery extremism of Seward and other northern Whigs. Many northern Democrats also opposed slavery, but they were not as outspoken as the northern Whigs who rejected compromise on the issue. This damaged party harmony to the point where southern Whigs began to question whether they belonged in a party with leaders like Seward. The sharp decline of the southern Whig vote in 1852 signaled that the breakup of the party had begun.

The disruption of the Whigs coincided with the unraveling of the Compromise of 1850. The sectional confrontation over slavery returned with a vengeance in 1854 when Congress took up the Kansas-Nebraska Bill. The Bill was the product of convoluted political arrangements made to clear the way for a transcontinental railroad linking California with the East. While the project had broad public support, there was sharp disagreement as to where it should be built. Geography favored a southern route between San Diego and New Orleans, but northern interests vigorously promoted a railroad linking San Francisco and Chicago. Proponents of the northern route had to overcome formidable political obstacles. The route ran through Nebraska, an unorganized territory inhabited mainly by Native Americans, from which slavery had been excluded by the Missouri Compromise. Building a great railroad through Nebraska would not be possible until a territorial government was established. Senator A. C. Dodge of Iowa, a backer of the northern route, introduced a bill to set up a territorial government. The bill was referred to the Senate Committee on Territories headed by Stephen A. Douglas of Illinois. Douglas's management of the proposal unleashed the furies that the Compromise of 1850 had temporarily held in check.

Kansas-Nebraska Act

Douglas, who strongly supported the northern route, knew that a political price would have to be paid to obtain it. The South would hardly agree to the organization of Nebraska as a free territory and thus set the stage for a northern railroad to the Pacific. In order to win southern support, he agreed to repeal the Missouri Compromise prohibition against slavery in the territory so that the status of slavery could be decided by the actual settlers in accordance with the principle of popular sovereignty. With the support of President Pierce, Douglas introduced his fateful Kansas-Nebraska Bill in place of the Dodge proposal. Besides opening Nebraska to slavery, it divided the territory into two parts, with the implicit understanding that the northern part, Nebraska, would become a free state, and the southern part, Kansas, a slave state.

Southerners supported the measure enthusiastically because it removed the last federal prohibition against slavery in the territories. But the North was outraged. To opponents of slavery, Douglas had betrayed a solemn pledge between the sections in opening up for slavery a territory from which the institution had long been excluded. The debate revived all the sectional animosity that the Compromise of 1850 had sought to lay to rest. Once raised, the issue again poisoned political life, and this time there would be no antidote. The South supported Douglas's bill as a matter of southern honor and constitutional rights; the North opposed it as an attempt to impose slavery on all the territories. Even with strong support from the administration, Douglas had difficulty getting the bill through Congress. Its final passage was a personal triumph, but with consequences disastrous both for Douglas and the nation.

Douglas's critics charged that he backed repeal of the Missouri Compromise to promote his presidential ambitions in the South. Douglas had been a contender for the Democratic nomination in 1852 and clearly wanted to be president. If winning southern support had been his goal, he succeeded completely. Passage of the Kansas-Nebraska Act made him widely popular in the South and improved his presidential prospects. Douglas defended the Act in the North as consistent with the Compromise of 1850. If popular sovereignty was acceptable for Utah and the New Mexico Territory, why not apply it in all the territories? Logically, he was right, but logic is not everything. Though a brilliant politician, Douglas was morally obtuse in failing to grasp what the debate was really about. It was not about slavery in the territories but about the morality of slavery as an institution. His failure to grasp what should have been obvious would cost the nation dearly.

The Kansas-Nebraska Act completed the destruction of the Whigs as a national political party. Already weakened by southern defections, the party now fell apart completely. Every northern Whig in Congress voted against the Act, and all but seven of the southern Whigs voted for it. The Whigs thereafter disintegrated into sectional coalitions. The Democrats also suffered losses as thousands of antislavery northerners left the party in protest. But Democratic losses in the North were offset by gains in the South as former Whigs joined the party in droves. The political realignment tilted the balance of party power southward and increased the influence of southerners in party councils. The Democrats remained a national party, but the tilt southward gave them less leeway on the slavery issue than before.

Emergence of the Modern Republican Party

The northern Whigs allied themselves with antislavery Democrats and Free-Soilers opposed to the Kansas-Nebraska Act, a coalition that evolved a year later into the modern Republican Party. The new party went considerably beyond opposition to the

Kansas-Nebraska Act. The Republican platform called for the prohibition of slavery in the territories, repeal of the Fugitive Slave Law, and abolition of slavery in the District of Columbia. The Republicans could afford to take strong antislavery stands because they were exclusively a northern party. With no southern wing to accommodate, they could appeal solely to northern concerns and interests. Unlike the Whigs, whose broader base had helped to hold the country together, they became a divisive force in national political life. The Republicans were originally stronger in the Northwest than in the East, but by the end of 1854 their organization had spread throughout the North. The party attracted both moderate and radical opponents of slavery, and its leaders had varied political backgrounds. Senator Charles Sumner, an antislavery Democrat, had helped organize the Free-Soil party, and Senator Seward had been an antislavery Whig for over a decade. The Republicans were joined by antislavery radicals like Salmon P. Chase and George Julian, and by conservatives like Edward Bates and Orville Browning. But wherever they stood on the Republican spectrum, all Republicans were anathema in the South.

Civil War in Kansas

Events in Kansas intensified the polarization of political life. Proslavery and antislavery forces poured into the territory determined to take control. Hostilities broke out, and Kansas was soon plunged into civil war. By the time federal troops moved in and restored order, the fighting had claimed over two hundred lives. The bloodshed put Democrats on the defensive. Although popular sovereignty had not worked, they could not disown it without antagonizing the South and admitting that their Nebraska policy had been a mistake. In 1856 the party convention endorsed popular sovereignty as "the only sound and safe solution of the slavery question," but the convention refused to nominate anyone connected with the situation in Kansas. This eliminated Douglas, who had sponsored the Kansas-Nebraska Act, as well as President Pierce, who had supported and signed it into law. The nomination went instead to James Buchanan, who had been ambassador to Great Britain during the period and therefore could not be blamed for the disorders in Kansas.

So vulnerable were the Democrats that the Republicans might have won in their first bid for national power had they united behind a strong candidate. An ideal candidate would have been Charles Francis Adams, whose political credentials were impeccable. The son of one president and grandson of another, Adams would have reassured northern conservatives that the Republicans could be trusted to govern responsibly. But instead the party nominated John C. Fremont, a former army officer and western explorer with a popular following but little political experience. The Republican platform denounced popular sovereignty as a failure and called for the admission of Kansas to the Union as a free state. Fremont ran a strictly northern campaign and offered no concessions to the South. Southerners reacted by threatening secession if the Republicans won the election. Concern for the Union and doubts about Fremont split the North and gave the election to Buchanan.

The results made it clear that the Republicans were strictly a sectional party. They carried eleven northern states but not a single slave state. Though still a national party, the Democrats emerged from the election more polarized than before. They carried nineteen states, but only five of them were free states. With their northern base weakened, the

Democrats tilted sharply southward. The complete sectionalization of one party and the growing sectionalization of the other put the Union in mortal peril. The national party system that had so long held the country together by compromise and accommodation was now a thing of the past. The polarization of the parties turned a system that had once promoted compromise and cohesion into a force for alienation and conflict.

Slavery and the Supreme Court

The slavery issue was fought out in the courts as well as in the political arena. In 1841 the Supreme Court delivered a sharp blow to the overseas slave trade in *United States v. The Schooner Amistad*. The *Amistad* was a Spanish slave ship which had sailed from Havana in 1839 with fifty-three African slaves bound for another Cuban port. The slaves mutinied, killing the captain and most of the crew. They spared only two whites to navigate and take the ship to Africa. The whites instead steered an erratic northern course until intercepted by a United States warship off Long Island. The *Amistad* was boarded and taken to Connecticut where the slaves were charged with murder and piracy.

The prisoners had reason to fear that they would be summarily surrendered to Spain. A treaty between Spain and the United States provided for the return of ships and merchandise seized on the high seas by robbers or pirates. The Van Buren administration hoped to end the affair quickly before it caused domestic political complications. The administration took the position that the Africans were admitted mutineers and murderers. But opponents of slavery in Connecticut insisted that the prisoners should not be surrendered to Spain without a judicial hearing. They engaged legal counsel to defend them and published newspaper accounts of their enslavement in Africa by slave traders. The publicity made it impossible for the administration to surrender them without a court order.

Expecting a favorable decision, the government made preparations for turning the captives over to Spain. A naval schooner was sent to take them on board as soon as the federal

---

Making the Case for the *Amistad* Africans

"This case is not only one of deep interest in itself, as affecting the destiny of the unfortunate Africans, whom I represent, but it involves considerations deeply affecting our national character in the eyes of the whole civilized world, as well as questions of power on the part of the government of the United States, which are regarded with anxiety and alarm by a large portion of our citizens. It presents, for the first time, the question whether the government, which was established for the promotion of JUSTICE, which was founded on the great principle of the Revolution, as proclaimed in the Declaration of Independence, can, consistently with the genius of our institutions, become a party to proceedings for the enslavement of human beings cast upon our shores, and found in the condition of freemen within the territorial limits of a FREE AND SOVEREIGN STATE?"

—Roger Sherman Baldwin, co-counsel for the *Amistad* Africans, *United States v. Libellants and Claimants of the Schooner Amistad* (1841)

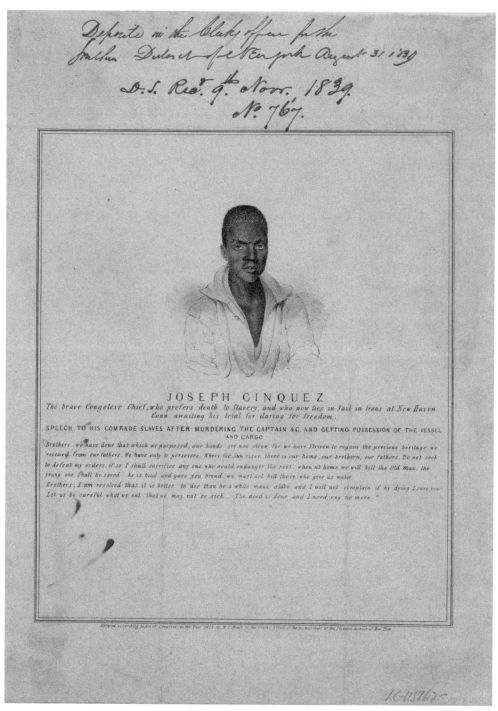

Figure IX.6 Portrait of Joseph Cinquez by Moses Yale Beach (1839). Cinquez led the mutiny against the captain and crew of the slaving vessel *Amistad* as the ship made its voyage to Cuba. Quoted beneath the portrait are the words Cinquez reportedly spoke to his fellow captives aboard the ship: "Brothers, we have done that which we purposed, our hands are now clean for we have Striven to regain the precious heritage we received from our fathers . . . I am resolved it is better to die than to be a white man's slave . . ."

Library of Congress, Prints and Photographs Division, LC-DIG-ppmsca-31280

district court in Connecticut ruled on the case. The treaty with Spain covered the case and seemingly mandated their surrender. But counsel for the Africans cleverly argued that since the slave trade was illegal under both American and Spanish law, they could not be "merchandise" within the terms of the treaty. Moreover, regardless of their status under Spanish law, they became free under state law the moment they landed in Connecticut. The court surprised the administration by freeing the Africans on the ground that they had been unlawfully kidnapped in Africa. The decision put the government in the embarrassing position of having to bring an appeal.

John Quincy Adams appeared as counsel for the Africans when the appeal was argued before the Supreme Court. The former president no longer engaged in private legal practice, but his opposition to slavery made it impossible for him to refuse the call. He covered the technical legal issues with great skill but relied principally on moral arguments to win the case. He argued that people have a natural right to defend their freedom and that what the prisoners had done could not be equated with piracy or murder. The argument that prevailed in the end, however, was the technical one on the "merchandise" issue. Justice Story held that the captives could not be merchandise, because the slave trade was illegal. If they were not merchandise, they were free and not subject to the terms of the treaty with Spain. Story said nothing about the applicability of Connecticut law or the natural law theory argued by Adams. But in any case, the Africans had won, and opponents of slavery were jubilant with the outcome. Only Justice Baldwin dissented from the decision.

Slavery and State Police Powers

Some of the domestic issues relating to slavery were more complicated than the slave trade issues. In *Groves v. Slaughter* (1841), the Court had to rule on a provision in the Mississippi state constitution prohibiting the importation of slaves for sale within the state. The importation of slaves had drained money from the state, and the prohibition sought to prevent the loss of more liquid capital. But imported slaves continued to be sold anyhow on credit extended by lenders in other states. Some borrowers refused to pay when the notes came due. They contended that the ban on imports made the transactions unlawful and the notes uncollectible. The resulting litigation attracted nationwide attention, partly because the sums involved were large, but also because Daniel Webster and Henry Clay represented the creditors. Seldom had so much legal talent and political power been brought to bear in a private litigation.

The case raised two issues. The first was whether the prohibition of slave imports invalidated the notes issued to pay for the imports. The second was whether the prohibition interfered with the constitutional power of Congress over interstate commerce. If the prohibition did not invalidate the notes, the Court would not have to rule on the constitutional issue. Such an outcome would be preferable to one that forced the Court to choose between upholding the commerce power of Congress or else subordinating it to the right of the states to exclude slaves. This was precisely how the Court attempted to dispose of the case. In a majority opinion delivered by Justice Thompson, but probably written by Chief Justice Taney, the validity of the notes was upheld on the ground that Mississippi law did not prohibit payment.

This would have ended the case had not Justice McLean surprised everyone by reading an opinion of his own from the bench. He conceded that the constitutional issue did not have to be decided, but declared it to be so important that he was compelled to give an opinion. He then delivered a highly political defense of the right of the states to exclude slaves. McLean, an opponent of slavery, contended that the right to exclude slaves was

> higher and deeper than the Constitution. The evil involves the prosperity and may endanger the existence of a State. Its power to guard against, or to remedy the evil, rests upon the law of self-preservation; a law vital to every community, and especially to a sovereign State.

Whether McLean's motives were idealistic or opportunistic cannot be determined, but probably they were a mixture of both. He was too ardent an opponent of slavery not to speak out on the issue, and too much the politician not to make the most of the opportunity to promote his presidential ambitions in the North.

Since McLean had politicized the case by referring to slavery as an evil, the other justices felt compelled to speak out on the issue. To say nothing might be taken for tacit agreement. While Taney agreed with McLean that the states could exclude slaves, he carefully avoided giving offense to the South. He said,

> The power over this subject is exclusively with the several states; and each of them has the right to decide for itself whether it will or will not allow persons of this description to be brought within its borders, from another State, either for sale, or for any other purpose.

Justice Baldwin sharply disagreed. He contended that slaves were property and that Congress had a duty under the Fifth Amendment to protect all property "from any state law which affects to prohibit its transmission for sale from one State to another." It therefore logically followed that the Amendment also prevented Congress from interfering in the interstate shipment of slaves. Justices Story and McKinley further complicated matters with dissenting opinions that the Mississippi prohibition was not only constitutional but barred the creditors from enforcing the notes.

Fugitive Slaves and Due Process of Law

No aspect of the slavery issue was more controversial than the capture and return of runaway slaves. Article IV of the Constitution provided that persons who fled from bondage across state lines "shall be delivered up on Claim of the Party to whom such Service or Labour may be due." In 1793 Congress gave effect to this provision by passing a fugitive slave law establishing federal procedures for the return of runaways. The law caused no controversy at the time because slavery had not yet emerged as a serious sectional issue. But by the 1820s both slavery and the law came under attack in the North. Northerners complained that the federal procedures for the return of runaways did not adequately protect free blacks in the North against unjust enslavement. The process was stacked outrageously against alleged runaways in fugitive slave proceedings. Federal judges had authority to issue certificates of return on the oath of the owner or his agent that the person claimed was a fugitive. The mere word of the claimant was enough to consign any African American to bondage.

The shortcomings of the federal process led northern states to pass so-called personal liberty laws. These laws made it a crime for claimants to remove alleged runaways without first obtaining an order of removal from a state court. The state court proceedings for obtaining the order were as heavily stacked against slaveholders as the federal proceedings were stacked in their favor. Some state judges refused to issue orders of removal regardless of the evidence. New York gave alleged runaways the right to a jury trial, and juries almost always brought in verdicts against the claimant. Despite their rights under federal law, slaveholders found it virtually impossible to recover their runaways through state court proceedings. But failure to comply with the state procedures could result in heavy fines and prison terms.

Prigg v. Pennsylvania

The constitutionality of the personal liberty laws was challenged in *Prigg v. Pennsylvania* (1842). Edward Prigg, a slave-catcher employed by a Maryland slaveholder, had been convicted by Pennsylvania for removing a runaway from the state without first obtaining a warrant from a state judge. When the Pennsylvania Supreme Court upheld his conviction, he appealed to the United States Supreme Court on the ground that Congress had exclusive jurisdiction over the return of fugitive slaves and that Pennsylvania therefore could not interfere in the matter. The Act of 1793 clearly preempted the subject as an area of federal jurisdiction. Pennsylvania's personal liberty law prescribed procedures different from the federal ones and was therefore unconstitutional.

The Court struck down the Pennsylvania law and overturned Prigg's conviction. Speaking for the majority, Justice Story held that the Fugitive Slave Law of 1793 preempted the subject as an area of federal jurisdiction and precluded state action. Even if Congress had not passed the 1793 Act, Article IV of the Constitution gave the federal government exclusive jurisdiction over runaway slaves. Story noted that before the Constitution was adopted, "no State had any power whatsoever over the subject, except within its own territorial limits, and could not bind the sovereignty or the legislation of other States." The holding invalidated not only the Pennsylvania law but also the personal liberty laws of every northern state. The federal procedures that favored slaveholders were now the only procedures applicable in the recovery of runaways.

But what Story gave to slaveholders with one hand, he took away from them with the other. He went on to say that because federal jurisdiction was exclusive, the states had no obligation to act at all, particularly with respect to the enforcement of federal laws on the subject. "The states cannot, therefore, be compelled to enforce them," he wrote,

> and it might well be deemed an unconstitutional exercise of the power of interpretation, to insist that the States are bound to provide means to carry into effect the

Justice Story on the Fugitive Slave Act

"The slave is to be delivered up on the claim. By whom to be delivered up? In what mode to be delivered up? How, if a refusal takes place, is the right of delivery to be enforced? Upon what proofs? What shall be the evidence of a rightful recaption or delivery? When and under what circumstances shall the possession of the owner, after it is obtained, be conclusive of his right[?] . . . These and many other questions will readily occur upon the slightest attention to the clause; and it is obvious that they can receive but one satisfactory answer. They require the aid of legislation to protect the right, to enforce the delivery, and to secure the subsequent possession of the slave. If, indeed, the Constitution guaranties the right, and if it requires the delivery upon the claim of the owner (as cannot well be doubted), the natural inference certainly is that the National Government is clothed with the appropriate authority and functions to enforce it. The fundamental principle, applicable to all cases of this sort, would seem to be that, where the end is required, the means are given; and where the duty is enjoined, the ability to perform it is contemplated to exist on the part of the functionaries to whom it is entrusted."

—Prigg v. Pennsylvania (1842)

duties of the national government, nowhere delegated or intrusted to them by the Constitution.

Story's invitation to noncompliance could not have been more explicit. He showed the states how to prevent the return of fugitive slaves without prohibitory legislation. The recovery of runaways could be made virtually impossible simply by not providing local police assistance. Without such assistance, slaveholders ran serious risks if they pursued runaways into the North.

Taney agreed with Story that the Pennsylvania law was unconstitutional, but he sharply disagreed that the states had no obligation to assist in the return of fugitives. Article IV expressly stated that runaways should be "delivered up" by the states to which they had fled, and this clearly imposed an obligation to cooperate in their recovery. "The language used in the constitution does not, in my judgment, justify the construction given to it by the court. It contains no words prohibiting the several states from passing laws to enforce this right." Only laws interfering with the right of recovery were unconstitutional. Taney contended that slaveholders were entitled to the same assistance in recovering runaway slaves as the owners of other property.

> I dissent therefore, upon these grounds, from that part of the opinion of the court which denies the obligation and right of the state authorities to protect the master . . . in pursuance of the right given to him by the Constitution of the United States.

Justice McLean wrote a highly political dissent upholding the constitutionality of the Pennsylvania law. He contended that it was a legitimate exercise of the state's police powers to regulate the way people were seized and removed from its jurisdiction. The law did not impair the claims of slaveholders but only sought to certify their authenticity. McLean noted that under Pennsylvania law every person was presumed to be free. This gave the state a legitimate interest in ascertaining the legal status of any person whose freedom was challenged. If in some cases the presumption of freedom turned out to be erroneous, he asked, "may not the assertion of the master be erroneous also; and if so, how is his act of force to be remedied?" Requiring the alleged owner to prove his claim before removal was the only way to protect the rights of the person claimed.

The opinions in *Prigg* accurately reflect how the justices personally stood on slavery. McLean detested the institution and never missed an opportunity to make his views known. Taney came from a slave state, and while not an apologist for slavery, he obviously found it acceptable. Their opinions were predictable, but Story's opinion came as a complete surprise. That so staunch a supporter of federal power would construe the Constitution in a way that permitted the states to withhold assistance in areas of federal jurisdiction could not have been anticipated. It seems highly unlikely that Story would have written such an opinion if slavery had not been the issue. Slavery had become the sort of issue that forced people, even great judges, into making moral choices. If the choice was sometimes bad law, it was because the moral aspect of the issue was so compelling.

The Dred Scott Case

The most important holding of the Court on slavery finally came in *Dred Scott v. Sandford* in 1857. The case involved the legal status of a Missouri slave named Dred Scott, whose owner, Dr. John Emerson, took him to Illinois, where slavery was prohibited by state law, and later to Wisconsin, where it was prohibited by the Missouri Compromise. When Emerson died after their return to Missouri, Scott sued Emerson's widow for his freedom. He contended that his residence in free territory made him a free man. The suit was brought in the state courts, and Scott won the first round when the trial court ruled in his favor. But the decision was reversed on appeal when the state supreme court ruled that under Missouri law he remained a slave.

What happened next is far from clear, except that Mrs. Emerson married Dr. Calvin Chaffee, a member of Congress from Massachusetts and a staunch opponent of slavery. Ownership of Scott was transferred to Mrs. Chaffee's brother, John Sanford (whose name is misspelled in the official reports), a resident of New York City. While there is no hard evidence, some commentators have suggested that the purpose of the transfer was to enable Scott to sue Sanford for his freedom in the federal courts. The transfer created the diversity of citizenship between the parties needed for the federal courts to take jurisdiction. But the collusion theory seems contradicted by the facts of the case. Scott had difficulty obtaining counsel for his Supreme Court appeal, and he sued Sanford for $9,000 in damages, a considerable sum not likely to be sought in a collusive action. Not that it matters in terms of its consequences, but the most disastrous case in the history of the federal courts appears at least to have been a real one.

Scott's suit raised two questions. Was he a citizen of Missouri with standing to sue in the federal courts, and did his residence in free territory make him a free man? The federal circuit court for Missouri ruled that he had standing to sue, but that under Missouri law he was still a slave. Scott then appealed to the United States Supreme Court and reiterated his claim that his residence in territory where slavery was prohibited by the Missouri Compromise altered his legal status as a slave. Partisans on both sides of the issue thought that the case would resolve once and for all whether Congress could constitutionally prohibit slavery in the territories. President Buchanan referred to the pending decision in his inaugural address and expressed confidence in the wisdom of the justices. "To their decision, in common with all good citizens, I shall cheerfully submit, whatever this may be."

Buchanan's willingness to accept any outcome certainly was not shared by most of the country. There was no chance that partisans on either side would "cheerfully submit" to a decision that went totally against them. The nation was too polarized by a decade of debate over the issue for a clear-cut judicial resolution to be acceptable to the losers. The prudent course would have been for the Court to avoid a constitutional ruling and leave the door open for political negotiation and compromise. In the earlier case of *Strader v. Graham* (1851) the Court had held that slave status depended on the law of the state of domicile. The *Strader* precedent could have disposed of the case without a ruling on the constitutionality of the Missouri Compromise. Scott was domiciled in Missouri, and under Missouri law he was a slave. Nothing more had to be decided.

A majority of the Court originally favored this prudent course. Even the five southern justices recognized the pitfalls of ruling on the power of Congress to prohibit slavery in the territories. The task of writing the Court's opinion was assigned to Justice Nelson, who favored a narrow decision based on *Strader*. But pressure both within and outside the Court steadily mounted for a broad decision covering all the issues. Southern political leaders urged the southern justices to rule once and for all that Congress could not exclude slavery from the national territories. Finally, on the motion of Justice Wayne, the Court

Figure IX.7 Portrait of Dred Scott by Louis Schultze (c. 1881). A group of African Americans commissioned Schultze to paint this portrait from the only known photograph of Scott. They presented it to the Missouri Historical Society in 1882.

Missouri History Museum, St. Louis

shifted gears, and the majority agreed that Chief Justice Taney should write an opinion dealing with all the issues raised by the case.

Why the Court threw caution to the wind has been argued as heatedly as the decision itself. Some commentators think that the consensus for moderation broke down when Justices Curtis and McLean announced that they would write opinions upholding the Missouri Compromise even if the rest of the Court did not take up the issue. This was the explanation given by Justices Catron and Grier for their change of heart. Not to take issue with Curtis and McLean might be mistaken as acceptance of their views. Although plausible, the Catron-Grier account of what happened was clearly self-serving. It was their defection that gave the southern justices more than a sectional majority, and both came under heavy pressure to justify their actions. Since they must have known from the outset where Curtis and McLean stood, their explanation has a hollow ring. What Curtis and McLean did really made no difference. They were a minority of two, and their dissents would have soon been forgotten.

Although Taney wrote the majority opinion, all the justices wrote concurring or dissenting opinions of their own. The profusion of opinions on the different issues made it difficult to ascertain what had actually been decided. Taney, along with Wayne and Daniel, held that Dred Scott was not a citizen of the United States. They argued that African Americans had not been citizens of their respective states when the Constitution was adopted, so it logically followed that the federal citizenship created by that document had been intended only for whites. Taney also held, and six other justices agreed, that Scott was not a citizen of Missouri and therefore lacked standing to sue in the federal courts. This should have ended the case, because if the Court lacked jurisdiction, nothing more

Citizen or Slave?

"The question before us is, whether the class of persons described in the plea in abatement compose a portion of this people, and are constituent members of this sovereignty? We think they are not, and that they are not included, and were not intended to be included, under the word "citizens" in the Constitution, and can therefore claim none of the rights and privileges which that instrument provides for and secures to citizens of the United States. On the contrary, they were at that time considered as a subordinate and inferior class of beings, who had been subjugated by the dominant race, and, whether emancipated or not, yet remained subject to their authority, and had no rights or privileges but such as those who held the power and the Government might choose to grant them . . . It is not the province of the court to decide upon the justice or injustice, the policy or impolicy, of these laws. The decision of that question belonged to the political or lawmaking power, to those who formed the sovereignty and framed the Constitution. The duty of the court is to interpret the instrument they have framed with the best lights we can obtain on the subject, and to administer it as we find it, according to its true intent and meaning when it was adopted."

—Chief Justice Roger Taney, *Dred Scott v. Sandford* (1857)

had to be decided. But Taney went on to rule that Scott's slave status did not change while he was in Wisconsin, because the Missouri Compromise prohibiting slavery there was unconstitutional. Congress had no power to prohibit slavery in the territories, because property in slaves was protected by the Fifth Amendment. Since five of the justices concurred, the Court stood six to three in holding the Missouri Compromise unconstitutional with respect to its slavery provisions. Only Justice Nelson stuck to his original decision to rule against Scott on the *Strader* precedent without taking up the explosive constitutional issues.

Not since *Marbury v. Madison* (1803) had the Court invalidated an act of Congress, so the decision hit the country like a bombshell. It infuriated the North and united all shades of antislavery opinion in common opposition. The decision, if fully implemented, might turn all the national territories into slave territories and ultimately into slave states. Critics pointed out that the constitutional holding on the Missouri Compromise was unnecessary. The Court could have ruled against Scott on the ground that Missouri law governed the case and that under Missouri law he was still a slave. This would have left the constitutional issues undecided and kept the door open for some sort of political compromise on the status of slavery in the territories. Slamming the door on compromise caused many to suspect a proslavery conspiracy.

Curtis and McLean wrote blistering dissents. They noted that many African Americans had state citizenship in the North when the Constitution was adopted, and that Taney's claim to the contrary was just bad history. They also upheld the Missouri Compromise and the authority of Congress to prohibit slavery in the national territories. The Constitution gave Congress complete power over the territories, including power to restrict or prohibit slavery. Moreover, the Court had no reason to rule on the constitutional issues. Whether Scott had standing to sue in the federal courts was all that had to be decided. Everything else was dicta and therefore not binding as judicial precedent. Nothing in the decision diminished in any way the power of Congress over the territories.

Both dissents were immediately put to political use. McLean, who hoped the Republicans would nominate him for president in 1860, told a northern newspaper editor how he would vote before the case was even argued. His dissent was published the day after the decision, well before the majority opinion was released to the press. Curtis gave a reporter a copy of his dissent immediately after reading it from the bench. Its publication before the majority opinion was released led to a bitter public dispute with Taney. Curtis accused Taney of altering the majority opinion in order to deal with points raised in his dissent. Taney denied any impropriety, but Curtis persisted in the charge. He compiled a list of eighteen pages of alleged differences between the opinion read from the bench and the version finally released for publication. The exchange was a sad footnote to a case that left the Court tarnished and in disarray.

Critics of the decision accused President Buchanan, who owed his election to the South, of collusion with the southern justices in opening the territories to slavery. Buchanan had pledged to support any decision in his inaugural address, but we now know that he had advance knowledge of what the decision would be. Justices Catron and Grier breached judicial ethics by informing him of the Court's intentions. So when he promised that he would "cheerfully submit" to the outcome, it is reasonable to assume that he was already smiling. The case was shot through with politics from beginning to end. The Court held off making a decision during its 1855–56 term in order not to influence the outcome of the presidential election. The delay, critics charged, had been intended to help the Democrats. If the decision had come down earlier, the backlash in the North might have given the election to the Republicans.

Republican leaders attacked the decision with partisan fervor. Some fell back on the old Jeffersonian-Jacksonian theory that constitutional interpretations of the Supreme Court do not bind the president and Congress. Nothing prevented Congress from ignoring the decision and banning slavery in the territories according to its own understanding of the Constitution. Some leaders, like Abraham Lincoln, pragmatically reasoned that what one court had done another could undo. Lincoln noted that the Court "has often overruled its own decisions, and we shall do what we can to have it overrule this." Others argued that since the constitutional holding was not essential to the decision, it was not binding under *stare decisis* in subsequent cases. Abolitionists drew renewed fervor from the decision. If an appeal could not be made to the Supreme Court, some argued, it would have to be made to God himself. In a speech to the American Anti-Slavery Society Frederick Douglass declaimed,

> The sun in the sky is not more palpable to the sight than man's right to liberty is to the moral vision. To decide against this right in the person of Dred Scott, or the humblest and most whip-scarred bondman in the land, is to decide against God. It is an open rebellion against God's government.

Whatever they thought of the decision, Republicans could not accept it without cutting the ground from under themselves as a political party.

The decision was praised in the South with the same partisan fervor that damned it in the North. Southern constitutional rights had been upheld, and the territories had been opened to slavery. Perhaps the worst effect of the decision was that it silenced southern moderates who had previously been a force for compromise. The proslavery extremists had been vindicated and moderates discredited. An issue previously open to political settlement had been transformed by judicial alchemy into a matter of southern constitutional rights. The South no longer had any reason to compromise on what the Constitution guaranteed. The decision set the stage for the final act of an unfolding national tragedy.

Ableman v. Booth

The Supreme Court dealt with slavery for the last time before the Civil War in *Ableman v. Booth* (1859). Although the case really had more to do with federal judicial authority than with slavery, critics of the *Dred Scott* decision cited it as another proof of the Court's proslavery bias. The case began with the arrest of a Wisconsin newspaper editor named Sherman Booth for assisting a runaway slave in violation of the federal fugitive slave law. Booth obtained a writ of habeas corpus from a state judge ordering his release from federal detention. The order was upheld by the state supreme court on the ground that the Fugitive

Slave Act of 1850 was unconstitutional. Ableman, the federal district marshal, appealed the order to the United States Supreme Court. In the meantime, Booth was convicted in the federal district court of Wisconsin and sentenced to prison. The state supreme court again ordered his release, and Ableman again appealed its order to the United States Supreme Court. Both appeals were combined and heard together.

Taney spoke for a unanimous Court in declaring the orders of the Wisconsin state courts unconstitutional. "No State judge or Court," he wrote, "after they are judicially informed that the party is imprisoned under the authority of the United States, has any right to interfere with him, or to require that he be brought before them." The Wisconsin supreme court had no more right to interfere "than it would have had if the prisoner had been confined in Michigan, or in any other State of the Union." Once the federal courts took jurisdiction, it was as though the case had been removed from the territory of the state. Even if the federal law was unconstitutional, the state courts could not intervene. The issue could be raised only in the federal courts.

Taney's opinion in *Ableman* was the most forceful assertion of federal judicial supremacy since *Cohens v. Virginia* (1821). The latter had brought down on the Court a storm of criticism in the South. *Ableman* had the same effect in the North. Opponents of slavery regarded it as another victory for the slave power. The Wisconsin legislature denounced it in resolutions upholding state sovereignty and the jurisdiction of Wisconsin's courts within the state's borders. Booth's supporters forcibly freed him and protected him from government agents. There were demands in Congress to rescind the Court's jurisdiction in slavery cases. The southern majority could not be trusted to deal fairly with such issues. The slavery question had not only polarized the country politically but turned nationalists into opponents of federal power. Those who had once defended federal judicial supremacy now became its most scathing critics. By 1860 the slavery issue had poisoned the wellsprings of national life, contaminating and discrediting all three branches of government.

The political storm dealt a sharp blow to the presidential ambitions of Stephen A. Douglas. The Dred Scott decision could not be reconciled with popular sovereignty, which was as far as Douglas and other northern Democrats dared go in accommodating the South. But if the Constitution protected slaveholding in the territories, slavery could not be prohibited by the settlers any more than by Congress. Douglas had staked his political future on the notion that popular sovereignty would be acceptable enough to northern and southern moderates to put him in the White House. But the Dred Scott decision changed the political arithmetic by undercutting the southern moderates. Having won the constitutional argument, the South now demanded not only toleration but full protection for slavery in the territories. This was more than Douglas and the northern Democrats could deliver without jeopardizing their political base in the North. The insistence of the South on what was politically impossible set in motion the disruption of the Democrats as a national political party.

The party split began in 1857 when a proslavery convention in Kansas drafted a constitution at Lecompton under which the territory would apply for admission to the Union as a state. The constitution gave the people of Kansas no real choice on whether slavery should be prohibited. They could vote only on whether the future importation of slaves should be prohibited, not on whether the institution should be banned completely.

A provision protecting the ownership of slaves already in the territory would go into effect automatically without being put to a vote. Refusing to play with a stacked deck, the antislavery forces boycotted the referendum. With only the proslavery settlers voting, the constitution was adopted in a form fully legalizing slavery. The proslavery legislature then applied to Congress for the admission of Kansas to the Union as a slave state.

The machinations of the slave power in Kansas caused a furor in the North. The backlash made President Buchanan waver before taking a position. The president finally gave in under southern pressure and supported the application for statehood. But Douglas broke ranks in the Senate and denounced the Lecompton constitution as a travesty of popular sovereignty and a fraud on the people of Kansas. His stand disappointed the South and embarrassed the administration. When the statehood application failed to pass, many of his southern supporters turned into bitter political enemies.

If Douglas hoped to win the presidency in 1860, he would have to mend his political fences in the South while keeping his northern base intact. Concern for northern public opinion had been a factor in his fight against the Lecompton constitution. Douglas had to walk a tightrope in balancing sectional interests or his national following would unravel. This would be no easy task, particularly because he had to run for reelection to the Senate in 1858 and take positions on risky issues. Even in winning, he might be forced into positions harmful to his presidential prospects two years later. The candidate chosen by Illinois Republicans to oppose Douglas was Abraham Lincoln.

Lincoln-Douglas Debates

Although long prominent in state politics, Lincoln was hardly known outside Illinois. The campaign against Douglas changed that and won him a national following. Because Douglas would likely be nominated for president in 1860, correspondents from all the major newspapers covered the campaign and gave both candidates national exposure. The campaign included a series of debates which gave the candidates an opportunity to discuss slavery and how they differed on the issue. Lincoln made a fine showing against his articulate and astute opponent. Avoiding radical antislavery positions, he still condemned the institution as "a moral, a social, and a political wrong." Douglas, knowing that he needed the South to be president, had to be more circumspect. He refused to take a stand against slavery, arguing that it was a local issue to be settled by the local inhabitants. Lincoln, who had only northern opinion to consider, won the high ground by default.

Lincoln inflicted heavy damage on Douglas at their famous Freeport debate. He asked Douglas whether the settlers in a territory could lawfully prohibit slavery. If Douglas answered yes, he would affirm his support of popular sovereignty but not of the Dred Scott decision, which held that the Constitution protected slavery in the national territories. If he answered no, he would endorse the decision but abandon popular sovereignty. An affirmative answer would ruin him in the South, and a negative answer would ruin him in the North. Douglas tried to come down on both sides with a compromise answer known as the Freeport Doctrine. He responded that the Dred Scott decision, which he accepted, made it unlawful for settlers in a territory to exclude slavery by proscriptive legislation. But they could still keep it out by denying it police protection. He declared that this would be as effective as outright prohibition, "for the reason that slavery cannot exist a day or an hour anywhere, unless it is supported by local police regulation." No slaveholder in his right mind would bring slaves into territory where the local police power would not protect him.

The Freeport Doctrine helped Douglas defeat Lincoln in Illinois, but it shattered what remained of his southern political base. The South demanded unequivocal support for the Dred Scott decision, and Douglas had not provided it. Douglas tried to reconcile the decision with de facto popular sovereignty, which was really the most any northern politician could offer. But it was not enough for the South. The southern reaction dealt a blow to Douglas's presidential chances and damaged party unity. If southern Democrats made demands that northern Democrats could not meet, the party's days as a national political organization were numbered.

Debating Liberty

"This declared indifference, but, as I must think, covert real zeal for the spread of slavery, I cannot but hate. I hate it because of the monstrous injustice of slavery itself. I hate it because it deprives our republican example of its just influence in the world—enables the enemies of free institutions, with plausibility, to taunt us as hypocrites—causes the real friends of freedom to doubt our sincerity, and especially because it forces so many really good men amongst ourselves into an open war with the very fundamental principles of civil liberty—criticizing the Declaration of Independence, and insisting that there is no right principle of action but self-interest."

—Abraham Lincoln, Debate at Ottawa, Illinois, August 21, 1858

Figure IX.8 Portrait of Abraham Lincoln (1858).

Library of Congress, Prints and Photographs Division, LC-USZ62-16377

"Mr. Lincoln, following the example and lead of all the little Abolition orators, who go around and lecture in the basements of schools and churches, reads from the Declaration of Independence, that all men were created equal, and then asks, how can you deprive a negro of that equality which God and the Declaration of Independence awards to him? . . . Now, I hold that Illinois had a right to abolish and prohibit slavery as she did, and I hold that Kentucky has the same right to continue and protect slavery that Illinois had to abolish it. I hold that New York had as much right to abolish slavery as Virginia has to continue it, and that each and every State of this Union is a sovereign power, with the right to do as it pleases upon this question of slavery, and upon all its domestic institutions . . . And why can we not adhere to the great principle of self-government, upon which our institutions were originally based."

—Stephen Douglas, Debate at Ottawa, Illinois, August 21, 1858

Figure IX.9 Portrait of Stephen Douglas (c. 1850–1852).

Library of Congress, Prints and Photographs Division, LC-USZ62-1754

The next two years were marked by sectional acrimony and political turmoil. The Republicans made rapid gains in the North, sweeping every state election except in Illinois and Indiana. Southern Democrats staked out increasingly radical positions that northern Democrats could not support. Some called for legalizing the overseas slave trade and extending federal police protection to slavery in the territories. Abolitionist John Brown's 1859 attempt to raise a slave revolt by raiding Harpers Ferry in Virginia enraged the South. Most Republicans unequivocally condemned the raid, but the affair exacerbated sectional tensions. Tempers were at a boiling point when Congress met in December, and insults were freely traded. Senator James Hammond of South Carolina reported that "every man in both Houses is armed with a revolver—some with two revolvers—and with a bowie knife." The time was drawing near when bullets would take the place of ballots.

John Brown at His Treason Trial

"Now, if it is deemed necessary that I should forfeit my life for the furtherance of the ends of justice, and mingle my blood further with the blood of my children and with the blood of millions in this slave country whose rights are disregarded by wicked, cruel, and unjust enactments,—I submit; so let it be done!"

—November 2, 1859

Figure IX.10 Portrait of John Brown (1859).

Library of Congress, Prints and Photographs Division, LC-USZ62-2472

The Democrats Divide

The Democrats were in a belligerent mood when they assembled for their national convention in 1860. Southern extremists warned of secession, and state legislatures in the Lower South authorized the raising of military forces. The southern delegates at the convention demanded a party platform calling for federal protection of slavery in the territories in accordance with the Dred Scott decision. The northern Democrats led by Douglas backed a platform calling for acceptance of all Supreme Court decisions but no federal action for or against slavery in the territories. When the Douglas forces prevailed, eight southern delegations walked out of the convention. In the presidential balloting, Douglas had a majority, but not the two-thirds majority needed for the nomination. After fifty-seven ballots the convention adjourned hopelessly deadlocked. A second convention met the following month and nominated Douglas on the second ballot. This led even more southerners to withdraw. The southern Democrats then held a convention of their own at which they adopted a platform supporting slavery in the territories and nominated Vice President John C. Breckinridge for president.

A new political coalition emerged on the heels of the Democratic split to add to the confusion. The remnants of the old Whig party merged with what remained of the American Party (an anti-Catholic, anti-immigrant movement) into the Constitutional Union party. The coalition made the preservation of the Union its single policy goal. Its strategy was to keep slavery out of the campaign so that supporters of the Union could buy time until a political settlement could be reached. The Constitutional Unionists endorsed the Constitution, enforcement of the laws, and preservation of the Union, a platform unlikely to be controversial. The party had strong support in the border states as well as the states of the Upper South where sentiment for the Union still ran strong. James Bell of Tennessee was nominated by the new party for president.

With the Democrats in disarray and the Constitutional Unionists likely to siphon off Democratic votes in the border states, the Republicans had every reason to feel confident when their convention met in May. The prospects were so good that party leaders wanted to ensure victory by nominating a moderate candidate with whom northern conservatives would feel comfortable. Senator Seward, the leading contender for the nomination and the most popular figure in the party, was not that sort of candidate. He had taken many controversial positions over the years and had numerous political enemies. His fierce opposition to slavery had also earned him a reputation for radicalism that might put off undecided voters. The party leaders opposing him blocked his nomination on the first two ballots by holding key delegations in line behind favorite-son candidates. Then, combining their forces on the third ballot, they nominated Abraham Lincoln.

The Republicans adopted a shrewd party platform. They took a moderate position on slavery, moderate at least by antislavery standards. They condemned proposals to reopen the foreign slave trade and declared that neither Congress nor territorial legislatures should legalize slavery in the national territories. This was a milder stand than calling for outright prohibition of slavery in the territories, though this is what they really had in mind. The platform also called for transportation improvements with federal assistance, including a railroad to the Pacific, and a homestead law for the distribution of federal land free to the settlers. The Republicans also endorsed tariff adjustments, by which they meant increases, to protect American industry. The tilt toward protectionism aimed at winning votes in key manufacturing states. With a "safe" candidate, an appealing platform, and a divided opposition, the Republicans were poised to sweep the North.

Election of 1860

The campaign was bitter, more like a war than an election. The South warned the North that a Republican victory would lead to secession and dissolution of the Union. Since Breckinridge and Bell lacked the broad popular base needed for an electoral victory, the election was really a contest between Lincoln and Douglas. But only Douglas had the national support needed to hold the country together. Never has the fate of the nation depended more clearly on the success of a particular candidate. Douglas was not a great man, but he was the one candidate who might have saved the Union. Lincoln, who later did save the Union, was in the 1860 election a force for its destruction. But the political arithmetic implacably favored the Republicans. Although he received less than forty percent of the popular vote, Lincoln won a decisive electoral victory over the divided opposition. But all his votes were northern votes, making the outcome a northern victory and southern defeat.

Secession and Disunion

South Carolina reacted by summoning a state convention to consider whether the situation justified secession. In states' rights theory, the convention was the ultimate source of sovereignty and political authority. The movement toward secession was abetted by the failure of the Republicans to take it seriously. They offered no assurances that southern rights and interests would be respected. Douglas, who understood the South better, knew that the threat to the Union was real. He did what Republican leaders should have done and made a hurried tour through six of the slave states in a last-ditch effort to prevent secession. He tried to convince southern leaders that the presidential election had changed nothing. The northern and southern Democrats still controlled Congress, so there was no way that Republicans could exclude slavery from the territories or even govern effectively without making compromises. Lincoln's hands would be tied unless he pursued a reasonable course. Douglas made perfect sense, but his arguments fell on deaf ears. Political reason no longer prevailed in the South. Passion and anger had taken over, and the extremists were in control. In December 1860 the South Carolina convention adopted an ordinance of secession, setting in motion the disruption of the Union.

The Crittenden Amendment

While he condemned secession, President Buchanan refused to act against South Carolina. The use of force might have driven the whole South into rebellion. The states of the Upper South had not seceded, but they threatened to do so if armed force was used against a sister state. Since he would soon leave office, Buchanan refused to take responsibility for provoking hostilities that would make things even worse. He left it to Lincoln and Congress to work out a political settlement. Senator John Crittenden of Kentucky took the lead and proposed a settlement in the form of an unamendable constitutional amendment. The amendment would restore the old Missouri Compromise line through all the national territories. Slavery would be prohibited north of latitude 36°30' and protected south of the line. This would permanently protect the interests of both sections.

Crittenden's amendment was probably the last chance for a political settlement. But Lincoln found it unacceptable, and he advised Republicans in Congress to reject it. While prepared to guarantee the rights of slaveholders in the slave states, he would make no concessions on the expansion of slavery into the territories. Keeping slavery out of the territories was a key Republican principle, and he would not split the party because the South was put out with the election returns. His refusal to compromise on the territories strengthened the hand of southern extremists. The secession of six more slave states in January 1861 put the situation beyond political settlement. The Union had been disrupted, and only force could now restore it.

Whether the tragedy about to happen might have been prevented is really a pointless question. But if an answer has to be given, it would probably be no. The causes of conflict were systemic and inseparable from the course of our national development. The inexorable march westward, particularly the last great push at the expense of Mexico, made sectional conflict inevitable. The war with Mexico brought the slavery issue into national politics and disrupted the party system that previously had held the country together. Expansion to the Pacific had been the Holy Grail of Manifest Destiny, but it turned out instead to be the poison cup of American history. The real price of the territories taken from Mexico by force would be paid on the battlefields of the Civil War. It all probably would have happened anyway, even without the push westward to the Pacific. Abolitionists had warned that the evil of slavery would eventually bring national calamity. The institution that had destroyed countless black lives had to be atoned in blood before the nation could be made whole.

Note

1. Nathaniel Appleton, *Considerations on Slavery: In a Letter to a Friend* (Boston, 1767).

December 20, 1860	February 18, 1861	March 4, 1861	March 11, 1861	April 12–13, 1861	April 19, 1861	April 27, 1861
South Carolina Leads the South into Secession	Jefferson Davis Elected President of the Confederate States of America	Abraham Lincoln Takes Office as President of the United States	Adoption of the Constitution of the Confederate States of America	Bombardment of Fort Sumter	Lincoln Proclaims a Blockade against Southern Ports	Lincoln Suspends Habeas Corpus in Maryland

July 17, 1862	July 21, 1862	September 24, 1862	December 10, 1862	January 1, 1863	March 3, 1863	March 10, 1863
Second Confiscation Act	Samuel F. Miller Becomes Associate Justice of Supreme Court	Lincoln's Proclamation Subjecting "Disloyal" Persons to Martial Law and Suspending Habeas Corpus in Such Cases	David Davis Becomes Associate Justice of Supreme Court	Emancipation Proclamation	Congress Passes Conscription Act and Habeas Corpus Suspension Act	The Prize Cases

April 14, 1865	April 15, 1865	December 18, 1865	April 3, 1866	August 20, 1866	March 6, 1871	April 3, 1871
Assassination of President Lincoln	Andrew Johnson Takes Office as President of the United States	Ratification of Thirteenth Amendment	Ex parte Milligan	President Johnson Declares the Civil War Ended	Virginia v. West Virginia	Miller v. United States

X   The Crisis of the Union

June 1, 1861	June 8, 1861	July 13, 1861	August 6, 1861	December 20, 1861	January 27, 1862	April 16, 1862
Ex parte Merryman	Tennessee Becomes Last Southern State to Secede from Union	Congress Authorizes Lincoln to Declare a State of Insurrection	Congress Retroactively Approves Lincoln's War Measures	First Meeting of Joint Committee on the Conduct of the War	Noah H. Swayne Becomes Associate Justice of Supreme Court	Abolition of Slavery in the District of Columbia

April 13, 1863	May 20, 1863	July 1–3, 1863	December 8, 1863	February 15, 1864	July 2, 1864	December 15, 1864
General Burnside Issues General Order No. 38	Stephen J. Field Becomes Associate Justice of Supreme Court	Battle of Gettysburg	Lincoln's Plan of Reconstruction	Ex parte Vallandigham	Congress Passes Wade-Davis Bill	Salmon P. Chase Becomes Chief Justice of the United States

"If I could save the Union without freeing *any* slave, I would do it; and if I could save it by freeing all the slaves, I would do it . . . What I do about slavery and the colored race, I do because I believe it helps to save this Union."
    —Abraham Lincoln to Horace Greeley (1862)

Southerners so revered the Constitution that the seceding states brought most of it with them when they left the Union. The constitution adopted by the Confederacy in 1861 was almost a carbon copy of the original document. But the preamble left no doubt that they considered it a compact for confederation, not a charter creating a sovereign national state. Instead of the ringing phrase "We the People of the United States," it began with "We the People of the Confederate States, each State acting in its sovereign and independent character," making it clear that the states surrendered none of their sovereign rights to the new Confederate government. Other significant changes reflected past southern grievances, such as the prohibition of protective tariffs and a ban on transportation improvements at public expense. There was also a provision limiting the president to a single six-year term. While it legalized slavery in any territories acquired by the Confederacy, it prohibited the maritime slave trade out of deference to public opinion in Europe. There were provisions for the separation of powers and for checks and balances, and all the rights guaranteed by the Bill of Rights were incorporated into the main body of the document. While the Constitution of the United States no longer applied in the eleven states of the Confederacy, the principles of constitutional government remained very much in force.

Northerners divided sharply on what to do about secession. A large and vocal body of public opinion favored doing nothing. Some argued that it was all for the best: Secession would rid the Union of slavery and free the North to pursue national goals long frustrated by the South. It had always been a bad marriage, the argument went, and a divorce between the sections was long overdue. Many white abolitionists welcomed secession as the only practical means of getting rid of slavery. Their goal had never been racial justice or the welfare of African Americans but rather the elimination of slavery as an institution. Getting rid of slavery by getting rid of the slave states was for some an acceptable solution. Horace Greeley, whose antislavery credentials were impeccable, opposed the use of force to bring the South back into the Union. "We hope never to live in a republic," he declared in a *New York Tribune* editorial, "where one section is pinned to the residue by bayonets." Better half a nation united in spirit and shared loyalties than one held together by military force. "Let the wayward sisters depart in peace," urged General Winfield Scott, who as army commander had no desire to lead Americans into fratricidal conflict with other Americans.

But many in the North were unwilling to write off the Union for any reason. They saw preserving it as a sacred trust and patriotic duty. President Lincoln shared this view, and his inaugural address on March 4, 1861 made it clear that he would hold the nation together regardless of the cost. He tried to reassure the South that his administration would not be hostile to southern interests, that he would not interfere with slavery in the slave states, and that the federal fugitive slave law would be vigorously enforced. He also promised not to oppose an unamendable constitutional amendment pending in Congress that would have permanently protected slavery in the South from federal interference. But Lincoln drew the line on secession, declaring that it was legally and constitutionally impossible. The Union was as permanent as the nation and not subject to dissolution by individual states. He warned the secessionists that resistance to national authority would be treated as "insurrectionary or revolutionary according to the circumstances." While his administration would not commence hostilities, he made it clear that acts of force would be met with force.

Lincoln used the occasion to refute the theory that secession was somehow constitutional. He pointed out that since the Constitution contains no provision for the dissolution of the Union, any attempt to dissolve it would necessarily be unconstitutional. But the heart of his argument was that the Union antedated and transcended even the Constitution. It began with the Articles of Association in 1774, which were confirmed by the Declaration of Independence two years later, and finally became perpetual under the Articles of Confederation in 1781. The Constitution adopted in 1787 did not create the Union, because the Union already existed. Its purpose was simply "to form a more perfect Union" than the existing one. To argue, as the secessionists argued, that the adoption of the Constitution somehow made the perpetual Union impermanent contradicted

Lincoln Pledges to Defend the Union

"I shall take care, as the Constitution itself expressly enjoins upon me, that the laws of the Union be faithfully executed in all the States . . . In doing this there needs to be no bloodshed or violence, and there shall be none unless it be forced upon the national authority. The power confided to me will be used to hold, occupy, and possess the property and places belonging to the Government and to collect the duties and imposts; but beyond what may be necessary for these objects, there will be no invasion, no using of force against or among the people anywhere."

—First Inaugural Address, March 4, 1861

the stated purpose of perfecting it. An impermanent Union would clearly be less perfect than a perpetual one. While the Constitution could be modified and changed, the Union itself was as indivisible and indestructible as the nation. This conception of the Union as anterior and superior to the Constitution provided the theoretical justification for many of the war measures of the Lincoln administration.

"The central idea of secession," Lincoln declared, "is the essence of anarchy." Far from being a tenable theory of government, it was really a formula for political disintegration. When a minority secedes rather than submits to the will of the majority, the precedent set will ultimately divide and ruin them. Why should a minority within the minority not secede if their demands are not met? The Confederacy could be divided and subdivided on the same theory on which the seceded states had left the Union. Lincoln upheld the principle of majority rule as "the only true sovereign for a free people. Whoever rejects it does, of necessity, fly to anarchy or to despotism." Since unanimity in political affairs is seldom possible, either the majority or the minority must prevail. No free people would tolerate the latter, nor would freedom long survive unlimited political devolution. The preservation of the Union, he declared, was the cause of free and representative government everywhere.

Attack on Fort Sumter

While most Northerners probably agreed with Lincoln in principle, they were uncertain what should be done about secession. Many were convinced that saving the Union was not worth a civil war. Lincoln spent his first month in office biding his time until he could build a political consensus. He had compelling reasons for caution. Precipitous military action against the Confederacy might provoke the slave states still in the Union into secession. But a stand had to be taken somewhere or secession would become a *fait accompli*. Forts, arsenals, and federal property were being seized throughout the South, and the longer the government waited, the more difficult it would become to act. Lincoln decided to take a stand at Fort Sumter, in Charleston Harbor, in the very cradle of secession. Supplies were running out, and evacuation of the garrison would be widely perceived as de facto recognition of the Confederacy. Over the objections of most of his cabinet, Lincoln decided to send supplies after informing the governor of South Carolina of his intentions. The announcement provoked southern agitators into forcing a confrontation. The Confederate authorities demanded the surrender of the fort, and when the deadline passed, the Charleston shore batteries began a bombardment that forced the garrison to capitulate on April 13. The Civil War had begun, and all the issues secession had raised would now be settled on the battlefield.

Lincoln's War Goals

The attack on Fort Sumter gave Lincoln the political consensus needed to take decisive action. An outburst of patriotic fervor swept the North for the defense of the Union. Lincoln used his mandate cautiously, making it clear that his only goal was the restoration of national authority in the seceded states. Pledging that the war would not be turned into a crusade against slavery, he outraged abolitionists by announcing that he recognized the legality of the institution in the states where it existed. This made good political sense, because those who saw the war as a moral crusade were then only a small minority. Whites willing to fight to save the Union were less willing to take up arms in order to free southern slaves. Always pragmatic, Lincoln made the restoration of the Union, a goal widely supported throughout the North, the unifying theme of the war effort.

Lincoln also had to take into account public opinion in the slave states that had not left the Union. Virginia, North Carolina, Tennessee, and Arkansas were lost when hostilities commenced, and Maryland, Kentucky, and Missouri might follow if antislavery became official policy. These states were politically and militarily important, because their defection to the Confederacy would have drastically altered the balance of forces. Those favoring secession contended that the national government planned to destroy slavery, so Lincoln had to be careful not to prove them right. He tried to reassure Unionists in the border states that slavery had nothing to do with the war, and that his sole aim was the restoration of the Union. If the southern states abandoned secession and returned to the fold, his administration would not interfere with their domestic institutions in any way.

Although Lincoln personally detested slavery, he thought that preventing its expansion into the national territories was the only constitutional way the federal government could act against it. Once slavery had been confined to the states where it already existed, he hoped it would eventually be abolished by voluntary state action, just as it had been abolished in the North in the late eighteenth century. At no point in his public career had Lincoln advocated immediate abolition or proposed equal legal status for African Americans. He made it clear during his Senate campaign against Stephen A. Douglas in 1858 that he regarded blacks as racially inferior to whites and that he endorsed white supremacy. He was nominated for the presidency in 1860 precisely because he was not identified with antislavery radicalism. Pessimistic about the prospects for race relations in the United States, Lincoln contemplated black colonization in Africa or Latin America as a possible solution. But even if his racial views had been more enlightened, he would not have allowed them to interfere with his goal of saving the Union. When Horace Greeley prodded him in 1862 to declare himself for emancipation, Lincoln refused. "If I could save the Union without freeing any slave," he replied,

> I would do it; and if I could save it by freeing all the slaves, I would do it; and if I could do it by freeing some and leaving others alone, I would also do that. What I do about slavery and the colored race, I do because I believe it helps to save this Union; and what I forbear, I forbear because I do *not* believe it would help to save the Union.

That the holder of such views went on to become the Great Emancipator would be just one of the war's many ironies.

The Radical Republicans

Lincoln's pragmatism struck many opponents of slavery as morally reprehensible. Radical members of his own party in Congress considered the destruction of slavery to be just as important as the restoration of the Union. Although they were a minority in the beginning, their dedication and political astuteness gave them influence beyond their numbers. They manipulated northern bitterness against the South and channeled it into antislavery. This was done by presenting emancipation not as racial justice for blacks but as a form of punishment for rebels. The last thing the Radicals wanted was a speedy restoration of the Union with no questions asked about slavery. They realized that time was on their side because military operations in the South would inevitably disrupt slavery and promote their antislavery agenda. By 1862 they had enough support in Congress to set up the Joint Committee on the Conduct of the War. Headed by Senator Benjamin Wade of Ohio, the Committee closely monitored military operations and the war policies of the Lincoln administration.

Generalizations about the Radical Republicans can be misleading, because they differed considerably on particular issues. Just to identify them as a group requires an analysis of roll-call votes in Congress. But the one issue on which all Radicals agreed was that the time had come to end slavery in the United States. They pressed hard to make emancipation a war goal even while President Lincoln insisted that restoration of the Union was the only goal of his administration. Although all Radicals supported emancipation, their reasons for doing so were not the same. Some, like Senator Charles Sumner and Thaddeus Stevens in the House of Representatives, were idealists primarily concerned with racial justice. Stevens, one of the most interesting figures of the era, was an ardent advocate of racial equality. The country not only owed blacks their freedom, he thought, but also a chance to share in the benefits of freedom as first-class citizens. On the other hand, some Radicals were less concerned with racial justice than with gaining political advantage. They saw an opportunity to alter the balance of party power in the United States by freeing and enfranchising southern blacks. From Jackson's administration to the election of Lincoln, southern Democrats had dominated national politics. They had shaped national policy to the disadvantage of the business and industrial classes represented by the Whigs and now by the Republicans. For thirty years the South had prevented transportation improvements, forced reductions in the protective tariff, and blocked a national banking system. The war had changed things temporarily by removing southerners from positions of power, a change that many Radicals hoped to make permanent by broadening the Republicans' voting base.

What the Radicals feared most was that the Union might be restored without any basic changes in the South. This would not only leave the national disgrace of slavery intact but probably restore the Democrats to power. A reunited and triumphant Democratic party would again vote down the business interests of the North as they had been voted down in the days of Clay and Webster. The political arithmetic of 1860 made it clear that the Republicans were currently a minority party with no base of support in the South. Lincoln polled only about 1,800,000 votes to 2,800,000 for his opponents, and only the secession of the southern Democrats had given the Republicans control of Congress. When the war ended, they could keep control only by broadening their electoral base. If the party acted boldly in support of emancipation and black enfranchisement, the grateful black masses

Senator Sumner Urges African Americans to Enlist

"Enlist at once. Now is the day, and now the fortunate hour. Help to overcome your cruel enemies battling against your country, and in this way you will surely overcome those other enemies, hardly less cruel, here at home, who still seek to degrade you . . . Do your duty to our common country, and you will set an example of generous self-sacrifice which must conquer prejudice and open all hearts."

—Letter of July 13, 1863

Figure X.1 Portrait of Abraham F. Brown (c. 1862–1863). Brown was a member of the Massachusetts 54th Infantry Regiment, the first black regiment of the Civil War.

Courtesy of the Massachusetts Historical Society

of the South would keep it in power permanently. Freedom and first-class citizenship for southern blacks would enable northern Republicans to retain control of the national government.

Radicals of every stripe agreed that the war should not end without emancipation. They wanted no political settlement that brought the South back into the Union with slavery intact. If the conflict "continues thirty years and bankrupts the nation," Senator Wade declared, "I hope to God there will be no peace until we can say there is not a slave in the land." The Radicals counted on a long war to force a change in war goals. "We don't want the war to be hurried," wrote Horace Greeley, who thought the Union not worth saving without emancipation. Some Radicals viewed Union defeats as blessings in disguise. Senator Sumner wrote that he feared victories more than defeats. "There must be more delay and more suffering – yet another 'plague' before all will agree to let my people go; and the war cannot, must not, end till then." Sumner thought that the use of black troops would force a change in war goals. He hoped for the day when the Union forces had "two hundred thousand Negroes with muskets in their hands, and then I shall not fear compromise." The Radicals finally prevailed when it became clear that the war would be a long one. As hopes for the quick restoration of the Union faded, Lincoln late in 1862 made emancipation one of his war objectives.

Lincoln's relations with the Radical Republicans have been the subject of much debate over the years. Some historians think there was no real conflict between him and the Radicals and that their disagreements involved only tactics and timing. There is a theory that the Congressional Radicals were really Lincoln's allies who promoted policies that he could not promote himself without undermining support for the war and risking the loss of the border states. But this view of their disagreements as a sort of political charade requires a suspension of disbelief. The record of the administration reveals Lincoln as a moderate under constant pressure from radical members of his own party in Congress. While he detested slavery personally, he resisted making emancipation a war goal until political necessity forced a change in policy. There seems no reason not to accept at face value what Lincoln wrote to Horace Greeley on the issue of emancipation. He would support it only to the extent that it assisted in the restoration of the Union.

Although Lincoln clearly had problems with Congress, it would be a mistake to exaggerate the depth of the rift between them. Lincoln maintained close personal ties with the

Senator Benjamin Wade on President Lincoln

"I never had a doubt of our ability to elect him by an overwhelming majority. I only wish we could do as well for a better man. But to save the nation I am doing all for him that I possibly could do for a better man . . . That stupid wilfulness cost this nation more than a hundred thousand men, as you well know and when I think of those things, I wish the d___l I had Old Abe. But the issue is now made up and we have either got to take him, or Jeff Davis . . ."

—Letter to Zachariah Chandler (1864)

Congressional Radicals. Senator Sumner was a family friend throughout the war years, and Owen Lovejoy, one of the most radical Republicans in Congress, was the president's closest political ally in the House of Representatives. That Congress was sometimes at odds with the administration probably had as much to do with Lincoln's Whig philosophy of government as with disagreements over emancipation. The Whigs had opposed Andrew Jackson's conception of the presidency as authoritarian and dictatorial, and they deplored his manipulation of Congress as invidious to the constitutional separation of powers. Lincoln never lost touch with his Whig political origins, particularly with respect to the separation of powers. The upshot was that he left Congress alone and did not interfere in legislative matters. "As a rule," he declared in 1861, "I think it better that Congress should originate, as well as perfect its measures, without external bias." Only with regard to the war powers did the Whigs concede the need for a strong executive, and these were the very powers that Lincoln invoked to justify the most controversial measures of his administration.

Legal and Constitutional Problems

The war posed legal and constitutional problems that might have affected its outcome. From the outset, Lincoln took the position that the conflict was not a war in the international sense but an internal insurrection. Neither the Confederacy nor the seceded states were recognized as political entities. The military operations undertaken were viewed as essentially a massive police action against lawless persons who had usurped power in the South. Except for the scale of what had happened, the situation was comparable with the events of the Whiskey Rebellion, when western farmers had defied the national government. Those in arms against the government were traitors without rights under the international laws of war. This theory of the war had the advantage of isolating the South diplomatically and cutting it off from needed foreign assistance. If the Confederacy had no standing under international law, recognition of it by foreign governments would have been an act of intervention in the internal affairs of the United States. Whether this theory of the war would be accepted abroad depended in large measure on what happened on the battlefield.

Some of the war measures adopted did not square with the theory that the war was a domestic insurrection. When Lincoln proclaimed a blockade of southern ports following the attack on Fort Sumter, he virtually conceded that a state of war existed in the international sense. A blockade is an act of war and cannot be justified on any other grounds under international law. Great Britain reacted by granting "belligerency" status to the Confederacy, but it stopped short of outright recognition. The Union itself granted the South de facto belligerency status in the treatment of Confederate prisoners. It really had no choice, for any other course would have resulted in reprisals against Union prisoners. Throughout the conflict both sides abided by the rules of war. Military protocol was observed, and prisoners were exchanged as in a war between sovereign nations. Despite the official theory that those in arms against the United States were rebels and traitors, no one was executed for treason as a result of the war.

Prize Cases

The legality of Lincoln's blockade proclamation was challenged in the *Prize Cases* (1863). The president had ordered the blockade in April 1861, but Congress did not approve his action until July. The owners of neutral ships that had been seized during the interim sued to recover their property on the ground that the president had no power to authorize acts of war without the consent of Congress. Blockades are lawful only in wartime, and only Congress can legally declare war. The owners argued that the United States had not legally been at war between April and July, and that the seizures were therefore illegal under international law. The outcome of the cases depended on how much war power the president had under the Constitution.

The Supreme Court began by declaring that all the seizures made after Congress had approved the blockade were legal. All the justices agreed that the war measures passed by Congress in July created a de facto state of war that legitimized the blockade under international law. The state of war had to be de facto, because a de jure state of war would have contradicted the theory that the conflict was not a war in the international sense. The key issue, however, was not the legality of the seizures made after July, but the legality of the seizures between April and July. On this the Court was sharply divided. In a 5–4 decision, with Chief Justice Taney dissenting, the majority upheld Lincoln's blockade proclamation as legal. Justice Robert Grier, speaking for the majority, declared that the president's duty to suppress insurrections implies the authority to take military measures deemed necessary without first consulting Congress. He noted that while Congress alone can declare war, insurrections do not begin with formal declarations. The president must have the power to act in such emergencies or the security of the nation might be fatally compromised. Thus was planted the seed of the almost limitless presidential war powers that would come to full fruition in the wars of the twentieth century.

Taney Dissents on Executive War Powers

"By the Constitution, Congress alone has the power to declare a national or foreign war. It cannot declare war against a State, or any number of States, by virtue of any clause in the Constitution. The Constitution confers on the President the whole Executive power. He is bound to take care that the laws be faithfully executed. He is Commander-in-chief of the Army and Navy of the United States, and of the militia of the several States when called into the actual service of the United States. He has no power to initiate or declare a war either against a foreign nation or a domestic State. But, by the Acts of Congress of February 28th, 1795, and 3d of March, 1807, he is authorized to call out the militia and use the military and naval forces of the United States in case of invasion by foreign nations, and to suppress insurrection against the government of a State or of the United States."

—The Prize Cases (1862)

Second Confiscation Act

Congress as well as the president stretched its war powers to the limit. The Second Confiscation Act passed in 1862 authorized *in rem* proceedings for the seizure of property belonging to Confederate supporters. Since obtaining personal jurisdiction over such persons would have been impossible in most cases, the federal courts were authorized to take jurisdiction over any property they owned in the North. Then, if they were adjudged disloyal in the proceedings, the property would be forfeited to the government. The problem with using *in rem* jurisdiction for this purpose was that accused persons were punished for alleged wrongdoing without a criminal conviction. No accused person can be criminally convicted by a court that does not have *in personam* jurisdiction to try the case. In effect, Congress had authorized the punishment of persons not subject to the jurisdiction of the courts that tried and convicted them in absentia. The measure was clearly unconstitutional, but Lincoln signed it anyway. Having stretched his own powers to the limit, he could hardly fault Congress for doing the same.

The legality of the *in rem* forfeitures finally came before the Supreme Court after the war in *Miller v. United States* (1871). Miller, a citizen of Virginia, had owned stock in several Michigan railroad corporations, and he challenged the constitutionality of the federal court order confiscating his stock. He contended that the forfeiture was a penalty imposed in violation of the Fifth and Sixth Amendments. The government had not indicted, tried, or convicted him of any crime, yet it had punished him for alleged wrongdoing. Miller was right about the constitutional issues, but he lost anyway. A divided Court upheld the forfeiture, not under the Constitution, but under the international rights of the United States as a belligerent in wartime. The law of war, the majority declared, confers upon the national government powers which supersede the peacetime guarantees of the Constitution. The decision legitimized the wartime seizure of property belonging to persons behind enemy lines and therefore beyond the personal jurisdiction of the courts.

Military Conscription

But the most controversial of all the war measures passed by Congress was the Conscription Act of 1863. The Act provided for the first military draft in American history. It made all able-bodied males between the ages of twenty and forty-five subject to military service at the call of the president. Compulsory service in the state militia had a history going back to colonial times, but the federal government had previously relied upon volunteers in wartime. Although Article I of the Constitution authorizes Congress "to raise and support armies," it does not specifically authorize conscription. Opponents of the draft cited this omission in challenging its constitutionality. They also attacked the unfairness of a provision that allowed those conscripted to avoid service by providing a substitute or paying $300. The provision favored the rich and was bitterly resented by those unable to buy exemptions. The first drawings caused riots in New York City, and federal troops had to be brought in to restore order. Disturbances also occurred in other cities, though on a much smaller scale.

Conscientious Objectors and the Draft

"[W]e were urged by our acquaintances to pay our commutation money; by some through well-meant kindness and sympathy; by others through interest in the war; and by others still through a belief they entertained it was our duty. But we confess a higher duty than that to country; and, asking no military protection of our Government and grateful for none, deny any obligation to support so unlawful a system, as we hold a war to be even when waged in opposition to an evil and oppressive power . . ."

—Diary of Cyrus Pringle, 1863

Opponents of conscription charged that Congress had encroached upon powers reserved to the states by the Constitution. The Act applied to members of the state militia and therefore interfered to some extent with the right of the states to maintain militias. Strict constructionists also argued that it was unconstitutional to conscript civilians, because Congress was not expressly authorized by the Constitution to do so. Northern Democrats used the issue to put Republicans on the defensive. Governor Horatio Seymour of New York denounced the draft and urged Lincoln not to enforce it. The debate raged in the press and in state legislatures. If reliance on the draft had been more extensive, the political backlash might have been disastrous. Actually, far more entered the armed forces as substitutes and volunteers than were drafted into military service. The constitutional issues raised did not reach the Supreme Court and so remained unsettled until the First World War.

Lincoln's Assumption of War Powers

Some of the powers assumed by Lincoln as commander in chief clearly belonged to Congress. Article I of the Constitution vests Congress with the power to raise armies and regulate the military and naval forces of the United States. After the attack on Fort Sumter in April 1861, Lincoln called on the governors of the loyal states to provide 75,000 volunteers from their state militias; he also proclaimed a blockade of the South, and authorized vast military and naval expenditures. In May he issued a call for 42,000 volunteers for the federal armed forces. Since Congress was not in session, he could plausibly claim that military necessity justified these actions. The claim would have been more convincing had he called Congress into session as quickly as possible. But he took his time in summoning Congress. The session he called for on July 4 left him in complete control of the government for more than two months. This gave him time to set the machinery of war inexorably in motion. By the time Congress finally met, the only choice open was to endorse what the president had done.

Despite serious doubts about the legality of all that Lincoln had done, Congress passed a law validating the measures taken "as if they had been issued and done under the previous express authority and direction of the Congress." Except for the summoning of the state militias, everything done by Lincoln probably would have been illegal without this retroactive approval. In 1827 the Supreme Court had held in *Martin v. Mott* that the president was the sole judge as to whether the situation justified calling out the state militias; but there were no precedents for the other actions taken by Lincoln. Relying solely on his powers as commander in chief, he plunged the nation into a war that Congress had not declared. He was the first president to do so, but he would not be the last.

While he welcomed the approval of Congress, Lincoln assumed that his war measures were constitutional without it. His oath to preserve and defend the Constitution, he thought, gave him implied authority to act in the emergency. "I felt that measures otherwise unconstitutional," he wrote, "might become lawful by becoming indispensable to the preservation of the Constitution through the preservation of the nation." If the nation unraveled, the Constitution would be lost with it. Lincoln would not permit that to happen, not even if he had to violate some of its provisions in order to save the whole Constitution. While he denied that he had acted unlawfully, he asserted the right, if necessary, to act unlawfully. If no president has ever claimed so much, it should be remembered that no other president has faced such a threat to the nation's survival.

The main problem with departures from strict legality, even for high-minded reasons, is that they tend to be habit-forming. The idea that special circumstances suspend the rule of law can lead those in power to confuse their own goals and interests with the interests of the nation. The admission of West Virginia to the Union as a separate state in 1863 provides a case in point. When Virginia seceded from the Union in 1861, its western counties, which never had much in common with the rest of the state, refused to go

Figure X.2 Etching of Lincoln as Quixote by Adalbert John Volck (1861). Lincoln is depicted as Cervantes's delusional idealist. As Lincoln drafts a list of Union defeats, his foot rests on books titled "Habeas Corpus," "Constitution," and "Law." An artillery mortar serves as his inkwell and a pike, a symbol of John Brown's rebellion, leans on the back of his chair. On the wall is a portrait of General Winfield Scott, Commander of the Union army.

National Portrait Gallery, Smithsonian Institution / Art Resource, NY

along. What followed confirmed Lincoln's warning in his inaugural address that secession begets secession. The Westerners held a convention at Wheeling, organized a Unionist government that claimed authority over the entire state, and elected Francis H. Pierpont as governor of Virginia. Then, acting in the name of Virginia, the Pierpont government authorized the western counties to draft a constitution for the new state of West Virginia. This political charade was necessary in order to satisfy the requirement in Article IV of the Constitution that states must consent to the organization of new states within their borders. Both the president and Congress endorsed the separation for political reasons. When challenged after the war in *Virginia v. West Virginia* (1871), the constitutionality of the separation was upheld by the Supreme Court.

Lincoln used his war powers aggressively in dealing with those who opposed the war. The enemies of the Union were not always visible nor were they all behind the Confederate lines. Thousands of northerners sympathized with the South and opposed the use of force to restore the Union. Reproached as "Copperheads" (from the Liberty penny they sometimes wore as an emblem), they were particularly strong in the Midwest. Politically, they allied themselves with the Democrats, but they also operated through secret organizations widely suspected of sabotage, spying, and recruiting for the enemy. Although some were indeed criminally disloyal, most confined themselves to lawful political opposition. They blamed Republicans for the war and urged negotiations with the South. To a beleaguered government, however, the distinction between legal and illegal opposition was sometimes difficult to make. There was a tendency to regard all opponents of the war effort as potential or actual traitors.

Suspension of Habeas Corpus

Lincoln from the outset acted decisively against those who threatened the Union. The situation in Maryland was particularly alarming. The secessionists there were organized and active, and the state was crucially important to the Union. On April 27, two weeks after the attack on Fort Sumter, Lincoln authorized his military commanders to suspend the writ of habeas corpus between Philadelphia and Washington, and the area covered was later extended north to New York City. He claimed constitutional authority to issue the order under Article I, which provides: "The Privilege of the Writ of Habeas Corpus shall not be suspended, unless when in Cases of Rebellion or Invasion the public Safety may require it." While the requisite state of rebellion certainly existed, it was arguable whether the president, acting without the approval of Congress, had the authority to suspend habeas corpus.

Ex parte Merryman

Lincoln's suspension of the writ precipitated a confrontation with the courts. The military authorities in Maryland arrested John Merryman, a leading secessionist, and confined him in Fort McHenry. Merryman applied to Chief Justice Taney, who was then on circuit court duty in Maryland, for a writ of habeas corpus. Taney issued the writ. It directed General George Cadwalader, who commanded Fort McHenry, to produce Merryman in court for a hearing on the legality of his detention. Cadwalader refused to comply on the ground that the president had suspended the writ. Taney thereupon cited the general for contempt of court and issued a warrant for his arrest. But arresting the uncooperative general was no easy matter. When the marshal sent to make the arrest was turned away, Taney relieved him of responsibility for enforcing the warrant. The chief justice then wrote a blistering opinion upholding Merryman's right to a habeas corpus hearing, and he sent a copy of the proceedings to the president.

Taney held that Lincoln's suspension of habeas corpus was unconstitutional. Citing both Marshall and Story, he ruled that Congress, not the president, has the power to suspend the writ. Taney noted that Article I, which authorizes suspension of the writ, covers the powers of Congress; the president's powers come from Article II, which says nothing about suspension of the writ. "If that high power over the liberty of the citizens now claimed was intended to be conferred on the president," Taney argued, "it would undoubtedly be found in plain words in this article." If the president could indeed suspend the writ, Taney concluded, "then the Constitution of the United States has conferred upon him more regal and absolute power over the liberty of the citizen than the people of England have thought it safe to entrust to the Crown."

Taney's opinion resonated with partisan politics. His scathing references to "regal" and "absolute" powers stung an administration already under fire for highhanded methods. He also excoriated the military for defying judicial authority. Taney warned that when the courts are disregarded by the military,

> the people of the United States are no longer living under a government of laws, but every citizen holds life, liberty, and property at the will and pleasure of the army officer in whose military district he may happen to be found.

The court had been defied by overwhelming military force, and he called upon the president to perform his constitutional duty to uphold the laws and judicial processes of the United States.

The highly charged political rhetoric does not detract from *Merryman* as one of Taney's best-reasoned opinions. Essentially, he reiterated and expanded upon Chief Justice Marshall's dicta in *Ex parte Bollman* (1807) that the power to suspend habeas corpus belongs exclusively to Congress. Since the authority of the federal courts to issue the writ derives from Congress, it logically follows that under the Suspension Clause only Congress can withdraw it. Habeas corpus is a judicial remedy, and Article III authorizes Congress alone to regulate what the judiciary may do. Apart from the president's Article II power to appoint federal judges, the executive branch has no role to play in judicial matters. These constitutional arrangements have roots that extend back to the colonial era when American resentment of the high-handed manipulation of the courts by royal governors helped exacerbate tensions with England. Indeed, interference by the executive branch with the administration of justice was one of the grievances cited in the Declaration of Independence. Taney's *Merryman* opinion essentially confirmed what had long been taken for granted about the constitutional separation of powers. Although never reviewed and affirmed by the Supreme Court, it has been accepted by most legal commentators as the definitive interpretation of the Suspension Clause.

But Lincoln did not accept the ruling. He reacted to it just as Andrew Jackson reacted to Marshall's holding in *Worcester v. Georgia*. He ignored it and left Merryman in military custody. His attorney general, Edward Bates, gave Lincoln the same advice that Taney as attorney general had given to Jackson: that the president is not subordinate to the judiciary and therefore not bound by its constitutional interpretations. As the head of a coequal branch of government, the president can judge for himself the scope of his constitutional authority and responsibilities. If the president thinks that suspension of habeas corpus is necessary, and that he has authority to suspend it, then he has a duty to suspend it. Lincoln took this position in his July message to Congress, declaring that the president has implied powers as commander in chief that go beyond the powers expressly granted by the Constitution. Authority to suspend habeas corpus in time of rebellion is one of these implied powers. Lincoln also pointed out that suspension of the writ was not punitive but only a precautionary measure taken to prevent the commission of criminal acts. Merryman was subsequently released when he was no longer considered dangerous by the government.

Support for Lincoln's view can be found in some of the questionable assumptions implicit in Taney's holding. He assumed that because the Suspension Clause appears in Article I, which deals with the powers of Congress, it necessarily follows that only Congress has authority to suspend habeas corpus. The problem here is that the powers and functions of the three branches of government are not limited to particular articles. Congress, for example, has powers beyond those listed in Article I. Its power to punish treason and the prohibition against bills of attainder and ex post facto laws are found in Article III, which deals with the federal judiciary. And the role of Congress with respect to executive and judicial appointments appears not in Article I but in Article II, which deals with the powers and duties of the president. The idea that Congress has exclusive power to suspend habeas corpus just because suspension of the writ is authorized in Article I arguably assumes too much. If the framers of Article I had indeed intended to entrust the power exclusively to Congress, would they not have made their intention clear in plain and unambiguous language? Taney posed the same question with respect to the president's authority to suspend the writ, and it is equally relevant to whether congressional authority was intended to be exclusive. From a practical standpoint, it seems implausible that the power to suspend habeas corpus was intended to be the exclusive prerogative of either the president or Congress. In time of rebellion or invasion, the branch of government having the ability to act must have authority to act. Since Congress was not in session when rebellion erupted, power to suspend the writ fell by default to the president as commander in chief.

Martial Law and Civilians

Lincoln asserted even more sweeping war powers the following year. On September 24, 1862, he issued a proclamation that

> all Rebels and Insurgents, their aiders and abettors, within the United States, and all persons discouraging volunteer enlistments, resisting militia drafts, or guilty of any disloyal practice . . . shall be subject to martial law and liable to trials and punishments by courts-martial or military commission.

The proclamation suspended habeas corpus for all persons arrested by the military or under sentence of a military court. Thus anyone arrested by the military would not have the right to a hearing in the regular federal courts. Since vague terms such as "disloyal practices" might mean almost anything, the military were granted virtual dictatorial power over civilians. Nor was the power limited to areas where military operations made it impossible for the regular courts to function. The proclamation applied everywhere, even far behind the lines where no military justification existed.

Critics of the administration contended that the proclamation set up a system of military despotism. The suspension of habeas corpus at least had a constitutional basis in Article I; but nowhere does the Constitution authorize military trials and punishments for civilians when the regular courts are open. The political backlash that followed caused Congress to review all the president's war measures. The review resulted in the passage of the Habeas Corpus Act of 1863, a measure designed to strike a balance between legal due process and the needs of wartime security. The Act authorized the president to suspend habeas corpus, which he had already done on his own authority, and to turn lists of prisoners being detained by the military over to the federal courts. Prisoners not indicted by the next grand jury following their arrest were to be released upon taking a loyalty oath. Congress thus endorsed the principle of preventive detention but put limits on its duration.

What the Habeas Corpus Act did not address was the president's proclamation authorizing military trials and punishments for civilians. The omission amounted to tacit approval of the order. Moreover, the Act immunized federal officials from later prosecution for enforcing any of the war measures, a provision likely to encourage abuses of power. The release provisions of the Act for prisoners not indicted were negated by the holding of Judge Advocate General Joseph Holt that they did not apply to persons triable by the military. Since anyone accused of "disloyal practices" fell into this category, most political prisoners were not protected by the Act. They could also be denied release by convicting them on some vague charge in a military court before the next grand jury met. A conviction made them ineligible for release regardless of the grand jury action.

The many abuses that occurred proved the accuracy of Lord Acton's maxim about absolute power and corruption. The president was not personally responsible for every arbitrary arrest, but the engine that he set in motion often ran roughshod over the rights of citizens. Democrats were detained to prevent them from opposing Republicans for office, and party leaders were harassed as rebel sympathizers. Those arrested for "disloyal practices" almost invariably turned out to be Democrats. Federal enforcement officials made no distinction between opposition to the Lincoln administration and disloyalty to the United States. Precise counts are unavailable, but official records indicate that at least 30,000 civilians were detained by the military during the war. The large numbers involved made a political backlash almost inevitable.

The Vallandigham Affair

The arrest of Clement L. Vallandigham, a leading Ohio Democrat, brought the issue to a head. Vallandigham, a former member of Congress, set out to make himself the leading spokesman for antiwar Democrats in the Midwest. He attacked Lincoln's war measures, particularly the military trial of civilians, and declared that a victory won at the cost of constitutional rights was not worth winning. His activities greatly annoyed General Ambrose Burnside, commander of the military department of Ohio. In April 1863 Burnside issued General Order No. 38, warning that

> all persons found within our lines who commit acts for the benefit of the enemies of our country will be tried as spies or traitors, and if convicted, will suffer death . . . The habit of declaring sympathies for the enemy will no longer be tolerated in this department. Persons committing such offenses will be at once arrested, with a view to being tried as above stated or sent beyond our lines into the lines of their friends. It must be distinctly understood that treason, expressed or implied, will not be tolerated.

The Order went beyond the "disloyal practices" standard of Lincoln's proclamation and invented the new crime of implied treason.

Vallandigham denounced Order No. 38 at a Democratic mass meeting. He then delivered a scathing denunciation of "King Lincoln" for the destruction of civil liberties by his administration. Burnside's agents were in the audience, and two days later the general ordered his arrest. A company of soldiers sent by special train broke into Vallandigham's home in Dayton in the early hours of the morning; he was taken to the train and brought to Burnside's headquarters in Cincinnati before his friends were aware of what had happened. These actions backfired badly. Vallandigham overnight became a political martyr, and he played the role to perfection. In a letter smuggled out of prison, he declared: "I am here in a military bastille for no other offense than my political opinions . . . I am a Democrat—for the Constitution, for law, for Union, for liberty—this is my only crime." The arrest provoked protest meetings and riots not only in Ohio but in other states as well.

Burnside appointed a military commission to try Vallandigham. The main charge against him was that he had defied General Order No. 38. Specifically, he was accused of

> publicly expressing . . . sympathies with those in arms against the Government of the United States, declaring disloyal sentiments and opinions, with the object and purpose of weakening the power of the Government in its efforts to suppress an unlawful rebellion.

No overt acts were charged, certainly none for which he could be prosecuted in the regular courts. Although he was allowed counsel, Vallandigham chose to conduct his own defense. He turned the tables on the prosecution and accused the administration and the military of acting unlawfully. The military had no jurisdiction to try him, he declared, and the charges against him were "not known to the Constitution nor to any law thereof." His only offense had been to criticize the Lincoln administration in an "open and public political meeting, lawfully and peaceably assembled." It was a good defense, though the verdict was a foregone conclusion. The commission found Vallandigham guilty and sentenced him to close confinement for the duration of the war.

Meanwhile, a petition for habeas corpus was filed on Vallandigham's behalf in the federal circuit court for Ohio. Judge Humphrey H. Leavitt, who presided, took the unusual step of inviting General Burnside to reply before ruling on the petition. Writs of habeas corpus are usually issued as a matter of right; only after producing the prisoner in court can the authorities argue the legality of his detention. But the federal courts in Ohio adopted the practice of giving the authorities advance notice in cases involving

Vallandigham's Protest Before the Military Commission

"Arrested without due "process of law," without warrant from any judicial officer, and now in a military prison, I have been served with a "charge and specifications," as in a Court-Martial or Military Commission . . . But the alleged "offense" is not known to the Constitution of the United States, nor to any law thereof. It is words spoken to the people of Ohio in an open and public political meeting, lawfully and peaceably assembled, under the Constitution and upon full notice. It is words of criticism of the public policy of the public servants of the people, but which policy it was alleged that the welfare of the country was not promoted. It was an appeal to the people to change that policy, not by force, but by free elections and the ballot-box. It is not pretended that I counseled disobedience to the Constitution, or resistance to the laws and lawful authority. I never have."

—May 7, 1863

Figure X.3 Portrait of Clement Vallandigham.
Collection of the U.S. House of Representatives

military arrests. Burnside submitted a statement defending General Order No. 38 and justifying Vallandigham's arrest on grounds of military necessity. This was enough for Judge Leavitt to refuse to issue the writ. He explained that it was not the practice of the court to grant habeas corpus in cases of military detention. Since the military almost certainly would not comply, he would not issue a writ "knowing it would not be respected, and that the court is powerless to enforce obedience." This capitulation to the military stands in sharp contrast with Taney's principled stand in the *Merryman* case. Whatever the merits of his holding, Taney did not flinch when confronted with raw power.

A petition for certiorari was then filed with the Supreme Court to review the proceedings of the military commission that tried Vallandigham. The petition argued that the military had no jurisdiction to try a civilian, and that the offenses charged were not crimes under the laws of the United States. The Court dismissed the petition on jurisdictional grounds without ruling on its merits. Justice James Wayne, speaking for the Court, explained that military commissions were not part of the regular judicial system over which the Court had appellate jurisdiction. However grave the constitutional issues raised, the case was outside the Court's jurisdiction. Wayne knew that the Court would be powerless to enforce an order against the military and, like Judge Leavitt, was reluctant to provoke a pointless confrontation. The ruling drove another nail in the coffin of wartime liberties and gave the military a free hand in security matters.

Although the administration had won a technical victory, the politics of the case were another matter. Vallandigham as a military prisoner became a symbol of political oppression. News that he would be confined at Fort Warren, in Boston Harbor, created a furor throughout the North. Governor Seymour of New York denounced his imprisonment as "cowardly, brutal, and infamous." Addressing a Democratic rally in Albany, he attacked those responsible and declared that ultimate responsibility lay with the president. "The perpetrators now seek to impose punishment, not for an offense against law, but for the disregard of an invalid order put forth in the utter disregard of the principles of civil liberty." The speech triggered a backlash against the administration. What had happened to Vallandigham could happen to anyone. Thousands of citizens had been arrested by the military, and even newspapers had been arbitrarily suppressed. Copies of Seymour's speech were sent to Democrats in every northern state, making it clear that the case would be an issue in the next elections.

Lincoln was furious at Burnside but could not disavow his actions without undermining the authority of all his military commanders. The general had managed to turn a local nuisance into a national political issue. Burnside proceeded to make things worse by suppressing the *Chicago Times* and banning the *New York World* in his department. But the key problem remained what to do about Vallandigham. General Order No. 38, the source of all the trouble, ironically provided the answer. Lincoln invoked the provision for transportation behind enemy lines as a way out of the dilemma. He commuted the sentence to banishment, and Vallandigham was passed through the Confederate lines. His release from military custody defused the issue, and the manner of his release suggested that he was now among friends. Vallandigham eventually went to Canada, and in 1864 he slipped back into the country. Left alone at the president's order, he renewed his political activities but never regained the importance he had as a political prisoner. The eagle when released from captivity turned out to be only a gadfly.

Ex parte Milligan

The constitutionality of trying civilians by military commissions came before the Supreme Court again in *Ex parte Milligan* (1866). The case involved Lambdin Milligan, a prominent citizen and one of the leaders of the Democratic Party in Indiana. Milligan, like many peace Democrats, engaged in secret as well as public political activities. He was a leader of the Sons of Liberty, an underground organization in the Midwest sympathetic to the South. The organization, which may have had as many as 500,000 members in Ohio, Indiana, and Illinois, was thoroughly infiltrated by spies of the War Department. Some extremist members, the government was informed, planned to incite disorders when the Democratic convention met in Chicago in 1864. The local arsenals would be seized, Confederate prisoners of war released, and an attack launched from the rear against Union forces in Kentucky and Missouri. The leaders of the alleged plot were arrested by the military in October 1864.

Milligan was one of those arrested. He and several other leaders of the Sons of Liberty were charged with conspiring against the government, inciting insurrection, and plotting attacks on the armed forces of the United States. Like Vallandigham, Milligan objected to being tried by the military; as a civilian, he claimed the right to be tried in the regular courts. The federal courts were open and functioning in Indiana, so there was no necessity for trial by the military. In overruling his objections, the military commission cited Lincoln's proclamation ordering such trials. All the defendants were convicted, and three, including Milligan, were sentenced to death.

Lincoln delayed approving the sentences for four months. He apparently planned to hold them in abeyance until the war ended and the prisoners could be safely released. But his assassination on April 14, 1865, changed everything. The North demanded vengeance, and clemency for Confederate sympathizers suddenly became unpopular. When the death sentences were submitted to President Andrew Johnson, he approved them. The order for carrying out the sentences directed that the prisoners were to be hanged on May 19, 1865. If the executions had been carried out, the prisoners would have been the first civilians put to death by the military for allegedly plotting against the United States.

The scheduling of the executions caused many to have second thoughts about the fairness of the trials and the severity of the sentences. The president was flooded with petitions from the Midwest urging clemency. Governor Oliver Morton of Indiana recommended that the sentences be commuted to life in prison. Morton was a Radical Republican, but he did not want to create political martyrs. The executions would cost the Republicans dearly in states where thousands openly sympathized with the condemned. Justice David

Davis, a close friend of Lincoln, urged Johnson to commute the sentences. The war was now over, and military executions could not be justified on grounds of necessity. The president wavered for a time but finally came down on the side of clemency. He postponed the executions and then commuted the sentences to life imprisonment.

Meanwhile, Milligan had petitioned the federal circuit court of Indiana for a writ of habeas corpus. Contending that the military had no jurisdiction to try him, he demanded his release under the release provisions of the Habeas Corpus Act of 1863. Since he had not been indicted by a grand jury within the time set by the Act, his detention was unlawful. The government took the position that the release provisions did not apply to prisoners tried by military commissions. So the case came down to two issues: whether the Habeas Corpus Act applied to Milligan, and whether the military had any right to try him. Because the issues were so important, the circuit court certified them to the Supreme Court for resolution. This gave the Court a second chance to rule on questions left unanswered in the *Vallandigham* case.

Both sides assembled an impressive array of legal talent to argue the case at the March term of the Court in 1866. Jeremiah S. Black, a former attorney general and secretary of state, James A. Garfield, the future president, and David Dudley Field, the great law modernizer and a brother of Justice Field, appeared on behalf of Milligan. The government was ably represented by General Benjamin Butler and Henry Stanbery, both brilliant lawyers. Black went right to the heart of the case, arguing that

> a person not in the military or naval service cannot be punished at all until he has had a fair, open, public trial before an impartial jury, in an ordained and established court, to which the jurisdiction has been given by law to try him for that specific offense.

Milligan had been denied these basic constitutional guarantees. Butler, speaking for the government, argued that the military trial of civilians had been justified by the wartime emergency. "When the nation is threatened," he declared,

> when the bayonet is called in as the final arbiter; when on its armed forces the Government must rely for all it has of power, authority and dignity . . . then we ask that martial law may so prevail, that the civil law may again live.

If the case had come before the Court in wartime, the outcome probably would have been the same as in *Vallandigham*. But the war was over, and the Court now gave less weight to claims of military necessity. Justice Davis, speaking for the Court, held that the military had no jurisdiction to try Milligan, and that he was entitled to a writ of habeas corpus. In what amounted to an apology for the *Vallandigham* decision, Davis noted that during the war "the temper of the times did not allow that calmness in deliberation and discussion so necessary to a correct conclusion of a purely judicial question." He declared that the president had no authority to order military trials for civilians in areas where the civil courts were open. "Martial law cannot arise from a *threatened* invasion," he said. "The necessity must be actual and present, the invasion real, such as effectually closes the courts and deposes the civil administration." He rejected the theory that the government's war powers supersede the guarantees of the Constitution.

> The Constitution of the United States is a law for rulers and people, equally in war and in peace, and covers with the shield of its protection all classes of men, at all times, and under all circumstances. No doctrine, involving more pernicious consequences, was ever invented by the wit of man than that any of its provisions can be suspended during any of the great exigencies of government. Such a doctrine leads directly to anarchy or despotism.

The Court was unanimous in holding that the president lacked authority to order the military trial of civilians. But it split sharply on whether the holding should apply to Congress as well. The authority of Congress was not at issue, because Congress had not authorized the military trials. But the Court took up the question anyway as too important to leave undecided. Five of the nine justices, with Davis again speaking for the majority, held that the guarantees of the Constitution are absolute and binding on all three branches of government. None of the safeguards of the Constitution, except for habeas corpus, can be suspended by the president, by Congress, or even by the Court itself. Chief Justice Salmon P. Chase, who had been appointed to the post after Taney's death in 1864, wrote a powerful dissent. He argued that the war power of Congress

> extends to all legislation essential to the prosecution of war with vigor and success . . . We cannot doubt that, in such time of public danger, Congress had power, under the Constitution, to provide for the organization of a military commission and for trial by that commission of persons engaged in this conspiracy.

Although Congress had not used its power, "that fact could not deprive Congress of the right to exercise it." Congress under the War Powers Clause had the power to do what the president could not do. It was a well-reasoned argument, but a majority of the justices rejected it.

The decision drew heavy political fire, particularly the holding that Congress could not order military trials in areas where the civil courts were open. This was precisely what the Radicals in Congress had in mind for the South as part of their Reconstruction program. If the military could not try civilians in wartime Indiana, how could they try them in the postwar South? President Johnson, who had broken with Congress over Reconstruction, relied on the decision to order the suspension of military trials in the southern states where Congress had declared a state of war still existed. The Court was accused of ignoring wartime realities, and there was even talk of impeaching the justices. Critics contended that if the decision had been handed down during the war, the war would have been lost. The *New York Times* charged that the Court had thrown "the great weight of its influence into the scale of those who assailed the Union and step after step impugned the constitutionality of nearly everything that was done to uphold it." But others praised the Court for delivering a needed rebuke to wartime abuses of power and for protecting citizens against future abuses.

Congress and Slavery

Some of the most difficult constitutional issues during the war years related to slavery. Although the conflict began as a war to save the Union, emancipation soon emerged as an equally important goal. In August 1861 Congress took the lead by including an emancipation provision in the First Confiscation Act. It freed slaves belonging to owners who required them to take up arms or assist the Confederacy in any way. In April 1862 Congress

Lincoln and Greeley Debate Emancipation

Horace Greeley to President Lincoln

"We think you are strongly and disastrously remiss in the discharge of your official and imperative duty with regard to the emancipating provisions of the new Confiscation Act. Those provisions were designed to fight Slavery with Liberty. They prescribe that men loyal to the Union, and willing to shed their blood on her behalf, shall no longer be held, with the nation's consent, in bondage to persistent, malignant traitors, who for twenty years have been plotting and for sixteen months have been fighting to divide and destroy our country. Why these traitors should be treated with tenderness by you, to the prejudice of the dearest rights of loyal men, we cannot conceive."

—*New-York Tribune*, August 19, 1862

Figure X.4 Portrait of Horace Greeley (c. 1860–1870).

Library of Congress, Prints and Photographs Division, LC-USZ62-122445

"I would save the Union. I would save it the shortest way under the Constitution If there be those who would not save the Union unless they could at the same time *save* Slavery, I do not agree with them. If there be those who would not save the Union unless they could at the same time *destroy* Slavery, I do not agree with them. My paramount object in this struggle *is* to save the Union, and is *not* either to save or destroy Slavery. If I could save the Union without freeing *any* slave, I would do it; and if I could save it by freeing *all* the slaves, I would do it; and if I could do it by freeing some and leaving others alone, I would also do that. Whatever I do about Slavery and the colored race, I do because I believe it helps to save this Union; and what I forbear, I forbear because I do *not* believe it would help to save the Union."

—President Lincoln to Greeley, August 22, 1862

Figure X.5 Portrait of Abraham Lincoln by Anthony Berger (1864).

Library of Congress, Prints and Photographs Division, LC-USP6-2415-A

abolished slavery in the District of Columbia with compensation for loyal slaveholders, and in June it freed slaves in the national territories without compensation to their owners. Both measures violated the *Dred Scott* decision and were probably unconstitutional. Slaveholders were deprived of their property in slaves without trial or hearing. Nevertheless, Congress showed much more initiative than the president in moving against slavery. Moderates as well as Radicals blamed it for the nation's problems, and many believed that the war would settle nothing unless slavery was abolished.

Congress moved aggressively against slavery in the Second Confiscation Act passed in July 1862. It emancipated slaves belonging to persons who supported the Confederacy. The Act also freed slaves captured by the armed forces as well as slaves who escaped through the enemy lines. These measures were probably unconstitutional, and it seems unlikely that they would have survived a challenge in the courts. Freeing slaves belonging to Confederate supporters was a criminal forfeiture, and forfeitures could be imposed only after conviction for a criminal offense. In ordering forfeitures without judicial proceedings, Congress also violated the constitutional prohibition against bills of attainder. Not even the law of war legitimized emancipation, because as civilian property slaves were not subject to confiscation. Lincoln had serious doubts about the constitutionality of the Act, but he signed it anyway to avoid a confrontation with Congress. However, he made no real effort to enforce its emancipation provisions.

The Emancipation Proclamation

Lincoln himself approached emancipation with considerable caution. Although he recognized by the spring of 1862 that slavery could not survive the war, he hoped to abolish it through voluntary state action with federal compensation for slaveholders. He tried this approach in the border states where he hoped it would serve as models for emancipation in the rest of the South. Congress approved a plan for compensated emancipation in April 1862, but the border states showed no enthusiasm for the idea. Despite personal appeals by the president, their senators and representatives refused to support it in Congress. The plan came under fire in the North as well. Abolitionists scorned the idea of voluntary state action and opposed compensation as a scheme to enrich slaveholders. When it became clear that the plan would not work, Lincoln took a more aggressive line. In July, following rejection of his plan by the representatives of the border states, he submitted a draft of his emancipation proclamation to the cabinet. It was approved, but Secretary of State Seward recommended holding it back until the North had won a major victory. Lincoln agreed, so the public remained unaware of the momentous change in policy until after the defeat of the Confederates at Antietam in September.

The Emancipation Proclamation

"And by virtue of the power, and for the purpose aforesaid, I do order and declare that all persons held as slaves within said designated States, and parts of States, are, and henceforward shall be free; and that the Executive government of the United States, including the military and naval authorities thereof, will recognize and maintain the freedom of said persons.

And I hereby enjoin upon the people so declared to be free to abstain from all violence, unless in necessary self-defence; and I recommend to them that, in all cases when allowed, they labor faithfully for reasonable wages.

And I further declare and make known, that such persons of suitable condition, will be received into the armed service of the United States to garrison forts, positions, stations, and other places, and to man vessels of all sorts in said service.

And upon this act, sincerely believed to be an act of justice, warranted by the Constitution, upon military necessity, I invoke the considerate judgment of mankind, and the gracious favor of Almighty God."

—Abraham Lincoln, January 1, 1863

The Preliminary Emancipation Proclamation, which was issued on September 23, 1862, gave the South one last chance to return to the Union with slavery intact. It provided that slaves in areas still in rebellion after January 1, 1863 would become legally free and discharged of all servile obligations. If the war had ended before that date, emancipation would not have taken effect. But the war did not end, so when the deadline passed Lincoln issued his formal Proclamation abolishing slavery in areas controlled by the Confederacy. He justified the Proclamation as "a fit and necessary war measure," which he had the power to take as commander in chief. As a war measure, it applied only in enemy territory and had no effect on slavery behind the Union lines. Lincoln specifically listed the occupied areas of the South not covered by the Proclamation. This did not please the abolitionists. Some charged that the president had freed slaves where they could not be freed but refused to free them where they could be freed.

While some Northerners thought that the Proclamation did not go far enough, others thought that it went too far. Many conservatives objected to the wholesale destruction of property rights by the federal government. The Proclamation not only destroyed the property rights of rebels but of loyal slaveholders as well. The Democrats criticized the administration for turning the war into a crusade against slavery. The Illinois legislature,

Figure X.6 *First Reading of the Emancipation Proclamation of President Lincoln* by Francis Bicknell Carpenter (1864). Lincoln is depicted among the members of his Cabinet. From left to right, they are Secretary of War Edwin M. Stanton, Secretary of Treasury Salmon P. Chase, Secretary of the Navy Gideon Welles, Secretary of the Interior Caleb B. Smith (standing), Secretary of State William H. Seward (seated), Postmaster General Montgomery Blair, and Attorney General Edward Bates.

Collection of the U.S. Senate

which they controlled, passed a resolution condemning the president for inciting slave rebellion. It declared Lincoln's Proclamation "an uneffaceable disgrace to the American people." But the administration gained more than it lost politically. The Proclamation closed the growing rift between Lincoln and the Radical Republicans over war goals. Both Congress and the president now shared the common goal of ending slavery in the United States. It also strengthened antislavery forces in the border states. It now became clear that the extinction of slavery in the South meant the end of slavery everywhere. By early 1865, Maryland, Missouri, and Tennessee had enacted emancipation laws, and abolition had begun in occupied areas of the South as well. For all its technical hedging, the Proclamation set slavery inexorably on the road to extinction in the United States.

Thirteenth Amendment

But even staunch supporters of the Proclamation had doubts about its constitutionality. Justifying it as a war measure would be difficult because it freed the slaves of loyal slaveholders as well as those belonging to rebels. Nor could it be justified as a penalty imposed on rebels, because not all slaveholders were rebels, and besides, it was up to Congress, not the president, to prescribe criminal penalties. Moreover, not even penalties prescribed by Congress are constitutional unless the person to be punished has been tried and convicted of some offense. When finally challenged in the courts, as it surely would be, the Proclamation might be declared unconstitutional. To preclude this possibility, but also to end slavery in areas not covered by the Proclamation, the Senate in April 1864 proposed the Thirteenth Amendment. The Amendment ran into considerable opposition in the House, and the required two-thirds majority could not be obtained until the following January. Even some opponents of slavery questioned using the amending process to change the domestic institutions of the states. But the argument for resolving all doubts about the legality of emancipation in the end carried the day. The amendment finally submitted to the states for ratification had two parts. The first abolished slavery and involuntary servitude except as punishment for crime, and the second authorized Congress to enforce the amendment by appropriate legislation. The enforcement provision opened the way for broad incursions by the federal government into the affairs of the states.

The Thirteenth Amendment marked the first use of the amending process for social reform. Apart from the Bill of Rights, which really guaranteed rights already taken for granted, the Constitution had been amended only two other times, and both amendments had been technical. The Eleventh restricted the jurisdiction of the federal courts, and the Twelfth corrected a defect in the election of the president and vice president. But the amending process was now being used to abolish a domestic state institution. The opponents of ratification argued that if one institution, admittedly a bad one, could be abolished in this way, why not others until the country finally became a unitary national state. Others objected that the provision for federal enforcement gave Congress too broad a mandate to interfere in the internal affairs of the states. The amendment could become the opening wedge for a vast expansion of federal power. Constitutional conservatives

The Thirteenth Amendment

Section 1. Neither slavery nor involuntary servitude, except as a punishment for crime whereof the party shall have been duly convicted, shall exist within the United States, or any place subject to their jurisdiction.

Section 2. Congress shall have power to enforce this article by appropriate legislation.

feared that it would end more than slavery in the United States. It would be far better, they argued, to abolish slavery by political action within the states than to create an engine of national power that might ultimately destroy the federal system of government.

Ratifying the Amendment required some questionable political arrangements. The votes of twenty-seven states were needed, but only twenty-five states had remained loyal to the Union. And two of them, Delaware and Kentucky, rejected the Amendment. That meant that at least four of the seceded states had to ratify in order to obtain the needed three-fourths majority. In the end, eight former states of the Confederacy were actually counted when the Amendment was declared ratified in December 1865. The problem with this was that the governments of these states had not been recognized by Congress as legitimate. Their senators and representatives had not been seated, and they existed in a sort of political limbo. If, as Congress claimed, they were not legitimate, how could they legally ratify the Amendment? But supporters of the Amendment were not concerned with logic or consistency, only with results. The practice of recognizing southern state governments as legal for some purposes but not legal for others was one of the anomalies of the Reconstruction era.

Presidential Reconstruction

In theory, the Civil War was fought not to bring the South back into the Union, which officially it had never left, but to suppress lawless groups resisting the authority of the national government. This theory gave the president an advantage over Congress in shaping Reconstruction policy. It would be up to him as commander in chief to determine when the rebellion had been crushed and loyal state governments had returned to power in the South. Meanwhile, occupied areas of the Confederacy would be under his control through the army. Lincoln claimed authority to manage the political details of Reconstruction under the Article IV provision of the Constitution guaranteeing every state a republican form of government. Although Article IV does not specifically make this a presidential responsibility, Lincoln assumed that his powers as commander in chief covered the situation. Whatever was done would have to be done through the army, and the president commanded the army.

Lincoln's policy called for setting up loyal state governments in the South as soon as possible. Carrying on political reorganization in tandem with military operations strengthened his role in managing things. In December 1863 he issued "A Proclamation of Amnesty and Reconstruction," offering a pardon to former supporters of the Confederacy who took an oath that they would be loyal to the United States and comply with all proclamations and acts of Congress relating to slavery. Although certain high-ranking Confederate officials were excluded, Lincoln made it clear that he planned to wipe the slate clear and restore civil government without sweeping changes in the South. The loyalty oath would start the process of political reorganization in states occupied by Union forces. When the number of persons who took the oath reached ten percent of the eligible voters in the state in 1860, the military commander would authorize the election of a convention to draft a new state constitution. The constitution would then be submitted to the loyal voters, and civil government would be restored upon ratification. Without making it a precondition, Lincoln made it clear that he favored the abolition of slavery by the new state governments. This would send a signal to the North that those in power could be trusted.

Loyal state governments were set up in Arkansas, Louisiana, and Tennessee. The new state constitutions adopted by the loyal voters repudiated secession and abolished slavery. So, counting West Virginia, four loyal state governments were in place by the time the war ended. But they were really only shadow governments with almost no popular support. They had been created by military force and would have collapsed without military backing. Congress, having Reconstruction plans of its own, treated them with contempt, and, with some exceptions, refused to seat their senators and representatives. Lincoln, however, insisted upon their legitimacy, though recognizing that some concessions would probably have to be made to make them acceptable to Congress. His immediate goal was political normalization. Only then would the South again be a functioning part of the Union and the wounds of war begin to heal.

Congressional Reaction

The Radicals in Congress took a dim view of Lincoln's Reconstruction policy. They wanted more basic changes in the South as a precondition for the restoration of civil government. Except for the abolition of slavery, the states reconstructed by Lincoln left the old power relationships essentially intact. What the Radicals wanted specifically were guarantees protecting the former slaves against substitute forms of bondage. They also wanted political rights for southern blacks, which, besides being fair, would give the Republicans a political base in the South. Returning power to former rebels would be disastrous both for the former slaves and for the Republican Party. The South would then return to the Union politically stronger than before, because all its black population would be counted for purposes of representation in Congress. The abolition of slavery meant additional votes in the House of Representatives, and the Radicals were determined that some of them should be Republican.

The Radicals began by asserting that the Constitution gave Congress control over Reconstruction. They argued that section 3 of Article IV, which gives Congress governing power in the national territories, applied also in the former states of the Confederacy. Two theories were advanced to support the claim. One was the "conquered provinces" theory of Thaddeus Stevens; the other was the "state suicide" theory of Senator Sumner. Stevens argued that whether it was constitutional or not, secession had actually occurred. The seceded states had severed all ties with the Union and waged war against it. Their defeat reduced them to the status of conquered territories subject to the Article IV jurisdiction of Congress. Sumner reached the same conclusion by a somewhat different route. He argued that while the southern states had never left the Union, their rebellion against the United States destroyed them as political entities. They had forfeited statehood and reverted to the status of national territories under the jurisdiction of Congress.

Wade-Davis Bill

In July 1864 Congress revealed its own plans for the South in the form of the Wade-Davis Bill. The Bill was supported by moderates as well as Radicals, and it provided that until military resistance had ended public affairs in the seceded states should be in the hands of provisional governors appointed by the president with the consent of Congress. The restoration of civil government would begin when a majority of the male white voters of the state took an oath of past and future loyalty to the Constitution. The provisional governor would then authorize the election of a convention to draft a new state constitution. The constitution would have to abolish slavery, repudiate the Confederate debt, and disfranchise the civil and military leaders of the Confederacy in order to be acceptable. When all these conditions had been met, the new state government set up under the constitution would be recognized by the president with the consent of Congress.

The Bill put Congress in charge of Reconstruction and made the president's role essentially ministerial. The preconditions for political normalization were stricter and more difficult to meet than the conditions set by Lincoln. No one who had served in the Confederate army or held civil office under the Confederacy would be eligible to take the required oath, so it would be virtually impossible to obtain the loyal white majority needed for the restoration of civil government. This would postpone the return to civil government almost indefinitely, or at least until Congress was sure that the old ruling class of the South was no longer in power. But the Bill did not make enfranchisement of African-Americans in the South a precondition of political normalization. This was partly a concession to the moderates, and partly because the Thirteenth Amendment had not yet been proposed. After slavery had been abolished the voting rights issue could be addressed. For the present, the important thing was for Congress to take control of Reconstruction.

Congress timed the measure badly. It passed just before adjournment, enabling Lincoln to kill it with a pocket veto. Bills not signed by the president within ten days, excepting Sundays, when Congress is in session, become law automatically; but any bills unsigned after ten days when Congress is not in session, simply die. The president in effect can veto bills when Congress is not in session just by keeping them in his pocket. Lincoln killed the Wade-Davis Bill this way with an explanation of his reasons for doing so. For one thing, he thought it impolitic "to be inflexibly committed to any single plan of restoration." This sent a conciliatory signal to Congress indicating his willingness to be flexible on the issue. But he was unwilling to have the reconstruction governments established under his plan "set aside and held for naught." While he was willing to be flexible, Lincoln had no intention of conceding all control of Reconstruction to Congress.

Lincoln's action enraged Wade and Davis. Rallying other supporters of the Bill, they issued a manifesto denouncing the veto. The manifesto was published in the *New York Times* and subsequently appeared in other leading newspapers. Its tone was personal and confrontational. The signers impugned Lincoln's motives in restoring civil government on such flimsy grounds in the South. They charged that he prized the electoral votes of his reconstructed states over the authority granted to Congress by the Constitution. They accused him of "dictatorial usurpation" and warned that the patience of Congress had limits. The manifesto declared:

> The President has greatly presumed on the forbearance which the supporters of his administration have so long practiced . . . But he must understand that our support is of a cause and not of a man; that the authority of Congress is paramount and must be respected . . . and if he wishes our support, he must confine himself to his executive duties – to obey and execute, not make the laws – to suppress by arms armed rebellion, and leave political reorganization to Congress.

The angry rhetoric exaggerates the seriousness of the rift between Lincoln and Congress. Senator Wade was one of the most combative figures in government and certainly not representative of most Republicans in Congress. The differences between the president and Congress at this point had more to do with timing than with basic Reconstruction policy. Like the Radicals, Lincoln wanted genuinely loyal governments established in the South. But he felt that his administration did not have all the time in the world to secure its political goals, particularly with respect to emancipation. The legality of the Emancipation Proclamation rested on the dubious claim of military necessity. If the war ended before the southern states abolished slavery through the reconstruction process, legal challenges in the courts might deal a fatal blow to the Proclamation. Any delay in

Reconstruction put emancipation at risk. It would be preferable to reconstruct the South imperfectly but quickly in order to make emancipation legal and permanent while the opportunity existed. Since the Thirteenth Amendment had not yet been proposed, the legal extinction of slavery could be accomplished with complete certainty only by the states themselves. That Lincoln coveted the electoral votes of his reconstructed states is probably correct, because these votes might be needed to prevent a peace Democrat from defeating him in 1864. If that happened, neither emancipation nor the restoration of the Union could be taken for granted.

The problems Lincoln had with Congress were institutional as well as political. Moderates in Congress were as determined as the Radicals that the legislative branch should have a voice in Reconstruction policy. This rift between the branches of government would widen into a chasm under Lincoln's successor. Had he lived, Lincoln would have had to cope with the same problems that ruined Andrew Johnson's administration, though he almost certainly would have handled them better. His political skills were incomparably better, and as an elected president, Lincoln would have had a stronger hand in dealing with Congress. It seems unlikely that he would have made Johnson's mistake of breaking openly with Congress. After killing the Wade-Davis Bill, he moved swiftly to repair his relations with Congress by conferring with Senator Sumner and other Radicals in order to work out a mutually acceptable plan of Reconstruction. He knew that compromise was necessary because Congress could nullify his political arrangements by refusing to seat the senators and representatives from his reconstructed states. It seems likely that under Lincoln some compromise plan would have emerged for the orderly restoration of the Union.

The Supreme Court Marginalized

While the president and Congress contended over political matters, the Supreme Court stood mainly on the sidelines. At the beginning of the war, most northerners viewed the Court with distrust. The *Dred Scott* decision not only gave it a proslavery reputation but raised suspicions about the loyalty of the chief justice. Taney's holding in the *Merryman* case seemed to confirm doubts about his loyalty to the Union. The Court almost overnight lost the public confidence that had been the mainstay of its power. Lincoln might have thought twice about defying Taney in the *Merryman* case had the chief justice been more popular. The northern press supported the president in the matter and showered abuse on the chief justice for siding with secessionists. At a time when constitutional liberties were most in peril, the Court had no popular mandate to defend them.

The Court carefully avoided confrontations with either the president or Congress. In the *Prize Cases*, it upheld the president's power to wage war on his own authority, and in the *Vallandigham* case it refused to rule on the jurisdiction of military commissions to try civilians. A challenge to any of the war measures might have brought political reprisals. The only challenge came from the chief justice in the *Merryman* case, and the outcome should have convinced the other justices of the futility of confronting the political branches on security issues. The situation called for judicial caution, and most of the justices accepted the wartime constraints. Taney himself feared that the loss of judicial independence might be permanent and complained that the Supreme Court might never regain "the authority and rank which the Constitution intended to confer on it." The Court of course did recover, but the chief justice would not live to witness its return to power.

Changes in Court Personnel

The recovery began with changes in Court personnel. The death or resignation of the justices who had participated in the *Dred Scott* case helped to clear the air. Change began with the resignation of Justice Curtis following his dispute with Taney over the alleged modification of the majority opinion. President Buchanan appointed Nathan Clifford of Maine, a loyal Democrat with the virtue of being uncontroversial. Buchanan had the opportunity to fill another vacancy when Justice Daniel died in May 1860, but he deliberated too long before nominating his Secretary of State, Jeremiah S. Black. By then, Lincoln had been elected and secession had begun. Although Black was highly qualified, Republicans in the Senate blocked his confirmation in order to keep the vacancy open for Lincoln to fill.

Lincoln waited almost a year before making an appointment. By then, two additional vacancies had occurred with the death of Justice McLean and the resignation of Justice Campbell, who returned to Alabama to serve in the Confederate government. One reason for the delay was Lincoln's preoccupation with military affairs; another was politics. If the South had returned to the Union, it would have been politic to appoint at least one southerner to the Court. By 1862, however, he could wait no longer. The Court was down to six members, four of whom were over the age of seventy, and the chief justice was in his eighties. The vacancy inherited from Buchanan was filled by Noah H. Swayne, an Ohio Republican, who as a lawyer had defended numerous fugitive slaves. Samuel F. Miller of Iowa and David Davis of Illinois, both prominent Republicans, filled the other two vacancies. Miller, a staunch opponent of slavery, had strong political backing; and Davis, a close friend of Lincoln, shared his views on most major issues. Congress created another vacancy the following year by increasing the membership of the Supreme Court to ten in order to accommodate the Far West. Lincoln appointed Stephen J. Field of California, a staunch Union supporter, to the new post.

Taney's death in 1864 gave Lincoln the opportunity to appoint a new chief justice. He chose his former Secretary of Treasury, Salmon P. Chase, an ardent abolitionist and leading Radical. A man of great ability and matching ambitions, Chase had long aspired to the presidency. He sought the Republican nomination in 1860 but was passed over by the convention as too radical on slavery. Although an excellent Treasury Secretary, his political ambitions created strains that led to his resignation from the cabinet. But he was too important to be denied high office; many Republicans thought that he would make a better president than Lincoln. Appointing him chief justice served the dual purpose of placating the Radicals and removing a rival from the political scene. Lincoln had no illusions that Chase would abandon his ambitions, but the new post would at least preclude him from active opposition.

Chase's appointment marked the beginning of the Court's recovery. His strong anti-slavery credentials helped bring it out of the shadow of the *Dred Scott* decision. While not an outstanding jurist, Chase was an able and astute chief justice. He avoided confrontations with the president and Congress that might have damaged the Court politically. But he was not overly deferential, for that would have been alien to his nature. A strong character, he infused the Court with a new sense of confidence and importance. Chase voted with the majority in the *Milligan* case, though he opposed extending the holding to Congress as well as the president. The Court became increasingly assertive under his leadership, though carefully avoiding serious confrontations. Reclaiming its old role as the arbiter of constitutionality, the Court declared ten acts of Congress and numerous state laws unconstitutional during his tenure. Since only two acts of Congress had been invalidated during the Marshall and Taney eras combined, this was a bold assertion of judicial power by a Court so recently in disrepute. Political ambition prevented Chase from becoming a great chief justice, but he was nevertheless a good one. He was the right man in the right job at the right time. Chase revived what Marshall had created and the blunder of the *Dred Scott* decision had nearly destroyed. The rapid recovery of judicial power in the United States owed much to his leadership.

Civil Liberties during the War

The Civil War was a watershed in the constitutional history of the United States. The war destroyed the states' rights doctrines that spawned secession but created others perhaps equally pernicious. Lincoln's theory that the nation is anterior and superior to the Constitution provided a durable rationale for massive assaults on civil liberties in wartime. Some historians have noted that constitutional rights were better protected in the South under Jefferson Davis than in the North under Lincoln. The Confederate Congress authorized the suspension of habeas corpus in 1862, but Davis used the power sparingly. Lincoln not only acted without the approval of Congress, but he suspended the writ in areas remote from military operations. Some of his wartime measures were probably justified by military necessity but others, such as the suspension of habeas corpus far behind the lines and the use of military trials for civilians, are difficult to justify. His administration used martial law for political purposes, and Democrats were harassed by the military to ensure Republicans victory at the polls. The popularity of secret organizations during the war may have reflected to some extent the risks of open political dissent. No previous administration had abused the power of government so flagrantly to promote partisan political goals.

But the wartime abuses of power were not fatal to constitutional government. Military arrests ceased with the defeat of the Confederacy, and political life in the North returned to normal. Moreover, most of the arrests made by the military during the war were not for political dissent; they were for real offenses such as blockade-running or involved the detention of suspicious Confederate civilians in areas occupied by the Union army. The *Merryman*, *Vallandigham*, and *Milligan* cases were exceptions, not the rule, with respect to

Civil Liberties in the Confederacy

"For proof of the sincerity of our purpose to maintain our ancient institutions, we may point to the constitution of the Confederacy and the laws enacted under it, as well as the fact that through all the necessities of an unequal struggle there has been no act on our part to impair personal liberty or the freedom of speech, of thought or of the press. The courts have been open, the judicial functions fully executed, and every right of the peaceful citizen maintained as securely as if a war of invasion had not disturbed the land."

—Jefferson Davis, Inaugural Address, February 22, 1862

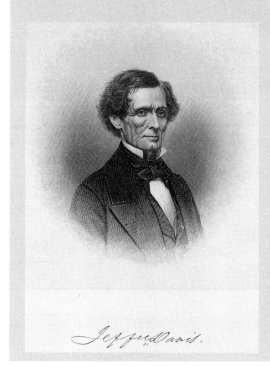

Figure X.7 Portrait of Jefferson Davis.

Library of Congress, Prints and Photographs Division, LC-USZ62-89800

the use of military power behind the lines. Most of the civilian cases tried by the military occurred in occupied areas of the Confederacy where conditions were far from normal. There is no question that serious abuses occurred, but this does not justify the conclusion that Lincoln was indifferent to civil liberties or imposed a quasi-military dictatorship on the North. That he subordinated everything to the restoration of the Union is undeniable, but this may well have been the margin of victory. If history teaches anything, it is that those who put anything above winning usually do not win. Lincoln did not become president to fail the nation by presiding over the dissolution of the Union. He did what had to be done in order to preserve it, and for that his greatness as a wartime leader is unassailable.

March 3, 1865	May 29, 1865	October 1865	November 1865	December 1865	February 19, 1866	April 9, 1866
Congress Establishes Freedmen's Bureau	President Johnson Issues Amnesty Proclamation	Florida Enacts Black Code	Mississippi Enacts Black Code	Alabama and South Carolina Enact Black Codes	President Johnson Vetoes Renewal of Freedmen's Bureau Bill	Civil Rights Act

March 23, 1867	April 15, 1867	February 10, 1868	March 2–3, 1868	May 26, 1868	July 1868	March 4, 1869
Second Reconstruction Act	Mississippi v. Johnson	Georgia v. Stanton	House of Representatives Draws Up Articles of Impeachment Against President Johnson	President Johnson Acquitted by the Senate	Ratification of Fourteenth Amendment	Ulysses S. Grant Takes Office as President of the United States

XI Reconstructing the Nation

May 1, 1866	July 16, 1866	July 30, 1866	January 14, 1867	February 5, 1867	March 2, 1867
Memphis Race Riot Begins	Congress Passes Freedmen's Bureau Bill Over President's Veto	New Orleans Race Riot	Test Oath Cases	Judiciary Act Habeas Corpus Act	First Reconstruction Act, Tenure of Office Act, and Command of the Army Act

April 12, 1869	October 25, 1869	February 3, 1870	April 20, 1871	March 1, 1875
Ex parte McCardle Texas v. White	Ex parte Yerger	Ratification of Fifteenth Amendment	Act to Enforce the Provisions of the Fourteenth Amendment	Civil Rights Act

> "[E]very man, no matter what his race or color; every earthly being who has an immortal soul, has an equal right to justice, honesty, and fair play with every other man; and the law should secure him those rights."
>
> —Thaddeus Stevens, in Congress (1867)

Lincoln's differences with Congress over Reconstruction flared into political warfare after his assassination in April 1865. His successor, Andrew Johnson, lacked the tact and political skill needed to lead the nation during the difficult postwar years. A Tennessee Democrat and opponent of secession, he had stayed in the Senate when his state seceded. Johnson served with distinction as military governor of Tennessee, and he was nominated as Lincoln's running mate on the National Union Party ticket in 1864. Republicans felt comfortable with a vice president who had urged Tennesseans to abolish slavery "because in the emancipation of slaves we break down an odious and dangerous aristocracy. I think we are freeing more whites than blacks in Tennessee." So it came as a shock when Johnson issued an amnesty proclamation in May 1865 pardoning former rebels who took an oath of future allegiance to the United States. The only persons excluded from the offer were high-ranking Confederate officials and persons owning more than $20,000 worth of taxable property. But those excluded from the general amnesty could apply to the president for individual pardons which would be considered separately. At the stroke of a pen, Johnson wiped the slate clean for the vast majority of southerners.

Johnson's Plan of Reconstruction

Johnson's plan for restoring civil government in the South accompanied his amnesty proclamation. Provisional governors appointed by the president would enroll the loyal voters in every southern state for the election of a state constitutional convention, and all pardoned rebels would be eligible to vote and participate in the process. The reconstructed state would be readmitted to the Union as soon as the new government repudiated the Confederate debt, abolished slavery as a domestic institution, and ratified the Thirteenth Amendment. When these conditions had been met, full control over internal affairs would be restored to the state along with the right to representation in Congress. His plan called for getting the South back into the Union quickly without sweeping political or social changes.

Radicals in Congress initially assumed that Johnson sided with them, and that Congress and the president would now work closely together to reconstruct the South. When he heard of Lincoln's death, Senator Zachariah Chandler of Michigan commented coarsely that God had kept Lincoln in office for as long as he was useful and then had put a better man in his place. Many other Radicals in Congress preferred Johnson to Lincoln. When the Joint Committee on the Conduct of the War called on Johnson shortly after the assassination, Senator Wade, its chairman, declared: "Johnson, we have faith in you. By the gods, there will be no trouble now in running the government." Johnson's reply to Wade probably reassured the Radicals: "I hold that robbery is a crime; rape is a crime; murder is a crime; treason is a crime and must be punished. Treason must be made infamous and traitors must be

Figure XI.1 Portrait of Andrew Johnson (c. 1855–1865).

Library of Congress, Prints and Photographs Division, LC-USZ62-13017

impoverished." A president who compared rebels with rapists and murderers would not likely bring the South back into the Union without major changes.

But Johnson's radical rhetoric did not accurately reflect his political views. The president actually had nothing in common with Republicans whose political agenda called for internal improvements, a national banking system, and high protective tariffs. A Jackson Democrat, he had spent his political life representing the small farmers and poor whites of Tennessee against the wealthy slaveholding interests. His distrust of the latter explains the $20,000 exception in his amnesty proclamation. He remained at heart a states' rights Democrat opposed to the nationalizing tendencies of the war years. He hoped to restore the Union essentially as it had been before secession but without slavery. Power would be transferred to the small farmers and non-slaveholding whites of the South, but the traditional relationship between the states and the federal government would remain unchanged. Moreover, the political and civil rights of the ex-slaves were matters for the southern states to settle for themselves without federal interference. To make voting rights for blacks a part of Reconstruction struck him as the height of folly.

Although Johnson's plan superficially resembled what Lincoln had proposed in 1863, circumstances had changed dramatically. For one thing, the war was over, and demands for racial justice no longer had to be subordinated to the restoration of the Union. For another, the freeing of hundreds of thousands of southern slaves raised race relations to the top of the political agenda. On this score, Lincoln's Reconstruction measures had achieved very little. The civil governments that he established in the South did nothing to reassure Congress that the rights of the ex-slaves would be protected. Even in Louisiana, where Lincoln took a personal hand in the restoration of state government, he had been unable to persuade the white Unionists to make any provision for the voting rights of blacks, not even blacks serving in the Union army. Lincoln expressed misgivings about the situation during the final weeks of the war. At a cabinet meeting on the day of his assassination, he approved a plan to halt the organization of civil governments in the former states of the Confederacy; they would be placed instead under military governors to ensure that the civil rights of ex-slaves were protected. By the time of his death, Lincoln had gone far to narrow the gap between himself and the Radicals in Congress. But Johnson now widened the gap by committing himself to policies no longer tenable.

The president's timing was better than his policies, because with Congress out of session he had a free hand to implement his plans. Lincoln had also recognized the advantage of proceeding while Congress was not in session. He declared it

> providential that this great rebellion is crushed out just as Congress has adjourned and there are none of the disturbing elements of that body to embarrass us. If we are wise and discreet we shall reanimate the states and get their governments in successful operation, with order prevailing and the Union reestablished before Congress comes together in December.

But Johnson was neither wise nor discreet. Had Lincoln lived, he probably would have put together a moderate-conservative coalition and isolated the extreme Radicals in Congress. But Johnson isolated no one, except possibly himself. He acted unilaterally without building political bridges or preparing the country for his program. Building alliances was indispensable, particularly for a nonelected president without a popular mandate. He counted instead on presenting Congress with a *fait accompli*, confident that it would have to accept the state governments he had already established. His worst mistake was to underestimate the skill and determination of the Radical leaders.

Congressional Reaction

Thaddeus Stevens led the counterattack in Congress, and his tactics were brilliant. The Republican caucus held on the day before Congress convened adopted his plan to set up a joint committee to investigate conditions in the South before any of the new southern senators and representatives were seated. So the southerners were omitted from the roll call and denied the seats to which they had been elected. The law required the entire roll to be called, but the Radicals simply ignored the requirement. Stevens then put through his resolution for a joint committee of nine representatives and six senators to investigate the Johnson-sponsored state governments. Senator William P. Fessenden of Maine, a moderate, headed the Committee, but Stevens was its most powerful member. Until the Committee submitted its report, no senators or representatives from the South would be seated by Congress. This left the Republicans firmly in power. If the southerners, all of whom were Democrats, had been seated, the Republican majority would have been precarious, and the power of the Radicals would have vanished.

Figure XI.2 Portrait of Thaddeus Stevens.

Library of Congress, Prints and Photographs Division, LC-USZC4-7987

By the beginning of 1866, public opinion in the North began to run strongly in favor of the Radicals. There was a growing conviction that Johnson had thrown away the victory won at such great cost on the battlefield. The old ruling class was back in power, and nothing had really changed in the South. Not one of the reconstructed states allowed African Americans to vote, and special police controls severely restricted their freedom. The election of so many ex-Confederate leaders to state and federal offices caused shock and indignation. Alexander H. Stephens, the Confederate vice president, was elected to the Senate, as were Benjamin F. Perry, a Confederate judge, and J. L. Manning, who had been an aide to General Beauregard at Fort Sumter and Bull Run. The contingent to the House of Representatives included Generals Cullen A. Battle, Phillip Cook, and W. T. Woffard, formerly of the Confederate Army. That the South should turn to its trusted leaders was understandable, but that so many of them had been prominent Confederates played into the hands of the Radicals.

Veto of the Freedmen's Bureau Bill

The first test of strength between Johnson and the Radicals came in January 1866 when Congress passed a bill extending the life of the Freedmen's Bureau. The Bureau was a wartime agency set up in 1865 to distribute emergency relief among the ex-slaves. The renewal bill greatly increased the Bureau's functions, essentially turning it into a political organization for the protection of the freedmen's rights. The bill ordered military trials for persons who deprived freedmen of their civil rights, thus putting such cases outside the jurisdiction of the regular courts. Johnson vetoed the bill on constitutional grounds, specifically because the provision for military trials violated due process guarantees. The veto, which was sustained by only a two-vote margin in the Senate, marked the beginning of open warfare between the president and Congress. Johnson had temporarily blocked the Radicals, but it turned out to be the last successful veto of his administration. In July 1866 Congress passed an almost identical Freedmen's Bureau Act over his veto.

Full Citizenship under the Civil Rights Act of 1866

"Be it enacted by the Senate and House of Representatives of the United States of America in Congress assembled, That all persons born in the United States and not subject to any foreign power, excluding Indians not taxed, are hereby declared to be citizens of the United States; and such citizens, of every race and color, without regard to any previous condition of slavery or involuntary servitude, except as a punishment for crime whereof the party shall have been duly convicted, shall have the same right, in every State and Territory in the United States, to make and enforce contracts, to sue, be parties, and give evidence, to inherit, purchase, lease, sell, hold, and convey real and personal property, and to full and equal benefit of all laws and proceedings for the security of person and property, as is enjoyed by white citizens, and shall be subject to like punishment, pains, and penalties, and to none other, any law, statute, ordinance, regulation, or custom, to the contrary notwithstanding . . ."

Civil Rights Act of 1866

The conflict between Johnson and the Radicals heated up in March 1866 when Congress passed the Civil Rights Act. Supported by moderates and Radicals alike, the Act sought to protect the ex-slaves against the infamous Black Codes enacted by Johnson's reconstructed states. The Act declared the freedmen citizens of the United States and forbade the states to discriminate against them on the basis of race or prior servitude. They were also guaranteed all the rights enjoyed by whites under the laws of their respective states. The Act authorized the president to use military force to enforce its provisions. Johnson vetoed the measure on the ground that the states alone had jurisdiction over rights not expressly protected by the Constitution. But the Radicals contended that the enforcement provision of the Thirteenth Amendment changed things by authorizing Congress to protect the freedom of the ex-slaves. When Congress overrode his veto, Johnson made the mistake of becoming involved in an acrimonious debate with the congressional leaders. Instead of cutting his losses and working for an accommodation, he painted himself into a political corner. His intemperate remarks alienated potential allies among moderates who might have been detached from the veto-proof majority in Congress.

The Black Codes more than any other development in the South helped to radicalize northern public opinion. They were so flagrantly racist that even moderates had to question the legitimacy of the Johnson state governments. The codes tended to be most draconian where the black population was largest. The Mississippi code prohibited African Americans from renting land or houses, intermarrying with whites, quitting a job without permission, or keeping arms and ammunition. They prescribed penalties for blacks convicted of "riots, affrays, trespasses, mischief, seditious speeches, insulting gestures, language or acts," with nothing said about similar conduct by whites. The obvious purpose of these laws was to keep the freedmen in regulatory chains. Such abuses of their state police powers put the Johnson governments in the worst possible light. Northerners viewed these measures as an attempt to negate the Thirteenth Amendment and subject former slaves to substitute forms of bondage.

The Black Code of Mississippi on Race Relations

"Be it further enacted, That all freedmen, free negroes and mulattoes in this State, over the age of eighteen years, found on the second Monday in January, 1866, or thereafter, without lawful employment or business, or found unlawfully assembling themselves together, either in the day or night time, and all white persons so assembling themselves with freedmen, free negroes or mulattoes, or usually associating with freedmen, free negroes or mulattoes, on terms of equality, or living in adultery or fornication with a freed woman, free negro or mulatto, shall be deemed vagrants, and on conviction thereof shall be fined in a sum not exceeding, in the case of a freedman, free negro, or mulatto, fifty dollars, and a white man two hundred dollars, and imprisoned, at the discretion of the court, the free negro not exceeding ten days, and the white man not exceeding six months."

—An Act to Amend the Vagrant Laws of the State (1865)

Fourteenth Amendment

Doubts that the courts would uphold the Civil Rights Act under the Thirteenth Amendment led the Radicals to incorporate its key provisions directly into the Constitution through the Fourteenth Amendment. The Amendment began by making all persons born or naturalized in the United States "citizens of the United States and of the State wherein they reside." This overturned the *Dred Scott* holding with respect to federal and state citizenship for African Americans. The Amendment also provided that

> No State shall make or enforce any law which shall abridge the privileges or immunities of citizens of the United States; nor shall any State deprive any person of life, liberty, or property, without due process of law; nor deny to any person within its jurisdiction the equal protection of the laws.

Other provisions dealt with state representation in Congress and the Electoral College, repudiation of the Confederate war debt, and the disfranchisement of ex-rebels. Like the Thirteenth Amendment, it contained an Enforcement Clause authorizing Congress to enforce its provisions. Approved by Congress in June 1866, the Amendment proposed the most sweeping changes in federal-state relations since the adoption of the Constitution.

The Radicals made ratification of the Amendment a precondition for recognition of the southern state governments. Moderates in Congress supported it as well, because the repression of blacks in the South demonstrated the need for federal constitutional protection. But Johnson denounced the Amendment as unconstitutional, and he urged southerners to reject it. This was a mistake because it put him in the position of opposing guarantees that on their face seemed fair and reasonable. A more flexible approach might have salvaged something. The president might have bargained acceptance of the Amendment for congressional recognition of his reconstructed state governments. But he chose

The Radical Position in the Debate on Southern Recognition

"I insist that the people who maintained constitutional State governments, who, during the entire war, were represented here, and who are now represented here, the people who maintained this national Government and put down the rebellion, have a right under the laws of war as conquerors to prescribe such conditions as in the judgment of the majority of this Congress are necessary for the national safety and the national security. This is the right of the conqueror under every law, human and divine. If this be not the true theory, then, indeed, is our national Government a rope of sand . . . The man who stands up and says that during the entire war the rebel States were entitled to be represented here lays down a proposition which would undermine and sap the very foundations of the Government. If these rebel States had the right to be represented here and had been represented here during this war, this Government would have been bound hand and foot, and we would have been incapable of resistance."

—Rep. James Ashley of Ohio, Debate on Proposed
Fourteenth Amendment, May 29, 1866

confrontation instead, and the southern states followed his lead. Only Tennessee ratified the Amendment, whereupon Congress seated its senators and representatives. The rest of the South counted on the coming congressional elections to repudiate the Radicals and vindicate Johnson's Reconstruction policy.

Both the president and the South miscalculated badly. The racial violence and disorders in the South had by now thoroughly discredited his reconstructed governments. A riot in Memphis in May 1866 claimed 46 black lives, and 200 blacks died in New Orleans during the July disorders. On the day after the New Orleans bloodbath, Horace Greeley's *New York Tribune* thundered: "The hands of the rebels are again red with loyal blood. Rebel armies have once more begun the work of massacre." Johnson made things worse by campaigning personally against his opponents in Congress, thus squandering what-ever remained of his presidential prestige. He was harassed at every stop by hecklers who drowned out what he had to say or provoked him into intemperate outbursts. The crush-ing defeat of Johnson's candidates enabled the Radicals to claim that the president himself had been repudiated by the voters. This was not necessarily true, because local politics also played a part in the outcome. But Johnson's intense personal involvement lent plau-sibility to the claim that he had been repudiated. The Radicals and their moderate allies came out of the elections with overwhelming majorities in both houses of Congress. Even more important, they now had a popular mandate to take direct control of Reconstruction.

Radical Reconstruction

Their first order of business was to sweep away the president's reconstructed state govern-ments. In March 1867 the outgoing Congress passed the First Military Reconstruction Act over Johnson's veto. Three supplementary Acts followed, but the First summed up most of the Radicals' program. The Act suspended civil government in the former states

First Military Reconstruction Act

"Whereas no legal State governments or adequate protections for life or property now exists in the rebel States of Virginia, North Carolina, South Carolina, Georgia, Mississippi, Alabama, Louisiana, Florida, Texas, and Arkansas; and whereas it is necessary that peace and good order should be enforced in said States until loyal and republican State governments can be legally established; Therefore . . . Be it Enacted, That said rebel States shall be divided into military districts and made subject to the military authority of the United States as herein prescribed."

—March 2, 1867

of the Confederacy and divided them into five military districts under the command of an army general appointed by the president. The general had authority to impose martial law and to order military trials for disturbers of the peace. Except for Tennessee, which had been rewarded with readmission for ratifying the Fourteenth Amendment, the southern states would be ruled by the military as though they were conquered provinces.

Civil government would be restored to the South only when the conditions set by Congress had been met. First, the military would enroll the loyal voters for the election of state constitutional conventions. There would be universal male suffrage, with blacks included, but large numbers of ex-Confederates barred from voting. The constitutions drafted would have to guarantee freedmen the right to vote and hold public office. After the constitution had been ratified by the voters and approved by Congress, elections would be held and civil government restored. The final hurdle would be ratification of the Fourteenth Amendment by the newly elected state legislature. The state would then be eligible for representation in Congress as soon as the Amendment became part of the Constitution. Until then, all political arrangements in the South would be temporary and provisional. The Radicals had no intention of readmitting the southern states until ratification of the Fourteenth Amendment had put the civil rights of the black population under federal protection.

The enfranchisement of African Americans and disfranchisement of numerous whites were essential parts of political reorganization. At least 200,000 southern whites were barred from voting or holding public office for having supported the Confederacy. Their exclusion gave blacks an overall voting majority that made the South temporarily Republican. One-third of the delegates elected to the state conventions were African Americans, and in South Carolina they were in the majority. Many northerners, derisively called "carpetbaggers," provided leadership in the work of political reorganization. They helped to draft the new state constitutions, which were usually based on northern models, and many of them were elected to high office in the new state governments. Large numbers of southern whites, the much scorned "scalawags," also played leading roles in organizing the new regimes. While blacks provided the votes needed for political reorganization, white carpetbaggers and scalawags controlled most of the public offices. But not all the offices went to whites. For the first time in the history of the South, African Americans filled positions in state and local government as mayors, sheriffs, and lawmakers, and some went on to serve as senators and representatives in the United States Congress.

The political dividends of Radical Reconstruction were not slow in coming. Grateful to the Republicans for emancipation and federal protection, southern blacks joined the party in droves. The work of organizing them as a political force was carried out by the Freedmen's Bureau and the Union and Loyal Leagues that sprang up in the South. The latter were local political action groups that put up candidates and got out the vote. The Bureau, though officially nonpolitical, became a conduit for federal patronage and money. The Bureau and the Leagues worked in tandem to build a Republican Party infrastructure in the South. But the political arrangements counted for less than the military support needed to keep the southern Radicals in power. Their governments were propped up by 20,000 federal troops and contingents of black militias. The troops were needed to protect black voters from disfranchised whites who increasingly resorted to violence and intimidation. Without them, the political structures would have collapsed like a house of cards.

By the summer of 1868, seven states had met all the conditions set for readmission to the Union. They had adopted constitutions which repudiated the Confederate debt, enfranchised blacks, and disfranchised ex-rebels. Only Mississippi, Texas, and Virginia

Figure XI.3 Group portrait of the first African American senator and representatives elected to Congress, by Currier and Ives (1872). In the front row, from left to right, are Sen. Hiram Revels (MS), Rep. Benjamin S. Turner (AL), Rep. Josiah T. Walls (FL), Rep. Joseph H. Rainey (SC), and Rep. Robert B. Elliot (SC). In the back row, from left to right, are Rep. Robert C. De Large (SC) and Rep. Jefferson F. Long (GA).

Library of Congress, Prints and Photographs Division, LC-USZC2-2325

remained unreconstructed, largely because of popular opposition to the harsh disfranchisement provisions of the proposed constitutions. Congress finally allowed these states to vote separately on disfranchisement, providing that the voting rights of blacks were recognized and protected. To make the protection ironclad, Congress also required them to ratify the Fifteenth Amendment in order to gain readmission to the Union. When the process was finally over, the South found itself with the most enlightened and progressive state constitutions in its history. If the northern states had been held to the same high standards, few would have qualified for admission to the Union.

The elections of 1868 demonstrated the importance of the southern black vote. General Ulysses S. Grant, the Republican candidate for president, defeated his Democratic opponent, Horatio Seymour, with a popular majority of only 306,000 out of a total of over 5,700,000 votes cast. Without the 700,000 votes cast by southern blacks, Grant would have lost the popular vote. The reconstructed South provided additional Republican senators and representatives, including African Americans who a decade earlier had been slaves, to strengthen the northern contingent in Congress. But the new Republican voting base in the

South might not be permanent. The Ku Klux Klan and other secret societies had already begun a campaign of political intimidation and terror to restore southern Democrats to power. Their strategy was to keep black Republicans from the polls and to win over southern white Republicans with appeals for racial solidarity. Combating terrorism and protecting their political base in the South became a high priority for Republicans in Congress.

Fifteenth Amendment

Political violence in the South convinced the Radicals that only a constitutional amendment could permanently guarantee black voting rights. The Fourteenth Amendment did not specifically protect the right to vote, and the suffrage guarantees of the southern state constitutions could be repealed if the old ruling class returned to power. If the latter happened, federal guarantees would be needed to protect blacks from disfranchisement. In February 1869 the Radicals pushed the Fifteenth Amendment through Congress in order to put black voting rights beyond the reach of state governments. The Amendment was concise and to the point: The right to vote "shall not be denied or abridged by the United States or by any State on account of race, color, or previous condition of servitude." As with the Thirteenth and Fourteenth Amendments, Congress was given authority to enforce the guarantee with appropriate legislation. Ratification of the Amendment in March 1870 put political rights for the first time under federal protection.

All the Reconstruction measures were passed by Congress over the president's veto. Although Johnson regarded them as unconstitutional, he implemented them nevertheless pursuant to his duty to enforce the laws. There were veto-proof majorities in both houses of Congress, and open defiance by the president would have invited impeachment. Moreover, Johnson was far from helpless; his patronage and removal powers could still be used to influence events. His position as commander in chief also gave him leverage in dealing with the military authorities responsible for the political reorganization of the South. Although his policies had been rejected by the voters in the congressional elections of 1866, the separation of powers kept his executive authority intact. From an institutional standpoint, the president remained a powerful force in government.

Marginalizing the President

The Radicals moved boldly to limit Johnson's powers. On March 2, 1867, the same day they passed the first Reconstruction Act, they pushed through two laws that challenged the constitutional separation of powers. The first, the Tenure of Office Act, provided that all officials appointed by the president with the consent of the Senate were protected against removal until a successor had been approved by the Senate. Anyone who accepted office in violation of the law would be guilty of a misdemeanor punishable by fine or imprisonment. Johnson vetoed the bill on the ground that it violated the separation of powers, but Congress overrode the veto. The second, generally known as the Command of the Army Act, forbade the president to issue orders to the military except through the commanding general of the army. This gave General Grant, the army commander, operational control of the military authorities responsible for implementing Reconstruction in

Figure XI.4 General Ulysses S. Grant at his headquarters in Cold Harbor, Virginia (1864).
Library of Congress, Prints and Photographs Division, LC-USZ61-903

the South. Johnson was also forbidden to remove the general or assign him to duties away from Washington except at his request or with the Senate's consent. Because the Act was attached as a rider to a needed military appropriation bill, Johnson did not veto it. But he made it clear that he regarded the encroachment upon his powers as commander in chief unconstitutional.

Johnson refused to submit to the constraints of the Tenure of Office Act. He proceeded to dismiss Secretary of War Edwin Stanton without the Senate's consent. Stanton supported the Radicals against Johnson, but he refused to leave the cabinet when the president requested his resignation. He kept the Radicals posted on cabinet deliberations and was generally a thorn in the side of the administration. Keeping him in office was important to the Radicals, because the War Department played a key role in military reconstruction. Johnson shrewdly suspended him in August 1867, when Congress was not in session, and he appointed General Grant as a temporary successor. When the Senate failed to approve the removal in December, Grant withdrew and Stanton resumed office. Johnson dismissed him unconditionally in February 1868, but Stanton stubbornly refused to give up office. In dismissing Stanton without the Senate's consent, Johnson gave his congressional foes the pretext they needed to begin impeachment proceedings against him.

Impeachment of Johnson

Three days after the dismissal of Stanton, the House of Representatives, with Thaddeus Stevens pulling the strings, began impeachment proceedings. Eleven articles of impeachment were agreed upon and passed by an overwhelming majority. The first eight cited specific violations of the Tenure of Office Act with respect to Stanton's dismissal. The ninth article accused the president of attempting to circumvent the Command of the Army Act by impugning its constitutionality to one of the army commanders. The tenth article was purely political, accusing him of attempting to bring "disgrace, ridicule, hatred, contempt, and reproach" on members of Congress. The eleventh article was the most dangerous of all, because it summed up the other ten in what amounted to a shotgun indictment of the president. Senators with doubts about particular articles could probably find enough in the cumulative charges to justify voting for conviction.

Johnson's trial by the Senate began on March 30, 1868, with Chief Justice Chase presiding. The House of Representatives, having brought the charges, appointed Thaddeus Stevens, Benjamin Butler, John Bingham, and George Boutwell to manage the prosecution. Johnson was represented by Henry Stanbery, Benjamin R. Curtis, and William M. Evarts, which gave him a clear edge in legal talent. Except for Butler, who was an excellent lawyer, the House managers were primarily politicians. But legal talent would not help much if the Senate decided that the trial was a political proceeding. If the Senate sat as a political rather than as a judicial body, it would not be bound by legal rules regarding the evidence; any evidence, including hearsay, would be admissible against the president. Nor would the Senate have to find him guilty of a specific crime or misdemeanor in order to convict him. A conviction could be justified on political grounds even if criminal charges could not be proved. Since no president had been impeached before, the nature of the process was an open question.

Counsel for Johnson argued persuasively that the trial was judicial, not political. The legal terminology of the Constitution describing impeachment proceedings suggested that the senators were to sit as judges rather than as politicians. Article I authorized them "to try" all impeachments, and Article II provided for removal of the president upon "Conviction" of "Treason, Bribery, or other high Crimes and Misdemeanors." The use of these terms indicated a clear intent that impeachments should be conducted as judicial trials. If impeachment became a political process, the independence of the executive branch would be destroyed. Any Congress with a sufficient majority would be able to remove a president for purely political reasons. This would destroy the constitutional separation of powers and create a parliamentary system of government under an all-powerful Congress.

The House managers were equally convinced that impeachment was more than just a judicial proceeding. If the president could be removed only for legal offenses, it would preclude the removal of palpably unfit chief executives. Would the nation have to endure a madman in the White House just because no laws had been broken? Judge John Pickering had been removed from the federal bench in 1804 more for his insane behavior than for any judicial misconduct. The Senate voted to remove him essentially because it was in the public interest. The same standard should apply to presidents as well. The analogy was persuasive but not really convincing. Although the Constitution authorizes the removal of judges for lapses from "good behavior" in office, it sets the higher standard of "high Crimes and Misdemeanors" for the removal of presidents. The House managers' response was that the issue before the Senate was not whether Johnson had committed specific crimes, but whether his continuance in office was harmful to the nation.

A procedural vote at the outset supported the defense theory that the trial was a judicial proceeding. The Senate voted 31 to 19 to allow the chief justice to settle all questions of law and evidence unless the senators overruled him. This suggested that the chief justice would act as a presiding judge in a court of law, and that the senators would act as associate judges. It also implied that rules of law applied, and that the president would have the benefit of legal presumptions available to ordinary defendants. Finally, it suggested that unless the legal offenses alleged in the articles of impeachment could be proved, the president should not be convicted. Proving him guilty of political offenses would not be enough to justify his removal from office.

The key to the case was Johnson's alleged violation of the Tenure of Office Act. The Act required the Senate's consent for the removal of Stanton, and Johnson had dismissed him without getting it. This was the only clear-cut violation of law alleged, and the president would have stood convicted by his own actions had the law not contained a loophole. The law provided that unless the Senate consented to their removal, cabinet officers were to hold office during the term of the president who appointed them and for one month thereafter. But since Stanton had been appointed by Lincoln, the law technically did not cover his dismissal by Johnson. In their haste to tie the president's hands, the Radicals had created a loophole that the defense exploited effectively. The House managers tried to make the best of things by arguing that Johnson was only serving out Lincoln's term and that the Act therefore did cover his dismissal of Stanton. But that they had to argue the point at all shifted the focus of the trial to whether the Tenure of Office Act even applied to Johnson.

Johnson's attorneys also argued that since the Act was clearly unconstitutional, a legal nullity, the president could not have broken it. The House managers replied that Congress is the proper judge of its legislative powers, and that all its enactments carry a presumption of constitutionality. They were right about this, because what the defense claimed gave too much power to the president. If the president can refuse to enforce laws just because he doubts their constitutionality, he would have a de facto veto not granted by the Constitution. But even if Johnson had violated the law, the defense contended that the violations were merely technical and designed only to raise the constitutional issue. The president had acted without criminal intent, his only purpose being to test the law in the courts. The prosecution replied that his motives were irrelevant; all that mattered was that he had violated the law, and the violation implied all the criminal intent needed to find him guilty of a legal offense.

The Senate voted first on Article 11, the shotgun article on which a guilty vote was most likely. Thirty-five of the fifty-four senators voted for conviction, just one short of the required two-thirds majority. Despite tremendous political pressure, seven Republicans broke ranks and joined the twelve Democrats who voted for acquittal. A second vote was taken ten days later on the second and third articles, but the seven Republicans held their ground and again prevented a conviction. These votes proved decisive, and the majority moved to break off the proceedings. Johnson had been saved by Republicans who put principle over party. They considered the Tenure of Office Act unconstitutional and refused to remove him for challenging it. But they paid a high price for their principled stand. Denounced as traitors to the Republican Party, six of the seven were defeated when they sought reelection.

Some of the senators who voted for acquittal probably preferred Johnson to the man who would have succeeded him. His successor would have been the ultra-radical Senator Wade, the president pro tempore of the Senate, whose position on a wide range of issues alarmed moderates and conservatives. Wade supported such causes as the free distribution of land to southern blacks and the extension of voting rights to women. Despite his many faults, Johnson's term of office was nearly over, and there was no conceivable way he could win reelection. Wade's situation was different. As an incumbent president with an enthusiastic following among the Radicals, he would have been a strong contender for the Republican nomination in 1868. The possibility of having Wade as president for four years or more seemed less desirable for some than putting up with Johnson for a few more months. Wade himself had fully expected to become president. He compiled a list

Attorney William Evarts for the Defense

"They wish to know whether the President has betrayed our liberties or our possessions to a foreign state. They wish to know whether he has delivered up a fortress or surrendered a fleet. They wish to know whether he has made merchandise of the public trust and turned the authority to private gain. And when informed that none of these things are charges, imputed, or even declaimed about, they yet seek further information and are told that he has removed a member of his cabinet."

Figure XI.5 Portrait of William Evarts.

Library of Congress, Prints and Photographs Division, LC-USZ62-83457

of cabinet appointments while the trial was in progress, and he helped his own cause by voting for conviction. Of all the Radicals, Wade was the biggest loser when Johnson was acquitted.

Although Johnson deserved acquittal, a conviction probably would not have altered our constitutional system in ways some commentators have suggested. The separation of powers would not suddenly have been replaced by a parliamentary system with Congress the dominant branch of government. Johnson's supporters raised this possibility during the trial, but the odds against this happening were overwhelming. For one thing, the powers of the president come directly from the Constitution, not from Congress; for another, he is elected by the people, not by Congress. The idea that impeachment could ever become equivalent to a no-confidence vote in the British parliament is farfetched. The constitutional separation of the legislative and executive branches protects the president against removal for merely political reasons. Impeachment is as traumatic for Congress as for the president and not likely to be undertaken lightly. Johnson's conviction would have had serious political consequences in making Wade president, but it would not have changed our constitutional separation of powers.

The Supreme Court during Reconstruction

What the Radicals feared most during Reconstruction was that the Supreme Court might declare their program unconstitutional. Since there was a real chance this might happen, they put the Court under heavy pressure not to interfere. When Justice Catron died in May 1865, Johnson appointed Attorney General Henry Stanbery to fill the vacancy. But the Senate did not act on the nomination; instead, Congress reduced the membership of the Court from ten justices to eight. This nullified the Stanbery nomination and deprived Johnson of the opportunity to fill the next vacancy as well. The Radicals wanted no Johnson appointees on the Court if the constitutionality of their program came up for review. They meant also to serve notice on the Court that judicial interference with Reconstruction would not be tolerated. When Justice Wayne died in 1867, the Court shrank to only eight justices. If another vacancy had occurred during Johnson's term, there almost certainly would have been further reductions.

The Radicals and their moderate allies had cause to be concerned. In December 1866 the Court held in *Milligan* that neither the president nor Congress could order military trials for civilians in areas where the civil courts were open. Since the Radicals planned to use martial law to effect political change in the South, the holding alarmed them. Equally alarming were two decisions handed down in the Test Oath Cases in January 1867. The first, in *Cummings v. Missouri*, invalidated provisions in the state constitution of Missouri requiring persons engaged in a wide range of occupations to take an oath that they had not supported the Confederacy and had always been loyal to the United States. Those unwilling or unable to take the oath were barred from voting, holding public office, or practicing their professions. In *Ex parte Garland*, decided on the same day, the Court invalidated a similar oath imposed by Congress on attorneys practicing before the federal courts.

Both cases were closely decided by 5–4 votes. The majority in both held that tests of past loyalty violated the constitutional prohibition against ex post facto laws and bills of attainder. Such tests imposed penalties not in force when the alleged offenses occurred, and they imposed them without any provision for a judicial hearing. The facts in *Cummings* may have influenced the outcome. Cummings was a Catholic priest who was tried and convicted in Missouri for preaching without taking the required oath. The *Garland* case involved a lawyer barred from practicing in the federal courts because his service in the Confederate army prevented him from taking the oath prescribed by Congress.

The Radicals in Congress attacked both decisions. They feared that the Court might be preparing to overturn their Reconstruction program. But the justices had no desire for political confrontations. In *Mississippi v. Johnson* (1867), the Court unanimously dismissed a suit brought by the state government of Mississippi to enjoin the president from enforcing the Reconstruction Acts. The Court held that the president's executive and political functions are not subject to judicial control. The opinion, written by Chief Justice Chase, made a distinction between the executive and ministerial duties of the president. Ministerial duties, according to Chase, are those prescribed by laws which leave the president no discretion. With respect to his executive duties, however, the president has considerable discretion as to how they shall be performed. While his ministerial duties are subject to judicial review, the Court may not interfere with his political discretion. Enforcement of the Reconstruction Acts involved political discretion and so put the case outside the Court's jurisdiction.

A second attempt was made to enjoin enforcement of the Reconstruction Acts in *Georgia v. Stanton* (1868). The suit was brought against Secretary of War Stanton on the theory that his duties as a department head were essentially ministerial. The state government of Georgia challenged the constitutional authority of Congress to put it out of office and subject the citizens of Georgia to military rule. The Court dismissed the suit on the ground that it involved political matters beyond the jurisdiction of the courts. Stanton's duties were not sufficiently fixed and ministerial to justify judicial intervention. The Court thought it germane that the suit did not involve individual rights but rather the corporate rights of a state as a political entity. The issues in the case were essentially political and therefore should be settled by the political branches of government. If personal rights rather than political interests had been at issue, the Court hinted, the outcome might have been different.

Ex parte McCardle

Such a case soon appeared, and the constitutional issues it raised could not be avoided. The case began in November 1867 with the arrest of William McCardle by the military authorities in Mississippi. McCardle was a newspaper editor who had staunchly opposed the Radical program and made himself a thorn in the side of General E.O.C. Ord, the commander responsible for the political reorganization of the state. When Ord imposed a tax to finance the state constitutional convention then in session, McCardle published an incendiary editorial urging resistance to the tax. He warned that persons who attempted to collect the tax would "be shot down like dogs, as they are! They will deserve to be shot, and we advise every man to resist the payment of such a tax by all the means God has given him." The provocation was too blatant to be ignored. General Ord had McCardle arrested and held for trial by a military court. This set the stage for a political and constitutional confrontation.

The case posed a threat to the whole program of military reconstruction in the South. The Supreme Court had held in *Milligan* that the trial of civilians by military courts was lawful only in war zones where the civil courts were closed. That decision weighed heavily on the Radicals. Thaddeus Stevens denounced it as more dangerous than *Dred Scott*, placing "the knife at the throat of every man who now or ever had declared himself a loyal Union Man." McCardle's pending trial by the military raised exactly the issues raised in the *Milligan* case. Unless the Court overruled *Milligan*, which seemed unlikely, one of the key provisions of the Reconstruction Acts would almost certainly be declared unconstitutional.

Opponents of Reconstruction recognized the importance of getting a ruling from the Court before the Radical program took hold in the South. Ironically, the Radicals had made access to the Court easier under the Judiciary Act of 1867. The Act revised the Judiciary Act of 1789 to authorize the federal courts to issue writs of habeas corpus and for the Supreme Court to review such cases on appeal. Previously, the Court only had jurisdiction to issue the writ in an original proceeding after remedies in the state courts had been exhausted. The revision had been enacted to protect federal officials and southern Radicals from legal harassment in the state courts. It guaranteed detained persons a speedy hearing in the federal courts and the right of appeal to the Supreme Court. Originally designed to protect Reconstruction, the procedure now threatened to destroy it.

Three days after his arrest, a petition for habeas corpus was filed on McCardle's behalf in the federal circuit court for Mississippi. The writ was issued by Judge Robert A. Hill, and the prisoner was produced in court for a hearing on the legality of his detention by the military. At issue was the constitutionality of the Reconstruction Acts, and the court upheld them as constitutional. McCardle was then remanded to the custody of the military for trial by a military court. The ruling had been anticipated, so McCardle's attorney immediately moved for permission to appeal to the Supreme Court. The court granted the motion and ordered McCardle released on bail of $1,000 pending the appeal. Everything was now in place for a Supreme Court decision that many expected would hold Radical Reconstruction unconstitutional.

McCardle was represented by Jeremiah S. Black, who had also represented Milligan, when the first arguments were heard. Black won the first round when the Court voted, 5–4, to advance the case on the calendar for an early hearing. Arguments were then set for March 1868, and it was generally assumed that the justices would vote the same way on the constitutional issues as they had on the calendar motion. The Radicals suffered another setback when Attorney General Stanbery informed the Court that he considered the Reconstruction Acts unconstitutional and therefore could not in good conscience argue to uphold them. His withdrawal compelled the War Department, whose jurisdiction to try

McCardle was being challenged, to engage outside counsel. Senator Lyman Trumbull, an outstanding Illinois lawyer, was retained to represent the government.

Trumbull tried to avoid a decision on the constitutional issues by challenging the Court's jurisdiction to hear the case. He argued that the issues were essentially political and that the Court should dismiss the case on the grounds given in *Mississippi v. Johnson* and *Georgia v. Stanton*. But this time there was no easy way out, and the Radicals had only themselves to blame. Chief Justice Chase, speaking for a unanimous Court, denied the motion, declaring that the Judiciary Act of 1867 not only authorized the appeal but required the Court to hear it. When it became clear that the constitutionality of the Reconstruction Acts would be tested, the War Department retained Matthew Hale Carpenter, a leading attorney, to assist Trumbull with the case.

Before the case was argued, David Dudley Field joined Black on behalf of McCardle. They had worked together in the *Milligan* case, and that decision provided the precedent with which they hoped to invalidate the Reconstruction Acts. Military rule destroyed the republican form of government guaranteed by the Constitution, they contended, because it denied southerners trial by jury and other due process guarantees. Carpenter, speaking for the government, argued that the Acts should be upheld under the belligerency powers of the United States. Secession had destroyed the southern states as political entities and put them under the direct authority of Congress. He also delivered what seemed to be a veiled warning. The Court was not equal to Congress, he declared, and certainly not above it. While the Court could not reorganize Congress or reduce its jurisdiction, Congress could do both to the Court. If the Court opposed Congress, Carpenter implied, political reprisals could be expected.

Figure XI.6 Portrait of Salmon Chase (c. 1860–1875).

Library of Congress, Prints and Photographs Division, LC-DIG-cwpbh-00687

That Congress might take reprisals seemed obvious. While the case was being argued, Chief Justice Chase had to divide his time between the Court and the Senate where he was also presiding over Johnson's impeachment trial. A Congress capable of impeaching a president was not likely to flinch from taking on the Court. The arguments in the case lasted until March 9 when the Court finally began deliberations. But the Radicals in Congress decided not to gamble on the outcome. They abridged the Court's appellate jurisdiction in a rider to another bill that did not attract the attention its importance demanded. The rider repealed the section of the Judiciary Act of 1867, which authorized the Court to hear appeals from the circuit courts in habeas corpus cases. They made the repeal retroactive in order to leave no doubt that it applied to the McCardle case. Senator Trumbull helped to draft the repeal, thus winning in Congress the jurisdictional argument that he had failed to win before the Court.

The bill to which it was attached passed both houses of Congress before the rider was discovered. Many moderates were outraged by the underhanded tactics employed by the Radicals to strip the Court of jurisdiction. The *New York Herald* declared: "The country is now in the hands of Congress. That Congress is the Radical majority, and that Radical majority is old Thad Stevens." The *Boston Post* urged the Court to decide the case anyway, "to show that the Court cannot be trifled with by reckless partisans who flippantly speak of 'clipping the wings of the Court.'" There was still time to hand down a decision before the law went into effect. Johnson delayed acting on the bill until the last day for exercising his veto in order to buy additional time for the Court. Actually, all that remained was for the Court to announce its decision. According to Justice Field, "The Judges had all formed their conclusions, and no excuse was urged that more time was wanted for examination." But no decision was announced. The majority voted instead to wait until the pending law had been disposed of one way or the other. As one Republican newspaper put it, the Court "decided that it would not run a race with Congress." Justices Field and Grier protested the delay and went on record against the postponement.

Johnson showed remarkable courage throughout the affair. Ignoring the impact on his impeachment trial, he vetoed the bill and sent a blistering message to Congress. He warned that the bill would create

> a precedent which, if followed, may eventually sweep away every check on arbitrary and unconstitutional legislation. Thus far during the existence of the government, the Supreme Court of the United States has been viewed by the people as the true expounder of their Constitution, and in the most violent party conflicts its judgments and decrees have always been sought and deferred to with confidence and respect.

But now a measure had been passed to silence the Court on an issue of great constitutional importance. What Congress had done, Johnson declared, would "be justly held by a large portion of the people as an admission of the unconstitutionality of the act on which its judgment may be forbidden or forestalled." But appearances no longer mattered. With congressional control of Reconstruction hanging in the balance, the Radicals and moderates together overrode the veto.

There was still a chance that the Court might hand down a decision despite the law. It had been passed after the case had been taken under deliberation and therefore might be held inapplicable. There were no precedents on this issue, and so for a time the Court did nothing. When no decision was announced on the next opinion day, McCardle's counsel moved for formal arguments on the effect of the law. The Court set the hearing for April 2, but arguments were postponed at the government's request until December. The Radicals' strategy was to stall and buy as much time as possible. The longer the decision was delayed, the more likely political changes in the South would render the issues moot.

The postponement infuriated Justices Field and Grier. The latter protested that a decision one way or the other was long overdue.

> By the postponement of the Case, we shall subject ourselves, whether justly or unjustly, to the imputation that we have evaded the performance of a duty imposed on us by the Constitution and waited for legislation to interpose and supersede our action and relieve us of our responsibility. I am not willing to be a partaker either of the eulogy or opprobrium that may follow.

He concluded with a quotation from Ovid's *Metamorphoses*: "It fills us with shame that these reproaches can be uttered, and cannot be repelled." Field, who translated the passage into English so that the point would not be missed, announced for the record that he shared Grier's sentiments completely on the handling of the case.

Final arguments were not heard until March 1869. Counsel for McCardle contended that because the Court had taken the case under advisement before the law had passed, it still had jurisdiction to hand down a decision. Congressional interference with cases *sub judice*, he argued, violated the constitutional separation of powers. This was a good point, because what Congress had done was essentially judicial, not legislative. It had directly intervened in the adjudication of a particular case. The government responded by citing the letter of the Constitution, pointing out that Article III grants the Court appellate jurisdiction "with such Exceptions, and under such Regulations as the Congress shall make." The Court got jurisdiction to hear McCardle's appeal only because Congress authorized the appeal under the Judiciary Act of 1867, and it lost jurisdiction by the same route when Congress revised the Act in 1868. Any cases that remained undecided could not be decided after the Court's jurisdiction had been taken away.

Chief Justice Chase, speaking for a unanimous Court, upheld the government. Even Field and Grier had to recognize that Congress had the power to do what had been done. Chase cited John Marshall's holding in *Durousseau v. United States* (1810) that even implied Congressional limitations of the Court's appellate jurisdiction are binding. While the Court's appellate jurisdiction comes from the Constitution, the extent to which it may be exercised is subject to such limitations as Congress may impose. "It is quite clear," Chase wrote, "that this court cannot proceed to pronounce judgment in this case, for it has no longer jurisdiction of the appeal." For McCardle, the outcome made no practical difference. The military charges against him were dropped, and he was never brought to trial. The last thing the government wanted was to keep the case alive.

Justice Chase on the Jurisdiction of the Supreme Court

"We are not at liberty to inquire into the motives of the legislature. We can only examine into its power under the Constitution; and the power to make exceptions to the appellate jurisdiction of this court is given by express words . . . What, then, is the effect of the repealing act upon the case before us? We cannot doubt as to this. Without jurisdiction the court cannot proceed at all in any cause. Jurisdiction is power to declare the law, and when it ceases to exist, the only function remaining to the court is that of announcing the fact and dismissing the cause. And this is not less clear upon authority than upon principle."

—Ex parte McCardle (1869)

Secession and Reconstruction

On the same day the Court dismissed McCardle's appeal, it handed down a decision in *Texas v. White* (1869) that rejected the Radicals' theory that secession had disrupted the Union and reduced the southern states to the status of conquered territories. The case involved the wartime sale by Texas officials of some federal bonds in the state treasury. The postwar government sued to recover the bonds on the ground that the secessionist government had no legal standing to sell them for the state. The Court upheld the claim, ruling that the sale had been illegal. Chief Justice Chase, speaking for a majority of the justices, used the case to comment generally on the nature of the Union, secession, and postwar reconstruction. He held that since the Union was permanent and secession impossible, Texas had never ceased being part of the United States. The secessionist government had been no more than an unlawful combination without authority to act for the state. The sale of the bonds was therefore illegal, so Texas could recover them.

Although ruling that the southern states had never left the Union, Chase nevertheless upheld the power of Congress to reconstruct them. The war had destroyed civil government in the South and created a political vacuum that the federal government had a constitutional duty to fill. He cited Taney's holding in *Luther v. Borden* (1849) that Congress has responsibility under Article IV to guarantee every state a republican form of government and to determine the legitimacy of particular state governments. It was ironical that Taney, who had been demonized by the Radicals, should be cited to uphold Radical Reconstruction. Chase did not uphold the constitutionality of what the Radicals were doing in the South, only that Congress had the power to supervise reconstruction there. Whether the measures adopted for political reorganization were constitutional was another matter. The holding was a clear victory for those who contended that Congress, not the president, had primary responsibility for reconstruction.

A case remarkably similar to *McCardle* came before the Court in *Ex parte Yerger* (1869). It involved a Mississippi newspaper editor who staunchly opposed Radical reconstruction in the state. Yerger was arrested by the military on charges of killing an army officer, and he was convicted by a military court. He thereupon applied to the Supreme Court for a writ of habeas corpus. But he applied not by way of appeal under the Judiciary Act of 1867, as McCardle had done, but by filing an original petition for the writ under the Judiciary Act of 1789. Although Congress had abolished habeas corpus appeals under the 1867 law in order to prevent a decision in *McCardle*, it had not deprived the Court of jurisdiction to issue writs on original petitions. So when the Court agreed to hear the case late in 1869, the Radicals were thoroughly alarmed. The petition raised the same issues left unsettled in *McCardle*, and a decision on the merits would probably overturn their reconstruction program.

Several measures were proposed in Congress to prevent a constitutional ruling. One would have deprived the Supreme Court of jurisdiction in any cases arising under the Reconstruction Acts. Another called for abolishing the Court's appellate jurisdiction in all habeas corpus cases. An even more drastic proposal called for ending judicial review of any acts passed by Congress. The measures proposed were much more drastic than what was done in *McCardle*. But a compromise was finally arranged that ended the crisis. The government agreed to turn Yerger over to the civil courts in return for withdrawal of his habeas corpus petition. Since this ended the judicial threat to Reconstruction, the anti-Court measures were dropped in Congress. The compromise served the interests of both sides but slammed the door on the last opportunity for a ruling on the constitutionality of the Reconstruction Acts.

The Court during Reconstruction

Although certainly cautious, the Court was by no means supine during the Reconstruction era. The justices backed away from political confrontations in some cases, but they stood their ground in others. The Court invalidated unconstitutional test oaths and protected the rights of individuals. While its handling of the *McCardle* case was questionable, the Court's options were really quite limited. A confrontation with Congress almost certainly would have brought reprisals that might have weakened the Court as an institution. By avoiding confrontation, the Court came out of the affair with its essential powers intact. This was more important in the long run than fighting political wars that probably could not be won. The Court had to walk a narrow line but managed to keep its balance remarkably well.

Far from reducing federal judicial power, the Radicals actually expanded it in order to implement their political program in the South. The expansion began during the war with the Habeas Corpus Act of 1863, which permitted the removal of habeas proceedings from the state courts to the federal courts in cases involving the exercise of federal authority. Removal of jurisdiction to the federal courts was also provided for in cases arising under the Civil Rights Act of 1866 and the Enforcement Act of 1871 on the assumption that the civil rights of blacks would be safer there than in the southern state courts. Finally, the Removal Act of 1875 authorized removal to the federal courts of all cases arising under the Constitution, laws, and treaties of the United States. The Act applied to cases in which the United States was the plaintiff as well as suits between citizens of different states. The habeas corpus jurisdiction of the federal courts also expanded. The Judiciary Act of 1789 had authorized writs of habeas corpus for persons under federal detention, but not for persons detained by the states. The Habeas Corpus Act of 1867 allowed the federal courts to issue the writ in all cases, state and federal, where release from detention was claimed under the Constitution, a law, or a treaty of the United States. Although *McCardle* deprived the Supreme Court of jurisdiction to review habeas corpus petitions on appeal, the habeas jurisdiction of the lower federal courts was left intact.

Failure of Radical Reconstruction

Despite all the efforts put into political reorganization, the Reconstruction governments set up in the South could not survive without federal military protection. This became apparent almost from the beginning. When federal troops were withdrawn from Georgia in 1868, blacks were expelled from the legislature, which caused Congress to return the state to military rule. The disfranchisement of southern whites in the reorganization process cost the Reconstruction governments any claim of political legitimacy. The fact that they were created and run mainly by carpetbaggers and scalawags voted into office by ex-slaves did not help their image much either. Opponents of the Reconstruction governments turned to the Democratic Party and worked to polarize southern politics along racial lines. In this they had the support of northern Democrats who needed the support of a Democratic South to oust the Republicans from national power. Disclosures of Republican corruption and mismanagement in the South also helped erode support for Radical Reconstruction in the North. The less publicized achievements of Reconstruction, particularly with respect to education and public services, went largely unnoticed. As time passed, the North increasingly viewed what went on in the South, including abridgments of the rights of southern blacks, as local and not national concerns.

By 1871 the Democrats had regained power in Virginia, Tennessee, North Carolina, and Georgia. The Democratic revival marked the end of the Radicals' hope for a solid Republican South. Republican moderates in Congress helped the process along by restoring

Democrats Oppose Radical Reconstruction

"And we do declare and resolve, That ever since the people of the United States threw off all subjection to the British crown, the privilege and trust of suffrage have belonged to the several States, and have been granted, regulated, and controlled exclusively by the political power of each State respectively, and that any attempt by congress, on any pretext whatever, to deprive any State of this right . . . will subvert our form of government, and can only end in a single centralized and consolidated government, in which the separate existence of the States will be entirely absorbed, and an unqualified despotism be established in place of a federal union of co-equal States; and that we regard the reconstruction acts so-called, of Congress, as such an usurpation, and unconstitutional, revolutionary, and void . . ."

—Democratic Party Platform, July 4, 1868

the political rights of most ex-Confederates. By 1872 all but about five hundred of the top leaders of the Confederacy had been amnestied. Their return to political life further destabilized the already wobbly Reconstruction governments. Carpetbaggers and scala-wags could not compete with the old leaders of the South in bidding for white votes. The failure of Congress to extend the life of the Freedmen's Bureau in 1872 sealed the fate of Reconstruction. The Bureau's demise deprived southern Radicals of the federal money and patronage needed for political organization. By 1875 the Democrats controlled eight southern states, leaving only Florida, Louisiana, and South Carolina under Radical rule.

Bullets as well as ballots helped bring down the Reconstruction governments. The Ku Klux Klan and other terrorist groups waged a campaign of intimidation and violence to keep African Americans from voting. Radical leaders were singled out for whipping, maiming, and hanging. Southern Democrats condoned the violence on the ground that law and order had broken down under the Radicals. Citizens had been forced to take mat-ters into their own hands against the rising tide of public disorders. There was no real political dialogue, only invective and vilification. The *Fairfield Herald* denounced Re-construction in South Carolina as "the rule of louse-eaten, devil-worshipping barbarians from the jungles of Dahomey, and peripatetic buccaneers from Cape Cod, Hell, and Bos-ton." The incendiary press gave terrorists a veneer of respectability. The political violence in some instances provided cover for criminal and antisocial elements. Although the Klan was formally disbanded in 1869, its place was taken by other vigilante groups who kept up the violence. Even where the Radicals had military protection, the troops were too widely dispersed to cope effectively with the terrorists.

Congress initially reacted to the violence by tightening federal control over the South. The Enforcement Acts of 1870 and 1871, known also as the Ku Klux Klan Acts, set federal penalties for the violation of rights guaranteed by the Fourteenth and Fifteenth Amendments. Congressional elections were placed under federal supervision, and it be-came a federal crime to prevent a citizen from voting. When it became clear that all the Reconstruction governments would eventually topple, Congress passed the Civil Rights Act of 1875 to put the civil rights of southern blacks under federal protection. The Act guaranteed African Americans equal access to hotels, theaters, and other places of public accommodation. The Removal Act, passed the same year, allowed cases involving federal rights to be transferred from the state courts to the federal courts. These measures were enacted as last-ditch efforts to protect blacks when the old ruling class returned to power in the South.

Radical Reconstruction failed in large measure because it was not radical enough. From the very beginning it was flawed by an overemphasis on political rights. What the freedmen needed far more than voting rights was the opportunity to become economically self-sufficient. The productive resources of the South remained firmly under the control of whites. Only the most extreme Radicals recognized the need for economic as well as political reorganization. Thaddeus Stevens proposed confiscating the property of lead-ing rebels and distributing the land among the ex-slaves to give them a fresh beginning. He hoped to turn them into citizen-farmers economically independent of their former masters. This would provide a firm foundation for making them first-class citizens with all the rights enjoyed by whites. But most Republicans rejected confiscation as incompatible with the rights of property everywhere. The Radicals could win the support of moderates only for the political side of their program. Failure to act on property rights left the blacks economically dependent and ultimately vulnerable to the loss of political rights as well.

But Radical Reconstruction was by no means a total failure. It gave blacks and countless poor whites their first practical experience with political affairs. Politics in the antebellum South had been dominated by the planter class, and that monopoly at least was permanently broken. Moreover, the Reconstruction governments fostered enlightened, progressive goals that greatly influenced southern thought and politics. They sponsored internal improvements and reformed tax systems that had undervalued land and unfairly taxed business and commerce. They also provided southerners with a wide range of public services that had not existed before. By 1876 the constitution of nearly every southern state made free public education for blacks and whites compulsory. That the Reconstruction governments were outrageously corrupt is undeniable, but corruption was rampant during the postwar years in the North as well. The scandals of the Grant administration and the Tweed Ring in New York City bear witness to the pervasiveness of the problem. Whatever their faults, the Reconstruction governments can claim credit for many real achievements. The Fourteenth and Fifteenth amendments could not have been ratified without them, and for that alone all Americans can be grateful.

Election of 1876

By the summer of 1876 only the Reconstruction governments of Florida, Louisiana, and South Carolina remained in power, and their days were clearly numbered. The presidential election of 1876 set the stage for the final overthrow of Reconstruction. Samuel Tilden, the Democratic candidate, won a popular majority of 250,000 votes over his Republican rival, Rutherford B. Hayes, but he fell one vote short of an electoral majority. The electoral results were bitterly disputed in Florida, Louisiana, South Carolina, and Oregon, all of which submitted double sets of returns. Republican election boards in the three southern states threw out enough Tilden votes to certify the states for Hayes. But if, as Democrats charged, these electoral votes were stolen from Tilden, one of Oregon's electoral votes seems to have been stolen from Hayes. The Republicans carried the state, but the Democratic governor disqualified one of the three Republican electors and appointed a Democrat in his place. This single electoral vote was all Tilden needed to become President.

No precedent existed for resolving the impasse. The outcome depended on which returns were certified by Congress, and it was not even clear how this should be done. The Constitution states only that "The President of the Senate shall, in the presence of the Senate and the House of Representatives, open all the Certificates, and the Votes shall then be counted." But who should do the counting—the Senate, the House of Representatives, or both bodies jointly? If counted by the Senate, which the Republicans controlled, the Hayes electors would be certified; if by the House, which the Democrats controlled, Tilden's electors would be certified. The deadlock split the country and put the political system itself on trial. Whatever irregularities occurred in state and local elections, Americans took the integrity of presidential elections for granted. But now a shadow had been cast over the legitimacy of the process. Unless it could be removed, constitutional government would be the permanent loser regardless of the outcome of the election.

After much haggling in Congress, both sides agreed to the appointment of an Electoral Commission to settle the dispute. The Commission consisted of five senators (three Republicans, two Democrats), five representatives (three Democrats, two Republicans), and four justices (two Republicans, two Democrats) of the Supreme Court. The four justices would then select a fifth justice, the tie-breaker, with the understanding that Justice Davis, an independent, would be chosen. Davis was chosen, but he soon resigned to accept election by the Illinois legislature to the United States Senate. His place on the Commission was taken by Justice Joseph Bradley, a Republican with a reputation for fairness. But Bradley in the end gave in to political pressure and voted with his fellow Republicans. By straight party votes of eight to seven, all the disputed ballots were awarded to Hayes, who defeated Tilden by an electoral majority of 185 to 184.

The Republicans on the Commission took the position that it would be impractical to go behind the returns officially certified by the states. They accepted the election returns certified by the Republican election boards of Florida, Louisiana, and South Carolina with no questions asked about the thousands of Democratic votes thrown out for alleged irregularities. But they did not follow this rule in the Oregon dispute where a Democratic elector had been officially certified. The Commission went behind the certification and determined that the Democrat had been improperly appointed. All three of the state's electoral votes were awarded to Hayes, giving him his one-vote margin of victory. If the Republicans did not "steal" the election, they certainly gave the appearance of having done so.

The findings of the Electoral Commission were not binding until accepted by Congress, and Democrats were loath to accept them. The transparent partisanship of the outcome threatened to worsen the political crisis. Even if Congress approved the results, an accommodation was needed in order to give Hayes a mandate to govern. It was the southern Democrats who finally broke the deadlock and made a settlement possible. Many of them were former Whigs who had nothing in common with northern Democrats. They had a conservative and pro-business outlook that made them Republican in everything but party label. Most Republicans had once been Whigs, and the party's platform was firmly grounded on Whig principles. If Reconstruction and racial politics had not gotten in the way, southern conservatives might have found a political home in the Republican Party. In any case, southern Democrats were more willing than northern Democrats to accept Hayes as president. A Republican administration under political obligation to the South would probably be more accommodating to southern interests that one controlled by northern Democrats.

Republican and southern Democratic leaders reached an accord early in 1877. In return for a promise that federal troops would be withdrawn, the southerners agreed not to block the orderly inauguration of Hayes. The troop withdrawal was the sort of concession that only Republicans could make without having their loyalty called into question. The agreement deprived northern Democrats of the votes needed to continue the deadlock and set the stage for approval of the Commission's findings just in time for the inauguration. Besides promising the withdrawal of federal troops, the Republicans agreed that at least one southerner would be appointed to the cabinet, and that the South would get appropriations for internal improvements and a share of the federal patronage. Hayes made good on these commitments by appointing David Key of Tennessee postmaster general; he also withdrew the Army from the South. By the spring of 1877 all the states of the former Confederacy had returned to Democratic control with the tacit blessing of northern Republicans.

Although Reconstruction failed to achieve its immediate goals, it effected the most significant changes in constitutional government in the United States since the ratification of the Constitution. It revolutionized relations between the national government and the states, and set the stage for the emergence of the unitary national state favored by the Hamiltonian Federalists. The new restraints on state sovereignty applied not only to the South but to the northern states as well. The Thirteenth, Fourteenth, and Fifteenth amendments vastly expanded the reach of the federal government over the civil rights and liberties of people in both sections. No longer would issues of legal due process, equal protection of law, and voting rights be exclusively the concern of the states. National constitutional standards now existed, and the national government had the power to enforce them. This power had been used vigorously during Reconstruction, and it would be used vigorously again when the struggle for civil rights and racial justice resumed a century later.

May 31, 1870	April 3, 1871	April 20, 1871	April 14, 1873	April 15, 1873	March 4, 1874
An Act to Enforce the Right of Citizens of the United States to Vote in the Several States of this Union, and for other Purposes.	Collector v. Day	Act to Enforce the Provisions of the Fourteenth Amendment to the Constitution of the United States, and for other Purposes	Slaughter-House Cases	Bradwell v. Illinois	Morrison R. Waite Becomes Chief Justice of the United States

March 1, 1880	March 4, 1881	September 19, 1881	January 22, 1883	October 15, 1883	March 3, 1884
Strauder v. West Virginia Virginia v. Rives	James A. Garfield Takes Office as President of the United States	Chester Arthur Takes Office as President of the United States	United States v. Harris	Civil Rights Cases	Ex parte Yarbrough

XII   Promises Betrayed

March 1, 1875	March 29, 1875	March 27, 1876	March 4, 1877	December 10, 1877	January 14, 1878
Civil Rights Act	Minor v. Happersett	United States v. Reese United States v. Cruikshank	Rutherford B. Hayes Takes Office as President of the United States	John Marshall Harlan Becomes Associate Justice of Supreme Court	Hall v. DeCuir

October 8, 1888	March 4, 1893	May 18, 1896	April 25, 1898	December 18, 1899
Melville Fuller Becomes Chief Justice of the United States	Grover Cleveland Takes Office as President of the United States	Plessy v. Ferguson	Williams v. Mississippi	Cumming v. Richmond County Board of Education

"Today, it is the colored race which is denied, by corporations and individuals wielding public authority, rights fundamental to their freedom and citizenship. At some future time, it may be that some other race will fall under the ban of race discrimination."
—Justice John M. Harlan, *Civil Rights Cases* (1883)

The Fourteenth and Fifteenth Amendments on paper altered the federal system of government of the United States. Previously, except for guarantees relating to contract rights, bills of attainder, and ex post facto laws, the Constitution had allowed the states almost unlimited power over the rights and liberties of their citizens. Freedom of speech, press, and religion, the right to counsel and jury trial, the privilege against compulsory self-incrimination, and the rule against double jeopardy were not binding on the state governments. The whole body of rights and liberties guaranteed by the federal Bill of Rights protected citizens only against the federal government. For protection against state power, citizens had to look to the guarantees of their own state constitutions. This had been settled constitutional law since the Marshall Court held in *Barron v. Baltimore* (1833) that the guarantees of the Bill of Rights did not apply to the states. What the states did with respect to civil rights and liberties was between them and their citizens.

In theory, all this changed with the adoption of the Civil War amendments. The Thirteenth Amendment abolished slavery whether the states wanted it or not, and the Fourteenth and Fifteenth Amendments put certain civil and political rights beyond state abridgment. The Fourteenth, if fully implemented, would have fundamentally changed federal-state relations. It granted state and federal citizenship to all persons born or naturalized in the United States, thereby overturning the citizenship holding of the *Dred Scott* decision, and prohibited state abridgment of the privileges or immunities of United States citizens. Many judges and lawyers thought that the latter overturned *Barron* and extended to the states the protection of the federal Bill of Rights. Nor could the states deny to any person equal protection of the law or deprive anyone of life, liberty, or property without due process of law. To many it all seemed to mean that rights formerly subject to state power had now become national rights protected by the United States Constitution.

Just how much had changed because of the Fourteenth Amendment was not immediately clear. What, for example, were the privileges and immunities of United States citizenship that might not be abridged by the states? When the question arose during a congressional debate in 1871, Representative John Bingham, the principal draftsman of the Amendment, declared that the purpose of the provision was to overturn *Barron v. Baltimore* and make the guarantees of the Bill of Rights applicable against the states. But whatever Bingham might have intended, it would ultimately be up to the Supreme Court to decide what the Amendment actually meant. Since most of the justices were constitutional conservatives with reservations about upsetting the traditional balance between federal and state government, their interpretation of the Amendment was likely to be less expansive. Federalism had served the nation too well in the past to be discarded even for the most laudable goals.

The Supreme Court and Federalism

The Court had already signaled its opposition to federal encroachments on state sovereignty in *Collector v. Day* (1871). The case invalidated a federal income tax on the salaries of state judges. Justice Nelson, speaking for the majority, declared that the state and federal governments "are separate and distinct sovereignties, acting separately and independently of each other, within their respective spheres." He held that the states "are as independent of the general government as that government within its sphere is independent of the states." Nelson cited the 1842 decision of the Court in *Dobbins v. Commissioners of Erie County* that the salaries of federal officials are not subject to state taxation. The same principle of sovereign immunity from taxation also barred federal taxation of state salaries. Neither government could tax officials of the other, because such power could be used to cripple or destroy governmental operations. The two governments were equal, Nelson ruled, with neither subordinate to the other for purposes of taxation. Whether this equality extended as well to federal-state relations under the Fourteenth Amendment remained to be seen. But the decision strongly suggested that the Court's answer would be yes.

Slaughter-House Cases

The Fourteenth Amendment came before the Court for the first time in the *Slaughter-House Cases* (1873), and a 5–4 majority narrowly interpreted its provisions. The cases began in 1869 when the Louisiana legislature granted a monopoly of the slaughterhouse business in New Orleans to a single firm. All livestock transported to New Orleans would have to be landed, kept, and slaughtered at a facility belonging to the Crescent City Live Stock Landing and Slaughter House Company. Although the monopoly was ostensibly for the purpose of protecting public health—an emergent public hygiene movement in the United States was pressing for reform in food production—the motives of the law-makers were palpably corrupt. They received stock in the monopoly and stood to profit handsomely. The arrangement was typical of the corrupt practices rampant in the South during Reconstruction. The measure put numerous independent slaughterhouses out of business and affected about 1,000 persons employed by them. When the details became known, there was a loud public outcry. Meanwhile, the independent butchers brought suit in the state courts to overturn the monopoly. They sought an injunction on the ground that the law creating the monopoly violated the Thirteenth and Fourteenth Amendments. Although both Amendments were cited, the key issue was whether the Privileges or Immunities Clause and other guarantees of the Fourteenth had been abridged by the Louisiana law.

After losing in the state courts, the butchers appealed to the United States Supreme Court. They were represented by former Justice John A. Campbell, who had resigned from the Court during the Civil War to return to Alabama. He held office in the Confederate government and settled in New Orleans after the war. Although in the past Campbell had strongly supported states' rights, he became convinced that only federal judicial intervention could save the South from the excesses of Reconstruction. Louisiana was represented by Matt H. Carpenter and Jeremiah S. Black. Carpenter, a former senator from Wisconsin, had helped draft the Fourteenth Amendment; Black, a former secretary of state and attorney general, had distinguished himself in the *Milligan* and *McCardle* cases. The array of legal talent on both sides matched the importance of the issues to be decided.

When the appeal was finally argued in January 1872, the absence of Justice Nelson from the bench prevented a clear-cut decision. The Court divided 4–4, so reargument was scheduled for later in the year before the full bench. But another postponement was ordered in November when Nelson resigned and Ward Hunt was appointed by President Grant to fill the vacancy. A full bench was not ready to hear final arguments until February 1873, a full three years after the monopoly had been created. But the issues at stake fully justified seeing the case through to a conclusion. The outcome would affect the rights of all Americans down to the present.

Campbell began by attacking the monopoly on Thirteenth Amendment grounds. He argued that it imposed a form of servitude on the independent butchers by requiring them to pay fees to the monopoly for the use of its facilities and services. Although probably worth making, this line of argument had little chance of success. The Louisiana law had nothing to do with slavery and involuntary servitude. While the monopoly had destroyed the businesses of the independent butchers, it had not destroyed their personal freedom. The Amendment protected only the latter, not the right to engage in a particular business.

Campbell's Fourteenth Amendment arguments were much more compelling. He contended that the Privileges or Immunities Clause had put the whole body of civil rights, including the right to earn a livelihood, beyond abridgment by the states. Its purpose, he said, was "to establish, through the whole jurisdiction of the United States, one people, and that every member of the Empire shall understand and appreciate the Constitutional fact that his privileges and immunities cannot be abridged by State authority." He argued in effect that the privileges and immunities of United States citizens are those rights which are protected against the federal government by the Constitution and Bill of Rights, and that the Fourteenth Amendment now protected these rights against the states. The states could no longer impose on their citizens any constraints forbidden to the federal government. The guarantees that prevented Congress from creating a slaughterhouse monopoly in New Orleans applied also to the Louisiana legislature.

Other Fourteenth Amendment rights had been violated as well. Campbell argued that the monopoly also violated the Equal Protection and Due Process Clauses of the Amendment. Equal protection of law meant equality of impact, he contended, and creating a monopoly by law had exactly the opposite effect by favoring one company at the expense of others. The law also deprived the independent butchers of property without due process of law by putting them out of business. Campbell rejected the idea that the monopoly was a constitutional exercise of state police power. That might have been true in the past, but the Fourteenth Amendment set a new standard of what was constitutionally permissible. The states no longer had a free hand in exercising their police powers but were now bound by the constraints of the Amendment.

The Court voted 5–4 to uphold the Louisiana law. Justice Miller, speaking for the majority, made short work of the Thirteenth Amendment issue. The Amendment prohibited only slavery and involuntary servitude, not state-created monopolies. Miller also rejected Campbell's expansive interpretation of the Fourteenth Amendment. He drew a sharp distinction between the privileges and immunities arising from state citizenship and those arising from federal citizenship. Only the latter were protected against abridgment by the states, and they were much less extensive than the former. They included the right to petition government, the right of access to American ports, and the right to federal protection on the high seas or within the territory of a foreign government. But they did not include the main body of rights and liberties enumerated in the Bill of Rights. These were incidents of state citizenship, and as such were subject to state regulation and abridgment. The *Barron* decision had not been overturned, and the states still had a free hand with respect to the rights and liberties of their citizens.

Nor did Miller think that the monopoly violated due process rights. He held that the Due Process Clause imposed no substantive constraints on the states; all it required was formal compliance with procedural proprieties. Since all the legislative formalities had been observed, the monopoly law met the requirements of due process. Finally, Miller held that the Equal Protection of the Laws Clause did not apply, because the case did not involve the rights of African Americans. He wrote,

> We doubt very much whether any action of a State not directed against the negroes as a class, or on account of their race, will ever be held to come within the purview

of this provision. It is so clearly a provision for that race and that emergency, that a strong case would be necessary for its application to any other.

Perhaps the most striking thing about Miller's opinion is that every issue would have been decided exactly the same if the Fourteenth Amendment had not been adopted. Miller's restrictive interpretation virtually repealed the Amendment.

Justice Field dissented sharply, taking issue particularly with Miller's narrow construction of the Privileges or Immunities Clause. He dismissed the distinction between state and federal citizenship as legal casuistry:

> A citizen of a State is now only a citizen of the United States residing in that State. The fundamental rights, privileges, and immunities which belong to him as a free

Justices Miller and Bradley on the Fourteenth Amendment

Justice Miller for the Majority, *Slaughter-House Cases*

It would be the vainest show of learning to attempt to prove by citations of authority, that up to the adoption of the recent amendments, no claim or pretence was set up that those rights depended on the Federal government for their existence or protection, beyond the very few express limitations which the Federal Constitution imposed upon the States—such, for instance, as the prohibition against ex post facto laws, bills of attainder, and laws impairing the obligation of contracts. But with the exception of these and a few other restrictions, the entire domain of the privileges and immunities of citizens of the States, as above defined, lay within the constitutional and legislative power of the States, and without that of the Federal government.

Figure XII.1 Portrait of Samuel Miller (c. 1870–1880).

Library of Congress, Prints and Photographs Division, LC-DIG-cwpbh-03988

Justice Bradley Dissents, *Slaughter-House Cases*

Admitting . . . that formerly the States were not prohibited from infringing any of the fundamental privileges and immunities of citizens of the United States, except in a few specified cases, that cannot be said now, since the adoption of the fourteenth amendment. In my judgment, it was the intention of the people of this country in adopting that amendment to provide National security against violation by the States of the fundamental rights of the citizen . . . It is futile to argue that none but persons of the African race are intended to be benefited by this amendment. They may have been the primary cause of the amendment, but its language is general, embracing all citizens, and I think it was purposely so expressed.

Figure XII.2 Portrait of Joseph Bradley (c. 1870–1880).

Library of Congress, Prints and Photographs Division, LC-BH826-3702

man and a free citizen, now belong to him as a citizen of the United States, and are not dependent upon his citizenship of any State.

Field declared that among the rights protected against state abridgment were "those *which of right belong to the citizens of all free governments.* Clearly among these must be placed the right to pursue a lawful employment in a lawful manner." Since the federal government could not abridge such a right, the states could not abridge it either without violating the Fourteenth Amendment.

Justice Bradley also dissented, and he took issue with nearly everything in Miller's opinion. He contended that the privileges and immunities of United States citizens are spelled out in the Declaration of Independence and the federal Bill of Rights. These are the rights protected by the Privileges or Immunities Clause of the Amendment against state abridgment.

He also rejected Miller's narrow interpretation of the Due Process and Equal Protection Clauses. "A law which prohibits a large class of citizens from adopting a lawful employment," he wrote, "does deprive them of liberty as well as property, without due process of law." He declared that such a prohibition "also deprives those citizens of the equal protection of the laws." Justice Swayne joined in the dissent, and he rebuked the majority for eviscerating the Fourteenth Amendment and turning "what was meant for bread into a stone."

Congressional Reaction

The decision angered many of the Radicals in Congress. Representative Bingham thought that the Privileges or Immunities Clause had been grossly misconstrued. He declared that his own intention had been to put the whole body of civil liberties under federal constitutional protection. Senator George Boutwell denounced as specious the notion that different rights arise from state and federal citizenship. The Fourteenth Amendment covered all rights, he insisted, federal and state alike. Senator George Edwards charged that the decision differed drastically "both to the intent of the framers and the construction of the language used by them." In other words, the majority justices had rewritten the Amendment to make it something quite different from what had been intended. If the decision had directly affected the rights of African Americans, Congress probably would have intervened to overturn it. But Justice Miller went out of his way to provide assurances that the rights of blacks were safe. His interpretation of the Equal Protection Clause singled them out for special protection, signaling that the Court would be vigilant in protecting them against racial discrimination. Since the case involved the economic interests of white butchers, it was not immediately apparent that it represented a major setback for the rights and liberties of all Americans.

Miller's narrow interpretation of the Privileges or Immunities Clause rendered its guarantees almost meaningless. He effectively killed the Clause by narrowly limiting the rights protected. Because his narrow interpretation appealed to constitutional conservatives concerned with protecting federalism, it soon settled into the bedrock of American constitutional law. There is today a mountain of case law supporting his holding that the Clause does not make rights guaranteed by the Bill of Rights applicable against the states. While most of the guarantees of the Bill of Rights now do apply against the states, they apply not through the Privileges or Immunities Clause but through an expanded interpretation of the Due Process Clause. The Privileges or Immunities Clause is as dead today as when Miller killed it in 1873. Along with Marshall's opinion in *Marbury v. Madison* and Taney's holding in the *Dred Scott* case, Miller's opinion is one of the most important constitutional holdings in the annals of the Court. Whether he was right or wrong cannot be proved one way or the other. What Congressman Bingham and other Radicals thought about the Clause is by no means conclusive. If they had made its meaning clear and unambiguous, Miller would not have had the opportunity to misconstrue it. The libertarian implications of the Clause have fueled the controversy, with conservatives generally siding with Miller. Liberals have tended to view it as a reactionary coup that nullified the most dynamic provision of the Fourteenth Amendment.

The truth probably lies somewhere in between. On the one hand, there is no evidence in the debates in Congress or in the state legislatures that the Clause was intended to override the traditional police powers of the states. Whatever the Radicals had to say later was not said when the Amendment was under consideration. The Radicals clearly intended to give southern blacks protection against state discrimination, but whether the protection given was meant to include all the guarantees of the federal Bill of Rights seems unlikely. Whites never had such protection before, and the goal was essentially to give blacks the same protection as whites. The equality of the races before the law could be achieved without extending the Bill of Rights to the states. Textual analysis of the Amendment also suggests that this was not intended. Why, for example, was the Due Process Clause included if the Privileges or Immunities Clause incorporated the Bill of Rights, which itself contains a due process guarantee in the Fifth Amendment? Reiterating the guarantee would have been redundant if the Clause had been intended to incorporate the federal guarantees. Had the Radicals intended to overturn *Barron v. Baltimore*, as Congressman Bingham declared, they probably would have done so clearly and unmistakably. Too much was at stake to leave anything so important open to judicial misconstruction. The Privileges or Immunities Clause probably meant more than Justice Miller concluded but also less than advocates of the total incorporation of the Bill of Rights have contended.

Race Relations in the South

The collapse of Reconstruction did not destroy the civil rights of southern blacks immediately. When conservative Democrats returned to power, the black vote was manipulated in the interests of conservative government. African Americans continued to vote as upper-class whites directed, and in return they received concessions. They were not treated as first-class citizens, but their basic rights were recognized and generally respected. Blacks continued to serve in state legislatures, and they were even elected to Congress until the end of the century. The worst immediate setback was in public education where the Reconstruction policy of equal access was scrapped in favor of racially segregated schools. But no laws were passed excluding blacks from public conveyances and accommodations used by whites. White supremacy was everywhere the rule, but it did not involve the virulent Negrophobia that later took hold. Blacks who did not challenge the status quo fared considerably better than had been expected.

But these arrangements began to break down in the late 1880s under the pressure of white populist politics. The depressed economic condition of poor white farmers turned them against the conservatives who had been running the southern state governments. The agrarian revolt caught blacks squarely in the middle of the struggle. If they made common cause with the poor whites, their upper-class patrons would disfranchise and abandon them. But if they sided with the conservatives and the populists came to power anyway, they also faced reprisals. In the end, neither side would allow black votes to tip the balance of power in favor of the other. Both resorted to racist politics in order to compete for white support. Demagogues on both sides denounced political coalitions with blacks as a threat to white supremacy and a form of racial treason. The upshot was the systematic disfranchisement of blacks, carried out in some states by conservatives, and in others by the populists. By the turn of the century, black voting rights had been virtually destroyed throughout the South.

More was lost than just the suffrage. Racist politics had such heady appeal that politicians vied with one another in stirring up hostility against African Americans. The civil

The Future of the South

"It has of late become the custom of the men of the South to speak with entire candor of the settled and deliberate policy of suppressing the negro vote. They have been forced to choose between a policy of manifest injustice toward the blacks and the horrors of negro rule. They chose to disfranchise the negroes. That was manifestly the lesser of two evils. In any community, North or South, or foreign, this course would have been adopted. It was the only way to avert civil destruction. Northern men who have an adequate knowledge of conditions at the South no longer denounce the suppression of the negro vote as it used to be denounced in the reconstruction days. The necessity of it under the supreme law of self-preservation is candidly recognized . . . The Republican Party committed a great public crime when it gave the right of suffrage to the blacks."

—*New York Times,* May 10, 1900

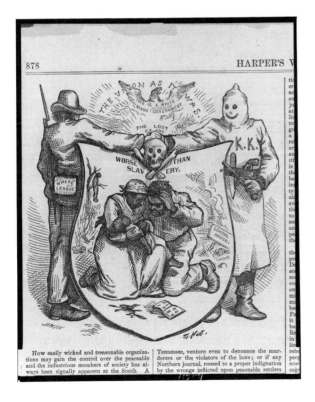

Figure XII.3 Political cartoon from *Harper's Weekly* titled "Worse than Slavery" (1874). A member of the White League shakes hands with a member of the Ku Klux Klan while an African American man, woman, and infant cower beneath. In the background, a man has been lynched and a school house burns.

Library of Congress, Prints and Photographs Division, LC-USZ62-128619

rights laws of the Reconstruction era were nullified by state legislation segregating every area of southern life. These "Jim Crow" laws, as they were called, set up barriers that neither race could cross without incurring criminal penalties. There had been almost no segregation in public transportation or places of public accommodation before 1890, but by the end of the century the forced separation of the races had become the rule throughout the South. Access to passenger trains, restaurants, hotels, theaters, and residential housing came to depend wholly upon race. Nowhere in the country were the two races closer together in everyday contacts but at the same time farther apart in everything that mattered.

New Court Appointments

The Supreme Court might have halted this assault on the civil rights of African Americans because what the southern states were doing was patently unconstitutional. But the justices appointed to the Court during the last three decades of the century were generally indifferent if not actually hostile to the civil rights of southern blacks. With one or two exceptions, they were all staunch conservatives committed to preserving the traditional powers of the states. After Johnson left the presidency in 1869, Congress increased the membership of the Court from seven to nine, allowing President Grant to make two new appointments. In 1870 he appointed William Strong of Pennsylvania and Joseph Bradley of New Jersey, both railroad lawyers. Bradley, who dissented in the *Slaughter-House Cases*, turned out to be one of the strongest members of the Court. Grant appointed Ward Hunt in 1872 upon the retirement of Justice Nelson. Hunt became mentally incompetent halfway through his nine-year tenure and played no significant part in Court decisions. He finally resigned in 1882 when Congress voted him a full salary for life.

The death of Chief Justice Chase in 1873 gave Grant the opportunity to make one more appointment. He first offered the chief justiceship to Senator Roscoe Conkling of New York, a close political ally whose talents were confined mainly to machine politics. Conkling had the good sense to decline the appointment. Grant then offered the post to another crony, Attorney General George Williams, who was already under fire for corruption in office. Williams did not decline, but his nomination thoroughly shocked the country. In the end, the nomination was withdrawn at his own request. Grant then nominated Caleb Cushing, a former member of the Massachusetts Supreme Judicial Court. Cushing was seventy-four years old and politically controversial, so again the nomination had to be withdrawn. Finally, as his fourth choice, Grant nominated Morrison W. Waite of Ohio. Waite, a successful Republican lawyer, was virtually unknown outside his state. But at least he was not controversial, and the Senate confirmed him quickly without difficulty. "After the previous shocks," the *New York Tribune* editorialized, "the people are prepared to accept, with something like equanimity, any appointment which should not be scandalous."

Waite had almost no public service prior to his appointment. A prominent corporation lawyer, he had served just one term in the Ohio legislature. Although his principal clients had been banks and railroads, Waite brought a liberal economic outlook to the Court. This liberalism was not matched, however, by his views on racial matters. While not intellectually the equal of Marshall or Taney, he was, on balance, a successful chief justice. His patience and tact made him more acceptable than some of his more gifted colleagues, such as Justices Miller or Field, would have been in his place. An advocate of judicial self-restraint, he believed that the Court should not substitute its judgment for the policy decisions made by the political branches of government. He represented what Justice Felix Frankfurter later described as "one of the greatest duties of a judge, the duty not to enlarge his authority."

When Justice Davis resigned in 1877 to enter the Senate, his place was taken by John M. Harlan of Kentucky. Although a slaveholder, Harlan had fought for the Union during the Civil War and had left the army with the rank of colonel. He drifted into the Republican Party after the war and soon became a convert to the cause of racial justice. Although twice defeated for the governorship in the 1870s, Harlan became the unquestioned leader of the Kentucky Republicans. He led the state's delegation to the Republican National Convention in 1876 and played a key role in the nomination of Rutherford B. Hayes. His reward came the following year when President Hayes appointed him to the Court. Of all the justices appointed during the postwar period, Harlan alone consistently championed the rights of African Americans.

In 1880 Hayes appointed William B. Woods of Alabama to fill the vacancy created by the retirement of Justice Strong. He also nominated Stanley Matthews of Ohio when Justice Swayne resigned because of disability. Matthews had helped to hammer out the political compromise that made Hayes president, and he had represented railroad interests as a lawyer and lobbyist. Both made him controversial, and the Senate refused to confirm his nomination. When President Garfield succeeded Hayes, the nomination was resubmitted and finally confirmed after a bitter debate. Horace Gray was appointed by President Arthur in 1882 after the resignation of Justice Clifford. Gray was a noted legal scholar and Chief Justice of Massachusetts. Arthur also appointed Samuel Blatchford of New York in 1882 to fill the seat vacated by Justice Hunt. Blatchford had previously served on the federal district and circuit courts. These then were the justices who would preside over the destruction of the civil rights of southern blacks.

Black Voting Rights

The disfranchisement of blacks began in 1876 in *United States v. Reese*. At issue in the case was the constitutionality of provisions in the Enforcement Act of 1870 making it a federal offense to prevent any qualified person from voting. The Act was passed pursuant to section 2 of the Fifteenth Amendment authorizing Congress to enforce the Amendment's provisions by appropriate legislation. Reese was one of two Kentucky election officials prosecuted for refusing to count the vote of an African American. The Court dismissed the prosecutions on the ground that the actions of the election officials were not subject to federal jurisdiction under the Amendment. Chief Justice Waite, speaking for the majority, held that the Fifteenth Amendment "does not confer the right of suffrage upon any one." It merely prevents the state and federal governments from disfranchising anyone because of race or prior servitude. Moreover, it applies only to official discrimination, not to the acts of discrimination by individuals. The election officials had acted unlawfully, but they had acted as individuals and therefore could not be punished by the federal government. They could be punished only by the state of Kentucky for their actions.

Waite's holding that the Fifteenth Amendment did not guarantee the right to vote set the stage for the wholesale abridgment of voting rights by the southern states. It meant that any voting restrictions not specifically based on race or prior servitude would be constitutional regardless of whether they had the practical effect of disfranchising blacks. Thus literacy tests and poll taxes were upheld by the Court in *Williams v. Mississippi* (1898). The law in question required voters to display a receipt for payment of a poll tax and to read and interpret a part of the state constitution as a prerequisite for voting. Although enforced in a way that discriminated against African Americans, the law was upheld as constitutional. The mere fact that blacks had been unable to meet its requirements did not make the law unconstitutional. Only discrimination expressly based on race violated the Fifteenth Amendment. Nor did the Amendment prevent bias by election officials, as in the *Reese* case, unless the state itself had officially mandated bias.

Somewhat different rules applied in federal elections. While allowing the states to set voter qualifications, the Constitution authorizes Congress to control the conduct of the elections. Article I provides that the times, places, and manner of electing United States senators and representatives shall be determined by the states, but that "Congress may at any time by Law make or alter such Regulations, except as to the Places of choosing Senators." Congress generally found it more convenient to use the election machinery of the states rather than set up separate election procedures. But in 1871, in order to protect black voters in the South, Congress made it a federal crime for state election officials to violate any federal or state law governing elections in which members of Congress were chosen. In 1880 the law was challenged in *Ex parte Siebold* by a Maryland official who was accused of stuffing a ballot box in a congressional election. The Court, speaking through Justice Bradley, upheld the conviction as constitutional. "To say that Congress is without power to pass appropriate legislation," he declared, "is to deny to the nation in a vital particular the power of self-preservation."

Four years later, in *Ex parte Yarbrough* (1884), the Court upheld the power of Congress to punish misconduct by individuals in federal elections. At issue was the constitutionality of a provision in the Enforcement Act of 1870 making it a crime to conspire "to prevent by force, intimidation, or threat, any citizen who is lawfully entitled to vote" from voting in a federal election. Yarbrough was convicted of conspiring to intimidate a black voter in a congressional election. He appealed his conviction on the ground that Congress had no authority to punish acts committed by individuals. The Court had so held in the *Reese* case, and the same principle applied, he contended, to his own case.

But the Court upheld the conviction. Justice Miller wrote a powerful opinion holding that the right to vote in federal elections is a right conferred by the Constitution. Although the states have power to set voting qualifications, once the qualifications are met, the right to vote becomes a federal right which Congress has the power to protect. The *Reese* decision, Miller declared, applied only in state elections. "[I]t is quite a different matter," he said, "when Congress undertakes to protect the citizen in the exercise of rights conferred by the Constitution of the United States." The power to act is not subject to the limitations of the Fifteenth Amendment but comes directly from Article I, which authorizes Congress to regulate federal elections. Without the power to regulate its own elections, the federal government would be "helpless before the two great natural and historical enemies of all republics, open violence and insidious corruption."

The Rights of Women

Although Fifteenth Amendment rights received limited protection in federal elections, the states had a virtually free hand with regard to Fourteenth Amendment rights. In *Bradwell v. Illinois* (1873), the Court held that the Amendment did not prevent the states from excluding women from the practice of law. The exclusion had been challenged under both the citizenship and privileges or immunities guarantees of the Amendment. The Court held that the right to practice law had nothing to do with the candidate's nationality or citizenship, noting that many foreigners had been admitted to practice law in the state courts of the United States. Nor was the right to practice law one of the privileges or immunities protected by the Amendment. Justice Miller's majority opinion noted that the limited protection afforded had been spelled out in the recently decided *Slaughter-House* cases and needed no reiteration. The Amendment created no new rights. Only existing rights were protected, and the practice of law was not one of them. The issue not having been raised in the pleadings, the Equal Protection Clause was not even discussed. Miller had done such a good job of making it a limited racial guarantee in his *Slaughter-House* opinion that rearguing the issue probably seemed a waste of time. Justice Bradley's concurring opinion makes it clear that the decision was less about the right of women to practice law than about their status in society. "Man is, or should be, women's protector and defender," he wrote. "The natural and proper timidity and delicacy which belongs to the female sex evidently unfits it for many of the occupations of civil life." That sort of chauvinism cloaked in chivalry made a virtue of gender discrimination.

Two years later, in *Minor v. Happersett* (1875), the Court upheld a state law denying women the right to vote. The law had been challenged as a violation of the citizenship guarantee of the Amendment on the theory that the right to vote inheres in the status of citizenship. The Court rejected the argument on the grounds that suffrage is distinct from citizenship and that the right of citizens to vote had always been subject to state regulation. The Amendment protected only rights predating its ratification, and therefore created no new classes of voters. Again, as in *Bradwell*, the Equal Protection Clause was not an issue. Today, the equal protection issue would be decisive, but the *Slaughter-House* decision had so weakened the guarantee that the issue was not even raised. Both *Bradwell* and *Minor* involved gender discrimination, but their racial implications were obvious. The Court made it unmistakably clear that conflicts between state police powers and rights claimed under the Fourteenth Amendment would be resolved against the latter.

In 1876 the Court dealt the Fourteenth Amendment another blow in *United States v. Cruikshank*. At issue was the constitutionality of a provision in the Enforcement Act of 1870 making it a federal offense to use force or intimidation to deprive anyone of rights

Figure XII.4 Portrait of Myra Bradwell (1870).
Photographer: C.D. Mosher. Chicago History Museum, ICHi-09585.

Chief Justice Waite on Suffrage and the Fourteenth Amendment

"The [Fourteenth A]mendment did not add to the privileges and immunities of a citizen. It simply furnished an additional guaranty for the protection of such as he already had. No new voters were necessarily made by it. Indirectly it may have had that effect, because it may have increased the number of citizens entitled to suffrage under the constitution and laws of the States, but it operates for this purpose, if at all, through the States and the State laws, and not directly upon the citizen . . . It is clear . . . that the Constitution has not added the right of suffrage to the privileges and immunities of citizenship as they existed at the time it was adopted. This makes it proper to inquire whether suffrage was coextensive with the citizenship of the States at the time of its adoption."

—Minor v. Happersett (1875)

guaranteed by the Constitution or by federal law. Congress had enacted the measure under the Enforcement Clause of the Fourteenth Amendment authorizing it to enforce the Amendment by appropriate legislation. For engaging in a racial massacre in Louisiana, Cruikshank and eight other white defendants were charged with plotting to deprive the murdered blacks of their lives in violation of the Due Process and Equal Protection Clauses of the Amendment. They were not indicted for murder, a crime which came under state jurisdiction, but for the federal offense of impairing Fourteenth Amendment rights in violation of the Enforcement Act. When they challenged the constitutionality of the Act, the federal trial court referred the case to the Supreme Court for determination of the constitutional issue.

The Supreme Court dismissed the indictment on the ground that the offenses charged were beyond federal jurisdiction. Chief Justice Waite, who wrote the opinion, followed the rationale of the *Reese* case. He held that Congress has no power under the Fourteenth Amendment to punish acts committed by individuals. The prohibitions of the Fourteenth Amendment, like those of the Fifteenth, apply only to governmental actions of the states, not to actions by individuals. The enforcement powers of Congress therefore could not be used against individuals. The latter were beyond the reach of the federal government. If they were to be punished for their actions it had to be by their state governments. But it was precisely because the states could not be relied upon to punish such crimes that Congress had made them federal offenses.

The Court used similar reasoning in *United States v. Harris* (1883) to invalidate key provisions of the Enforcement Act of 1871. The Act prohibited conspiracies for the purpose of impeding or obstructing "the due course of justice in any State or Territory, with intent to deny any citizen of the United States the due and equal protection of the laws." Harris had joined a Tennessee lynch mob and helped seize four black prisoners from the custody of a deputy sheriff. The prisoners were beaten so severely that one of them died. When Harris was indicted for conspiring to deny the blacks their constitutional rights, he challenged the indictment on the grounds cited in the *Cruikshank* decision. Justice Woods, speaking for the majority, dismissed the indictment, declaring that the Fourteenth Amendment was "a guarantee of protection against the acts of the State Government itself . . . not a guarantee against the commission of individual offenses." The latter were beyond the enforcement powers of Congress under the Amendment.

Civil Rights Cases

The Court followed the same narrow reasoning in the *Civil Rights Cases* (1883) to invalidate key provisions of the Civil Rights Act of 1875. The Act, which had been passed to protect African Americans against the return of white rule to the South, prescribed penalties for the denial of equal access to public conveyances and accommodations because of race or prior servitude. It also provided that no citizen should be barred from jury service on account of race. The public accommodations provisions were challenged in five separate suits. In each, a black had been denied access to some accommodation or privilege because of race. Since they raised the same constitutional issue, the cases were consolidated and brought up on appeal together.

The Court declared the public accommodations provisions of the Act unconstitutional. Justice Bradley, speaking for the majority, held that the Fourteenth Amendment prohibited the states from discriminating against blacks but did not prohibit private discrimination by individuals. Congress therefore had no authority under the Enforcement Clause of the Amendment to punish acts committed by individuals. The Amendment, he said, "nullifies and makes void all State legislation, and State action of every kind, which impairs the privileges and immunities of citizens of the United States . . . or which denies to any of them the equal protection of the laws." But similar action by an individual is simply "a private wrong" not punishable under federal law. What might not be done lawfully by a state might be done with impunity by an individual.

Justice Harlan filed an eloquent dissent. "I cannot resist the conclusion," he declared, "that the substance and spirit of the recent amendments of the Constitution have been sacrificed by a subtle and ingenious verbal criticism." Harlan could not have been more correct. The amendments had been eviscerated by brilliant but pernicious semantics. He chided the majority for not adhering to the rule that in interpreting provisions of the Constitution "full effect be given to the intent with which they were adopted." To distinguish between wrongs committed by states and those committed by individuals was specious. The analysis adopted by the majority was a formula for destroying rights guaranteed by the Constitution, turning them into "splendid baubles, thrown out to delude those who deserved fair and generous treatment at the hands of the nation."

Harlan thought that even the most narrow and technical construction of the Fourteenth Amendment authorized prohibitions against discrimination in public conveyances and accommodations. Facilities used by the public which operate under governmental licenses are agents of the states and therefore subject to the same constitutional constraints as the states. Their wrongs become state wrongs and fall within the enforcement provisions of the Amendment. Harlan's technical analysis was impeccable, but his main theme was racial justice. He urged recognition of

> the legal right of the black race to take the rank of citizens, and to secure the enjoyment of privileges belonging, under the law, to them as a component part of the people for whose welfare and happiness government is ordained.

Harlan denounced the tyranny of race as the worst of all tyrannies. "Today, it is the colored race which is denied," he warned. "At some future time, it may be that some other race will fall under the ban of race discrimination."

Justice Harlan on the Civil Rights Act of 1875

"It is, I submit, scarcely just to say that the colored race has been the special favorite of the laws. The statute of 1875, now adjudged to be unconstitutional, is for the benefit of citizens of every race and color. What the nation, through Congress, has sought to accomplish in reference to that race, is—what had already been done in every State of the Union for the white race—to secure and protect rights belonging to them as freemen and citizens; nothing more . . . The one underlying purpose of congressional legislation has been to enable the black race to take the rank of mere citizens. The difficulty has been to compel a recognition of the legal right of the black race to take the rank of citizens, and to secure the enjoyment of privileges belonging, under the law, to them as a component part of the people for whose welfare and happiness government is ordained."

—Civil Rights Cases (1883)

Civil rights won a minor victory in *Strauder v. West Virginia* (1880), when the Court invalidated a statute barring blacks from jury service. The exclusion was such a flagrant violation of the Equal Protection Clause of the Fourteenth Amendment that no other outcome was possible. But the practical effect of the decision was undermined by *Virginia v. Rives* (1880), a companion case. The Court upheld the conviction of a black by an all-white jury despite the fact that no blacks had been enrolled for jury service. But because Virginia had not expressly excluded them by statute, nothing unconstitutional could be inferred from their absence. The defendant had the burden of proving that their absence from the rolls was the result of official state policy. Proving that was virtually impossible, because the law gave local officials broad discretion with respect to jury qualifications. The decision in effect approved the *de facto* exclusion of blacks from jury service.

The Fourteenth Amendment decisions of the 1870s and 1880s had at least one positive aspect: They all recognized that the Amendment prohibited official state discrimination based on race. The Court consistently held that racial discrimination by government was unconstitutional. While private citizens had the right to discriminate, the states were forbidden to do so as a matter of constitutional law. This distinction was important, because it was the difference between permissive and compulsory racism. If blacks could be protected against the latter, the cause of racial justice would be far from hopeless. Without the force of law behind them, the racial barriers erected by individuals might be overcome. Only the law could institutionalize and give permanence to the system. But this could not happen, the Court held in case after case, because it was expressly prohibited by the Amendment. If the justices had stuck to that position, the racist tendencies of the period would not have escalated into the abomination of state-sponsored racism.

Conservatives Appointed to the Court

Sweeping changes in Court personnel set the stage for the final assault on the civil rights of African Americans. Eight new justices were appointed between 1888 and 1896, all conservative and all inclined to regard race relations as essentially a local concern. This new majority would preside over the destruction of all that remained of the Reconstruction program. When Justice Woods died in 1887, President Grover Cleveland replaced him with Lucius Q.C. Lamar, a former Confederate colonel and senator from Mississippi. The appointment, which a decade earlier would have been unthinkable, caused hardly a political ripple. The death of Chief Justice Waite the following year gave Cleveland the opportunity to fill that post as well before his term expired. After several other candidates had been eliminated for one reason or another, he nominated Melville W. Fuller, an Illinois Democrat. Fuller, like his predecessor, had only limited experience in public office before becoming chief justice.

Benjamin Harrison, who defeated Cleveland in 1888, made four appointments during his four years as president. He appointed David J. Brewer of Kansas to fill the vacancy created by the death of Justice Matthews in 1889. Brewer was a nephew of Justice Field, and he had served as both a state and federal judge. Like his uncle, he was a thoroughgoing conservative. After Justice Miller's death in 1890, Harrison appointed Henry B. Brown of Michigan. Brown, a former senator and judge, was competent and conservative, but he lacked the brilliance of the man he replaced. When Justice Bradley died in 1892, Harrison nominated George Shiras, Jr., a Pittsburgh railroad lawyer. Shiras was controversial, and his nomination was confirmed only after bitter debate. Harrison's last appointment was made after his defeat by Cleveland in the 1892 election. He appointed Howell E. Jackson, a Tennessee Democrat, to replace Justice Lamar, who died after only five years on the bench.

Cleveland appointed two justices during his second term. He appointed Senator Edward D. White of Louisiana after Justice Blatchford's death in 1893. White, a wealthy sugar planter and former Confederate officer, remained in the Senate for two weeks after his confirmation in order to participate in debates over the sugar bounty, a matter in which he had a personal interest. When Justice Jackson died in 1895, Cleveland appointed Rufus H. Peckham of New York to succeed him. Peckham, a member of the New York Court of Appeals, continued to serve as a trustee of a major insurance company for more than a decade after joining the Supreme Court. He resigned his post only after disclosures of improper and unethical practices by the company. This, then, was the cast of corporation lawyers and political conservatives who would complete the destruction of the rights of African Americans under the Fourteenth Amendment.

Plessy v. Ferguson

The final blow fell in *Plessy v. Ferguson* (1896) when the Supreme Court held that the Fourteenth Amendment did not prevent the states from ordering racial segregation. The earlier cases had upheld only racial discrimination by individuals, but the Court now crossed that line and upheld state-ordered discrimination as well. At issue was an 1890 Louisiana law requiring separate railroad accommodations for blacks and whites. All railroads within the state were ordered to provide "equal but separate accommodations for the white, and colored races, by providing two or more passenger coaches for each passenger train, or by dividing the passenger coaches by a partition so as to secure separate accommodations." Any member of either race using the accommodations reserved for the other race would be punished by a $25 fine or 20 days in jail. The law was typical of other legislation being passed in the South to exclude blacks from schools, parks, and other public accommodations reserved for whites. A group of New Orleans residents formed the Comité des Citoyens to oppose the law, and they organized a test case to challenge its constitutionality. Their plaintiff was Homer Plessy, a freeborn man who was one-eighth African American and thus classified as black under Louisiana law. Plessy challenged the law by refusing to move when ordered to leave the white compartment of a railroad car. Tried and convicted in the state courts, he appealed to the United States Supreme Court on the grounds that the law violated the guarantees of both the Thirteenth and Fourteenth Amendments.

Plessy contended that state-ordered segregation imposed on blacks a badge of servitude in violation of the Thirteenth Amendment, and that it also violated the due process and equal protection guarantees of the Fourteenth. Justice Brown, speaking for the majority, rejected both claims. There had been no violation of the Thirteenth Amendment, he held, because that Amendment prohibited only slavery and involuntary servitude. The Louisiana law imposed neither and therefore did not violate the Amendment. Nor did it violate the Fourteenth Amendment, because no one had been deprived of life, liberty, or property, nor had anyone been denied equal protection of the laws. Brown noted that the Louisiana law applied equally to both races, excluding whites from black railroad compartments under the same penalties that blacks were excluded from white compartments. The Equal Protection of the Laws Clause required only the equal legal treatment of the races, and the Louisiana law did precisely that.

Brown upheld the right of the states to take race into account in regulating places of public accommodation. He cited an 1849 holding by Chief Justice Lemuel Shaw of Massachusetts that legal distinctions based on race were compatible with state constitutional guarantees of legal equality. Shaw ruled in *Roberts v. City of Boston* that racial segregation in the public schools did not violate a provision in the state constitution that all persons were equal before the law. He held that this guarantee of legal equality did not prevent the state from making reasonable distinctions based on age, sex, and race. It was a bad decision by a great judge, but Brown relied on it heavily to bolster his own arguments. He contended that distinctions based on race were similarly compatible with the Fourteenth Amendment. The Amendment had not been intended to abolish racial distinctions or enforce social equality or the commingling of the races. Brown noted that Congress had established separate schools for blacks in the District of Columbia. He wrote,

> We cannot say that a law which authorizes or even requires the separation of the two races in public conveyances is unreasonable or more obnoxious to the Fourteenth Amendment than the acts of Congress requiring separate schools for colored children in the District of Columbia, the constitutionality of which does not seem to have been questioned.

That the constraints placed upon the states by the Fourteenth Amendment did not apply to Congress was ignored by Brown in his haste to justify the decision.

Brown scorned the claim that forced segregation stamped blacks with a badge of inferiority. "If this be so," he wrote, "it is not by reason of anything found in the act, but solely because the colored race chooses to put that construction upon it." He thought that regulations based on race "do not necessarily imply the inferiority of either race to the other, and have been generally, if not universally, recognized as within the competency of the state legislatures in the exercise of their police power." Racial animosities and prejudices could not be overcome by the forced commingling of the races, he declared. "Legislation is powerless to eradicate racial instincts or to abolish distinctions based upon physical differences . . . If one race be inferior to the other socially, the Constitution of the United States cannot put them upon the same plane." But Brown misstated the issue. The case had nothing to do with forced integration but rather with the right of both races to commingle voluntarily.

Only Justice Harlan dissented, and he wrote one of the most memorable dissents in the history of the Court. He began by condemning the notion that the states could take race into account for any lawful purpose. "Our Constitution is color-blind," he wrote, "and neither knows nor tolerates classes among citizens." The failure of the Court to invalidate the Louisiana law would, he predicted, "prove to be quite as pernicious as the decision made by this tribunal in the *Dred Scott case.*" The decision would "encourage the belief that it is possible, by means of state enactments, to defeat the beneficent purposes which the people of the United States had in view when they adopted the recent amendments of the Constitution." The two races were inextricably linked, Harlan declared, "and the interests of both require that the common government of all shall not permit the seeds

Justices Brown and Harlan on Separate but Equal

Justice Brown for the Majority, *Plessy v. Ferguson*

We consider the underlying fallacy of the plaintiff's argument to consist in the assumption that the enforced separation of the two races stamps the colored race with a badge of inferiority. If this be so, it is not by reason of anything found in the act, but solely because the colored race chooses to put that construction upon it . . . The argument also assumes that social prejudices may be overcome by legislation, and that equal rights cannot be secured to the negro except by an enforced commingling of the two races. We cannot accept this proposition. If the two races are to meet upon terms of social equality, it must be the result of natural affinities, a natural appreciation of each other's merits and a voluntary consent of individuals . . . If one race be inferior to the other socially, the Constitution of the United States cannot put them upon the same plane . . ..

Figure XII.5 Portrait of Henry Billings Brown.

Library of Congress, Prints and Photographs Division, LC-USZ62-90766

Justice Harlan Dissents, *Plessy v. Ferguson*

If evils will result from the commingling of the two races upon public highways established for the benefit of all, they will be infinitely less than those that will surely come from state legislation regulating the enjoyment of civil rights upon the basis of race. We boast of the freedom enjoyed by our people above all other peoples. But it is difficult to reconcile that boast with a state of the law which, practically, puts the brand of servitude and degradation upon a large class of our fellow citizens, our equals before the law.

Figure XII.6 Portrait of John Marshall Harlan.

Library of Congress, Prints and Photographs Division, LC-DIG-cwpbh-04615

of race hate to be planted under the sanction of law." He dismissed with scorn Justice Brown's reasoning that the Louisiana law treated both races equally. "The thin disguise of 'equal' accommodations for passengers," he wrote, "will not mislead any one, nor atone for the wrong this day done."

Except for the *Dred Scott* case, *Plessy* is arguably the worst decision in the history of the Supreme Court. The test of reasonableness upon which the majority placed so much emphasis had nothing to do with the case. Even the most reasonable laws are invalid if they violate express provisions of the Constitution. All sorts of things considered reasonable in the antebellum period became unconstitutional with the adoption of the Civil War Amendments. That applied to the segregation in Boston's public schools upheld by Chief Justice Shaw of Massachusetts in 1849. Nor did the acts of Congress for segregated schools in the District of Columbia have anything to do with the case. Since the Fourteenth Amendment applied only to the states, what the federal government did had no bearing on the case. Congress was not limited by the Equal Protection Clause as the states were limited. While the Due Process Clause of the Fifth Amendment would later be held to subsume equal protection of law, the linkage did not then exist. Justice Brown probably cited what Congress had done in order to obscure the real issue. The issue was not what Congress had done but what Louisiana had done, and that was clearly unconstitutional.

Harlan's prediction that the decision would encourage assaults on the rights of blacks tragically proved correct. The "separate but equal" doctrine became the cornerstone for a vast edifice of racist legislation that made compulsory segregation settled policy in the South for the next half-century. Nor would it be limited only to public accommodations. In *Berea College v. Kentucky* (1908), the Court held that even private schools could be compelled by the states to separate the races. Thus the wheel came full circle. Beginning in the 1870s with decisions that upheld the right of individuals to discriminate, the Court by the turn of the century was upholding laws that took away even the right not to discriminate.

Separate and Unequal

Harlan was also correct about the hypocrisy of the "separate but equal" doctrine. In practice, it became a shabby pretext for the unequal treatment of the races. In subsequent cases the Court adopted the rule that separate facilities for blacks would be constitutional if "substantially" equal to those provided for whites. Exact or mathematical equality was not a constitutional requirement. And "substantial" equality could be anything or nothing depending on what the states wanted to spend on separate facilities. In *Cumming v. Richmond County Board of Education* (1899), the Court held that a poor school district could constitutionally bar black children from a white high school without providing them with a high school of their own. The Court accepted the argument that the school district would be unable to operate a separate elementary school for blacks if school funds had to be used to maintain a separate high school. The alternative of admitting the blacks to the white school apparently did not occur to the justices. The sliding-scale approach to equality continued well into the twentieth century. In *Gong Lum v. Rice* (1927), the Court upheld the order of a school district barring a Chinese girl from a white school in her own district. The Court held that her assignment to a school for blacks in a neighboring school district met the standard of substantial equality.

By the turn of the century the Supreme Court had put the stamp of legality on one of the most shameful chapters in American history. Systematically denied their constitutional rights, African Americans entered the twentieth century as second-class citizens. They were isolated socially, barred from economic opportunities, and deprived of the chance to develop their talents or improve their condition. Their powerlessness made them convenient scapegoats for demagogues who found it safe and politically profitable to pillory them. Those striving for something better were insulted and threatened, in some cases beaten and murdered, for questioning the place assigned to them. The justices of the Supreme Court cannot be blamed for every outrage, but they do deserve blame for legitimizing what happened. Racism in the United States would have been less virulent had the Court not given it the gloss of legality.

The racial biases of the justices obviously had something to do with these decisions. The state police powers that the Court upheld when used to promote segregation were struck down when used to promote integration. In 1869, for example, the Reconstruction government of Louisiana passed a law prohibiting discrimination in all forms of transportation. The Court declared the law unconstitutional in *Hall v. DeCuir* (1878) on the ground that the state had encroached upon the power of Congress to regulate interstate commerce. "If the public good requires such legislation," Chief Justice Waite declared, "it must come from Congress and not from the States." If the Court had been consistent in its Commerce Clause jurisprudence, it would also have struck down state laws segregating the races on interstate carriers. But state laws enforcing segregation were routinely upheld. In *Louisville, New Orleans & Texas Railway Co. v. Mississippi* (1890), the Court held that state-ordered segregation on the intrastate operations of interstate carriers was constitutional. The decision was inconsistent with the holding in *Hall v. DeCuir*, so much so that Justice Bradley joined Justice Harlan in dissenting. When the casuistry and legalese are stripped away, it becomes fairly obvious that most of the justices shared to some extent the racist views of the segregationists.

While no single justice can be blamed for everything that happened, a large share of the responsibility belongs to Justice Miller for his opinion in the *Slaughter-House Cases*. Described by Chief Justice Chase as the dominant personality on the Court, Miller provided the legal reasoning that made the majority's narrow construction of the Fourteenth Amendment intellectually tenable. His interpretation of the Privileges or Immunities Clause denied whites and blacks alike the protection of the federal Bill of Rights against state government. The opinion sent a message to the states that they were free to regulate the whole body of civil rights and liberties without serious interference from the Court. "The only thing slaughtered in the Slaughterhouse Cases," one commentator has noted, "was the right of the Negro to equality."[1] Miller cannot be blamed for what the Court later did to the Equal Protection Clause. His own views on race were enlightened for the time and he probably would have joined in Harlan's dissent had he lived. Nevertheless, his *Slaughter-House* opinion signaled the beginning of the era of Fourteenth Amendment jurisprudence that produced the *Plessy* decision.

Some of the blame for what happened rests squarely with Congress. After the collapse of Reconstruction, no political action of any sort was taken to protect the civil rights of African Americans in the South. The Fourteenth Amendment authorized the reduction of the congressional representation of states that abridged the suffrage rights of male citizens. Whites in the South might have thought twice before disfranchising blacks if it had meant the loss of seats in Congress. In 1890 such reductions were proposed by Representative Henry Cabot Lodge of Massachusetts, but Congress failed to act. By then enthusiasm for racial justice had waned, and most congressmen had no desire to upset existing political arrangements. A new era had begun, and idealism was as dead as the old Radical leaders. To a new generation of politicians obsessed with patronage and power the rights of black citizens hardly mattered. The struggle for racial justice would not reclaim a place on the national agenda until well into the next century.

Note

1. Leo Pfeffer, *This Honorable Court* (Boston: Beacon Press, 1967), 200.

February 25, 1862	July 11, 1862	March 3, 1863	1868	February 7, 1870	April 3, 1871
First Legal Tender Act	Second Legal Tender Act	Third Legal Tender Act	Thomas M. Cooley Publishes *A Treatise on the Constitutional Limitations which Rest upon the Legislative Power of the States of the American Union*	Hepburn v. Griswold	Collector v. Day

February 4, 1887	March 24, 1890	July 2, 1890	May 11, 1894	May 26, 1894	August 27, 1894
Interstate Commerce Act	Chicago, Milwaukee & St. Paul Railway Co. v. Minnesota	Sherman Anti-Trust Act	Pullman Strike Begins	Reagan v. Farmers' Loan & Trust Co.	Wilson-Gorman Tariff Act

November 8, 1897	February 28, 1898	May 31, 1898	April 17, 1905	February 24, 1908	April 9, 1917
Interstate Commerce Commission v. Alabama Midland Railway Co.	Holden v. Hardy	Smyth v. Ames	Lochner v. New York	Muller v. Oregon	Bunting v. Oregon

XIII Property Rights and Judicial Activism

May 1, 1871	March 1, 1877	January 24, 1881	March 3, 1884	May 10, 1886	October 25, 1886
Knox v. Lee; Parker v. Davis	Munn v. Illinois; Peik v. Chicago & Northwestern Railway Co.	Springer v. United States	Hurtado v. California Juilliard v. Greenman	Santa Clara County v. Southern Pacific Railroad	Wabash v. Illinois

January 21, 1895	April 8, 1895	May 27, 1895	March 30, 1896	March 1, 1897	May 24, 1897
United States v. E.C. Knight Co.	Pollock v. Farmers' Loan & Trust Co.	In re Debs	Cincinnati, New Orleans & Texas Pacific Railway Co. v. Interstate Commerce Commission	Allgeyer v. Louisiana; Chicago, Burlington & Quincy Railroad Co. v. Chicago	Interstate Commerce Commission v. Cincinnati, New Orleans & Texas Pacific Railway Co.

"Under the mere guise of police regulations, personal rights and private property cannot be arbitrarily invaded, and the determination of the legislature is not final or conclusive. If it passes an act ostensibly for the public health . . . it is for the courts to scrutinize the act to see whether it really relates to and is convenient and appropriate to promote the public health."

—Judge Robert Earle *In re Jacobs* (1885), New York Court of Appeals

The protection of property in the late nineteenth century had a higher priority with the Supreme Court than the protection of civil rights and liberties. Following the Civil War the Court increasingly intervened in matters formerly left to Congress and state legislatures in order to protect business and property interests against public regulation. A dozen acts of Congress and over one hundred state laws were declared unconstitutional between 1874 and 1898, more than double the number invalidated previously. The

Fourteenth Amendment provided a powerful weapon against state regulation after the holding in *Santa Clara County v. Southern Pacific Railroad* (1886) that it protected corporations as well as natural persons. The same was true on the federal level. Over a nine-year period, the Chase Court struck down more congressional legislation than during the Marshall and Taney eras combined. The conservative stance extended to every area of public policy. Constitutional interpretation became a pretext for policy-making as the justices imposed their views upon the country in everything from race relations to protecting business against public regulation. Final say over public policy shifted away from the political branches of government until by the end of the century the United States had what many regarded as government by the judiciary.

Legal Tender Cases

In 1870 the Court boldly intervened in monetary policy to declare the Legal Tender Acts of 1862 and 1863 unconstitutional. To cover wartime expenditures, Congress had authorized the issuance of large amounts of paper currency, known as greenbacks, to serve as legal tender for the payment of all debts. The measures were immediately challenged by creditors seeking to enforce preexisting debt provisions for payment in gold and silver. In the first of the cases, *Hepburn v. Griswold*, the Court voted 5–3 to invalidate the laws on the ground that Congress's monetary power could not be used to abridge the contract rights of creditors. Chief Justice Chase, speaking for the majority, noted that while the Contract Clause applied only to the states, federal violation of it would be inconsistent with the spirit of the Constitution. He held also that the laws violated the Due Process Clause of the Fifth Amendment by scaling down the value of gold and silver obligations to the depreciated level of paper money.

The decision, if allowed to stand, would have caused economic havoc. Over $400 million in legal tender would have been removed from circulation to the utter ruin of countless debtors. The currency contraction would have plunged the country into a deflationary spiral driving large numbers of farmers and businessmen into bankruptcy. Chase, as secretary of treasury, had been the chief architect of the Legal Tender Acts, and critics of the decision understandably attacked him for changing his position. So almost immediately the political wheels began turning to bring about a reversal. This became feasible when Justice Grier, who had voted with the majority, resigned from the Court, leaving the justices divided 4–3 on the issue. Since Congress had increased the membership of the Court to nine in 1869, two vacancies were available for President Grant to fill. On the very day the decision came down, he appointed Justices Bradley and Strong to the posts. As soon as they were confirmed, the government filed a motion to reconsider the issue. Chase opposed the motion, but Bradley and Strong voted with the three dissenting justices to form a 5–4 majority for reconsideration.

The same 5–4 majority proceeded to overturn the decision in the *Second Legal Tender Cases* (*Knox v. Lee* and *Parker v. Davis*) in 1871. Justice Strong, speaking for the new majority, upheld the Acts as a constitutional exercise of national power in time of emergency. While the War Powers clause was not specifically invoked, Strong noted that paper currency had been crucially important in financing military operations during the Civil War. Even if contract rights had been abridged, the abridgment was technical and did not violate the spirit of the Contract Clause. "Contracts must be understood as made in reference to the possible exercise of the rightful authority of the government," he wrote, "and no obligation of a contract can extend to the defeat of legitimate government authority." Strong declared that while Congress had no express power to make paper money legal tender, the power to do so is implicit in other functions expressly delegated to it by the Constitution.

That Grant deliberately packed the Court to secure a reversal of *Hepburn* seems fairly obvious. While there is no evidence that he received prior assurances from his appointees, he certainly had reason to believe that they were with him on the issue. Strong had already voted to uphold the Legal Tender Acts while on the Pennsylvania Supreme Court, and Bradley's close ties to the business community virtually guaranteed that he would do the same. Grant did what any president would have done in similar circumstances. If the means employed to overturn *Hepburn* were political, so were the means employed to uphold it. Chief Justice Chase used all his considerable political skills to prevent the new appointees from voting on the issue. "The Chief Justice has resorted to all the stratagems of the lowest political trickery to prevent their being heard," Justice Miller wrote, "and the fight has been bitter in the conference room . . . such a strain on my brain and nervous system as I never wish to encounter again." The reversal of *Hepburn* did not give Congress a free hand to issue paper money. The Court held only that the Acts were constitutional as wartime measures, not that Congress had unlimited power with respect to monetary policy. Thirteen years would elapse before that issue was settled in Congress's favor in *Juilliard v. Greenman* (1884), which again underscored the role of the Court in defining the limits of congressional power.

Social and Economic Changes

The growth of judicial power was concomitant with an unparalleled prosperity that transformed American life in the late nineteenth century. With no foreign enemies to contend with, the country was able to reduce military expenditures and funnel national resources into productive enterprises. The population more than doubled to 70 million by the end of the century, and the proportion of people living in cities increased from 16 to over 50 percent of the population. The demand for consumer goods soared as the population grew, and great railway networks sprang up linking the country together and creating national markets. Capital for development flowed in from abroad, and the state and federal governments were generous in granting rights to natural resources. The country turned its full attention to economic development with spectacular results. Investors made unprecedented profits, and wage rates were higher than at any previous time. For some the changes brought economic hardship, but for most the era was one of increasing material abundance. By the end of the century the United States had become the greatest industrial nation on earth, producing more iron and steel than any other two countries combined.

Most Americans viewed their prosperity as a triumph of laissez-faire capitalism. Entrepreneurs and private investors, not government planners, were responsible for the astonishing transformation of the country. Some were self-serving and corrupt, but even the worst of them quickened the pace of economic progress. They started new industries and revitalized old ones, ruthlessly and without regard to the environment, but creating new sources of wealth in the process. During the last three decades of the century the country produced an array of business talent greater than the world had ever seen. The drive to maximize profits increased the mechanization of industry and agriculture and intensified the specialization of labor. Mass markets were created for a seemingly endless stream of goods and services in an emergent consumer economy. For better or worse, the modern era of American life had begun.

But so much change also produced social and economic hardship that aggrieved groups sought to redress by political means. They pressed for laws that would bring the new and enormous power of giant corporations under public regulation. The great leaders of industry and commerce were both envied and feared by ordinary citizens. They dictated prices and wage rates, created monopolies in key industries, and ran their businesses with scant regard for the public interest. Decisions made in the boardrooms of Boston and New York City determined the cost of shipping corn in Iowa, the price of heating oil in Cleveland, and sometimes whether whole communities remained economically viable. The making of corporate decisions affected the lives of millions of people. The real issue for groups pressing for public regulation was not the wealth of the corporations but the power they wielded over the life of the nation.

The railways in particular were targeted for regulation. Abusive practices and monumental arrogance pervaded the industry. Some lines granted rebates to large shippers, and others rewarded favored shippers with drawbacks on the freight charges paid by their competitors. The rebates and drawbacks would be recouped by charging farmers and small businessmen all that the traffic would bear. Shippers in towns not served by competing lines were charged higher rates than those served by more than one carrier. Long- and short-haul price discrimination was widespread, and whole communities suffered economically. Towns with no transportation alternatives were at the mercy of the railways serving them. Since the public interest was real and the abuses undeniable, the case for some form of public regulation was compelling.

Due Process and Regulation

Railroad regulation began in the Midwest with the enactment of the so-called Granger laws. The granges, which were originally social and educational farm organizations, evolved into a political movement which won control of several state legislatures. Between 1870 and 1874 Illinois, Minnesota, Wisconsin, and Iowa passed laws fixing railway rates and warehouse charges. State commissions were set up to enforce the regulations and deal with violations. Prior to the Civil War such measures would have raised no constitutional issues, except possibly with respect to their impact on interstate commerce. The states then had the power to use their police powers unconditionally to promote the general welfare of their citizens. But the Fourteenth Amendment now limited what the states might do within their own borders. While the Supreme Court had ruled that state police powers remained virtually intact with regard to civil rights and liberties, it remained to be seen how the Court would react to laws restricting the rights of property.

The constitutionality of the Granger legislation came before the Court in *Munn v. Illinois* (1877). At issue was an Illinois law fixing maximum charges for the storage of grain in cities with a population of 100,000 or more. The measure was aimed at Chicago, the only city in the state with that many people. The fourteen warehouses there controlled the city's grain storage business and served as conduits for the shipment of western grain to eastern markets. The constitutionality of the statute was challenged on three grounds: first, that it encroached upon the commerce power of Congress under Article I; second, that it granted preferences to the ports of one state over those of others in violation of the same Article; and third, that it violated the Due Process Clause of the Fourteenth Amendment by depriving the owners of the warehouses of property without due process of law. The Illinois state courts upheld the law, and the case was taken on appeal to the United States Supreme Court.

Chief Justice Waite, speaking for the majority, dismissed the Article I objections as inapplicable. The rate regulations did not affect interstate commerce or grant port preferences. That the warehouses were used by shippers doing business across state lines did not make them a part of interstate commerce. They were no more a part of interstate commerce than the local wagons used to transfer grain from one railroad to another. Their regulation was a domestic matter within the police powers of the state. That the regulations might have an indirect or marginal impact on interstate commerce did not invalidate them. Until Congress acted on the commerce issue, Illinois had concurrent jurisdiction to use its police powers to regulate such matters.

The due process issue was more complicated. Just what limitations, if any, did the due process guarantee of the Fourteenth Amendment impose upon the police powers of the states? Due process had traditionally been regarded as a guarantee against arbitrary punishment in criminal cases; it meant only that a defendant's life, liberty, or property might not be taken away except pursuant to the law of the land. The guarantee had nothing to do with the substance or effect of the law; it required only that government should act lawfully. Due process was essentially a matter of observing procedural formalities. But there was an alternative view that due process was not just procedural but imposed substantive limits on the power of government itself. The Supreme Court declared the Missouri Compromise unconstitutional in the *Dred Scott* case (1857) on the ground that it deprived slaveholders of property by preventing them from bringing their slaves into the national territories. Similarly, due process was cited by the Court in *Hepburn v. Griswold* as a ground for invalidating the Legal Tender Acts. The issue in both cases was not whether the government had acted lawfully but whether it had the power to act at all. In both cases the answer was no. Although the procedural formalities of due process had been complied with, the substantive effect of the laws rendered them unconstitutional.

But the case law on due process was far from clear. *Dred Scott* was an odious precedent, and *Hepburn* had been overturned the following year in the Second Legal Tender Cases.

Moreover, when the due process guarantee of the Fourteenth Amendment came before the Court for the first time in the *Slaughter-House Cases*, the majority treated it as an essentially procedural guarantee that imposed no substantive restraints on the police powers of the states. Due process meant only that established legal procedures had to be observed. So the outcome of *Munn v. Illinois* depended largely on which theory of due process was adopted by the Court. Since the Illinois law met all the procedural requirements, only a substantive interpretation of the guarantee could invalidate it.

Waite upheld the law under what amounted to a modified theory of substantive due process. He cited the rule propounded by the seventeenth-century English jurist Sir Matthew Hale that when private property is affected with a public interest it becomes subject to public regulation. Waite wrote,

> It has been customary in England from time immemorial, and in this country from its first colonization, to regulate ferries, common carriers, hackmen, bakers, millers, wharfingers, innkeepers, etc., and in doing so to fix a maximum charge to be made for services rendered . . . and we think it has never yet been successfully contended that such legislation came within any of the constitutional prohibitions against interference with private property.

By putting his property to a public use, the owner must submit to having it regulated for the common good. He may withdraw it from public control by discontinuing its public use; but while its public use continues, it remains subject to public regulation.

For the next sixty years Waite's "public interest" doctrine became the threshold test of the constitutionality of public regulation. Not until *Nebbia v. New York* (1934) was the test abandoned as an issue for judicial determination. The test established an essentially substantive standard of due process for determining whether a business was subject to governmental regulation. Making this determination would ultimately be up to the Court's interpretation of the Due Process Clause. The states could legislate the nature and form of the regulations, but the Court would ultimately have to decide whether the

---

Chief Justice Waite on the Public Interest Doctrine

"Looking, then, to the common law, from whence came the right which the Constitution protects, we find that when private property is "affected with a public interest, it ceases to be *juris privati* only." This was said by Lord Chief Justice Hale more than two hundred years ago . . . and has been accepted without objection as an essential element in the law of property ever since. Property does become clothed with a public interest when used in a manner to make it of public consequence, and affect the community at large. When, therefore, one devotes his property to a use in which the public has an interest, he, in effect, grants to the public an interest in that use, and must submit to be controlled by the public for the common good, to the extent of the interest he has created. He may withdraw his grant by discontinuing the use; but, so long as he maintains the use, he must submit to the control . . ."

—Munn v. Illinois (1877)

businesses regulated were of the sort subject to regulation. Since the commercial storage of grain clearly met that test, the Illinois law was upheld as constitutional.

Although the reasonableness of the storage rates set by Illinois was not an issue, Waite held that such matters were within the legislative discretion of the states. All that the Court could determine was whether a state had the power to regulate, and that depended on whether the business regulated was affected with a public interest. If the power to regulate existed, the Court could not second-guess the states as to how it should be exercised. While the owners of the property were entitled to a reasonable return on their investment, what was reasonable was ultimately a matter to be determined by lawmakers, not judges. "In countries where the common law prevails," the chief justice wrote, "it has been customary from time immemorial for the legislature to declare what shall be a reasonable compensation." As Waite saw it, the reasonableness of regulatory legislation was not a matter to be determined by judges. "For protection against abuses by legislatures," he said, "the people must resort to the polls, not to the courts."

Justice Field, with Justice Strong concurring, wrote a spirited dissent. He began by refuting Waite's understanding of the English common law regarding the public regulation of private property. Field contended that in England public use of or reliance upon the use of private property had never been sufficient to affect property with a public interest that subjected it to public regulation. The kind of property that Hale had in mind was property that had been dedicated by its owners to public use, such as inns, ferries, toll bridges, and the like, businesses that operated under a governmental license. The idea that private property becomes subject to public regulation simply because it proves useful or important to the public struck Field as an astonishing proposition, at odds with the English common law and incompatible with the due process guarantee of the Fourteenth Amendment. "If this be sound law," he wrote,

> if there be no protection, either in the principles upon which our republican government is founded, or in the prohibitions of the Constitution against such invasion of private rights, all property and all business in the State are held at the mercy of a majority of its legislature.

He also disagreed with Waite that the reasonableness of the public regulation of private property was up to the legislative branch of government and not a matter for judicial determination. Field contended that the Due Process Clause made the reasonableness of regulatory measures a constitutional issue to be determined by the Court as the guarantor of rights protected by the Constitution.

Field did not contend that property had absolute rights, only that under the Fourteenth Amendment it had some rights that were constitutionally protected against the states. The *Munn* case convinced him that state police powers had been invoked to deprive the warehouse owners of their property without just compensation. If the state wanted to regulate private property in the public interest, the proper course was to assert eminent domain with compensation to the owners. The state could not arbitrarily regulate it as an exercise of police powers in ways that diminished or destroyed its value. Illinois naturally did not want to invoke eminent domain, because this would have imposed upon it the cost

Figure XIII.1 Portrait of Stephen Field (c. 1870–1880).

Library of Congress, Prints and Photographs Division, LC-DIG-cwpbh-03993

and difficulty of taking over and managing the warehouses. So the burden of serving the public interest was simply shifted to the private owners by fixing the rates that they might charge. The state in effect got the benefits of eminent domain without any of its costs and bother. Legal title to the warehouses remained with the owners but subject to regulations that greatly reduced the value of their property.

Field's substantive interpretation of due process extended to liberty as well as property. He declared,

> By the term liberty, something more is meant than mere freedom from physical restraint or the bonds of a prison. It means the freedom to go where one may choose, and to act in such manner, not inconsistent with the equal rights of others, as his judgment may dictate for the promotion of his happiness.

He had dissented from the Court's narrow interpretation of due process in the *Slaughter-House Cases*, and his opposition to that decision never wavered. Nor would he accept the *Munn* holding as final. He kept the issue alive in dissent after dissent, hammering away with brilliantly reasoned arguments that due process meant something more than due procedure, enough at least for courts to review the reasonableness of state constraints on the rights of property.

One of the reasons the issue remained alive was that the *Munn* majority had left the door open by failing to come down unequivocally on the side of procedural due process. Waite's "public interest" doctrine conceded that there were at least some substantive constraints on the regulatory powers of the states, so it was essentially a question of how far the constraints extended. Waite took a pragmatic approach: The Court would determine whether under the public interest test the state had the power to regulate certain types of property; if the state indeed had the power, the details of regulation would then be entirely up to the state lawmakers. As a practical matter, getting into the details was simply beyond the technical competency of the courts. Field, on the other hand, ignored the practical difficulties and insisted upon full judicial protection against possible abuses of state regulatory power.

Trend toward Substantive Due Process

Powerful forces at work in American society favored Field's theory of substantive due process. The great corporate interests that emerged in the late nineteenth century feared the consequences of unrestricted governmental regulation. Because of their scale and the increased interdependence of economic relations, most of these enterprises met the "public interest" test and therefore stood well within the shadow of state regulation. These powerful interests, thoroughly alarmed by the implications of the *Munn* decision, saw possible salvation in Field's spirited dissent. If the courts reviewed the reasonableness of how the states regulated property and business, their interests would be better protected than if left to the discretion of state lawmakers whose concerns were more political than constitutional. So Field did not wage a lonely crusade; his position was applauded and encouraged by powerful and vocal elements in the business community and legal profession. Contemporary trends in constitutional theory also favored Field's ideas. Thomas M. Cooley's *Constitutional Limitations*, first published in 1868, had become an authoritative text for judges, much as Justice Story's *Commentaries* had been in the antebellum period. That Cooley's position on due process was essentially substantive added the gloss of scholarly acceptance to Field's dissents, making them historically plausible and logically compelling.

The trend toward substantive due process began at the state level as conservative judges put brakes on what state legislatures could do in exercising their police powers. In the case of *In re Jacobs* (1885), the New York Court of Appeals, a leader among state courts in the development of substantive due process, struck down a state health law prohibiting the manufacture of cigars in tenement houses in New York City and Brooklyn. Judge Robert Earle, speaking for the Court, held that the law deprived cigarmakers of liberty and property without due process of law. Earle declared,

> Under the mere guise of police regulations personal rights and private property cannot be arbitrarily invaded, and the determination of the legislature is not final or exclusive. If it passes an act ostensibly for the public health, and thereby destroys or takes away the property of a citizen, or interferes with his personal liberty, then it is for the courts to scrutinize the act and see whether it really relates to and is convenient and appropriate to promote health.

Earle found that the law in question failed this test. "It is plain that this is not a health law, and has no relation to public health," he declared. The measure was an arbitrary and unconstitutional abuse of state police powers.

Thomas M. Cooley on Property Rights and Substantive Due Process

"The principles, then, upon which the process is based, are to determine whether it is "due process" or not, and not any considerations of mere form . . . [W]hen the government, through its established agencies, interferes with the title to one's property, or with his independent enjoyment of it . . . we are to test its validity by those principles of civil liberty and constitutional protection which have become established in our system of laws, and not generally by the rules that pertain to forms of procedure merely."

—*A Treatise on Constitutional Limitations*

Figure XIII.2 Portrait of Thomas M. Cooley.

Bentley Historical Library, University of Michigan, BL003507

State Regulation and Interstate Commerce

Besides the constraints of the Fourteenth Amendment, state lawmakers had to take the Commerce Clause into account in exercising their police powers. The public interests doctrine was cited by the Court in *Peik v. Chicago & Northwestern Railway Co.* in 1877 in upholding the power of the states to fix maximum railway rates. Railway operations so clearly affected the public interest that the right of the states to regulate them was fairly obvious. But more serious than the due process issue was whether such regulations encroached upon the commerce power of Congress. Waite, speaking for the majority, held that in the absence of federal legislation the states could regulate the intrastate operations of interstate railroads. The theory that the states had concurrent jurisdiction to regulate commerce had been propounded by Taney before the Civil War to allow state regulation where no federal legislation had been enacted. Whatever its original merits, the theory posed problems after the war when the intrastate and interstate operations of railroads were difficult to separate. Still, given the choice between state regulation and no regulation, the Waite Court regarded the former as the lesser evil. The upshot was a rash of state legislation subjecting the railways to widely different rules and regulations.

The adverse impact of these regulations on interstate commerce finally forced the Court to reconsider the matter. In 1886 a decade of state regulation of interstate carriers came to a crashing halt in *Wabash v. Illinois.* At issue was an Illinois law prohibiting rate discrimination between Illinois and New York City. Justice Miller, speaking for the majority, declared the law unconstitutional on the ground that it encroached upon the commerce power of Congress. It made no difference that Congress had not legislated; all that mattered was that the business regulated fell exclusively within the jurisdiction of the federal government. Miller wrote,

> It is not, and never has been, the deliberate opinion of a majority of this Court that a statute of a State which attempts to regulate the fares and charges by railroad companies within its limits, for a transportation which constitutes a part of commerce among the States, is a valid law.

By putting all interstate rail operations beyond the jurisdiction of the states, the decision made the enactment of federal regulations imperative. Without them, interstate carriers would be free to do as they pleased.

The need for federal regulation extended beyond the railroads. State regulation of big business had never been really effective. The giant corporations of the late nineteenth century transacted business across state lines, and the scale of their operations put them beyond the regulatory power of individual states. The problems that arose were national in scope and required national solutions. But federal regulatory intervention raised serious constitutional issues. The federal government, unlike the states, has no general police powers to provide for the common welfare; it has only powers expressly granted to it by the Constitution and powers necessarily implied by those expressly granted. Providing for the general welfare had always been considered the responsibility of state government, a responsibility expressly affirmed in the Tenth Amendment. The only clear grant of federal regulatory power can be found in the Commerce Clause, and the Clause would have to be stretched considerably if the regulatory functions of state government were to be shifted to the national level.

Triumph of Substantive Due Process

Changes in Court personnel set the stage for the triumph of Justice Field's expansive views about due process. Five of the nine justices who participated in the *Munn* decision died or resigned in the 1880s, and by 1890 only two of them remained. Their places were taken by corporation lawyers who viewed public regulation with suspicion and distrust. The departing justices were constitutional conservatives who construed the Fourteenth

Amendment narrowly both with respect to civil rights and the rights of property. They did not want the Amendment used to destroy the traditional police powers of the states and thereby undermine our federal system of government. While the justices who replaced them would continue to construe the Amendment narrowly with respect to civil rights, they would broaden the protection it afforded property rights. Given their professional background, the new justices tended to regard public regulation as the opening wedge of a radical assault on the free enterprise system and private property. Convinced that constitutional government could not survive the destruction of property rights, they deployed every weapon in their legal arsenal to keep the regulators at bay. Field's theory of substantive due process would prove to be the most powerful weapon of all.

The trend toward substantive due process became clear in 1886 when the Court decided *Stone v. Farmers' Loan & Trust Co.* At issue was a Mississippi statute creating a railway commission with authority to set rates for intrastate operations. While Chief Justice Waite, speaking for the Court, upheld the law under the public interest doctrine, he departed from his *Munn* opinion in one important respect. He now took the position that the public regulation of private property had to be reasonable in order to satisfy the due process requirement. He declared that to deny the owner a fair rate of return would amount to "a taking of private property for public use without just compensation, or without due process of law." The holding did not affect the outcome of the case, because the reasonableness of the rates had not been challenged. But it represented a departure from the *Munn* holding that the reasonableness of public regulations was not for the courts but for the legislature to determine.

Full vindication of Field's due process theory came four years later in *Chicago, Milwaukee & St. Paul Railway Co. v. Minnesota* (1890). By then, only two of the justices who had participated in *Munn* remained on the Court, and Melville Fuller had replaced Waite as chief justice. At issue was a Minnesota statute creating a rail and warehouse commission with authority to fix rates on intrastate operations. The rates set by the commission were to be final, and there was no provision for notice and a hearing for the carriers. Justice Blatchford, speaking for the majority, held that failure to provide for a hearing or review of the commission's findings was unreasonable, and therefore unconstitutional. The reasonableness of the rates was not at issue, only the method prescribed for setting them. Blatchford declared that the matter could not be left to the discretion of the commission. "The question of the reasonableness of a rate of charge," he wrote, "is eminently a question for judicial investigation, requiring due process of law for its determination." The holding drastically reduced the regulatory power of state legislatures. If reasonableness was ultimately a judicial question, then judges, not lawmakers, would be the final arbiters of regulatory policy.

Justice Bradley, the only surviving member of the majority that had decided *Munn*, filed a sharp dissent. He contended that the Court had practically overruled *Munn* and other cases involving regulatory issues. "The governing principle of those cases was that the regulation and settlement of the fares of railroads and other public accommodations is a legislative prerogative and not a judicial one." Bradley was in no way disturbed that the rates set by the Minnesota commission were final and not reviewable. "There must be a

Judicial Review of Public Regulation

"If the company is deprived of the power of charging reasonable rates for the use of its property, and such deprivation takes place in the absence of an investigation by judicial machinery, it is deprived of the lawful use of its property, and thus, in substance and effect, of the property itself, without due process of law and in violation of the Constitution of the United States; and in so far as it is thus deprived, while other persons are permitted to receive reasonable profits upon their invested capital, the company is deprived of the equal protection of the laws."

—Justice Samuel M. Blatchford, *Chicago,
Milwaukee & St. Paul Railway Co. v. Minnesota* (1890)

final tribunal somewhere for deciding every question in the world," he noted. "Injustice may take place in all tribunals. All human institutions are imperfect—courts as well as commissions and legislatures." The Court was wrong to assume that the latter could not be trusted. He thought them actually far more competent than judges to deal with complicated economic and regulatory matters requiring technical expertise.

The new emphasis on judicial review as an essential part of the regulatory process was affirmed in *Reagan v. Farmers' Loan & Trust Co.* (1894). The Court upheld the order of a federal circuit court in Texas for an inquiry into the rates set by the state railway commission. The order had been appealed because the law creating the commission did not authorize federal court reviews. The reasonableness of the rates was not at issue, only the jurisdiction of the federal courts to review the matter. Justice Brewer, speaking for the majority, held that federal courts had jurisdiction to review rates whether authorized by the states or not. While they could not revise rates set by state legislatures or commissions, they had the power to review their reasonableness. "There is nothing new or strange in this," Brewer declared.

> It has always been a part of the judicial function to determine whether the act of one party (whether that party be a single individual, an organized body, or the public as a whole) operates to divest the other party of any rights of person or property.

Having equated reasonableness with due process, the courts now had jurisdiction to intervene routinely.

The Court did not actually invalidate a rate schedule as unreasonable until four years later in *Smyth v. Ames* (1898). At issue was a Nebraska statute setting railway rates at a much lower level than the rates previously in effect. Bondholders of the railroads sought an injunction in the federal circuit court to restrain management from implementing the new schedule. The injunction was granted, and an appeal was taken to the Supreme Court. Justice Harlan, speaking for the Court, upheld the injunction on the ground that the rates were indeed unreasonable. They were unreasonable for failing to provide owners with a "fair return" on the "fair value" of their property. He wrote,

> ### Justice Brewer on Judicial Review
>
> "[I]t is within the scope of judicial power and a part of judicial duty to restrain anything which, in the form of a regulation of rates, operates to deny to the owners of property invested in the business of transportation that equal protection which is the constitutional right of all owners of other property. There is nothing new or strange in this. It has always been a part of the judicial function to determine whether the act of one party . . . operates to divest the other party of any rights of person or property. In every constitution is the guarantee against the taking of private property for public purposes without just compensation. The equal protection of the laws which, by the Fourteenth Amendment, no State can deny to the individual, forbids legislation, in whatever form it may be enacted, by which the property of one individual is, without compensation, wrested from him for the benefit of another, or of the public."
>
> —Reagan v. Farmers' Loan & Trust Co. (1894)

In order to ascertain that value, the original cost of construction, the amount expended in permanent improvements, the amount and market value of its bonds and stocks, the present as compared with the original cost of construction, the probable earning capacity of the property, under particular rates prescribed by statute, and the sum required to meet operating expenses, are all matters for consideration, and are to be given such weight as may be just and right in each case.

What it all came down to was that the states now had to follow rate-setting criteria approved by the Court.

The Court's "fair return" doctrine was easier to articulate than to implement. Since a rate of return that was fair and reasonable for one business might be unfair for another, the matter had to be determined on a case-by-case basis. In *Wilcox v. Consolidated Gas Co.* (1909), the Court held that a six percent rate of return on invested capital was reasonable for a gas utility, but in *United Railways & Electric Co. v. West* (1930) a return of eight percent was held necessary for a street railway company. The latter was riskier than a gas utility, so investors were entitled to a higher rate of return. Such distinctions, however valid economically, had nothing to do with law or with the traditional role of the courts. They required the evaluation of masses of business and economic data better left to other departments of government having greater access to the necessary technical expertise.

Why the Court took on this difficult task is fairly obvious. It simply did not trust the political branches of government to be fair and reasonable. The legislative branch in particular was subject to pressures that the judiciary could safely ignore. The political fires burned exceedingly hot in the late nineteenth century, as radicals of every stripe attacked capitalism and the rights of property in general. A siege mentality took hold among conservatives who came to regard reform as a pretext for radicalism. Many believed that the public regulation of property would inevitably lead to confiscation. What began with railroads and other businesses affected with a public interest would inexorably grind down all private enterprise and destroy the rights of property. At the end of the road lay socialism, economic stagnation, and the loss of political freedom. The justices shared these apprehensions. While conscious of the need for some regulation, they were determined to keep the extent of the regulation firmly under judicial control.

Laissez-faire economics had now found a judicial corollary in laissez-faire constitutionalism among conservatives on the Court. This approach to constitutional interpretation was rooted in nineteenth-century theories that viewed economic activity as subject to laws as immutable as the laws of nature. Some things were beyond political manipulation and regulation. The law of supply and demand could no more be suspended than the law of gravity. The best formula for economic growth was for government to allow market forces to play out with minimal interference. Supply and demand would fairly determine the value of goods and services, and scarcity during economic downturns would stimulate production and innovation. From the standpoint of laissez-faire constitutionalism, the only justification for regulatory legislation was to insure that market forces operated freely. No regulation that interfered with free markets would pass constitutional muster.

Substantive Due Process and the Bill of Rights

The shift to substantive due process paved the way for extending the guarantees of the federal Bill of Rights to the states. The guarantees were substantive safeguards that could not have been extended to the states via due process by a purely procedural approach. Once a federal guarantee had been identified as an essential part of due process, it could be applied to the states through the Due Process Clause of the Fourteenth Amendment. The business interests of the country were the immediate beneficiaries of the new approach, because the first rights protected were the rights of property. But the protection of property would eventually open the way for the protection of other rights as well. The protection of liberty would inevitably follow the protection of property, because both were included in the due process guarantee.

The breakthrough in extending Bill of Rights guarantees to the states came in *Chicago, Burlington & Quincy Railroad Co. v. Chicago* (1897). At issue was Chicago's use of eminent domain to condemn railroad property for the purpose of laying out streets across tracks within the city. The Illinois eminent domain statute required payment of just compensation to the owners of property condemned, and it provided that in case of disagreement the amount of compensation would be determined by the local county court. The railroad contended that compensation should reflect all the possible commercial uses of the property, while Chicago contended that the property should be valued at only its current use-value for railroad tracks. The county court agreed with the city, and in each instance the jury awarded the railroad only one dollar for the land condemned. Apart from any bias this may have reflected against railroads in general, the jurors apparently concluded that constructing streets over tracks only nominally impaired the value of the property. But the railroad disagreed, and after losing appeals in the state courts, brought the case to the United States Supreme Court on the ground that the nominal award deprived it of property without due process of law.

Counsel for the railroad argued that the Due Process Clause of the Fourteenth Amendment extended the just compensation guarantee of the Fifth Amendment to the states and that the nominal award violated the guarantee. Illinois responded that the Amendment did not extend any of the federal guarantees to the states, because that would destroy our federal system of government and turn state sovereignty into a political fiction. Illinois also argued that the state proceedings had fully protected the due process rights of the railroad. There had been a trial at which both sides presented their evidence, after which the jury brought in a verdict awarding compensation. That the verdict might be wrong or the compensation inadequate did not amount to the denial of due process. Due process required only fair process, not a fair result.

Justice Harlan, speaking for a unanimous Court, agreed with the railroad that the Due Process Clause of the Fourteenth Amendment bound the states to the just compensation guarantee of the Fifth Amendment. For the first time one of the federal guarantees, not surprisingly a property guarantee, had been extended to the states through the Fourteenth Amendment. Although the railroad had won on the constitutional issue, it turned out to be a hollow victory. Harlan went on to rule that the Seventh Amendment prevented the Court from overturning the compensation awarded by the Chicago jury. The Amendment provides that "no fact tried by a jury shall be otherwise re-examined in any court of the United States than according to the rules of the common law." Since the common law limits appellate review to questions of law, the Court could not set aside the factual findings of the jury on the value of the property condemned. In effect, the railroad's Fourteenth Amendment right to just compensation was trumped by the Seventh Amendment provision protecting jury verdicts.

A Double Standard of Due Process

Although the Fourteenth Amendment might incorporate the federal just compensation guarantee, it did not immediately incorporate any of the guarantees protecting the rights of criminal defendants. In *Hurtado v. California* (1884), the Court held that the Due Process Clause of the Fourteenth Amendment did not give defendants the right to a grand jury hearing in state criminal proceedings. Hurtado had been convicted of murder under a provision in the California state constitution that permitted defendants to be tried after a preliminary hearing and commitment by a magistrate. He appealed the conviction on the ground that due process of law requires a grand jury indictment prior to trial. Chief Justice Waite, speaking for the majority, rejected the claim. He pointed out that the Fifth Amendment, from which the Due Process Clause of the Fourteenth is derived, treats grand jury indictment and due process as separate guarantees. The latter therefore could not have been intended to encompass the former, not unless the framers of the Fifth Amendment had been intentionally redundant. Since the grand jury guarantee had been left out of the Fourteenth Amendment, it had to be assumed that it had been omitted deliberately. The states therefore were not bound by the grand jury guarantee of the Fifth Amendment. Criminal due process under the Fourteenth Amendment required only that the procedures adopted by the states were fair and reasonable.

Had this reasoning been applied in property cases, the states would have had the same free hand in dealing with regulatory issues. The reasonableness doctrine assumed that property could not be taken or regulated in the public interest without just compensation. But just compensation, like grand jury indictment, is a specific guarantee of the Fifth Amendment, separate and distinct from the guarantee of due process. If due process did not encompass grand jury indictment, then by the same reasoning neither did it encompass just compensation. Since the latter does not appear in the Fourteenth Amendment, it must be assumed, as with grand jury indictment, that it had been deliberately omitted. That the Court nevertheless read it into the due process guarantee underscores its acute concern for the rights of property. Justice Harlan alone was consistent on the issue. He voted to overturn Hurtado's conviction on the ground that all the guarantees of the Fifth Amendment applied to the states through the Fourteenth Amendment.

The Court showed much less enthusiasm for protecting liberty than property. Not surprisingly, the first form of liberty protected by the Court had a property aspect in freedom of contract. In *Allgeyer v. Louisiana* (1897) the Court invalidated a statute that prohibited owners of property in Louisiana from insuring it with companies not authorized to do business in the state. Justice Peckham, speaking for the Court, held that the Due Process Clause protects the right of citizens to be left alone and free of unreasonable restraints by government over their lives and personal freedom. His opinion was a virtual restatement of what Justice Field had said in his *Munn* dissent twenty years earlier. The liberty protected by due process included more than the right to be free of physical restraint and arbitrary imprisonment. In Peckham's view, it included the right of every citizen

> to be free in the enjoyment of all his faculties; to be free to use them in all lawful ways; to live and work where he will; to earn his livelihood by any lawful calling; to pursue any livelihood or avocation, and for that purpose to enter into all contracts which may be proper, necessary, and essential to his carrying out to a successful conclusion the purposes above mentioned.

The same reasonableness standard that protected property now applied also to laws imposing restraints on personal liberty.

Although the specific issue in *Allgeyer* was freedom of contract, the decision was a major breakthrough for personal liberty. The traditional view had been that the only liberty protected by due process was the right not to be arbitrarily deprived of physical liberty by government. It was a safeguard for persons accused of crimes, not a restriction on the general police powers of the states. *Allgeyer* broadened the concept of personal freedom and gave it a libertarian dimension. The states could no more restrict a citizen's personal liberty than take away his property. Laws seeking to regulate either liberty or property had to be reasonable in order to be constitutional. The idea that state police powers had to be exercised reasonably had far-reaching implications. Did this mean that laws against abortion, homosexuality, miscegenation, and other condemned forms of social behavior had to pass the reasonableness test? These issues were not immediately addressed, because the case involved only the liberty to contract freely. But the other aspects of liberty now stood waiting in the wings until changing times and mores brought them on stage as hot-button constitutional issues.

The expansion of due process in *Allgeyer* had little immediate impact on the protection of other Bill of Rights guarantees. In *Maxwell v. Dow* (1900) the Court affirmed *Hurtado* and further limited the due process rights of criminal defendants. At issue was a provision in Utah's State constitution authorizing criminal trials with juries of fewer than twelve members. While defendants in capital cases had the right to twelve-member juries, lesser offenses were tried by juries of eight. Nor did Utah require a grand jury indictment for bringing accused persons to trial. Maxwell, who had been convicted of robbing a bank, appealed on the grounds that denial of a grand jury hearing and a twelve-member trial jury violated Fifth and Sixth Amendment rights that were applicable to the states through the Fourteenth Amendment.

The Court made short work of the grand jury issue. Justice Peckham, speaking for the majority, held that *Hurtado* settled that issue: Grand jury indictment was not an essential element of due process of law. He held also that Utah was not bound by the Sixth Amendment jury trial guarantee. Citing the *Slaughter-House Cases*, he ruled that the guarantees of the federal Bill of Rights did not extend to the states, and that nothing in the Constitution or the Bill of Rights required the states to provide defendants trial by a common-law jury of twelve members. They were bound only to provide due process, and due process required only a fair trial. Since there was no showing that trial by an eight-member jury was inherently unfair, Maxwell's due process rights had not been violated.

Freedom of Contract

The freedom of contract protected in *Allgeyer* was nevertheless subject to reasonable limitations. In *Holden v. Hardy* (1898), the Court upheld a Utah statute prohibiting the employment of workers in mines, smelters, or ore refineries for more than eight hours a day. Justice Brown, speaking for the majority, noted that while workers

> may engage in ordinary employments more than eight hours per day without injury to their health, it does not follow that labor for the same length of time is innocuous when carried on beneath the surface of the earth, when the operative is deprived of fresh air and sunlight, and is frequently subjected to foul atmosphere and a very high temperature, or to the influence of noxious gases, generated by the processes of refining and smelting.

The hazardous nature of the employment made the law a reasonable and constitutional exercise of the state's police powers.

Since reasonableness is inherently subjective, the outcome of cases in which it was an issue would be difficult to predict. In *Lochner v. New York* (1905), the Court invalidated by a 5–4 vote a statute limiting employment in bakeries to sixty hours a week or ten hours in any one day. Justice Peckham, speaking for the majority, held that the law unreasonably restricted the workers' freedom of contract:

> In every case that comes before this court, the question necessarily arises: Is this a fair, reasonable and appropriate exercise of the police power of the State, or is it an unreasonable, unnecessary and arbitrary interference with the right of the individual to his personal liberty or to enter into contracts in relation to labor which may seem to him appropriate or necessary for the support of himself and his family?

Peckham struck down the law on the ground that employment in bakeries posed no health hazards justifying interference by the state.

Justice Harlan wrote a strong dissent refuting Peckham's assumptions about commercial bakeries. He cited an impressive array of medical and public health data showing that long hours of employment in bakeries caused injury to workers. Since the health issue was at least arguable, Harlan thought that the New York legislature deserved the benefit of the doubt. Due process demanded only that lawmakers act reasonably; it did not require infallibility. He cited the rule that all laws are presumably constitutional and that the burden of proof lies with those challenging their constitutionality. The majority had turned things upside down by resolving doubtful matters against the state. A state should be allowed to exercise its police powers as it sees fit, Harlan wrote, "so long as it does not appear beyond all question that it has violated the Federal Constitution."

Justice Holmes joined in the dissent and questioned the right of the Court to meddle at all in state regulatory matters. He accused the majority of writing a particular political and social philosophy into the Constitution under the pretext of interpreting it. The decision had more to do with laissez-faire economics than with principled constitutional interpretation. "A constitution is not intended to embody a particular economic theory," he wrote.

> It is made for people of fundamentally differing views, and the accident of our finding certain opinions natural and familiar, or novel, and even shocking, ought not to conclude our judgment upon the question whether statutes embodying them conflict with the Constitution of the United States.

Even the most foolish laws are not necessarily unconstitutional, he argued, and for the Court to bend public policy to its views of the general welfare amounted to judicial usurpation of legislative functions.

Holmes's views on judicial self-restraint would ultimately prevail, but Harlan's factual focus had greater immediate impact. It emphasized the importance of assembling data showing that the law in question was not unreasonable. This was the sort of thing usually done by legislatures considering regulatory measures but now it was judicially relevant since the courts had assumed the functions of legislatures. Louis D. Brandeis made effective use of this strategy three years later in *Muller v. Oregon* (1908) when he appeared on behalf of Oregon to defend a law prohibiting the employment of women in factories and laundries for more than ten hours in any one day. Instead of citing legal precedents, which is the way appeals are usually argued, he relied instead on factual evidence. His brief contained only two pages of legal arguments but over two hundred pages of medical, social, and statistical data supporting the argument that laws limiting the workday of women were both reasonable and in the public interest.

The sheer weight of evidence made it impossible for the Court to rule that Oregon had acted unreasonably. Justice Brewer, speaking for a unanimous Court, upheld the statute. His opinion incorporated whole portions of Brandeis's brief. "That a woman's physical structure and the performance of maternal functions place her at a disadvantage in the struggle for subsistence is obvious," he wrote.

> This is especially true when the burdens of motherhood are upon her. Even when they are not, by abundant testimony of the medical fraternity continuance for a long time on her feet at work, repeating this from day to day, tends to injurious effects upon the body, and, as healthy mothers are essential to vigorous offspring, the physical well-being of woman becomes an object of public interest and care in order to preserve the strength and vigor of the race.

Brewer carefully distinguished the case from *Lochner*. Regulations unreasonable for the protection of one sex might be reasonable and constitutional for the protection of the other. He made it clear that issues of reasonableness would be decided on a case-to-case basis according to the nature and purpose of the regulation.

While *Lochner* had not been overruled by *Muller*, its precedential authority had been weakened. It became only a question of time until factual evidence could be assembled that excessive hours of labor were injurious to men as well as to women. The opportunity came in *Bunting v. Oregon* (1917) when the Court reviewed the constitutionality of an Oregon law which limited the hours of labor for all workers in mills and factories to ten hours a day. Felix Frankfurter, the attorney for Oregon, presented a "Brandeis brief"

Figure XIII.3 Portrait of Louis Brandeis (1915).
Library of Congress, Prints and Photographs Division, LC-B2-3747-9

showing that long hours of industrial employment were harmful to both sexes. The strategy worked, and the Court upheld the law as a reasonable exercise of the state's police powers. *Lochner* was thereafter ignored as a precedent, which led some commentators to conclude that the holding had been quietly abandoned. But bad law dies hard, and the judicial reaction of the 1920s would demonstrate that *Lochner* was no exception.

The Origins of Federal Regulation

The regulation of business by the states had never been really effective. Corporations that did business across state lines posed problems that required national solutions beyond the patchworks of regulations in force at the state level. The interstate railways were the first enterprises targeted for federal regulation. Their business practices were corrupt, and their operations affected the economic life of the entire nation. Nor was there any constitutional obstacle to federal regulation, because the Commerce Clause gave Congress indisputable power over them. Railway legislation had been considered as early as 1872 when the Senate appointed a committee to investigate industry abuses. Bills against rate discrimination were proposed from time to time, but no real progress was made until 1886 when the *Wabash* decision put interstate carriers beyond the reach of state regulators. This made some form of federal regulation imperative, because the idea of allowing railroads to operate completely unregulated was unthinkable. The following year Congress began the era of national regulation by passing the Interstate Commerce Act.

The Act sought to make all interstate rail charges reasonable and just. Rate schedules had to be published and adhered to by carriers; all rebates, rate discrimination, and rate-fixing agreements between railroads were also prohibited. These provisions were to be enforced by a five-member Interstate Commerce Commission (ICC) appointed by the president with the consent of the Senate. The Commission had authority to hear complaints, examine books and accounts, and compel the attendance of witnesses at its hearings. It could disallow rates found to be unreasonable and issue orders enforceable in the federal courts.

As the first permanent regulatory agency created by Congress, the ICC served as a model for all the federal regulatory bodies that followed. It operated differently from the traditional departments of government, combining executive, legislative, and judicial functions within one agency. The traditional separation of powers was waived in order to promote administrative efficiency. The regular departments of government were not structured to deal with complex regulatory problems. It was one thing for Congress to prohibit carriers from charging unreasonable rates, but quite another to determine whether the rates were reasonable or not. The ICC amounted to a fourth branch of government staffed by technical experts responsible for implementing the policy goals set by Congress.

The ICC and the Courts

The Supreme Court took a dim view of the ICC from the outset. Its very novelty caused alarm. Such an agency could conceivably usurp the functions of Congress and the courts. By narrowly construing the Act that created it and broadly interpreting the due process guarantee of the Fifth Amendment, the Court weakened the agency at every turn. In *Cincinnati, New Orleans & Texas Pacific Railway Co. v. Interstate Commerce Commission* (1896), the Court, speaking through Justice Shiras, ruled that the Commission had no power to disallow rates and set new ones pending judicial determination of the reasonableness of the rates in force. The following year, in *Interstate Commerce Commission v. Cincinnati, New Orleans & Texas Pacific Railway Co.* (1897), the Court held that the Commission could not set maximum rates even after the rates in force had been found unreasonable. Justice Brewer, speaking for the majority, ruled that the power to set rates was a legislative function which Congress had not expressly delegated to the Commission. "No just rule of construction would tolerate," he wrote, "a grant of such power by mere implication." This meant that the Commission would have to disallow one unreasonable rate after another until the railroad itself finally set a reasonable one. Justice Harlan filed a dissent protesting that the decision would fatally undermine the effectiveness of the Commission as a regulatory body.

An even worse blow came in *Interstate Commerce Commission v. Alabama Midland Railway Co.* (1897). The Court, again speaking through Justice Shiras, held that findings of fact by the Commission were not final and conclusive. Its findings of fact had standing as prima facie evidence, but the courts could review them as well as admit new evidence on the issue of reasonableness. Justice Harlan, again dissenting, declared that the decision "goes far to make that Commission a useless body for all practical purpose . . . It has been shorn, by judicial interpretation, of authority to do anything of an effective character." The ruling allowed the railroads to delay implementation of new rates by tying the Commission up in court on every factual issue. As the judges sifted through masses of technical data, the regulatory process would grind to a halt. Keeping the Commission under control seemed to have a higher priority with the Court than controlling the railroads.

By the turn of the century the ICC had been reduced to a mere fact-gathering agency without real power. The Supreme Court ruled against it in fifteen of the first sixteen cases brought up on appeal. Its most essential functions were transferred by judicial interpretation to the courts. There was virtually nothing that could be done without direct judicial supervision. The Court clearly regarded the agency as potentially more dangerous than the abuses it had been created to prevent. It represented the faceless sort of bureaucratic power that, given a foothold, might grow and eventually supersede traditional forms of government. The ICC gave the Court a glimpse of the future, and the justices did not like what they saw.

Regulating Big Business

The railroads were only part of the larger problem of regulating monopoly in general. The powerful combinations that emerged in the late nineteenth century dominated key sectors of the nation's economy. Beginning with the Standard Oil Trust in 1879, monopolies were created in many essential industries. They controlled production, dictated prices, and wielded tremendous economic power. In size and wealth they dwarfed even the largest corporations of the antebellum period. Their control of whole industries enabled them to operate free of ordinary market constraints. The main issue was not their size and wealth but the enormous power they exerted over the lives of millions of Americans. Submitting to unaccountable power in any form was not in the nation's traditions.

Popular resentment against these combinations resulted in the enactment of antimonopoly laws in a dozen states and territories. But such measures were generally ineffective, because their national scope of operations put most monopolies beyond local control. Some of them were wealthier than the states attempting to regulate them. It soon became obvious that only federal regulation could be really effective. The demand for action at the federal level had broad bipartisan support. In 1888 both the Republicans and Democrats went on record against the abuses of monopoly at their national party conventions. Both adopted party platforms calling upon Congress to intervene. The joint pledge was honored two years later when the Sherman Anti-Trust Act passed both houses without serious opposition.

The Sherman Act outlawed contracts, combinations, and conspiracies in restraint of interstate or foreign commerce. Civil and criminal penalties were prescribed for violations, and the federal courts were authorized to dissolve illegal combinations. But the law unfortunately had many loopholes and ambiguities. Congress failed to define such key terms as "combination," "monopoly," and "restraint of trade." Nor was it clear whether the Act applied to combinations of labor as well as capital. Far too much was left for the courts to clarify or fill in by judicial interpretation. Some critics contended that the Act had not been intended to be really effective, that it was essentially a cosmetic measure passed to appease public opinion. "The whole effort," said Senator Orville Platt, "has been to get some bill headed: 'A Bill to Punish Trusts' with which to go to the country."

The Act had little immediate impact on business practices. Of the eighteen antitrust suits brought between 1890 and 1901, four were against labor unions. The hostility of the courts to the Act was evident from the outset, particularly with regard to breaking up large corporations. Although the government won some suits against big business, the courts refused to order the outright dissolution of key monopolies. When a federal district court dismissed proceedings for the breakup of the whisky trust, the government dropped suits against other monopolies. The Act promised much but actually delivered little. It neither broke up existing monopolies nor prevented new ones from being formed.

The Supreme Court dealt the Sherman Act a particularly heavy blow in *United States v. E.C. Knight Co.* (1895). The government had brought suit to dissolve the American Sugar Refining Company, a combination that controlled between 90 and 98 percent of the sugar refined in the United States. Chief Justice Fuller, speaking for the majority, held that the Act applied only to commerce and that to extend it to manufacturing or processing would be unconstitutional. He took the position that the commerce power of Congress extended only to combinations directly engaged in interstate or foreign commerce. Although sugar was refined for distribution across state lines, the refining itself was not a part of commerce and therefore not subject to regulation by Congress. "That which belongs to commerce is within the jurisdiction of the United States," Fuller wrote, "that which does not belong to commerce is within the jurisdiction of the police power of the State."

Eviscerating the Sherman Anti-Trust Act

"Doubtless the power to control the manufacture of a given thing involves in a certain sense the control of its disposition, but this is a secondary and not the primary sense; and although the exercise of that power may result in bringing the operation of commerce into play, it does not control it, and affects it only incidentally and indirectly. The power to regulate commerce is the power to prescribe the rule by which commerce shall be governed, and is independent of the power to suppress monopoly."

—Chief Justice Melville Fuller, *United States v. E.C. Knight Co.* (1895)

Figure XIII.4 Portrait of Melville Fuller (1908).

Library of Congress, Prints and Photographs Division, LC-USZ62-95658

Justice Harlan alone dissented. He argued that a categorical distinction between commerce and manufacturing was specious, and that anything manufactured for shipment in interstate or foreign commerce fell under the federal commerce power.

> Whatever improperly obstructs the free course of interstate intercourse and trade, as involved in the buying and selling of articles to be carried from one State to another, may be reached by Congress, under its authority to regulate commerce among the States.

To deny Congress authority to act meant surrendering to monopoly. It put the public at the mercy of manufacturing combinations beyond the effective reach of state government. "In my judgment," Harlan wrote, the general government is not placed by the Constitution in such a condition of helplessness that it must fold its arms and remain inactive while capital combines, under the name of a corporation, to destroy competition, not in one State only, but throughout the entire country.

The *Knight* decision effectively eviscerated the Sherman Act with respect to manufacturing and processing monopolies. The only successful prosecutions for many years thereafter were against railroads engaged in interstate commerce. But productive enterprises went almost completely unregulated, and the Act had little effect on business practices. The Court's hostility to the Act had more to do with the political conservatism of the justices than with the finer points of constitutional interpretation. Monopoly was bad, but giving a blank check to regulators might turn out to be even worse. So, as with the Interstate Commerce Act, judicial constraints were imposed on what sort of regulation was permissible. The courts, not the politicians, would be the final arbiters of how much regulation was in the public interest.

Organized Labor and the Courts

The demands of organized labor in the late nineteenth century alarmed the courts far more than the abuses of big business. The latter at least gave lip service to traditional values, whereas the former seemed threatening and in some ways un-American. Political radicalism and a proclivity for violence gave organized labor a bad public image in the post–Civil War period. A series of strikes paralyzed the nation's rail centers in 1877, and over one hundred deaths were reported in Chicago alone. Pitched battles were fought with Pinkerton guards during the Homestead steel strike in 1892, and violence between striking miners and strikebreakers brought federal troops into Idaho the same year. Conservatives viewed these developments in the light of the class turbulence rampant in Europe in the late nineteenth century. More seemed to be at stake in the bloody confrontations than just wages and hours. Many feared that the real goal of union activists was social revolution and the destruction of capitalism.

The Strike Injunction

The most potent weapon available to companies threatened by strikes was the labor injunction. The injunction is a device used by courts to enforce their orders in equity cases. Since the device originated in chancery proceedings where historically juries were not employed, everything in such cases was decided by a judge. If it appeared that irreparable harm would result from a strike, the company could obtain a temporary injunction without notice or a hearing. Until a hearing was held to determine whether the injunction should be made permanent, the union had to halt all strike activity. If it did not, its officers could be summarily fined or imprisoned for contempt of court.

The constitutionality of antistrike injunctions was challenged in *In re Debs* (1895). The case grew out of the violent Pullman strike of 1894 and the refusal of the American Railway

Union, led by Eugene V. Debs, to handle Pullman cars. The strike paralyzed major rail centers and obstructed delivery of the federal mails in the Chicago area. President Grover Cleveland, over the objections of Illinois Governor John Altgeld, dispatched federal troops to protect interstate commerce. In the meantime, Attorney General Richard Olney obtained an injunction against the union on the ground that the strike prevented delivery of the federal mails. The injunction not only prohibited any obstruction of the mails but declared the strike illegal under the Sherman Act. The court held it an unlawful combination in restraint of trade and enjoined the union against any form of strike activity. For defying the order, Debs was sentenced to six months in prison for contempt of court.

Debs challenged the sentence in a habeas corpus petition to the Supreme Court. Represented by Clarence Darrow, he argued that contempt proceedings were criminal in nature and therefore not within the equity jurisdiction of the courts. That sort of jurisdiction exists only to protect property and to remedy civil wrongs, not to punish criminal acts. The latter can be punished only in courts of law where the accused has the right to a jury trial. The Court rejected this argument and unanimously upheld his conviction. Justice Brewer, speaking for the Court, conceded that only the need to protect property justified the use of injunctions, but he denied that the courts lose their equity jurisdiction simply because the acts enjoined are also violations of criminal law. Debs had been sentenced for defying the court, not for some criminal act requiring a jury trial. While not disputing the finding that the strike violated the Sherman Act, Brewer upheld the injunction on the broader ground that agencies of the federal government have power to do all things necessary, including issue injunctions, in order to protect interstate commerce. He wrote: "If the emergency arises, the army of the Nation, and all its militia, are at the service of the Nation to compel obedience to its laws."

Figure XIII.5 Portrait of Eugene Debs.

Library of Congress, Prints and Photographs Division, LC-B2-6091-11

Clarence Darrow on the *Debs* Case

"The Supreme Court held, among other things, that there was an allegation in the bill in reference to the obstruction of mail; but while there was such an allegation, and while Judge Woods, in deciding the case, said he supposed the United States Government owned the mail bags and had property interest in the mail bags, still there was no claim upon anybody's part that any mail bag was interfered with or anything of that sort, and when the Federal troops were sent to Chicago they were all sent to the stock-yards district, where there were no mail trains and nothing except the strike. That course was not taken on account of any mail; it was taken because it was a great strike; that is all . . . [I]t is very easy for courts to give good excuses for any act which they are willing to justify or think they ought to justify."

—Testimony before the Senate Judiciary Committee, March 23, 1900

The decision was a major setback for organized labor. Nothing matched injunctions as devices for breaking strikes. They could be adapted to any situation and directed against almost any union activity. In theory, management had to show that irreparable harm would result if an injunction was not issued, but the standard was so vague that judges could safely issue them without fear of reversal. Both state and federal courts issued injunctions in all sorts of labor disputes. So routine did they become on the side of management that the courts came under political fire. The Democrats made it a national issue in the 1896 election by adopting a party platform which denounced the injunction as "a new and highly dangerous form of oppression." But the Republican victory in the general election stalled proposals for its abolition. It would remain for well into the twentieth century the most powerful antistrike weapon available to management.

Proposals for a Federal Income Tax

Proposals for tax reform in the late nineteenth century alarmed conservatives as a threat to constitutional government. Soaring incomes brought such vast increases in the personal wealth of individuals that the great fortunes of the antebellum period were dwarfed by comparison. The earning power of the economic elite went untaxed at the federal level where nearly all the government's revenue came from excise taxes and tariffs, which disproportionately fell upon the lower economic classes. Proponents of tax reform urged shifting some of the burden to a tax on incomes. Taxing incomes would be more equitable, they contended, because it would make people contribute to the cost of government according to their means. The fact that enormous incomes went untaxed while tariffs and excises picked the pockets of the poor created a broad constituency for reform. The movement made so much headway that in the 1870s more than a dozen income tax measures were proposed in Congress. But conservative opponents of the idea prevented any legislation from being enacted.

Some conservatives feared that a tax on incomes would become a device for the leveling of society through the redistribution of wealth to the less-favored classes. The process, once begun, would turn class against class as demagogues bid for popular support by raising tax rates to higher and higher levels. What began at reasonable rates would end in confiscation. Government would then avidly pick the pockets of the middle class once the wealthy had been squeezed dry. Excess income would be earmarked for social programs until nothing remained for capital investment. Stagnation and economic collapse would follow as the country sank inevitably into the quagmire of socialism. The class equality that finally prevailed would take the form of national poverty and political tyranny.

The nation's experience with income taxes had been limited. Congress enacted a mildly progressive levy on incomes during the Civil War, but the tax expired in 1872 and was not renewed. The constitutionality of the levy had been challenged in *Springer v. United States* (1881) on the ground that income taxes were direct taxes and therefore had to be apportioned among the states on the basis of population. Opponents argued that a tax which falls on an individual and cannot be passed on is a direct tax, in contrast with an indirect tax, such as a sales tax, which can be passed on to the ultimate consumer in the form of higher prices. Justice Swayne, speaking for a unanimous Court, rejected the argument. He cited *Hylton v. United States* (1796) and ruled that only head taxes and taxes on real estate are direct taxes under Article I of the Constitution. The power of Congress with respect to other forms of taxation is not subject to apportionment.

With the constitutional issue apparently settled, proponents of tax reform shrewdly linked the income tax to demands for reductions in the protective tariff. The opportunity came when Treasury deficits caused by the business depression of 1893 forced Congress to consider new forms of taxation. Since a tax on incomes would not pass standing alone, it was attached as a rider to the Wilson-Gorman Tariff in 1894. The protectionists were forced to accept the tax in order to get the votes needed to enact the tariff. The rider called for a two percent levy on all income over $4,000 a year. That was a considerable income in the 1890s, so only the fairly affluent would be affected.

Pollock v. Farmers' Loan & Trust Co.

The constitutionality of the tax was immediately challenged in *Pollock v. Farmers' Loan & Trust Co.* (1895). Pollock, who owned stock in the bank, sued to enjoin it from paying the tax. By suing the bank he managed to circumvent a statute prohibiting suits to restrain the collection of taxes. Since he sued to restrain payment rather than collection of the tax, his suit did not run afoul of the statute. But the suit still smacked of collusion because the bank also had an interest in having the tax invalidated. The alternative would have been to pay the tax and then sue the government for a refund on the ground that the tax was unconstitutional. But this would have been more time consuming than a suit to enjoin payment and not the best way to get the case before the Supreme Court for an immediate decision.

Pollock attacked the law on political as well as constitutional grounds. The $4,000 exemption demonstrated that it was a class tax directed against the middle and upper classes. If upheld, he argued, it would be followed by further invasions of private and property rights, as one vice follows another, and very soon we should have, possibly, only one per cent of the people paying the taxes, and finally a provision that only the twenty people who have the greatest estates should bear the whole taxation, and after that communism, anarchy, and then, the ever following despotism.

The case was not just about taxes, but about whether freedom and constitutional government would survive in the United States.

Because illness kept Justice Jackson from the bench, the case was argued before only eight of the justices. Pollock challenged the law on three constitutional grounds: first, that the exemption for incomes of less than $4,000 violated the Article I provision that taxes must be uniform throughout the United States; second, that the tax was a direct tax and therefore subject to the apportionment provision of Article I; and third, that Congress had encroached upon the sovereignty of the states by taxing income from state and municipal bonds. The first two objections challenged the constitutionality of the law completely, while the third sought to limit its application.

All eight justices held the law invalid with respect to income from state and municipal bonds. The holding was consistent with the principle of intergovernmental tax immunity endorsed by the Court in *Collector v. Day* (1871). The immunity is an aspect of state and federal sovereignty within their respective spheres of operation. A majority of the justices also invalidated the taxation of income from real estate. The Court divided 6–2 on the issue. Chief Justice Fuller, speaking for the majority, held that taxes on income from land, like taxes on land itself, are direct taxes and therefore subject to the apportionment provisions of the Constitution. Justices Harlan and White dissented, arguing that taxes on income from land are different from taxes on the land itself and therefore not direct taxes within the meaning of the Constitution. Finally, the Court deadlocked 4–4 on the constitutionality of taxing income from salaries, professional fees, and personal property.

The deadlock had the effect of leaving the tax on salaries and personal income standing while invalidating the rest. The outcome satisfied no one, so a rehearing was ordered after Justice Jackson returned to the bench. This time the Court voted 5–4 to invalidate the entire law. Fuller, who again wrote the majority opinion, expanded the definition of direct taxes to include taxes on income from personal property as well taxes on income from land. He then proceeded to invalidate the tax on salaries and fee income by invoking a rule of statutory construction. "It is elementary," he wrote, "that the same statute may be in part constitutional and in part unconstitutional, and, if the parts are wholly independent of each other, that which is constitutional may stand while that which is unconstitutional will be rejected." But if the constitutional and unconstitutional parts are inextricably connected and interdependent, both must fall together. Fuller found that to be the case here and so invalidated the entire law.

Proponents of tax reform assailed the decision as bad law. They pointed out that the Court had ignored the *Springer* decision and overturned a century of constitutional precedent on the limited nature of direct taxes. That one of the justices changed sides between the two hearings also caused controversy. Since Jackson voted with the minority, one of the justices who had voted to uphold the law with respect to income from salaries and personal property obviously changed his mind at the second hearing. Because there are no written opinions when the Court deadlocks, it is impossible to be certain who shifted sides. But the field can be narrowed to three of the justices. Harlan and White voted at the first hearing to uphold the law with respect to income from land, so it can be safely assumed that they also voted to uphold it with respect to income from salaries and fees. Fuller and Field made it clear at the first hearing that they opposed the entire law, which makes it likely that either Brewer, Gray, or Shiras changed sides at the second hearing. In any case, one switched vote made the difference.

A strictly legal analysis of *Pollock* is pointless. The case was shot through with politics and ideology from the outset. Justice Field made this clear at the first hearing when he declared:

> The present assault upon capital is but the beginning. It will be but the stepping-stone to others, larger and more sweeping, till our political contests will become a war of the poor against the rich; a war constantly growing in intensity and bitterness. If the Court sanctions the power of discriminating taxation, and nullifies the uniformity mandate of the Constitution . . . it will mark the hour when the sure decadence of our government will commence.

In Field's view, the real issue was not taxation but the survival of constitutional government.

The dissenting justices were equally passionate about the outcome. Justice Harlan wrote: "The practical effect of the decision to-day is to give to certain kinds of property a position of favoritism and advantage inconsistent with the fundamental principles of our social organization." Justice Jackson considered the decision a blow against "the great principle of equality in taxation . . . the most disastrous blow ever struck at the constitutional power of Congress." Justice Brown found the politics of the case deeply disturbing. "[T]he decision involves nothing less than a surrender of the taxing power to the moneyed class," he wrote.

> Even the spectre of socialism is conjured up to frighten Congress from laying taxes upon the people in proportion to their ability to pay them . . . I hope it may not prove the first step towards the submergence of the liberties of people in a sordid despotism of wealth.

Members of the Court talking politics not surprisingly sound just like politicians.

Government by Judiciary

More important than the outcome of particular cases in the late nineteenth century was the Court's assumption of policy-making functions formerly left to the political branches of government. In case after case, the justices substituted their views for those of elected lawmakers on matters of public policy. Every measure enacted by state legislatures and Congress to serve the general welfare had to meet their standards of reasonableness in order to pass constitutional muster. They turned what were clearly political issues into constitutional ones by judicial fiat. But political involvement brought with it a loss of consistency and principled jurisprudence. The hasty rehearing and reversal in the *Legal Tender Cases*, the shifting standards of reasonableness with respect to public regulation, and the politics of the *Pollock* decision marked the beginning of an era of increased judicial uncertainty. The volume of Court business not only increased, but the issues addressed were often so political and technically complicated that the justices could seldom agree. Concurring and dissenting opinions proliferated to the point where the Court seldom spoke with a single voice. The Court under Fuller had more power than it had in the days of Marshall and Taney, but it also had far less institutional credibility.

This expansion of judicial power did not occur in a vacuum. It was part of a general expansion of governmental power following the Civil War. The states became more involved with new social and economic problems, and Congress had to come to grips with issues posed by monopoly and big business. Had the role of government in the life of the nation not grown dramatically, most of the regulatory issues brought before the Supreme Court would not have arisen. Currency debasement led to the *Legal Tender Cases*, and a tax law with radical political implications led to the *Pollock* decision. As the shadow of government lengthened, the Court was increasingly called upon to set limits. The alternative would have been to stand on the sidelines and trust the politicians completely. Such a course would have been incompatible with the Court's traditions. As guardians of constitutional government, the justices considered it their duty not to greet Leviathan gladly.

Recommended Reading

Primary Sources and Basic Secondary Works

The basic texts of American constitutionalism can be found in Francis N. Thorpe, ed., *The Federal and State Constitutions, Colonial Charters, and Other Organic Laws*, 7 vols. (1909). To supplement the texts, Leonard W. Levy and Kenneth L. Karst, eds., *Encyclopedia of the American Constitution*, 6 vols. (2000), a comprehensive collection of essays dealing with every aspect of United States constitutional law from the Constitutional Convention of 1787 to the Clinton impeachment, is highly recommended. The primary sources for State constitutional developments are Robert L. Maddex, *State Constitutions of the United States* (2d ed., 2005), a topical summary of the key provisions of the current constitutions of the fifty states, United States territories, and the District of Columbia; and William F. Swindler, comp., *Sources and Documents of United States Constitutions*, 11 vols. (1973–88), an annotated collection of State constitutions to 1988. The decisions and opinions of the United States Supreme Court not only provide gloss to the texts but comprise the overwhelming bulk of our constitutional law. They are available in the *United States Reports*, the official publication, and in the *Lawyers' Edition* and the *Supreme Court Reporter*, both privately published. The name of the Court reporter is used in volumes 1 through 90 (23 Wallace), and beginning with volume 91 in 1875 the reporter's name is omitted. The most recent decisions of the Court are published by the government in pamphlets known as advance sheets about one to two months after the case is decided and are available electronically almost immediately on the Court's website.

While technically not sources of law, some commentaries on the Constitution have had a direct impact on constitutional developments. Next to the Constitution itself, *The Federalist Papers* of Madison, Hamilton, and Jay is our most important textual source of constitutional law. Some decisions of the Supreme Court not only cite it as authoritative but accord it almost equal standing with the Constitution. While far less authoritative, several other commentaries are very useful. The most important for the antebellum period are Joseph Story's *Commentaries on the Constitution of the United States*, 2 vols. (1833), which is particularly valuable for the Marshall Court; James Kent's *Commentaries on American Law*, 4 vols., preferably the 12th edition (1873) edited by Oliver Wendell Holmes, Jr.; and Nathaniel Chipman, *Principles of Government, a Treatise on Free Government, Including the Constitution of the United States* (1833). Thomas M. Cooley, *Treatise on the Constitutional Limitations Which Rest Upon the Legislative Power of the States of the American Union*, 2 vols. (1927), and Christopher G. Tiedeman, *A Treatise on the Limitations of Police Power in the United States, Considered both from a Civil and Criminal Standpoint* (1886) cover the limitations imposed on state sovereignty under our federal system of government. Useful commentaries from the standpoint of the national government include Edward Dumbauld, *The Constitution of the United States* (1964); Bernard Schwartz, *A Commentary on the Constitution of the United States*, 5 vols. (1963–68), a work of painstaking scholarship; and the more recent work by Ronald D. Rotunda and John E. Nowak, *Treatise on Constitutional Law: Substance and Procedure*, 5 vols. (3d ed., 1999), which is regularly updated by pocket additions.

Excellent general coverage of the Constitution can be found in Edward S. Corwin, *The Constitution and What It Means Today* (1958), a one-volume classic by the foremost constitutional scholar of the twentieth century; Andrew C. McLaughlin, *A Constitutional History of the United States* (1935), which stops before the New Deal Court but is nevertheless still useful for its historical insights; William W. Crosskey, *Politics and the Constitution of the United States*, 2 vols. (1953), a nationalist interpretation which argues that the Founding Fathers intended to create a unitary national state; Arthur E. Sutherland, *Constitutionalism in America: Origin and Evolution of Its Fundamental Ideas* (1965), which emphasizes our common-law heritage; and Carl B. Swisher, *American Constitutional Development* (1954), a work of outstanding scholarship. Highly reliable accounts of United States constitutional history can be found in Alfred H. Kelly, Winfred A. Harbison, and Herman Belz, *The American Constitution*, 2 vols. (1991), and Melvin I. Urofsky and Paul Finkelman, *A March of Liberty*, 2 vols. (2011); both have been widely adopted as college texts. Michael Kammen's *A Machine That Would Go of Itself* (1986), an excellent cultural history of American constitutionalism, is highly recommended. A brief but quite engaging narrative account is Forrest McDonald's *A Constitutional History of the United States* (1982). Akhil Reed Amar's *America's Constitution: A Biography* (2006) is the best of the most recent books on the subject. Journal articles and essays contain a wealth of information on particular constitutional issues. Some of the best can be found in Kermit L. Hall, ed., *United States Constitutional and Legal History* (1987), a collection of over 450 important articles, and Richard Loss, ed., *Corwin on the Constitution*, 3 vols. (1981), a collection of articles by Edward S. Corwin on political and constitutional matters. Similarly, David M. O'Brien, ed., *Civil Rights and Civil Liberties* (2003) provides a varied and excellent selection of readings by legal historians, political scientists, sociologists, attorneys, and journalists on a wide range of contemporary issues.

The authoritative work on the place of the Supreme Court in our constitutional system is the Oliver Wendell Holmes Devise *History of the Supreme Court of the United States*, now in the course of publication by the Cambridge University Press. The volumes already in print provide a comprehensive survey of the Court from the beginning to the Warren Court and are a major achievement of American legal and historical writing. While containing little on twentieth-century developments, Charles Warren's *The Supreme Court in United States History*, 3 vols. (1922) is still an excellent introduction to the subject. Written from a Federalist point of view, it is indispensable for nineteenth-century developments. Also useful are Alpheus T. Mason and William H. Beaney, *The Supreme Court in a Free Society* (1959), excellent for theory and analysis; Leo Pfeffer, *This Honorable Court* (1965), remarkably complete for a one-volume study; and David M. O'Brien's *Storm Center: The Supreme Court in American Politics* (1986), which sets the Court squarely at the center of American law and politics.

Some of the best constitutional writing deals with the theory and practice of judicial review. Charles A. Miller, *The Supreme Court and the Uses of History* (1968), focuses on the use and misuse of history for judicial purposes, while Charles P. Curtis, *Lions under the Throne* (1947), views adjudication as essentially part of the political process. The perennial debate over judicial review has contributed significantly to American intellectual history. A good starting point is Charles A. Beard's still useful *The Supreme Court and the Constitution* (1912), which argues persuasively for the legitimacy of judicial review, and Edwin S. Corwin, *The Doctrine of Judicial Review* (1914), which offers a well-reasoned and equally persuasive rebuttal. Raoul Berger's *Government by Judiciary* (2d ed., 1997) has become a rallying text for opponents of judicial review as a pretext for judicial activism via free-wheeling interpretation of the Fourteenth Amendment. An accessible collection of essays on nonjudicial factors involved in how cases are decided can be found in Cornell W. Clayton and Howard Gillman, eds., *Supreme Court Decision-Making: New Institutionalist Approaches* (1999), and the essays compiled by Ronald Kahn and Ken I. Kersch, eds., in *The Supreme Court and American Political Development* (2006). Together, the volumes provide balance to the overemphasis social scientists sometimes place on the ideology of particular justices. An excellent volume by Christopher Wolfe, *The Rise of Modern Judicial Review* (2d ed., 1994), traces the evolution of judicial review from traditional textual exegesis to the modern era of judge-made law. For a compelling explanation of why the political branches of government conceded responsibility for constitutional interpretation to the Supreme Court, see Keith E. Whittington's *Political Foundations of Judicial Supremacy* (2009).

Studies of the justices of the Supreme Court often throw light on particular aspects of constitutional developments. The best general coverage can be found in Leon Friedman, *The Justices of the United States Supreme Court: Their Lives and Major Opinions*, 4 vols. (1995), and Melvin I. Urofsky, ed., *Supreme Court Justices: A Biographical Dictionary* (1994), the latter a collection of analytic and interpretive essays by sixty-seven eminent scholars covering the members of the Court from John Jay, the first chief justice, to the appointment of Ruth Bader Ginsburg by President Clinton. Peter Fish's *The Office of Chief Justice* (1984) deals with the role and influence of the chief justice in shaping constitutional developments, while Henry J. Abraham, *Justices, Presidents, and Senators: A History of the U.S. Supreme Court Appointments from Washington to Clinton* (1999), examines the politics of the selection and confirmation process. Equally recommended, particularly for more recent Court appointments, is Christine L. Nemacheck, *Strategic Selection: Presidential Nomination of Supreme Court Justices from Herbert Hoover to George W. Bush* (2007). Finally, David N. Atkinson's *Leaving the Bench: Supreme Court Justices at the End* (1999) considers the impact of illness and debility on the institutional efficiency of the Court.

I English and Colonial Origins

Excellent general surveys of the English origins of American constitutionalism can be found in J.E.A. Jolliffe, *The Constitutional History of Medieval England* (1967); F.W. Maitland, *Constitutional History of England* (1908); Bryce Lyon, *Constitutional and Legal History of Medieval England* (1960); and David L. Keir, *The Constitutional History of*

Modern Britain since 1485 (1967). Any edition of William Stubbs's *Constitutional History of England in Its Origin and Development*, 3 vols. (1878) is highly recommended and should be supplemented with Charles E. Petit-Dutaillis, *Studies and Notes Supplementary to Stubbs' Constitutional History* (1930). The constitution of England is inseparable from the development of the English common law, and the best one-volume introduction to the latter is Arthur R. Hogue, *Origins of the Common Law* (1966). Theodore F.T. Plucknett's *A Concise History of the Common Law* (1956) is indispensible for legal and procedural developments which shaped particular constitutional principles. Three excellent comprehensive accounts are William S. Holdsworth's *A History of English Law*, 13 vols. (1952); James F. Stephens's *History of the Criminal Law of England*, 3 vols. (1883); and J.H. Baker's *Introduction to English Legal History* (1990), together with Baker and S.F.C. Milsom's *Sources of English Legal History* (1986). All are works of impeccable scholarship.

The writ system through which the common law superseded rival systems of law is covered in R.C. Van Caenegem, *Royal Writs in England from the Conquest to Glanvill* (1954), while S.B. Chrimes, *An Introduction to the Administration of Justice in Medieval England* (1952) deals with the courts of the Middle Ages. Michael Dalton's *The Country Justice*, available in several editions, is the best contemporary summary of English law and practice in the seventeenth century. Information on the local customary law of England familiar to the early settlers in New England can be found in J. Tait, *British Borough Charters, 1216–1307* (1923). John H. Langbein's *Torture and the Law of Proof* (2006) remains the definitive work on the subject. The historical development of the jury from an evidentiary to decision-making body is discussed in Thomas Andre Green, *Verdict According to Conscience: Perspectives on the English Criminal Trial Jury, 1200–1800* (1985).

The impact of political events on English constitutional development is covered in H.G. Richardson and G.O. Sayles, *The Governance of Mediaeval England* (1963), and Christopher Daniell, *From Norman Conquest to Magna Carta: England from 1066–1215* (2003). The legal and administrative innovations of Henry II are dealt with in Emilie Amt, *The Accession of Henry II in England: Royal Government Restored, 1149–1159* (1993), and Christopher Harper Bill and Nicholas Vincent, eds., *Henry II: New Interpretations* (2007). For the Magna Carta, see Geoffrey Hindley, *A Brief History of the Magna Carta: The Story of the Origins of Liberty* (2008); J.C. Holt, *Magna Carta* (1965); A.E. Dick Howard, *Magna Carta: Text and Commentary* (1998); and William S. McKechnie, *Magna Carta: A Commentary on the Great Charter of King John with an Historical Introduction* (1905), an older but still useful treatment of the subject. Constitutional documents from the Tudor and Stuart periods can be found in G.R. Elton, *The Tudor Constitution* (1982) and J.P Kenyon, *The Stuart Constitution* (1966). The victory of Parliament over divine right monarchy in the 1640s is covered by Martyn Bennett, *The English Civil War: A Historical Companion* (2004); Peter Gaunt, ed., *The English Civil War: The Essential Readings* (2000); and Keith Lindley, ed., *The English Civil War and Revolution: A Source Book* (1998). C.V. Wedgewood's *The Trial of Charles I* (1964) provides a compelling account of the regicide, especially when supplemented by David Lagomarsino and Charles T. Wood, *The Trial of Charles I: A Documentary History* (1989). The final triumph of Parliament over monarchy with the deposition of James II is dealt with in Eveline Cruickshanks, *The Glorious Revolution* (2000), and John Miller, *The Glorious Revolution* (1997). The best general work on society and politics in England during the period of English settlement in America is George M. Trevelyan, *England under the Stuarts* (1949), an authoritative treatment of developments from the accession of James I to the death of Queen Anne in 1714. Finally, Wallace Notestein's *The English People on the Eve of Colonization, 1603–1630* (1954) sets the stage for bringing English constitutional traditions to this side of the Atlantic.

A good introduction to the English colonies can be found in Peter Charles Hoffer, *The Brave New World: A History of Early America* (2006); Steven Sarson, *British America, 1500–1800: Creating Colonies, Imagining an Empire* (2005); and Bruce Catton and William B. Catton, *The Bold and Magnificent Dream: America's Founding Years, 1492–1815* (1978). Earlier works that continue to be useful for institutional developments are Charles M. Andrews, *The Colonial Period of American History*, 4 vols. (1939), and Herbert L. Osgood, *The American Colonies in the Seventeenth Century*, 3 vols. (1930). Both cover the emergence of political and governmental institutions. Osgood's *The American Colonies in the Eighteenth Century*, 4 vols. (1924) carries developments forward to the end of the colonial period. Oliver M. Dickerson, *American Colonial Government, 1696–1765* (1962), and Leonard W. Labaree, *Royal Government in America* (1930) provide excellent coverage of political developments. For information on the legislative branch of government, see Mary P. Clarke, *Parliamentary Privilege in the American Colonies* (1943). George A. Washburne, *Imperial Control of the Administration of Justice in the Thirteen Colonies, 1684–1776* is valuable for the colonial judiciary.

The growth of colonial political autonomy is described by Michael Kammen in *Deputyes & Libertyes: The Origins of Representative Government in Colonial America* (1969) and by Wesley Frank Craven, *The Colonies in Transition, 1660–1713* (1968). David S. Lovejoy, *The Glorious Revolution in America* (1972), and Lois G. Carr and David W. Jordan, *Maryland's Revolution in Government, 1689–1692* (1974), examine the impact of England's Glorious Revolution on politics and government in America. Max Savelle's *Seeds of Liberty: The Genesis of the American Mind* (1948), Clinton L. Rossiter's *Seedtime of the Republic* (1953), and Bernard Bailyn's *The Origins of American Politics* (1968) are excellent for an understanding of colonial political thought.

How the constitutional traditions of England took root and flourished in the colonial environment is covered in journal articles and essays on particular topics. The following are especially valuable: H.D. Hazeltine, "The Influence of Magna Carta on American Constitutional Development," 17 *Columbia Law Review* 1 (1917); Paul S. Reinsch, "The English Common Law in the Early American Colonies," in *Select Essays in Anglo-American Legal History*, 3 vols. (1909), I, 376–415; Richard B. Morris, "Massachusetts and the Common Law: The Declaration of 1646," 31 *American Historical Review* 443 (1926); George L. Haskins, "A Problem in the Reception of the Common Law in the Colonial Period," 97 *University of Pennsylvania Law Review* 842 (1949); and Zechariah Chafee, Jr., "Colonial Courts and the Common Law," 68 *Massachusetts Historical Society Proceedings* 132 (1945). Edward J. White, "Benefit of Clergy," 46 *American Law Review* 78 (1912), examines one of the archaisms of English felony law, and Julius Goebel, Jr., "King's Law and Local Custom in Seventeenth Century New England," 31 *Columbia Law Review* 416 (1931), emphasizes the importance of English customary law as well as the common law in American legal development. The colonial judiciary is examined in Erwin C. Surrency, "The Courts in the American Colonies," 11 *American Journal of Legal History* 253, 347 (1967), and an important branch of judicial power is treated in Stanley N. Katz, "The Politics of Law in Colonial America: Controversies over Chancery Courts and Equity Law in the Eighteenth Century," 5 *Perspectives in American History* 257 (1971). In *The Province of Legislation Determined* (1989), David Leiberman provides a compelling account of the eighteenth-century British legal thought so influential in the colonies.

Richard B. Morris's *Studies in the History of American Law* (1930) is still the best introduction to the subject. The more recent studies by Lawrence M. Friedman, A *History of American Law* (1986), and William E. Nelson, *Americanization of the Common Law* (1974), are also useful. Bradley Chapin, *Criminal Justice in Colonial America, 1606–1660* (1983), has valuable information on early criminal procedures. Material on particular colonies can be found in Edgar J. McManus, *Law and Liberty in Early New England: Criminal Justice and Due Process, 1620–1692* (1993), which focuses on the criminal justice system; George L. Haskins, *Law and Authority in Early Massachusetts* (1960), a work of impeccable scholarship with a wealth of information on the early legal institutions of the Bay Colony; David T. Konig, *Law and Society in Puritan Massachusetts: Essex County, 1629–1692* (1979); Edwin Powers, *Crime and Punishment in Early Massachusetts, 1620–1692* (1966), useful for criminal law in Massachusetts and New Plymouth; Julius Goebel, Jr. and T. Raymond Naughton, *Law Enforcement in Colonial New York* (1944), a comprehensive work covering the subject from the New Netherland period through the eighteenth century; Paul M. Hamlin and Charles Baker, *The Supreme Court of Judicature of the Province of New York, 1691–1704*, 3 vols. (1959), a valuable but highly technical resource; Arthur P. Scott, *Criminal Law in Colonial Virginia* (1930), which covers the English contributions to Virginia's criminal laws; and Marilyn L. Geiger, *The Administration of Justice in Colonial Maryland, 1632–1689* (1987), a study of the Maryland judiciary in the seventeenth century. The specialized studies in David H. Flaherty, ed., *Essays in the History of Early American Law* (1969), and George A. Billias, ed., *Law and Authority in Colonial America* (1965), are also recommended.

Law in the seventeenth century took race, status, and gender into account in both civil and criminal matters. Crimes by women are dealt with in N.E.H. Hull, *Female Felons: Women and Serious Crime in Colonial Massachusetts* (1987), and Peter C. Hoffer and N.E.H. Hull, *Murdering Mothers: Infanticide in England and New England, 1558–1803* (1981). Both are excellent, though the latter offers some questionable conclusions about infanticide convictions on the basis of circumstantial evidence. Roger Thompson's *Women in Stuart England and America: A Comparative Study* (1974) is useful for the social and cultural subordination of women in the seventeenth century. How gender discrimination related to the prosecution of women for witchcraft is dealt with in Carol F. Karlsen's *The Devil in the Shape of a Woman: Witchcraft in Colonial New England* (1987), a book filled with valuable leads and insights. Richard B. Morris's *Studies in the History of American Law*, already cited, has a useful chapter on the legal treatment of women in colonial times.

Several books deal with the legal treatment of Africans and Native Americans. The best work on blacks is Lorenzo J. Greene's *The Negro in Colonial New England, 1620–1776* (1942), which covers both slaves and free blacks in the New England colonies. Useful information can also be found in Edgar J. McManus, *Black Bondage in the North* (1973), which covers the Middle Colonies as well as New England. For the southern colonies, see Thomas B. Morris, *Southern Slavery and the Law, 1619–1869* (1996), which covers both the colonial and national periods. Paul Finkelman's *The Law of Freedom and Bondage* (1986) provides a fine overview of the subject. Historians disagree, sometimes sharply, on the treatment of the Native Americans. Alden T. Vaughan, *The New England Frontier: Puritans and Indians, 1620–1675* (1965), takes the view that the Puritan justice system treated them fairly. Others disagree. Yasuhide Kawashima, *Puritan Justice and the Indian: White Man's Law in Massachusetts* (1986), Francis Jennings, *The Invasion of America: Indians, Colonialism, and the Cant of Conquest* (1975), and Wilcomb E. Washburn, *Red Man's Land/White Man's Law: A Study of the Past and Present Status of the American Indian* (1971), contend that colonial law was an instrument of repression and that white chauvinism and cultural arrogance made equitable relations between the two races impossible.

The colonial version of rights later incorporated into the United States Constitution can be found in monographs and journal articles. On the guarantees of the Bill of Rights in the colonial period, see the excellent studies by Leonard W. Levy, *Origins of the Bill of Rights* (1999), and *Origins of the Fifth Amendment: The Right against Self-Incrimination* (1968). E.M. Morgan, "The Privilege against Self-Incrimination," 34 *Minnesota Law Review* 1 (1949–50), and R. Carter Pittman, "The Colonial and Constitutional History of the Privilege against Self-Incrimination in America," 21 *Virginia Law Review* 763 (1935), are also recommended. Fourth Amendment rights are covered in William Cuddihy and B. Carmon Hardy, "A Man's House Was Not His Castle: Origins of the Fourth Amendment to the United States Constitution," 37 *William and Mary Quarterly*, 3d ser. 371 (1980), and Julius J. Marke, "Of Smugglers, Free Trade, and the Revolution, 12 *New York University Law Center Bulletin* 8 (1964). The Sixth Amendment right to counsel is dealt with in Nathan Matthews, "The Results of the Prejudice against Lawyers in Massachusetts in the 17th Century," 13 *Massachusetts Law Quarterly* 73 (1928), and Max Radin, "The Ancient Grudge: A Study in the Public Relations of the Legal Profession," 32 *Virginia Law Review* 734 (1946). On press freedom, see Leonard H. Levy, "Did the Zenger Case Really Matter? Freedom of the Press in Colonial New York," 17 *William and Mary Quarterly*, 3d ser. 35 (1960), which argues that the significance of the case has been exaggerated, and Julius J. Marke, "Peter Zenger's Trial and Freedom of the Press," 10 *New York University Law Center Bulletin* 4 (1961), which takes the opposite view. Paul Finkelman, ed., *A Brief Narrative of the Tryal of John Peter Zenger* (1997) is highly recommended. The colonial right of habeas corpus is dealt with by A.H. Carpenter in "Habeas Corpus in the Colonies," 8 *American Historical Review* 18 (1902).

II Independence and Nationhood

The events leading up to the American Revolution from the British point of view can be found in Lawrence H. Gipson, *The Coming of the Revolution, 1765–1775* (1954), and Charles M. Andrews, *The Colonial Background of the American Revolution* (1924), written from an American perspective. Merrill Jensen's *The Founding of a Nation, 1763–1776* (1968) examines the interaction of social and political forces contributing to the conflict, and John C. Miller's *Origins of the American Revolution* (1948) provides an excellent general survey of the underlying sources of conflict. Robert Middlekauff, *The Glorious Cause: The American Revolution, 1763–1789* (1982), is a first-rate account of events from the French and Indian War to 1789, and Pauline Maier's *From Resistance to Revolution: Colonial Radicals and the Development of American Opposition to Britain, 1765–1776* (1972) traces how American resistance to Great Britain rapidly escalated during the decade preceding the outbreak of hostilities.

John Phillip Reid's four-volume *Constitutional History of the American Revolution* (2003) provides an authoritative account of the constitutional issues at the heart of the Revolution. Two major American grievances along the road to conflict are covered in Edmund S. Morgan and Helen M. Morgan, *The Stamp Act Crisis: Prologue to Revolution* (1953), and Peter G.D. Thomas, *The Townshend Duties Crisis: The Second Phase of the American Revolution, 1767–1773* (1987). Benjamin W. Labaree's *The Boston Tea Party* (1964) treats that incident as the point of no return in the disruption of Anglo-American relations. On the role of ideology in the conflict, the following are useful: Bernard Bailyn, *The Ideological Origins of the American Revolution* (1967); H. Trevor Colbourn, *The Lamp of Experience: Whig History and the Intellectual Origins of the American Revolution* (1965); Charles H. McIlwaine, *The American Revolution: A Constitutional Interpretation* (1961); and Randolph G. Adams, *Political Ideas of the American Revolution* (1958). Carl L. Becker's *The Eve of the Revolution* (1918) is still the best account of the struggle between American moderates and radicals during the critical period from 1774 to 1775.

Political developments during the Revolutionary War are tracked by Elisha P. Douglass in *Rebels and Democrats: The Struggle for Equal Political Rights and Majority Rule During the American Revolution* (1955). Jackson T. Main, *The Sovereign States, 1775–1783* (1973), provides an excellent account of state government during the war years, and Edmund C. Burnett's *The Continental Congress* (1941) is the definitive work on our first agency of central government. On the Declaration of Independence, see Pauline Maier's *American Scripture: Making the Declaration of Independence* (1998) on the drafting of the Declaration and its significance as a legal and political document; Carl L. Becker's *The Declaration of Independence* (1956), a classic work that views the document as an expression of eighteenth-century liberal political theory; Edward Dumbauld, *The Declaration of Independence and What It Means Today* (1950), a line-by-line commentary on the document; and John H. Hazelton's *The Declaration of Independence* (1906), an older but still valuable study of the document. The drafting and adoption of state constitutions during the war is covered in Allan Nevins, *The American States During and After the Revolution, 1775–1789* (1969); Donald S. Lutz, *Popular Consent and Popular Control: Whig Political*

Theory in the Early State Constitutions (1980); and Willi Paul Adams, *The First American Constitutions: Republican Ideology and the Making of the State Constitutions in the Revolutionary Era* (2001), an updated edition of the authoritative account of how the Revolutionary generation instituted republican government by constitutional means.

III A More Perfect Union

Two excellent works on the Articles of Confederation, our first national constitution, are Merrill Jensen's *The Articles of Confederation: An Interpretation of the Socio-Constitutional History of the American Revolution, 1774–1781* (1940) and *The New Nation: A History of the United States during the Confederation, 1781–1789* (1967). Jensen offers a positive view of the period and emphasizes the ideological continuity between the Revolutionary and Confederation eras. For an opposite view, see John Fiske's *The Critical Period of American History, 1783–1789* (1898), a classic work written from a nationalist perspective, and Andrew C. McLaughlin's *The Confederation and the Constitution, 1781–1789* (1905), which emphasizes the weaknesses of the Confederation government. Both fault the Articles for failing to provide the sort of government able to deal effectively with the challenges confronting the Young Republic in the postwar years. The persistence of the debate is reviewed by Richard B. Morris in "The Confederation and the American Historian," 13 *William and Mary Quarterly,* 3d ser. 139 (1956).

The national government during the Confederation period is covered in Edmund C. Burnett, *The Continental Congress* (1941), a standard work; H. James Henderson, *Party Politics in the Continental Congress* (1974); and Jack N. Rakove, *The Beginnings of National Politics: An Interpretive History of the Continental Congress* (1979). The executive functions of government are dealt with in Jennings B. Sanders, *Evolution of Executive Departments of the Continental Congress, 1774–1789* (1935); Charles C. Thach, Jr., *The Creation of the Presidency, 1775–1789* (1922); and Jennings B. Sanders, *The Presidency of the Continental Congress, 1774–1789* (1930). Judicial functions of the Confederation government are covered in Henry J. Bourguignon, *The First Federal Court: The Federal Appellate Prize Court of the American Revolution, 1775–1787* (1977), and in the first volume of the Oliver Wendell Holmes Devise *History of the Supreme Court of the United States* by Julius Goebel, Jr., *Antecedents and Beginnings to 1801* (1971).

Charles Warren's *The Making of the Constitution* (1937) is still the best work on the Philadelphia Constitutional Convention. The records of the Convention, including Madison's notes, are available in Max Farrand, ed., *The Records of the Federal Convention of 1787,* 4 vols. (1937). James Hutson's *Supplement to Max Farrand's Records of the Federal Convention of 1787* (1987) contains new documentary material discovered since the 1937 edition. Farrand's *The Framing of the Constitution of the United States* (1913) covers the issues debated at the Convention, and his *The Fathers of the Constitution* (1921) describes the Convention through the eyes of its leading personalities. Other useful accounts include Carl Van Doren, *The Great Rehearsal: The Story of the Making and Ratifying of the Constitution of the United States* (1948); Clinton Rossiter, *1787: The Grand Convention* (1966); and Robert L. Schuyler, *The Constitution of the United States* (1923), still the best work on the actual drafting of the Constitution. For intellectual sketches of the Founders who played a central role in defining American political liberties, see Richard B. Morris, *Witnesses at the Creation: Hamilton, Madison, Jay and the Constitution* (1985). Biographies of leading Convention figures contain valuable information. The most useful are volume I of Broadus Mitchell's *Alexander Hamilton*, 2 vols. (1957); vol. III of Irving Brant's *James Madison*, 6 vols. (1961); Charles P. Smith's *James Wilson: Founding Father, 1742–1798* (1967); Marvin R. Zahniser, *Charles Cotesworth Pinckney: Founding Father* (1967); and William Howard Adams, *Gouverneur Morris: An Independent Life* (2003).

The motives and aims of the Founding Fathers were widely debated during the struggle for ratification. Charles A. Beard brought the debate into the twentieth century with the publication of his *An Economic Interpretation of the Constitution of the United States* (1913), a groundbreaking analysis of the class interests present or represented at the Philadelphia Convention. His conclusion that the delegates were at least partly motivated by economic self-interest has been challenged by Robert E. Brown, *Charles Beard and the Constitution: A Critical Analysis of an Economic Interpretation of the Constitution* (1956), and by Forrest McDonald, *We the People: The Economic Origins of the Constitution* (1958). Robert E. Thomas, "A Reappraisal of Charles A. Beard's *An Economic Interpretation of the Constitution of the United States*," 57 *American Historical Review* 370 (1952), defends Beard's thesis, while Douglass Adair, "The Tenth Federalist Revisited," 8 *William and Mary Quarterly*, 3d ser. 48 (1951), rejects it. The pros and cons of the debate are considered in Richard Hofstadter, "Beard and the Constitution: The History of an Idea," 2 *American Quarterly* 195 (1950); Cecilia M. Kenyon, "An Economic Interpretation of the Constitution after Fifty Years," 7 *Centennial Review of Arts & Science* 327 (1963); E. James Ferguson, "The Nationalists of 1781–1783 and the Economic Interpretation of the Constitution," 56 *Journal of American History* 241 (1969); and John P. Diggins, "Power and Authority in American History: The Case of Charles A. Beard and His Critics," 86 *American Historical Review* 701 (1981). Leonard W. Levy, ed., *Essays on the Making of the Constitution* (1987), provides useful summaries of the opposing views.

Topical studies explore the issues that confronted the Convention. How the delegates handled, or mishandled, the slavery issue is covered in William W. Freehling, "The Founding Fathers and Slavery," 77 *American Historical Review* 81 (1972); Calvin Jillson and Thornton Anderson, "Realignments in the Convention of 1787: The Slave Trade Compromise," 34 *Journal of Politics* 712 (1977); and Howard A. Ohline, "Republicans and Slavery: Origins of the Three-Fifths Clause in the United States Constitution," 28 *William and Mary Quarterly*, 3d ser. 563 (1971). Lawrence Goldstone's *Dark Bargain: Slavery, Profits, and the Struggle for the Constitution* (2005) provides a useful synthesis of historical research on the subject. On the Commerce Clause, see Frederick H. Cooke, *The Commerce Clause of the Federal Constitution* (1908), and M. Ramaswamy, *The Commerce Clause in the Constitution of the United States* (1948). Information on the Contract Clause can be found in Benjamin F. Wright, *The Contract Clause of the Constitution* (1938), and William W. Crosskey, "The Ex-Post-Facto and Contract Clauses in the Federal Constitution: A Note on the Editorial Genius of James Madison," 35 *University of Chicago Law*

Review 248 (1968). Robert H. Jackson's *Full Faith and Credit: The Lawyer's Clause of the Constitution* (1945) deals with the issue of interstate comity under the Constitution.

The best general account of the struggle for ratification can be found in Robert A. Rutland, *The Ordeal of the Constitution* (1966). Orin G. Libby's *The Geographical Distribution of the Vote of the Thirteen States on the Federal Constitution 1787–8* (1894) is indispensable for the political demographics of ratification. The question of popular representation in the ratifying conventions is dealt with in Charles W. Roll, Jr., "We, Some of the People: Apportionment in the Thirteen State Conventions Ratifying the Constitution," 56 *Journal of American History* 21 (1969). For the struggle in particular states, see Robin Brooks, "Alexander Hamilton, Melancton Smith, and the Ratification of the Constitution in New York," 24 *William and Mary Quarterly*, 3d ser. 339 (1967); Albert R. Newsome, "North Carolina's Ratification of the Federal Constitution," 17 *North Carolina Historical Review* 287 (1940); and Charles Warren, "Elbridge Gerry, James Warren, Mercy Warren, and the Ratification of the Federal Constitution in Massachusetts," 64 *Massachusetts Historical Society Proceedings* 143 (1932).

The polemics on both sides of the ratification debate can be sampled in Jonathan Elliot, ed., *The Debates in the Several State Conventions on the Adoption of the Federal Constitution*, 5 vols. (1907). The best arguments in favor of ratification were made by Hamilton, Madison, and Jay in *The Federalist*, available in many editions, though the volume edited by Jacob E. Cooke for the Wesleyan University Press is particularly recommended. But opponents of ratification had able and articulate spokesmen as well. The case against ratification can be found in Ralph Ketcham, ed., *The Anti-Federalist Papers and the Constitutional Convention Debates* (1986). Just as *The Federalist Papers* defended the Constitution and its strong central government, the *Anti-Federalist Papers* voiced the dissenting opinions of Patrick Henry, George DeWitt, and other Revolutionary leaders who saw threats in the Constitution to the rights and liberties so recently won from England. Useful information can also be found in John Strong, ed., *The Antifederalist* (1985); Cecilia M. Kenyon, ed., *The Antifederalists* (1961); and M. Borden, ed., *The Antifederalist Papers* (1965). Jackson T. Main, *The Antifederalists* (1961), presents the opponents of the Constitution in a favorable light, and Herbert J. Storing, *What the Antifederalists Were For: The Political Thought of the Opponents of the Constitution* (1981), thinks they should be counted among the Founding Fathers because their reservations about the original Constitution set off a debate that culminated in the Bill of Rights. Saul Cornell's *The Other Founders: Anti-Federalism and the Dissenting Tradition in America, 1788–1828* (1999) gives them high marks as spokesmen for an alternative constitutional tradition. But Cecilia M. Kenyon, "Men of Little Faith: The Anti-Federalists on the Nature of Representative Government," 12 *William and Mary Quarterly*, 3d ser. 3 (1955), is sharply critical of them.

IV Launching the New Government

The first decade of the new national government is brilliantly described by John C. Miller in *The Federalist Era, 1789–1801* (1960). Problems of organization and administration are described in Leonard D. White, *The Federalists: A Study in Administrative History*

(1948), and Lloyd M. Short, *The Development of National Administrative Organization in the United States* (1923). For developments in the executive branch, see James Hart, *The American Presidency in Action, 1789: A Study in Constitutional History* (1948); Forrest McDonald, *The Presidency of George Washington* (1974); and Stephen G. Kurtz, *The Presidency of John Adams: The Collapse of Federalism, 1795–1800* (1957). The emergence of national political parties is described in Joseph Charles, *The Origins of the American Party System* (1956); Noble E. Cunningham, *The Jeffersonian Republicans* (1957); and William N. Chambers, *Political Parties in a New Nation* (1963). The first four chapters of Wilfred E. Binkley's *American Political Parties* (1954) are also useful.

The adoption of the Bill of Rights receives excellent coverage in Irving Brant's *The Bill of Rights: Its Origin and Meaning* (1965) and Robert A. Rutland's *The Birth of the Bill of Rights, 1776–1791* (1962). The best book on the legislative history of the Bill of Rights is Robert A. Goldwin's *From Parchment to Power: How James Madison Used the Bill of Rights to Save the Constitution* (1997), which describes the key role played by Madison in drafting and getting the first ten amendments through Congress. Documentary material on the legislative background can be found in Helen E. Veit, Kenneth R. Bowling, and Charles B. Bickford, eds., *Creating the Bill of Rights: The Documentary Record of the First Federal Congress* (1991). Useful information is also available in Richard Labunski, *James Madison and the Struggle for the Bill of Rights* (2006), and John F. Kaminski, "The Making of the Bill of Rights, 1776–1791," in Stephen L. Schechter and Richard B. Bernstein, eds., *Contexts of the Bill of Rights* (1990). The central importance ascribed to the First Amendment is discussed by Leonard W. Levy in "Liberty and the First Amendment, 1790–1800," 68 *American Historical Review* 22 (1962). Richard Epstein's *Takings: Private Property and the Power of Eminent Domain* (1985) is an excellent introduction to the Just Compensation Clause of the Fifth Amendment. An original and controversial theory of the Bill of Rights has been advanced by Akhil Reed Amar, *The Bill of Rights: Creation and Reconstruction* (1998), who challenges the traditional understanding that its purpose was to protect individual liberty. Amar argues that its real purpose was the protection of federalism and states' rights.

Information on the organization and work of the early Supreme Court can be found in Richard B. Morris, *John Jay, the Nation, and the Court* (1967), and Julius Goebel, Jr., *History of the Supreme Court: Antecedents and Beginnings to 1801* (1971). Biographies of the first justices are also useful. The best are Charles P. Smith, *James Wilson, Founding Father* (1956); Griffith J. McRee, ed., *The Life and Correspondence of James Iredell*, 2 vols. (1949), an account of the justice whose dissent in *Chisholm v. Georgia* became the basis of the Eleventh Amendment; and William G. Brown, *Life of Oliver Ellsworth* (1905), which describes Ellsworth's role in passing the Judiciary Act of 1789 and his tenure as third chief justice of the United States. Francis F. Beirne, "Sam Chase–'Disturber'," 57 *Maryland Historical Magazine* 78 (1962) contains material on the most controversial of the justices and the only member of the Court impeached by the House of Representatives. How the judiciary operated is covered in John P. Frank, "Historical Bases of the Federal Judicial System," 23 *Indiana Law Journal* 236 (1948); Erwin C. Surrency, "A History of the Federal Courts," 28 *Missouri Law Review* 214 (1963); and Kermit L. Hall, "The Children of the Cabins: The Lower Federal Judiciary, Modernization, and the Political Culture, 1789–1899," 75 *Northwestern University Law Review* 423 (1980). The conversion of the judiciary into a Federalist stronghold is covered in Kathryn Turner, "Federalist Policy and the Judiciary Act of 1801," 22 *William and Mary Quarterly*, 3d ser. 3 (1965).

V Jeffersonian Republicanism

The standard work on Jefferson's presidency is Henry Adams, *History of the United States during the Administrations of Thomas Jefferson*, 2 vols. (1986), one of the classic works of American history, but to be read carefully because of the author's issues with Jefferson's character. Other useful accounts include Robert W. Tucker and David C. Hendrickson, *Empire of Liberty: The Statecraft of Thomas Jefferson* (1990); Marshall Smelser, *The Democratic Republic, 1801–1815* (1968); Charles M. Wiltse, *The New Nation, 1800–1845* (1961); and Leonard D. White, *The Jeffersonians: A Study in Administrative History, 1801–1829* (1959). Political developments are covered in Dumas Malone, *Thomas Jefferson as Political Leader* (1963), and David H. Fischer, *The Revolution of American Conservatism* (1965), which describes attempts by some Federalists to broaden their party's political base. Jefferson's political thought is examined in Charles M. Wiltse, *The Jeffersonian Tradition in American Democracy* (1935); Adrienne Koch, *The Philosophy of Thomas Jefferson* (1943); and Merrill D. Peterson, *The Jefferson Image in the American Mind* (1960). For Jefferson's vision of what he thought America should stand for, see Joyce Appleby, *The Jeffersonian Tension in American Nationalism* (1992). Gilbert Chinard's *Thomas Jefferson: The Apostle of Americanism* (1957) is a highly readable and sympathetic treatment of the third president.

Jefferson's assault on the Federalist-controlled judiciary is covered in Edward S. Corwin's *John Marshall and the Constitution* (1919). The impeachment trial of Justice Chase is described in William H. Rehnquist, *Grand Inquests: The Historic Impeachments of Justice Samuel Chase and President Andrew Johnson* (1999); Irving Brant, *Impeachment: Trials and Errors* (1972); and Richard Lillich, "The Chase Impeachment," 4 *American Journal of Legal History* 49 (1960). The removal of Judge Pickering from the federal bench is covered in Lynn W. Turner, "The Impeachment of John Pickering," 54 *American Historical Review* 49 (1960), and Jerry W. Knudson, "The Jeffersonian Assault on the Federalist Judiciary, 1802–1805: The Political Forces and Press Reaction," 14 *American Journal of Legal History* 55 (1970). On Jefferson and civil liberties, see Adrienne Koch and Harry Ammon, "The Kentucky and Virginia Resolutions: An Episode in Jefferson's and Madison's Defense of Civil Liberties," 5 *William and Mary Quarterly,* 3d ser. 145 (1948), which links the resolutions to Jefferson's support for civil liberties generally, and Leonard W. Levy, *Jefferson and Civil Liberties: The Darker Side* (1963), which contends that Jefferson, except for his stand on church-state separation, was no friend of civil liberties. Jefferson's role in Aaron Burr's treason trial is described by Thomas P. Abernethy in *The Burr Conspiracy* (1954), and in Bradley Chapin's *The American Law of Treason: Revolutionary and Early National Origins* (1964).

Events leading up to the War of 1812 are covered in Bradford Perkins, *Prologue to War: England and the United States, 1805–1812* (1961), and Julius W. Pratt, *Expansionists of*

1812 (1957). The best accounts of the War are Francis F. Beirne, *The War of 1812* (1949); Harry F. Coles, *The War of 1812* (1965); Roger H. Brown, *The Republic in Peril: 1812* (1964); and Patrick C.T. White, *A Nation on Trial: America and the War of 1812* (1965). George Dangerfield's *The Era of Good Feelings* (1952) provides excellent coverage on the peace negotiations that ended the conflict. Dangerfield's *The Awakening of American Nationalism, 1815–1828* (1965) has a detailed account of postwar developments. Monroe's administration is covered by Irving Brant, *The Fourth President: A Life of James Madison* (1970), which is excellent for political events. The demise of the Federalist party is described by Shaw Livermore in *The Twilight of Federalism: The Disintegration of the Federalist Party, 1815–1830* (1962), and in Charles S. Sydnor, "The One-Party Period in American History," 51 *American Historical Review* 439 (1946).

VI John Marshall and Judicial Nationalism

The literature on the Marshall Court is extensive and overwhelmingly favorable to the great chief justice. The best general coverage can be found in George L. Haskins and Herbert A. Johnson, *Foundations of Power: John Marshall, 1801–1815* (1981); G. Edward White, *The Struggle for Nationalism: The Marshall Court, 1815–1825* (1987); and White, *The Challenge of Jacksonian Democracy: The Marshall Court, 1826–1835* (1987). All three volumes are part of the Oliver Wendell Holmes Devise *History of the Supreme Court of the United States*. Also recommended are Edward S. Corwin, *John Marshall and the Constitution* (1919); volume I of Charles Warren, *The Supreme Court in United States History*, 3 vols. (1922); and volumes III and IV of Albert Beveridge, *The Life of John Marshall*, 4 vols. (1919). Samuel J. Konefsky's *John Marshall and Alexander Hamilton: Architects of the American Constitution* (1964) traces the incorporation of Hamiltonian principles of government into constitutional law by the Marshall Court. R. Kent Newmyer's *John Marshall and the Heroic Age of the Supreme Court* (2001) is an indispensible personal and intellectual biography of the chief justice. For a more critical treatment of Marshall, see volume I of Louis Boudin's *Government by Judiciary*, 2 vols. (1932). Justice Story's contributions to the Marshall Court are described in Gerald T. Dunne, *Justice Joseph Story and the Rise of the Supreme Court* (1971). Daniel Webster was by far the most important attorney to practice before the Marshall Court, and his influence on the Court is analyzed in Maurice G. Baxter's *Daniel Webster and the Supreme Court* (1966). The career and legal thought of the first Republican justice appointed to the Court are treated by Donald G. Morgan in *Justice William Johnson, the First Dissenter* (1954).

Particular areas of constitutional law during the Marshall era are covered in topical monographs and journal articles. On the Contract Clause, see Benjamin F. Wright, *The Contract Clause of the Constitution* (1938); C. Peter Magrath, *Yazoo: Law and Politics in the New Republic* (1966), an excellent account of *Fletcher v. Peck*; and Francis N. Stites, *Private Interest and Public Gain: The Dartmouth College Case, 1819* (1972). The Commerce Clause is examined in Felix Frankfurter, *The Commerce Clause under Marshall, Taney and Waite* (1937); Maurice G. Baxter, *The Steamboat Monopoly* (1972), an account of *Gibbons v. Ogden*; and George L. Haskins, "John Marshall and the Commerce Clause of the Constitution," 104 *University of Pennsylvania Law Review* 23 (1955). The contro-versy over appeals to the Supreme Court from the state courts is discussed in William E. Dodd, "Chief Justice Marshall and Virginia, 1813–1821," 12 *American Historical Review* 776 (1907), and Margaret E. Horsnell, *Spencer Roane: Judicial Advocate of Jeffersonian Principles* (1987), a study of Marshall's great antagonist on the issue. Both are excellent for background information on *Martin v. Hunter's Lessee* and *Cohens v. Virginia*.

Judicial review was the most important issue of the Marshall years and also the most controversial. The political ramifications of the doctrine are examined by Donald O. Dewey in *Marshall v. Jefferson: The Political Background of Marbury v. Madison* (1970). Volume VII of Kermit L. Hall, ed., *United States Constitutional and Legal History*, 20 vols. (1987) has some excellent articles on the subject. The most useful are Henry Steele Commager, "Judicial Review and Democracy," 19 *Virginia Quarterly Review* 417 (1943), which is harshly critical of the doctrine; Wallace Mendelson, "Jefferson on Judicial Review: Consistency Through Change," 29 *University of Chicago Law Review* 327 (1962); William E. Nelson, "Changing Conceptions of Judicial Review: The Evolution of Con-stitutional Theory in the United States, 1790–1860," 120 *University of Pennsylvania Law Review* 1166 (1972); Eugene Rostow, "The Democratic Character of Judicial Review," 66 *Harvard Law Review* 193 (1952); and D.O. Wagner, "Some Antecedents of the American Doctrine of Judicial Review," 40 *Political Science Quarterly* 561 (1925). William Michael Treanor's "Judicial Review Before Marbury," 58 *Stanford Law Review* 455 (2005) is also strongly recommended.

VII Majority Rule and Sectional Rights

The localizing tendencies in politics after 1815 are described by Charles S. Sydnor's *The Development of Southern Sectionalism, 1819–1848* (1948). The particular issues that di-vided the nation are treated in several excellent monographs. Ralph C.H. Catterall, *The Second Bank of the United States* (1902), Walter B. Smith, *Economic Aspects of the Sec-ond Bank of the United States* (1953), and Jean A. Wilburn, *Biddle's Bank: The Crucial Years* (1967), cover the national bank debate. The tariff controversy is examined in Wil-liam W. Freehling, *Prelude to Civil War: The Nullification Controversy in South Carolina, 1816–1836* (1966), and Richard E. Ellis, *The Union at Risk: Jacksonian Democracy, States' Rights and the Nullification Crisis* (1987). Calhoun's nullification theory is discussed in August O. Spain, *The Political Theory of John C. Calhoun* (1951), and his role in the South Carolina nullification crisis is described by Charles M. Wiltse, *John C. Calhoun*, 3 vols. (1951), a favorable account of the great spokesman for states' rights. The emergence of slavery as a national political issue is traced by Glover Moore in *The Missouri Compromise, 1819–1821* (1953), an account of events leading up to the first and most durable of the slavery compromises.

The best general surveys of Jacksonian Democracy are Glyndon G. Van Dusen's *The Jacksonian Era, 1828–1848* (1959), and the classic study by Arthur M. Schlesinger, Jr., *The Age of Jackson* (1945). Harold C. Syrett, *Andrew Jackson: His Contribution to the American Tradition* (1953), Michael F. Holt, *Political Parties and American Political*

Development: From the Age of Jackson to the Age of Lincoln (1992), and Sean Wilentz, *The Rise of American Democracy: Jefferson to Lincoln* (2005), are also recommended. The chapter on Jackson in Richard Hofstadter's *The American Political Tradition* (1948) contains useful insights on the era. Jackson's victory at the polls in 1828 is described by Robert V. Remini in *The Election of Andrew Jackson* (1963). Jacksonian political thought is discussed in Marvin Meyers, *The Jacksonian Persuasion: Politics and Belief* (1957), and John W. Ward, *Andrew Jackson, Symbol of an Age* (1955). Politics and party organization are covered in Richard P. McCormick, *The Second American Party System: Party Formation in the Jacksonian Era* (1966); Robert V. Remini, *Martin Van Buren and the Making of the Democratic Party* (1959); and Chilton Williamson. *American Suffrage: From Property to Democracy, 1760–1860* (1960).

Jackson's presidency has been the subject of numerous studies. Richard B. Latner, *The Presidency of Andrew Jackson* (1979), describes rivalries among the Jacksonians, and Matthew A. Crenson, *The Federal Machine* (1975), examines the beginnings of bureaucracy under the Jacksonians. Jon Meacham's Pulitzer Prize-winning *American Lion: Andrew Jackson in the White House* (2009) is a highly readable account of Jackson's presidency. On Jackson's Indian policy, see Ronald N. Satz, *American Indian Policy in the Jacksonian Era* (1974); Wilson Lumpkin, *The Removal of the Cherokee Indians from Georgia*, 2 vols. (1907), an account by a contemporary Georgia political leader; and Marion L. Starkey, *The Cherokee Nation* (1946). Jackson's relations with the Supreme Court are covered in Richard Longaker, "Andrew Jackson and the Judiciary," 71 *Political Science Quarterly* 341 (1956), and Joseph C. Burke, "The Cherokee Cases: A Study in Law, Politics, and Morality," 21 *Stanford Law Review* 500 (1969). The political reaction against Jackson is treated in Eber M. Carroll, *Origins of the Whig Party* (1925); George R. Poage, *Henry Clay and the Whig Party* (1936); and Michael F. Holt, *The Rise and Fall of the American Whig Party: Jacksonian Politics and the Onset of the Civil War* (1999). The economic consequences of the bank war are examined in Reginald C. McGrane, *The Panic of 1837* (1924), an account of the financial collapse that undermined the Jacksonians politically, and Robert G. Gunderson, *The Log-Cabin Campaign* (1957), which describes the Whig victory in the 1840 elections.

VIII More Power to the States

The standard work on the Taney Court and the shift of power to the states is volume V of the Oliver Wendell Holmes Devise *History of the Supreme Court of the United States* by Carl B. Swisher, *The Taney Period, 1836–1864* (1974). The consolidation of Jacksonian power on the Court is described by Charles G. Haines and Foster H. Sherwood in *The Role of the Supreme Court in American Government and Politics, 1835–1864* (1957), and by R. Kent Newmyer, *The Supreme Court under Marshall and Taney* (1968), who traces the emergence of the Court from the long shadow cast by Marshall. On Taney and the Contract Clause, see Stanley I. Kutler, *Privilege and Creative Destruction: The Charles River Bridge Case* (1971), and Benjamin F. Wright's *The Contract Clause of the Constitution* (1938), a comparative study emphasizing continuity between the Marshall and Taney

Courts on the subject. The Commerce Clause is treated in Edward S. Corwin, *The Commerce Power versus States' Rights* (1938); Elizabeth K. Bauer, *Commentaries on the Constitution, 1790–1860* (1952); and Felix Frankfurter, "Taney and the Commerce Clause," 49 *Harvard Law Review* 1286 (1936).

IX Slavery and the Constitution

The polarization of the nation by the slavery controversy has been covered by historians from virtually every standpoint. The *Narrative of the Life of Frederick Douglass, An American Slave*, first published in 1845, is a compelling firsthand account of slavery. The Yale University Press edition (2001) is particularly recommended. Kenneth M. Stampp's *The Peculiar Institution* (1955) is still the best general survey of the American slave system. John Hope Franklin's *From Slavery to Freedom* (1963) is also recommended. Information on particular aspects of the institution can be found in Stanley M. Elkins, *Slavery: A Problem in American Institutional and Intellectual Life* (1961), which draws upon modern psychology and sociology to describe the experience of being a slave; David B. Davis, *The Problem of Slavery in Western Culture* (1966), which traces the rationales supporting the institution from ancient to modern times; and Winthrop D. Jordan, *White over Black* (1965), a comprehensive study of racial attitudes from colonial times to the nineteenth century. Henry Weincek's *An Imperfect God* (2003) explores the contradictions of race and slavery during the Revolution and founding through the figure of George Washington. John W. Blassingame's *The Slave Community* (1972) offers a rich historical account of slavery, race, and society in the antebellum South. Race and slavery outside the South are covered in Edgar J. McManus, *Black Bondage in the North* (1973), and Leon F. Litwack, *North of Slavery: The Negro in the Free States, 1790–1860* (1961). The complexity of the slave system is described in Robert S. Starobin, *Industrial Slavery in the Old South* (1970), and Richard C. Wade, *Slavery in the Cities* (1967). Black resistance to slavery is treated by Herbert Aptheker in *American Negro Slave Revolts* (1943), a useful account of a neglected subject.

How slavery became a political and constitutional issue is traced in Richard H. Sewell, *Ballots for Freedom: Antislavery Politics in the United States, 1837–1860* (1976); William M. Wiecek, *The Sources of Antislavery Constitutionalism in America, 1760–1848* (1977); and Donald L. Robinson, *Slavery in the Structure of American Politics, 1765–1820* (1971). The fugitive slave issue that sharply divided the nation is dealt with in Thomas D. Morris, *Free Men All: The Personal Liberty Laws of the North, 1780–1861* (1974); Allen Johnson, "The Constitutionality of the Fugitive Slave Acts," 31 *Yale Law Journal* 161 (1921); and Paul Finkelman, "*Prigg v. Pennsylvania* and Northern State Courts: Anti-Slavery Uses of a Pro-Slavery Decision," 25 *Civil War History* 5 (1979). Mark Tushnet's *The American Law of Slavery, 1810–1860* (1981) is an excellent survey of the legal status and treatment of slaves. Particular aspects of slave law are examined in Daniel J. Flanigan, "Criminal Procedure in Slave Trials in the Antebellum South," 40 *Journal of Southern History* 537 (1974); Wilbert E. Moore, "Slave Law and the Social Structure," 26 *Journal of Negro History* 171 (1941); and Walter Berns, "The Constitution and the Migration of Slaves," 78

Yale Law Journal 198 (1968). Howard Jones, *Mutiny on the Amistad* (1987), describes the impact of that celebrated slave mutiny on the antislavery movement in the United States.

The best studies of the antislavery movement are Louis Filler, *The Crusade Against Slavery, 1830–1860* (1960), an excellent general account; Gilbert H. Barnes, *The Anti-Slavery Impulse, 1830–1844* (1964), which emphasizes the role of Midwestern opponents of slavery; and Dwight L. Dumond's *Antislavery: The Crusade for Freedom in America* (1961), very useful for the politics of antislavery in the North. Particular aspects of the movement are treated in Betty Fladeland, "Who Were the Abolitionists?" 49 *Journal of Negro History* 99 (1964); Leon F. Litwack, "The Abolitionist Dilemma: The Antislavery Movement and the Northern Negro," 34 *New England Quarterly* 50 (1961), which deals with the problem of reconciling antislavery with racism in the North; William H. Pease and Jane H. Pease, "Antislavery Ambivalence: Immediatism, Expediency, Race," 17 *American Quarterly* 682 (1965), a study of the divisions within the movement; and Larry Garza, "The Professional Fugitive in the Abolition Movement," 48 *Wisconsin Magazine of History* 196 (1965). How the South reacted to the antislavery agitation is treated in William J. Cooper, *The South and the Politics of Slavery, 1828–1856* (1978); Clement Eaton, "Censorship of the Southern Mails," 48 *American Historical Review* 266 (1943); and Robert P. Ludlum, "The Antislavery 'Gag-Rule': History and Argument, 26 *Journal of Negro History* 203 (1941), which covers the attempt to halt congressional debate over slavery.

The controversy over the extension of slavery into the national territories was a direct consequence of American expansionism in the antebellum period. The best treatment of the subject can be found in Alfred H. Bill, *Rehearsal for Conflict: The War with Mexico, 1846–1848* (1947); K. Jack Bauer, *The Mexican War, 1846–1848* (1974); and Holman Hamilton, *Prologue to Conflict: The Crisis and Compromise of 1850* (1964). Mark Stegmaier, *Texas, New Mexico, and the Compromise of 1850: Boundary Dispute and Sectional Crisis* (1996), and Michael F. Holt, *The Fate of Their Country: Politicians, Slavery Extension and the Coming of the Civil War* (2005), which holds the politicians responsible for precipitating the crisis, are also recommended. Robert R. Russel, "Constitutional Doctrines with Regard to Slavery in the Territories," 32 *Journal of Southern History* 466 (1966), is useful for the constitutional issues. On the Kansas-Nebraska Act, see George F. Milton, *The Eve of Conflict: Stephen A. Douglas and the Needless War* (1923), and Perley O. Ray, *The Repeal of the Missouri Compromise* (1909), for opposing interpretations of that fateful measure. The political consequences of the Act are described in volume II of William W. Freehling, *The Road to Disunion: Secessionists Triumphant, 1854–1861* (2007); Roy F. Nichols, *The Disruption of American Democracy* (1948); and David M. Potter, *The Impending Crisis, 1848–1861* (1976), which was awarded a Pulitzer Prize. Roy F. Nichols, "The Kansas-Nebraska Act: A Century of Historiography," 43 *Mississippi Valley Historical Review* 187 (1956), is also useful.

Historians generally agree that the *Dred Scott* decision marked the point of no return in the slavery controversy, and the case has been the subject of intense political and legal analysis. Three excellent studies are Don E. Fehrenbacher, *The Dred Scott Case: Its Significance in American Law and Politics* (1981); Austin Allen, *Origins of the Dred Scott*

Case: Jacksonian Jurisprudence and the Supreme Court, 1837–1857 (2006); and Vincent C. Hopkins, *Dred Scott's Case* (1951). Helen T. Catterall, "Some Antecedents of the Dred Scott Case," 30 *American Historical Review* 56 (1924), is useful for the state court background of the case. Particular aspects of the decision are discussed in Edward S. Corwin, "The Dred Scott Decision, in the Light of Contemporary Legal Doctrines," 17 *American Historical Review* 52 (1911); F.H. Hodder, "Some Phases of the Dred Scott Case," 16 *Mississippi Valley Historical Review* 3 (1929), which focuses on the dissenting justices; and Richard H. Leach, "Justice Curtis and the Dred Scott Case," 94 *Essex Institute Historical Collection* 37 (1958). Mark Tushnet, ed., I *Dissent: Great Opposing Opinions in Landmark Supreme Court Cases* (2008), covers the Curtis dissent. Francis P. Weisenburger, *The Life of John McLean, a Politician on the United States Supreme Court* (1937), is useful for McLean's dissenting opinion.

The events leading up to the secession crisis are described in Avery O. Craven, *The Growth of Southern Nationalism, 1848–1861* (1953); Arthur C. Cole, *The Irrepressible Conflict, 1850–1865* (1934); and David H. Donald, *Charles Sumner and the Coming of the Civil War* (1960). The influence of the Republican Party on political polarization is covered in Eric Foner, *Free Soil, Free Labor, Free Men: The Ideology of the Republican Party before the Civil War* (1995); William E. Gienapp, *The Origins of the Republican Party, 1852–1856* (1988); and James D. Bilotta, *Race and the Rise of the Republican Party, 1848–1865* (1992). Two useful studies of the 1860 election are Richard H. Luthin, *The First Lincoln Campaign* (1944), and Ollinger Crenshaw, *The Slave States in the Presidential Election of 1860* (1945). Particular aspects of the secession crisis are described in Norman A. Graebner, ed., *Politics and the Crisis of 1860* (1961), a collection of essays on that fateful year; David M. Potter, *Lincoln and His Party in the Secession Crisis* (1962); Kenneth M. Stampp, *And the War Came* (1950), an account of the crisis from a Northern perspective; and Ralph A. Wooster, *The Secession Conventions in the South* (1962), a study of the politics of secession. Dwight L. Dumond's *The Secession Movement, 1860–1861* (1931) is still the best general account of how the South left the Union. Robert G. Gunderson's *Old Gentlemen's Convention: The Washington Peace Conference of 1861* (1961) describes the final unsuccessful effort for a political settlement between North and South.

X The Crisis of the Union

Volumes V and VI of Allan Nevins, *The Ordeal of the Union*, 6 vols. (1947–60), provide excellent general coverage of the Civil War, and the two-volume accounts by James M. McPherson, *Ordeal by Fire: The Civil War and Reconstruction* (1982), and James G. Randall and David H. Donald, *The Civil War and Reconstruction* (1969), are also recommended. James M. McPherson, *Battle Cry of Freedom: The Civil War* (1988), is an excellent one-volume account of the conflict. Lincoln's wartime leadership is covered in David H. Donald's prize-winning *Lincoln* (1995); Doris Kearns Goodwin's *Team of Rivals: The Political Genius of Abraham Lincoln* (2006); and James M. McPherson's *Tried by War: Abraham Lincoln as Commander in Chief* (2008). For a fine collection of original essays on Lincoln, see Eric Foner, ed., *Our Lincoln: New Perspectives on Lincoln and His World*

(2008). The political problems confronting Lincoln are dealt with in T. Harry Williams, *Lincoln and the Radicals* (1941), an account of his difficulties with Republican extremists; William B. Hesseltine, *Lincoln and the War Governors* (1948), which deals with the expansion of federal power at the expense of the states; and Burton J. Hendrick, *Lincoln's War Cabinet* (1946), an account of political infighting within the administration. The contribution of African Americans to the Union victory is treated in Benjamin Quarles, *The Negro in the Civil War* (1953).

Northern opposition to the war is treated in Frank L. Klement, *The Copperheads in the Middle West* (1960); Wood Gray, *The Hidden Civil War: The Story of the Copperheads* (1942); and George F. Milton, *Abraham Lincoln and the Fifth Column* (1942). The resulting suppression of civil liberties is covered in James G. Randall, *Constitutional Problems under Lincoln* (1951), an account critical of the administration for alleged abuses of power. The charge that Lincoln ran roughshod over civil liberties is rejected by Harold M. Hyman, *A More Perfect Union: The Impact of the Civil War and Reconstruction on the Constitution* (1973); Mark E. Neely, Jr., *The Fate of Liberty* (1991); and Michael Les Benedict, *The Blessings of Liberty: A Concise History of the Constitution of the United States* (1996). Particular constitutional issues are dealt with in Sherill Halbert, "The Suspension of the Writ of Habeas Corpus by President Lincoln," 2 *American Journal of Legal History* 95 (1958); Thomas F. Carroll, "Freedom of Speech and of the Press during the Civil War," 9 *Virginia Law Review* 516 (1923); and Patricia L.M. Lucie, "Confiscation: Constitutional Crossroads," 23 *Civil War History* 307 (1977), which describes the wartime seizure of enemy property. The conscription issue is covered by Eugene C. Murdock, *One Million Men: The Civil War Draft in the North* (1971). For emancipation and the Thirteenth Amendment, see Herman Belz, *Emancipation and Equal Rights: Politics and Constitutionalism in the Civil War Era* (1978); John Hope Franklin, *The Emancipation Proclamation* (1963); and Eric Foner, *Forever Free: The Story of Emancipation and Reconstruction* (2005).

XI Reconstructing the Nation

An excellent account of the Reconstruction Era can be found in Eric Foner's prize-winning *Reconstruction: America's Unfinished Revolution, 1863–1877* (1988). Also recommended are Rembert W. Patrick, *The Reconstruction of the Nation* (1967); E. Merton Coulter, *The South During Reconstruction: 1865–1877* (1947); John Hope Franklin, *Reconstruction: After the Civil War* (1961); and Kenneth M. Stampp, *The Era of Reconstruction, 1865–1877* (1965). The moderate presidential phase of Reconstruction is covered in William B. Hesseltine, *Lincoln's Plan of Reconstruction* (1960), and Eric McKitrick, *Andrew Johnson and Reconstruction* (1960). The plight of the ex-slaves during this period is dealt with in Theodore B. Wilson, *The Black Codes of the South* (1965). For the radical congressional phase, see William Brock, *An American Crisis: Congress and Reconstruction, 1865–1867* (1963); James M. McPherson, *The Struggle for Equality: Abolitionists and the Negro in the Civil War and Reconstruction* (1964); and David H. Donald, *The Politics of Reconstruction, 1863–1867* (1965). Fawn Brodie's *Thaddeus Stevens, Scourge of the South* (1959) is useful background on the leading congressional radical. Two interesting accounts of the era from a Marxist standpoint are James S. Allen, *Reconstruction: The Battle for Democracy* (1937), and W.E.B. DuBois, *Black Reconstruction* (1935), the latter a work of sound scholarship and still useful for the role played by the freedmen in the postwar South.

The constitutional issues raised by Reconstruction are addressed in numerous topical studies of the era. John Hart's *Tenure of Office Act under the Constitution* (1930) examines congressional encroachments upon the executive branch, and David M. DeWitt's *The Impeachment and Trial of Andrew Johnson, Seventeenth President of the United States* (1967) describes the attempt of the congressional radicals to remove President Johnson from office. Hans L. Trefousse, *Impeachment of a President* (1975), is also an excellent account of Johnson's impeachment and trial. Habeas corpus in the South is treated in William M. Wiecek, "The Great Writ and Reconstruction: The Habeas Corpus Act of 1867," 36 *Journal of Southern History* 530 (1970), which describes how the Act of 1867 expanded the jurisdiction of federal courts to review state court criminal proceedings. On bills of attainder and ex post facto laws, see Harold M. Hyman, *Era of the Oath: Northern Loyalty Tests during the Civil War and Reconstruction* (1954). The reach of federal judicial power during Reconstruction is treated in Stanley I. Kutler, *Judicial Power and Reconstruction Politics* (1968), and William M. Wiecek, "The Reconstruction of Federal Judicial Power, 1863–1875," 13 *American Journal of Legal History* 333 (1969). The latter describes how technical jurisdictional statutes paved the way for a vast expansion of federal judicial power over both the states and Congress.

Accounts of the Fourteenth Amendment can be found in Jacobus ten Broek, *The Antislavery Origins of the Fourteenth Amendment* (1965); Joseph B. James, *The Framing of the Fourteenth Amendment* (1956); and Michael Kent Curtis, *No State Shall Abridge: The Fourteenth Amendment and the Bill of Rights* (1990), the last a highly readable account of the Amendment's ideological context and the sources the Thirty-ninth Congress drew upon in framing its provisions. Suffrage guarantees for African Americans are dealt with in William Gillette, *The Right to Vote: Politics and the Passage of the Fifteenth Amendment* (1965). The end of Reconstruction is dealt with in Paul H. Buck, *The Road to Reunion, 1865–1900* (1937), and C. Vann Woodward, *Reunion and Reaction: The Compromise of 1877 and the End of Reconstruction* (1951). Stanley P. Hirshson's *Farewell to the Bloody Shirt: Northern Republicans and the Southern Negro, 1877–1893* (1962) is a thoughtful account of the political abandonment of African Americans in the South after 1877.

XII Promises Betrayed

Two excellent studies of how the Supreme Court dealt with the Fourteenth Amendment can be found in Jonathan Lurie and Ronald Labbe, *The Slaughterhouse Cases: Reconstruction, Regulation and the Fourteenth Amendment* (2003), and Michael A. Ross, *Justice of Shattered Dreams: Samuel Freeman Miller and the Supreme Court during the Civil War Era* (2003), which focuses on the author of the *Slaughterhouse* decision. Charles Fairman's *Justice Miller and the Supreme Court, 1862–1890* (1939) is also useful for understanding the justice whose views had such a decisive effect on the interpretation of the Fourteenth

Amendment. Edward M. Gaffney, Jr., "History and Legal Interpretation: The Early Distortion of the Fourteenth Amendment by the Gilded Age Court," 25 *Catholic University of America Law Review* 207 (1976); J. David Hoeveler, Jr., "Reconstruction and the Federal Courts: The Civil Rights Act of 1875," 31 *Historian* 604 (1969); Michael Les Benedict, "Preserving Federalism: Reconstruction and the Waite Count," 1978 *Supreme Court Review* 39; and Loren P. Beth, "The Slaughter-House Cases–Revisited," 23 *Louisiana Law Review* 487 (1963) are also recommended.

For an excellent overview of racism C. Vann Woodward's prize-winning *The Strange Career of Jim Crow* (1955) continues to be useful. The "separate but equal" doctrine is treated in Harvey Fireside, *Separate and Unequal: Homer Plessy and the Supreme Court Decision that Legalized Racism* (2003); Keith Weldon Medley, *We as Freemen: Plessy v. Ferguson* (2003); and Brook Thamas, ed., *Plessy v. Ferguson: A Brief History with Documents* (1997). For the theory that Jim Crow statutes frequently reflected rather than fostered Jim Crow attitudes, see Michael J. Klarman, "The Plessy Era," 1998 *Supreme Court Review* 303 (1998). A case-by-case account of the erosion of Fourteenth and Fifteenth Amendment guarantees in the South can be found in Robert J. Harris, *The Quest for Equality: The Constitution, Congress, and the Supreme Court* (1960). The disfranchisement of African Americans in the South is dealt with in Frederic D. Ogden, *The Poll Tax in the South* (1958), and J. Morgan Kousser, *The Shaping of Southern Politics: Suffrage Restriction and the Establishment of the One-Party South, 1880–1910* (1974). The experience of racial segregation is described by Neil R. McMillen, *Dark Journey: Black Mississippians in the Age of Jim Crow* (1989), and Leon F. Litwack, *Trouble in the Mind: Black Southerners in the Age of Jim Crow* (1998), a moving account of what it must have been like to be black in the post-Reconstruction period.

XIII Property Rights and Judicial Activism

Social and economic change in the later nineteenth century is dealt with in Thomas C. Cochran and William Miller, *The Age of Enterprise: A Social History of Industrial America* (1961), and Edward C. Kirkland, *American Economic History since 1860* (1971). The rise of the railroads is covered in Robert F. Himmelberg, ed., *The Rise of Big Business and the Beginning of Antitrust and Railroad Regulation, 1870–1900* (1994), an excellent collection of essays on the transformation of the economy. George R. Taylor and Irene D. Neu, *The American Railroad Network, 1861–1890* (1956); John F. Stover, *American Railroads* (1961); and Robert W. Fogel, *Railroads and American Economic Growth* (1964), are also recommended. The political response to abuses by the railroad monopolies is described in Solon J. Buck, *The Granger Movement* (1963); John D. Hicks, *The Populist Revolt* (1931); and Nathan Fine, *Labor and Farmer Parties in the United States, 1828–1928* (1961). How the regulatory measures that resulted fared in the courts is covered in James W. Ely, Jr., *Railroads and American Law* (2001), and Richard C. Cortner's *The Iron Horse and the Constitution* (1993).

The problems of organized labor are examined in Howard Kimeldorf, *Battling for American Labor: Wobblies, Craft Workers, and the Making of the Union Movement* (1999), and Bruce Laurie, *Artisans into Workers: Labor in Nineteenth-Century America* (1989). Norman J. Ware's *The Labor Movement in the United States, 1860–1895* (1928) also continues to be useful. For labor and political activism, see Kim Voss, *The Making of American Exceptionalism: The Knights of Labor and Class Formation in the Nineteenth Century* (1993); Matthew Hild, *Greenbackers, Knights of Labor, and Populists: Farmer-Labor Insurgency in the Late Nineteenth-Century South* (2007); Joseph Gerteis, *Class and the Color Line: Interracial Class Coalition in the Knights of Labor and the Populist Movement* (2007); and Richard Schneirov, *Labor and Urban Politics: Class Conflict and the Origins of Modern Liberalism in Chicago, 1864–97* (1998). Patrick Renshaw, *The Wobblies: The Story of the IWW and Syndicalism in the United States* (1999), and Paul F. Brissenden, *The I.W.W.: A Study of American Syndicalism* (1957), deal with radical responses to the problems confronting American workers. One of the often violent confrontations of labor with management is described by Paul Avrich in *The Haymarket Tragedy* (1984).

Volume I of Isaiah L. Sharfman's *The Interstate Commerce Commission*, 4 vols. (1931–1937) provides a useful introduction to the era of federal railroad regulation. The judicial response to the measure is covered in Arnold M. Paul, *Conservative Crisis and the Rule of Law* (1960); Edward S. Corwin, *Court over Constitution* (1938); and Loren P. Peth, *The Development of the American Constitution, 1877–1917* (1971). The history of the Sherman Anti-Trust Act is tracked in Hans B. Thorelli, *The Federal Antitrust Policy: Origination of an American Tradition* (1954), and John D. Clark, *The Federal Trust Policy* (1931). For judicial enforcement of the Sherman Act, see William Howard Taft, *The Anti-Trust Act and the Supreme Court* (1914); Milton Handler, *A Study of the Construction and Enforcement of the Federal Antitrust Laws* (1941); and William Letwin, *Law and Economic Policy in America: The Evolution of the Sherman Anti-Trust Act* (1965). Tony A. Freyer's "Economic Liberty, Antitrust, and the Constitution," in Ellen Frankel Paul and Howard Dickman, eds., *Liberty, Property, and Government: Constitutional Interpretation before the New Deal* (1989) is also recommended. For the decision that rendered the measure virtually useless as a restraint on manufacturing monopolies, see Charles W. McCurdy, "The *Knight* Sugar Decision of 1895 and the Modernization of American Corporation Law, 1869–1903," 53 *Business History Review* 304 (1979). Robert H. Bork's *The Antitrust Paradox: A Policy at War with Itself* (1993) is an excellent overview of the Act and its contradictions.

How laissez-faire political thinking influenced constitutional interpretation in the late nineteenth century is discussed in Benjamin R. Twiss, *Lawyers and the Constitution: How Laissez Faire Came to the Supreme Court* (1942), and William F. Swindler, *Court and Constitution in the Twentieth Century: The Old Legality, 1889–1932* (1969). Alan Jones, "Thomas M. Cooley and 'Laissez Faire Constitutionalism': A Reconsideration," 53 *Journal of American History* 751 (1967), is also recommended. Thorough discussions of the historical development of laissez-faire constitutionalism can be found in Michael Les Benedict's article, "Laissez-Faire and Liberty: A Re-Evaluation of the Meaning and Origins of Laissez-Faire Constitutionalism," 3 *Law and History Review* 293 (1985), and Matthew J. Lindsay's "In Search of 'Laissez-Faire Constitutionalism'," 123 *Harvard Law Review* 55 (2010). David M. Gold discusses the relationship between the growth of railroads in the United States and the rise of laissez-faire constitutionalism in

"Redfield, Railroads, and the Roots of 'Laissez-Faire Constitutionalism'," 27 *American Journal of Legal History* 254 (1983). On the role of the courts in labor-management disputes, Edward Berman, *Labor and the Sherman Act* (1930), and Felix Frankfurter and Nathan Greene, *The Labor Injunction* (1930), continue to be useful. For the shift from procedural to substantive due process, see Maurice Finkelstein, "From *Munn v. Illinois* to *Tyson v. Banton*: A Study in the Judicial Process," 27 *Columbia Law* Review 769 (1927), and Charles Fairman, "The So-Called Granger Cases, Lord Hale, and Justice Bradley," 5 *Stanford Law* Review 587 (1953). Both emphasize the "public interest" doctrine adopted in Munn as the opening wedge for the transition to substantive due process. Also recommended are John V. Orth, *Due Process of Law: A Brief History* (2003); Michael J. Phillips, *The Lochner Court, Myth and Reality: Substantive Due Process from the 1890s to the 1930s* (2001); and Edward Keynes, *Liberty, Property, and Privacy: Toward a Jurisprudence of Substantive Due Process* (1996). Kenneth W. Dam's article, "The Legal Tender Cases," 1981 *Supreme Court* Review 367 (1981), discusses the cases' significance in the economic context of the period. The fate of the federal income tax in the *Pollock* case is covered in Robert Stanley, *Dimensions of Law in the Service of Order: Origins of the Federal Income Tax, 1861–1913* (1993), and John Witte's *The Politics and Development of the Federal Income Tax* (1985). The tactics of the attorney general who defended the tax are examined by Gerald G. Eggert in "Richard Olney and the Income Tax Cases," 48 *Mississippi Valley Historical Review* 24 (1961).

Appendix I:
Glossary of Legal Terms

ACTION IN REM A legal proceeding against property rather than against the owner of the property. Typical actions in rem are condemnation and forfeiture.

APPELLANT The party who appeals from a lower court's decision to a higher court.

APPELLATE JURISDICTION The power vested in a superior court to review and revise the decisions of a lower court.

APPELLEE The party who defends the decision of a lower court against an appeal.

ATTAINT To pass an act or bill of attainder.

BILL OF ATTAINDER A legislative act imposing penalties on a person not convicted in a court of law.

BRIEF A memorandum of fact or law submitted to the court in support of oral arguments.

CASE LAW Law based on court decisions and rulings, as distinct from statute law passed by legislatures.

CERTIFICATION *See* writ of certification.

CERTIORARI *See* writ of certiorari.

CIVIL LAW The body of law governing the private rights of individuals. The law of contracts, torts, and copyright are examples.

CLASS ACTION A legal proceeding on behalf of all members of a group having an interest in the outcome.

COMITY Cooperation between sovereigns. Typical examples are the enforcement of court decisions and the extradition of fugitives.

COMMON LAW The general body of Anglo-American law, except as modified by statute. Often synonymous with case law.

CONCURRING OPINION The opinion of a judge who agrees with the decision but not with the reasoning of the majority.

CORRUPTION OF BLOOD A feudal law doctrine that treason so corrupts a traitor's blood that his property cannot pass to his heirs but escheats to the Crown.

CRIMINAL LAW The body of public law prescribing penalties for prohibited offenses.

DE FACTO In fact, actually; but without a legal basis.

DE JURE By law or by right; having a legal basis.

DICTA *See* obiter dictum.

DISSENTING OPINION The opinion of a judge who disagrees with the decision of the majority.

DOUBLE JEOPARDY Prosecuting the accused a second time for the same offense.

EMINENT DOMAIN The power of the government, state or federal, to seize private property without the consent of the owner.

EQUITY The branch of Anglo-American law governing cases where the legal remedies are inadequate. Equitable remedies are typically more flexible than legal ones.

EX PARTE A petition or application to the court by one of the parties.

EX POST FACTO LAW A statute imposing or increasing penalties for something done in the past. A measure criminalizing past conduct retroactively.

EX REL. (EX RELATIONE) On the relation or information of. Although the relator upon whose information the legal action is brought is the actual plaintiff, for technical reasons the suit must be brought in the name of the sovereign or some designated public official. For example, *Illinois ex rel. McCollum v. Board of Education*, 333 U.S. 203 (1948).

GRAND JURY A common law panel of from twelve to twenty-three persons convened to determine whether the evidence is sufficient to indict and bring the accused to trial.

HABEAS CORPUS *See* write of habeas corpus.

INDICTMENT A grand jury finding that the evidence justifies bringing the accused to trial.

INJUNCTION An equitable remedy prohibiting the enjoined person from doing something. Its opposite is the mandatory injunction ordering the performance of some act.

INTERNATIONAL LAW A general body of rules, including treaty and custom, observed by nations in their relations with one another.

JURISDICTION The authority of the court over the parties or subject matter of the case.

JUSTICIABLE Subject to judicial determination. Hypothetical cases and those brought to resolve political issues are not justiciable and therefore are subject to dismissal.

MAJORITY OPINION The opinion of a majority of the judges participating in the case.

MANDAMUS *See* writ of mandamus.

MOOT Rendered nonjusticiable by altered circumstances.

MOTION An application to the court for a ruling incidental to a trial or appeal.

MUNICIPAL LAW The domestic law of a particular state or nation.

NATURAL LAW Universal legal principles prescribed by nature rather than by man.

OBITER DICTUM An incidental statement or finding by a judge in the course of his opinion. If not essential to the decision, it is not binding in future cases.

ORIGINAL JURISDICTION A court's trial jurisdiction. Any jurisdiction not appellate is original.

PER CURIAM By the court. An unsigned opinion by the court as a whole.

PETIT JURY A common law jury of twelve members impaneled to try the defendant. It is "petty" from the standpoint of size in relation to the grand jury.

PETITIONER A person seeking judicial action or relief. The party opposing the petition is the respondent.

PLURALITY OPINION An opinion by less than a majority of the judges deciding the case.

POLITICAL QUESTION One involving the political functions of government and therefore not suitable for judicial determination. Cases raising such questions are deemed nonjusticiable.

RATIO DECIDENDI The reason or legal principle at the heart of the decision. The part of the opinion that is binding in future cases.

REMAND An order returning the case to a lower court for proceedings consistent with the findings of the superior court.

REMITTITUR The order of reversal issued by an appellate court overturning a decision.

Respondent The party opposing the petitioner's motion or application.

Stare decisis "Let the decision stand." The judicial doctrine that the ratio decidendi of a case becomes a binding precedent for the courts in future cases. The doctrine does not apply to dicta not essential to the decision.

Statutes Laws passed by legislative bodies. The courts construe statutes narrowly if they modify or change the common law.

Sub judice Under judicial consideration.

Subpoena An order to appear before a court or some legislative body to provide needed testimony.

Subpoena duces tecum A subpoena to produce specified evidence relevant to the inquiry.

Writ A court order.

Writ of assistance A court order in colonial times authorizing customs officers to search any premises for smuggled goods.

Writ of certification An order for a superior court to provide a lower court with clarification on a point of law.

Writ of certiorari An order granted by an appellate court for the review of a lower court's ruling or decision.

Writ of error An order by an appellate court for the review of the trial record for legal errors by the lower court. The courts have less discretion with respect to this writ than in the case of review by certiorari.

Writ of habeas corpus "You have the body." A writ directing the person having custody of the prisoner to produce him in court for a hearing to determine the legality of his detention. As a fundamental safeguard of personal liberty, it is the only writ specifically guaranteed by the Constitution.

Writ of mandamus "We command." An order directing a public officer to perform some duty connected with his office. It is issued if the official fails or refuses to perform that duty.

Writ of prohibition An order from a superior court directing a lower court to halt proceedings in a case beyond its jurisdiction.

Year Books The earliest reports of decisions of the courts of England from the reign of Edward I to the time of Henry VIII.

Appendix II: Declaration of Independence

In Congress, July 4, 1776

The Unanimous Declaration of the Thirteen United States of America

When in the Course of human events, it becomes necessary for one people to dissolve the political bands which have connected them with another, and to assume among the powers of the earth, the separate and equal station to which the Laws of Nature and of Nature's God entitle them, a decent respect to the opinions of mankind requires that they should declare the causes which impel them to the separation.

We hold these truths to be self-evident, that all men are created equal, that they are endowed by their Creator with certain unalienable Rights, that among these are Life, Liberty and the pursuit of Happiness.—That to secure these rights, Governments are instituted among Men, deriving their just powers from the consent of the governed,—That whenever any Form of Government becomes destructive of these ends, it is the Right of the People to alter or to abolish it, and to institute new Government, laying its foundation on such principles and organizing its powers in such form, as to them shall seem most likely to effect their Safety and Happiness. Prudence, indeed, will dictate that Governments long established should not be changed for light and transient causes; and accordingly all experience hath shewn, that mankind are more disposed to suffer, while evils are sufferable, than to right themselves by abolishing the forms to which they are accustomed. But when a long train of abuses and usurpations, pursuing invariably the same Object evinces a design to reduce them under absolute Despotism, it is their right, it is their duty, to throw off such Government, and to provide new Guards for their future security.—Such has been the patient sufferance of these Colonies; and such is now the necessity which constrains them to alter their former Systems of Government. The history of the present King of Great Britain is a history of repeated injuries and usurpations, all having in direct object the establishment of an absolute Tyranny over these States. To prove this, let Facts be submitted to a candid world.

He has refused his Assent to Laws, the most wholesome and necessary for the public good.

He has forbidden his Governors to pass Laws of immediate and pressing importance, unless suspended in their operation till his Assent should be obtained; and when so suspended, he has utterly neglected to attend to them.

He has refused to pass other Laws for the accommodation of large districts of people, unless those people would relinquish the right of Representation in the Legislature, a right inestimable to them and formidable to tyrants only.

He has called together legislative bodies at places unusual, uncomfortable, and distant from the depository of their public Records, for the sole purpose of fatiguing them into compliance with his measures.

He has dissolved Representative Houses repeatedly, for opposing with manly firmness his invasions on the rights of the people.

He has refused for a long time, after such dissolutions, to cause others to be elected; whereby the Legislative powers, incapable of Annihilation, have returned to the People at large for their exercise; the State remaining in the mean time exposed to all the dangers of invasion from without, and convulsions within.

He has endeavoured to prevent the population of these States; for that purpose obstructing the Laws for Naturalization of Foreigners; refusing to pass others to encourage their migrations hither, and raising the conditions of new Appropriations of Lands.

He has obstructed the Administration of Justice, by refusing his Assent to Laws for establishing Judiciary powers.

He has made Judges dependent on his Will alone, for the tenure of their offices, and the amount and payment of their salaries.

He has erected a multitude of New Offices, and sent hither swarms of Officers to harass our people, and eat out their substance.

He has kept among us, in times of peace, Standing Armies without the Consent of our legislatures.

He has affected to render the Military independent of and superior to the Civil power.

He has combined with others to subject us to a jurisdiction foreign to our constitution, and unacknowledged by our laws; giving his Assent to their Acts of pretended Legislation:

For Quartering large bodies of armed troops among us:

For protecting them, by a mock Trial, from punishment for any Murders which they should commit on the Inhabitants of these States:

For cutting off our Trade with all parts of the world:

For imposing Taxes on us without our Consent:

For depriving us in many cases, of the benefits of Trial by Jury:

For transporting us beyond Seas to be tried for pretended offences

For abolishing the free System of English Laws in a neighbouring Province, establishing therein an Arbitrary government, and enlarging its Boundaries so as to render it at once an example and fit instrument for introducing the same absolute rule into these Colonies:

For taking away our Charters, abolishing our most valuable Laws, and altering fundamentally the Forms of our Governments:

For suspending our own Legislatures, and declaring themselves invested with power to legislate for us in all cases whatsoever.

He has abdicated Government here, by declaring us out of his Protection and waging War against us.

He has plundered our seas, ravaged our Coasts, burnt our towns, and destroyed the lives of our people.

He is at this time transporting large Armies of foreign Mercenaries to compleat the works of death, desolation and tyranny, already begun with circumstances of Cruelty & perfidy scarcely paralleled in the most barbarous ages, and totally unworthy the Head of a civilized nation.

He has constrained our fellow Citizens taken Captive on the high Seas to bear Arms against their Country, to become the executioners of their friends and Brethren, or to fall themselves by their Hands.

He has excited domestic insurrections amongst us, and has endeavoured to bring on the inhabitants of our frontiers, the merciless Indian Savages, whose known rule of warfare, is an undistinguished destruction of all ages, sexes and conditions.

In every stage of these Oppressions We have Petitioned for Redress in the most humble terms: Our repeated Petitions have been answered only by repeated injury. A Prince whose character is thus marked by every act which may define a Tyrant, is unfit to be the ruler of a free people.

Nor have We been wanting in attentions to our British brethren. We have warned them from time to time of attempts by their legislature to extend an unwarrantable jurisdiction over us. We have reminded them of the circumstances of our emigration and settlement here. We have appealed to their native justice and magnanimity, and we have conjured them by the ties of our common kindred to disavow these usurpations which, would inevitably interrupt our connections and correspondence. They too have been deaf to the voice of justice and of consanguinity. We must, therefore, acquiesce in the necessity, which denounces our Separation, and hold them, as we hold the rest of mankind, Enemies in War, in Peace Friends.

We, therefore, the Representatives of the United States of America, in General Congress, Assembled, appealing to the Supreme Judge of the world for the rectitude of our intentions, do, in the Name, and by Authority of the good People of these Colonies, solemnly publish and declare, That these United Colonies are, and of Right ought to be Free and Independent States; that they are Absolved from all Allegiance to the British Crown, and that all political connection between them and the State of Great Britain, is and ought to be totally dissolved; and that as Free and Independent States, they have full Power to levy War, conclude Peace, contract Alliances, establish Commerce, and to do all other Acts and Things which Independent States may of right do. And for the support of this Declaration, with a firm reliance on the protection of divine Providence, we mutually pledge to each other our Lives, our Fortunes and our sacred Honor.

The 56 signatures on the Declaration appear in the positions indicated:

Column 1
Georgia:

Button Gwinnett
Lyman Hall
George Walton

Column 2
North Carolina:

William Hooper
Joseph Hewes
John Penn

South Carolina:

Edward Rutledge
Thomas Heyward, Jr.
Thomas Lynch, Jr.
Arthur Middleton

Column 3
Massachusetts:

John Hancock

Maryland:

Samuel Chase
William Paca
Thomas Stone
Charles Carroll of Carrollton

Virginia:

George Wythe
Richard Henry Lee
Thomas Jefferson
Benjamin Harrison
Thomas Nelson, Jr.
Francis Lightfoot Lee
Carter Braxton

Column 4
Pennsylvania:

Robert Morris
Benjamin Rush
Benjamin Franklin
John Morton
George Clymer
James Smith
George Taylor
James Wilson
George Ross

Delaware:

Caesar Rodney
George Read
Thomas McKean

Column 5
New York:

William Floyd
Philip Livingston
Francis Lewis
Lewis Morris

New Jersey:

Richard Stockton
John Witherspoon
Francis Hopkinson
John Hart
Abraham Clark

Column 6
New Hampshire:

Josiah Bartlett
William Whipple

Massachusetts:

Samuel Adams
John Adams
Robert Treat Paine
Elbridge Gerry

Rhode Island:

Stephen Hopkins
William Ellery

Connecticut:

Roger Sherman
Samuel Huntington
William Williams
Oliver Wolcott

New Hampshire:

Matthew Thornton

Appendix III: Articles of Confederation

The Articles of Confederation

Agreed to by Congress November 15, 1777; ratified and in force, March 1, 1781.

Preamble

To all to whom these Presents shall come, we the undersigned Delegates of the States affixed to our Names send greeting.

Whereas the Delegates of the United States of America in Congress assembled did on the fifteenth day of November in the Year of our Lord One Thousand Seven Hundred and Seventy-seven, and in the Second Year of the Independence of America agree to certain articles of Confederation and perpetual Union between the States of New Hampshire, Massachusetts bay, Rhode Island and Providence Plantations, Connecticut, New York, New Jersey, Pennsylvania, Delaware, Maryland, Virginia, North Carolina, South Carolina and Georgia in the Words following, viz.

Articles of Confederation and perpetual Union between the States of New Hampshire, Massachusetts bay, Rhode Island and Providence Plantations, Connecticut, New York, New Jersey, Pennsylvania, Delaware, Maryland, Virginia, North Carolina, South Carolina and Georgia.

Article I. The Stile of this Confederacy shall be "The United States of America."

Article II. Each state retains its sovereignty, freedom, and independence, and every power, jurisdiction, and right, which is not by this Confederation expressly delegated to the United States, in Congress assembled.

Article III. The said States hereby severally enter into a firm league of friendship with each other, for their common defense, the security of their liberties, and their mutual and general welfare, binding themselves to assist each other, against all force offered to, or attacks made upon them, or any of them, on account of religion, sovereignty, trade, or any other pretense whatever.

Article IV. The better to secure and perpetuate mutual friendship and intercourse among the people of the different States in this Union, the free inhabitants of each of these States, paupers, vagabonds, and fugitives from justice excepted, shall be entitled to all privileges and immunities of free citizens in the several States; and the people of each State shall have free ingress and regress to and from any other State, and shall enjoy therein all the privileges of trade and commerce, subject to the same duties, impositions, and restrictions as the inhabitants thereof respectively, provided that such restrictions shall not extend so far as to prevent the removal of property imported into any State, to any other State, of which the owner is an inhabitant; provided also that no imposition, duties or restriction shall be laid by any State, on the property of the United States, or either of them.

If any person guilty of, or charged with, treason, felony, or other high misdemeanor in any State, shall flee from justice, and be found in any of the United States, he shall, upon demand of the Governor or executive power of the State from which he fled, be delivered up and removed to the State having jurisdiction of his offense.

Full faith and credit shall be given in each of these States to the records, acts, and judicial proceedings of the courts and magistrates of every other State.

Article V. For the most convenient management of the general interests of the United States, delegates shall be annually appointed in such manner as the legislatures of each State shall direct, to meet in Congress on the first Monday in November, in every year, with a power reserved to each State to recall its delegates, or any of them, at any time within the year, and to send others in their stead for the remainder of the year.

No State shall be represented in Congress by less than two, nor more than seven members; and no person shall be capable of being a delegate for more than three years in any term of six years; nor shall any person, being a delegate, be capable of holding any office under the United States, for which he, or another for his benefit, receives any salary, fees or emolument of any kind.

Each State shall maintain its own delegates in a meeting of the States, and while they act as members of the committee of the States.

In determining questions in the United States in Congress assembled, each State shall have one vote.

Freedom of speech and debate in Congress shall not be impeached or questioned in any court or place out of Congress, and the members of Congress shall be protected in their persons from arrests or imprisonments, during the time of their going to and from, and attendance on Congress, except for treason, felony, or breach of the peace.

Article VI. No State, without the consent of the United States in Congress assembled, shall send any embassy to, or receive any embassy from, or enter into any conference, agreement, alliance or treaty with any King, Prince or State; nor shall any person holding any office of profit or trust under the United States, or any of them, accept any present, emolument, office or title of any kind whatever from any King, Prince or foreign State; nor shall the United States in Congress assembled, or any of them, grant any title of nobility.

No two or more States shall enter into any treaty, confederation or alliance whatever between them, without the consent of the United States in Congress assembled, specifying accurately the purposes for which the same is to be entered into, and how long it shall continue.

No State shall lay any imposts or duties, which may interfere with any stipulations in treaties, entered into by the United States in Congress assembled, with any King, Prince or State, in pursuance of any treaties already proposed by Congress, to the courts of France and Spain.

No vessel of war shall be kept up in time of peace by any State, except such number only, as shall be deemed necessary by the United States in Congress assembled, for the defense of such State, or its trade; nor shall any body of forces be kept up by any State in time of peace, except such number only, as in the judgment of the United States in Congress assembled, shall be deemed requisite to garrison the forts necessary for the defense of such State; but every State shall always keep up a well-regulated and disciplined militia, sufficiently armed and accoutered, and shall provide and constantly have ready for use, in public stores, a due number of field pieces and tents, and a proper quantity of arms, ammunition and camp equipage.

No State shall engage in any war without the consent of the United States in Congress assembled, unless such State be actually invaded by enemies, or shall have received certain advice of a resolution being formed by some nation of Indians to invade such State, and the danger is so imminent as not to admit of a delay till the United States in Congress assembled can be consulted; nor shall any State grant commissions to any ships or vessels of war, nor letters of marque or reprisal, except it be after a declaration of war by the United States in Congress assembled, and then only against the Kingdom or State and the subjects thereof, against which war has been so declared, and under such regulations as shall be established by the United States in Congress assembled, unless such State be infested by pirates, in which case vessels of war may be fitted out for that occasion, and kept so long as the danger shall continue, or until the United States in Congress assembled shall determine otherwise.

Article VII. When land forces are raised by any State for the common defense, all officers of or under the rank of colonel, shall be appointed by the legislature of each State respectively, by whom such forces shall be raised, or in such manner as such State shall direct, and all vacancies shall be filled up by the State which first made the appointment.

Article VIII. All charges of war, and all other expenses that shall be incurred for the common defense or general welfare, and allowed by the United States in Congress assembled, shall be defrayed out of a common treasury, which shall be supplied by the several States in proportion to the value of all land within each State, granted or surveyed for any person, as such land and the buildings and improvements thereon shall be estimated according to such mode as the United States in Congress assembled, shall from time to time direct and appoint.

The taxes for paying that proportion shall be laid and levied by the authority and direction of the legislatures of the several States within the time agreed upon by the United States in Congress assembled.

Article IX. The United States in Congress assembled, shall have the sole and exclusive right and power of determining on peace and war, except in the cases mentioned in the sixth article—of sending and receiving ambassadors—entering into treaties and alliances, provided that no treaty of commerce shall be made whereby the legislative power of the respective States shall be restrained from imposing such imposts and duties on foreigners, as their own people are subjected to, or from prohibiting the exportation or importation of any species of goods or commodities whatsoever—of establishing rules for deciding in all cases, what captures on land or water shall be legal, and in what manner prizes taken by land or naval forces in the service of the United States shall be divided or appropriated—of granting letters of marque and reprisal in times of peace—appointing courts for the trial of piracies and felonies committed on the high seas and establishing courts for receiving and determining finally appeals in all cases of captures, provided that no member of Congress shall be appointed a judge of any of the said courts.

The United States in Congress assembled shall also be the last resort on appeal in all disputes and differences now subsisting or that hereafter may arise between two or more States concerning boundary, jurisdiction or any other causes whatever; which authority shall always be exercised in the manner following. Whenever the legislative or executive authority or lawful agent of any State in controversy with another shall present a petition to Congress stating the matter in question and praying for a hearing, notice thereof shall be given by order of Congress to the legislative or executive authority of the other State in controversy, and a day assigned for the appearance of the parties by their lawful agents, who shall then be directed to appoint by joint consent, commissioners or judges to constitute a court for hearing and determining the matter in question: but if they cannot agree, Congress shall name three persons out of each of the United States, and from the list of such persons each party shall alternately strike out one, the petitioners beginning, until the number shall be reduced to thirteen; and from that number not less than seven, nor more than nine names as Congress shall direct, shall in the presence of Congress be drawn out by lot, and the persons whose names shall be so drawn or any five of them, shall be commissioners or judges, to hear and finally determine the controversy, so always as a major part of the judges who shall hear the cause shall agree in the determination: and if either party shall neglect to attend at the day appointed, without showing reasons, which Congress shall judge sufficient, or being present shall refuse to strike, the Congress shall proceed to nominate three persons out of each State, and the secretary of Congress shall strike in behalf of such party absent or refusing; and the judgement and sentence of the court to be appointed, in the manner before prescribed, shall be final and conclusive; and if any of the parties shall refuse to submit to the authority of such court, or to appear or defend their claim or cause, the court shall nevertheless proceed to pronounce sentence, or judgement, which shall in like manner be final and decisive, the judgement or sentence and other proceedings being in either case transmitted to Congress, and lodged among the acts of Congress for the security of the parties concerned: provided that every commissioner, before he sits in judgement, shall take an oath to be administered by one of the judges of the supreme or superior court of the State, where the cause shall be tried, 'well and truly to hear and determine the matter in question, according to the best of his judgement, without favor, affection or hope of reward': provided also, that no State shall be deprived of territory for the benefit of the United States.

All controversies concerning the private right of soil claimed under different grants of two or more States, whose jurisdictions as they may respect such lands, and the States which passed such grants are adjusted, the said grants or either of them being at the same time claimed to have originated antecedent to such settlement of jurisdiction, shall on the petition of either party to the Congress of the United States, be finally determined as near as may be in the same manner as is before prescribed for deciding disputes respecting territorial jurisdiction between different States.

The United States in Congress assembled shall also have the sole and exclusive right and power of regulating the alloy and value of coin struck by their own authority, or by that of the respective States—fixing the standards of weights and measures throughout the United States—regulating the trade and managing all affairs with the Indians, not members of any of the States, provided that the legislative right of any State within its own limits be not infringed or violated—establishing or regulating post offices from one State to another, throughout all the United States, and exacting such postage on the papers passing through the same as may be requisite to defray the expenses of the said office—appointing all officers of the land forces, in the service of the United States, excepting regimental officers—appointing all the officers of the naval forces, and commissioning all officers whatever in the service of the United States—making rules for the government and regulation of the said land and naval forces, and directing their operations.

The United States in Congress assembled shall have authority to appoint a committee, to sit in the recess of Congress, to be denominated 'A Committee of the States', and to consist of one delegate from each State; and to appoint such other committees and civil officers as may be necessary for managing the general affairs of the United States under their direction—to appoint one of their members to preside, provided that no person be allowed to serve in the office of president more than one year in any term of three years; to ascertain the necessary sums of money to be raised for the service of the United States, and to appropriate and apply the same for defraying the public expenses—to borrow money, or emit bills on the credit of the United States, transmitting every half-year to the respective States an account of the sums of money so borrowed or emitted—to build and equip a navy—to agree upon the number of land forces, and to make requisitions from each State for its quota, in proportion to the number of white inhabitants in such State; which requisition shall be binding, and thereupon the legislature of each State shall appoint the regimental officers, raise the men and cloath, arm and equip them in a solid-like manner, at the expense of the United States; and the officers and men so cloathed, armed and equipped shall march to the place appointed, and within the time agreed on by the United States in Congress assembled. But if the United States in Congress assembled shall, on consideration of circumstances judge proper that any State should not raise men, or should raise a smaller number of men than the quota thereof, such extra number shall be raised, officered, cloathed, armed and equipped in the same manner as the quota of each State, unless the legislature of such State shall judge that such extra number cannot be safely spread out in the same, in which case they shall raise, officer, cloath, arm and equip as many of such extra number as they judge can be safely spared. And the officers and men so cloathed, armed, and equipped, shall march to the place appointed, and within the time agreed on by the United States in Congress assembled.

The United States in Congress assembled shall never engage in a war, nor grant letters of marque or reprisal in time of peace, nor enter into any treaties or alliances, nor coin money, nor regulate the value thereof, nor ascertain the sums and expenses necessary for the defense and welfare of the United States, or any of them, nor emit bills, nor borrow money on the credit of the United States, nor appropriate money, nor agree upon the number of vessels of war, to be built or purchased, or the number of land or sea forces to be raised, nor appoint a commander in chief of the army or navy, unless nine States assent to the same: nor shall a question on any other point, except for adjourning from day to day be determined, unless by the votes of the majority of the United States in Congress assembled.

The Congress of the United States shall have power to adjourn to any time within the year, and to any place within the United States, so that no period of adjournment be for a longer duration than the space of six months, and shall publish the journal of their proceedings monthly, except such parts thereof relating to treaties, alliances or military operations, as in their judgement require secrecy; and the yeas and nays of the delegates of each State on any question shall be entered on the journal, when it is desired by any delegates of a State, or any of them, at his or their request shall be furnished with a transcript of the said journal, except such parts as are above excepted, to lay before the legislatures of the several States.

Article X. The Committee of the States, or any nine of them, shall be authorized to execute, in the recess of Congress, such of the powers of Congress as the United States in Congress assembled, by the consent of the nine States, shall from time to time think expedient to vest them with; provided that no power be delegated to the said Committee, for the exercise of which, by the Articles of Confederation, the voice of nine States in the Congress of the United States assembled be requisite.

Article XI. Canada acceding to this confederation, and adjoining in the measures of the United States, shall be admitted into, and entitled to all the advantages of this Union; but no other colony shall be admitted into the same, unless such admission be agreed to by nine States.

Article XII. All bills of credit emitted, monies borrowed, and debts contracted by, or under the authority of Congress, before the assembling of the United States, in pursuance of the present confederation, shall be deemed and considered as a charge against the United States, for payment and satisfaction whereof the said United States, and the public faith are hereby solemnly pledged.

Article XIII. Every State shall abide by the determination of the United States in Congress assembled, on all questions which by this confederation are submitted to them. And the Articles of this Confederation shall be inviolably observed by every State, and the Union shall be perpetual; nor shall any alteration at any time hereafter be made in any of them; unless such alteration be agreed to in a Congress of the United States, and be afterwards confirmed by the legislatures of every State.

And Whereas it hath pleased the Great Governor of the World to incline the hearts of the legislatures we respectively represent in Congress, to approve of, and to authorize us to ratify the said Articles of Confederation and perpetual Union. Know Ye that we the undersigned delegates, by virtue of the power and authority to us given for that purpose, do by these presents, in the name and in behalf of our respective constituents, fully and entirely ratify and confirm each and every of the said Articles of Confederation and perpetual Union, and all and singular the matters and things therein contained: And we do further solemnly plight and engage the faith of our respective constituents, that they shall abide by the determinations of the United States in Congress assembled, on all questions, which by the said Confederation are submitted to them. And that the Articles thereof shall be inviolably observed by the States we respectively represent, and that the Union shall be perpetual.

In Witness whereof we have hereunto set our hands in Congress. Done at Philadelphia in the State of Pennsylvania the ninth day of July in the Year of our Lord One Thousand Seven Hundred and Seventy-Eight, and in the Third Year of the independence of America.

On the part and behalf of the State of New Hampshire:

Josiah Bartlett
John Wentworth Junr. August 8th 1778

On the part and behalf of The State of Massachusetts Bay:

John Hancock
Samuel Adams
Elbridge Gerry
Francis Dana
James Lovell
Samuel Holten

On the part and behalf of the State of Rhode Island and Providence Plantations:

William Ellery
Henry Marchant
John Collins

On the part and behalf of the State of Connecticut:

Roger Sherman
Samuel Huntington
Oliver Wolcott
Titus Hosmer
Andrew Adams

On the Part and Behalf of the State of New York:

James Duane
Francis Lewis
Wm Duer
Gouv Morris

On the Part and in Behalf of the State of New Jersey, November 26, 1778.

Jno Witherspoon
Nath. Scudder

On the part and behalf of the State of Pennsylvania:

Robt Morris
Daniel Roberdeau
John Bayard Smith
William Clingan
Joseph Reed 22nd July 1778

On the part and behalf of the State of Delaware:

Tho Mckean February 12, 1779
John Dickinson May 5th 1779
Nicholas Van Dyke

On the part and behalf of the State of Maryland:

John Hanson March 1 1781
Daniel Carroll

On the Part and Behalf of the State of Virginia:

Richard Henry Lee
John Banister
Thomas Adams
Jno Harvie
Francis Lightfoot Lee

On the part and Behalf of the State of No Carolina:

John Penn July 21st 1778
Corns Harnett
Jno Williams

On the part and behalf of the State of South Carolina:

Henry Laurens
William Henry Drayton
Jno Mathews
Richd Hutson
Thos Heyward Junr

On the part and behalf of the State of Georgia:

Jno Walton 24th July 1778
Edwd Telfair
Edwd Langworthy

Appendix IV: The Constitution of the United States

We the People of the United States, in Order to form a more perfect Union, establish Justice, insure domestic Tranquility, provide for the common defense, promote the general Welfare, and secure the Blessings of Liberty to ourselves and our Posterity, do ordain and establish this Constitution for the United States of America.

Article I

Section 1. All legislative Powers herein granted shall be vested in a Congress of the United States, which shall consist of a Senate and House of Representatives.

Section 2. The House of Representatives shall be composed of Members chosen every second Year by the People of the several States, and the Electors in each State shall have the Qualifications requisite for Electors of the most numerous Branch of the State Legislature.

No Person shall be a Representative who shall not have attained to the Age of twenty five Years, and been seven Years a Citizen of the United States, and who shall not, when elected, be an Inhabitant of that State in which he shall be chosen.

Representatives and direct Taxes shall be apportioned among the several States which may be included within this Union, according to their respective Numbers, which shall be determined by adding to the whole Number of free Persons, including those bound to Service for a Term of Years, and excluding Indians not taxed, three fifths of all other Persons. The actual Enumeration shall be made within three Years after the first Meeting of the Congress of the United States, and within every subsequent Term of ten Years, in such Manner as they shall by Law direct. The Number of Representatives shall not exceed one for every thirty Thousand, but each State shall have at Least one Representative; and until such enumeration shall be made, the State of New Hampshire shall be entitled to chuse three, Massachusetts eight, Rhode-Island and Providence Plantations one, Connecticut five, New-York six, New Jersey four, Pennsylvania eight, Delaware one, Maryland six, Virginia ten, North Carolina five, South Carolina five, and Georgia three.

When vacancies happen in the Representation from any State, the Executive Authority thereof shall issue Writs of Election to fill such Vacancies.

The House of Representatives shall chuse their Speaker and other Officers; and shall have the sole Power of Impeachment.

Section 3. The Senate of the United States shall be composed of two Senators from each State, chosen by the Legislature thereof for six Years; and each Senator shall have one Vote.

Immediately after they shall be assembled in Consequence of the first Election, they shall be divided as equally as may be into three Classes. The Seats of the Senators of the first Class shall be vacated at the Expiration of the second Year, of the second Class at the Expiration of the fourth Year, and of the third Class at the Expiration of the sixth Year, so that one third may be chosen every second Year; and if Vacancies happen by Resignation, or otherwise, during the Recess of the Legislature of any State, the Executive thereof may make temporary Appointments until the next Meeting of the Legislature, which shall then fill such Vacancies.

No Person shall be a Senator who shall not have attained to the Age of thirty Years, and been nine Years a Citizen of the United States, and who shall not, when elected, be an Inhabitant of that State for which he shall be chosen.

The Vice President of the United States shall be President of the Senate, but shall have no Vote, unless they be equally divided.

The Senate shall chuse their other Officers, and also a President pro tempore, in the Absence of the Vice President, or when he shall exercise the Office of President of the United States.

The Senate shall have the sole Power to try all Impeachments. When sitting for that Purpose, they shall be on Oath or Affirmation. When the President of the United States is tried, the Chief Justice shall preside: And no Person shall be convicted without the Concurrence of two thirds of the Members present.

Judgment in Cases of Impeachment shall not extend further than to removal from Office, and disqualification to hold and enjoy any Office of honor, Trust or Profit under the United States: but the Party convicted shall nevertheless be liable and subject to Indictment, Trial, Judgment and Punishment, according to Law.

Section 4. The Times, Places and Manner of holding Elections for Senators and Representatives, shall be prescribed in each State by the Legislature thereof; but the Congress may at any time by Law make or alter such Regulations, except as to the Places of chusing Senators.

The Congress shall assemble at least once in every Year, and such Meeting shall be on the first Monday in December, unless they shall by Law appoint a different Day.

Section 5. Each House shall be the Judge of the Elections, Returns and Qualifications of its own Members, and a Majority of each shall constitute a Quorum to do Business; but a smaller Number may adjourn from day to day, and may be authorized to compel the Attendance of absent Members, in such Manner, and under such Penalties as each House may provide.

Each House may determine the Rules of its Proceedings, punish its Members for disorderly Behaviour, and, with the Concurrence of two thirds, expel a Member.

Each House shall keep a Journal of its Proceedings, and from time to time publish the same, excepting such Parts as may in their Judgment require Secrecy; and the Yeas and Nays of the Members of either House on any question shall, at the Desire of one fifth of those Present, be entered on the Journal.

Neither House, during the Session of Congress, shall, without the Consent of the other, adjourn for more than three days, nor to any other Place than that in which the two Houses shall be sitting.

Section 6. The Senators and Representatives shall receive a Compensation for their Services, to be ascertained by Law, and paid out of the Treasury of the United States. They shall in all Cases, except Treason, Felony and Breach of the Peace, be privileged from Arrest during their Attendance at the Session of their respective Houses, and in going to and returning from the same; and for any Speech or Debate in either House, they shall not be questioned in any other Place.

No Senator or Representative shall, during the Time for which he was elected, be appointed to any civil Office under the Authority of the United States, which shall have been created, or the Emoluments whereof shall have been encreased during such time; and no Person holding any Office under the United States, shall be a Member of either House during his Continuance in Office.

Section 7. All Bills for raising Revenue shall originate in the House of Representatives; but the Senate may propose or concur with Amendments as on other Bills.

Every Bill which shall have passed the House of Representatives and the Senate, shall, before it become a Law, be presented to the President of the United States: If he approve he shall sign it, but if not he shall return it, with his Objections to that House in which it shall have originated, who shall enter the Objections at large on their Journal, and proceed to reconsider it. If after such Reconsideration two thirds of that House shall agree to pass the Bill, it shall be sent, together with the Objections, to the other House, by which it shall likewise be reconsidered, and if approved by two thirds of that House, it shall become a Law. But in all such Cases the Votes of both Houses shall be determined by yeas and Nays, and the Names of the Persons voting for and against the Bill shall be entered on the Journal of each House respectively. If any Bill shall not be returned by the President within ten Days (Sundays excepted) after it shall have been presented to him, the Same shall be a Law, in like Manner as if he had signed it, unless the Congress by their Adjournment prevent its Return, in which Case it shall not be a Law.

Every Order, Resolution, or Vote to which the Concurrence of the Senate and House of Representatives may be necessary (except on a question of Adjournment) shall be presented to the President of the United States; and before the Same shall take Effect, shall be approved by him, or being disapproved by him, shall be repassed by two thirds of the Senate and House of Representatives, according to the Rules and Limitations prescribed in the Case of a Bill.

Section 8. The Congress shall have Power To lay and collect Taxes, Duties, Imposts and Excises, to pay the Debts and provide for the common Defence and general Welfare of the United States; but all Duties, Imposts and Excises shall be uniform throughout the United States;

To borrow Money on the credit of the United States;

To regulate Commerce with foreign Nations, and among the several States, and with the Indian Tribes;

To establish an uniform Rule of Naturalization, and uniform Laws on the subject of Bankruptcies throughout the United States;

To coin Money, regulate the Value thereof, and of foreign Coin, and fix the Standard of Weights and Measures;

To provide for the Punishment of counterfeiting the Securities and current Coin of the United States;

To establish Post Offices and post Roads;

To promote the Progress of Science and useful Arts, by securing for limited Times to Authors and Inventors the exclusive Right to their respective Writings and Discoveries;

To constitute Tribunals inferior to the supreme Court;

To define and punish Piracies and Felonies committed on the high Seas, and Offences against the Law of Nations;

To declare War, grant Letters of Marque and Reprisal, and make Rules concerning Captures on Land and Water;

To raise and support Armies, but no Appropriation of Money to that Use shall be for a longer Term than two Years;

To provide and maintain a Navy;

To make Rules for the Government and Regulation of the land and naval Forces;

To provide for calling forth the Militia to execute the Laws of the Union, suppress Insurrections and repel Invasions;

To provide for organizing, arming, and disciplining, the Militia, and for governing such Part of them as may be employed in the Service of the United States, reserving to the States respectively, the Appointment of the Officers, and the Authority of training the Militia according to the discipline prescribed by Congress;

To exercise exclusive Legislation in all Cases whatsoever, over such District (not exceeding ten Miles square) as may, by Cession of particular States, and the Acceptance of Congress, become the Seat of the Government of the United States, and to exercise like Authority over all Places purchased by the Consent of the Legislature of the State in which the Same shall be, for the Erection of Forts, Magazines, Arsenals, dock-Yards, and other needful Buildings;—And

To make all Laws which shall be necessary and proper for carrying into Execution the foregoing Powers, and all other Powers vested by this Constitution in the Government of the United States, or in any Department or Officer thereof.

Section 9. The Migration or Importation of such Persons as any of the States now existing shall think proper to admit, shall not be prohibited by the Congress prior to the Year one thousand eight hundred and eight, but a Tax or duty may be imposed on such Importation, not exceeding ten dollars for each Person.

The Privilege of the Writ of Habeas Corpus shall not be suspended, unless when in Cases of Rebellion or Invasion the public Safety may require it.

No Bill of Attainder or ex post facto Law shall be passed.

No Capitation, or other direct, Tax shall be laid, unless in Proportion to the Census or enumeration herein before directed to be taken.

No Tax or Duty shall be laid on Articles exported from any State.

No Preference shall be given by any Regulation of Commerce or Revenue to the Ports of one State over those of another; nor shall Vessels bound to, or from, one State, be obliged to enter, clear, or pay Duties in another.

No Money shall be drawn from the Treasury, but in Consequence of Appropriations made by Law; and a regular Statement and Account of the Receipts and Expenditures of all public Money shall be published from time to time.

No Title of Nobility shall be granted by the United States: And no Person holding any Office of Profit or Trust under them, shall, without the Consent of the Congress, accept of any present, Emolument, Office, or Title, of any kind whatever, from any King, Prince, or foreign State.

Section 10. No State shall enter into any Treaty, Alliance, or Confederation; grant Letters of Marque and Reprisal; coin Money; emit Bills of Credit; make any Thing but gold and silver Coin a Tender in Payment of Debts; pass any Bill of Attainder, ex post facto Law, or Law impairing the Obligation of Contracts, or grant any Title of Nobility.

No State shall, without the Consent of the Congress, lay any Imposts or Duties on Imports or Exports, except what may be absolutely necessary for executing it's inspection Laws: and the net Produce of all Duties and Imposts, laid by any State on Imports or Exports, shall be for the Use of the Treasury of the United States; and all such Laws shall be subject to the Revision and Controul of the Congress.

No State shall, without the Consent of Congress, lay any Duty of Tonnage, keep Troops, or Ships of War in time of Peace, enter into any Agreement or Compact with another State, or with a foreign Power, or engage in War, unless actually invaded, or in such imminent Danger as will not admit of delay.

Article II

Section 1. The executive Power shall be vested in a President of the United States of America. He shall hold his Office during the Term of four Years, and, together with the Vice President, chosen for the same Term, be elected, as follows:

Each State shall appoint, in such Manner as the Legislature thereof may direct, a Number of Electors, equal to the whole Number of Senators and Representatives to which the State may be entitled in the Congress: but no Senator or Representative, or Person holding an Office of Trust or Profit under the United States, shall be appointed an Elector.

The Electors shall meet in their respective States, and vote by Ballot for two Persons, of whom one at least shall not be an Inhabitant of the same State with themselves. And they shall make a List of all the Persons voted for, and of the Number of Votes for each; which List they shall sign and certify, and transmit sealed to the Seat of the Government of the United States, directed to the President of the Senate. The President of the Senate shall, in the Presence of the Senate and House of Representatives, open all the Certificates, and the Votes shall then be counted. The Person having the greatest Number of Votes shall be the President, if such Number be a Majority of the whole Number of Electors appointed; and if there be more than one who have such Majority, and have an equal Number of Votes, then the House of Representatives shall immediately chuse by Ballot one of them for President; and if no Person have a Majority, then from the five highest on the List the said House shall in like Manner chuse the President. But in chusing the President, the Votes shall be taken by States, the Representation from each State having one Vote; A quorum for this purpose shall consist of a Member or Members from two thirds of the States, and a Majority of all the States shall be necessary to a Choice. In every Case, after the Choice of the President, the Person having the greatest Number of Votes of the Electors shall be the Vice President. But if there should remain two or more who have equal Votes, the Senate shall chuse from them by Ballot the Vice President.

The Congress may determine the Time of chusing the Electors, and the Day on which they shall give their Votes; which Day shall be the same throughout the United States.

No Person except a natural born Citizen, or a Citizen of the United States, at the time of the Adoption of this Constitution, shall be eligible to the Office of President; neither shall any Person be eligible to that Office who shall not have attained to the Age of thirty five Years, and been fourteen Years a Resident within the United States.

In Case of the Removal of the President from Office, or of his Death, Resignation, or Inability to discharge the Powers and Duties of the said Office, the Same shall devolve on the Vice President, and the Congress may by Law provide for the Case of Removal, Death, Resignation or Inability, both of the President and Vice President, declaring what Officer shall then act as President, and such Officer shall act accordingly, until the Disability be removed, or a President shall be elected.

The President shall, at stated Times, receive for his Services, a Compensation, which shall neither be increased nor diminished during the Period for which he shall have been elected, and he shall not receive within that Period any other Emolument from the United States, or any of them.

Before he enter on the Execution of his Office, he shall take the following Oath or Affirmation:—"I do solemnly swear (or affirm) that I will faithfully execute the Office of President of the United States, and will to the best of my Ability, preserve, protect and defend the Constitution of the United States."

Section 2. The President shall be Commander in Chief of the Army and Navy of the United States, and of the Militia of the several States, when called into the actual Service of the United States; he may require the Opinion, in writing, of the principal Officer in each of the executive Departments, upon any Subject relating to the Duties of their respective Offices, and he shall have Power to grant Reprieves and Pardons for Offences against the United States, except in Cases of Impeachment.

He shall have Power, by and with the Advice and Consent of the Senate, to make Treaties, provided two thirds of the Senators present concur; and he shall nominate, and by and with the Advice and Consent of the Senate, shall appoint Ambassadors, other public Ministers and Consuls, Judges of the supreme Court, and all other Officers of the United States, whose Appointments are not herein otherwise provided for, and which shall be established by Law: but the Congress may by Law vest the Appointment of such inferior Officers, as they think proper, in the President alone, in the Courts of Law, or in the Heads of Departments.

The President shall have Power to fill up all Vacancies that may happen during the Recess of the Senate, by granting Commissions which shall expire at the End of their next Session.

Section 3. He shall from time to time give to the Congress Information of the State of the Union, and recommend to their Consideration such Measures as he shall judge necessary and expedient; he may, on extraordinary Occasions, convene both Houses, or either of them, and in Case of Disagreement between them, with Respect to the Time of Adjournment, he may adjourn them to such Time as he shall think proper; he shall receive Ambassadors and other public Ministers; he shall take Care that the Laws be faithfully executed, and shall Commission all the Officers of the United States.

Section 4. The President, Vice President and all civil Officers of the United States, shall be removed from Office on Impeachment for, and Conviction of, Treason, Bribery, or other high Crimes and Misdemeanors.

Article III

Section 1. The judicial Power of the United States shall be vested in one supreme Court, and in such inferior Courts as the Congress may from time to time ordain and establish. The Judges, both of the supreme and inferior Courts, shall hold their Offices during good Behaviour, and shall, at stated Times, receive for their Services a Compensation, which shall not be diminished during their Continuance in Office.

Section 2. The judicial Power shall extend to all Cases, in Law and Equity, arising under this Constitution, the Laws of the United States, and Treaties made, or which shall be made, under their Authority;—to all Cases affecting Ambassadors, other public Ministers and Consuls;—to all Cases of admiralty and maritime Jurisdiction;—to Controversies to which the United States shall be a Party;—to Controversies between two or more States;—between a State and Citizens of another State;—between Citizens of different States;—between Citizens of the same State claiming Lands under Grants of different States, and between a State, or the Citizens thereof, and foreign States, Citizens or Subjects.

In all Cases affecting Ambassadors, other public Ministers and Consuls, and those in which a State shall be Party, the supreme Court shall have original Jurisdiction. In all the other Cases before mentioned, the supreme Court shall have appellate Jurisdiction, both as to Law and Fact, with such Exceptions, and under such Regulations as the Congress shall make.

The Trial of all Crimes, except in Cases of Impeachment, shall be by Jury; and such Trial shall be held in the State where the said Crimes shall have been committed; but when not committed within any State, the Trial shall be at such Place or Places as the Congress may by Law have directed.

Section 3. Treason against the United States, shall consist only in levying War against them, or in adhering to their Enemies, giving them Aid and Comfort. No Person shall be convicted of Treason unless on the Testimony of two Witnesses to the same overt Act, or on Confession in open Court.

The Congress shall have Power to declare the Punishment of Treason, but no Attainder of Treason shall work Corruption of Blood, or Forfeiture except during the Life of the Person attainted.

Article IV

Section 1. Full Faith and Credit shall be given in each State to the public Acts, Records, and judicial Proceedings of every other State. And the Congress may by general Laws prescribe the Manner in which such Acts, Records and Proceedings shall be proved, and the Effect thereof.

Section 2. The Citizens of each State shall be entitled to all Privileges and Immunities of Citizens in the several States.

A Person charged in any State with Treason, Felony, or other Crime, who shall flee from Justice, and be found in another State, shall on Demand of the executive Authority of the State from which he fled, be delivered up, to be removed to the State having Jurisdiction of the Crime.

No Person held to Service or Labour in one State, under the Laws thereof, escaping into another, shall, in Consequence of any Law or Regulation therein, be discharged from such Service or Labour, but shall be delivered up on Claim of the Party to whom such Service or Labour may be due.

Section 3. New States may be admitted by the Congress into this Union; but no new State shall be formed or erected within the Jurisdiction of any other State; nor any State be formed by the Junction of two or more States, or Parts of States, without the Consent of the Legislatures of the States concerned as well as of the Congress.

The Congress shall have Power to dispose of and make all needful Rules and Regulations respecting the Territory or other Property belonging to the United States; and nothing in this Constitution shall be so construed as to Prejudice any Claims of the United States, or of any particular State.

Section 4. The United States shall guarantee to every State in this Union a Republican Form of Government, and shall protect each of them against Invasion; and on Application of the Legislature, or of the Executive (when the Legislature cannot be convened), against domestic Violence.

Article V

The Congress, whenever two thirds of both Houses shall deem it necessary, shall propose Amendments to this Constitution, or, on the Application of the Legislatures of two thirds of the several States, shall call a Convention for proposing Amendments, which, in either Case, shall be valid to all Intents and Purposes, as Part of this Constitution, when ratified by the Legislatures of three fourths of the several States, or by Conventions in three fourths thereof, as the one or the other Mode of Ratification may be proposed by the Congress; Provided that no Amendment which may be made prior to the Year One thousand eight hundred and eight shall in any Manner affect the first and fourth Clauses in the Ninth Section of the first Article; and that no State, without its Consent, shall be deprived of its equal Suffrage in the Senate.

Article VI

All Debts contracted and Engagements entered into, before the Adoption of this Constitution, shall be as valid against the United States under this Constitution, as under the Confederation.

This Constitution, and the Laws of the United States which shall be made in Pursuance thereof; and all Treaties made, or which shall be made, under the Authority of the United States, shall be the supreme Law of the Land; and the Judges in every State shall be bound thereby, any Thing in the Constitution or Laws of any State to the Contrary notwithstanding.

The Senators and Representatives before mentioned, and the Members of the several State Legislatures, and all executive and judicial Officers, both of the United States and of the several States, shall be bound by Oath or Affirmation, to support this Constitution; but no religious Test shall ever be required as a Qualification to any Office or public Trust under the United States.

Article VII

The Ratification of the Conventions of nine States, shall be sufficient for the Establishment of this Constitution between the States so ratifying the Same.

Done in Convention by the Unanimous Consent of the States present the Seventeenth Day of September in the Year of our Lord one thousand seven hundred and Eighty seven and of the Independence of the United States of America the Twelfth. In Witness whereof We have hereunto subscribed our Names.*

George Washington–President and deputy from Virginia

New Hampshire

John Langdon
Nicholas Gilman

Massachusetts

Nathaniel Gorham
Rufus King

Connecticut

>William Samuel Johnson
>Roger Sherman

New York

>Alexander Hamilton

New Jersey

>William Livingston
>David Brearley
>William Paterson
>Jonathan Dayton

Pennsylvania

>Benjamin Franklin
>Thomas Mifflin
>Robert Morris
>George Clymer
>Thomas FitzSimmons
>Jared Ingersoll
>James Wilson
>Gouverneur Morris

Delaware

>George Read
>Gunning Bedford, Jr.
>John Dickinson
>Richard Bassett
>Jacob Broom

Maryland

>James McHenry
>Daniel of Saint Thomas
>Jenifer
>Daniel Carroll

Virginia

>John Blair
>James Madison Jr.

North Carolina

>William Blount
>Richard Dobbs Spaight
>Hugh Williamson

South Carolina

>John Rutledge
>Charles Cotesworth Pinckney
>Charles Pinckney
>Pierce Butler

Georgia

>William Few
>Abraham Baldwin

Amendments to the Constitution**

Amendment I

Congress shall make no law respecting an establishment of religion, or prohibiting the free exercise thereof; or abridging the freedom of speech, or of the press; or the right of the people peaceably to assemble, and to petition the Government for a redress of grievances.

Amendment II

A well regulated Militia, being necessary to the security of a free State, the right of the people to keep and bear Arms, shall not be infringed.

Amendment III

No Soldier shall, in time of peace be quartered in any house, without the consent of the Owner, nor in time of war, but in a manner to be prescribed by law.

Amendment IV

The right of the people to be secure in their persons, houses, papers, and effects, against unreasonable searches and seizures, shall not be violated, and no Warrants shall issue, but upon probable cause, supported by Oath or affirmation, and particularly describing the place to be searched, and the persons or things to be seized.

Amendment V

No person shall be held to answer for a capital, or otherwise infamous crime, unless on a presentment or indictment of a Grand Jury, except in cases arising in the land or naval forces, or in the Militia, when in actual service in time of War or public danger; nor shall any person be subject for the same offense to be twice put in jeopardy of life or limb; nor shall be compelled in any criminal case to be a witness against himself, nor be deprived of life, liberty, or property, without due process of law; nor shall private property be taken for public use, without just compensation.

Amendment VI

In all criminal prosecutions, the accused shall enjoy the right to a speedy and public trial, by an impartial jury of the State and district wherein the crime shall have been committed, which district shall have been previously ascertained by law, and to be informed of the nature and cause of the accusation; to be confronted with the witnesses against him; to have compulsory process for obtaining witnesses in his favor, and to have the Assistance of Counsel for his defence.

Amendment VII

In Suits at common law, where the value in controversy shall exceed twenty dollars, the right of trial by jury shall be preserved, and no fact tried by a jury, shall be otherwise re-examined in any Court of the United States, than according to the rules of the common law.

Amendment VIII

Excessive bail shall not be required, nor excessive fines imposed, nor cruel and unusual punishments inflicted.

Amendment IX

The enumeration in the Constitution, of certain rights, shall not be construed to deny or disparage others retained by the people.

Amendment X

The powers not delegated to the United States by the Constitution, nor prohibited by it to the States, are reserved to the States respectively, or to the people.

Amendment XI (Ratified January 8, 1798)

The Judicial power of the United States shall not be construed to extend to any suit in law or equity, commenced or prosecuted against one of the United States by Citizens of another State, or by Citizens or Subjects of any Foreign State.

Amendment XII (Ratified September 25, 1804)

The Electors shall meet in their respective states, and vote by ballot for President and Vice-President, one of whom, at least, shall not be an inhabitant of the same state with themselves; they shall name in their ballots the person voted for as President, and in distinct ballots the person voted for as Vice-President, and they shall make distinct lists of all persons voted for as President, and of all persons voted for as Vice-President and of the number of votes for each, which lists they shall sign and certify, and transmit sealed to the seat of the government of the United States, directed to the President of the Senate;

The President of the Senate shall, in the presence of the Senate and House of Representatives, open all the certificates and the votes shall then be counted;

The person having the greatest Number of votes for President, shall be the President, if such number be a majority of the whole number of Electors appointed; and if no person have such majority, then from the persons having the highest numbers not exceeding three on the list of those voted for as President, the House of Representatives shall choose immediately, by ballot, the President. But in choosing the President, the votes shall be taken by states, the representation from each state having one vote; a quorum for this purpose shall consist of a member or members from two-thirds of the states, and a majority of all the states shall be necessary to a choice. And if the House of Representatives shall not choose a President whenever the right of choice shall devolve upon them, before the fourth day of March next following, then the Vice-President shall act as President, as in the case of the death or other constitutional disability of the President.

The person having the greatest number of votes as Vice-President, shall be the Vice-President, if such number be a majority of the whole number of Electors appointed, and if no person have a majority, then from the two highest numbers on the list, the Senate shall choose the Vice-President; a quorum for the purpose shall consist of two-thirds of the whole number of Senators, and a majority of the whole number shall be necessary to a choice. But no person constitutionally ineligible to the office of President shall be eligible to that of Vice-President of the United States.

Amendment XIII (Ratified December 18, 1865)

Section 1. Neither slavery nor involuntary servitude, except as a punishment for crime whereof the party shall have been duly convicted, shall exist within the United States, or any place subject to their jurisdiction.

Section 2. Congress shall have power to enforce this article by appropriate legislation.

Amendment XIV (Ratified July 28, 1868)

Section 1. All persons born or naturalized in the United States, and subject to the jurisditcion thereof, are citizens of the United States and of the State wherein they reside. No State shall make or enforce any law which shall abridge the privileges or immunities of citizens of the United States; nor shall any State deprive any person of life, liberty, or property, without due process of law; nor deny to any person within its jurisdiction the equal protection of the laws.

Section 2. Representatives shall be apportioned among the several States according to their respective numbers, counting the whole number of persons in each State, excluding Indians not taxed. But when the right to vote at any election for the choice of electors for President and Vice-President of the United States, Representatives in Congress, the Executive and Judicial officers of a State, or the members of the Legislature thereof, is denied to any of the male inhabitants of such State, being twenty-one years of age, and citizens of the United States, or in any way abridged, except for participation in rebellion, or other crime, the basis of representation therein shall be reduced in the proportion which the number of such male citizens shall bear to the whole number of male citizens twenty-one years of age in such State.

Section 3. No person shall be a Senator or Representative in Congress, or elector of President and Vice-President, or hold any office, civil or military, under the United States, or under any State, who, having previously taken an oath, as a member of Congress, or as an officer of the United States, or as a member of any State legislature, or as an executive or judicial officer of any State, to support the Constitution of the United States, shall have engaged in insurrection or rebellion against the same, or given aid or comfort to the enemies thereof. But Congress may by a vote of two-thirds of each House, remove such disability.

Section 4. The validity of the public debt of the United States, authorized by law, including debts incurred for payment of pensions and bounties for services in suppressing insurrection or rebellion, shall not be questioned. But neither the United States nor any State shall assume or pay any debt or obligation incurred in aid of insurrection or rebellion against the United States, or any claim for the loss or emancipation of any slave; but all such debts, obligations and claims shall be held illegal and void.

Section 5. The Congress shall have power to enforce, by appropriate legislation, the provisions of this article.

Amendment XV (Ratified March 30, 1870)

Section 1. The right of citizens of the United States to vote shall not be denied or abridged by the United States or by any State on account of race, color, or previous condition of servitude.

Section 2. The Congress shall have power to enforce this article by appropriate legislation.

Amendment XVI (Ratified February 25, 1913)

The Congress shall have power to lay and collect taxes on incomes, from whatever source derived, without apportionment among the several States, and without regard to any census or enumeration.

Amendment XVII (Ratified May 31, 1913)

The Senate of the United States shall be composed of two Senators from each State, elected by the people thereof, for six years; and each Senator shall have one vote. The electors in each State shall have the qualifications requisite for electors of the most numerous branch of the State legislatures.

When vacancies happen in the representation of any State in the Senate, the executive authority of such State shall issue writs of election to fill such vacancies: Provided, That the legislature of any State may empower the executive thereof to make temporary appointments until the people fill the vacancies by election as the legislature may direct.

This amendment shall not be so construed as to affect the election or term of any Senator chosen before it becomes valid as part of the Constitution.

Amendment XVIII (Ratified January 29, 1919)

Section 1. After one year from the ratification of this article the manufacture, sale, or transportation of intoxicating liquors within, the importation thereof into, or the exportation thereof from the United States and all territory subject to the jurisdiction thereof for beverage purposes is hereby prohibited.

Section 2. The Congress and the several States shall have concurrent power to enforce this article by appropriate legislation.

Section 3. This article shall be inoperative unless it shall have been ratified as an amendment to the Constitution by the legislatures of the several States, as provided in the Constitution, within seven years from the date of the submission hereof to the States by the Congress.

Amendment XIX (Ratified August 26, 1920)

The right of citizens of the United States to vote shall not be denied or abridged by the United States or by any State on account of sex.

Congress shall have power to enforce this article by appropriate legislation.

Amendment XX (Ratified February 6, 1933)

Section 1. The terms of the President and Vice President shall end at noon on the 20th day of January, and the terms of Senators and Representatives at noon on the 3d day of January, of the years in which such terms would have ended if this article had not been ratified; and the terms of their successors shall then begin.

Section 2. The Congress shall assemble at least once in every year, and such meeting shall begin at noon on the 3d day of January, unless they shall by law appoint a different day.

Section 3. If, at the time fixed for the beginning of the term of the President, the President elect shall have died, the Vice President elect shall become President. If a President shall not have been chosen before the time fixed for the beginning of his term, or if the President elect shall have failed to qualify, then the Vice President elect shall act as President until a President shall have qualified; and the Congress may by law provide for the case wherein neither a President elect nor a Vice President elect shall have qualified, declaring who shall then act as President, or the manner in which one who is to act shall be selected, and such person shall act accordingly until a President or Vice President shall have qualified.

Section 4. The Congress may by law provide for the case of the death of any of the persons from whom the House of Representatives may choose a President whenever the right of choice shall have devolved upon them, and for the case of the death of any of the persons from whom the Senate may choose a Vice President whenever the right of choice shall have devolved upon them.

Section 5. Sections 1 and 2 shall take effect on the 15th day of October following the ratification of this article.

Section 6. This article shall be inoperative unless it shall have been ratified as an amendment to the Constitution by the legislatures of three-fourths of the several States within seven years from the date of its submission.

Amendment XXI (Ratified December 5, 1933)

Section 1. The eighteenth article of amendment to the Constitution of the United States is hereby repealed.

Section 2. The transportation or importation into any State, Territory, or possession of the United States for delivery or use therein of intoxicating liquors, in violation of the laws thereof, is hereby prohibited.

Section 3. The article shall be inoperative unless it shall have been ratified as an amendment to the Constitution by conventions in the several States, as provided in the Constitution, within seven years from the date of the submission hereof to the States by the Congress.

Amendment XXII (Ratified February 27, 1951)

Section 1. No person shall be elected to the office of the President more than twice, and no person who has held the office of President, or acted as President, for more than two years of a term to which some other person was elected President shall be elected to the office of the President more than once. But this Article shall not apply to any person holding the office of President, when this Article was proposed by the Congress, and shall not prevent any person who may be holding the office of President, or acting as President, during the term within which this Article becomes operative from holding the office of President or acting as President during the remainder of such term.

Section 2. This article shall be inoperative unless it shall have been ratified as an amendment to the Constitution by the legislatures of three-fourths of the several States within seven years from the date of its submission to the States by the Congress.

Amendment XXIII (Ratified March 29, 1961)

Section 1. The District constituting the seat of Government of the United States shall appoint in such manner as the Congress may direct:

A number of electors of President and Vice President equal to the whole number of Senators and Representatives in Congress to which the District would be entitled if it were a State, but in no event more than the least populous State; they shall be in addition to those appointed by the States, but they shall be considered, for the purposes of the election of President and Vice President, to be electors appointed by a State; and they shall meet in the District and perform such duties as provided by the twelfth article of amendment.

Section 2. The Congress shall have power to enforce this article by appropriate legislation.

Amendment XXIV (Ratified January 23, 1964)

Section 1. The right of citizens of the United States to vote in any primary or other election for President or Vice President, for electors for President or Vice President, or for Senator or Representative in Congress, shall not be denied or abridged by the United States or any State by reason of failure to pay any poll tax or other tax.

Section 2. The Congress shall have power to enforce this article by appropriate legislation.

Amendment XXV (Ratified February 10, 1967)

Section 1. In case of the removal of the President from office or of his death or resignation, the Vice President shall become President.

Section 2. Whenever there is a vacancy in the office of the Vice President, the President shall nominate a Vice President who shall take office upon confirmation by a majority vote of both Houses of Congress.

Section 3. Whenever the President transmits to the President pro tempore of the Senate and the Speaker of the House of Representatives his written declaration that he is unable to discharge the powers and duties of his office, and until he transmits to them a written declaration to the contrary, such powers and duties shall be discharged by the Vice President as Acting President.

Section 4. Whenever the Vice President and a majority of either the principal officers of the executive departments or of such other body as Congress may by law provide, transmit to the President pro tempore of the Senate and the Speaker of the House of Representatives their written declaration that the President is unable to discharge the powers and duties of his office, the Vice President shall immediately assume the powers and duties of the office as Acting President.

Thereafter, when the President transmits to the President pro tempore of the Senate and the Speaker of the House of Representatives his written declaration that no inability exists, he shall resume the powers and duties of his office unless the Vice President and a majority of either the principal officers of the executive department or of such other body as Congress may by law provide, transmit within four days to the President pro tempore of the Senate and the Speaker of the House of Representatives their written declaration that the President is unable to discharge the powers and duties of his office. Thereupon Congress shall decide the issue, assembling within forty eight hours for that purpose if not in session. If the Congress, within twenty one days after receipt of the latter written declaration, or, if Congress is not in session, within twenty one days after Congress is required to assemble, determines by two thirds vote of both Houses that the President is unable to discharge the powers and duties of his office, the Vice President shall continue to discharge the same as Acting President; otherwise, the President shall resume the powers and duties of his office.

Amendment XXVI (Ratified June 30, 1971)

Section 1. The right of citizens of the United States, who are eighteen years of age or older, to vote shall not be denied or abridged by the United States or by any State on account of age.

Section 2. The Congress shall have power to enforce this article by appropriate legislation.

Amendment XXVII (Ratified May 14, 1992)

No law varying the compensation for the Services of the Senators and Representatives shall take effect, until an election of Representative shall have intervened.

Notes

* Abbreviated signatures spelled out.
** First ten amendments (Bill of Rights) declared ratified on December 15, 1791.

Appendix V: Justices of the United States Supreme Court

(Chief Justice in Italics)

Justice	Appointed by	Term of Service
1. *John Jay*	George Washington	1789–1795
2. John Rutledge[1]	"	1789–1791
3. William Cushing	"	1789–1810
4. James Wilson	"	1789–1798
5. John Blair	"	1789–1796
6. Robert H. Harrison[2]	"	1789–1790
7. James Iredell	"	1790–1799
8. Thomas Johnson	"	1791–1793
9. William Paterson	"	1793–1806
10. *John Rutledge[3]*	"	1795
11. Samuel Chase	"	1796–1811
12. *Oliver Ellsworth*	"	1796–1811
13. Bushrod Washington	John Adams	1798–1829
14. Alfred Moore	"	1799–1804
15. *John Marshall*	"	1801–1835
16. William Johnson	Thomas Jefferson	1804–1834
17. Brockholst Livingston	"	1806–1823
18. Thomas Todd	"	1807–1826
19. Joseph Story	James Madison	1811–1845
20. Gabriel Duvall	"	1812–1835
21. Smith Thompson	James Monroe	1823–1843
22. Robert Trimble	John Quincy Adams	1826–1828
23. John McLean	Andrew Jackson	1829–1861
24. Henry Baldwin	"	1830–1844
25. James M. Wayne	"	1835–1867
26. Philip P. Barbour	"	1836–1841
27. *Roger B. Taney*	"	1836–1864
28. John Catron	"	1837–1865

(*Continued*)

Justice	Appointed by	Term of Service
29. John McKinley	Martin Van Buren	1837–1852
30. Peter V. Daniel	"	1841–1860
31. Samuel Nelson	John Tyler	1845–1872
32. Levi Woodbury	James K. Polk	1845–1851
33. Robert C. Grier	"	1846–1870
34. Benjamin R. Curtis	Millard Fillmore	1851–1857
35. John A. Campbell	Franklin Pierce	1853–1861
36. Nathan Clifford	James Buchanan	1858–1881
37. Noah H. Swayne	Abraham Lincoln	1862–1881
38. Samuel F. Miller	"	1862–1890
39. David Davis	"	1862–1877
40. Stephen J. Field	"	1863–1897
41. *Salmon P. Chase*	"	1864–1873
42. William Strong	Ulysses S. Grant	1870–1880
43. Joseph P. Bradley	"	1870–1892
44. Ward Hunt	"	1873–1882
45. *Morrison R. Waite*	"	1874–1888
46. John M. Harlan	Rutherford B. Hayes	1877–1911
47. William B. Woods	"	1881–1887
48. Stanley Matthews	James A. Garfield	1881–1889
49. Horace Gray	Chester A. Arthur	1882–1902
50. Samuel Blatchford	"	1882–1902
51. Lucius Q. C. Lamar	Grover Cleveland	1888–1893
52. *Melville Fuller*	"	1888–1910
53. David J. Brewer	Benjamin Harrison	1890–1910
54. Henry B. Brown	"	1891–1906
55. George Shiras, Jr.	"	1892–1903
56. Howell E. Jackson	"	1893–1895
57. Edward D. White	Grover Cleveland	1894–1910
58. Rufus W. Peckham	"	1896–1909
59. Joseph McKenna	William McKinley	1898–1925
60. Oliver W. Holmes, Jr.	Theodore Roosevelt	1902–1932
61. William R. Day	"	1903–1922
62. William H. Moody	"	1906–1910
63. Horace H. Lurton	William H. Taft	1910–1914
64. Charles E. Hughes	"	1910–1916
65. Willis Van Devanter	"	1911–1937
66. Joseph R. Lamar	"	1911–1916

(Continued)

Justice	Appointed by	Term of Service
67. *Edward D. White*[4]	William H. Taft	1910–1921
68. Mahlon Pitney	"	1912–1922
69. James C. McReynolds	Woodrow Wilson	1914–1941
70. Louis D. Brandeis	"	1916–1939
71. John H. Clarke	"	1916–1922
72. *William H. Taft*	Warren G. Harding	1921–1930
73. George Sutherland	"	1922–1938
74. Pierce Butler	"	1922–1939
75. Edward T. Sanford	"	1923–1930
76. Harlan F. Stone	Calvin Coolidge	1925–1941
77. *Charles E. Hughes*	Herbert Hoover	1930–1941
78. Owen J. Roberts	"	1930–1945
79. Benjamin N. Cardozo	"	1932–1938
80. Hugo L. Black	Franklin D. Roosevelt	1937–1971
81. Stanley F. Reed	"	1938–1957
82. Felix Frankfurter	"	1939–1962
83. William O. Douglas	"	1939–1975
84. Frank Murphy	"	1940–1949
85. *Harlan F. Stone*[5]	"	1941–1946
86. James F. Byrnes	"	1941–1942
87. Robert H. Jackson	"	1941–1954
88. Wiley B. Rutledge	"	1943–1949
89. Harold H. Burton	Harry S. Truman	1945–1958
90. *Fred M. Vinson*	"	1946–1953
91. Tom C. Clark	"	1949–1967
92. Sherman Minton	"	1949–1956
93. *Earl Warren*	Dwight D. Eisenhower	1953–1969
94. John M. Harlan, II	"	1955–1971
95. William J. Brennan	"	1956–1990
96. Charles E. Whittaker	"	1957–1962
97. Potter Stewart	"	1958–1981
98. Byron White	John F. Kennedy	1962–1993
99. Arthur J. Goldberg	"	1962–1965
100. Abe Fortas	Lyndon B. Johnson	1965–1969
101. Thurgood Marshall	"	1967–1991
102. *Warren E. Burger*	Richard M. Nixon	1969–1986
103. Harry A. Blackmun	"	1970–1994
104. Lewis F. Powell, Jr.	"	1972–1987

(Continued)

Justice	Appointed by	Term of Service
105. William H. Rehnquist	Richard M. Nixon	1972–1986
106. John Paul Stevens	Gerald Ford	1975–2010
107. Sandra Day O'Connor	Ronald Reagan	1981–2006
108. *William H. Rehnquist*[6]	"	1986–2006
109. Antonin Scalia	"	1986–
110. Anthony M. Kennedy	"	1987–
111. David H. Souter	George H.W. Bush	1990–2009
112. Clarence Thomas	"	1991–
113. Ruth Bader Ginsburg	William Clinton	1993–
114. Steven Breyer	"	1994–
115. *John Roberts*	George W. Bush	2006–
116. Samuel Alito	"	2006–
117. Sonia Sotomayor	Barack Obama	2009–
118. Elena Kagan	"	2010–

Notes

1. Resigned without sitting.
2. Returned commission.
3. Recess appointment rejected by the Senate.
4. Promoted from Associate Justice to Chief Justice.
5. Promoted from Associate Justice to Chief Justice.
6. Promoted from Associate Justice to Chief Justice.

Table of Cases

Index

Note: Page numbers in *italics* indicate image and timeline entries.